Lecture Notes in Computer

Commenced Publication in 1973
Founding and Former Series Editors:
Gerhard Goos, Juris Hartmanis, and Jan van Leeuwen

Editorial Board

David Hutchison
  Lancaster University, UK
Takeo Kanade
  Carnegie Mellon University, Pittsburgh, PA, USA
Josef Kittler
  University of Surrey, Guildford, UK
Jon M. Kleinberg
  Cornell University, Ithaca, NY, USA
Friedemann Mattern
  ETH Zurich, Switzerland
John C. Mitchell
  Stanford University, CA, USA
Moni Naor
  Weizmann Institute of Science, Rehovot, Israel
Oscar Nierstrasz
  University of Bern, Switzerland
C. Pandu Rangan
  Indian Institute of Technology, Madras, India
Bernhard Steffen
  University of Dortmund, Germany
Madhu Sudan
  Massachusetts Institute of Technology, MA, USA
Demetri Terzopoulos
  University of California, Los Angeles, CA, USA
Doug Tygar
  University of California, Berkeley, CA, USA
Moshe Y. Vardi
  Rice University, Houston, TX, USA
Gerhard Weikum
  Max-Planck Institute of Computer Science, Saarbruecken, Germany

4071

Lecture Notes in Computer Science

Editorial Board

Hari Sundaram   Milind Naphade
John R. Smith   Yong Rui (Eds.)

Image and Video Retrieval

5th International Conference, CIVR 2006
Tempe, AZ, USA, July 13-15, 2006
Proceedings

 Springer

Volume Editors

Hari Sundaram
Arizona State University
Arts Media and Engineering Program
Tempe AZ 85281, USA
E-mail: Hari.Sundaram@asu.edu

Milind Naphade
John R. Smith
IBM T.J. Watson Research Center
Intelligent Information Management Department
19 Skyline Drive, Hawthorne, NY 10532, USA
E-mail: {naphade,jrsmith}@us.ibm.com

Yong Rui
Microsoft China R&D Group, China
E-mail: yongrui@microsoft.com

Library of Congress Control Number: 2006928858

CR Subject Classification (1998): H.3, H.2, H.4, H.5.1, H.5.4-5, I.4

LNCS Sublibrary: SL 3 – Information Systems and Application, incl. Internet/Web
and HCI

ISSN   0302-9743
ISBN-10   3-540-36018-2 Springer Berlin Heidelberg New York
ISBN-13   978-3-540-36018-6 Springer Berlin Heidelberg New York

This work is subject to copyright. All rights are reserved, whether the whole or part of the material is
concerned, specifically the rights of translation, reprinting, re-use of illustrations, recitation, broadcasting,
reproduction on microfilms or in any other way, and storage in data banks. Duplication of this publication
or parts thereof is permitted only under the provisions of the German Copyright Law of September 9, 1965,
in its current version, and permission for use must always be obtained from Springer. Violations are liable
to prosecution under the German Copyright Law.

Springer is a part of Springer Science+Business Media

springer.com

© Springer-Verlag Berlin Heidelberg 2006
Printed in Germany

Typesetting: Camera-ready by author, data conversion by Scientific Publishing Services, Chennai, India
Printed on acid-free paper   SPIN: 11788034   06/3142   5 4 3 2 1 0

Preface

This volume contains the proceeding of the 5th International Conference on Image and Video Retrieval (CIVR), July 13–15, 2006, Arizona State University, Tempe, AZ, USA: http://www.civr2006.org. Image and video retrieval continues to be one of the most exciting and fast-growing research areas in the field of multimedia technology. However, opportunities for exchanging ideas between researchers and users of image and video retrieval systems are still limited. The International Conference on Image and Video Retrieval (CIVR) has taken on the mission of bringing together these communities to allow researchers and practitioners around the world to share points of view on image and video retrieval. A unique feature of the conference is the emphasis on participation from practitioners. The objective is to illuminate critical issues and energize both communities for the continuing exploration of novel directions for image and video retrieval.

We received over 90 submissions for the conference. Each paper was carefully reviewed by three members of the program committee, and then checked by one of the program chairs and/or general chairs. The program committee consisted of more than 40 experts in image and video retrieval from Europe, Asia and North America, and we drew upon approximately 300 high-quality reviews to ensure a thorough and fair review process. The paper submission and review process was fully electronic, using the EDAS system.

The quality of the submitted papers was very high, forcing the committee members to make some difficult decisions. Due to time and space constraints, we could only accept 18 oral papers and 30 poster papers. These 48 papers formed interesting sessions on Interactive Image and Video Retrieval, Semantic Image Retrieval, Visual Feature Analysis, Learning and Classification, Image and Video Retrieval Metrics, and Machine Tagging. To encourage participation from practitioners, we also had a strong demo session, consisting of 10 demos, ranging from VideoSOM, a SOM-based interface for video browsing, to collaborative concept tagging for images based on ontological thinking. Arizona State University (ASU) was the host of the conference, and has a very strong multimedia analysis and retrieval program. We therefore also included a special ASU session of 5 papers.

We would like to thank the Local Chair, Gang Qian; Finance Chair, Baoxin Li; Web Chair, Daniel Gatica-Perez; Demo Chair, Nicu Sebe; Publicity Chairs, Tat-Seng Chua, Rainer Lienhart and Chitra Dorai; Poster Chair, Ajay Divakaran; and Panel Chair John Kender, without whom the conference would not have been possible. We also want to give our sincere thanks to the three distinguished keynote speakers: Ben Shneiderman ("Exploratory Search Interfaces to Support Image Discovery"), Gulrukh Ahanger ("Embrace and Tame the Digital Content"), and Marty Harris ("Discovering a Fish in a Forest of Trees. False Positives and User Expectations in Visual Retrieval. Experiments in CBIR and the

Visual Arts"), whose talks highlighted interesting future directions of multimedia retrieval.

Finally, we wish to thank all the authors who submitted their work to the conference, and the program committee members for all the time and energy they invested in the review process. The quality of research between these covers reflects the efforts of many individuals, and their work is their gift to the multimedia retrieval community. It has been our pleasure and privilege to accept this gift.

May 2006

John Smith and Yong Rui
General Co-Chairs

Hari Sundaram and Milind R. Naphade
Program Co-Chairs

Table of Contents

Session O4: Learning and Classification

Session O5: Image and Video Retrieval Metrics

Session O6: Machine Tagging

Session P1: Poster I

Session P2: Poster II

Session A: ASU Special Session

Session D: Demo Session

Invited Talks

Interactive Experiments in Object-Based Retrieval

Sorin Sav, Gareth J.F. Jones, Hyowon Lee,
Noel E. O'Connor, and Alan F. Smeaton

Adaptive Information Cluster & Centre for Digital Video Processing
Dublin City University, Glasnevin, Dublin 9, Ireland
sorinsav@eeng.dcu.ie

Abstract. Object-based retrieval is a modality for video retrieval based on segmenting objects from video and allowing end-users to use these objects as part of querying. In this paper we describe an empirical TRECVid-like evaluation of object-based search, and compare it with a standard image-based search into an interactive experiment with 24 search topics and 16 users each performing 12 search tasks on 50 hours of rushes video. This experiment attempts to measure the impact of object-based search on a corpus of video where textual annotation is not available.

1 Introduction

The main hurdles to greater use of objects in video retrieval are the overhead of object segmentation on large amounts of video and the issue of whether objects can actually be used efficiently for multimedia retrieval. Despite much focus and attention, fully automatic object segmentation is far from completely solved. Despite this there are already some examples of work which supports retrieval based on video objects. The notion of using objects in video retrieval has been seen as desirable for some time e.g [1], but only very recently has technology started to allow even very basic object-location functions on video.

In previous work we developed a video retrieval and browsing system which allowed users to search using the text of closed captions, using the whole keyframe and using a a set of pre-defined video objects [2]. We evaluated our system on the content of several seasons of the Simpsons TV series in order observe the ways in which different video retrieval modalities (text search, image search, object search) were used and we concluded that certain queries can benefit from using object presence as part of their search, but this is not true for all query types. In retrospect this may seem obvious but we are all learning that different query types need different combinations of video search modalities, aspect best illustrated in the work of the Informedia group at ACM Multimedia 2004 [3].

Our hypothesis in this paper is that there are certain types of information need which lend themselves to expression as queries where objects form a central part of the query. We have developed and implemented a system which can support object-based matching of video shots by using a semi-automatic segmentation process described in [4]. In this paper we investigate how useful this

H. Sundaram et al. (Eds.): CIVR 2006, LNCS 4071, pp. 1–10, 2006.
© Springer-Verlag Berlin Heidelberg 2006

technique is for for searching and browsing very unstructured video, specifically the TRECVid BBC 2005 rushes corpus [5].

Research related to object-based retrieval is described in [6] where a set of homogeneous regions are grouped into an ad-hoc "object" in order to retrieve similar objects on a content of animated cartoons. Similarly in [7] there is another proposal for locating arbitrary-shaped objects in video sequences. Although these are not true object-based video retrieval systems they demonstrate video retrieval based on groups of segmented regions and are functionally identical to video object retrieval. In another approach in [8] object segmentation is performed on the query keyframe and this object is then matched and highlighted against similar objects appearing in video shots. This approach compensates for changes in the appearance of an object due to various artifacts presented in the video. Work reported in [9] addresses a complex approach to motion representation and object tracking and retrieval without actually segmenting the semantic object. Similar work, operating on video rather than video keyframes, is reported in [10] where video frames are automatically segmented into regions based on colour and texture, and then the largest of these is tracked through a video sequence.

The remainder of this paper is organised as follows. In the next section we outline the architecture of our object-based video retrieval system and briefly introduce its functionality. In section 3 we present the evaluation of object-based search functionality in an interactive search experiment on a test corpus of rushes video. The results derived from this evaluation are described and discussed in Section 4. Section 5 completes the paper summarising the conclusions of this study.

2   System Description

In this section we outline the architecture of our object-based video retrieval system. Our system begins by analysing raw video data in order to determine shots. For this we use a standard approach to shot boundary determination, basically comparing adjacent frames over a certain window using low-level colour features in order to determine boundaries [11]. From the 50 hours of BBC rushes video footage we detected 8,717 shots, or 174 keyframes per hour, much less than for post-produced video such as broadcast TV news. For each shot we extracted a single keyframe by examining the whole shot for levels of visual activity using features extracted directly from the video bitstream. Rushes video is raw video footage which is unedited and contains lots of redundancy, overlap and wasted material in which shots are generally much longer than in post-produced video. The regular approach of choosing the first, last or middle frames as the keyframe within a shot would be quite inappropriate given the amount of "dead" time that is in shots within rushes video. Thus an approach to keyframe selection based on choosing the frame where the greatest amount of action is happening seems reasonable, although this is not always true and is certainly a topic for further investigation.

Each of the 8,717 keyframes was then examined to determine if there was at least one significant object present in the frame. For such keyframes one or more objects were semi-automatically segmented from the background using a segmentation tool we had developed and used previously [12]. This is based on performing an RSST-based [13] homogeneous colour segmentation. A user then scribbles on-screen using a mouse to indicate the region inside, and the region outside the dominant object. This process is very quick for a user to perform, requires no specialist skills and yielded 1,210 such objects since not all keyframes contained objects.

Once the segmentation process is completed, we proceed to extract visual features from keyframes making use of several MPEG-7 XM [14] visual descriptors. These descriptors have been implemented as part of the aceToolbox [15] image analysis toolkit developed as part of the aceMedia project [16]. The descriptors used in our experiments were Dominant Colour, Texture Browsing and Shape compactness. The detailed presentation of these descriptors can be found in [17]. We extracted dominant colour and texture browsing features for all keyframes and dominant colour, texture browsing, and shape compactness features for all segmented objects. This effectively resulted in two separate representations of each keyframe/shot. We then pre-computed two 8,717 x 8,717 matrices of keyframe similarities using colour and texture for the whole keyframe and three 1,210 x 1,210 matrices of similarities between those keyframes with segmented objects using colour, texture and shape.

For retrieval or browsing of this or any other video archive with little metadata to describe it, we cannot assume that the user knows anything about its content since it is not catalogued in the conventional sense. In order to kick-start a search we ask the user to locate one or more images from outside the system using some other image searching resource. The aim here is to find one or more images, or even better one or more video objects, which can be used for searching. In our experiments our users use Google image search [18] to locate such external images but any image searching facility could be used. Once external images are found and downloaded they are analysed in the same way as the keyframes and the user is allowed to semi-automatically segment one object in the external image if they wish.

When these seed images have been ingested into our system the user is asked to indicate which visual characteristics make each seed image a good query image - colour or texture in the case of the whole image and colour, shape or texture in the case of segmented objects in the image. Once this is done the set of query images is used to perform retrieval and the user is presented with a list of keyframes from the archive. For keyframes where there is a segmented object present (1,210 of our 8,717 keyframes) the object is highlighted when the keyframe is presented. The user is asked to browse these keyframes and can either play back the video, save the shot, or add the keyframe (and its object, if present) to the query panel and the process of querying and browsing can continue until the user is satisfied. The overall architecture of our system is shown as Figure 1.

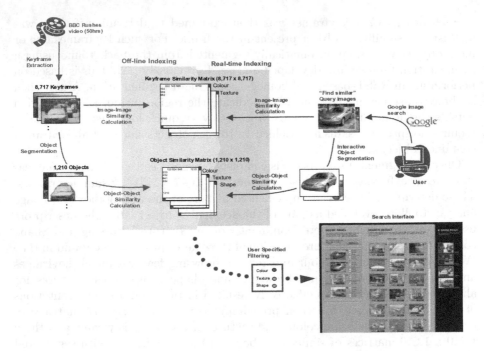

Fig. 1. System architecture overview

3   Experiments

In our experiments we aimed to evaluate how real users make use of object-based search functionality in contrast with image-based search. For this purpose we asked the users to perform a set of video searches with our system by using two identical looking search interfaces (like the one depicted at the bottom right in Figure 1). In one interface allowing object-based search users could use a combination of object and image searching, whereas in the other interface they were restricted (by disabling the object functionality) to using only whole image searching. For the reminder of this paper we refer to these interfaces as object-based interface and respectively image-based interface. The task given to the users is to find as many relevant shots for each predefined topic as possible. The effectiveness of a search interface being regarded as proportional with the number of relevant shots retrieved with that interface.

Each user was asked to perform a set of 6 separate search tasks with the object-based interface and a different set of 6 search tasks using the image-based interface. The users selected seed images from the Google image search and could semi-automatically segment objects in these images if they considered that useful for their search. The segmentation step is not performed when using the image interface. The users were instructed to save all relevant shots retrieved. At any stage during the search the user can add or remove images from the query either from the retrieved images or from the external resource.

We allocated only a 5 minute period for task completion for each of the 12 searches completed by each user. The objective of the time limit is was to put participants under pressure to complete the task within the available time. Users were offered the chance to take a break at session's half-time should they feel fatigued.

3.1 Search Topics Formulation

As described earlier in the paper, running shot boundary detection on the rushes corpus returned 8,717 shots with one keyframe per shot. 1,200 representative objects were selected and subsequently extracted from these keyframes.

For this experiment we required a set of realistic search topics. We based our formulation of the search topics on a set of over 1,000 real queries performed by professional TV editors at RTÉ, the Irish national broadcaster's video archive. These queries had previously been collected for another research project. The BBC rushes corpus consists of video recorded for a holiday program. One member of our team played through all the video and then eliminated queries which we knew could not be answered from the rushes collection. We then removed duplicate queries and similar, subsumed or narrow topics, ending with a set of 26 topics for which it is likely to find a reasonable number of relevant shots within this collection. Of these, 24 topics where used as search tasks and the other 2 as training during our users' familiarisation with the system. In the selection of search topics we did not consider whether they would be favorably inclined towards a particular search modality (object-based or image-based).

3.2 Experimental Design Methodology

In our experimental investigation we followed the guidelines for design of user experiments recommended by TRECVid [5]. These guidelines were developed in order to minimise the effect of user variability and possible noise in the experimental procedure. The guidelines outline the experimental process to be followed when measuring and comparing the effectiveness of two system variants (object/image based search versus image-only based search) using 24 topics and either 8, 16 or 24 searchers, each of whom searches 12 topics. The distribution of searchers against topics assumes a Latin-square configuration where a searcher performs a given topic only once and completes all work on one system variant before beginning any work on the other variant.

We chose to run the evaluation with 24 search topics and 16 users, with each user searching for 12 topics, 6 with the object/image based search and another 6 with the image-only based search. Our users were 16 postgraduate students and postdoctoral researchers: 8 people from within our research group with some prior exposure to video search interfaces and video retrieval experiments and another 8 people from other research fields with no exposure to video retrieval. Topics were assigned randomly to searchers. This design allows the estimation of the difference in performance between the two system variants free from the main (additive) effects of searcher and topic.

3.3   Experimental Procedure

In order to accommodate the schedules of users we ran experimental sessions with 4 users at a time. The search interface and segmentation tool were demonstrated to the users and we explained how the system worked and how to use all of its features. We then conducted a series of test searches until the users felt comfortable working with the retrieval system. Following these, the main search tasks began.

Users were handed a written description of the search topics. The topics were introduced one at a time at the beginning of each search task such that users would not be exposed to the next search topic in advance. This was done in order to reduce the influence that the current query and retrieved shots may have in revealing clues for the subsequent search topics. As previously stated, users were given 5 minutes for each topic and were offered the chance to take a break after completing 6 search topics. At the end of the two sessions (object/image and image-only based searching), each user was asked to complete a post-experiment questionnaire.

Each individual's interactions were logged by the system and one member of our team was present for the duration of each of the sessions to answer questions or handle any unexpected system issues. The results of users' searching (i.e. saved shots) were collected and formed the ground-truth for evaluation. The rationale behind doing this is that the shots saved by a user are assumed to be relevant and in terms of retrieval effectiveness for each system what we measure is how many shots, all assumed to be relevant, have users managed to locate and to explicitly save as relevant.

4   Results Derived from Experiments

For each topic we have collected a time-stamp log of the composition of each search at each iteration. Additionally in order to complement the understanding of objective measures we collected subjective observations from users through post-experiment questionnaires.

4.1   Evaluation Metrics

Since we did not have a manual relevance ground-truth for our topics, we assumed the shots saved by users during the interactive search to be relevant and used them as our recall baseline. Although we do not have any independent third party validation of the relevance of the saved shots our users were under instruction to only save shots they felt were relevant to the search topic, so this is not as unreasonable assumption. Naturally there may be other relevant shots in the collection, which were not retrieved by our users, but in the absence of exhaustive ground-truth we cannot know how many such shots are there. However our goal was to observe how real users make use of the object-based search functionality and that can be inferred even without an absolute ground-truth.

Table 1. Size-bounded recall by search topic

Topic no #	Topics	Shots retrieved		Distinct retrieved		Unique retrieved	
		Cumulative	Distinct	Object interface	Image interface	Object interface	Image interface
1	helicopter	32	7	7	5	2	0
2	people walking on the beach	72	18	16	12	2	2
3	fish market	20	8	4	6	1	3
4	boats at sea or in harbour	124	29	27	19	11	2
5	fresh vegetables or fruits	28	9	5	7	1	3
6	bridge	16	5	4	3	2	1
7	farm animals	56	14	13	8	5	1
8	palm trees	108	23	21	15	10	2
9	people in urban settings	140	29	27	19	9	2
10	nightclub life	44	15	8	12	1	5
11	camels	44	12	11	7	5	1
12	people in traditional dress	52	16	13	10	6	2
13	flying birds	52	11	10	8	3	1
14	cars in urban settings	96	21	21	13	5	1
15	people in the pool or sea	68	17	14	11	5	1
16	historic buildings	60	14	11	12	2	3
17	people sunbathing	108	22	19	16	4	2
18	skyscrapers	40	9	8	7	2	1
19	people inside a restaurant/bar	24	8	6	5	2	2
20	pigeons in a plaza	40	9	8	6	2	1
21	shoes in a shop window	64	18	17	8	12	2
22	people wind-surfing	40	11	10	6	3	1
23	elephant	28	6	6	4	2	0
24	plane in flight	56	12	11	9	3	1
	Average	59	14	12	10	4	2

From the logged data we derived the set of measures presented in Tables 1 and 2. The measures are shown for each search topic separately. The *shots retrieved* measure represents the total number of shots saved by all users for each search topic irrespective of the search interface used. The *cumulative* column gives the sum of shots saved by all users including the duplication of shots when saved by different users. The *distinct* value is obtained from the above cumulative number by removing duplicate shots. This value shows how many relevant shots were found for each topic. The *distinct retrieved* shots are then divided into shots saved with the object-based and with the image-based interface respectively. The *unique retrieved* value gives the number of distinct shots retrieved with only one of the search interfaces.

Table 2 shows the average values obtained during the 4 executions (by 4 users) of a search topic and each interface. All values are rounded to the nearest integer value. The *average retrieved* shots gives the mean number of distinct shots saved. The *average query length* shows how many images/objects have been used for each query, and *average iterations* presents the number of iteration runs for each search task. The last distinct column of this table measures the *average utilisation of object functionality* in terms of average number of images

Table 2. Average size-bounded recall by search topic

Topic no #	Average retrieved		Average query length		Average iterations		Average utilisation of object functionality	
	Object interface	Image interface	Object interface	Image interface	Object interface	Image interface	Object features	Image features
1	5	3	2	2	4	7	2	0
2	11	7	2	3	6	9	2	1
3	2	3	3	2	6	7	3	2
4	20	11	2	3	7	9	2	1
5	3	4	3	3	3	6	3	2
6	3	1	2	2	6	9	2	1
7	10	4	2	3	4	6	2	1
8	18	9	2	3	6	8	2	1
9	23	12	3	4	8	9	3	1
10	5	6	2	3	4	6	2	2
11	8	3	2	2	5	8	1	1
12	8	5	3	2	7	9	3	1
13	8	5	3	3	7	8	2	2
14	18	6	2	2	7	9	2	1
15	11	6	3	2	8	9	3	1
16	7	8	2	2	6	8	2	2
17	16	11	3	3	7	9	3	1
18	6	4	2	2	4	6	2	1
19	4	2	3	3	8	9	3	1
20	7	3	2	2	5	9	2	2
21	14	2	2	3	6	9	2	1
22	8	2	3	4	4	7	3	1
23	5	2	2	2	6	9	2	0
24	9	5	1	2	4	7	1	1
Average	10	5	2	3	6	8	2	1

for which object features and/or global image features have been used within the object-based search interface.

4.2   Results Interpretation

As shown by the *shots retrieved* values in Table 1 from the comparison between the *cumulative* and *distinct* values the sets of shots saved by different users largely overlap, which means that most users were able to find the same relevant shots although they may have used a different combination of query images or features. However during the experiments we observed that most users tended to initiate the search tasks from the same Google retrieved images, usually those found on the first page. Thus it is likely that most users have followed closely related search paths.

The number of *distinct retrieved* shots, given in Table 1 provides a measure of recall bound by the number of saved shots. By comparing the number of distinct shots retrieved with each search interface it can be observed that users found more relevant shots with the object-based interface. However that is not true for all search topics. For few search topics such as *fish market, bridge, nightclub life* and *historic building* searching on the image-based interface seemed to provide better results. These topics seem to be more suited to global image feature searching and although such features were also available on the object-based interface, users made only limited use of them, focusing mostly on object features. Additionally it is clear that except for the *bridge* topic, for the other three topics it is relatively difficult to define what images/objects will provide a good initial query. The object-based retrieval seems to provide not only better recall but also helps with locating shots that are not found by using image-only searching.

The average number of retrieved shots shows that object features provide better searching power than global features alone. The *average query length* and *average iterations* values are somehow correlated since performing an object-based search involves some time dedicated to segmenting objects which invariably reduces the time allocated to actually searching and therefore decreases the query length and the number of search iterations a user will be able to perform. The results shows that although using shorter queries and less iterations, object-based search compensates through the additional discerning capacity provided by the object's features. The *average utilisation of object functionality* shows that searchers have largely employed object-based features when available. This was confirmed as well by users' feedback provided in the post-experiment questionnaire.

5   Conclusions

In this paper we have described an empirical TRECVid-like evaluation of object-based video search functionality in an interactive search experiment. This was done in an attempt to isolate the impact of object-based search taking as an experimental collection the BBC rushes video corpus where text from automatic speech recognition (ASR), from video OCR, and from closed captions is not available. Sixteen users each completed 12 different searches, each in a controlled and measured environment with a 5 minutes time limit to complete each search.

The analysis of logged data corroborated with observations of user's behaviour during the search and with the feedback provided by users show that object-based searching consistently outperforms the image-based search. This result goes some way towards validating the approach of allowing users to select objects as a basis for searching video archives when the search dictates it as appropriate, though the technology to do this, is still under development for larger scale video collections.

Acknowledgments

BBC 2005 Rushes video is copyright for research purposes by the BBC through the TRECVid IR research collection. Part of this work was supported by Science Foundation Ireland under grant 03/IN.3/I361. We are grateful for the support of the *aceMedia* project which provided the aceToolbox image analysis toolkit.

References

1. E. Oomoto and K. Tanaka. Ovid: Design and implementation of a video-object database system. In IEEE Transactions on Knowledge and Data Engineering, vol 5, no.4, 1993.
2. A.F. Smeaton and P. Browne. A Usage Study of Retrieval Modalities for Video Shot Retrieval. Information Processing and Management (in press), 2006.
3. A. Hauptmann and M. Christel. Successful Approaches in the TREC Video Retrieval Evaluations. In Proceedings of ACM Multimedia, 2004.
4. S. Sav, H. Lee, A.F. Smeaton, N.E. O'Connor, and N. Murphy. Using Video Objects and Relevance Feedback in Video Retrieval. In Proceedings of the SPIE Conference on Multimedia Systems and Applications VIII, Boston, Mass., November 2005.
5. TRECVid Evaluation, available at http://www-nlpir.nist.gov/projects/trecvid
6. L. Hohl, F. Souvannavong, B. Merialdo, and B. Huet. Enhancing latent semantic analysis video object retrieval with structural information. In ICIP 2004 - International Conference on Image Processing, 2004.
7. B. Erol and F. Kossentini. Shape-based retrieval of video objects. In IEEE Transactions on Multimedia, vol 7, no.1, 2005.
8. J. Sivic, F. Shaffalitzky, and A. Zisserman. Efficient object retrieval from videos. In EUSIPCO 2004 - European Signal Processing Conference, 2004.
9. C.-B. Liu and N. Ahuja. Motion based retrieval of dynamic objects in videos. In Proceedings of ACM Multimedia, 2004.
10. M. Smith and A. Khotanzad. An object-based approach for digital video retrieval. In ITCC 2004 - International Conference on Information Technology: Coding and Computing, 2004.
11. P. Browne, C. Gurrin, H. Lee, K. McDonald, S. Sav, A.F. Smeaton, and J. Ye. Dublin City University Video Track Experiments for TREC 2001. In TREC 2001 - Proceedings of the Text REtrieval Conference, 2001.
12. T. Adamek and N.E. O'Connor. A Multiscale Representation Method for Non-rigid Shapes With a Single Closed Contour. In IEEE Transactions on Circuits and Systems for Video Technology, vol. 14, no. 5, May 2004.
13. E. Tuncel, L. Onural. Utilization of the recursive shortest spanning tree algorithm for video-object segmentation by 2D affine motion modelling. In IEEE Transactions on Circuits and Systems for Video Technology, vol. 10, no. 5, August 2000.
14. MPEG-7(xm) version 10.0, ISO/IEC/JTC1/SC29/WG11, N4062, 2001.
15. N.E. O'Connor, E. Cooke , H. LeBorgne , M. Blighe and T. Adamek. The AceToolbox: Low-Level Audiovisual Feature Extraction for Retrieval and Classification. In IEE European Workshop on the Integration of Knowledge, Semantic and Digital Media Technologies, London, UK, 2005.
16. The AceMedia project, available at http://www.acemedia.org
17. B. Manjunath, P. Salembier, and T. Sikora. Introduction to MEPG: Multimedia Content Description Standard. New York: Wiley, 2001.
18. The Google image search page, available at http://images.google.com

Learned Lexicon-Driven Interactive Video Retrieval

Cees Snoek*, Marcel Worring, Dennis Koelma, and Arnold Smeulders

Intelligent Systems Lab Amsterdam, University of Amsterdam,
Kruislaan 403, 1098 SJ Amsterdam, The Netherlands
{cgmsnoek, worring, koelma, smeulders}@science.uva.nl
http://www.mediamill.nl

Abstract. We combine in this paper automatic learning of a large lexicon of semantic concepts with traditional video retrieval methods into a novel approach
to narrow the semantic gap. The core of the proposed solution is formed by the
automatic detection of an unprecedented lexicon of 101 concepts. From there,
we explore the combination of query-by-concept, query-by-example, query-by-
keyword, and user interaction into the *MediaMill* semantic video search engine.
We evaluate the search engine against the 2005 NIST TRECVID video retrieval
benchmark, using an international broadcast news archive of 85 hours. Top ranking results show that the lexicon-driven search engine is highly effective for interactive video retrieval.

1 Introduction

For text collections, search technology has evolved to a mature level. The success has
whet the appetite for retrieval from video repositories, yielding a proliferation of commercial video search engines. These systems often rely on filename and accompanying
textual sources only. This approach is fruitful when a meticulous and complete description of the content is available. It ignores, however, the treasure of information available
in the visual information stream. In contrast, the image retrieval research community
has emphasized a visual-only analysis. It has resulted in a wide variety of efficient image and video retrieval systems e.g. [1,2,3]. A common denominator in these prototypes
is their dependence on color, texture, shape, and spatiotemporal features for representing video. Users query an archive with stored features by employing visual examples.
Based on user-interaction the query process is repeated until results are satisfactory. The
visual query-by-example paradigm is an alternative for the textual query-by-keyword
paradigm.

Unfortunately, techniques for image retrieval are not that effective yet in mining the
semantics hidden in video archives. The main problem is the semantic gap between
image representation and their interpretation by humans [4]. Where users seek high-
level semantics, video search engine technology offers low-level abstractions of the data
instead. In a quest to narrow the semantic gap, recent research efforts have concentrated
on automatic detection of semantic concepts in video [5, 6, 7, 8]. Query-by-concept
offers users an additional entrance to video archives.

---

* This research is sponsored by the BSIK MultimediaN project.

H. Sundaram et al. (Eds.): CIVR 2006, LNCS 4071, pp. 11–20, 2006.
© Springer-Verlag Berlin Heidelberg 2006

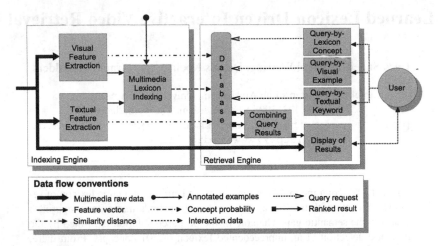

Fig. 1. General framework for an interactive video search engine. In the indexing engine, the system learns to detect a lexicon of semantic concepts. In addition, it computes similarity distances. A retrieval engine then allows for several query interfaces. The system combines requests and displays results to a user. Based on interaction a user refines search results until satisfaction.

State-of-the-art video search systems, e.g. [9, 10, 11, 6], combine several query interfaces. Moreover, they are structured in a similar fashion. First, they include an engine that indexes video data on a visual, textual, and semantic level. Systems typically apply similarity functions to index the data in the visual and textual modality. Video search engines often employ a semantic indexing component to learn a lexicon of concepts, such as *outdoor*, *car*, and *sporting event*, and accompanying probability from provided examples. All indexes are typically stored in a database at the granularity of a video shot. A second component that all systems have in common is a retrieval engine, which offers users an access to the stored indexes and the video data. Key components here are an interface to select queries, e.g. query-by-keyword, query-by-example, and query-by concept, and the display of retrieved results. The retrieval engine handles the query requests, combines the results, and displays them to an interacting user. We visualize a general framework for interactive video search engines in Fig. 1.

While proposed solutions for effective video search engines share similar components, they stress different elements in reaching their goal. Rautiainen *et al.* [9] present an approach that emphasizes combination of query results. They extend query-by-keyword on speech transcripts with query-by-example. In addition, they explore how a limited lexicon of 15 learned concepts may contribute to retrieval results. As the authors indicate, inclusion of more accurate concept detectors would improve retrieval results. The web-based MARVEL system extends classical query possibilities with an automatically indexed lexicon of 17 semantic concepts, facilitating query-by-concept with good accuracy [6]. In spite of this lexicon, however, interactive retrieval results are not competitive with [10, 11]. This indicates that much is to be gained when, in addition to query-by-concept, query-by-keyword, and query-by-example, more advanced interfaces for query selection and display of results are exploited for interaction.

Christel *et al.* [10] explain their success in interactive video retrieval as a consequence of using storyboards, i.e. a grid of key frame results that are related to a keyword-based query. Adcock *et al.* [11] also argue that search results should be presented in semantically meaningful units. They stress this by presenting query results as story key frame collages in the user interface. We adopt, extend, and generalize the above solutions.

The availability of gradually increasing concept lexicons, of varying quality, raises the question: how to take advantage of query-by-concept for effective interactive video retrieval? We advocate that the ideal video search engine should emphasize off-line learning of a large lexicon of concepts, based on automatic multimedia analysis, for the initial search. Then, the ideal system should employ query-by-example, query-by-keyword, and interaction with an advanced user interface to refine the search until satisfaction. To that end, we propose the *MediaMill* semantic video search engine. The uniqueness of the proposed system lies in its emphasis on automatic learning of a lexicon of concepts. When the indexed lexicon is exploited for query-by-concept and combined with query-by-keyword, query-by-example, and interactive filtering using an advanced user interface, a powerful video search engine emerges. To demonstrate the effectiveness of our approach, the interactive search experiments are evaluated within the 2005 NIST TRECVID video retrieval benchmark [12].

The organization of this paper is as follows. First, we present our semantic video search engine in Section 2. We describe the experimental setup in which we evaluated our search engine in Section 3. We present results in Section 4.

2   The MediaMill Semantic Video Search Engine

We propose a lexicon-driven video search engine to equip users with semantic access to video archives. The aim is to retrieve from a video archive, composed of n unique shots, the best possible answer set in response to a user information need. To that end, the search engine combines learning of a large lexicon with query-by-keyword, query-by-example, and interaction. The system architecture of the search engine follows the general framework as sketched in Fig. 1. We now explain the various components of the search engine in more detail.

2.1   Indexing Engine

Multimedia Lexicon Indexing. Generic semantic video indexing is required to obtain a large concept lexicon. In literature, several approaches are proposed [5, 6, 7, 8]. The utility of supervised learning in combination with multimedia content analysis has proven to be successful, with recent extensions to include video production style [7] and the insight that concepts often co-occur in context [5, 6]. We combine these successful approaches into an integrated video indexing architecture, exploiting the idea that the essence of produced video is its creation by an author. Style is used to stress the semantics of the message, and to guide the audience in its interpretation. In the end, video aims at an effective semantic communication. All of this taken together, the main focus of generic semantic indexing must be to reverse this authoring process, for which we proposed the semantic pathfinder [7].

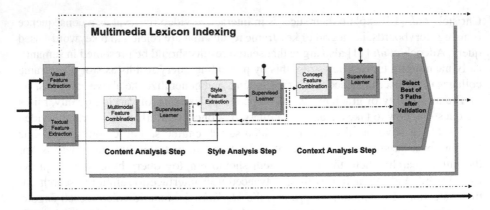

Fig. 2. Multimedia lexicon indexing is based on the semantic pathfinder [7]. In the detail from Fig. 1 we highlight its successive analysis steps. The semantic pathfinder selects for each concept a best path after validation.

The semantic pathfinder is composed of three analysis steps, see Fig. 2. The output of an analysis step in the pathfinder forms the input for the next one. We build this architecture on machine learning of concepts for the robust detection of semantics. The semantic pathfinder starts in the *content analysis step*. In this stage, it follows a data-driven approach of indexing semantics. It analyzes both the visual data and textual data to extract features. In the learning phase, it applies a support vector machine to learn concept probabilities. The *style analysis step* addresses the elements of video production, related to the style of the author, by several style-related detectors, i.e. related to layout, content, capture, and context. They include shot length, frequent speakers, camera distance, faces, and motion. At their core, these detectors are based on visual and textual features also. Again, a support vector machine classifier is applied to learn style probabilities. Finally, in the *context analysis step*, the probabilities obtained in the style analysis step are fused into a context vector. Then, again a support vector machine classifier is applied to learn concepts. Some concepts, like *vegetation*, have their emphasis on content thus style and context do not add much. In contrast, more complex events, like *people walking*, profit from incremental adaptation of the analysis by using concepts like *athletic game* in their context. The semantic pathfinder allows for generic video indexing by automatically selecting the best path of analysis steps on a per-concept basis.

Textual and Visual Feature Extraction. To arrive at a similarity distance for the textual modality we first derive words from automatic speech recognition results. We remove common stop words using the SMART's English stop list [13]. We then construct a high dimensional vector space based on all remaining transcribed words. We rely on latent semantic indexing [14] to reduce the search space to 400 dimensions. While doing so, the method takes co-occurrence of related words into account by projecting them onto the same dimension. The rationale is that this reduced space is a better representation of the search space. When users exploit query-by-keyword as similarity measure, the terms of the query are placed in the same reduced dimensional space. The most similar shots, viz. the ones closest to the query in that space, are returned, regardless of whether they contain the original query terms. In the visual modality the similarity query is by example. For all key frames in the video archive, we compute the perceptually uniform *Lab* color histogram using 32 bins for each color channel. Users compare key frames with Euclidean histogram distance.

2.2   Retrieval Engine

To shield the user from technical complexity, while at the same time offering increased efficiency, we store all computed indexes in a database. Users interact with the search engine based on query interfaces. Each query interface acts as a ranking operator on the multimedia archive. After a user issues a query it is processed and combined into a final result, which is presented to the user.

Query Selection. The set of concepts in the lexicon forms the basis for interactive selection of query results. Users may rely on direct query-by-concept for search topics related to concepts from this lexicon. This is an enormous advantage for the precision of the search. Users can also make a first selection when a query includes a super-class or a sub-class of a concept in the lexicon. For example, when searching for *sports* one can use the available concepts *tennis*, *soccer*, *baseball*, and *golf* from a lexicon. In a similar fashion, users may exploit a query on *animal* to retrieve footage related to *ice bear*. For search topics not covered by the concepts in the lexicon, users have to rely on query-by-keyword and query-by-example. Applying query-by-keyword in isolation allows users to find very specific topics if they are mentioned in the transcription from automatic speech recognition. Based on query-by-example, on either provided or retrieved image frames, key frames that exhibit a similar color distribution can augment results further. This is especially fruitful for repetitive key frames that contain similar visual content throughout the archive, such as previews, graphics, and commercials. Naturally, the search engine offers users the possibility to combine query interfaces. This is helpful when a concept is too general and needs refinement. For example when searching for Microsoft stock quotes, a user may combine query-by-concept *stock quotes* with query-by-keyword *Microsoft*. While doing so, the search engine exploits both the semantic indexes and the textual and visual similarity distances.

Combining Query Results. To rank results, query-by-concept exploits semantic probabilities, while query-by-keyword and query-by-example use similarity distances. When users mix query interfaces, and hence several numerical scores, this introduces the question how to combine the results. In [10], query-by-concept is applied after query-by-keyword. The disadvantage of this approach is the dependence on keywords for initial search. Because the visual content is often not reflected in the associated text, user-interaction with this restricted answer set results in limited semantic access. Hence, we opt for a combination method exploiting query results in parallel. Rankings offer us a comparable output across various query results. Therefore, we employ a standard approach using linear rank normalization [15] to combine query results.

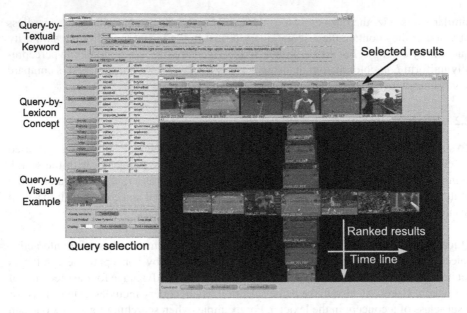

Query-by-Textual Keyword

Selected results

Query-by-Lexicon Concept

Query-by-Visual Example

Ranked results

Time line

Query selection

Fig. 3. Interface of the *MediaMill* semantic video search engine. The system allows for interactive query-by-concept using a large lexicon. In addition, it facilitates query-by-keyword, and query-by-example. Results are presented in a cross browser.

Display of Results. Ranking is a linear ordering, so ideally should be visualized as such. This leaves room to use the other dimension for visualization of the chronological series, or story, of the video program from which a key frame selected. This makes sense as frequently other items in the same broadcast are relevant to a query also [10, 11]. The resulting *cross browser* facilitates quick selection of relevant results. If requested, playback of specific shots is also possible. The interface of the search engine, depicted in Fig. 3, allows for easy query selection and swift visualization of results.

3   Experimental Setup

We performed our experiments as part of the interactive search task of the 2005 NIST TRECVID benchmark to demonstrate the significance of the proposed video search engine. The archive used is composed of 169 hours of US, Arabic, and Chinese broadcast news sources, recorded in MPEG-1 during November 2004. The test data contains approximately 85 hours. Together with the video archive came automatic speech recognition results and machine translations donated by a US government contractor. The Fraunhofer Institute [16] provided a camera shot segmentation. The camera shots serve as the unit for retrieval.

We detect in this data set automatically an unprecedented lexicon of 101 concepts using the semantic pathfinder. We select concepts by following a predefined concept ontology for multimedia [17] as leading example. Concepts in this ontology are chosen

Fig. 4. Instances of the 101 concepts in the lexicon, as detected with the semantic pathfinder

based on presence in WordNet [18] and extensive analysis of video archive query logs. Where concepts should be related to program categories, setting, people, objects, activities, events, and graphics. Instantiations of the concepts in the lexicon are visualized in Fig. 4. The semantic pathfinder detects all 101 concepts with varying performance, see [8] for details.

The goal of the interactive search task, as defined by TRECVID, is to satisfy an information need. Given such a need, in the form of a search topic, a user is engaged in an interactive session with a video search engine. Based on the results obtained, a user rephrases queries; aiming at retrieval of more and more accurate results. To limit the amount of user interaction and to measure search system efficiency, all individual search topics are bounded by a 15-minute time limit. The interactive search task contains 24 search topics in total. They became known only few days before the deadline of submission. Hence, they were unknown at the time we developed our 101 semantic concept detectors. In line with the TRECVID submission procedure, a user was allowed to submit, for assessment by NIST, up to a maximum of 1,000 ranked results for the 24 search topics.

We use *average precision* to determine the retrieval accuracy on individual search topics, following the standard in TRECVID evaluations [12]. The average precision is a single-valued measure that is proportional to the area under a recall-precision curve. As an indicator for overall search system quality, TRECVID reports the mean average precision averaged over all search topics from one run by a single user.

4   Results

The complete numbered list of search topics is plotted in Fig. 5. Together with the topics, we plot the benchmark results for 49 users using 16 present-day interactive video search engines. We remark that most of them exploit only a limited lexicon of concepts, typically in the range of 0 to 40. The results give insight in the contribution of the proposed system for individual search topics. At the same time, it allows for comparison against the state-of-the-art in video retrieval.

The user of the proposed search engine scores excellent for most search topics, yielding a top 3 average precision for 17 out of 24 topics. Furthermore, our approach obtains the highest average precision for five search topics (Topics: 3, 8, 10, 13, 20). We explain the success of our search engine, in part, by the lexicon used. In our lexicon, there was an (accidental) overlap with the requested concepts for most search topics. Examples are *tennis*, *people marching*, and *road* (Topics: 8, 13, 20), where performance is very good. The search engine performed moderate for topics that require specific instances of a concept, e.g. maps with Bagdhad marked (Topic: 7). When search topics contain combinations of several concepts, e.g. meeting, table, people (Topic: 15), results are also not

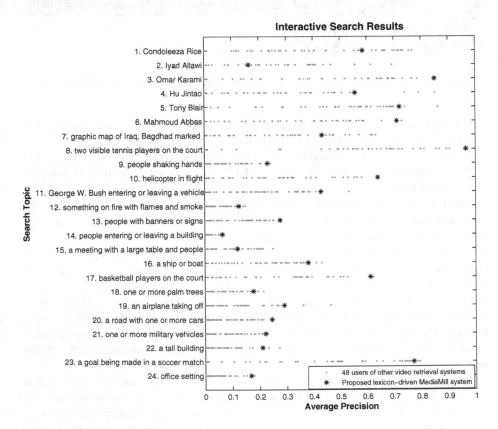

Fig. 5. Comparison of interactive search results for 24 topics performed by 49 users of 16 present-day video search engines

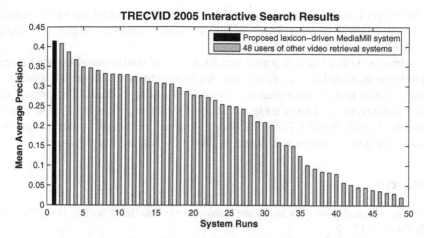

Fig. 6. Overview of all interactive search runs submitted to TRECVID 2005, ranked according to mean average precision

optimal. This indicates that much is to be expected from a more intelligent combination of query results. When a user finds an answer to a search topic in a repeating piece of footage, query-by-example is particularly useful. A typical search topic profiting from this observation it the one related to Omar Karami (Topic: 3), who is frequently interviewed in the same room. Query-by-keyword is especially useful for specific information needs, like person X related inquiries. It should be noted that although we have a large lexicon of concepts, performance of them is far from perfect, often resulting in noisy detection results. We therefore grant an important role to the interface of the video search engine. Because our user could quickly select relevant segments of interest, the search engine aided for search topics that could not be addressed with (robust) concepts from the lexicon.

To gain insight in the overall quality of our lexicon-driven approach to video retrieval, we compare the mean average precision results of using our search engine with 48 other users that participated in the interactive retrieval task of the 2005 TRECVID benchmark. We visualize the results for all submitted interactive search runs in Fig. 6. The results show that the proposed search engine obtains a mean average precision of 0.414, which is the highest overall score. The benchmark results demonstrate that lexicon-driven interactive retrieval yields state-of-the-art accuracy.

5 Conclusion

In this paper, we combine automatic learning of a large lexicon of semantic concepts with traditional video retrieval methods into a novel approach to narrow the semantic gap. The foundation of the proposed approach is formed by a learned lexicon of 101 semantic concepts. Based on this lexicon, query-by-concept offers users a semantic entrance to video repositories. In addition, users are provided with an entry in the form of textual query-by-keyword and visual query-by-example. Interaction with the various query interfaces is handled by an advanced display of results, which provides feedback in the form of a cross browser. The resulting *MediaMill* semantic video search engine limits the influence of the semantic gap.

Experiments with 24 search topics and 85 hours of international broadcast news video indicate that the lexicon of concepts aids substantially in interactive search performance. This is best demonstrated in a comparison among 49 users of 16 present-day retrieval systems, none of them using a lexicon of 101 concepts, within the interactive search task of the 2005 NIST TRECVID video retrieval benchmark. In this comparison, the user of the lexicon-driven search engine gained the highest overall score.

References

1. Flickner, M., et al.: Query by image and video content: The QBIC system. IEEE Computer **28**(9) (1995) 23–32
2. Chang, S.F., Chen, W., Men, H., Sundaram, H., Zhong, D.: A fully automated content-based video search engine supporting spatio-temporal queries. IEEE TCSVT **8**(5) (1998) 602–615
3. Rui, Y., Huang, T., Ortega, M., Mehrotra, S.: Relevance feedback: A power tool in interactive content-based image retrieval. IEEE TCSVT **8**(5) (1998) 644–655
4. Smeulders, A., Worring, M., Santini, S., Gupta, A., Jain, R.: Content based image retrieval at the end of the early years. IEEE TPAMI **22**(12) (2000) 1349–1380
5. Naphade, M., Huang, T.: A probabilistic framework for semantic video indexing, filtering, and retrieval. IEEE Trans. Multimedia **3**(1) (2001) 141–151
6. Amir, A., et al.: IBM research TRECVID-2003 video retrieval system. In: Proc. TRECVID Workshop, Gaithersburg, USA (2003)
7. Snoek, C., Worring, M., Geusebroek, J., Koelma, D., Seinstra, F., Smeulders, A.: The semantic pathfinder: Using an authoring metaphor for generic multimedia indexing. IEEE TPAMI (2006) in press.
8. Snoek, C., et al.: The MediaMill TRECVID 2005 semantic video search engine. In: Proc. TRECVID Workshop, Gaithersburg, USA (2005)
9. Rautiainen, M., Ojala, T., Seppänen, T.: Analysing the performance of visual, concept and text features in content-based video retrieval. In: ACM MIR, NY, USA (2004) 197–204
10. Christel, M., Huang, C., Moraveji, N., Papernick, N.: Exploiting multiple modalities for interactive video retrieval. In: IEEE ICASSP. Volume 3., Montreal, CA (2004) 1032–1035
11. Adcock, J., Cooper, M., Girgensohn, A., Wilcox, L.: Interactive video search using multilevel indexing. In: CIVR. Volume 3569 of LNCS., Springer-Verlag (2005) 205–214
12. Smeaton, A.: Large scale evaluations of multimedia information retrieval: The TRECVid experience. In: CIVR. Volume 3569 of LNCS., Springer-Verlag (2005) 19–27
13. Salton, G., McGill, M.: Introduction to Modern Information Retrieval. McGraw-Hill, New York, USA (1983)
14. Deerwester, S., Dumais, S., Furnas, G., Landauer, T., Harshman, R.: Indexing by latent semantic analysis. J. American Soc. Inform. Sci. **41**(6) (1990) 391–407
15. Lee, J.: Analysis of multiple evidence combination. In: ACM SIGIR. (1997) 267–276
16. Petersohn, C.: Fraunhofer HHI at TRECVID 2004: Shot boundary detection system. In: Proc. TRECVID Workshop, Gaithersburg, USA (2004)
17. Naphade, et al.: A light scale concept ontology for multimedia understanding for TRECVID 2005. Technical Report RC23612, IBM T.J. Watson Research Center (2005)
18. Fellbaum, C., ed.: WordNet: an electronic lexical database. The MIT Press, Cambridge, USA (1998)

Mining Novice User Activity with TRECVID Interactive Retrieval Tasks

Michael G. Christel and Ronald M. Conescu

School of Computer Science, Carnegie Mellon University
Pittsburgh, PA, U.S.A. 15213
christel@cs.cmu.edu, rconescu@andrew.cmu.edu

Abstract. This paper investigates the applicability of Informedia shot-based interface features for video retrieval in the hands of novice users, noted in past work as being too reliant on text search. The Informedia interface was redesigned to better promote the availability of additional video access mechanisms, and tested with TRECVID 2005 interactive search tasks. A transaction log analysis from 24 novice users shows a dramatic increase in the use of color search and shot-browsing mechanisms beyond traditional text search. In addition, a within-subjects study examined the employment of user activity mining to suppress shots previously seen. This strategy did not have the expected positive effect on performance. User activity mining and shot suppression did produce a broader shot space to be explored and resulted in more unique answer shots being discovered. Implications for shot suppression in video retrieval information exploration interfaces are discussed.

1 Introduction

As digital video becomes easier to create and cheaper to store, and as automated video processing techniques improve, a wealth of video materials are now available to end users. Concept-based strategies, where annotators carefully describe digital video with text concepts that can later be used for searching and browsing, are powerful but expensive. Users have shown that they are unlikely to invest the time and labor to annotate their own photograph and video collections with text descriptors. Prior evaluations have shown that annotators do not often agree on the concepts used to describe the materials, so the text descriptors are often incomplete.

To address these shortcomings in concept-based strategies, content-based strategies work directly with the syntactic attributes of the source video in an attempt to derive indices useful for subsequent browsing and retrieval, features like color, texture, shape, and coarse audio attributes such as speech/music or male/female speech. These lowest level content-based indexing techniques can be automated to a high degree of accuracy, but unfortunately in practice they do not meet the needs of the user, reported often in the multimedia information retrieval literature as the semantic gap between the capabilities of automated systems and the users' information needs. Pioneer systems like IBM's QBIC demonstrated the capabilities of color, texture, and shape search, while also showing that users wanted more.

Continuing research in the video information indexing and retrieval community attempts to address the semantic gap by automatically deriving higher order features,

H. Sundaram et al. (Eds.): CIVR 2006, LNCS 4071, pp. 21–30, 2006.
© Springer-Verlag Berlin Heidelberg 2006

e.g., outdoor, building, face, crowd, and waterfront. Rather than leave the user only with color, texture, and shape, these strategies give the user control over these higher order features for searching through vast corpora of materials. The NIST TRECVID video retrieval evaluation forum has provided a common benchmark for evaluating such work, charting the contributions offered by automated content-based processing as it advances [1].

To date, TRECVID has confirmed that the best performing interactive systems for news and documentary video leverage heavily from the narration offered in the audio track. The narration is transcribed either in advance for closed-captioning by broadcasters, or as a processing step through automatic speech recognition (ASR). In this manner, text concepts for concept-based retrieval are provided for video, without the additional labor of annotation from a human viewer watching the video, with the caveat that the narration does not always describe the visual material present in the video. Because the text from narration is not as accurate as a human annotator describing the visual materials, and because the latter is too expensive to routinely produce, subsequent user search against the video corpus will be imprecise, returning extra irrelevant information, and incomplete, missing some relevant materials as some video may not have narrative audio. Interfaces can help the interactive user to quickly and accurately weed out the irrelevant information and focus attention on the relevant material, addressing precision. TRECVID provides an evaluation forum for determining the effectiveness of different interface strategies for interactive video retrieval. This paper reports on a study looking at two interface characteristics:

1. Will a redesigned interface promote other video information access mechanisms besides the often-used text search for novice users?
2. Will mining user interactions, to suppress the future display of shots already seen, allow novice users to find more relevant video footage than otherwise?

The emphasis is on novice users: people who are not affiliated with the research team and have not seen or used the system before. Novices were recruited as subjects for this experiment to support the generalization of experimental results to wider audiences than just the research team itself.

2   Informedia Retrieval Interface for TRECVID 2005

The Informedia interface since 2003 has supported text query, image color-based or texture-based query, and browsing actions of pre-built "best" sets like "best road shots" to produce sets of shots and video story segments for subsequent user action, with the segments and shots represented with thumbnail imagery often in temporally arranged storyboard layouts [2, 3, 4]. Other researchers have likewise found success with thumbnail image layouts confirmed with TRECVID studies [5, 6, 7]. This paper addresses two questions suggested by earlier TRECVID studies.

First, Informedia TRECVID 2003 experiments suggested that the usage context from the user's interactive session could improve one problem with storyboard interfaces on significantly sized corpora: there are too many shot thumbnails within candidate storyboards for the user's efficient review. The suggestion was to mark all shots seen by a user pursuing a topic, and suppress those shots from display in subsequent interactions regarding the topic [4]. Mining the users' activity in real time can reduce the number of shots shown in subsequent interactions.

Second, Informedia TRECVID 2004 experiments found that novice users do not pursue the same solution strategies as experts, using text query for 95% of their investigations even though the experts' strategy made use of image query and "best" set browsing 20% of the time [3]. The Informedia interface for TRECVID 2005 was redesigned with the same functionality as used in 2003 and 2004, but with the goal of promoting text searches, image searches, and visual feature browsing equally. Nielsen's usability heuristics [8] regarding "visibility of system status" and "recognition over recall," and guidelines for clarifying search in text-based systems [9] were consulted during the updating, with the redesigned Informedia interface as used for TRECVID 2005 shown in Fig. 1.

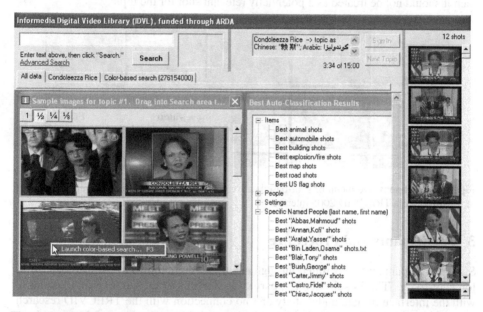

Fig. 1. 2005 Informedia TRECVID search interface, with text query (top left), image query (middle left), topic description (top middle), best-set browsing (middle), and collected answer set display (right) all equally accessible

Fig. 2 illustrates a consistency in action regarding the thumbnail representations of shots. The shot can be captured (saved as an answer for the topic), used to launch an image query, used to launch a video player queued to that shot's start time, used to launch a storyboard of all the shots in the shot's story segment, or used to show production metadata (e.g., date of broadcast) for the segment. New for 2005 was the introduction of 2 capture lists supporting a ranked answer set: the "definite" shots in the "yes" list, and the "possible" answers put to a "maybe" secondary list. The six actions were clearly labeled on the keyboard by their corresponding function keys.

As an independent variable, the interface was set up with the option to aggressively hide all previously "judged" shots. While working on a topic, the shots seen by the user as thumbnails were tracked in a log. If the user captured the shot to either the "yes" or "maybe" list, it would not be shown again in subsequent text and image queries, or subsequent "best" set browsing, as these shots were already judged positively for the topic. In addition, all shots skipped over within a storyboard while capturing a shot were assumed to be implicitly judged negatively for the topic, and would not be shown again in subsequent user actions on that topic. So, for the topic of "tanks or military vehicles", users might issue a text search "tank" and see a storyboard of shots as in Fig. 2. They capture the third shot on the top row. That shot, and the first 2 shots in that row marked as "implicitly judged negatively", are now no longer shown in subsequent views. Even if those 3 shots discuss "soldier", a subsequent search on "soldier" would not show the shots again. The "implicitly judged negatively" shots, henceforth labeled as "overlooked" shots, are not considered further, based on the assumption that if a shot was not good enough for the user to even capture as "maybe", then it should not be treated as a potentially relevant shot for the topic.

Fig. 2. Context-sensitive menu of shot-based actions available for all thumbnail representations in the Informedia TRECVID 2005 interface

3 Participants and Procedure

Study participants were recruited through electronic communication at Carnegie Mellon University. The 24 subjects who participated in this study had no prior experience with the interface or data under study and no connection with the TRECVID research group. The subjects were 11 female and 13 male with a mean age of 24 (6 subjects less than 20, 4 30 or older); 9 undergraduate students, 14 graduate students, and 1 university researcher. The participants were generally familiar with TV news. On a 5-point scale responding to "How often do you watch TV news?" (1=*not at all*, 5=*more than once a day*), most indicated some familiarity (distribution for 1-5 were 6-3-8-5-2). The participants were experienced web searchers but inexperienced digital video searchers. For "Do you search the web/information systems frequently?" (1=*not at all*, 5= *I search several times daily*), the answer distribution was 0-1-3-7-13 while for "Do you use any digital video retrieval system?" with the same scale, the distribution was 15-7-1-1-0. These characteristics are very similar to those of novice users in a TRECVID 2004 published study [3]. Each subject spent about 90 minutes in the study and received $15 for participation.

Participants worked individually with an Intel® Pentium® 4 class machine, a high resolution 1600 x 1200 pixel 21-inch color monitor, and headphones in a Carnegie Mellon computer lab. Participants' keystrokes and mouse actions were logged within the retrieval system during the session. They first signed a consent form and filled out a questionnaire about their experience and background. During each session, the participant was presented with four topics, the first two presented with one system ("Mining" or "Plain") and the next two with the other system. The "Mining" system kept track of all captured shots and overlooked shots. Captured and overlooked shots were not considered again in subsequent storyboard displays, and overlooked shots were skipped in filling out the 1000-shot answer set for a user's graded TRECVID submission. The "Plain" system did not keep track of overlooked shots and did not suppress shots in any way based on prior interactions for a given topic.

24 subject sessions produced 96 topic answers: 2 Mining and 2 Plain for each of the 24 TRECVID 2005 search topics. The topics and systems were counter-balanced in this within-subjects design: half the subjects experienced Mining first for 2 topics, and then Plain on 2 topics, while the other half saw Plain first and then Mining. For each topic, the user spent exactly 15 minutes with the system answering the topic, followed by a questionnaire. The questionnaire content was the same as used in 2004 across all of the TRECVID 2004 interactive search participants, designed based on prior work conducted as part of the TREC Interactive track for several years [10]. Participants took two additional post-system questionnaires after the second and fourth topics, and finished with a post-search questionnaire.

Participants were given a paper-based tutorial explaining the features of the system with details on the six actions in Figure 2, and 15 minutes of hands-on use to explore the system and try the examples given in the tutorial, before starting on the first topic.

4 Results

Transaction log analysis shows that the interface changes illustrated in Fig. 1 had their intended effect: novice users made much more frequent use of image search and the "best" sets browsing rather than relying almost exclusively on text search, as was found in the TRECVID 2004 experiment [3]. Table 1 summarizes the results, including an extra column showing the statistics from the TRECVID 2004 experiment. Since the topics, corpus, and features for "best" sets changed between TRECVID 2004 and 2005, the reader is cautioned against making too many inferences between corpora. For example, the increase in segment count per text query from 2004 to 2005 might be due to more ambiguous queries of slightly longer size, but could also be due to the TRECVID 2005 overall corpus being larger. The point emphasized here is that with the 2004 interface, novices were reluctant to interact with the Informedia system aside from text search, while in 2005 the use of "best" set browsing increased ten-fold and image queries three-fold.

Table 2 shows the access mechanism used to capture shots and the distribution of captured correct shots as graded against the NIST TRECVID pooled truth [1]. While "best" browsing took place much less than image search (see Table 1), it was a more precise source of information, producing a bit more of the captured shots than image search and an even greater percentage of the correct shots. This paper focuses on novice user performance; the expert's performance is listed in Table 2 only to show the relative effects of interface changes on novice search behavior compared to the expert. In 2004, the expert relied on text query for 78% of his correct shots, with image query shots contributing 16% and "best" set browsing 6%. The novice users' interactions were far different, with 95% of the correct shots coming from text search and near nothing coming from "best" set browsing. By contrast, the same expert in

2005 for the TRECVID 2005 topics and corpus drew 53% of his correct shots from text search, 16% from image query, and 31% from "best" set browsing. The novice users with the same "Mining" interface as used by the expert produced much more similar interaction patterns to the expert than was seen in 2004, with image query and "best" set browsing now accounting for 35% of the sources of correct shots.

Table 1. Interaction log statistics for novice user runs with TRECVID data

	TRECVID 2005		TRECVID 2004 Novice ([3])
	Novice Plain	Novice Mining	
Number of users	24	24	24
Number of topics	48	48	48
Fixed minutes spent per topic	15	15	15
Avg. (average) feature "best" sets browsed per topic	1.38	1.13	0.13
Avg. image queries per topic	3.27	4.19	1.23
Avg. text queries per topic	5.67	7.21	9.04
Word count per text query	2.31	2.19	1.51
Avg. number of video segments returned by each text query	194.7	196.8	105.3
Query/browse actions per topic	10.32	12.53	10.4

Table 2. Percentages of submitted shots and correct shots from various groups

	Access Mechanism	TRECVID 2005			TRECVID 2004 ([3])	
		Novice Plain	Novice Mining	Expert Mining	Expert	Novice
Shots Submitted	Text query	48%	65%	54%	81%	95%
	Image query	25%	17%	20%	12%	5%
	"Best" browse	27%	18%	26%	7%	0%
Shots Judged Correct	Text query	47%	65%	53%	78%	95%
	Image query	24%	14%	16%	16%	5%
	"Best" browse	29%	21%	31%	6%	0%

Overall performance for the novice runs was very positive, with the mean average precision (MAP) for four novice runs of 0.253 to 0.286 placing the runs in the middle of the 44 interactive runs for TRECVID 2005, with all of the higher scoring runs coming from experts (developers and colleagues acting as users of the tested systems). Hence, these subjects produced the top-scoring novice runs, with the within-subjects study facilitating the comparison of one system vs. another, specifically the relative merits of Plain vs. Mining based on the 96 topics answered by these 24 novice users.

There is no significant difference in performance as measured by MAP for the 2 Plain and 2 Mining runs: they are all essentially the same. Mining did not produce the effect we expected, that suppressing shots would lead to better average precision for a topic within the 15-minute time limit. The users overwhelmingly (18 of 24) answered "no difference" to the concluding question "Which of the two systems did you like best?" confirming that the difference between Plain and Mining was subtle (in deciding *what* to present) rather than overt in *how* presentation occurs in the GUI. The Mining interface did lead to more query and browsing interactions, as shown in the final row of Table 1, and while these additional interactions did not produce an overall better MAP, they did produce coverage changes as discussed below.

5 Discussion

TRECVID encourages research in information retrieval specifically from digital video by providing a large video test collection, uniform scoring procedures, and a forum for organizations interested in comparing their results. TRECVID benchmarking covers interactive search, and the NIST TRECVID organizers are clearly cognizant of issues of ecological validity: the extent to which the context of a user study matches the context of actual use of a system, such that it is reasonable to suppose that the results of the study are representative of actual usage and that the differences in context are unlikely to impact the conclusions drawn. Regarding the task context, TRECVID organizers design interactive retrieval topics to reflect many of the various sorts of queries real users pose [1]. Regarding the user pool, if only the developers of the system under study serve as the users, it becomes difficult to generalize that novices (non-developers and people outside of the immediate research group) would have the same experiences and performance. In fact, a study of novice and expert use of the Informedia system against TRECVID 2004 tasks shows that novice search behavior is indeed different from the experts [3]. Hence, for TRECVID user studies to achieve greater significance and validity, they should be conducted with user pools drawn from communities outside of the TRECVID research group, as done for the study reported here, its predecessor novice study reported in [3], and done with [11].

The interface design can clearly affect novice user interaction. A poor interface can deflate the use of potentially valuable interface mechanisms, while informing the user as to what search variants are possible and all aspects of the search (in line with [9]) and promoting "visibility of system status" and "recognition over recall" [8] can produce a richer, more profitable set of user interactions. The Informedia TRECVID 2005 interface succeeded in promoting the use of "best" browsing and image search nearly to the levels of success achieved by an expert user, closing the gulf between novice and expert interactions witnessed with a TRECVID 2004 experiment.

As for the Mining interface, it failed to produce MAP performance improvements. The TRECVID 2005 interactive search task is specified to allow the user 15 minutes on each of 24 topics to identify up to 1000 relevant shots per topic from among the 45,765 shots in the test corpus. As discussed in [5], MAP does not reward returning a short high precision list over returning the same list supplemented with random choices, so the search system is well advised to return candidate shots above and beyond what the user identifies explicitly. For our novice runs, the "yes" primary captured shot set was ranked first, followed by the "maybe" secondary set of captured shots (recall Fig. 2 options), followed by an automatic expansion seeded by the user's captured set, to produce a 1000 shot answer set. For the Mining treatment, the overlooked shots were never brought into the 1000 shot answer set during the final automatic expansion step. A post hoc analysis of answer sets shows that this overly aggressive use of the overlooked shots for Mining was counterproductive. The user actually identified more correct shots with Mining than with Plain. Table 3 summarizes the results, with the expert run from a single expert user with the Mining system again included to illustrate differences between performances obtained with the Mining and Plain system. Novices for both named specific topics and generic topics, as classified by the TRECVID organizers [1], had better recall of correct shots in their primary sets with Mining versus Plain. However, the precision was less with Mining, perhaps because when shots are suppressed, the user's expectations are confounded and the temporal flow of thumbnails within storyboards is broken up by the removal of overlooked shots. Suppressing information has the advantage of stopping the cycle of constant rediscovery of the same information, but has the disadvantage of removing navigation cues and the interrelationships between data items [12], in our case shots. Coincidentally, the novices did use the secondary capture set as intended, for lower precision guesses or difficult-to-confirm-quickly shots: the percentage correct in the secondary set is less than the precision of the primary capture set.

Table 3. Primary and secondary captured shot set and overlooked shot set sizes, with percentage of correct shots, for named and generic TRECVID 2005 topics

TREC-VID 2005	Shot Set	Avg. Shot Count Per Topic			% Correct in Shot Set		
		Novice Plain	Novice Mining	Expert Mining	Novice Plain	Novice Mining	Expert Mining
6 Named Topics	Primary	53.9	64.8	67.2	92.4	72.1	97.0
	Secondary	5.3	5.2	12.2	31.3	46.8	93.2
	Overlooked	n/a	372.0	223.7	n/a	5.8	8.6
18 Generic Topics	Primary	41.9	47.9	55.7	78.3	74.9	91.2
	Secondary	5.7	3.8	11.9	42.2	26.8	65.1
	Overlooked	n/a	649.8	503	n/a	4.2	6.5

The most glaring rows from Table 3 address the overlooked shot set (suppressed shots that are not in the primary or secondary capture sets): far from containing no information, they contain a relatively high percentage of correct shots. A random pull of shots for a named topic would have 0.39% correct shots, but the novices' overlooked set contained 5.8% correct items. A random pull of generic shots would contain 0.89% correct shots, but the novices' overlooked set contained 4.2% correct shots. Clearly, the novices (and the expert) were overlooking correct shots at a rate higher than expected.

Fig. 3 shows samples of correct shots that were overlooked when pursuing the topic "Condoleezza Rice." They can be categorized into four error types: (a) the shot was mostly of different material that ends up as the thumbnail representation, but started or ended with a tiny bit of the "correct" answer, e.g., the end of a dissolve out of a Rice shot into an anchor studio shot; (b) an easily recognizable correct shot based on its thumbnail, but missed by the user because of time pressure, lower motivation than the expert "developer" users often employed in TRECVID runs, and lack of time to do explicit denial of shots with "implicitly judged negatively" used instead to perhaps too quickly banish a shot into the overlooked set; (c) incorrect interpretation of the query (Informedia instructions were to ignore all still image representations and only return video sequences for the topic); and (d) a correct shot but with ambiguous or incomplete visual evidence, e.g., back of head or very small. Of these error classes, (a) is the most frequent and easiest to account for: temporal neighbors of correct shots are likely to be correct because relevant shots often occur in clumps and the reference shot set may not have exact boundaries. Bracketing user-identified shots with their neighbors during the auto-filling to 1000 items has been found to improve MAP by us and other TRECVID researchers [5, 7]. However, temporally associated shots are very likely to be shown in initial storyboards based on the Informedia storyboard composition process, which then makes neighbor shots to correct shots highly likely to be passed over, implicitly judged negatively, and, most critically, never considered again during the auto-filling to 1000 shots. So, the aggressive mining and overlooking of shots discussed here led to many correct shots of type (a) being passed over permanently, where bracketing strategies as discussed in [5] would have brought those correct shots back into the final set of 1000.

Fig. 3. Sample of overlooked but correct shots for Condoleezza Rice topic, divided into 4 error classes (a) - (d) described above

One final post hoc analysis follows the lines of TRECVID workshop inquiries into unique relevant shots contributed by a run. Using just the 4 novice runs and one expert run per topic from the Informedia interactive system, the average unique relevant shots in the primary capture set contributed by the novices with Plain was 5.1 per topic, novices with Mining contributed 7.1, and the expert with Mining for reference contributed 14.9. Clearly the expert is exploring video territory not covered by the novices, but the novices with the Mining interfaces are also exploring a broader shot space with more unique answer shots being discovered.

6 Summary and Acknowledgements

Video retrieval achieves higher rates of success with a human user in the loop, with the interface playing a pivotal role in encouraging use of different access mechanisms by novices. A redesigned Informedia interface succeeded in promoting the use of image search and "best" shot set browsing in addition to text search, as evidenced by 24 novice user sessions addressing 4 TRECVID 2005 topics each. These sessions also served as a within-subjects experiment to test whether an aggressive strategy for hiding previously captured and passed over shots would produce better performance. The Mining interface with such shot suppression did not perform better than the control Plain interface using the TRECVID metric of MAP. However, the Mining strategy appears promising where diversity in answer sets is rewarded, e.g., if finding 3 answer shots from 3 different sources on different reporting days is more important than finding a clump of 3 answer shots temporally adjacent to one another. Also, by relaxing the aggressive restriction of overlooked shots, the Mining strategy can be adjusted to still encourage more diverse exploration by the user, but then to recover suppressed shots that are temporal neighbors to answer shots (as shown in Fig. 3a). Our revised Mining strategy will still suppress overlooked shots during the user interaction period, but then will not ignore the overlooked shots during the auto-filling to the complete (1000) TRECVID answer set, reverting back to the temporal bracketing [5] that has proven useful in the past.

This material was made possible by the NIST assessors and the TRECVID community. It is based on work supported by the Advanced Research and Development Activity (ARDA) under contract number H98230-04-C-0406 and NBCHC040037, and supported by the National Science Foundation under Grant No. IIS-0535056.

References

1. Over, P., Ianeva, T., Kraaij, W., Smeaton, A.F.: TRECVID 2005 An Introduction. TRECVID 2005 Proceedings, http://www-nlpir.nist.gov/projects/trecvid
2. Hauptmann, A.G.: Lessons for the Future from a Decade of Informedia Video Analysis Research. Proc. CIVR (Singapore, July 2005), LNCS 3568: 1-10
3. Christel, M., Conescu, R.: Addressing the Challenge of Visual Information Access from Digital Image and Video Libraries. Proc. ACM/IEEE JCDL (Denver, June 2005), ACM Press, 69-78
4. Christel, M., Moraveji, N.: Finding the Right Shots: Assessing Usability and Performance of a Digital Video Library Interface. Proc. ACM Multimedia (New York, Oct. 2004), ACM Press, 732–739
5. Adcock, J., Cooper, M., Girgensohn, A., Wilcox, L.: Interactive Video Search Using Multilevel Indexing. Proc. CIVR (Singapore, July 2005), LNCS 3568: 205-214
6. Snoek, C., Worring, M., et al.: MediaMill: Exploring News Video Archives based on Learned Semantics. Proc. ACM Multimedia (Singapore, Nov. 2005), ACM Press, 225-226.
7. Hauptmann, A., Christel, M.: Successful Approaches in the TREC Video Retrieval Evaluations. Proc. ACM Multimedia (New York, Oct. 2004), ACM Press, 668-675
8. Nielsen, J.: Heuristic Evaluation. In Nielsen, J., and Mack, R.L. (eds.), Usability Inspection Methods. John Wiley & Sons, New York, NY, 1994
9. Shneiderman, B., Byrd, D., Croft, W.B.: Clarifying Search: A User-Interface Framework for Text Searches. D-Lib Magazine, 3, 1 (January 1997), http://www.dlib.org
10. Kraaij, W., Smeaton, A.F., Over, P., Arlandis, J.: TRECVID 2004 – An Introduction. In TRECVID'04 Proc., http://www-nlpir.nist.gov/projects/tvpubs/tvpapers04/ tv4overview.pdf
11. Yang, M., Wildemuth, B., Marchionini, G.: The Relative Effectiveness of Concept-based Versus Content-based Video Retrieval. Proc. ACM Multimedia 2004, ACM Press 368-371
12. Golovchinsky, G.: Queries? Links? Is there a difference? Proc. CHI '97, ACM Press (1997), 407-414

A Linear-Algebraic Technique with an Application in Semantic Image Retrieval

Jonathon S. Hare[1], Paul H. Lewis[1],
Peter G.B. Enser[2], and Christine J. Sandom[2]

[1] School of Electronics and Computer Science, University of Southampton, UK
{jsh2, phl}@ecs.soton.ac.uk
[2] School of Computing, Mathematical and Information Sciences,
University of Brighton, UK
{p.g.b.enser, c.sandom}@bton.ac.uk

Abstract. This paper presents a novel technique for learning the underlying structure that links visual observations with semantics. The technique, inspired by a text-retrieval technique known as cross-language latent semantic indexing uses linear algebra to learn the semantic structure linking image features and keywords from a training set of annotated images. This structure can then be applied to unannotated images, thus providing the ability to search the unannotated images based on keyword. This *factorisation* approach is shown to perform well, even when using only simple global image features.

1 Introduction

Automatic annotation of images has come to the fore as a means of trying to achieve the integration of content-based and text-based image retrieval. An overview of the techniques which have been used in auto-annotation has been provided by Hare et al [1], and we are currently exploring how such techniques can meet the real needs of image searchers in limited domains. This work is being undertaken within the Bridging the Semantic Gap Project, as described by Enser et al [2].

In this paper, we propose a linear algebraic method for *learning* the semantic structure between terms in an annotated training set of images. Unannotated images can then be projected into the structure. The resulting space is unique in that it allows images to be ranked on their relevance to terms that may not have been explicitly assigned to the images, even though the image is relevant to the term.

2 Using Linear-Algebra to Associate Images and Terms

Latent Semantic Indexing (LSI) [3] is a technique in text-retrieval for indexing documents in a dimensionally-reduced semantic vector space. Landauer and Littman [4], demonstrate a system based on LSI for performing text searching

H. Sundaram et al. (Eds.): CIVR 2006, LNCS 4071, pp. 31–40, 2006.
© Springer-Verlag Berlin Heidelberg 2006

on a set of French and English documents where the queries could be in either French or English (or conceivably both), and the system would return documents in both languages which corresponded to the query. Landauer's system negated the need for explicit translations of all the English documents into French; instead, the system was trained on a set of English documents and versions of the documents translated into French, and through a process called 'folding-in', the remaining English documents were indexed without the need for explicit translations. This idea has become known as *Cross-Language Latent Semantic Indexing* (CL-LSI).

Monay and Gatica-Perez [5] attempted to use straight LSI with simple cross-domain vectors for auto-annotation. They first created a training matrix of cross-domain vectors and applied LSI. By querying the left-hand subspace they were able to rank an un-annotated query document against each annotation term in order to assess likely annotations to apply to the image.

Our approach, based on a generalisation of CL-LSI, is different because we do not explicitly annotate images. The technique works by placing unannotated images in a semantic-space which can be queried by keyword.

In general, any document (be it text, image, or even video) can be described by a series of observations, or measurements, made about its content. We refer to each of these observations as terms. Terms describing a document can be arranged in a vector of term occurrences, i.e. a vector whose i-th element contains a count of the number of times the i-th term occurs in the document. There is nothing stopping a term vector having terms from a number of different modalities. For example a term vector could contain term-occurrence information for both 'visual' terms and textual annotation terms.

Given a corpus of n documents, it is possible to form a matrix of m observations or measurements (i.e. a term-document matrix). This $m \times n$ observation matrix, $\mathbf{O}$, essentially represents a combination of terms and documents, and can be factored into a separate term matrix, $\mathbf{T}$, and document matrix, $\mathbf{D}$:

$$\mathbf{O} = \mathbf{TD} \ . \tag{1}$$

These two matrices can be seen to represent the structure of a semantic-space co-inhabited by both terms and documents. Similar documents and/or terms in this space share similar locations. The advantage of this approach is that it doesn't require *a-priori* knowledge and makes no assumptions of either the relationships between terms or documents. The primary tool in this factorisation is the Singular Value Decomposition. This factorisation approach to decomposing a measurement matrix has been used before in computer vision; for example, in factoring 3D-shape and motion from measurements of tracked 2D points using a technique known as Tomasi-Kanade Factorisation [6].

The technique presented here consists of two steps. In the first step, a fully-observed *training* observation matrix is created and decomposed into separate term and document matrices. For example, the observations may consist of both 'visual' terms and annotations from a set of training images. The second step consists of assembling an observation matrix for the documents which are to be indexed. These documents need not be fully observed; for example, they may consist of only 'visual' terms. Any unobserved terms are represented by zeros. The document-space of this second observation matrix is then created using the term matrix from the first stage as a basis. The idea behind this is that any term-term relationships that were uncovered in the training stage will be applied to the test data, thus giving the test data *pseudo*-values for the unobserved terms. The net result is that we are left with a new document-space which can be searched by any of the terms used in the training set, even if they were not directly observed in the test set.

2.1 Decomposing the Observation Matrix

Following the reasoning of Tomasi and Kanade [6], although modified to fit measurements of terms in documents, we first show how the observation matrix can be decomposed into separate term and document matrices.

Lemma 1 (The rank principle for a noise-free term-document matrix). *Without noise, the observation matrix, $\mathbf{O}$, has a rank at most equal to the number of independent terms or documents observed.*

The rank principle expresses the simple fact that if all of the observed terms are independent, then the rank of the observation matrix would be equal to the number of terms, m. In practice, however, terms are often highly dependent on each other, and the rank is much less than m. Even terms from different modalities may be interdependent; for example a term representing the colour *red*, and the word "Red". This fact is what we intend to exploit.

In reality, the observation term-document matrix is not at all noise free. The observation matrix, $\mathbf{O}$ can be decomposed using SVD into a $m \times r$ matrix $\mathbf{U}$, a $r \times r$ diagonal matrix $\mathbf{\Sigma}$ and a $r \times n$ matrix $\mathbf{V}^T$, $\mathbf{O} = \mathbf{U}\mathbf{\Sigma}\mathbf{V}^T$, such that $\mathbf{U}^T\mathbf{U} = \mathbf{V}\mathbf{V}^T = \mathbf{V}^T\mathbf{V} = \mathcal{I}$, where $\mathcal{I}$ is the identity matrix. Now partitioning the $\mathbf{U}$, $\mathbf{\Sigma}$ and $\mathbf{V}^T$ matrices as follows:

$$\mathbf{U} = \left[\,\mathbf{U}_k | \mathbf{U}_N\,\right] \ \}m, \quad \mathbf{\Sigma} = \left[\begin{array}{c|c} \mathbf{\Sigma}_k & 0 \\ \hline 0 & \mathbf{\Sigma}_N \end{array}\right] \begin{array}{l} \}k \\ \}r-k \end{array}, \quad \mathbf{V}^T = \left[\begin{array}{c} \mathbf{V}_k^T \\ \hline \mathbf{V}_N^T \end{array}\right] \begin{array}{l} \}k \\ \}r-k \end{array}, \tag{2}$$

$$\underbrace{}_{k}\underbrace{}_{r-k} \qquad \underbrace{}_{k}\underbrace{}_{r-k} \qquad \underbrace{}_{n}$$

we have, $\mathbf{U}\mathbf{\Sigma}\mathbf{V}^T = \mathbf{U}_k\mathbf{\Sigma}_k\mathbf{V}_k^T + \mathbf{U}_N\mathbf{\Sigma}_N\mathbf{V}_N^T$.

Assume $\mathbf{O}^*$ is the ideal, *noise-free* observation matrix, with k independent terms. The rank principle implies that the singular values of $\mathbf{O}^*$ are at most k. Since the singular values of $\mathbf{\Sigma}$ are in monotonically decreasing order, $\mathbf{\Sigma}_k$ must contain all of the singular values of $\mathbf{O}^*$. The consequence of this is that $\mathbf{U}_N\mathbf{\Sigma}_N\mathbf{V}_N^T$ must be entirely due to noise, and $\mathbf{U}_k\mathbf{\Sigma}_k\mathbf{V}_k^T$ is the best possible approximation to $\mathbf{O}^*$.

Lemma 2 (The rank principle for a noisy term-document matrix). *All of the information about the terms and documents in $\mathbf{O}$ is encoded in its k largest singular values together with the corresponding left and right eigenvectors.*

We now define the estimated noise-free term matrix, $\hat{\mathbf{T}}$, and document matrix, $\hat{\mathbf{D}}$, to be $\hat{\mathbf{T}} \stackrel{\text{def}}{=} \mathbf{U}_k$, and, $\hat{\mathbf{D}} \stackrel{\text{def}}{=} \boldsymbol{\Sigma}_k \mathbf{V}_k^T$, respectively. From Equation 1, we can write

$$\hat{\mathbf{O}} = \hat{\mathbf{T}}\hat{\mathbf{D}}, \tag{3}$$

where $\hat{\mathbf{O}}$ represents the estimated noise-free observation matrix.

Interpreting the Decomposition. The two vector bases created in the decomposition form an aligned vector-space of terms and documents. The rows of the term matrix create a basis representing a position in the space of each of the observed terms. The columns of the document matrix represent positions of the observed documents in the space. Similar documents and terms share similar locations in the space.

2.2 Using the Terms as a Basis for New Documents

Theorem 1 (Projection of partially observed measurements). *The term-matrix of a decomposed fully-observed measurement matrix can be used to project a partially observed measurement matrix into a document matrix that encapsulates estimates of the unobserved terms.*

Manipulating Equation 3 gives us a method of projecting a partially-observed observation matrix, $\mathbf{P}$ into the basis created by the term matrix, $\hat{\mathbf{T}}$. The underlying assumption is that if we were to project the original fully-observed observation matrix (i.e. $\mathbf{P} = \hat{\mathbf{O}}$), then we should get the same document basis.

$$\mathbf{P} = \hat{\mathbf{T}}\hat{\mathbf{D}}$$
$$\therefore \hat{\mathbf{D}} = \hat{\mathbf{T}}^{-1}\mathbf{P} = \hat{\mathbf{T}}^T\hat{\mathbf{T}}\hat{\mathbf{T}}^{-1}\mathbf{P} = \hat{\mathbf{T}}^T\mathbf{P} \tag{4}$$

Therefore, to project a new partially observed measurement matrix into a basis created from a fully observed training matrix, we need only pre-multiply the new observation matrix by the transpose of the training term matrix. The columns of this new document matrix represent the locations in the semantic space of the documents. In order to query the document set for documents relevant to a term, we just need to rank all of the documents based on their position in the space with respect to the position of the query term in the space. The cosine similarity is a suitable measure for this task.

Thus far, we have ignored the value of k. The rank principle states that k is such that all of the semantic structure of the observation matrix, minus the noise is encoded in the singular values and eigenvectors. k is also the number of independent, un-correlated terms in the observation matrix. In practice, k will vary across data-sets, and so we have to estimate its value empirically.

3   Experimental Results

In this section, we present experiments using real images from both the Washington data-set [7] and the Corel data-set proposed in [8]. Because all of the images in these data-sets have ground truth annotations, it is possible to automatically assess the performance of the retrieval. By splitting the data-sets into a training set and testing set, it is possible to attempt retrieval for each of the keyword terms and mark test images as relevant if they contained the query term in their annotations. Results from this technique are presented against results using the *hard* annotations from the vector-space propagation technique described in [9].

3.1 Experiments with the Washington Data-Set and SIFT 'Visual' Terms

We split the Washington data-set [7] into a training set of 349 images, and a test set of 348 images. Each of the images was indexed using 'visual' terms from quantised local SIFT descriptors about interest points picked from peaks in a difference-of-Gaussian pyramid [9, 10]. The size of the visual vocabulary was fixed to 3000 terms [10].

Choosing a Good Value for k. In order to select a value for k, we need to try and optimise the retrieval. A good statistic of overall retrieval performance is the Mean Average Precision (MAP). Plots of the average precision versus varying values of k for four different queries in the test set are shown in Figure 1. A plot of the MAP over all possible queries in the training set, is shown in Figure 2.

Figure 1 shows that there is a very large amount of variation of average precision across different queries. This is in a large part due to biases in both the training set of images and in the test set. For example, both the training set and test set contain an approximately equal number of images of a football stadium, however, the number of *stadium* images in the training set is quite large in comparison to many of the other queries. The net effect is that the "Stadium" query is particularly well trained. Well trained queries can also result from few training images when the training image is sufficiently visually dissimilar to the other images (i.e. it contains a fairly unique combination of visual terms).

Unfortunately, Figure 2 doesn't show a peak from which to select a good value of k, instead it is asymptotic to a mean average precision of about 0.38. However, given the constraint that we want to choose k such that it is the smallest it can be whilst still giving good retrieval, we chose a value of $k = 100$ for the following experiments.

Overall Retrieval Effectiveness. The overall retrieval effectiveness of the technique is characterised in Figure 3. As can be seen, the factorisation approach outperforms the propagation approach at all values of recall.

The precision-recall curves in Figure 3 don't truly reflect the whole performance of the approach because certain queries are better performing than others. Figure 5 illustrates this by showing the average precision for each of the queries, sorted by decreasing precision. For clarity, only queries yielding an average precision of above 0.5 are shown.

Example: Querying for "Bridge". We now take an example query using the term "Bridge" to investigate the performances of the approaches in more detail.

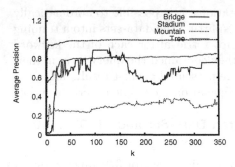

Fig. 1. The effect of k on average precision for four different queries

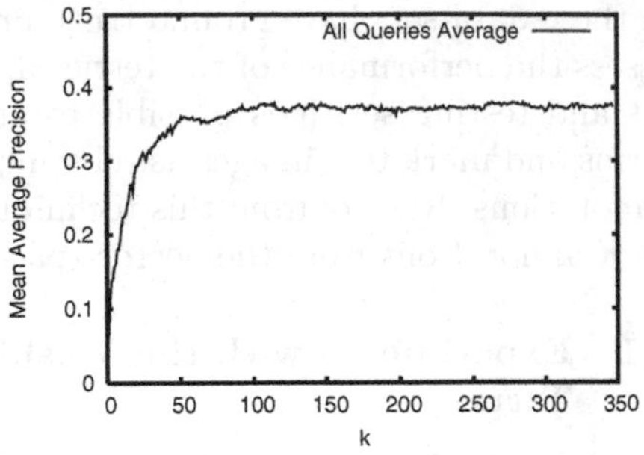

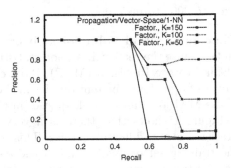

Fig. 2. The effect of k on the Mean-Average Precision over all queries

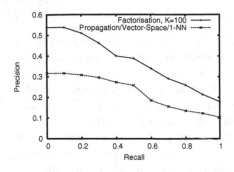

Fig. 3. Average precision-recall curves for the different algorithms over all queries

Fig. 4. Precision-Recall curves for querying with the keyword "Bridge"

There are ten occurrences of the annotation keyword "Bridge" in the Washington data-set. Of these ten occurrences, four images are in the test set and six in the training set. One of the training images has been labelled with "Bridge", although it doesn't actually appear to contain a bridge. This mislabelling of images corresponds to noise, and the algorithms need to be robust to noise within the data-set. The training images are shown in Figure 6. Figure 4 illustrates the effect on precision over different recall values using both the Factorisation algorithm and the vector-space propagation algorithm. Three different values of k for the factorisation algorithm are shown in the figure. The precision recall curves show that both of the algorithms exhibit perfect precision up to recall values of 0.5, but then tend to drop off.

Figure 7 shows the test images containing the "Bridge" keyword, along with the rank-position of the images using the factorisation and propagation techniques. The images were retrieved in the same order by the two algorithms, however, the positions at which they occur varies greatly. The factorisation approach retrieved all four relevant images within the top five images, whilst the propagation approach didn't achieve full recall until 332 images had been retrieved.

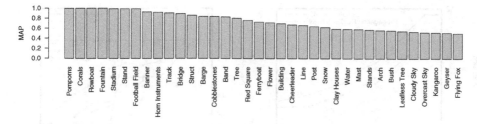

Fig. 5. Average precision of all queries with precision > 0.5, sorted by decreasing precision

Fig. 6. Training images containing the "Bridge" keyword

3.2 The Corel Data-Set

In the previous subsection we proposed using SIFT visual terms to model the image content. However, this is not the only option; the observation matrix could conceivably contain observations of any type of feature. In order to demonstrate the power of the factorisation technique, we use a much simpler feature; a 64-bin global RGB histogram. We use the training set of 4500 images and test set of 500 images from the Corel data-set described in [8].

Following the methodology for optimising k based on MAP described previously, we set $k = 43$. Overall averaged precision-recall curves of the factorisation and propagation approaches are shown in Figure 8. As before, the factorisation approach outperforms the propagation approach. Whilst the overall averaged precision-recall curve doesn't achieve a very high recall and falls off fairly rapidly, this isn't indicative of all the queries; some query terms perform much better than others. Figure 9 shows precision-recall curves for some queries with *good* performance.

Ideally, we would like to be able to perform a direct comparison between our factorisation method and the results of the statistical machine-translation (MT)

Factorisation (k=100)	1	2	3	5
Vector-space Prop. (1NN)	1	2	125	332

Fig. 7. Test Images and the rank-order in which they were retrieved by the two algorithms

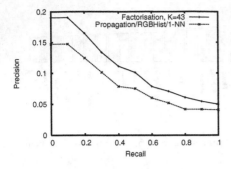 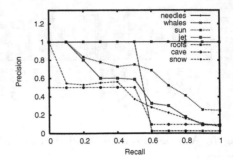

Fig. 8. Average Precision-Recall plots for the Corel data-set using RGB-Histogram descriptors for both the factorisation and propagation algorithms

Fig. 9. Precision-Recall curves for the top seven Corel queries using factorisation $(k = 43)$

model presented by Duygulu et al [8], which has become a benchmark against which many auto-annotation systems have been tested. Duygulu et al present their precision and recall values as single points for each query, based on the number of times the query term was predicted throughout the whole test set. In order to compare results it should be fair to compare the precision of the two methods at the recall given in the MT results. Table 1 summarises the results over the 15 *best* queries found by the MT system (base results), corresponding to recall values greater than 0.4.

Table 1 shows that nine of of the fifteen queries had better precision for the same value of recall with the Factorisation algorithm. This higher precision at

Table 1. Comparison of precision values for equal values of recall between the machine translation model [8] and the factorisation approach

Query Word	Recall	Precision	
		Machine Translation Base Results, th=0	Factorisation, RGB Histogram, K=43
petals	0.50	1.00	0.13
sky	0.83	0.34	0.35
flowers	0.67	0.21	0.26
horses	0.58	0.27	0.24
foals	0.56	0.29	0.17
mare	0.78	0.23	0.19
tree	0.77	0.20	0.24
people	0.74	0.22	0.29
water	0.74	0.24	0.34
sun	0.70	0.28	0.52
bear	0.59	0.20	0.11
stone	0.48	0.18	0.22
buildings	0.48	0.17	0.25
snow	0.48	0.17	0.54

the same recall can be interpreted as saying that more relevant images are retrieved with the factorisation algorithm for the same number of images retrieved as with the machine learning approach. This result even holds for Duygulu et al's slightly improved *retrained* result set. This implies, somewhat surprisingly, that even by just using the rather simple RGB Histogram to form the visual observations, the factorisation approach performs better than the machine translation approach for a number of queries. This, however does say something about the relative simplicity of the Corel dataset [11]. Because not all of the top performing results from the factorisation approach are reflected in the *best* results from the machine translation approach, it follows that the factorisation approach may actually perform better on a majority of *good* queries compared to the machine translation model.

4   Conclusions and Future Work

This paper presented a novel approach to building a semantic space for image retrieval using a linear algebraic factorisation. Performance of the technique is good, even when using a simple global image feature such as the RGB histogram. The approach is exciting because it models the semantic gap between image descriptors and keywords in a flexible way. The factorisation technique does not produce equal performance for all queries. The reasons for this are most likely two-fold; firstly, the visual features used to represent the image may not have been sufficient to represent the keyword. Secondly, the training data may not have been sufficient to learn a good representation for the term. In terms of the Corel data-set using RGB histogram features, the factorisation approach works particularly well with annotations that can be described globally across the image by colour alone. For example, searching for 'sun' returns images with many warm yellow tones, and searching for 'snow' returns images with lots of white colours.

More experimentation needs to be performed to investigate the performance of the factorisation approach. In particular, it would be interesting to use the image descriptors created by [8] to build our observation matrix, and then to directly compare retrieval results with other automatic annotation approaches. It would also be interesting to investigate the scalability of the approach.

In the 'Bridging the semantic gap' project, we aim to test this approach more extensively with picture librarians, in an attempt to establish its ability as a system offering the potential of semantic search.

Acknowledgements

The 'Bridging the semantic gap in information retrieval' project is funded by the Arts and Humanities Research Council (MRG-AN6770/APN17429), whose support is gratefully acknowledged. We are also grateful to the EPSRC and Motorola UK Research Laboratory for their support of parts of this work.

References

[1] Hare, J.S., Lewis, P.H., Enser, P.G.B., Sandom, C.J.: Mind the gap. In Chang, E.Y., Hanjalic, A., Sebe, N., eds.: Multimedia Content Analysis, Management, and Retrieval 2006. Volume 6073., San Jose, California, USA, SPIE (2006) 607309-1–607309-12

[2] Enser, P.G.B., Sandom, C.J., Lewis, P.H.: Surveying the reality of semantic image retrieval. In Bres, S., Laurini, R., eds.: VISUAL 2005. Volume 3736 of LNCS., Amsterdam, Netherlands, Springer (2005) 177–188

[3] Deerwester, S.C., Dumais, S.T., Landauer, T.K., Furnas, G.W., Harshman, R.A.: Indexing by latent semantic analysis. Journal of the American Society of Information Science **41** (1990) 391–407

[4] Landauer, T.K., Littman, M.L.: Fully automatic cross-language document retrieval using latent semantic indexing. In: Proceedings of the Sixth Annual Conference of the UW Centre for the New Oxford English Dictionary and Text Research, Waterloo, Ontario, Canada (1990) 31–38

[5] Monay, F., Gatica-Perez, D.: On image auto-annotation with latent space models. In: MULTIMEDIA '03: Proceedings of the eleventh ACM international conference on Multimedia, ACM Press (2003) 275–278

[6] Tomasi, C., Kanade, T.: Shape and motion from image streams under orthography: a factorization method. IJCV **9** (1992) 137–154

[7] University of Washington: Ground truth image database. http://www.cs.washington.edu/research/imagedatabase/groundtruth/ (2004)

[8] Duygulu, P., Barnard, K., de Freitas, J.F.G., Forsyth, D.A.: Object recognition as machine translation: Learning a lexicon for a fixed image vocabulary. In: ECCV '02: Proceedings of the 7th European Conference on Computer Vision-Part IV, London, UK, Springer-Verlag (2002) 97–112

[9] Hare, J.S., Lewis, P.H.: Saliency-based models of image content and their application to auto-annotation by semantic propagation. In: Proceedings of the Second European Semantic Web Conference (ESWC2005), Heraklion, Crete (2005)

[10] Hare, J.S., Lewis, P.H.: On image retrieval using salient regions with vector-spaces and latent semantics. In Leow, W.K., Lew, M.S., Chua, T.S., Ma, W.Y., Chaisorn, L., Bakker, E.M., eds.: Image and Video Retrieval. Volume 3568 of LNCS., Singapore, Springer (2005) 540–549

[11] Yavlinsky, A., Schofield, E., Rüger, S.: Automated Image Annotation Using Global Features and Robust Nonparametric Density Estimation. In Leow, W.K., Lew, M.S., Chua, T.S., Ma, W.Y., Chaisorn, L., Bakker, E.M., eds.: Image and Video Retrieval. Volume 3568 of LNCS., Singapore, Springer (2005) 507–517

Logistic Regression of Generic Codebooks for Semantic Image Retrieval

João Magalhães and Stefan Rüger

Department of Computing, South Kensington Campus
Imperial College London, London SW7 2AZ, UK
{j.magalhaes, s.rueger}@imperial.ac.uk

Abstract. This paper is about automatically annotating images with keywords in order to be able to retrieve images with text searches. Our approach is to model keywords such as 'mountain' and 'city' in terms of visual features that were extracted from images. In contrast to other algorithms, each specific keyword-model considers not only its own training data but also the whole training set by utilizing correlations of visual features to refine its own model. Initially, the algorithm clusters all visual features extracted from the full imageset, captures its salient structure (e.g. mixture of clusters or patterns) and represents this as a generic codebook. Then keywords that were associated with images in the training set are encoded as a linear combination of patterns from the generic codebook. We evaluate the validity of our approach in an image retrieval scenario with two distinct large datasets of real-world photos and corresponding manual annotations.

1 Introduction

The growing interest in managing multimedia collections effectively and efficiently has created new research interest that arises as a combination of multimedia understanding, information extraction, information retrieval and digital libraries. In this paper we focus on information extraction algorithms that model keywords such as 'sky' and 'beach' in terms of visual features that were extracted from images. These models return the probability of a keyword being present in new unseen images and thus enabling text searches on collections of images.

Most of the existing approaches just model the visual features of images containing a given keyword ignoring the presence of other keywords in the same image and their cross-interference. Some keywords such as 'bird' or 'plane' have a visual representation too complex to be captured by just its training data: the presence of different concepts and their cross-interference increases the uncertainty of the extracted information. For example, concepts such as 'sun', 'outdoor' or 'indoor' may be easy to detect but concepts such as 'bird', 'boat' or 'insect' may be more reliably detected if other, more basic and correlated concepts were detected previously.

Thus, we advocate that one should first detect the most salient low-level visual patterns of the full image dataset in the feature space and then learn the causality relation between these low-level visual pattern co-occurrences and the keywords. To achieve

H. Sundaram et al. (Eds.): CIVR 2006, LNCS 4071, pp. 41–50, 2006.
© Springer-Verlag Berlin Heidelberg 2006

this goal, we formulate the following hypothesis: *"Given a common generic codebook of patterns (codewords) of the full imageset, the keywords can be encoded as a low-complexity linear combination of codewords and exhibit a competitive retrieval performance"*. With this hypothesis we aim to achieve a fast, simple, scalable algorithm capable of annotating images with keywords at high precision. The codebook lists the low-level visual patterns of the full image dataset and its contents will be interchangeably referred to as patterns, clusters or codewords.

Section 2 describes related work on image-semantic annotation, Section 3 the proposed algorithm, Section 4 presents the experiments and results, and Section 5 discusses the generic codebook generation and the algorithm characteristics.

2   Related Work

Several algorithms have been proposed to extract semantic information from multimedia content. Single-class-model approaches estimate an individual distribution function for each keyword. Other types of approaches are based on a translation model between keywords and images features (global, tiles or regions). These two groups of approaches assume a minimal relation between the various elements of the same image (words, blobs, tiles). Hierarchical models consider the hierarchical relation or the inter-dependence relation between the elements of an image (words and blobs or tiles) and reflect it in the statistical model.

Single-class-models are a straight-forward approach to the semantic analysis of multimedia content. The idea behind is to learn a class-conditional probability distribution of each single keyword w of the semantic vocabulary given its training data x. Bayes law is used to invert the problem and model $p(x \mid w)$ the features data density distribution of a given keyword. Several techniques to model the $p(x \mid w)$ with a simple density distribution have been proposed: Yavlinsky et al. [1] deployed a non-parametric distribution; Carneiro and Vasconcelos [2] a semi-parametric density estimation; Westerveld and de Vries [3] a finite-mixture of Gaussians; while Mori et al. [4], and Vailaya et al. [5] apply different flavours of vector quantization techniques. This type of approach only considers the class's own data ignoring the co-occurrence of classes, while the present approach takes that into consideration.

Other types of approaches are based on a translation model between keywords and images (global, tiles or regions). Inspired by machine translation research, Duygulu et al. [6] developed a method of annotating image regions with words. First, regions are created using a segmentation algorithm like normalized cuts. For each region, features are computed and then blobs are generated by clustering the image features for these regions across an image collection. The problem is then formulated as learning the correspondence between the discrete vocabulary of blobs and the image keywords. Following a translation model Jeon et al. [7], Lavrenko et al. [8] and Feng et al. [9] studied a model where blob features $b_I^{(r)}$ of an image I are conditionally independent of keywords w_i. Jeon et al. [7] recast the image annotation as a cross-lingual information retrieval problem applying a cross-media relevance model based on a discrete codebook of regions. Lavrenko et al. [8] continued previous work by Jeon et al. [7]

and described the process of generating blob features with continuous probability density functions $P(b_I^{(r)} \mid J)$ to avoid the loss of information related to the generation of the codebook. Prolonging their previous work Feng et al. [9] replace blobs with tiles and model image keywords with a Bernoulli distribution. These methods have the mathematical form of kernel density estimation – the model corresponds to the entire training data – making them computationally very demanding: in contrast our model uses a linear combination of a common codebook for all classes, which is by its very nature computationally much simpler.

In the hierarchical models group Barnard and Forsyth [10] studied a generative hierarchical aspect model, inspired by a hierarchical clustering/aspect model. The data are assumed to be generated by a fixed hierarchy of nodes with the leaves of the hierarchy corresponding to soft clusters. Blei and Jordan [11] describe three hierarchical mixture models to annotate image data, culminating in the correspondence latent Dirichlet allocation model. This model specifies a Bayesian model for capturing the relations between regions, words and latent variables. It combines the advantages of probabilistic clustering for dimensionality reduction with an explicit model of the conditional distribution from which image keywords are generated. In our approach we do not create a fixed hierarchy of nodes/clusters that decreases the flexibility of the method.

3 Algorithm Description

The dataset is composed of a training set and a test set of images, and each image is manually annotated with a vocabulary of keywords corresponding to the visual content of that particular image. The image dataset is initially processed to extract a set of low-level visual features from all images. Once the low-level visual features and the manual annotations are loaded the features are further processed.

The generic codebook is produced with an unsupervised learning algorithm that returns a finite mixture of clusters modelling the full dataset feature space. The set of clusters of the finite mixture is then stored in the generic codebook as K codewords, each of which is defined by a set of parameters θ_k. The notation for the probability of a codeword k for an image i, $q(x^{(i)} \mid \theta_k)$, will be abbreviated as $q_k(x^{(i)})$.

Only in the final step of the algorithm are the annotations used to learn the keyword-model of each keyword w_t, i.e., the weight $\beta_k^{w_t}$ of each codeword θ_k. The model $p(w_t \mid x)$ expresses the probability of a word w_t given the low-level visual features x of an unseen image. This model is defined as a generalized linear model:

$$g\left(E\left[w_t \mid x^{(i)}\right]\right) = \beta_0^{w_t} + \beta_1^{w_t} q_1\left(x_1^{(i)}\right) + \ldots + \beta_K^{w_t} q_K\left(x_K^{(i)}\right), \tag{1}$$

where the link function $g(\cdot)$ allows to model non-linear relations between and the features $x^{(i)} = \left[1, x_1^{(i)}, \ldots, x_K^{(i)}\right]$, or a transformation of it e.g. $q_n(x_n)$, and the $E[w_t \mid X]$. Typical link functions are the identity function for normal linear regression, the *logit* function for logistic regression and the *log* function for log-linear regression. In this paper we consider the logistic regression model.

3.1 Features Processing

The feature processing step normalises the features and creates smaller-dimensional subspaces from the original feature-spaces. Three different low-level features are used in our implementation: **marginal HSV distribution moments**, a 12 dimensional colour **feature** that captures the histogram of 4 central moments of each colour component distribution; **Gabor texture**, a 16 dimensional texture feature that captures the frequency response (mean and variance) of a bank of filters at different scales and orientations; and **Tamura texture**, a 3 dimensional texture feature composed by measures of image's coarseness, contrast and directionality. We used $N=15$ feature sub-spaces. As a common practice we tiled the images in 3 by 3 parts before extracting the low-level features. This has two advantages: it adds some locality information and it greatly increases the amount of data used to learn the generic codebook.

3.2 Learning the Generic Codebook

In the algorithm's second step, the features subspace clustering is done under the assumption that the subspaces are independent. That is, each feature subspace n is processed individually and modelled as a Gaussian mixture model (GMM)

$$p\left(x \mid \theta_n\right) = \sum_{m=1}^{M_n} \alpha_{n,m} p\left(x \mid \mu_{n,m}, \sigma_{n,m}^2\right), \tag{2}$$

where M_n is the number of Gaussians (clusters) in feature subspace n, x is the low-level visual feature, and θ_n represents the complete set of model parameters with mean $\mu_{n,m}$, covariance $\sigma_{n,m}^2$, and component prior $\alpha_{n,m}$. The components priors have the convexity constraint $\alpha_{n,1},...,\alpha_{n,m} \geq 0$ and $\sum_{m=1}^{M_n} \alpha_{n,m} = 1$. We implemented the mixture learning algorithm as proposed by Figueiredo et al. in [12] in C++. Each codeword $q\left(\cdot \mid \theta_k\right)$ correspond to a certain cluster $p\left(x \mid \theta_{n,m}\right)$.

The algorithm starts with a number of clusters that is much larger than the real number and gradually eliminates the clusters that start to get few support data (singularities). This avoids the initialization problem of EM since the algorithm only produce mixtures with clusters that have enough support data. This strategy can cause a problem when the initial number of clusters is too large: no cluster receives enough initial support causing the deletion of all clusters. To avoid this situation, cluster parameters are updated sequentially and not simultaneously as in standard EM. That is: first update cluster 1 parameters $\left(\mu_1, \sigma_1^2\right)$, then recompute all posteriors, update cluster 2 parameters $\left(\mu_2, \sigma_2^2\right)$, recompute all posteriors, and so on.

After finding a good fit for a GMM with k clusters, the algorithm deletes the weakest cluster and restarts itself with $k-1$ Gaussians and repeats the process until a minimum number of clusters is reached. Each fitted GMM is stored and in the end the set of fitted models describe the feature subspace at different levels of granularities. We can then consider generic codebooks with different levels of complexities.

3.3 Learning Keyword-Models: A Logistic Model

As mentioned before, we cast the keyword-models as a generalized linear model. The codebook of clusters modelled the features sub-spaces with great detail so that it can be used now as smoothing functions on the logistic model. The link function $g(x) = \text{logit}(p) = \log\big(p/(1-p)\big)$ defines the log-posterior odds between positive examples and negative examples of a keyword as a linear combination of the codebook output:

$$\text{logit}(E[w_t \mid x]) = \beta_0^{w_t} + \beta_1^{w_t} q_1(x_1) + \ldots + \beta_K^{w_t} q_K(x_K). \tag{3}$$

Assuming a matrix notation we define the codebook and the parameters as $Q(x) = [1, q_1(x_1), \ldots, q_K(x_K)]$ and $\beta^{w_t} = [\beta_0^{w_t}, \beta_1^{w_t}, \ldots, \beta_K^{w_t}]$, respectively. This allows writing the logistic model as:

$$p(w_t \mid x) = \frac{1}{1 + e^{\beta^{w_t} Q(x)}}. \tag{4}$$

We implemented the binomial logistic regression model where one class is always modelled relatively to all other classes. With this choice we achieve some independence between keywords because they only depend on their own β^{w_t}: once the codebook is computed, it is the same for all classes and only the β^{w_t} weights are specific of each class. A second reason for choosing the binomial approach is due to the complexity of the algorithms for fitting multinomial models and their requirements. We tested several methods to compute the β^{w_t} weights, and discuss two of the methods.

3.3.1 Parameter Estimation Using L-BFGS

The only variables we now need to compute using the annotations are the priors β^{w_t} which can be computed by minimizing the log-likelihood of the above model over the entire data set:

$$\beta^{w_t} = \arg\max_{\beta^{w_t}} \sum_{i \in I} l(\beta^{w_t}), \tag{5}$$

where $l(\beta)$ is the log-likelihood function, and I is the entire training set. We used a Gaussian prior with σ^2 variance to prevent the optimization procedure from overfitting. Thus the log-likelihood function for a binomial logistic model becomes:

$$l(\beta) = \sum_{i \in I}\left\{ y_{w_t}^{(i)} \beta^T Q(x^{(i)}) - \log\big(1 + e^{\beta^T Q(x^{(i)})}\big)\right\} - \frac{\beta^T \beta}{2\sigma^2}, \tag{6}$$

where $y_{w_t}^{(i)}$ is 1 if the image i has the keyword w_t and 0 otherwise, $x^{(i)}$ is the low-level visual features of the image i. To maximize the log-likelihood of each keyword model, we set its gradient to zero and proceed with a Quasi-Newton optimization algorithm:

$$\frac{\partial l(\beta)}{\partial \beta} = \sum_{i \in I} Q(x^{(i)})\big(y_{w_t}^{(i)} - p(w_t \mid x^{(i)}, \beta)\big) - \frac{\beta}{\sigma^2} = 0. \tag{7}$$

Because the dataset is quite large and the codebook might hold up to 10000 codewords, algorithms that depend on the computation of the Hessian would require too much memory. It has been shown that for this type of models the limited-memory BFGS algorithm [13] is the best solution. We use the implementation provided by Liu and Nocedal [13].

3.3.2 Parameter Estimation Using Codewords Log-Odds

A simpler and computationally less demanding algorithm is based on the codewords's log-odds. Since we have a fixed codebook with predefined parameters θ_k we estimate the $\beta_k^{w_j}$ weights individually as the corresponding codeword log-odds. The prior of each codeword is then given by the logarithm of the proportion of positive versus negative examples:

$$\beta_k^{w_t} = \log \frac{E[q_k \mid w = w_t]}{1 - E[q_k \mid w = w_t]} = \log \frac{E[q_k \mid w = w_t]}{E[q_k \mid w \neq w_t]}. \tag{8}$$

The expected values of the above expressions are:

$$E[q_k \mid w] = \frac{1}{|I_w|} \sum_{i \in I_w} q_k \left(x_k^{(i)} \right), \tag{9}$$

where the set $i \in I_w$ represents the set of images annotated with the keyword w, and $x_k^{(i)}$ is the low-level visual feature k of the image i. The interpretation of Equation (8) is straightforward: if the codeword is more relevant for negative examples the proportion will be < 1 and thus its log will be negative, if the codeword is more relevant for positive examples the proportion will be > 1 and thus its log will be also positive. This way, when evaluating unseen samples each codeword will have a low or high contribution to the overall model probability.

4 Experiments and Results

The algorithm was tested with a subset of the COREL Stock Photo CDs [6] and a subset of Getty Images [1] in a typical information retrieval scenario to evaluate its mean average precision. We conducted an evaluation of our model with a view to study the influence of the granularity of the generic codebook.

COREL Dataset. This dataset was compiled by Duygulu et al. [6] from a set of COREL Stock Photo CDs. The dataset has some visually similar concepts (jet, plane, Boeing), and some concepts have a limited number examples (10 or less). In their seminal paper, the authors acknowledge that fact and ignored the classes with these problems. In this paper we use the same setup as in [1], [2], [7], [8] and [9], which differs slightly from the one used in the dataset original paper, [6]. The retrieval evaluation scenario consists of a training set of 4500 images and a test set of 500 images. Each image is annotated with 1-5 keywords from a vocabulary of 371 keywords. Only keywords with at least 2 images in the test set were evaluated which reduced the number of vocabulary to 179 keywords. Retrieval lists have the same length as the test set, i.e. 500 items.

Fig. 1 depicts the evolution of the mean average precision with the complexity of the generic codebook. On the test set the maximum achieved MAP was 27.7% with an average codebook complexity of 45 clusters per feature per tile – note that these clusters are common to all keywords. The different codebook sizes reflect the different levels of model granularities of the features-subspaces. The different granularities are based on model complexity (number of parameters) of each feature subspace (other criteria could have been used such as likelihood or MDL).

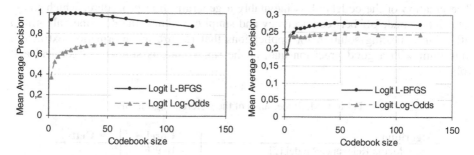

Fig. 1. Evolution of the MAP vs codewords per feature per tile for the Corel collection on the training (left) and on the test set (right)

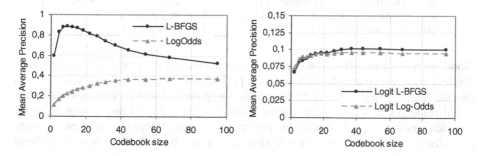

Fig. 2. Evolution of the MAP vs codewords per feature per tile for the Getty-Images collection on the training (left) and on the test set (right)

Getty Images Dataset. This dataset compiled by Yavlinsky et al. [1] is a selection of photographs retrieved by submitting queries with a given selection that result in a random selection of photos, which excludes any non-photographic content, any digitally composed or enhanced photos and any photos taken in unrealistic studio settings. The resulting dataset contains pictures from a number of different photo vendors, which reduces the chance of unrealistic correlations between keywords and image contents. Keywords for Getty images can express subjects (e.g. 'tiger'), concepts (e.g. 'emptiness') or styles (e.g. 'panoramic photograph').

The retrieval evaluation scenario consisted in a training set of 5000 images and a test set of 2560 images. Only keywords with at least 2 images in the test set were evaluated which results in a vocabulary of 184 keywords. Retrieval lists have the same length as the test set, 2560 items. We use the same setup as in [1].

Fig. 2 depicts the evolution of the mean average precision with the different complexities of the generic codebook. On the test set, the maximum achieved MAP was 10.2% with an average codebook complexity of 36 clusters per feature per tile – note that these clusters are common to all keywords.

5 Discussion

The creation of the codebook is inevitably a generalization procedure, which translates into a trade-off between accuracy and simplicity. Thus, the described algorithm offers an appealing solution for applications that require an information extraction algorithm with a good precision that, at the same time, is simple, economical and robust.

Table 1. MAP measures of the different algorithms

Algorithm	Corel	Getty
Cross-Media Relevance Model [7]	16.9%	-
Continuous-space Relevance Model [8]	23.5%	-
Logistic regression (Log-Odds)	**24.6%**	**9.6%**
Logistic regression (L-BFGS)	**27.7%**	**10.2%**
Nonparametric Density Distribution [1]	28.6%	9.2%
Multiple-Bernoulli Relevance Model [9]	30.0%	-
Mixture of Hierarchies [2]	31.0%	-

Good retrieval precision. The retrieval performance of our approach is competitive: Table 1 compares our algorithm retrieval performance against others. Note that our method uses a simple set of features, a basic tiling method and requires less computational resources than any other method (both in terms of CPU and memory), and it still delivers a competitive retrieval performance. The differences in mean average precision between these two datasets show that Getty dataset is much more difficult than Corel dataset.

Inference scalability. Since the generic codebook is common to all keywords the clusters must be computed only once for all keywords. Thus, the resources required to evaluate the relevancy of an image for each keywords are relatively modest. Apart from the mixture of hierarchies [2] all other methods are some sort of nonparametric density distributions. It is well known [14] that the nonparametric nature of these methods makes the task of running these models on new data computationally demanding: the model corresponds to the entire training set meaning that the demand on CPU time and memory increases with the training data. To infer all the keywords with our best model requires only 36 to 45 clusters per feature-subspace per tile, while method [9] requires 1 Gaussian kernel per tile (24 tiles) per training image (4000). For example, to evaluate all 179 keywords of the Corel dataset our model needs to compute $36 \times 15 \times 9 = 4,860$ Gaussians plus a linear combination for each keyword, while method [9] needs to compute $4000 \times 24 = 96,000$ Gaussian kernels plus a linear combination for each keyword.

Keywords scalability. Assuming that the used set of keywords is a faithful sample of a larger keyword vocabulary it is expected that one can use the same codebook to learn the logistic model of new random keywords and preserve the same retrieval performance. Note that the codebook is a representation of the data feature space: it is selected based on the set keywords.

Little overfitting. The MAP curve on the test set remains quite stable as the common model complexity increases depicting the algorithm's immunity to overfitting. Our model can be interpreted as ensemble methods (additive models) if we consider that each cluster is a weak learner and the final model a linear combination of those weak learners. This means that our model has some of the characteristics of additive models namely the observed immunity to overfitting. It is interesting to note that the simple log-odds estimation of the parameters appears more immune to overfitting than the l-bfgs algorithm. This fact occurs because the optimization procedure fits the model tightly to the training data (favouring large $\beta_k^{w_t}$), while the log-odds estimation avoids overfitting by computing weighted average the expected value of all codewords. Note that when fitting the model we are minimizing a measure of the average classification residual error (model log-likelihood) and not a measure of how documents are ranked in a list (Mean Average Precision). The mean average precision is the mean of the accumulated precision over a ranked list. This contributes to the large difference between the training set MAP and the test set MAP. To the best of our knowledge there are no published results assessing the training set MAP versus the test set MAP at different model complexities and therefore we cannot compare our results with others.

6   Conclusions

This paper's novelty resides in the simplicity of the linear combination of a generic visual vocabulary for image retrieval and the keyword's parameters estimation process: the results show that such a low complexity approach compares competitively with much more complex approaches. This has a bearing on the design of image search engines, where scalability and response time is as much of a factor as the actual mean average precision of the returned results. It is also important to stress the little-overfitting exhibited by the algorithm.

Our aim was to explore the most salient low-level visual patterns of the full dataset feature space and learn the causality relation between these patterns' co-occurrence and the keywords. To achieve this goal, we formulated a hypothesis: *"Given a common generic codebook of patterns (codewords) of the full imageset, the keywords can be encoded as a low-complexity linear combination of codewords and exhibit a competitive retrieval performance"*. The evaluation results allow us to conclude that the initial hypothesis is valid.

Acknowledgements. We thank Alexei Yavlinsky for having provided us with the Getty Images dataset low-level visual features and its annotations. This work was partially funded by the Portuguese Foundation for Science and Technology.

References

[1] A. Yavlinsky, E. Schofield, and S. Rüger, "Automated image annotation using global features and robust nonparametric density estimation," Int'l Conference on Image and Video Retrieval, Singapore, 2005.

[2] G. Carneiro and N. Vasconcelos, "Formulating semantic image annotation as a supervised learning problem," IEEE Conference on Computer Vision and Pattern Recognition, San Diego, CA, USA, 2005.

[3] T. Westerveld and A. P. de Vries, "Experimental result analysis for a generative probabilistic image retrieval model," ACM SIGIR Conference on research and development in information retrieval, Toronto, Canada, 2003.

[4] Y. Mori, H. Takahashi, and R. Oka, "Image-to-word transformation based on dividing and vector quantizing images with words," Int'l Workshop on Multimedia Intelligent Storage and Retrieval Management, Orlando, FL, USA, 1999.

[5] A. Vailaya, M. Figueiredo, A. K. Jain, and H. J. Zhang, "Image classification for content-based indexing," *IEEE Transactions on Image Processing*, vol. 10, pp. 117-130, 2001.

[6] P. Duygulu, K. Barnard, N. de Freitas, and D. Forsyth, "Object recognition as machine translation: Learning a lexicon for a fixed image vocabulary," European Conference on Computer Vision, Copenhagen, Denmark, 2002.

[7] J. Jeon, V. Lavrenko, and R. Manmatha, "Automatic image annotation and retrieval using cross-media relevance models," ACM SIGIR Conference on research and development in information retrieval, Toronto, Canada, 2003.

[8] V. Lavrenko, R. Manmatha, and J. Jeon, "A model for learning the semantics of pictures," Neural Information Processing System Conference, Vancouver, Canada, 2003.

[9] S. L. Feng, V. Lavrenko, and R. Manmatha, "Multiple Bernoulli relevance models for image and video annotation," IEEE Conference on Computer Vision and Pattern Recognition, Cambridge, UK, 2004.

[10] K. Barnard and D. A. Forsyth, "Learning the semantics of words and pictures," Int'l Conference on Computer Vision, Vancouver, Canada, 2001.

[11] D. Blei and M. Jordan, "Modeling annotated data," ACM SIGIR Conference on research and development in information retrieval, Toronto, Canada, 2003.

[12] M. Figueiredo and A. K. Jain, "Unsupervised learning of finite mixture models," *IEEE Transactions on Pattern Analysis and Machine Intelligence*, vol. 24, pp. 381-396, 2002.

[13] D. C. Liu and J. Nocedal, "On the limited memory method for large scale optimization," *Mathematical Programming B*, vol. 45, pp. 503-528, 1989.

[14] T. Hastie, R. Tibshirani, and J. Friedman, *The elements of statistical learning: Data mining, inference and prediction*: Springer, 2001.

Query by Semantic Example

Nikhil Rasiwasia[1], Nuno Vasconcelos[1], and Pedro J. Moreno[2]

[1] Statistical Visual Computing Lab,
University of California, San Diego
nikux@ucsd.edu, nuno@ece.ucsd.edu
[2] Google, Inc. 1440 Broadway, 21st Floor New York, NY USA
pedro@google.com

Abstract. A solution to the problem of image retrieval based on query-by-semantic-example (QBSE) is presented. QBSE extends the idea of query-by-example to the domain of semantic image representations. A semantic vocabulary is first defined, and a semantic retrieval system is trained to label each image with the posterior probability of appearance of each concept in the vocabulary. The resulting vector is interpreted as the projection of the image onto a semantic probability simplex, where a suitable similarity function is defined. Queries are specified by example images, which are projected onto the probability simplex. The database images whose projections on the simplex are closer to that of the query are declared its closest neighbors. Experimental evaluation indicates that 1) QBSE significantly outperforms the traditional query-by-visual-example paradigm when the concepts in the query image are known to the retrieval system, and 2) has equivalent performance even in the worst case scenario of queries composed by unknown concepts.

1 Introduction

Content-based image retrieval (CBIR), has been the subject of a significant amount of computer vision research in the recent past [6]. Two main retrieval paradigms have evolved over the years: one based on visual queries, here referred to as *query-by-visual-example* (QBVE), and the other based on text, here denoted as *semantic retrieval*. Under the QBVE paradigm, each image is decomposed into a number of low-level visual features (e.g. a color histogram) and image retrieval is formulated as the search for the best database match to the feature vector extracted from a user-provided query image. It is, however, well known that strict visual similarity is, in most cases, weakly correlated with the measures of similarity adopted by humans for image comparison. This motivated the more ambitious goal of designing retrieval systems with support for semantic queries [4]. The basic idea is to annotate images with semantic keywords, enabling users to specify their queries through a natural language description of the visual concepts. Because manual image labeling is a labor intensive process, the goal of semantic retrieval generated significant interest in the problem of the automatic extraction of semantic descriptors, by the application of machine learning algorithms. Early efforts targeted the extraction of specific semantics,

H. Sundaram et al. (Eds.): CIVR 2006, LNCS 4071, pp. 51–60, 2006.
© Springer-Verlag Berlin Heidelberg 2006

more recently there has been an effort to solve the problem in greater generality, through techniques capable of learning relatively large semantic vocabularies from informally annotated training image collections with resort to unsupervised [1,2,5] and weakly supervised learning [9].

When compared to QBVE, semantic retrieval has the advantages of 1) image similarity at a higher level of abstraction, and 2) support for the natural language queries. However, the performance of semantic retrieval systems tends to degrade for semantic classes that were not identified as potentially interesting during training, and can lead to less intuitive interaction with retrieval systems (especially during query refinement) than QBVE. In this work, we show that it is possible to combine the advantages of the two formulations by extending the query-by-example paradigm to the semantic domain. We refer to the combination of the two paradigms as query-by-semantic-example (QBSE), and compare its performance to QBVE. Our results indicate that QBSE can perform significantly better for queries composed of concepts known to the semantic retrieval system, and achieves equivalent performance in the worst case scenario of queries composed by concepts outside of the semantic vocabulary.

2 Motivation

2.1 Generalization

In terms of generalization, the performance of QBVE and semantic retrieval systems can be quite distinct. On one hand, natural language queries enable a much higher level of *query abstraction*, and therefore exhibit much better generalization along *the dimension of image similarity*. For example, a query for "sky" will return scenes of both daytime (where sky is mostly blue) and sunsets (where sky tends to be orange) with equal ease. QBVE can be quite limited in this respect, since most concepts of interest exhibit a great diversity of visual appearance. It is usually quite difficult to design a set of visual features that captures all the relevant dimensions of image variability (e.g. that sky can be both blue or orange). On the other hand, semantic retrieval can be quite brittle, due to the need to pre-learn appearance models for all visual concepts of interest [8]. Learning large vocabularies is a difficult task, which requires large corpuses of manually labeled data that are usually not available. In result, it is not uncommon to find scenes for which the most obvious semantic classes are not even defined in the supported semantic vocabulary. For these queries, the performance of semantic retrieval systems can degrade quite dramatically. Other problems include the fact that many scenes do not have a unique interpretation[1] (e.g. a picture of a lake may evoke the "fishing" descriptor for fishing aficionados, the "wind-surfing" label for fans of this sport, and the simple "lake" characterization for most other users), and the fact that it is possible to miss images that use different synonyms in their descriptions (e.g. when faced with a query for "sea", the retrieval system must assign a non-zero relevance to classes

---

[1] It is commonly said that "a picture is worth a thousand words".

such as "ocean", "shore", "waves", "coast", or "beach"). None of these problems affect QBVE, which places very few constraints on the supported queries and, therefore, generalizes much better along the *dimension of query diversity*.

2.2   User Interaction

A second metric of retrieval system performance where QBVE and semantic retrieval differ significantly, is that of user-interaction. Natural language queries are the easiest form of *query specification* for most naive users. By definition, QBVE requires an example similar to the desired image, which is typically not easy to find. Furthermore, due to the different measures of similarity implemented by users and retrieval system, there can be a significant difference in the retrieval efficiency achieved by power and naive users. Successful interaction with a QBVE system typically requires some ability, by the user, to "think" in terms of low-level properties such as color or texture. On the other hand, QBVE systems tend to enable a more intuitive *user interaction*. This is particularly true when the desired image is not immediately found, and there is a need for *query refinement*. The refinement of a natural language query is usually not trivial, and can be particularly challenging when the supported semantic vocabulary is small. In QBVE systems, interaction proceeds by 1) visual inspection of the top results to the current query and 2) selection of a number of examples for the subsequent query. This builds on the ability of the human visual system to quickly scan through a screen of images and select those that are most like the image of interest. Furthermore, assuming that the database is large enough, there is never a shortage of subsequent examples with which to refine the query.

2.3   Query by Semantic Example

From the discussion above, it follows that QBVE and semantic retrieval are, in many respects, *complementary*. While semantic retrieval generalizes better along the dimension of image similarity, QBVE supports a much broader query diversity. While the former enables easier query specification, the latter allows more intuitive interaction. In fact, the advantages of each paradigm are not mutually exclusive: *while those of semantic retrieval are indisputably connected to the semantic representation, the limitations of this paradigm are mostly due to the desire for an unambiguous query specification, as a short natural language description.* Let us assume, for an instant, that instead of a few keywords, 1) the user specifies the query as *a vector of weights for all the keywords in the semantic vocabulary* supported by the retrieval system, and 2) each weight represents the *relevance, to the query, of the associated keyword.*

Clearly, because the representation is still of semantic level, none of the advantages of semantic retrieval are compromised. On the other hand, most of its limitations are eliminated. First, synonyms are no longer a problem, since all the semantic classes that could be relevant receive a non-zero weight. Second, even if the semantic class of interest is not part of the semantic vocabulary, there may still be various semantic concepts that are relevant for the query. For example, "fishing" images are likely to be returned in response to a query composed of fishing-related terms, e.g. "lake", "boats", "nets", "water", and "people", even if an appearance model for the fishing class has never been explicitly learned. Finally, it may suffice to specify the weights qualitatively, by *equating the relevance weights with the probability of the concept appearing in the desired image* Given that concepts of small weight will penalize potential false-positives (e.g. a zero weight for "beach" scenes will filter out a large number of possible false-positives for the "fishing" query), it may not be necessary to specify the concept probabilities with great accuracy.

2.4   Implementation

It is obviously not feasible to ask a user to explicitly provide all the probabilities required to make this type of query practical. The user can, nevertheless, provide these probabilities *indirectly*, through the adoption of the query-by-example paradigm. The basic idea is to, as in QBVE systems, let users specify the query in visual terms, by providing query images. These images are then classified by the semantic retrieval system which returns a vector of probabilities, where each component is the posterior probability of a semantic concept satisfying the query. This probability vector is then compared to the set of similar probability vectors previously computed for each of the images in the database, in the standard query-by-example fashion. Note that, because from the user point of view the interaction really occurs at the visual level, this shares all the user-interaction advantages of QBVE. In fact, the combination of query by example with the semantic representation even allows a combination of the interaction modes, e.g. user starts with a traditional natural language query and switches to QBSE for query refinement.

An interesting interpretation QBSE, is that of *query-by-example on a semantic feature space*. The space is the simplex of posterior concept probabilities, and each image is represented as a point in this simplex, as illustrated by Fig. 1 a). Image similarity is measured by evaluating distances in this space. When the user selects a query image, the computation of the posterior probabilities for that image can be seen as a (highly non-linear) *projection* of the image into this semantic space. Each probability can be thought of as a *semantic feature*. Features (semantic concepts) that are not part of the semantic vocabulary define directions that are orthogonal to the semantic space. While it is impossible to recover their values exactly, they can still be approximated by their closest projection in the space. The traditional specification of the query by a short natural language description can also be mapped to the space: it is equivalent to the adoption of a binary probability vector where a few concepts are assigned non-zero posterior probabilities and all other probabilities are set to zero. This restricts the area populated by the images to the sides, and most frequently the corners, of the simplex, as illustrated by Figure 1 b). Under QBSE, images can be projected onto the entire simplex, enabling a much richer representation.

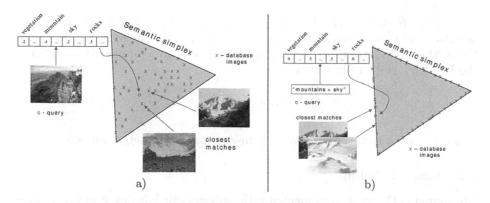

Fig. 1. Semantic image retrieval. a) Under QBSE the user provides a query image, posterior probabilities (given the image) are computed for all concepts, and the image represented by the concept probability distribution. b) Under the traditional semantic retrieval paradigm, the user specifies a short natural language description, and only a small number of concepts are assigned a non-zero posterior probability.

3 Query by Semantic Example

3.1 Definitions

The starting point for the design of a QBSE retrieval system is the combination of an image database $\mathcal{I} = \{\mathcal{I}_1, \ldots, \mathcal{I}_D\}$ and a vocabulary $\mathcal{L} = \{w_1, \ldots, w_L\}$ of semantic labels or keywords w_i. All database images are annotated with a caption composed of words from $\mathcal{L}$, i.e the caption $\mathbf{c}_i$ that (in the judgment of a human labeler) best describes image I_i is available for all i. Note that $\mathbf{c}_i$ is a binary L-dimensional vector such that $\mathbf{c}_{i,j} = 1$ if the ith image was annotated with the jth keyword in $\mathcal{L}$. The training set $\mathcal{D} = \{(\mathcal{I}_1, \mathbf{c}_1), \ldots, (\mathcal{I}_D, \mathbf{c}_D)\}$ of image-caption pairs is said to be weakly labeled if the absence of a keyword from caption $\mathbf{c}_i$ does not necessarily mean that the associated concept is not present in $\mathcal{I}_i$. This is usually the case in practical scenarios, since each image is likely to be annotated with a small caption that only identifies the semantics deemed as most relevant to the labeler. We assume weak labeling in the remainder of this work.

The design of a QBSE retrieval systems requires two main components. The first is a semantic image labeling system that, given a novel image $\mathcal{I}$, produces a vector of posterior probabilities $\pi = (\pi_1, \ldots, \pi_L)^T$ for the concepts in $\mathcal{L}$. This can be seen as a feature transformation, from the space of image measurements $\mathcal{X}$ to the L-dimensional probability simplex $\mathcal{S}_L$, i.e. a mapping $\mathbf{\Pi} : \mathcal{X} \rightarrow \mathcal{S}_L$ such that $\mathbf{\Pi}(\mathcal{I}) = \pi$. Each image can, therefore, be seen as a point π in $\mathcal{S}_L$, i.e. the probability distribution of a multinomial random variable defined on the space of semantic concepts. We will refer to this representation as the *semantic multinomial* (SMN) that characterizes the image. The second component is a query-by-example function on $\mathcal{S}_L$. This is a function that, given the SMN that characterizes a query image, returns the most similar SMN among those derived from all database images, i.e. $f : \mathcal{S}_L \rightarrow \{1, \ldots, D\}$ such that

$f(\pi) = \arg\max_i s(\pi, \pi_i)$ where π is the query SMN, π_i the SMN that characterizes the ith database image, and $s(\cdot, \cdot)$ an appropriate similarity function. Given that SMNs are probability distributions, a natural similarity function is the Kullback-Leibler divergence

$$s(\pi, \pi') = KL(\pi||\pi_i) = \sum_{i=1}^{L} \pi_i \log \frac{\pi'_i}{\pi_i}, \tag{1}$$

which we adopt in this work. We next present our implementation of $\mathbf{\Pi}$.

3.2   Image Labeling

The mapping $\mathbf{\Pi}$ can be implemented with any semantic labeling system that produces posterior probabilities for the concepts in $\mathcal{L}$ given an image $\mathcal{I}$. We build on our previous work in the area, by adopting the weakly supervised method of [9], briefly reviewed in the remainder of this section. This method formulates semantic image labeling as an L-ary classification problem. Images are represented as bags of localized measurements $I = \{\mathbf{x}_1, \ldots, \mathbf{x}_n\}$, where $\mathbf{x}_i \in \mathcal{X}$ is a vector of image measurements (or *visual features*), and semantic labeling is achieved through the introduction of 1) a random variable W, which takes values in $\{1, \ldots, L\}$, so that $W = i$ if and only if $\mathbf{x}$ is a sample from the concept w_i, and 2) a set of class-conditional distributions $P_{\mathbf{X}|W}(\mathbf{x}|i), i \in \{1, \ldots, L\}$ for visual features given the semantic class.

For all i, the semantic class density $P_{\mathbf{X}|W}(\mathbf{x}|i)$ is learned from a training set $\mathcal{D}_i$ of images labeled with the annotation w_i, using a *hierarchical estimation* procedure first proposed, in [7], for image indexing. This procedure is itself composed of two steps. First, a Gaussian mixture model is learned for each image in $\mathcal{D}_i$, using the classical expectation-maximization (EM) algorithm. This originates a sequence of mixture density estimates $P_{\mathbf{X}|L,W}(\mathbf{x}|l, i) = \sum_k \pi_{i,l}^k \mathcal{G}(\mathbf{x}, \mu_{i,l}^k, \Sigma_{i,l}^k)$, where $\pi_{i,l}^k$ is a probability mass function such that $\sum_k \pi_{i,l}^k = 1$, $\mathcal{G}(\mathbf{x}, \mu, \Sigma)$ a Gaussian density of mean μ and covariance Σ, and L a hidden variable that indicates the image number. Omitting, for brevity, the dependence of the mixture parameters on the semantic class i, and assuming that each mixture has K components, this produces $D_i K$ mixture components of parameters $\{\pi_j^k, \mu_j^k, \Sigma_j^k\}, j = 1, \ldots, D_i, k = 1, \ldots, K$. The second step is an extension of the EM algorithm, which clusters the Gaussian components into a T-component mixture, where T is the desired number of components at the semantic class level. Denoting by $\{\pi_c^t, \mu_c^t, \Sigma_c^t\}, t = 1, \ldots, T$ the parameters of the class mixture, this algorithm iterates between the following steps.

E-step: compute

$$h_{jk}^t = \frac{\left[\mathcal{G}(\mu_j^k, \mu_c^t, \Sigma_c^t) e^{-\frac{1}{2} trace\{(\Sigma_c^t)^{-1} \Sigma_j^k\}} \right]^{\pi_j^k N} \pi_c^t}{\sum_l \left[\mathcal{G}(\mu_j^k, \mu_c^l, \Sigma_c^l) e^{-\frac{1}{2} trace\{(\Sigma_c^l)^{-1} \Sigma_j^k\}} \right]^{\pi_j^k N} \pi_c^l}, \tag{2}$$

where N is a user-defined parameter (see [7] for details).

M-step: set

$$(\pi_c^t)^{new} = \frac{\sum_{jk} h_{jk}^t}{PK} \tag{3}$$

$$(\mu_c^t)^{new} = \sum_{jk} w_{jk}^t \mu_j^k, \text{ where } w_{jk}^t = \frac{h_{jk}^t \pi_j^k}{\sum_{jk} h_{jk}^t \pi_j^k} \tag{4}$$

$$(\Sigma_c^t)^{new} = \sum_{jk} w_{jk}^t \left[\Sigma_j^k + (\mu_j^k - \mu_c^t)(\mu_j^k - \mu_c^t)^T \right]. \tag{5}$$

Notice that the number of parameters in each image mixture is orders of magnitude smaller than the number of feature vectors in the image itself. Hence the complexity of estimating the class mixture parameters is negligible when compared to that of estimating the individual mixture parameters for all images in the class. It follows that the overall training complexity is equivalent to that required to train a QBVE retrieval system based on the minimum probability of error cost [10].

4 Experimental Evaluation

In this section we present results of an evaluation of QBSE on a number of databases. The goal is to answer two main questions. The first is how well QBSE performs, comparatively to QBVE, in the standard scenario where the queries are from classes which belong to the semantic space on which the system was trained. The second deals with generalization, namely how well QBSE performs on images from classes outside this space.

4.1 Experimental Protocol

In all experiments the semantic feature space was learned from the Corel database used in [3,5]. This database, henceforth called *Corel50*, consists of 5,000 images from 50 Corel Stock Photo CDs, divided into a training set of 4,500, and a test set of 500 images. Each CD includes 100 images of the same topic, and each image is labeled with 1-5 semantic concepts. Overall there are 371 keywords in the data set, leading to a 371-dimensional semantic simplex. In terms of image representation, all images were normalized to size 181×117 or 117×181 and converted from RGB to the YBR color space. Image observations were derived from 8×8 patches obtained with a sliding window, moved in a raster fashion. A feature transformation was applied to this space by computing the 8×8 discrete cosine transform (DCT) of the three color components of each patch. The parameters of the semantic class mixture hierarchies were learned in the subspace of the resulting 192-dimension feature space composed of the first 21 DCT coefficients from each channel. For all experiments, the SMN associated with each image was computed with these semantic class distributions.

To evaluate retrieval performance, we relied on the standard precision/recall (PR) curves and carried out tests on three databases *Corel50*, *Flickr18* and

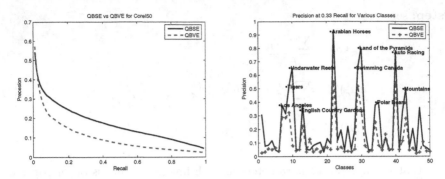

Fig. 2. Left: average PR for QBSE and QBVE on *Corel50*. Right: Precision for 50 classes of the *Corel50* database.

Corel15. In all cases there is a clear ground truth regarding which images are relevant to a given query (e.g., images labeled as belonging to the same Topic on *Corel50* data set.). The first set of experiments were done using the 500 test images of *Corel50* as the *query database* and the 4500 training images as the *retrieval database*. The closest match in the retrieval database was found for each image in the query database, PR measured, and averaged over all queries. Note that, in this experiment, the query images belong to the semantic classes that the system was trained to recognize, i.e. they are in the semantic simplex. This is the usual evaluation scenario for semantic image retrieval [3,5]. To analyze the generalization ability of QBSE, we have also used two completely new image databases. The first, *Flickr18*, was built with 1,800 images from 18 classes downloaded from `www.flickr.com`. These were classified according to the manual annotations provided by the online users. The second, *Corel15*, consisted of 1,500 images from another These were classified based on the CD themes, which were non-overlapping with the semantic class learned from *Corel50*. For both databases, 20% of randomly selected images served as the *query database* and the remaining 80% as the *retrieval database*.

4.2 Performance Within the Semantic Simplex

Figure 2 a) presents the PR curves obtained on *Corel50* with QBVE and QBSE. It can be seen that the precision of QBSE is significantly higher than that of QBVE at most levels of recall. QBVE performs well at low-levels of recall, confirming its well known ability to generalize along the *dimension of query diversity*, i.e. to find most images that are *visually similar* to the query. However, its performance is dramatically inferior to that of QBSE, which is able to generalize much more broadly along the *dimension of image similarity*. Figure 2 presents a comparison of the relative performance for individual classes, namely the precision at 0.33 recall. It is clear that QBSE outperforms QBVE for almost all classes. In 5 classesthe absolute precision gain is greater than 0.30. The benefits of QBSE are illustrated in Fig. 3, where we present the results for some queries

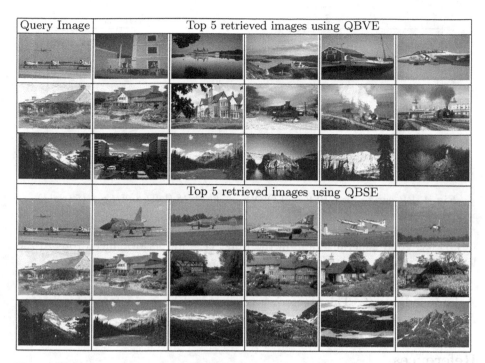

Fig. 3. QBVE and QBSE retrieval from *Corel50*. The first column shows the query image and columns 2 − 6 the top 5 database matches.

under both QBVE and QBSE. Note, for example, that for the query image containing *yellow airplanes* and a large area of *blue sky*, QBVE tends to retrieve images with *yellowish* foregrounds, against a the backdrop of *blue*, that have little connection to the *airplane* theme. Due to its higher level of abstraction, QBSE is successfully able to generalize the main semantic concepts of *airplanes, ground* and *sky*.

4.3   Semantic Simplex Mismatch

One question which is always of relevance for semantic retrieval systems is that of how well they generalize for image classes not seen during training. QBVE is obviously not affected by this problem, and provides a good comparative benchmark. To address this question, we tested QBSE on two other image sets (*Flickr18* and *Corel15*) with a significant number of semantic classes that are not covered by *Corel50*. Note that this is true for both the *query* and *retrieval* databases constructed. While there is a semantic space associated with these databases, and this space necessarily has some overlap with that of *Corel50* (e.g., all databases contain images with "sky"), these two datasets were explicitly constructed to minimize this overlap insofar as possible. Figure 4 presents the PR curves obtained in *Flickr18* and *Corel15*. It can be seen that, in both cases, the performance of QBSE is equivalent to that of QBVE. This indicates that

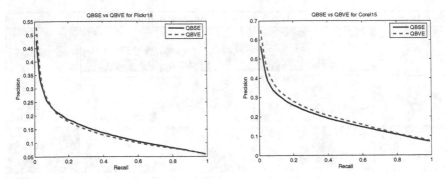

Fig. 4. PR curves for QBSE and QBVE on *Flickr18* (left) and *Corel15* (right)

QBSE has good generalization: in the worst case its performance drops to the levels that were possible with visual similarity.

Acknowledgment. This research was supported by a gift from Google Inc., NSF Career award IIS-0448609, and NSF award IIS-0534985.

References

1. K. Barnard, P. Duygulu, N. de Freitas, D. Forsyth, D. Blei, and M. I. Jordan. Matching words and pictures. *JMLR*, 3:1107–1135, 2003.
2. D. Blei and M. I. Jordan. Modeling annotated data. In *Proceedings of the 26th Intl. ACM SIGIR Conf.*, pages 127–134, 2003.
3. V. Lavrenko, R. Manmatha, and J. Jeon. A model for learning the semantics of pictures. In *NIPS*, 2003.
4. R. Picard. Digital Libraries: Meeting Place for High-Level and Low-Level Vision. In *Proc. Asian Conf. on Computer Vision*, December 1995, Singapore, USA.
5. S.L.Feng, R. Manmatha, and V. Lavrenko. Multiple bernoulli relevance models for image and video annotation. In *CVPR*, 2004.
6. A. Smeulders, M. Worring, S. Santini, A. Gupta, and R. Jain. Content-based image retrieval: the end of the early years. In *PAMI*, 22(12):1349–1380, 2000.
7. N. Vasconcelos. Image Indexing with Mixture Hierarchies. In *CVPR.*, Kawai, Hawaii, 2001.
8. S. Sclaroff, M. L. Cascia, S. Sethi, and L. Taycher. Unifying textual and visual cues for content-based image retrieval on the world wide web. *Computer Vision and Image Understanding*, 75(1-2):8698, 1999.
9. G. Carneiro and N. Vasconcelos. Formulating Semantics Image Annotation as a Supervised Learning Problem. In *CVPR*, San Diego, 2005.
10. N. Vasconcelos. Minimum Probability of Error Image Retrieval., In *IEEE Transactions on Signal Processing* Vol. 52, NO. 8, 2004

Corner Detectors for Affine Invariant Salient Regions: Is Color Important?

Nicu Sebe[1], Theo Gevers[1], Joost van de Weijer[2], and Sietse Dijkstra[1]

[1] Faculty of Science, University of Amsterdam, The Netherlands
[2] INRIA Rhone-Alpes, France

Abstract. Recently, a lot of research has been done on the matching of images and their structures. Although the approaches are very different, most methods use some kind of point selection from which descriptors or a hierarchy are derived. We focus here on the methods that are related to the detection of points and regions that can be detected in an affine invariant way. Most of the previous research concentrated on intensity based methods. However, we show in this work that color information can make a significant contribution to feature detection and matching. Our color based detection algorithms detect the most distinctive features and the experiments suggest that to obtain optimal performance, a tradeoff should be made between invariance and distinctiveness by an appropriate weighting of the intensity and color information.

1 Introduction

Corner detection can be traced back to Moravec [1] who measured the average change of intensity by shifting a local window by a small amount in different directions. Harris and Stephens [2] improved the repeatability of Moravec detector under small image variations and near edges. By an analytic expansion of the Moravec detector the local autocorrelation matrix is derived using first order derivatives. The Harris detector, in combination with a rotational invariant descriptor, was also used by Schmid and Mohr [3] when they extended local feature matching to general object recognition.

A low-level approach to corner finding is proposed by Smith and Brady: the SUSAN detector [4]. Their corner detector compares the intensity of a pixel with the intensities of neighboring pixels. If few of the neighboring pixels have approximately the same value, the center pixel is considered a corner point.

Lindeberg [5] proposed an "interesting scale level" detector which is based on determining maxima over scale of a normalized blob measure. The Laplacian-of-Gaussian (LoG) function is used for building the scale space. Mikolajczyk [6] showed that this function is very suitable for automatic scale selection of structures. An efficient algorithm for use in object recognition was proposed by Lowe [7]. This algorithm constructs a scale space pyramid using difference-of-Gaussian (doG) filters. The doG are used to obtain an efficient approximation of the LoG. From the local 3D maxima a robust descriptor is build for matching purposes. The disadvantage of using doG or LoG is that the repeatability is

H. Sundaram et al. (Eds.): CIVR 2006, LNCS 4071, pp. 61–71, 2006.
© Springer-Verlag Berlin Heidelberg 2006

not optimal since they not only respond to blobs, but also to high gradients in one direction. Because of this, the localization of the features may not be very accurate.

An approach that intuitively arises from this observation, is the separation of the feature detector and the scale selection. The original Harris detector [2] shows to be robust to noise and lighting variations, but only to a very limited extend to scale changes [8]. To deal with this Dufournoud et al. [9] proposed the scale adapted Harris operator. Given the scale adapted Harris operator, a scale space can be created. Local 3D maxima in this scale space can be taken as salient points. Mikolajczyk points out that the scale adapted Harris operator rarely attains a maximum over scales [6]. This results in very few points, which are not representative enough for the image. To address this problem, Mikolajczyk [6] proposed the Harris-Laplace detector that merges the scale-adapted Harris corner detector and the Laplacian based scale selection.

All the approaches presented above are intensity based. Since the luminance axis is the major axis of color variation in the RGB color cube, most salient points are found using just intensity. The additional color based salient points might not dramatically increase the number of salient points. The distinctiveness of these color based salient points is however much larger, and therefore color can be of great importance when matching images. Furthermore, color plays an important role in the pre-attentive stage in which features are detected. This means that the saliency value of a point also depends on the color information that is present. Very relevant to our work is the research of van de Weijer et al. [10]. They aim at incorporating color distinctiveness into the design of salient point detectors. In their work, the color derivatives form the basis of a color saliency boosting function since they are used in both the detection of the salient points, and the determination of the information content of the points. Furthermore, the histograms of color image derivatives show distinctive statistical properties which are used in a color saliency boosting function.

Our contribution is twofold. First of all, we are comparing the Harris corner detector used by Mikolajczyk [11] with the SUSAN corner detector [4]. Second we are investigating the use of color in extracting corners. We first used the color extended Harris detector [10] which operates on the same principle as the intensity based Harris detector. The extension to color consists of a transformation of the color model to decorrelate common photometric variations and a saliency boosting function that takes into account the statistics of color image derivatives. Later, we investigate the use of invariant color ratios and we show that by using color information the distinctiveness of the regions is increased, whereas the desirable properties are preserved. The incorporation of color information however increases the detection complexity.

2   Corners Detectors in the Affine Invariant Framework

In the affine invariant region detection algorithm [6], an initial point with a corresponding detection scale is assumed. Based on the region defined by the initial location and scale, the point is subject to an iterative procedure in which the parameters of the region are adapted until convergence is reached. The affine invariance is obtained by combining a number of existing algorithms. The characteristic scale of a structure is selected using the Laplacian scale selection. The location of a region is determined using the Harris corner detector, and the affine deformation of a structure is obtained by using certain properties of the second moment matrix. Because all parameters (scale, location, and shape) influence each other, they all need to be adjusted in every iteration. If the algorithm converges towards a stable region, the adjustments become smaller. If they become small enough the algorithm halts, and the next initial region is processed. More details on the framework can be found in [11,6]. Note that we are using this framework as a baseline and we "plug-in" several corner detectors (Harris [2], SUSAN [4], and two color variants of Harris corner detector).

To extend the Harris detector to incorporate color information, the second moment matrix used in the detector should be based on color information. Because of common photometric variations in imaging conditions such as shadows and illumination, we use two invariant color spaces i.e. the opponent color space [10] for the colOppHarris detector and the m-color ratio space [12] for the colRatHarris detector. The reason for choosing these color spaces is to investigate whether color invariance plays a role in the repeatability and distinctiveness of the detectors. It has been shown that there exists a trade-off between color invariant models and their discriminative power [12]. While the opponent color space has limited invariance and the intensity information is still present, the color ratio is independent of the illumination, changes in viewpoint, and object geometry [12].

The second moment matrix is computed as follows. The first step is to determine the gradients of RGB by using a convolution with the differentiation kernels of size σ_D. The gradients are then transformed into the desired color system (i.e. opponent or color ratio system). By the multiplication and summation of the transformed gradients, the components of the second moment matrix are computed. The values are averaged by a Gaussian integration kernel with size σ_I. Scale normalization is done again using a factor σ_D^2. This procedure is shown in Eq. 1 where a general notation is used. Color space C is used with its components $[c_1, \ldots, c_n]^T$, where n is the number of color system components and $c_{i,x}$ and $c_{i,y}$ denote the components of the transformed RGB gradients, with $i \in [1, \ldots, n]$, and the subscript x or y indicating the direction of the gradient.

$$\mu(\mathbf{x}) = \sigma_D^2 g_{\sigma_I} \begin{bmatrix} C_x^T(\mathbf{x})C_x(\mathbf{x}) & C_x^T(\mathbf{x})C_y(\mathbf{x}) \\ C_x^T(\mathbf{x})C_y(\mathbf{x}) & C_y^T(\mathbf{x})C_y(\mathbf{x}) \end{bmatrix} \tag{1}$$

If the distribution of the transformed image derivatives is observed for a large set of images, regular structures are formed by points of equal frequency [10]. The planes of these structures are called isosalient surfaces. These surfaces are formed by connecting the points in the histogram that occur the same number of times. Based on the observed statistics a saliency measure can be derived in which vectors with an equal information content have an equal effect on the saliency function. This is called the color saliency boosting function which is based on rotation and normalization [10]. The components of the second moment matrix that incorporate the rotation and normalization, are shown in Eq. 2. The components of the rotated transformed image derivatives are denoted by $\tilde{c}_{i,x}$ and $\tilde{c}_{i,y}$. The normalization of the ellipsoid is done using the diagonal matrix Λ.

$$C_x^T(\mathbf{x})C_x(\mathbf{x}) = \sum_{i=1}^{n} \Lambda_{ii}^2 \tilde{c}_{i,x}^2(\mathbf{x}, \sigma_D)$$

$$C_x^T(\mathbf{x})C_y(\mathbf{x}) = \sum_{i=1}^{n} \Lambda_{ii}^2 \tilde{c}_{i,x}(\mathbf{x}, \sigma_D) \tilde{c}_{i,y}(\mathbf{x}, \sigma_D) \qquad (2)$$

$$C_y^T(\mathbf{x})C_y(\mathbf{x}) = \sum_{i=1}^{n} \Lambda_{ii}^2 \tilde{c}_{i,y}^2(\mathbf{x}, \sigma_D)$$

Note that in the case of color ratios, the derivatives are already incorporated in the way the ratios are computed. A brief description is given below.

We focus on the following color ratio [12]:

$$M(c_{\boldsymbol{x}_1}^i, c_{\boldsymbol{x}_2}^i, c_{\boldsymbol{x}_1}^j, c_{\boldsymbol{x}_2}^j) = \frac{c_{\boldsymbol{x}_1}^i c_{\boldsymbol{x}_2}^j}{c_{\boldsymbol{x}_2}^i c_{\boldsymbol{x}_1}^j}, c^i \neq c^j, \qquad (3)$$

expressing the color ratio between two neighboring image locations $\boldsymbol{x}_1$ and $\boldsymbol{x}_2$, for $c^i, c^j \in C$ giving the measured sensor response obtained by a narrow-band filter with central wavelengths i and j.

For a standard RGB color camera, we have:

$$m_1(R_{\boldsymbol{x}_1}, R_{\boldsymbol{x}_2}, G_{\boldsymbol{x}_1}, G_{\boldsymbol{x}_2}) = \frac{R_{\boldsymbol{x}_1} G_{\boldsymbol{x}_2}}{R_{\boldsymbol{x}_2} G_{\boldsymbol{x}_1}} \qquad (4)$$

$$m_2(R_{\boldsymbol{x}_1}, R_{\boldsymbol{x}_2}, B_{\boldsymbol{x}_1}, B_{\boldsymbol{x}_2}) = \frac{R_{\boldsymbol{x}_1} B_{\boldsymbol{x}_2}}{R_{\boldsymbol{x}_2} B_{\boldsymbol{x}_1}} \qquad (5)$$

$$m_3(G_{\boldsymbol{x}_1}, G_{\boldsymbol{x}_2}, B_{\boldsymbol{x}_1}, B_{\boldsymbol{x}_2}) = \frac{G_{\boldsymbol{x}_1} B_{\boldsymbol{x}_2}}{G_{\boldsymbol{x}_2} B_{\boldsymbol{x}_1}}. \qquad (6)$$

Taking the natural logarithm of both sides of Eq. 4 results for m_1 (a similar procedure is used for m_2 and m_3) in:

$$\ln m_1(R_{\boldsymbol{x}_1}, R_{\boldsymbol{x}_2}, G_{\boldsymbol{x}_1}, G_{\boldsymbol{x}_2}) = \ln(\frac{R_{\boldsymbol{x}_1} G_{\boldsymbol{x}_2}}{R_{\boldsymbol{x}_2} G_{\boldsymbol{x}_1}}) = \ln(\frac{R_{\boldsymbol{x}_1}}{G_{\boldsymbol{x}_1}}) - \ln(\frac{R_{\boldsymbol{x}_2}}{G_{\boldsymbol{x}_2}})$$

Hence, the color ratios can be seen as differences at two neighboring locations $\boldsymbol{x}_1$ and $\boldsymbol{x}_2$ in the image domain of $\ln(R/G)$:

$$\nabla_{m_1}(\boldsymbol{x}_1, \boldsymbol{x}_2) = (\ln(\frac{R}{G}))_{\boldsymbol{x}_1} - (\ln(\frac{R}{G}))_{\boldsymbol{x}_2}. \qquad (7)$$

Differentiation is obtained by computing the difference in a particular direction between neighboring pixels of $\ln R/G$. The resulting derivation is independent of the illumination color, changes in viewpoint, the object geometry, and illumination intensity. To obtain the gradient magnitude, the Canny's edge detector is taken (derivative of the Gaussian with $\sigma = 1.0$).

3   Experiments

In this section we compare the different corner detectors according to three criteria: repeatability, information content, and complexity. We are interested in comparing the intensity and color based detectors and in investigating the role color invariance plays in the performance of color based detectors.

3.1   Repeatability

The repeatability is measured by comparing the regions that are detected in an image I_R, and in a transformed copy of it, I_L. The localizations and shapes of the structures in the images are related by a homography H. By comparing the correspondences between the detected regions that cover the same part of the depicted scene, the repeatability rate can be computed as [6]:

$$r = \frac{n_m}{\min(n_R, n_L)} \times 100\%$$

where n_R is the number of regions in the common part of I_R, n_L is the number of regions in the common part of I_L, and n_m is the number of matches.

In order to determine the robustness of the detectors, the repeatability is measured under common variations in the imaging conditions. For each transformation the detectors are evaluated using a set of images in which in every successive image the transformation is increased a little. The dataset used, is the one used in [6] for determining the repeatability. Test sets are provided for blur, zoom & rotation, viewpoint changes, light changes, and JPEG compression. All images are taken with a digital camera that introduced JPEG compression artifacts.

Blur. The blur testset consists of two sets of 6 images. In both sets the focus of the camera is gradually varied from sharp in the first image to unsharp in the last image. The successive images are also translated.

For most of the images (see Fig. 1(a)), the color-based Harris detectors performed best. The intensity based Harris detector performs about 10% worse for images 2 to 5. The SUSAN based detector performs worse over the whole set of images. This poor performance might be due to the scale of the detectable

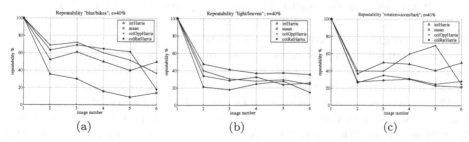

Fig. 1. Repeatability for different detectors on the blur set (a), the lighting set (b), and the rotation and scaling set (c)

structures that increases as the images get more blurred. The localization of the SUSAN based detector gets worse as the scale increases. Note that the color Harris detectors have similar repeatability and they only need a fraction of the number of regions that the other detectors need to achieve a similar repeatability.

Lighting. In this test set the aperture of the camera is varied. This results in a sequence of images that range from light to dark. In theory, this should only affect the intensity component, but since the camera pre-processes the image additional variations might be present. The successive images in this set are also slightly translated. In the test set only the intensity is changed and no other lighting changes like shadow and highlights are present.

The intHarris detector performs best on this test set (Figure 1(b)). This is probably due to the fact that the Harris corner detector is based on the derivatives of the image instead of on the actual pixel values. The SUSAN detector uses its brightness threshold to determine whether something qualifies as a corner. If the overall image intensity gets lower, the variations in brightness also get lower. As a result the SUSAN detector will pick up less corners. The repeatability of the colOppHarris based detector is similar to that of the SUSAN detector, although it is also based on derivatives. ColRatHarris detector performs the worst probably due to the invariant properties imposed on it. The number of regions needed is the highest for the intHarris detector, whereas the SUSAN and color Harris detectors need a lower number of regions.

Rotation and Scaling. Invariance against rotation and scaling is very important in detecting the same regions in different images of the same scene. Any multi-scale interesting point detector should have good results on this.

The "bark" test set consists of a number of rotated and zoomed images depicting a natural structure. Although corners and edges are present, most of them are found in the texture. Color information is present, be it in a modest way.

The colOppHarris based detector performs best (Figure 1(c)). This might be due to the fact that it only detects 10 regions in the reference image; which might be too few for matching. The intensity based Harris detector also performs well, using more regions. The SUSAN based detector needs the most regions and achieves the lowest repeatability comparable to the one of colRatHarris detector. Note again that by using a more invariant color space (as is the case for colRatHarris detector) we tend to lose in repeatability performance.

Viewing Angle. The "graffiti" test set depicts a planar scenes from different viewpoints and its images contain regions of equal color that have distinctive edges and corners. The images bear similarities to synthetic images as those images in general also have sharp edges and colors with high saturation.

The repeatability results are shown in Figure 2(a). All detectors perform similar. Overall the repeatability of the SUSAN detector is a few percents lower than those of the other detectors. Again, the number of regions used by the color Harris detectors to achieve this repeatability, is much lower than that of the other detectors.

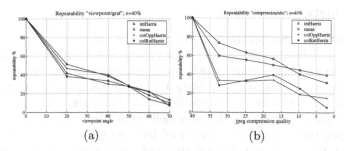

Fig. 2. Repeatability for different detectors on the viewpoint set (a) and the compression set (b)

JPEG Compression. The JPEG compression artefacts introduced are all rectangular regions. These rectangles introduce many additional corners in the image. All salient point detection methods used in the experiments rely on corners. Therefore, these artefacts might have a significant impact on the repeatability. When dealing with color and JPEG compression it is important to know that the lossy compression aims at discarding information the human cannot easily see. The human eye is more sensitive to variations in intensity than to variations in color. This is therefore also used in the JPEG compression scheme.

In the test set the reference image is compressed at a quality of 40%. In the successive images the quality is decreased to 2%. Note that most JPEG compressed images are compressed at a higher quality level; low quality values like these are in practice only used under special circumstances like low bandwidth video.

The intHarris and SUSAN detectors perform similar under compression in this test set, as is shown in Figure 2(b). The intensity based detectors deal significantly better with the artefacts than the color Harris detectors do. The color Harris detectors are clearly confused by the (color) artefacts introduced by the high JPEG compression. This might be due to the fact that the JPEG encoding is more conservative in varying the intensity information than it is with varying the color information of an image.

Discussion. Overall, from the experiments can be concluded that regions can be detected more reliable under some transformations when using just intensity information. The opponent color model that is used in the colorOppHarris detector decorrelates the intensity and color information. It is possible that by varying the ratio of these two different components, the tradeoff between invariance and distinctiveness can be made. If the weighting of the intensity component is increased, probably more regions are detected. Although the information content of these additional regions might not be very high, they can be detected reliable under varying imaging conditions. On the other extreme, the colRatHarris detector does not use any intensity information and this is reflected in the poor results under most of the transformations. However, this is compensated by a higher distinctiveness of the descriptors as it will be illustrated in the next section.

3.2   Information Content

The information content of the detected regions is measured using the entropy. The entropy is defined as the average information content of all "messages". The information content of one message i can be computed from the probability of the message p_i according to $I_i = -\log(p_i)$. From the information content of one message, the average information content of all messages can be derived. The entropy of a set of messages is therefore defined as $I = -\sum_i p_i \log(p_i)$.

To estimate the entropy of a number of detected regions, the regions need to be described. In this context, the descriptor of a region acts as the "message" in the entropy estimation. There are numerous ways of describing a region; in this research two common methods are used to describe regions. Both methods are based on convolutions with Gaussian derivatives.

A method to describe a region using derivatives is the "local jet" of order N at point $\mathbf{x}$ [13]. In this research rotational differential invariants up to the second order are used to create the intensity based descriptor $\mathbf{v}_i$ (similar to [8] and [6]):

$$\mathbf{v}_i = \begin{bmatrix} L_x^2 + L_y^2 \\ L_{xx}L_x^2 + 2L_{xy}L_xL_y + L_{yy}L_y^2 \\ L_{xx} + L_{yy} \\ L_{xx}^2 + 2L_{xy}^2 + L_{yy}^2 \end{bmatrix} \tag{8}$$

To determine the entropy of a set of descriptors, the probabilities of the descriptors have to be determined. We implemented the method proposed in [8]. Due to the space limitation we refer the reader to the original work for more details.

The color based descriptor $\mathbf{v}_c$ as used in [10] is given by:

$$\mathbf{v}_c = \begin{bmatrix} R, G, B, R_x, G_x, B_x, R_y, G_y, B_y \end{bmatrix}^T \tag{9}$$

This descriptor uses only derivatives up to the first order. Montesinos et al. [14] argue that due to the additional color information the color 1-jet is sufficient for local structure description. Note that this descriptor is not invariant to rotation. To keep the probabilities of the descriptors computable, the probabilities of the $zero^{th}$ order signal and the first order derivatives are assumed independent, as is done in [10]. The probability of descriptor $\mathbf{v}_c$ becomes:

$$p(\mathbf{v}_c) = p((R, G, B)^T)p((R_x, G_x, B_x)^T)p((R_y, G_y, B_y)^T) \tag{10}$$

The information content of such a descriptor can be computed by summing the information content of the three independent components. This is shown in Eq. 11, where $I(L)$, $I(L_x)$, and $I(L_y)$ represent the information content of the $zero^{th}$ and first order color derivatives.

$$I(\mathbf{v}_c) = I(L) + I(L_x) + I(L_y) \tag{11}$$

Since the Harris and SUSAN detector are based on intensity and the other detectors are color based we use two information content measures. The intensity based descriptors are computed as described in [8] (cf. Eq. 8). The color based descriptors are computed according to [10] (cf. Eq. 9).

Evaluation. A large number of points has to be considered in order to get a statistically significant measure. For this purpose a random selection of 300 images from the Corel dataset was made. The images both depict man made objects as well as images of natural scenes.

After normalization the descriptor space is partitioned in order to determine the probabilities of the descriptors. Because of normalization the same partition size can be used in all dimensions. The size of the partitions is determined by the largest absolute descriptor value of the normalized descriptors. In the experiments, each dimension of the normalized descriptor space is divided into 20 partitions.

For intensity based entropy calculation, the results are shown in Table 1. Note that in this experiments, for each corner detected by one of the methods (intensity or color based detectors), we used the descriptors calculated from derivatives of the intensity function up to the second order (cf. Eq. 8).

Table 1. The intensity and color information content for different detectors

Detector	Entropy				
	intensity	L	L_x	L_y	Total (color)
SUSAN	3.1146	4.9321	3.3366	2.9646	11.2333
Harris	3.3866	4.9799	3.2160	3.2132	11.4091
colOppHarris	2.5541	5.4367	4.0040	3.9659	13.4066
colRatHarris	2.4505	5.4153	4.2644	4.2865	13.9662
Random	2.3654	4.8754	2.1534	2.2183	9.2470

Although the color Harris detectors are included here, the intensity based descriptors are too restrictive to draw conclusions since no color information is considered in characterizing the regions. A region that is of equal intensity might be a high salient red-green corner. The color Harris detectors are included here since the occurrence of such corners is quite rare in natural images. Most color corners are also visible in the intensity image, be it with a lower gradient.

As expected, the regions that are detected using the random region generator have the lowest average information content. Also, the intensity based entropies of the regions detected by the color Harris are low. The intensity based descriptor is unable to describe the features that are detected by the color Harris detectors. The entropy of the regions detected by the Harris and SUSAN detectors are the highest.

Although the Harris and SUSAN detector are intensity based we can still use a color descriptor to compare the detected features. These detectors do not only detect pure black/white/gray corners but to a certain extent also color corners. The results for the color based entropy calculation are summarized in Table 1. The columns L, L_x and L_y correspond to the components of Eq. 11. The total entropy is computed from this by summing the components.

Again, the regions detected by the random region generator have the lowest entropy. The Harris and SUSAN based detectors perform also approximately the same. The regions detected by the color Harris detectors are by far the most distinctive according to the color based entropy calculation.

Discussion. The color Harris detectors in combination with the intensity based descriptors are not good choices, as expected. The intensity descriptor is unable to represent the additional color information that is present; an opposite effect can be seen in the results of the color based entropy calculation.

It is clear that a good balance between repeatability and distinctiveness has to be made. By increasing the repeatability, the distinctiveness of the regions decreases. To make the regions more distinctive, color information can be used to describe the regions. When introducing the color information in the descriptor, the detector becomes less invariant to changes in illumination. By using a color model in the detector that is invariant to common changes in illumination, a tradeoff between invariance and distinctiveness can be made. This is exactly what the colRatHarris detector does. The experiments clearly show the advantages of this approach. If color information is used to describe the regions, the color Harris regions are significantly more distinctive than the regions detected by the intensity based detectors.

3.3 Complexity

The complexity of the complete system depends on two parameters: color or intensity framework; and Harris or SUSAN corner detector. The complexity of the color based framework is due to the additional color channels, about 3 times larger than that of the intensity based framework.

Computing the Harris cornerness measure is equally expensive in the color or intensity based framework. The SUSAN corner detector is only used in the intensity based framework. In the intensity based framework, the SUSAN corner detector operates the fastest. The Harris corner detector needs to perform more and larger convolutions to determine the cornerness measure of one pixel. If recursive filters are used to perform the convolutions, the size of the kernel does not matter anymore. In this case, the difference in speed between the detectors within the framework becomes very small.

The greater part of the total running time is spent in the framework. Also, the SUSAN and Harris corner detectors (intensity) perform similar in terms of speed. For these two reasons the choice of the corner detector should be based on performance in terms of repeatability and entropy.

The choice between using color or intensity information depends on more criteria. The complexity is increased by a factor of 3 compared to the intensity based framework. At this cost the distinctiveness of the regions is increased whereas the repeatability is decreased. Possibly, the matching complexity should also be considered, since this involves the number of regions needed for matching. The experiments have shown that when using the color information, less regions are needed to obtain a similar repeatability.

4 Conclusion

Based on our extensive experiments a number of conclusions can be drawn. The invariance to common image transformations is in general similar for the intensity and color Harris detectors. The intensity based detectors have the lowest computational cost. The color based detection algorithms detect the most distinctive features. Furthermore, the experiments suggest that to obtain optimal performance, a tradeoff can be made between invariance and distinctiveness by an appropriate weighting of the intensity and color information. To conclude, color information can make a significant contribution to (affine invariant) feature detection and matching.

References

1. Moravec, H.: Visual mapping by a robot rover. In: Int. Joint Conf. on Artif. Intell. (1979) 598–600
2. Harris, C., Stephens, M.: A combined corner and edge detector. In: 4th Alvey Vision Conf. (1988) 147–151
3. Schmid, C., Mohr, R.: Local grayvalue invariants for image retrieval. PAMI **19** (1997) 530–535
4. Smith, S., Brady, J.: SUSAN - a new approach to low level image processing. IJCV **23** (1997) 45–78
5. Lindeberg, T.: Feature detection with automatic scale selection. IJCV **30** (1998) 79–116
6. Mikolajczyk, K., Schmid, C.: Scale & affine invariant interest point detectors. IJCV **60** (2004) 63–86
7. Lowe, D.: Distinctive image features from scale-invariant keypoints. IJCV **60** (2004) 91–110
8. Schmid, C., Mohr, R., Bauckhage, C.: Evaluation of interest point detectors. IJCV **37** (2000) 151–172
9. Dufournaud, Y., Schmid, C., Horaud, R.: Matching images with different resolutions. In: CVPR. (2000) 612–618
10. van de Weijer, J., Gevers, T., Geusebroek, J.M.: Edge and corner detectors by photometric quasi-invariants. PAMI **27** (2005) 625–630
11. Mikolajczyk, K., Schmid, C.: An affine invariant interest point detector. In: ECCV. Volume 1. (2002) 128–142
12. Gevers, T., Smeulders, A.: Color based object recognition. Patt. Recogn. **32** (1999) 453–464
13. Koenderink, J., van Doorn, A.: Representation of local geometry in the visual system. Biol. Cybern. **55** (1987) 367–375
14. Montesinos, P., Gouet, V., Deriche, R.: Differential invariants for color images. In: ICPR. (1998) 838–840

Keyframe Retrieval by Keypoints: Can Point-to-Point Matching Help?

Wanlei Zhao, Yu-Gang Jiang, and Chong-Wah Ngo

Department of Computer Science
City University of Hong Kong, Kowloon, Hong Kong
{wzhao2, yjiang, cwngo}@cs.cityu.edu.hk

Abstract. Bag-of-words representation with visual keypoints has recently emerged as an attractive approach for video search. In this paper, we study the degree of improvement when point-to-point (P2P) constraint is imposed on the bag-of-words. We conduct investigation on two tasks: near-duplicate keyframe (NDK) retrieval, and high-level concept classification, covering parts of TRECVID 2003 and 2005 datasets. In P2P matching, we propose a one-to-one symmetric keypoint matching strategy to diminish the noise effect during keyframe comparison. In addition, a new multi-dimensional index structure is proposed to speed up the matching process with keypoint filtering. Through experiments, we demonstrate that P2P constraint can significantly boost the performance of NDK retrieval, while showing competitive accuracy in concept classification of broadcast domain.

1 Introduction

Keyframe based retrieval is one of the earliest studied topics in video search. In large video corpus, keyframe retrieval can aid in the threading of stories with similar content [1], and the tracking of shots with similar concepts [2]. Two recent related efforts are the retrieval of near-duplicate keyframes [3] and the extraction of high-level features in TRECVID [4]. To date, retrieving keyframes with region or object-of-interest is still challenging since video frames are more easily affected by various factors. These factors include the variations in lighting and viewpoint, the artifacts due to motion-blur and compression, and the presence of background clutter.

Recently, retrieval with local keypoints emerges as a promising approach for the aforementioned problems [5]. Keypoints are salient regions detected over image scales and their descriptors are invariant to certain transformations exist in different images. In [6], Sivic & Zisserman show the effectiveness of keypoints for object matching and mining in movies. In [7], Ke & Sukthankar demonstrate the advantage of keypoints over global features such as color histogram in retrieving near-duplicate high-resolution art images. Nevertheless, the number of keypoints in a keyframe can range from a few up to several thousands. The matching of keypoints in two keyframes can consume a significant amount of time which makes efficient on-line retrieval intractable. To tackle this problem,

H. Sundaram et al. (Eds.): CIVR 2006, LNCS 4071, pp. 72–81, 2006.
© Springer-Verlag Berlin Heidelberg 2006

the offline quantization of keypoints is adopted in [6] where a visual dictionary is constructed. Each keyframe is indexed with a vector of keypoints. Comparison of two keyframes can be as simple as the dot product of two vectors. In contrast to [6], [7] speeds up the search of nearest keypoints with locality sensitive hashing (LSH). Intuitively, [7] is more effective than [6] due to the engagement of point-to-point matching during search. However, [7] is still slower despite the fact that the large amount of keypoints can be pruned with LSH.

This paper investigates the role of point-to-point (P2P) matching in keypoint-based retrieval. We study this topic for two problems: (i) near-duplicate keyframe (NDK) retrieval, and (ii) high-level concept classification, by contrasting the performances of with and without P2P matching. We examine *when* and *how* the P2P matching can boost the performance of these two tasks. In P2P, we propose a new index structure, namely LIP-IS, for fast matching and effective filtering. Under our investigation, LSH is not effective for filtering in noisy environment. As demonstrated in our experiments with TRECVID datasets, LSH indeed deteriorates the performance of matching because the chance of returning nearest neighbors is practically not high. In non-P2P matching, as in [6], we generate a dictionary of visual keypoints by clustering. Each keyframe is represented as a point in the vector space model of dictionary. Thus, the nearest neighbor search is not an issue in this strategy. The potential risk, however, is the difficulty in determining the number of clusters during quantization. In addition, the co-occurrence and distribution of keypoints are inherently neglected.

The usefulness of point-to-point matching is also studied in [8] for three datasets with scenes (from the sitcom *Friends*), objects (from ETH-80) and textures (from VisTex) respectively. Empirically, [8] shows that P2P matching is useful for retrieving keyframes with similar scenes, but not always so for objects and textures. The success of P2P matching also largely depends on the underlying matching strategy. In [8], the embedded Earth Mover's Distance (eEMD) with LSH filtering support is employed. Basically eEMD projects keypoints to a high dimensional feature space, and LSH utilizes this sparseness property to increase the chance of finding the nearest neighbors in high speed. The eEMD belongs to multi-point matching technique, and is susceptible to noise if no proper mechanism is used to constrain the flow of mass from one keypoint to the other [9]. Under the presence of background clutter, the matching can become random simply to meet the goal of minimizing the amount of efforts in transforming one signature to another. For robustness consideration, we use a relatively simple one-to-one symmetric (OOS) keypoints matching strategy to reduce as many false matches as possible. Empirically we find that OOS outperforms the nearest neighbor search with many-to-one matching strategy [7].

The remainder of this paper is organized as follows. Section 2 compares different keypoint detectors and their descriptors. Section 3 details the proposed one-to-one symmetric matching algorithm and its filtering support. Section 4 describes the construction of visual dictionary with keypoints. Section 5 and Section 6 present the experimental results, and Section 7 concludes our findings.

2   Keypoint Detectors and Descriptors

There are numerous keypoint detectors and descriptors in the literature. A good survey of these works can be found in [10], [11]. The detectors basically locate stable keypoints (and their support regions) which are invariant to certain variations introduced by geometric and photometric changes. Popular detectors include Harris-Affine [10], Hessian-Affine [10], Difference of Gaussian (DoG) [12], and Maximal Stable Extreme Region (MSER) [13]. Harris-Affine, which is derived from Harris-Laplace, estimates the affine neighborhood by the affine adaptation process based on the second moment matrix. Keypoints of Hessian-Laplace are points which reach the local maxima of Hessian determinant in space and fall into the local maxima of Laplacian-of-Gaussian in scale. DoG uses the similar method as Hessian-Laplace to localize the keypoint at local space-scale maxima of the difference of Gaussian. MSER is detected by a watershed like process and is invariant to affine transformations and robust to viewpoint changes.

In [14], SIFT (scale-invariant feature transform) has shown to be one of the best descriptors for keypoints. SIFT is a 128-dimensional feature vector that captures the spatial structure and the local orientation distribution of a patch surrounding keypoints. PCA-SIFT, proposed in [15], is a compact version of SIFT with principal component analysis. In this paper, we adopt the 36-dimensional PCA-SIFT as the descriptors of keypoints due to its compactness and retrieval effectiveness, as indicated in [15]. Based on PCA-SIFT, we use Cosine similarity to measure the closeness of two keypoints.

3   Keypoint Matching and Filtering

3.1   One-to-One Symmetric Keypoint Matching

Given two sets of keypoints respectively from two keyframes, the alignment between them can be solved with bipartite graph matching algorithms. Depending on the mapping constraint being imposed, we can categorize them as many-to-many (M2M), many-to-one (M2O), one-to-many (O2M) and one-to-one (O2O) matching. The factors that affect the choice of matching strategy include noise tolerance, similarity measure, matching effectiveness and efficiency. In videos, frames are always suffering from low-resolution, motion-blur and compression artifact. Noise becomes a crucial factor in selecting matching algorithm, particularly when the matching decision is made upon a small local patch surrounding keypoints. Noise can affect the performance of keypoint detectors [12]. The localization errors caused by detectors can deteriorate the distinctiveness of PCA-SIFT. It becomes very common that a keypoints fails to find its corresponding neighbor in another keyframe, and on the other extreme, a keypoint can simply match to many other keypoints due to mapping ambiguity. In principle, to suppress faulty matches, O2O matching appears to be noise tolerant although some correct matches may be missed.

For effective keyframe retrieval, in our opinion, the false matches should be filtered off as many as possible. To retain only the most reliable matches for retrieval, we introduce a new scheme – namely one-to-one symmetric (OOS) matching. OOS ensures all the matches are the nearest neighbors. The symmetric property is also emphasized so that if keypoint P matches to Q, then P is the nearest neighbor of Q (i.e., $P \rightarrow Q$) and similarly $P \leftarrow Q$. This property indeed makes OOS stable and unique, i.e., the result of matching a keypoint set A to set B is exactly the same as B to A, unless there are keypoints that have more than one nearest neighbor. Generally speaking, O2O matching cannot guarantee each matched keypoints pair to be meaningful. Some false matches indeed could exist with high similarity value. But it becomes a rare case for these false matches to be symmetrically stable and paired to each other in both directions.

3.2   Fast Keypoint Filtering

Point-by-point matching between two sets is generally a time consuming task especially when the set cardinality is high. To allow fast retrieval of OOS, we perform approximate nearest neighbor search by indexing PCA-SIFT descriptors in a multi-dimensional structure called LIP-IS. The structure is a group of 36 histograms formed independently by every components of PCA-SIFT. LIP-IS is constructed by equally and independently quantizing each histogram into 8 bins, with a resolution of $\Delta = 0.25$ (the range of a PCA-SIFT components is [-1,1]). Given $P = [p_1, p_2, ..., p_i, ..., p_{36}]$, the index of P in dimension i is defined as

$$\mathcal{H}(p_i) = \lfloor \frac{p_i + 1}{\Delta} \rfloor \qquad (1)$$

Totally, this index structure is composed of 8×36 bins. During indexing, a keypoint P is repeatedly indexed into the corresponding bins of 36 histograms, according to its quantized value in particular dimension. Thus, each keypoint is hashed and then distributed into 36 bins in this structure. In principle, the structure encodes the keypoints of a keyframe by decomposing the PCA-SIFT components and modeling them as 36 independent distributions. This structure is intuitive and reasonable since the PCA-SIFT components are orthogonal to each other. Based on this structure, we define the function that any two keypoints P and Q collide in dimension i if

$$\mathcal{C}(q_i, p_i) = \begin{cases} 1 \text{ if } |\mathcal{H}(q_i) - \mathcal{H}(p_i)| \leq 1 \\ 0 \text{ Otherwise} \end{cases} \qquad (2)$$

When searching for the nearest neighbor of a query keypoint Q, the structure will return a candidate set $A(Q)$ which includes the points collide with Q across all the 36 dimensions. Then we search for Q's nearest neighbor from the set $A(Q)$ by OOS matching algorithm. This structure has the merit that it is efficient and easy to implement with simple bit operation.

With LIP-IS, basically two keypoints which are similar to each other are more likely to collide in every dimension. And in contrast, the dissimilar keypoints have a relatively lower chance of collision. Since each component of PCA-SIFT descriptors is theoretically Gaussian distributed, the probability that any two keypoints collide in a dimension can be estimated. The probability that a keypoint Q will collide with P in i dimension, in its best ($\mathbf{P}_b$) and worst ($\mathbf{P}_w$) cases, can be estimated as follows

$$\mathbf{P}_b = 2 \int_0^{2\Delta} \frac{1}{\sqrt{2\pi}\sigma_i} \exp\{-\frac{q_i^2}{4\sigma_i^2}\} \, dq_i \tag{3}$$

$$\mathbf{P}_w = 2 \int_0^{\Delta} \frac{1}{\sqrt{2\pi}\sigma_i} \exp\{-\frac{q_i^2}{4\sigma_i^2}\} \, dq_i \tag{4}$$

Then, the probability that a point will collide with Q in 36 dimensions can be expressed as

$$\mathbf{P}_f = \mathbf{P}_b^{36} \tag{5}$$

Notice that $\mathbf{P}_f \ll 1$ in general. This also implies that the cardinality of $A(Q)$ can be very small, i.e., $\mathbf{P}_f \times n$, where n is the total number of keypoints to be searched. The probability of missing the nearest neighbor can also be estimated. Suppose M is the maximum number of dimensions that the nearest neighbor $\hat{P}$ and Q will not collide, the worst case probability is

$$\mathbf{P}_{miss} = \sum_{i=1}^{M} \binom{M}{i} \mathbf{P}_w^{M-i}(1 - \mathbf{P}_w)^i = 1 - \mathbf{P}_w^M \tag{6}$$

In theory, M can be estimated (and this value is much smaller than 36), if we set a threshold to exclude keypoints with low similarity from consideration. In our simulation, when searching for a nearest neighbor from a 1000 keypoint set, LIP-IS is often capable of filtering 99.5% of the points without missing the real candidate for OOS matching.

4   Visual Keywords Generation

We generate a visual dictionary based on [6]. We select approximately 900 keyframes from TRECVID-2005 development set, with about 70% of them containing the 39 high-level concepts specified in TRECVID [4]. In total, there are about 490,000 keypoints extracted. Empirically we quantize these keypoints into 5,000 clusters, and each cluster represents a visual keyword. Instead of employing K-means for clustering, we adopt a faster clustering algorithm based on the recent work in [16]. With this visual dictionary, the classical *tf-idf* is used to weight the importance of keywords. A keyframe is then represented as a vector of keywords, analogous to the traditional text-based vector space model.

5   Experiment-I: Near-Duplicate Keyframe Retrieval

We conduct experiments on the near-duplicate keyframe (NDK) dataset given by [3]. The dataset contains 150 NDK pairs and 300 non-NDKs selected from

TRECVID 2003 video corpus. We evaluate the retrieval performance with the probability of the successful top-k retrieval, defined as

$$\mathbf{P}(k) = \frac{Q_c}{Q_t}, \tag{7}$$

where Q_c is the number of queries that find its duplicate in the top k list, and Q_t is the total number of queries. In this experiment, we use all NDKs (300 keyframes) as queries. The ranking is based on the cardinality of keypoints being matched. In case the cardinality is the same, the average similarity of matched keypoints is further used. In the dataset, the number of keypoints per keyframe varies depending on the detectors and keyframe content. DoG, on average, detects 1000 keypoints per keyframe. In contrast, Harris-Affine, Hessian-Affine and MSER detectors only extract few hundreds of keypoints respectively.

5.1   Keypoint Comparison

We first compare the retrieval effectiveness of different keypoints under the one-to-one symmetric matching scheme. Figure 1(a) shows the performance of different detectors, and (b) shows the performance when re-ranking the top-k lists of two detectors with equal weight. Overall, DoG achieves the best performance, followed by Hessian Affine. Both detectors indeed win a large margin over Harris Affine as well as MSER. This is mainly because both DoG and Hessian Affine are capable of detecting more distinctive keypoints than Harris Affine and MSER. These two detectors are more reliable in the presence of partial occlusion and background clutter. Since there is no detector alone that is robust enough to against all kinds of transformations, we also attempt the fusion of two detectors by re-ranking their retrieved lists, as shown in Figure 1(b). We find that the combination of DoG with Hessian Affine detectors performs the best. However, this comes with the cost of time since the speed is basically double of the DoG and Hessian Affine alone. For this reason, we only use DoG for testing in the remaining experiments.

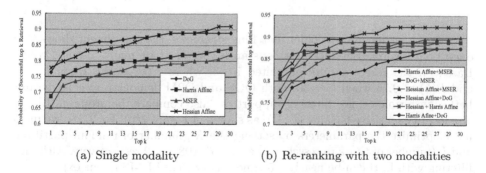

(a) Single modality   (b) Re-ranking with two modalities

Fig. 1. Comparison of different keypoint detectors

5.2   Effectiveness of Point-to-Point Matching

We mainly compare the effectiveness of OOS matching (OOS) and visual keywords (VK). In addition, we contrast their performances with many-to-one (M2O) matching based on the nearest neighbor search in [7], block-based color moment (CM), and global color histogram (CH). For CM, we use the first three color moments extracted in *Lab* color space over 5×5 grid partitions. In CH, we use HSV color space with 64 bins of H, 8 bins of S, and 4 bins of V.

Figure 2(a) shows the comparison of five different approaches. OOS outperforms all other methods across all k (from 1 to 30) being tested. Moreover, the strategies based on point-to-point matching (OOS and M2O) significantly outperforms others. VK performs poorly and shows lower $P(k)$ than the baselines CM and CH. In VK, we find that although the small patches in a cluster tend to have high similarity value, they actually appear differently based on human perception. This may due to the problems of polysemy and synonymy as previously mentioned by [17] when constructing the visual dictionary. Our dictionary is generated based on TRECVID 2005 corpus, it may have certain impact when applying to 2003 corpus. In addition, the selection of clustering parameters (e.g. number of clusters) can also affect the final results.

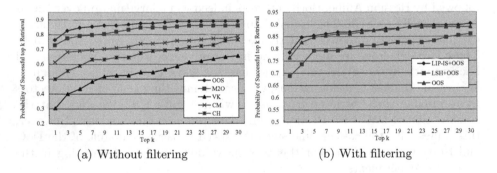

(a) Without filtering   (b) With filtering

Fig. 2. Performance Comparison of different retrieval techniques

Comparing the point-to-point matching strategies, the experiment shows that one-to-one symmetric (OOS) is constantly better than many-to-one (M2O). Based on the recent results presented in [3] where $P(k) \approx 0.6$ when $k = 1$ and $P(k) \approx 0.76$ when $k = 30$, both OOS and O2M demonstrate considerably better performance. For filtering support, we also compare the proposed LIP-IS and locality sensitive hashing (LSH), as shown in Figure 2(b). For LSH, we manually optimize the parameters by setting the K (number of random partition) and L (number of times to tessellate a set) with 108 and 2 respectively. Although filtering with LSH can be nearly 2.5 times faster than LIP-IS in our experiment, its performance is relatively poor since the nearest neighbors are not always returned with LSH. In contrast, our proposed scheme (LIP-IS+OOS) shows nearly the same retrieval performance with pure OOS.

5.3 Speed Efficiency

With large amount of keypoints in keyframes, speed becomes a critical concern for online retrieval. Table 1 shows the average time for comparing two keyframes with different features. All the approaches are tested on a Pentium-4 machine with 3G Hz CPU and 512M main memory in Windows-XP environment. LIP-IS is able to speed up OOS matching by 12.5 times. Apparently, the methods without point-to-point matching such as VK are faster since the comparison only requires the manipulation of two feature vectors.

Table 1. Speed efficiency for comparing two keyframes

Method	LIP-IS+OOS	OOS	VK	O2M	CM	CH
Time (s)	0.028	0.35	0.93×10^{-4}	0.34	10^{-5}	10^{-5}

6 Experiment-II: High-Level Concept Classification

In this experiment, we compare OOS and VK in classifying keyframes according to high-level concepts. We construct a dataset of four concepts containing 5589 keyframes extracted from the TRECVID 2005 common development feature annotation (by CMU and IBM tools) and test sets. The dataset is composed of 901 keyframes with US-flag, 2816 keyframes with maps, 910 keyframes with computer/TV screen, and 962 keyframes with waterscape/waterfront. We manually select 430 keyframes covering the four concepts for training, and leave the remaining keyframes as testing set. Figure 3 shows some samples with water and US-flag concepts. The targeted concepts in keyframes appear in varying forms in terms of lighting, viewpoint, color and scale changes. Some concepts are partially occluded and present in background clutter.

We train two types of classifiers for testing: k-NN and support vector machines (SVM). For OOS matching, we perform 1-NN classification. The similarity is based on the cardinality of matched keypoints found in a comparison. For visual keywords (VK), we construct 1, 3-NN classifiers, and a multi-class SVM. We use CCR (correct classification rate) to evaluate the accuracy of classification:

$$CCR = \frac{\text{number of correctly classified keyframes in class } i}{\text{number of keyframes in class } i}. \tag{8}$$

Fig. 3. Keyframes from two semantic concepts

Table 2. Classification rate of OOS and variant of VK classifiers

Methods	US-Flag	Maps	Screen	Water
OOS (1-NN)	0.645	0.810	0.723	0.790
VK (1-NN)	0.441	0.603	0.441	0.570
VK (3-NN)	0.347	0.567	0.244	0.475
VK (SVM)	0.445	0.527	0.126	0.723

Table 2 shows the classification performance of OOS and VK. Overall, point-to-point matching outperforms all runs based on VK. However, when we repeat 3-NN for OOS, surprisingly the results are less satisfactory. We investigate the results and find that indeed there are many duplicate keyframe pairs with common concepts in the broadcast videos. With 1-NN, OOS has an excellent success rate of classifying a keyframe if its near-duplicate version is also found in the training set. However, when the number of near-duplicate samples is less than k, k-NN does not perform well. This probably concludes that OOS is effective in finding near-duplicate keyframes, rather than the targeted concepts appeared in varying forms. Compared to OOS, VK is poorer partially because the co-occurrence of keypoints in a concept is not fully exploited under this representation. It is susceptible to noise due to the problems of polysemy and synonymy. Moreover, due to the limited amount of training samples, the CCR of 1-NN indeed works better than 3-NN and SVM classifiers.

7   Discussion and Conclusion

We have presented the proposed point-to-point (P2P) matching algorithm and compared its performance with visual keyword (VK) generation. Overall, P2P matching significantly outperforms VK in both tasks we investigate. VK, despite its simplicity and efficiency, has the deficiencies that it neglects the co-occurrence and distribution of keypoints, is vulnerable to the potential risks of polysemy and synonymy, and could be sensitive to the setting of parameters during clustering. P2P matching, in contrast, is relatively slower but much stable due to the fact that constraints can be easily imposed during matching. In addition, variant matching strategies exhibit different retrieval effectiveness in our experiments, however, overall they demonstrate the advantage of matching over VK. In NDK retrieval, our proposed OOS matching shows superior performance over all other methods. When LIP-IS is used for filtering support, OOS still performs consistently better with more than 10 times of speed up. In concept classification, OOS matching is still better than VK with k-NN and SVM classifiers. Nevertheless, we only conclude that OOS is effective in broadcast domain where the near-duplicate version of keyframes has a higher chance to be found in both testing and training samples. Other than that, we have no enough empirical evidence to support that P2P is a winner over VK. Basically, when the targeted concepts appear in quite different scales under background clutter, only few matches can be found with P2P. With these few matches, it becomes difficult to distinguish keyframes of different concepts.

Acknowledgements

The work described in this paper was fully supported by a grant from the Research Grants Council of the Hong Kong Special Administrative Region, China (Project No. CityU 118905).

References

1. Wu, X., Ngo, C.-W., Li, Q.: Threading and Autodocumenting News Videos. IEEE Signal Processing Magazine. **23** no.2 (2006) 59–68
2. Chang, S.-F. et. al: Columbia University TRECVID-2005 Video Search and High-Level Feature Extraction. TRECVID Online Proceedings. (2005)
3. Zhang, D.-Q., Chang, S.-F.: Detecting Image Near-Duplicate by Stochastic Attributed Relational Graph Matching with Learning. ACM International Conference on Multimedia. (2004) 877–884
4. TREC Video Retrieval Evaluation. In *http://www-nlpir.nist.gov/projects/trecvid/*.
5. Csurka, G., Dance, C., Fan, L. et. al: Visual Categorization with Bags of Keypoints. ECCV2004 Workshop on Statistical Learning in Computer Vision. (2004) 59–74
6. Sivic, J., Zisserman, A.: Video Google: A Text Retrieval Approach to Object Matching in Videos. International Conference on Computer Vision. (2003) 1470–1477
7. Ke, Y., Suthankar, R., Huston L.: Efficient Near-Duplicate Detection and Sub-image Retrieval. ACM International Conference on Multimedia. (2004) 869–876
8. Grauman, K., Darrell, T.: Efficient Image Matching with Distributions of Local Invariant Features. Computer Vision and Pattern Recognition. (2005) 627–634
9. Rubner, Y., Tomasi, C., Guibas, L.J.: The Earth Mover's Distance as a Metric for Image Retrieval. International Journal of Computer Vision. **40** (2000) 99–121
10. Mikolajczyk, K., Schmid, C.: Scale and Affine Invariant Interest Point Detectors. International Journal of Computer Vision. **60** (2004) 63–86
11. Mikolajczyk., K., Tuytelaars, T., Schmid, C. et. al: A Comparison of Affine Region Detectors. International Journal on Computer Vision **65** no.1-2 (2005) 43–72
12. Lowe, D.: Distinctive Image Features from Scale-Invariant Key Points. International Journal of Computer Vision. **60** (2004) 91–110
13. Matas, J., Chum O., Urban, M. et. al: Robust Wide Baseline Stereo from Maximally Stable Extremal Regions. British Machine Vision Conference. (2002) 384–393
14. Mikolajczyk, K., Schmid, C.: A Performance Evaluation of Local Descriptors. Computer Vision and Pattern Recognition. (2003) 257–263
15. Ke, Y., Sukthankar, R.: PCA-SIFT: A More Distinctive Representation for Local Image Descriptors. Computer Vision and Pattern Recognition. **2** (2004) 506–513
16. Zhao, Y., Karypis, G.: Empirical and Theoretical Comparisons of Selected Criterion Functions for Document Clustering. Machine Learning. **55** (2004) 311–331
17. Quelhas, P., Monay, F., et al.: Modeling Scenes with Local Descriptors and Latent Aspects. International Conference on Computer Vision. (2005) 883–890

Local Feature Trajectories for Efficient
Event-Based Indexing of Video Sequences

Nicolas Moënne-Loccoz, Eric Bruno, and Stéphane Marchand-Maillet*

University of Geneva 24, rue General Dufour - 1211 Geneva 4, Switzerland
Nicolas.Moenne-Loccoz@cui.unige.ch
http://viper.unige.ch/

Abstract. We address the problem of indexing video sequences according to the events they depict. While a number of different approaches have been proposed in order to describe events, none is sufficiently generic and computationally efficient to be applied to event-based retrieval of video sequences within large databases. In this paper, we propose a novel index of video sequences which aims at describing their dynamic content. This index relies on the local feature trajectories estimated from the spatio-temporal volume of the video sequences. The computation of this index is efficient, makes assumption neither about the represented events nor about the video sequences. We show through a batch of experimentations on standard video sequence corpus that this index permits to classify complex human activities as efficiently as state of the art methods while being far more efficient to retrieve generic classes of events.

1 Introduction

Event-based indexing of video sequences aims at describing the events sequences depict, *i.e.* the different actions that involve the captured visual entities. Such events may be more formally defined as *long-term spatio-temporal objects* [20]. These objects may be local within the spatio-temporal volume of the sequences. Their appearance is highly variable due to partial occlusion or varying capture conditions (*e.g.* lighting, point of view) or varying scale of occurence (spatial and temporal).

Thus, an event-based index has to represent complex local spatio-temporal patterns. For the sake of genericity and robustness, it should make as few assumptions as possible on the characterized events and on the video sequences content.

Previous works include models of the global motion (see *e.g.* Fablet *et al* [7] and Bruno *et al* [3]), dense local motions representation (Chomat *et al* [5] and Manor and Irani [20]) and more recently, sparse local motions representation (Laptev *et al* [9,10]). The latter, being based on invariant spatio-temporal local features, is the best-suited to the problem we address since it is able to richly

---

* This work is funded by EU-FP6 IST-NoE SIMILAR (www.similar.cc) and the Swiss NCCR IM2 (Interactive Multimodal Information Management).

H. Sundaram et al. (Eds.): CIVR 2006, LNCS 4071, pp. 82–91, 2006.
© Springer-Verlag Berlin Heidelberg 2006

describe local motions while being robust to most transformations of their appearance. However, this approach does not capture all kinds of local motions but only those that are local extrema of a specific functional. Moreover, it has a very high computational complexity because it handles the complete spatio-temporal volume of a video sequence at once.

In this paper, we propose to sparsely describe the local motions of video sequences using invariant spatial local feature trajectories. Spatial invariant local features are atomic parts of an image that cover its main visual entities. Such features have been extensively used for image and video sequences indexing [18,15]. Their invariance properties make the estimation of their motion reliable. Their extraction is also efficient and makes very few assumptions about the events and the video sequences. Hence, they are particularly well-suited to index video sequences for event-based retrieval.

The section 2 details the estimation of spatial local feature trajectories from the spatio-temporal volume of the video sequences. The section 3 presents how, from this bag of trajectories, a multi-scale histogram is used as an event-based index of these sequences. Finally, the approach is experimentally validated in section 4.

2 Local Feature Trajectories

Given the set of invariant local features (*e.g.* affine invariant interest points [13]) that are detected for every frame of a video sequence, the trajectories are estimated by matching features of successive frames as proposed by C. Tomasi *et al* [17]. Matching the elements of the two successive sets of local features W_t and $W_{t+\delta t}$ consists for every feature $w_t \in W_t$, defined by its position $\mathbf{v}_t$ in the image-space V, its scale s_t in the scale-space S and its supporting region $\mathcal{V}_t \subset V \times S$, in determining the feature $w_{t+\delta t}$ that is detected on the same visual entity within the next frame.

The feature trajectories are eventually compensated according to the estimated affine global motion in order to obtain descriptions that are nearly invariant to the camera motion.

2.1 Matching Likelihood

To match local features between successive frames, a likelihood measure of a potential match $(w_t, w_{t+\delta t})$ is defined. It takes into account not only the similarity of the visual appearance of the feature supporting regions $(D_{\mathcal{F}})$ but also the likelihood of the corresponding trajectory $(D_V \,\&\, D_S)$ in a weighted average of the form:

$$D = \alpha_{\mathcal{F}} D_{\mathcal{F}} + \alpha_V D_V + \alpha_S D_S \tag{1}$$

where the weights are used to normalize the different measures.

More precisely, the similarity between the feature supporting regions is characterized by the distance between their local descriptors :

$$D_{\mathcal{F}}(w_t, w_{t+\delta t}) = \|\mathcal{F}(\mathcal{S}(\mathcal{V}_t, t)) - \mathcal{F}(\mathcal{S}(\mathcal{V}_{t+\delta t}, t + \delta t))\| \tag{2}$$

As the description space $\mathcal{F}$ of the supporting region $\mathcal{V}$, we use the $SIFT$ [12] that has been shown to be one of the most robust.

Because some very similar features may be detected within the same frame, in order to disambiguate the potential matches, a measure of the trajectory likelihood in the image-space V is used:

$$D_V(w_t, w_{t+\delta t}) = \|(\mathbf{v}_t + \tilde{\mathbf{u}}_t) - \mathbf{v}_{t+\delta t}\| \tag{3}$$

where $\mathbf{v}_t + \tilde{\mathbf{u}}_t$ is the predicted position at time $t + \delta t$ of the feature w_t. The predicted motion $\tilde{\mathbf{u}}_t$ is simply the repetition of the motion estimated in the previous frame, $i.e.$ at time $t - \delta t$.

Similarly, and as proposed by L. Bretzner and T. Lindeberg [2], the matching distance takes into account the likelihood of the trajectory in the scale-space S:

$$D_S(w_t, w_{t+\delta t}) = \left|\log \frac{s_t}{s_{t+\delta t}}\right| \tag{4}$$

It penalized high scale motions ($ds_t = \frac{s_t}{s_{t+\delta t}}$), $i.e.$ matches whose features have been extracted at highly different scales.

2.2 Matching Algorithm

Given the likelihood of all potential matches between the two sets W_t and $W_{t+\delta t}$, the problem of determining the ones that correspond to actual trajectories of visual entities, may be formalized as finding the solution of :

$$\pi^* = \arg\min_\pi \left(\sum_{w_t^i \in W_t} D\left(w_t^i, w_{t+\delta t}^{\pi(i)}\right) \right) \tag{5}$$

where π is an injection from $[1..|W_t|]$ to $[1..|W_{t+\delta t}|]$.

Finding the optimal function π^* corresponds to the bipartite graph matching problem that may be solved in $O(n^3)$ by the $Hungarian\ algorithm$ (H. W. Kuhn [8]). Alternatively, the $greedy$ algorithm permits to find a suboptimal $\hat{\pi}$ with a $O(n)$ complexity. It is also more robust because it considers only locally the match distances disregarding the global matching cost.

By matching features from frame to frame along the whole video sequence, a set Z of local feature trajectories $z_{[t_z, t_z+\tau_z]} = \{w_{t_z}, w_{t_z+\delta t}, ..., w_{t_z+\tau_z}\}$ is obtained, as illustrated in the figure 1.

2.3 Global Motion Cancellation

The local feature trajectories $z_{[t_z, t_z+\tau_z]} \in Z$ may be reduced to :

$$z_{[t_z, t_z+\tau_z]} = \{(\mathbf{u}_{t_z}, ds_{t_z}), (\mathbf{u}_{t_z+\delta t}, ds_{t_z+\delta t}), ..., (\mathbf{u}_{t_z+\tau_z}, ds_{t_z+\tau_z})\} \tag{6}$$

where $\mathbf{u}$ is the motion of the feature within V, and ds its motion within S. These motions include a global component that mainly comes from the camera motion. Hence, in order to obtain trajectory invariant to such motions, we estimate the global component of the trajectories, modeled as an affine planar motion as presented in [14], and we compensate $\mathbf{u}$ and ds accordingly.

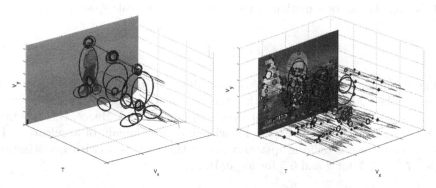

Fig. 1. Examples of local feature trajectories: C. Schüldt *et al* [16] corpus (left) and TrecVid'03 [19] corpus (right)

3   Event-Based Indexing

The *bags of keypoints* paradigm (G. Csurka *et al* [6]) has been proposed as an extension of the *bags of keywords* approach, in the context of local features-based image indexing. It has been shown to be very efficient despite the fact that it does not consider the relative position of the features. Applying this paradigm to our problem, we define a set of local motion models $\mathcal{M}$. Every bag of local feature trajectories Z, which describe the events depicted by the video sequence, is thus projected into a vector representing the number of occurrences of each local motion model of $\mathcal{M}$. However, when considering trajectories, we are faced to the problem of their variable length, different temporal scale and alignment. Furthermore, events may involve different local motions at different temporal scales. In our model, the quantization is performed on multi-scale sliding segments of the trajectories. A set of local motion models is thus obtained for different temporal positions and scales. As an initial result, by determining a minimal scale for these segments, the noisy trajectories are filtered out.

3.1   Quantization of Local Trajectories

A temporal segment of a local feature trajectory $z \in Z$ is described by a vector $\mathbf{z}$ representing the overall motion at the temporal position t and for the temporal scale τ :

$$\mathbf{z}_{[t,t+\tau]} = \left(\rho_{[t,t+\tau]}, \theta_{[t,t+\tau]}, ds_{[t,t+\tau]} \right) \tag{7}$$

where $(\rho_{[t,t+\tau]}, \theta_{[t,t+\tau]})$ are the polar coordinates of the total motion vector $\mathbf{u}_{[t,t+\tau]}$ of the segment in the image-space V :

$$\mathbf{u}_{[t,t+\tau]} = \sum_{i=t}^{t+\tau} \mathbf{u}_i \tag{8}$$

and $ds_{[t,t+\tau]}$ is the total motion of the segment in the scale-space S :

$$ds_{[t,t+\tau]} = \prod_{i=t}^{t+\tau} ds_i \qquad (9)$$

The quantization function Q that maps all trajectory representations $\mathbf{z}$ into the vocabulary $\mathcal{M}$ should be such that the local motion models are able to characterize the motions involved in the events to be retrieved. Hence, this function should be defined from the expert knowledge of the domain of application. In this paper we use a uniform quantization of the vectors $\mathbf{z}$ (with quantization steps : 7 for ρ, $\frac{\pi}{4}$ for θ and 0.5 for $\log(ds)$).

3.2   Multi-scale Histogram of Local Motions

As discussed by L. Chen *et al* in [4], multi-scale histograms of trajectories are able to cope with the time shifting and scaling problems. Therefore, we adopt a similar approach to describe bags of local feature trajectories.

The underlying idea is, for a given temporal segment, to quantize parts of the trajectories taken on a sliding window at different sizes. More formally, given the temporal segment $[t, t + \tau]$, the set of local features trajectories Z is projected into an histogram $H(Z)$ which entry for every local motion model $\hat{m}^i \in \mathcal{M}$ is computed as:

$$H_i(Z) = \sum_{t_k=t}^{t+\tau} \sum_{\tau_k=\delta t}^{\tau} \sum_{z^j \in Z} \delta(\hat{m}^i, Q_{t_k,\tau_k}(z^j)) \qquad (10)$$

where $\delta(x, y) = 1$ iff $x = y$ and the temporal quantization function is defined as:

$$Q_{t_k,\tau_k}(z^j) = \begin{cases} Q(\mathbf{z}^j_{[t_k,t_k+\tau_k]}) & \text{if } z^j \text{ is defined on } [t_k, t_k + \tau_k] \\ 0 & \text{otherwise} \end{cases} \qquad (11)$$

The histogram $H(Z)$ represents the bag of local motion models, *i.e.* the index of the video sequence that characterizes the events it depicts.

4   Experimental Evaluation

We have conducted two sets of experimentations. The first one aims at evaluating the richness of the proposed event representation. For that purpose the event recognition capabilities of our model are compared to state-of-the-art approaches. The second test is designed to evaluate our model's retrieval capabilities in the context of generic classes of events.

4.1   Human Activities Recognition

Event representations have been mainly studied for recognizing complex human activities. Such activities are characterized by the complexity of their spatio-temporal signature. In that context, event representations have to be sufficiently rich to recognize these patterns.

Experimental Corpus and Protocol. We use the database presented by C. Schüldt *et al* in [16]. It is made out of 2391 video sequences depicting 6 different complex human activities. These events are performed by 25 different subjects and are captured in varying conditions (*e.g.* camera motions, backgrounds) as illustrated in tabe 1.

Table 1. Examples of the 6 human activities of the C. Schüldt *et al* [16] corpus

Boxing	Jogging	Walking	Running	HandWaving	HandClapping

For every activity, a batch of 30 learning processes is performed with random training sets (20 positive examples and 40 negative ones). The three following event representations associated to their best-suited (according to our experimentations) classification algorithm are compared :

- LFT - χ^2 SVM : multi-scale histogram of local motion models (affine invariant interest point trajectories) - SVM with a χ^2 kernel
- MGH - χ^2 SVM : multi-scale spatio-temporal gradients histogram of the sequence (see L. Zelnik-Manor and M. Irani [20]) - SVM with a χ^2 kernel
- HMH - RBF SVM : *Hu* statistical moments of the motion history image (see J. Davis and A. Bobick [1]) - SVM with a *RBF* kernel

Results. Figure 2 (a) presents the mean *ROC* curves obtained for all concepts with the different event representation methods. It shows that the proposed one (*LFT*) performs only slightly worse than the two other state-of-the-art approaches. However, by considering the detailed performances for every activity (see figure 2 (b)), no significant difference between the *LFT* and the others representations may be observed.

These results show that the proposed event representation has the same representation capabilities as state-of-the-art activities recognition approaches while being much more robust. Effectively, the *MGH* and *HMH* representations rely on some crude assumptions about the video sequences such as the uniqueness of the activity within their spatio-temporal volume and the absence of any camera motion.

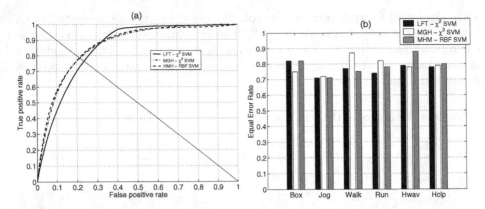

Fig. 2. Human activities recognition: (a) mean ROC curves for all activities - (b) detailed equal error rate for every activity

Table 2. Examples of the 6 classes of events used for our experimentation with the TrecVid'03 [19] corpus

Crowd	People Event	Male & Female Face	Basketball	Meeting	Sport Events

4.2 Event-Based Video Retrieval

Event-based retrieval of video sequences is the task of learning generic classes of events. In general, the learning problem is difficult because there is a large amount of variation in the event appearances within real databases. Moreover, only few learning examples are usually available.

Experimental Corpus and Protocol. For these experimentations, we use the TrecVid'03 [19] training corpus which contains almost 60 hours of broadcast news video sequences. These sequences are provided with their temporal segmentation and the manual annotations of the temporal segments [11]. We use a subset of 1550 of such segments (randomly chosen from the whole corpus) and we select 6 different concepts (see table 2) to perform the experimentations.

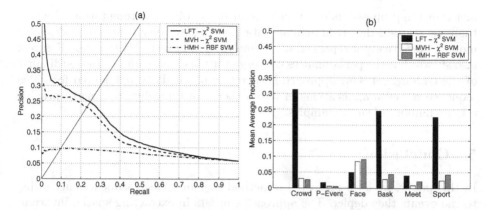

Fig. 3. Event-based video retrieval: (a) mean *Precision/Recall* curves for all classes - (b) detailed mean average precision (at 100) for every activity

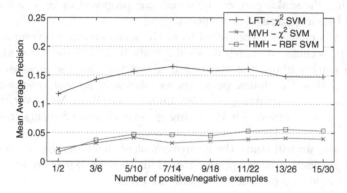

Fig. 4. Retrieval of classes of events: mean average precision (at 100) according to the number of positive and negative training examples

For every classe of events, a batch of 30 experiments is performed with random training sets (3 positive video sequences and 9 negative ones) and the three following event representations (again associated to their best-suited classification algorithm) are compared :

- LFT - χ^2 SVM (proposed representation, see 4.1)
- MVH - χ^2 SVM : histogram of the MPEG motion vectors - SVM with a χ^2 kernel (events retrieval baseline representation)
- HMH - RBF SVM (events recognition baseline representation, see 4.1)

Results. Figure 3 (a) presents the mean *Precision/Recall* curves obtained for all classes of events. This clearly shows that the proposed event representation (*LFT*) outperforms the two others approaches. Moreover, the figure 3 (b) shows that this observation is valid for all the considered concepts (except for the *Face* one which is mainly characterized by an overall null motion). This is due to the fact that the proposed index provides a far more robust representation of events than the state-of-the-art human activities representations. It also provides a far more expressive event representation than the too generic *MVH* index. Figure 4 also shows that the performances converge very fast according to the cardinality of the training set. Our approach is therefore particularly well-suited for video sequence retrieval applications in which users are typically not able to provide a large number of such examples.

5   Conclusion

In this paper, we have presented a method to index video sequences according to the events they depict. The approach consists in extracting spatial invariant local features in every frame of the video sequence. The trajectories of these features are estimated and compensated w.r.t. the affine global motion. From these compensated trajectories which characterize the displacements of the visual entities within the scale-space of the scene, the proposed index is a multi-scale histogram of their quantized description.

This index is efficiently computed from the spatio-temporal volume of video sequences. It permits to represent local events in space and time and makes assumption neither about the events nor about the video sequences. We have demonstrated that this index performs as efficiently as state-of-the-art event representations for recognizing complex human activities. Moreover, it further outperforms other methods for retrieving generic classes of events from within large corpus.

As extension, we will study the improvement of this index by considering the evolution of the local feature appearances. This way, we expect to obtain a more robust index able to represent more complex events.

References

1. Aaron F. Bobick and James W. Davis. The recognition of human movement using temporal templates. *IEEE Trans. Pattern Anal. Mach. Intell.*, 23(3):257–267, 2001.
2. Lars Bretzner and Tony Lindeberg. Feature tracking with automatic selection of spatial scales. *Computer Vision and Image Understanding: CVIU*, 71(3):385–392, 1998.
3. Éric Bruno, Nicolas Moënne-Loccoz, and Stéphane Marchand-Maillet. Unsupervised event discrimination based on nonlinear temporal modelling of activity. *Pattern Analysis and Application (PAA)*, 7(4):402–410, december 2004.
4. Lei Chen, M. Tamer Özsu, and Vincent Oria. Using multi-scale histograms to answer pattern existence and shape match queries. In *SSDBM*, pages 217–226, 2005.
5. Olivier Chomat and James L. Crowley. Probabilistic recognition of activity using local appearance. In *CVPR*, pages 2104–2109, 1999.
6. G. Csurka, C. Dance, L. Fan, J. Williamowski, and C. Bray. Visual categorization with bags of keypoints. In *Workshop on Statistical Learning in Computer Vision*, 2004.

7. R. Fablet, P. Bouthemy, and P. Pérez. Non-parametric motion characterization using causal probabilistic models for video indexing and retrieval. *IEEE Trans. on Image Processing*, 11(4):393–407, April 2002.
8. H. W. Kuhn. The hungarian method for the assignment problem. *Naval Research Logistics Quaterly*, 2:83–97, 1955.
9. Ivan Laptev and Tony Lindeberg. Space-time interest points. In *ICCV*, pages 432–439, 2003.
10. Ivan Laptev and Tony Lindeberg. Velocity adaptation of space-time interest points. In *ICPR (1)*, pages 52–56, 2004.
11. Ching-Yung Lin, Belle L. Tseng, and John R. Smith. Video collaborative annotation forum: Establishing ground-truth labels on large multimedia datasets. In *Proceedings of the TRECVID 2003 Workshop*, 2003.
12. David G. Lowe. Distinctive image features from scale-invariant keypoints. *International Journal of Computer Vision*, 60(2):91–110, 2004.
13. Krystian Mikolajczyk and Cordelia Schmid. Scale and affine invariant interest point detectors. *International Journal of Computer Vision*, 60(1):63–86, 2004.
14. Nicolas Moënne-Loccoz, Eric Bruno, and Stéphane Marchand-Maillet. Video content representation as salient regions of activity. In *Proceedings of the Third International Conference on Image and Video Retrieval, CIVR 2004*, pages 384–392, Dublin, Ireland, July 2004.
15. Nicolas Moënne-Loccoz, Eric Bruno, and Stéphane Marchand-Maillet. Interactive partial matching of video sequences in large collections. In *IEEE International Conference on Image Processing*, Genova, Italy, 11-14 September 2005.
16. Christian Schüldt, Ivan Laptev, and Barbara Caputo. Recognizing human actions: A local svm approach. In *ICPR (3)*, pages 32–36, 2004.
17. Jianbo Shi and Carlo Tomasi. Good features to track. In *CVPR*, Seattle, june 1994.
18. J. Sivic and A. Zisserman. Video Google: A text retrieval approach to object matching in videos. In *ICCV*, October 2003.
19. Alan F. Smeaton, Wessel Kraaij, and Paul Over. TRECVID 2003 - An Introduction. In *Proceedings of the TRECVID 2003 Workshop*, 2003.
20. Lihi Zelnik-Manor and Michal Irani. Event-based analysis of video. In *CVPR (2)*, pages 123–130, 2001.

A Cascade of Unsupervised and Supervised Neural Networks for Natural Image Classification

Julien Ros, Christophe Laurent, and Grégoire Lefebvre

France Télécom R&D - TECH/IRIS/CIM
4, rue du Clos Courtel
35512 Cesson Sévigné Cedex - France
{julien.ros, christophe2.laurent, gregoire.lefebvre}@francetelecom.com

Abstract. This paper presents an architecture well suited for natural image classification or visual object recognition applications. The image content is described by a distribution of local prototype features obtained by projecting local signatures on a self-organizing map. The local signatures describe singularities around interest points detected by a wavelet-based salient points detector. Finally, images are classified by using a multilayer perceptron receiving local prototypes distribution as input. This architecture obtains good results both in terms of global classification rates and computing times on different well known datasets.

1 Introduction

With the dramatic increase of available digital contents, advanced content management solutions become essential. If we focus on the particular situation of digital images (Infotrends[1] expects that the number of images captured on camera phones will reach 227 billion by 2009), efficient images management solutions such that supervised image classification have to be found.

The goal of a supervised image classification system is to group images into semantic categories giving thus the opportunity of fast and accurate image search. To achieve this goal, these applications should be able to group a wide variety of unlabelled images by using both the information provided by unlabelled query image as well as the learning databases containing different kind of images labelled by human observers.

In practice, a supervised image classification solution requires three main steps [1]: pre-processing, feature extraction and classification. Based on this architecture, many image classification systems have been proposed, each one distinguished from others by the method used to compute the image signature and/or the decision method used in the classification step. Regarding the signature computation, the most efficient methods are probably the local aproaches firstly introduced in [2]. In this case, local signatures are computed around some interest points and their values are chosen in a dictionnary obtained from the training

---

[1] http://www.infotrends-rgi.com/home/Press/itPress/2005/1.11.05.html

H. Sundaram et al. (Eds.): CIVR 2006, LNCS 4071, pp. 92–101, 2006.
© Springer-Verlag Berlin Heidelberg 2006

database. Local signatures are used to represent the image by a distribution of local image features easily classifiable as in [3,4] or are directly used to learn a model used for the next recognition step [5,6,7].

In the state of the art, the dictionnary is classically computed thanks to a K-means algorithm [5] or by a bottom-up clustering procedure[8]. We propose here to use a self organizing map [9] to generate the visual dictionnary. Furthermore, in our approach, a Multilayer Perceptron classifier is built with the training dataset and is used for the last classification step.

The paper is organized as follows. Section 2 describes the method which was introduced earlier in [10] to detect interest points and extract local image features. Section 3 presents the self-organizing map algorithm, the construction of the vocabulary of local descriptors and the construction of the image feature vector. The design of the Multilayer Perceptron classifier and the decision rule are explained in detail in section 4. Experiments are presented in section 5 and finally, section 6 concludes the paper.

2 Local Features Extraction

The goal of feature extraction is to reduce the amount of data contained in an image by extracting relevant and discriminating features. In local approaches, this extraction phase results in feature vectors computed around interest points and an image I_j is thus represented by a set of local signatures $S(I_j) = \{s_{1j}, \ldots, s_{nj}\}$. It is important to mention here that local approaches result in a lack of ordering between signatures.

2.1 Interest Points Detection

The goal of interest point detectors is to find image locations that are perceptually relevant for the next recognition step. Many detectors have been proposed in the literature, each one focusing on a particular local property of the image content such as contrast [11], corners [12,13], edges [10,14], etc.

The salient points detector presented in [10] uses a wavelet analysis in order to find relevant pixels located on sharp region boundaries. The use of wavelet analysis is motivated by observing that multi-resolution, orientation and frequency analysis are of prime importance for the human visual system during the recognition step. This detector has proven its efficiency in many vision applications[10] and thus will be used in the present work.

2.2 Description of Local Singularities

Most local descriptors describe the local neighborhood of salient points by characterizing edges in this area. Edge information thus appears fundamental in the process of local neighborhood description. To describe edges, gradient orientation and magnitude are generally used. Nevertheless, from a mathematical point of view, an edge or more generally a singularity can also be efficiently characterized by considering its Hölder exponents. We propose to use this mathematical notion to design our local descriptor.

Definition 1. $f : [a, b] \rightarrow \mathbb{R}$ *is Hölder* $\alpha \geq 0$ *at* $x_0 \in \mathbb{R}$ *if* $\exists K > 0, \delta > 0$ *and a polynom* P *of degree* $m = \lfloor \alpha \rfloor$: $\forall x, x_0 - \delta \leq x \leq x_0 + \delta, |f(x) - P(x - x_0)| \leq K|x - x_0|^{\alpha}$.

Definition 2. *The Hölder exponent* $h_f(x_0)$ *of* f *at* x_0 *is the superior bound value of all* α. $h_f(x_0) = sup\{\alpha, f$ *is Hölder* α *at* $x_0\}$.

The local regularity of a function at a point x_0 is thus measured by the value $h_f(x_0)$. It is worth noting that the smaller $h_f(x_0)$, the more singular is the signal at the point considered. For example, the Hölder exponent of a Dirac impulse is -1 and 0 for a step function. For an image, the Hölder exponent is measured in the direction of the minimal regularity of the singularity (in the gradient direction). The different singularities met in an image are shown on figure 1. To

Original Image $-0.2 \leq h \leq 0.2$ $-1.2 \leq h \leq -0.8$

Fig. 1. Different Type of Singularities

describe an ROI associated to an interest point in an image I_j, both orientation and Hölder regularity of singularities contained in that ROI are characterized. For this purpose, orientation $\theta(x, y)$ and gradient magnitude $m(x, y)$ at each pixel location (x, y) of the ROI are first computed:

$$m(x, y)^2 = (I_j(x + 1, y) - I_j(x - 1, y))^2 + (I_j(x, y + 1) - I_j(x, y - 1))^2 \quad (1)$$

$$\theta(x, y) = tan^{-1} \left(\frac{I_j(x, y + 1) - I_j(x, y - 1)}{I_j(x + 1, y) - I_j(x - 1, y)} \right). \quad (2)$$

Then, for each singularity, the Hölder exponent h is estimated with foveal wavelets as presented in [15]. Orientations and Hölder exponents maps are then conjointly used to construct different 3D histograms. To build such histograms, each ROI is first partitionned into 4×4 blocks and each histogram is computed in a particular block before being normalized by the block size (See figure 2). This last step of the signature design is realized in the same spirit as the construction of the SIFT descriptor presented in [16]. Finally, the signature is obtained by concatenating the different 3D histograms and thus has a size of $n \times r \times o$ where n is the number of subregions (i.e. the number of interest points), r is the number of Hölder exponents bins into the range $[-1.5, 1.5]$ and o is the number of orientations bins into $[-\frac{\pi}{2}, \frac{\pi}{2}]$. We typically use 4 orientations, 16 subregions and 3 Hölder exponents bins resulting in a signature size of 192.

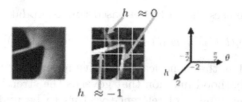

Fig. 2. Principle of the Singularity Descriptor

3 Image Representation

To use a classical machine learning methods for the last classification step, images must be represented by a vector of equal size. When local image descriptors have been extracted, a powerful and recent method is to represent the image by an histogram of local descriptors, this is the "bag of keypoints" representation introduced in [3]. Nevertheless, it supposes that local descriptors are quantized into a visual dictionnary of fixed size. We propose to build such a dictionnary by using a self-organizing-map.

3.1 Self Organizing Map Learning

The self-organizing map (SOM) is an unsupervised classification algorithm based on competitive learning[9]. It is a variant of the k-means algorithm that has the advantage of preserving the topology of input datas $X = \{x(t), t = 1, 2, \ldots\}$ with $x(t) \in D \subset \mathbb{R}^n$ and providing thus a better description of them.

The SOM aims at projecting the input data space D into a lower dimensionnal space (1D, 2D,...) defined by a regular discrete lattice L composed of N nodes. Therefore, it is a vector quantization algorithm which preserves the topology of the input space because each node c of the lattice is a neuron with a codebook vector $w_c \in \mathbb{R}^n$ such that if c_1 and c_2 are close then w_{c_1} and w_{c_2} are close in $\mathbb{R}^n$. For this purpose, the SOM is trained thanks to a competitive learning algorithm

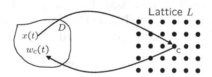

Fig. 3. General Principle of a Self Organizing Map

which supposes first that the SOM has been correctly initialized. For example, $w_i(0)$ could have been initialized randomly $\forall i = 1, 2, \ldots, N$. At epoch t of the learning step, $x(t)$ is compared simultaneously to all $w_i(t)$ by using a distance measure $d(x(t), w_i(t))$ on the input space D and the best candidate vector $w_c(t)$ associated to the node c (the best matching unit or BMU) is chosen such that:

$$w_c(t) = arg \min_i d(x(t),\ w_i(t)) i = 1, 2, \ldots, N. \tag{3}$$

The learning scheme uses then a kernel based rule to update the weights:

$$w_i(t+1) = w_i(t) + \alpha(t)h_{ci}(t)[x(t) - w_i(t)] \tag{4}$$

where $0 < \alpha(t) < 1$ is the monotically decreasing learning rate. Furthermore, h_{ci} denotes a neighborhood function that governs the strength of weight adaptation as well as the number of reference vectors to be updated (generally, a gaussian function is used). It is worth noting that a good choice for the number of iterations during the learning is 500 times the number of cells in the SOM.

3.2 Bag of Local Descriptors Representation

As previously emphasized, at this stage of the algorithm, an image I_j is described by a set of local signatures $S(I_j) = \{s_{1j}, \ldots, s_{nj}\}$ representing $3D$ histograms around interest points presented in section 2.2. Thus, this kind of representation could not be directly interpreted by a classifier because of the lack of ordering between signatures. Moreover, the number of signatures could be different for two images (due to different number of interest points detected). Thus, to build and use an image classifier, the image I_j should be represented by a feature vector $H(I_j) = [h_{1j}, \ldots, h_{Nj}]$. For this purpose, an indexing step should be used to transform the set of local signatures into a precise and compact representation of the image content.

This is a classical problem met in text categorization where a document composed of a set of words has to be characterized by a vector describing its content. For this purpose, a text is often represented by a vector of term weights, where the terms are chosen in the codebook (a set of meaningful words for the understanding of texts); this is the well known "Bag of Words" representation. This approach has influenced the work presented in [3] and denoted "Bag of Keypoints" which proposed to adapt text categorization methods to the computer vision problems.

Similarly, we propose to represent the image content by the probabilistic distribution H over local images features. This distribution is in fact the activation histogram of the SOM previously learned. For this purpose, each local signature of the image activates a particular cell (The BMU) and participates to an update of the histogram $H(I_j)$. The bins h_{lj} are defined as follow:

$$h_{lj} = card\{s_k \in I_j, ||s_k - w_l|| < ||s_k - w_i|| \forall l \neq j, k \in \{1, \ldots, n\}\}. \tag{5}$$

4   Neural Network Classification

At this stage of the algorithm, each image is represented by a unique feature vector denoted H. The natural image classification problem is thus reduced to a multi-class supervised classification problem. For this purpose, we have tested a multilayer perceptron (MLP), a Radial Basis Function network classifier (RBF) and a Support Vector Machine classifier (SVM). Experimentally MLP exhibited better results than the RBF and equivalent results than the SVM. Thus we restrict our discussion on this classifier.

MLPs can be used for classification problems and are multi layers feedforward neural networks fully connected. Thanks to their fundamental property of parcimonious approximation, they are well suited to modelize any continuous function $g : \mathbb{R}^N \to \mathbb{R}^p$, where N is the dimension of the input space and p is the number of classes. However, it supposes that sufficient neurons are chosen during the definition of the network architecture. A three layer perceptron architecture with N intputs, n_h hidden neurons and p output neurons is presented on figure 4.

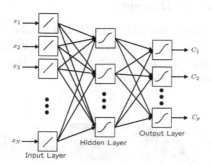

Fig. 4. General Principle of a Multilayer Perceptron

For an input data $X = [x_1, \ldots, x_N] \in \mathbb{R}^N$, the output of the kth output neuron of this MLP is given by the discriminant function:

$$g_k(X, W) = \varphi \left(\sum_{j=1}^{n_h} w_{kj} \varphi \left(\sum_{i=1}^{N} w_{ji} x_i + w_{j0} \right) + w_{k0} \right) \forall k \in \{1, \ldots, p\} \quad (6)$$

where $W = \{w_{ij}\}$ is the set of weights of the neural network considered and φ is the activation of the neurons of both the hidden and ouput layer. This one should be non-linear allowing the MLP networks to model nonlinear mappings well and is the standart sigmoidal function in the following.

MLPs are trained with the backpropagation algorithm which adapts the weights of the network in W to their optimal values for the given pairs $(X_l, t(X_l)) \forall l \in \{1, \ldots, N_L\}$ in the training dataset. If the target vector $t(X_l)$ gives the correct class of X_l and is such that $t_k(X_l) = 1$ if $X_l \in C_k$ and 0 otherwise then the trained network approximates the correct a posteriori probabilities concerning the classification problem: $g_k(X, W) \approx P(C_k|X)$. An input data X can thus be easily classified by regarding the maximal value of the output neurons.

5   Experimental Results

In this section, the system scheme is tested on different well known datasets. The experiments particularly emphasize on the influence of the vocabulary size (i.e. the size of the SOM) on the classification results. These results are analyzed by evaluating global classification rates. Furthermore, the analysis of ROC curves by computing the area under curve (AUC) for the best parameters will be presented providing a direct comparison to other algorithms. It is worth noting that the MLPs used in the experiments have a number of nodes in the hidden layer which is the mean of the number of nodes in the input and ouput layer $n_h = \frac{N+p}{2}$. It permits to achieve good classification results in reasonable computing times.

5.1   Presentation of the Datasets

The first dataset is extracted from the SIMPLICITY database[2]. It contains 500 images of size 384×256 and is divided into a learning dataset of 250 images and a test dataset of 250 images. There are five clusters: beaches, buildings, buses, elephants and flowers as shown on figure 5.

Fig. 5. Images from the SIMPLICITY Database

The Pascal database[3] is used to compare results with other major approaches of the state of the art presented during the PASCAL visual object classes challenge 2005. It is composed of four clusters (bikes, bicycles, persons and cars) as shown on figure 6. The test set contains 688 images whereas the training set contains 684 images. This base is representative of what a person has on his computer, they are of various sizes and have been shot from various viewpoints.

Fig. 6. Images from the PASCAL Database

5.2   Influence of the Self Organizing Map Size

The influence of the vocabulary size on the classification results is conjointly tested with the number of interest points extracted from the image. The SOM is rectangular and its size varies from 5×5 to 15×15 which constitutes a vocabulary from 25 to 225 prototypes. On figure 7, the global classification rates are shown.

---

[2] http://wang.ist.psu.edu/ jwang/test1.tar
[3] http://www.pascal-network.org/challenges/VOC/

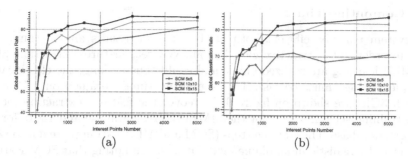

Fig. 7. Global Classification Rates for SIMPLICITY (a) and Pascal (b) datasets

For the two dataset used, the optimal SOM size is 15×15 which constitutes a small dictionnary of 250 prototypes. Nevertheless, the results between 15×15 and 10×10 are not so different compared from those obtained with a 5×5 lattice. Moreover, a study has shown that the quantization error does not decay very fast if the SOM is larger. It is thus not necessary to improve the dictionnary size.

For the two dataset, 3000 interest points are a good compromise in term of computing times and global classification rates. In this case, the method obtains a global classification rate of 86.4% for the SIMPLICITY dataset (86.4% for the SVM and 82% for the RBF) and 82.9% for the PASCAL database (81.7% for the SVM and 75% for the RBF).

5.3 ROC Curve Analysis and Confusion Matrix

On figure 8, AUC and confusion matrix are displayed for the parameters exhibited in the previous section. For the PASCAL dataset, the results are good and comparable to those obtained during the PASCAL 2005 recognition challenge.

Class	AUC
Beaches	0.9125
Buildings	0.9330
Buses	0.9959
Elephants	0.9844
Flowers	0.9971

Beach	Buildings	Buses	Elephants	Flowers	classified as
37	6	2	3	2	Beach
8	37	0	4	1	Buildings
2	1	47	0	0	Buses
4	1	0	45	0	Elephants
0	0	0	0	50	Flowers

Class	AUC
Bicycles	0.926
Cars	0.9622
Motorbikes	0.9793
People	0.8862

Bicycles	Cars	Motorbikes	People	classified as
71	23	14	6	Bicycles
7	252	5	11	Cars
7	3	202	4	Motorbikes
13	18	7	46	People

Fig. 8. AUC and Confusion Matrix for the SIMPLICITY and Pascal Dataset

5.4   Computing Times

The system must be efficient both in classification results and in computing times in order to be attractive for a human. Whereas features extraction, SOM and MLP learning are realized offline and could thus be long, the classification of a query image must be fast. The computing times obtained on a Pentium IV with 3Ghz are shown on figure 9. Moreover the features extraction for the entire training set takes $290s$ for the SIMPLICITY database and $1301s$ for the PASCAL database. The training steps (SOM and MLP learning) are not too long and so totally realistic in an offline mode. It is worth noting that SOM learning does not depend on the database size and the interest point number but only on the dimension of the SOM as emphasized in section 3.1 because the number of iterations is 500 times the number of cells in the SOM. The classification of a new instance is very fast and could thus be realized online in a professional application.

Dataset	SIMPLICITY			PASCAL		
Size of the SOM	5×5	10×10	15×15	5×5	10×10	15×15
SOM learning	4s	46s	185s	5s	46s	195s
MLP learning	12s	127s	665s	30s	413s	1706s
MLP classification	0.00012s	0.00064s	0.00244s	0.00012s	0.00073s	0.00232s

Fig. 9. Computing Times

6   Conclusion

This paper presents a neural network architecture for natural image classification using local images features. It has been shown that a self organizing map could learn a small visual dictionnary subsequently used to represent the image content by a distribution over the prototypes. Moreover, a classification step based on a multilayer perceptron has shown to be efficient. The approach exhibits high classification rates and small computing times. Its implementation in a professional application is thus possible. The perspectives are to use the Growing Hierarchical Self Organizing Map to generate the codebook [17] and to represent the image as a "bags of graphs" generated by grouping interest points which could be learned thanks to a SOM for structured datas [18].

References

1. Duda R.O, Hart P.E., Stork D.G.: Pattern Classification. 2nd edition edn. John Wiley & Sons (2001)
2. Schmid C., Mohr R.: Local grayvalue invariants for image retrieval. IEEE Transaction on Pattern Analysis and Machine Intelligence 19(5) (1997) 530–535
3. Csurka G., Bray C., Dance C., Fan L.: Visual categorization with bags of keypoints. In: The 8th European Conference on Computer Vision, Prague, Czech Republic (2004) 327–334

4. Jurie F., Triggs B.: Creating efficient codebooks for visual recognition. In: International Conference on Computer Vision, Beijing, China (2005) 604–610
5. Weber M., Welling M., Perona P.: Unsupervised learning of models for recognition. In: The 6th European Conference on Computer Vision, London, UK, Springer-Verlag (2000) 18–32
6. Fei-Fei L., Perona P.: A hierarchical bayesian model for learning natural scene categories. In: International Conference on Computer Vision and Pattern Recognition. Volume 2., San Diego, CA, USA (2005) 524–531
7. Marée R., Geurts P., Piater J., Wehenkel L.: Random subwindows for robust image classification. In: International Conference on Computer Vision and Pattern Recognition. Volume 1. (2005) 34–40
8. Agarwal S., Awan A., Roth D.: Learning to detect objects in images via a sparse, part-based representation. IEEE Transactions on Pattern Analysis and Machine Intelligence $26(11)$ (2004) 1475–1490
9. Kohonen T.: Self-Organizing Maps. Springer-Verlag, Berlin, Heidelberg, New York (2001)
10. Laurent C., Laurent N., Maurizot M., Dorval T.: In depth analysis and evaluation of saliency-based color image indexing methods using wavelet salient features. Multimedia Tools and Application (2004)
11. Bres S., Jolion J.M.: Detection of interest points for image indexation. In: 3rd International Conference on Visual Information Systems, Amsterdam, The Netherlands (1999) 427–434
12. Harris C., Stephens M.: A combined corner and edge detector. In: 4th Alvey Vision Conference. (1988) 147–151
13. K. Mikolajczyk, Schmid C.: Scale and affine invariant interest point detectors. International Journal of Computer Vision $60(1)$ (2004) 63–86
14. Loupias E., Sebe N., Bres S., Jolion J.M.: Wavelet-based salient points for image retrieval. In: IEEE International Conference on Image Processing, Vancouver, Canada (2000) 518–521
15. Mallat S.: Foveal Approximations for Singularities. Applied and Computational Harmonic Analysis $14(2)$ (2003) 133–180
16. Lowe D.G.: Distinctive image features from scale-invariant keypoints. International Journal of Computer Vision $60(2)$ (2004) 91–110
17. Rauber A., Merkl D., Dittenbach M.: The growing hierarchical self-organizing maps: Exploratory analysis of high-dimensional data. IEEE Transactions on Neural Networks $13(6)$ (2002) 1331–1341
18. Hagenbuchner M., Sperduti A.: A self-organizing map for adaptive processing of structured data. IEEE Transactions on Neural Networks $14(3)$ (2003) 491–505

Bayesian Learning of Hierarchical Multinomial Mixture Models of Concepts for Automatic Image Annotation

Rui Shi[1], Tat-Seng Chua[1], Chin-Hui Lee[2], and Sheng Gao[3]

[1] School of Computing, National University of Singapore, Singapore 117543
[2] School of ECE, Georgia Institute of Technology, Atlanta, GA 30332, USA
[3] Institute for Infocomm Research, Singapore 119613
{shirui, chuats}@comp.nus.edu.sg, chl@ece.gatech.edu,
gaosheng@i2r.a-star.edu.sg

Abstract. We propose a novel Bayesian learning framework of hierarchical mixture model by incorporating prior hierarchical knowledge into concept representations of multi-level concept structures in images. Characterizing image concepts by mixture models is one of the most effective techniques in automatic image annotation (AIA) for concept-based image retrieval. However it also poses problems when large-scale models are needed to cover the wide variations in image samples. To alleviate the potential difficulties arising in estimating too many parameters with insufficient training images, we treat the mixture model parameters as random variables characterized by a joint conjugate prior density of the mixture model parameters. This facilitates a statistical combination of the likelihood function of the available training data and the prior density of the concept parameters into a well-defined posterior density whose parameters can now be estimated via a maximum a posteriori criterion. Experimental results on the Corel image dataset with a set of 371 concepts indicate that the proposed Bayesian approach achieved a maximum F_1 measure of 0.169, which outperforms many state-of-the-art AIA algorithms.

1 Introduction

It is said that "a picture is worth a thousand words". Following the advances in computing and Internet technologies, the volume of digital image and video is increasing rapidly. The challenge is how to use these large and distributed image collections to increase human productivity in the reuse of valuable assets and the retrieval of information in domains such as crime prevention, medicine and publishing. Thus effective tools to automatically index images are essential in order to support applications in image retrieval. In particular, automatic image annotation has become a hot topic to facilitate content-based indexing of images.

Automatic image annotation (AIA) refers to the process of automatically labeling the image contents with a predefined set of keywords or concepts representing image semantics. It is used primarily for image database management. Annotated images can be retrieved using keyword-based search, while non-annotated images can only be found using content-based image retrieval (CBIR) techniques whose performance levels are still not good enough for practical image retrieval applications. Thus AIA aims to annotate the images as accurately as possible to support keyword-based image

H. Sundaram et al. (Eds.): CIVR 2006, LNCS 4071, pp. 102–112, 2006.
© Springer-Verlag Berlin Heidelberg 2006

search. In this paper, we loosely use the term *word* and *concept* interchangeably to denote text annotations of images.

Most approaches to AIA can be divided into two categories. The AIA models in the first category focus on finding joint probabilities of images and concepts. Co-occurrence model (CO) [12], translation model (TR) [3], and cross-media relevance model (CMRM) [7] are a few examples in this category. To represent an image, those models first segment the image into a collection of regions and quantize the visual features from image regions into a set of region clusters (so-called blobs). Given a training image corpus represented by a collection of blobs, many learning algorithms have been developed to estimate the joint probability of the concepts and blobs. In the annotation phase, the top concepts that maximize such a joint probability are assigned as concept associated with the test image. To simplify the joint density characterization, the concepts and blobs for an image are often assumed to be mutually independent [7]. As pointed out in [2], there is some contradiction with this naïve assumption because the annotation process is based on the Bayes decision rule which relies on the dependency between concepts and blobs.

In the second category of approaches, each concept corresponds to a class typically characterized by a mixture model. AIA is formulated as a multi-class classification problem. In [2], the probability density function for each class was estimated by a tree structure which is a collection of mixtures organized hierarchically. Given a predefined concept hierarchy, the approach in [4] focused on finding an optimal number of mixture components for each concept class. Different from approaches in [2] and [4], ontologies are used in [14] to build a hierarchical classification model (HC) with a concept hierarchy derived from WordNet [11] to model concept dependencies. Only one mixture component was used to model each concept class. An improved estimate for each leaf concept node was obtained by "shrinking" its ML (maximum likelihood) estimate towards the ML estimates of all its ancestors tracing back from that leaf to the root. A multi-topic text categorization (TC) approach to AIA was proposed in [5] by representing an image as a high-dimension document vector with associations to a set of multiple concepts.

When more mixture components are needed to cover larger variations in image samples, it often leads to poor AIA performance due to the insufficient amount of training samples and inaccurate estimation of a large number of model parameters. To tackle this problem, we incorporate prior knowledge into the hierarchical concept representation, and propose a new Bayesian learning framework called BHMMM (Bayesian Hierarchical Multinomial Mixture Model) to estimate the parameters of these concept mixture models. This facilitates a statistical combination of the likelihood function of the available training data and the prior density of the concept parameters into a well-defined posterior density whose parameters can now be estimated via a maximum a posteriori (MAP) criterion. Experimental results on the Corel image dataset with 371 concepts indicate that our proposed framework achieved an average per-concept F_1 measure of 0.169 which outperforms many state-of-the-art AIA techniques.

The rest of the paper is organized as follows. In Section 2 we address the key issues in general mixture models and formulate the AIA problem using hierarchical Bayesian multinomial mixture models. In Section 3 we discuss building concept hierarchies from WordNet. Two concept models, namely two-level and multi-level hierarchical models, or TL-HM and ML-HM for short, are proposed to specify the hyperparameters needed to define the prior density and perform the MAP estimation of the concept parameters. Experimental results for a 371-concept AIA task on the Corel dataset and performance comparisons are presented in Section 4. Finally we conclude our findings in Section 5.

2   Problem Formulation

Since mixture models are used extensively in our study, we first describe them in detail. In [3, 7], any image can be represented by an image vector $I = (n_1, n_2, ..., n_L)$, where L is the total number of blobs, and $n_l (1 \leq l \leq L)$ denotes the observed count of the lth blob in image I. Given a total of J mixture components and the ith concept c_i, the observed vector I from the concept class c_i is assumed to have the following probability:

$$p(I \mid \Lambda_i) = \sum_{j=1}^{J} w_{i,j} p(I \mid \theta_{i,j}) \tag{1}$$

where $\Lambda_i = \{W_i, \Theta_i\}$ is the parameter set for the above mixture model, including mixture weight set $W_i = \{w_{i,j}\}_{j=1}^{J}$ ($\sum_{j=1}^{J} w_{i,j} = 1$), and mixture parameter set $\Theta_i = \{\theta_{i,j}\}_{j=1}^{J}$. $p(I \mid \theta_{i,j})$ is the jth mixture component to characterize the class distribution. In this paper, we use θ_i to denote the mixture parameters of concept class c_i and $\theta_{i,j}$ to denote the parameters of the jth mixture component of the concept class c_i. In this study, we assume that each mixture component is modeled by multinomial distribution as follows:

$$p(I \mid \theta_{i,j}) \propto \prod_{l=1}^{L} \theta_{i,j,l}^{n_l} \tag{2}$$

where $\theta_{i,j} = (\theta_{i,j,1}, \theta_{i,j,2}, ..., \theta_{i,j,L})$, $\theta_{i,j,l} > 0$, $\sum_{l=1}^{L} \theta_{i,j,l} = 1$, and each element $\theta_{i,j,l} (1 \leq l \leq L)$ represents the probability of the lth blob occurring in the jth mixture component of the ith concept class. Now for a total of N concepts, we are given a collection of independent training images D_i ($I_{i,t} \in D_i$) for each concept class c_i, the parameters in set Λ_i can be estimated with a maximum likelihood (ML) criterion as follows:

$$\overline{\Lambda}_i^{ml} = \arg\max_{\Lambda_i} \log p(D_i \mid \Lambda_i) = \arg\max_{\Lambda_i} \log \prod_{t=1}^{|D_i|} p(I_{i,t} \mid \Lambda_i) \tag{3}$$

We followed the EM algorithm [13] to estimate the model parameter Λ_i with ML criterion. In this following, we will use this model as our baseline. Although the mixture model is a simple way to combine multiple simpler distributions to form more complex ones, the major shortcoming of mixture model is that there are usually too many parameters to be estimated but not enough training images for each concept. In cases when there are larger variations among the image examples, more mixture components are needed to cover such diversities. This problem is particularly severe for natural images that tend to have large variations among them. Furthermore, for more general concepts, there are likely to be larger variations among the images, too. Figure 1 shows some images from the general 'hawaii' concept class. It is clear a large-scale mixture model is needed to model this particular concept.

Fig. 1. Image examples from 'hawaii'

One way to enhance the ML estimates is to incorporate prior knowledge into modeling by assuming the mixture parameters in $\theta_{i,j}$ as random variables with a joint prior density $p_0(\theta_{i,j} \mid \varphi_i)$ with a set of parameters φ_i (often referred to as *hyperparameters*). The posterior probability of observing the training set can now be evaluated as:

$$p(\Lambda_i \mid D_i) = a * \{\prod_{t=1}^{|D_i|} \sum_{j=1}^{J} [w_{i,j} p(I_{i,t} \mid \theta_{i,j})]\} * p_0(\Theta_i \mid \varphi_i) \qquad (4)$$

where a is a scaling factor that depends on D_i. In contrast to conventional ML estimation shown in Eq. (3), we can impose a maximum a posterior (MAP) criterion to estimate the parameters as follows:

$$\bar{\Lambda}_i^{map} = \arg\max_{\Lambda_i} \log p(\Lambda_i \mid D_i) = \arg\max_{\Lambda_i} \log\{\prod_{t=1}^{|D_i|} \sum_{j=1}^{J} [w_{i,j} p(I_{i,t} \mid \theta_{i,j})]\} * p_0(\Theta_i \mid \varphi_i) \qquad (5)$$

Generally speaking, the definition of the prior density p_0 may come from subject matter considerations and/or from previous experiences. Due to the complexity of the data set for new applications, we often do not have enough experiences to specify the hyperparameters. However, in most practical settings, we do have prior domain knowledge which describes the dependencies among concepts often in terms of a hierarchical structure. Thus based on the posteriori density in Eq. (4), we propose a new Bayesian hierarchical multinomial mixture model (BHMMM) to characterize the hierarchical concept structure. The basic idea behind the proposed BHMMM is that the mixtures from the most dependent concepts share the same set of hyperparameters and these concept mixture models are constrained by a common prior density parameterized by this set. This is reasonable since given a concept (say, 'leopard') the images from its most dependent concepts (say, 'tiger') are often related and can be used as prior knowledge. Obviously how to define 'most dependent' depends on our prior domain knowledge. For example, Fig.2a shows the simplest two-level concept hierarchy in which all the concepts (c_1, c_2, ... , c_N) are derived from the root node labeled 'entity'. The structure of this two-level hierarchical model (TL-HM) is shown in Fig.2b, in which all the mixture parameters share only one common prior density with the same hyperparameter set φ_0.

The advantage of using such a two-level concept hierarchy is that we don't need any prior domain knowledge. However, the two-level concept hierarchy can not capture all the concept dependencies accurately. For instance, there is not much

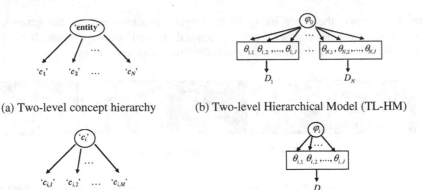

(a) Two-level concept hierarchy   (b) Two-level Hierarchical Model (TL-HM)

(c) Sub-tree of multi-level concept hierarchy   (d) Multi-level HM (ML-HM)

Fig. 2. An illustration of the proposed BHMMM

dependency between the concepts of 'buildings', 'street' and the concept of 'tiger'. To better model the concept dependencies, we first derive a concept hierarchy through WordNet in Section 3.1. Fig. 2c shows a sub-tree of multi-level concept hierarchy in which the concepts ($c_{i,1}$, $c_{i,2}$, ... , $c_{i,M}$) are derived from their parent node labeled 'c_i'. We then extend the two-level to multi-level hierarchical model (ML-HM) by characterizing the prior density parameters for the ith concept mixture model with a separate set of hyperparameters φ_i, as shown in Fig 2d. Then the mixtures from concepts $c_{i,1}$, $c_{i,2}$, ... , $c_{i,M}$ share the same set of hyperparameters φ_i. Clearly more hyperparameters are needed in ML-HM than in TL-HM. We will compare the two models in Section 3.

3   Hierarchical Models

3.1   Building Concept Hierarchy

As discussed in Section 2, we are interested in accurately model the concept dependencies which requires finding relationships between concepts. Ontologies, such as the WordNet [11], are convenient specifications of such relationships. WordNet is an electronic thesaurus to organize the meaning of English nouns, verbs, adjectives and adverbs into synonym sets, and are used extensively in lexical semantics acquisition [9]. Every word in WordNet has one or more senses, each of which has a distinct set of related words through other relations such as hypernyms, hyponyms or holonyms. For example, the word 'path' is a concept in our corpus. 'Path' has four senses in WordNet and each sense is characterized by a sequence of words (hypernyms): (a) path←course ←action←activity←abstract←entity; (b) path←way←artifact←object←entity; (c) path, route←line←location←object←entity, and (d) path, track←line←location← object←entity. Thus the key for building a concept hierarchy is to disambiguate the senses of words.

Since the words used as annotations in our data set (Corel CD) are nouns, we only use the 'hypernym' relation which points to a word that is more generic than a given word in order to disambiguate the sense of words. We further assume that one word corresponds to only one sense in the whole corpus. This is reasonable as a word naturally has only one meaning within a context. With this assumption, we adopt the basic idea that the sense of a word is chosen if the hypernyms that characterize this sense are shared by its co-occurred words in our data set. For example, the co-occurred words of 'path' are 'tree', 'mountain', 'wall', 'flower' and so on. Thus path←way←artifact←object←entity is chosen since this sense is mostly shared by these co-occurred words of 'path'. Our approach for disambiguating the senses of words is similar to that used in [1]. After this step of word sense disambiguation, every word is assigned a unique sense characterized by its hypernyms. Thus, we can easily build a multi-level concept hierarchy with 'entity' as the root node of the overall concept hierarchy.

3.2 Definition of Prior Density

Based on the MAP formulation in Eq. (5), three key issues need to be addressed: (i) choosing the form of the prior density, (ii) specification of the hyperparameters, and (iii) MAP estimation. It is well-known that a Dirichlet density is the conjugate prior for estimating the parameters of multinomial distributions so that the posterior distribution has a similar form to the Dirichlet density, which makes it easy to estimate its parameters. Such methods have been used successfully in automatic speech recognition for adaptive estimation of histograms, mixture gains, and Markov chains [6, 9]. We adopt Dirichlet distribution as the prior distribution p_0 with hyperparameter φ (as in Figures 2b and 2d), as follows:

$$p_0(\theta_{i,j} \mid \varphi_0) = \frac{\Gamma(\sum_{l=1}^{L} \varphi_{0,l})}{\prod_{l=1}^{L} \Gamma(\varphi_{0,l})} \prod_{l=1}^{L} \theta_{i,j,l}^{(\varphi_{0,l}-1)} \quad \text{or} \quad p_0(\theta_{i,j} \mid \varphi_i) = \frac{\Gamma(\sum_{l=1}^{L} \varphi_{i,l})}{\prod_{l=1}^{L} \Gamma(\varphi_{i,l})} \prod_{l=1}^{L} \theta_{i,j,l}^{(\varphi_{i,l}-1)} \quad (6)$$

where $\varphi_i = (\varphi_{i,1}, \varphi_{i,2}, ..., \varphi_{i,L})$, $\varphi_{i,l} > 0, 1 \leqslant l \leqslant L$, and the hyperparameter $\varphi_{i,l}$ can be interpreted as 'prior observation counts' for the lth blob occurring in the ith concept class, and $\Gamma(x)$ is the Gamma function. As discussed in Section 2, the performances of the proposed BHMMM framework depend on the structure of the concept hierarchy. This is related to how we intend to specify the hyperparameters. The remaining issue is the estimation of hyperparameters which will be addressed next.

3.3 Specifying Hyperparameters Based on Concept Hierarchy

We first discuss how to specify hyperparameters based on two-level concept hierarchy as shown in Figures 2a and 2b. If we assume that all mixture parameters $\theta_{i,j}$ share the same set of hyperparameters, φ_0, we can then adopt an empirical Bayes approach [6] to estimate these hyperparameters. Let $\overline{\Theta}_0 = \{\overline{\theta}_1^{ml}, \overline{\theta}_2^{ml}, ..., \overline{\theta}_N^{ml}\}$ denote the mixture parameter set estimated with ML criterion as in Eq. (3). We then pretend to view $\overline{\Theta}_0$ as a set of random samples from the Dirichlet prior $p_0(\varphi_0)$ in Eq. (6). Thus the ML estimate of φ_0 maximizes the logarithm of the likelihood function, $\log p_0(\overline{\Theta}_0 \mid \varphi_0)$. As pointed out in [10], there exists no closed-form solution to this ML estimate, and the fixed-point iterative approach [10] can be adopted to solve for the ML estimate based on a preliminary estimate of φ_0^{old} that satisfies the following:

$$\Psi(\varphi_{0,l}^{new}) = \Psi(\sum_{l=1}^{L} \varphi_{0,l}^{old}) + \frac{1}{N \times J} \sum_{i=1}^{N} \sum_{j=1}^{J} \log \overline{\theta}_{i,j,l}^{ml} \tag{7}$$

where $\Psi(x) = \dfrac{d\Gamma(x)}{dx}$ is known as the digamma function. More details can be found in [10].

For characterizing multi-level concept hierarchy, we assume that all mixture parameters $\theta_{i,j}$ in the ith concept share the same set of hyperparameters, φ_i, then we can use the data in D_i to obtain a preliminary ML estimate $\overline{\theta}_i$ and pretend to view $\overline{\theta}_i$ as a set of random samples from the Dirichlet prior $p_0(\varphi_i)$ in Eq. (6). Then the ML estimate of φ_i can be solved by maximizing the log-likelihood $\log p_0(\overline{\theta}_i | \varphi_i)$. The above fixed-point iterative approach [10] can again be adopted to solve for the ML estimate based on a preliminary estimate of φ_i^{old} that satisfies the following:

$$\Psi(\varphi_{i,l}^{new}) = \Psi(\sum_{l=1}^{L} \varphi_{i,l}^{old}) + \frac{1}{J} \sum_{j=1}^{J} \log \overline{\theta}_{i,j,l}^{ml} \tag{8}$$

It is clear that the concept-specific hyperparameter estimate φ_i uses less data in Eq. (8) than those in Eq. (7) for general hyperparameter estimate φ_0.

3.4 MAP Estimation of Mixture Model Parameters

With the prior density given in Eq. (6) and the hyperparameters specified in Eq. (7) or (8), we are now ready to solve MAP estimation in Eq. (5) as follows:

By traversing the nodes one by one from left to right in the same level, and from root level down to the leaf level, for each node c_i in the concept hierarchy:

♦ Let c_{ip} denote the parent node of c_i and $p_0(\overline{\varphi}_{ip}^{ml})$ denote the prior density function for the mixture model parameters of c_{ip}, we have:

$$\overline{\Lambda}_i^{map} = \arg \max_{\Lambda_i} \log p(\Lambda_i | D_i) = \arg \max_{\Lambda_i} \log \{ \prod_{t=1}^{|D_i|} [\sum_{j=1}^{J} [w_{i,j} p(I_{i,t} | \theta_{i,j})]] * p_0(\Theta_i | \overline{\varphi}_{ip}^{ml}) \tag{9}$$

where $\overline{\varphi}_{ip}^{ml} = (\overline{\varphi}_{ip,1}^{ml}, \overline{\varphi}_{ip,2}^{ml}, ..., \overline{\varphi}_{ip,L}^{ml})$, $\overline{\varphi}_{ip,l}^{ml} > 0, 1 \leqslant l \leqslant L$.

♦ If c_i has the child node, then the prior density function $p_0(\varphi_i)$ for mixture parameters of c_i can be calculated by the approach described in Section 4.

$$\overline{\varphi}_i^{ml} = \arg \max_{\varphi_i} \log \prod_j p_0(\overline{\theta}_{i,j}^{ml} | \varphi_i)$$

We simply extend the EM algorithm in [13] to solve Eq. (9). Given a preliminary estimate of Λ_i^{new}, the EM algorithm can be described as follows:

E-step: $w_{i,j}^{old} = w_{i,j}^{new}, \quad \theta_{i,j}^{old} = \theta_{i,j}^{new}, \quad \Lambda_i^{old} = \{\{w_{i,j}^{old}\}_{j=1}^J, \{\theta_{i,j}^{old}\}_{j=1}^J\},$

$$p(j|I_{i,t}, \Lambda_i^{old}) = \frac{p(I_{i,t}|\theta_{i,j}^{old})p_0(\theta_{i,j}^{old}|\overline{\varphi}_{ip}^{ml})w_{i,j}^{old}}{\sum_{j=1}^J p(I_{i,t}|\theta_{i,j}^{old})p_0(\theta_{i,j}^{old}|\overline{\varphi}_{ip}^{ml})w_{i,j}^{old}} = \frac{w_{i,j}^{old}\prod_{l=1}^L (\theta_{i,j,l}^{old})^{n_{i,t,l}+\overline{\varphi}_{ip,l}^{ml}-1}}{\sum_{j=1}^J w_{i,j}^{old}\prod_{l=1}^L (\theta_{i,j,l}^{old})^{n_{i,t,l}+\overline{\varphi}_{ip,l}^{ml}-1}}.$$

M-step: $\quad w_{i,j}^{new} = \dfrac{\sum_{t=1}^{|D_i|} p(j|I_{i,t}, \Lambda_i^{old})}{|D_i|}, \quad \theta_{i,j,l}^{new} = \dfrac{\sum_{t=1}^{|D_i|} p(j|I_{i,t}, \Lambda_i^{old})\times(n_{i,t,l}+\overline{\varphi}_{ip,l}^{ml}-1)}{\sum_{t=1}^{|D_i|}\sum_{l=1}^L p(j|I_{i,t}, \Lambda_i^{old})\times(n_{i,t,l}+\overline{\varphi}_{ip,l}^{ml}-1)}.$

Here $|D_i|$ denotes the size of training set D_i for c_i, $n_{i,t,l}$ ($1 \leqslant l \leqslant L$) denotes the observed count of the lth blob in the image $I_{i,t} \in D_i$, and $p(j|I_{i,t}, \Lambda_i^{old})$ is the probability that the jth mixture component fits the image $I_{i,t}$, given the parameter Λ_i^{old}.

4   Testing Setup and Experimental Results

Following [3, 7], we conduct our experiments on the same Corel CD data set, consisting of 4500 images for training and 500 images for testing. The total number of region clusters (blobs) is $L=500$. In this corpus, there are 371 concepts in the training set but only 263 such concepts appear in the testing set, with each image assigned 1-5 concepts. After the derivation of concept hierarchy as discussed in Section 3.1, we obtained a concept hierarchy containing a total of 513 concepts, including 322 leaf concepts and 191 non-leaf concepts. The average number of children of non-leaf concepts is about 3. If a non-leaf concept node in the concept hierarchy doesn't belong to the concept set in Corel CD corpus, then its training set will consist of all the images from its child nodes. As with the previous studies on this AIA task, the AIA performance is evaluated by comparing the generated annotations with the actual image annotations in the test set. We assign a set of five top concepts to each test image based on their likelihoods.

Table 1. Performances of our approaches

Models (mixture number)	Baseline ($J=5$)	Baseline ($J=25$)	TL-HM ($J=5$)	TL-HM ($J=25$)	ML-HM ($J=5$)	ML-HM ($J=25$)
# of concepts (recall>0)	104	101	107	110	117	122
Mean Per-concept metrics on all 263 concepts on the Corel dataset						
Mean Precision	0.102	0.095	0.114	0.121	0.137	0.142
Mean Recall	0.168	0.159	0.185	0.192	0.209	0.225
Mean F1	0.117	0.109	0.133	0.140	0.160	0.169

We first compare the performances of TL-HM and ML-HM with the baseline mixture model. In order to highlight the ability to cover large variations in the image set, we select two different numbers of mixtures (5 and 25) to emulate image variations.

These two numbers are obtained by our empirical experiences. The results in terms of averaging precision, recall and F1 are tabulated in Table 1. From Table 1, we can draw the following observations: (a) The performance of baseline (J=25) is worse than that of baseline (J=5). This is because the number of training image examples are same in both cases and we are able to estimate the small number of parameters for baseline (J=5) more accurately. This result highlights the limitation of mixture model when there are large variations in image samples. (b) The F1 performances of TL-HM and ML-HM are better than that of the baseline (J=5). This indicates that the proper use of prior information is important to our AIA mixture model. (c) Compared with TL-HM (J=5, 25), ML-HM (J=5, 25) achieves about 20% and 21% improvements on F1 measure. This shows that the use of concept hierarchy in ML-HM results in more accurate estimate of prior density, since ML-HM permits a concept node to only inherit the prior information from its parent node. Overall, ML-HM achieves the best performance of 0.169 in terms of F1 measure.

Table 2. Performances of state-of-the-art AIA models

Models	CO [8,12]	TR [3,8]	CMRM [7,8]	HC [14]
#concepts with recall>0	19	49	66	93
Mean per-concept results on all 263 concepts on the Corel dataset				
Mean Per-concept Precision	0.020	0.040	0.090	0.100
Mean Per-concept Recall	0.030	0.060	0.100	0.176

For further comparison, we tabulate the performances of a few representative state-of-the-art AIA models in Table 2. These are all *discrete* models which used the same experimental settings as in Table 1. From Table 2, we can draw the following observations: (a) Among these models, HC achieved the best performance in terms of precision and recall measures, since HC also incorporated the concept hierarchy derived from the WordNet into the classification. This further reinforces the importance of utilizing the hierarchical knowledge for AIA task. (b) Compared with HC which used only one mixture for each concept class and adopted ML criterion to estimate the parameters, HM-ML (J=25) achieved about 40% and 28% improvements on the measure of mean per-concept precision and mean per-concept recall respectively. This demonstrates again that HM-ML is an effective strategy to AIA task.

To analyze the benefits of our strategies, we perform a second test by dividing the testing concepts into two sets – designated as primitive concept (PC) and

Table 3. Performances of our approaches in PC and NPC

Models (mixture components)	Baseline (J=5)	TL-HM (J=25)	ML-HM (J=25)	Baseline (J=5)	TL-HM (J=25)	ML-HM (J=25)
Concept Split	Results with 137 concepts in **PC**			Results with 126 concepts in **NPC**		
#concepts (recall>0)	44	45	49	60	65	73
Mean Per-concept F1	0.099	0.116	0.141	0.133	0.162	0.196

non-primitive concept (NPC) sets. The PC concepts, such as 'tiger', 'giraffe' and 'pyramid', have relatively concrete visual forms. On the other hand the NPC concepts, such as 'landscape', 'ceremony' and 'city', do not exhibit concrete visual descriptions. The total number of concepts is 137 and 126 for NPC and PC sets respectively. We expect the use of ML-HM that utilizes the concept hierarchy to be more beneficial to the concepts in the NPC set than those in the PC set. In this test, we select the best performing system in each category, namely Baseline (J=5), TL-HM (J=25) and ML-HM (J=25). The results on the PC and NPC sets are presented in Table 3 for the F1 measure. It is clear that ML-HM (J=25) achieves the best performance on the NPC set among the three cases. ML-HM can detect 13 more concepts on the NPC set as compared to the baseline but only 5 more concepts on the PC set. In terms of the F1 measure, ML-HM achieves about 47% and 42% improvement over the baseline on the NPC and PC sets respectively. Overall, both ML-HM and TL-HM outperform the Baseline on both the PC and NPC sets. The ML-HM model, being able to take full advantage of the multi-level concept structure to model the concepts in the NPC set, performs better than TL-HM model.

Table 4. Mean number of training examples

Concept Split	(1) NPC #concepts (recall>0)	(2) NPC #concepts (recall=0)	(3) PC #concepts (recall>0)	(4) PC #concepts (recall=0)
Number of concept classes in each group	77	49	54	83
Mean number of training examples for each concept class	103.34	19.25	98.11	12.35

To analyze the effect of the number of training examples on the performances, we further analyze the results by splitting the testing concepts into four groups, two concept groups for NPC with recall>0 and recall=0, and two concept groups for PC with recall>0 and recall=0. In arriving at the number of concept classes of 77 (or 54) for NPC (or PC), we simply combine all the classes with recall>0 obtained from the three methods (Baseline TL-HM and ML-HM). From the results presented in Table 4, the mean number of training examples from (1) and (3) is significantly more than that in (2) and (4). Although we didn't investigate the qualitative relationships between the number of training examples and the performances, this result clearly states that if the number of training examples is too small, our proposed BHMMM could not achieve good performances. So from this perspective, how to acquire more training examples for concept classes is an important problem which we will tackle in our future work.

5 Conclusion

In this paper, we incorporated prior knowledge into hierarchical representation of concepts to facilitate modeling of multi-level concept structures. To alleviate the potential difficulties arising in estimating too many parameters with insufficient training images, we proposed a Bayesian hierarchical mixture model framework. By treating the mixture model parameters as random variables characterized by a joint conjugate prior density, it facilitates a statistical combination of the likelihood function of the available training data and the prior density of the concept parameters into a well-defined posterior density whose parameters can now be estimated via a maximum a posteriori criterion. On the one hand when no training data are used, MAP estimate is the mode of the prior density. On the other hand when a large of amount of training data is available the MAP estimate can be shown to asymptotically converge to the conventional maximum likelihood estimate. This desirable property makes the MAP estimate an ideal candidate for estimating a large number of unknown parameters in large-scale mixture models. Experimental results on the Corel image dataset show that the proposed BHMMM approach, using a multi-level structure of 371 concept with a maximum of 25 mixture components per concept, achieves a mean F_1 measure of 0.169, which outperforms many state-of-the-art techniques for automatic image annotation.

References

[1] K. Barnard, P. Duygulu and D. Forsyth, "Clustering Art", In *Proceedings of CVPR*, 2001.

[2] G. Carneiro and N. Vasconcelos, "Formulating Semantic Image Annotation as a Supervised Learning Problem", In *Proceedings of CVPR*, 2005.

[3] P. Duyulu, K. Barnard, N. de Freitas, and D. Forsyth, "Object Recognition as Machine Translation: Learning a Lexicon for a Fixed Image Vocabulary", In *Proc. of ECCV*, 2002.

[4] J. P. Fan, H. Z. Luo and Y. L. Gao, "Learning the Semantics of Images by Using Unlabeled Samples", In *Proceedings of CVPR*, 2005.

[5] S. Gao, D.-H. Wang and C.-H. Lee, "Automatic Image Annotation through Multi-Topic Text Categorization", In *Proceedings of. ICASSP*, Toulouse, France, May 2006.

[6] Q. Huo, C. Chan and C.-H. Lee, "Bayesian Adaptive Learning of the Parameters of Hidden Markov Model for Speech Recognition", *IEEE Trans. Speech Audio Processing*, vol. 3, pp. 334-345, Sept. 1995.

[7] J. Jeon, V. Lavrenko, and R. Manmatha, "Automatic Image Annotation and Retrieval Using Cross-Media Relevance Models", In *Proceedings of the 26th ACM SIGIR*, 2003.

[8] V. Lavrenko, R. Manmatha and J. Jeon, "A Model for Learning the Semantics of Pictures", In *Proceedings of the 16th Conference on NIPS*, 2003.

[9] C.-H. Lee and Q. Huo, "On Adaptive Decision Rules and Decision Parameter Adaptation for Automatic Speech Recognition", In *Proceedings of the IEEE*, vol. 88, no. 8, Aug, 2000.

[10] T. Minka, http://www.stat.cmu.edu/~minka/papers/dirichlet, "Estimating a Dirichlet Distribution", 2003.

[11] G. A. Miller, R. Beckwith, C. Fellbaum, D. Gross and K. J. Miller, "Introduction to WordNet: an on-line lexical database", *Intl. Jour. of Lexicography*, vol. 3, pp. 235-244, 1990.

[12] Y. Mori, H. Takahashi, and R. Oka, "Image-to-Word Transformation Based on Dividing and Vector Quantizing Images with Words", In *Proceedings of MISRM*, 1999.

[13] J. Novovicova and A. Malik, "Application of Multinomial Mixture Model to Text Classification", *Pattern Recognition and Image Analysis*, LNCS 2652, pp. 646-653, 2003.

[14] M. Srikanth, J. Varner, M. Bowden and D. Moldovan, "Exploiting Ontologies for Automatic Image Annotation", In *Proceedings of the 28th ACM SIGIR*, 2005.

Efficient Margin-Based Rank Learning Algorithms for Information Retrieval

Rong Yan and Alexander G. Hauptmann

School of Computer Science
Carnegie Mellon University
Pittsburgh PA, 15213, USA
{yanrong, alex+}@cs.cmu.edu

Abstract. Learning a good ranking function plays a key role for many applications including the task of (multimedia) information retrieval. While there are a few rank learning methods available, most of them need to explicitly model the relations between every pair of relevant and irrelevant documents, and thus result in an expensive training process for large collections. The goal of this paper is to propose a general rank learning framework based on the margin-based risk minimization principle and develop a set of efficient rank learning approaches that can model the ranking relations with much less training time. Its flexibility allows a number of margin-based classifiers to be extended to their rank learning counterparts such as the ranking logistic regression developed in this paper. Experimental results show that this efficient learning algorithm can successfully learn a highly effective retrieval function for multimedia retrieval on the TRECVID'03-'05 collections.[1]

1 Introduction

Many applications have to present their results in form of ranked lists, such as information retrieval that sorts documents according to their relevance to the query and collaborative filtering that sorts items for a user based on the rating provided by other users. All of these applications can benefit if we can automatically learn a better ranked list from some given training examples. In this paper, we specifically consider such a rank learning problem in the context of information retrieval and evaluate it using multimedia retrieval collections. Typically, the training data of a retrieval system include a set of queries, a set of retrieved documents for each query and relevance judgments that manually label some pairs of queries and retrieved documents as relevance and others as irrelevance. Our task is to learn a retrieval utility function to rank the documents using the manual relevance judgments of the training queries.

Previous retrieval models usually cast rank learning into a binary classification problem that treats the relevant query-document pairs as positive data and

---

[1] This research is partially supported by Advanced Research and Development Activity (ARDA) under contract number H98230-04-C-0406 and NBCHC040037, and by the National Science Foundation under Grant No. IIS-0535056.

H. Sundaram et al. (Eds.): CIVR 2006, LNCS 4071, pp. 113–122, 2006.
© Springer-Verlag Berlin Heidelberg 2006

irrelevant pairs as negative data. Some examples include the generative models used in the binary independence model [1] and the discriminative models such as the maximum entropy model [2]. Despite its great successfulness, converting retrieval into classification might suffer from several disadvantages. For example, since the classification accuracy has no direct relationship with the retrieval measure, a learning algorithm that can achieves a high classification accuracy might not produce a good performance in terms of ranking. Therefore, there are a few recent attempts to develop learning algorithms that can explicitly account for ranking relations in information retrieval [3,4,5,6,7]. Most of these rank learning approaches attempt to model the pairwise ranking preferences between every pair of relevant and irrelevant training examples. They are built on a solid foundation because it has been shown that minimizing the discordant pairs of examples are closely related to the commonly used ranking criteria. However, the effort of modeling every pair of examples often leads to a prohibitive learning process and thus limits their applications in practice.

In this paper, we propose a general rank learning framework based on the principle of margin-based risk minimization, which can be generalized to a large family of rank learning approaches such as Ranking SVMs [3] and RankBoost [4]. To make the optimization less computational intensive but still keep the ability to model the ranking relations between examples, we further propose an approximate but efficient rank learning framework by bounding the pairwise risk function. In particular, we designed a new learning algorithm called ranking logistic regression(RLR) by plugging in the logit loss function. Experiments show that this efficient learning algorithm can successfully learn a highly effective retrieval function for multimedia retrieval on the TRECVID'03-'05 collections.

2   Related Work

The wide range of applications for rank learning has inspired numeric approaches to handle this problem especially in the context of information retrieval. One typical direction of rank learning is to formulate it into an ordinal regression problem, i.e., mapping the labels to an ordered set of numerical ranks. Herbrich et al. [8] model the ranks as intervals on the real line, and optimize the loss function based on the true ranks and features. Following the similar idea, "PRank" [9] is developed based on an online linear learning algorithm called perceptron that uses one example at a time to update the linear feature weights. The ordinal regression formulation has been proven to be effective in the task of collaborative filtering. However, it might not be suitable for retrieval because the absolute rankings over documents are usually expensive to collect and users are less willing to provide such a detailed feedback in practice. Moreover, all the objects in ordinal regression have to be ranked in the same scale. But for retrieval, the ranking relationships only need to be consistent within a query which can greatly reduce the number of constraints.

As an alternative of learning the absolute numerical ranks, the approaches that model the relative ranking preferences between pairs of training data has also been investigated recently. In the setting of collaborative filtering, Freund et al. [4] proposed the RankBoost algorithm which learns to rank a set of objects by combining multiple "weak" classifiers to build up a more accurate composite classifiers. The ranking SVMs proposed by Joachims [3] is constructed on a risk-minimization framework with the goal to minimize the number of misorderings between the predicted ranks and target ranks. Bearing resemblance to the common classification SVMs, ranking SVMs can be solved with similar optimization techniques. Based on a simple probabilistic cost function, Burges et al. [5] investigated a gradient descent method called RankNet to learn ranking functions with a neural network implementation. More recently, Chua et al. [6] developed a ranking maximal figure-of-merit(MFoM) algorithm by maximizing the area under the ROC curve. This approach has gained its success in the domain of video semantic feature extraction. In essence, aforementioned rank learning algorithms transform ranks into a set of pairwise relationships between relevant and irrelevant examples and thus cast it into a classification problem built on example pairs. However, above algorithms usually suffer from a expensive training process due to the explosive amount of training data after coupling each relevant and irrelevant documents, especially when the number of underlying training documents is large. For example, a query with 100 relevant documents and 900 irrelevant ones will result in 90,000 pairs of training examples, which is computationally intensive for many learning algorithms. It would be helpful to develop an efficient rank learning algorithm that is able to capture the ranking relationship while with a less learning time.

3 A Margin-Based Framework for Learning Ranks

We begin by introducing the basic notations and terminologies used in this work. The term *document* is referred to as the basic unit of retrieval throughout this paper. For example, in the TRECVID video retrieval task, the documents stands for video shots. A query collection $\mathcal{Q}$ contains a set of queries $\{q_1, ..., q_t, ..., q_{M_Q}\}$ where q_t can have either a set of keywords, a detailed text descriptions or even possibly image, audio, video query examples. A search collection $\mathcal{D}$ contains a set of documents $\{d_1, ..., d_j, ..., d_{M_D}\}$. D_q^+ is the collection of relevant documents and D_q^- is the collection of irrelevant documents for query q. M_D^+ and M_D^- are the number of documents in each collection. For each query q and document d, we can generate a bag of ranking features denoted as $f_i(d, q), i = 1..N$. For instance, in the context of multimedia retrieval, the features can be generated from multiple knowledge sources including either the uni-modal retrieval experts built from various modalities or the indexing of predefined semantic video concepts.

Formally, a ranking (partially ordered list) is a binary relation defined on $D \times D$ with the properties of weak ordering. The goal of a retrieval system is to find a ranking function r_f to approximate the optimal ranking r^*, where r_f means the documents are sorted in a descending order of the retrieval function $f(d_i, q)$. But the prerequisite of optimizing the ranking function is to define an appropriate similarity measure between two rankings. As pointed out by

Joachims [3], Kendall's τ is one of the most frequently used criteria to compare ordinal correlations of two random variables. To explain the Kendall's τ measure, let us define concordant pairs as the document pair (d_i, d_j) when r_1 and r_2 agree on their orders, otherwise discordant pairs. Based on the number of discordant pairs Q, Kendall's τ can be defined as $\tau(r_1, r_2) = 1 - \frac{4Q}{M_D(M_D-1)}$. In the case of binary relevance scale, i.e., all of the documents are judged as either relevant or irrelevant, maximizing $\tau(r_1, r_2)$ is the same as minimizing the average ranks of relevant documents. Since the definition of Kendall's τ only depends on Q, maximizing the $\tau(r_1, r_2)$ is also equivalent to minimizing the number of inversions Q. More importantly, the inverse of Q provides a lower bound of another frequently used performance measure in information retrieval called average precision [3]. Therefore, it is reasonable to develop a rank learning algorithm that attempts to minimize the number of inversions between the predicted ranking r_f and the target ranking r^* in the training data.

In information retrieval, most of the learning approaches simplify the rank learning to be a binary classification problem and many of them can be derived from a learning framework that aims at minimizing the following regularized empirical risk [10],

$$\min_f R_{reg}(f) = \sum_{t=1}^{M_Q} \sum_{j=1}^{M_D} L(y_j f(d_j, q_t)) + \nu \Omega(\|f\|_{\mathcal{H}}), \qquad (1)$$

where y_j is the binary relevance label for j^{th} training document d_j, L is the empirical loss function, $\Omega(\cdot)$ is some monotonically increasing regularization function and ν is the regularization constant. The component of $yf(d, q)$ is usually called "margin" in the literature [10] and hence the learning framework is called *margin-based risk minimization* framework. However, such a classification framework might have difficulties in dealing with the retrieval task. For example, because there are only a small fraction of relevant examples in the collection and many others are left as irrelevant ones, a classification algorithm that always provides negative prediction will unfortunately achieve a high predictive accuracy. Moreover, the classification accuracy has no relationship with the retrieval measure such as average precision. Maximizing the classification accuracy does not necessarily imply a higher ranking effectiveness. To address this issue, we can consider switching the learning criterion to optimize the number of discordant pairs Q between the predicted ranking and the target ranking, i.e., $\sum_{q_t} \sum_{d_j \in D_{qt}^+} \sum_{d_k \in D_{qt}^-} I(f(d_j, q_t) - f(d_k, q_t))$ where $I(\cdot)$ is the indicator function. Unfortunately, a direct optimization on the general form of above equation has been shown to be NP-hard. But following the similar idea of margin-based risk minimization, we can replace the binary misclassification error $I(\cdot)$ into a continuous, convex and monotonically decreasing loss function $L(\cdot)$ in an attempt to facilitate the learning process. By introducing an additional regularization term, we can obtain the following unified margin-based rank learning framework,

$$\min_f RR_{reg}(f) = \sum_{q_t \in Q} \sum_{d_j \in D_{qt}^+} \sum_{d_k \in D_{qt}^-} L(f(d_j, q_t) - f(d_k, q_t)) + \nu \Omega(\|f\|_{\mathcal{H}})$$

$$= \sum_{q_t \in Q} \sum_{d_j \in D_{qt}^+} \sum_{d_k \in D_{qt}^-} L\left(\sum_{i=1}^n \lambda_i [f_i(d_j, q_t) - f_i(d_k, q_t)]\right) + \nu \Omega(\|f\|_\mathcal{H}), \quad (2)$$

where the retrieval function $f(d_j, q)$ is expressed as a linear function of the ranking features due to its retrieval effectiveness and simple presentation, i.e., $f(d_j, q) = \sum_{i=1}^n \lambda_i f_i(d_j, q)$. By optimizing the risk function, we can compute the risk minimization estimator λ_i^* for each ranking feature $f_i(d_j, q)$. With different choices of loss functions and regularization terms, a large family of rank learning algorithms can be derived from Eqn(2). For example, ranking support vector machines can be obtained by setting loss function to be the hinge loss and regularization factor to be $\|w\|_2^2$. RankBoost can be viewed as a rank learning algorithm with the exponential loss function. A recent proposed linear discriminant ranking model(LDM) [7] can be derived by using a binary loss function without regularization terms and setting $f(d_j, q)$ to be a linear function.

The rank learning framework presented in Eqn(2) lends itself to another advantage over the margin-based classification framework. Before further discussions, let us define a useful property called rank consistency,

Definition 1 (Rank consistency). *If a risk minimization estimator λ_i^* satisfies the following conditions: 1) $\lambda_i^* \geq 0$ when $\forall d_j \in D_q^+, \forall d_k \in D_q^-, f_i(d_j, q) \geq f_i(d_k, q)$, and similarly 2) $\lambda_i^* \leq 0$ when $f_i(d_j, q) \leq f_i(d_k, q)$, we will call the estimator is consistent with the data ranking. Note that we assume $f_i(\cdot)$ does not take a trivial constant value.*

It is intuitive to expect the parameters estimated from a rank learning algorithm to satisfy the property of rank consistency. For instance, let us assume the binary outputs of an anchor person detector is one of the ranking features in the multimedia retrieval system, where $f_a = 0$ means no anchor available and $f_a = 1$ otherwise. For a specific query, if we find all of the relevant documents do not contain any anchor shots, i.e., $f_a(d_j, q) \leq f_a(d_k, q)$, then it is naturally to expect the corresponding weight λ_a to be lower than 0, because a negative λ_a can push the relevant examples closer to the top ranked positions.

Unfortunately, simple margin-based classifiers do not offer any guarantees on this intuitive property. In other words, for a ranking feature, even when its values in the relevant documents are always lower than that in the irrelevant documents, the corresponding weight estimator can still be positive. This is because general classification algorithms did not take the ranking information into consideration and the violation of rank consistency might sometimes provide better separability between positive/negative examples rather than better retrieval performance. In contrast, the proposed margin-based rank learning framework preserves such a property, namely, the λ^* learned from Eqn(2) is always consistent with the data ranking if $L(\cdot)$ is a monotonically decreasing function. The proof is given in Appendix. This fact further explains why the proposed margin-based rank learning framework is a better candidate for the retrieval problem.

4 Efficient Rank Learning Algorithms

The above margin-based rank learning framework is quite general, but as mentioned before, optimizing the pairwise risk function in Eqn(2) in a brute force manner need to take care of an explosive number of training pairs between every relevant and irrelevant documents. Therefore, it is desirable to develop a more efficient algorithm to speed up the learning process. In this section, we will describe one of such types of efficient learning algorithms derived from the general rank learning framework. Unless stated otherwise, the following discussions assume the loss function $L(\cdot)$ is convex and satisfies $2L(x/2) \geq L(x)$. Under this assumption[2], we can have the following inequality,

$$RR_{prox}(f) \geq RR'_{reg}(f) \geq \frac{1}{2}[RR_{prox}(f) - RR_{prox}(-f)], \qquad (3)$$

where $RR'_{reg}(f)$ is the pairwise ranking risk defined in Eqn(2) without the regularization factor and $RR_{prox}(f)$ is the approximate ranking risk function based on a shifted retrieval function $f^\alpha(d_j, q) = \sum_{i=1}^n \lambda_i[f_i(d_j, q) - \alpha_i]$,

$$RR_{prox}(f) = \sum_{q_t} \left\{ \sum_{d_j \in D_{qt}^+} M_D^- L\left(f^\alpha(d_j, q_t)\right) + \sum_{d_k \in D_{qt}^-} M_D^+ L\left(-f^\alpha(d_k, q_t)\right) \right\}. \,(4)$$

The proof of inequality Eqn(3) is provided in the Appendix. Both bounds are tight in the sense that all three parts are equal when $L(\cdot)$ is a linear function. Therefore, in lieu of optimizing the pairwise ranking function, we can consider minimizing the $RR_{prox}(f)$ as a reasonable surrogate. Meanwhile, it is instructive to compare and contrast $RR_{prox}(f)$ with the margin-based classification risk function presented in Eqn(1). As can be seen, if we set the label y of d_j to be $+1$ and that of d_k to be -1 in Eqn(1), these two risk functions have a similar form with each other. Therefore, minimizing $RR_{prox}(f)$ has a small computational complexity $O(M_D^+ + M_D^-)$, which is much faster than minimizing the pairwise ranking risk function with a complexity $O(M_D^+ M_D^-)$. However, $RR_{prox}(f)$ also bears some major differences with the classification risk R_{reg}, because (1) it weights the relevant documents more heavily by a ratio of M_D^-/M_D^+; (2) it drops the constant feature term, which is usually available for classification to capture the shifts of decision boundary; 3) it shifts each feature vector by the parameter α_i. These differences has made the $RR_{prox}(f)$ a better choice for the rank learning such as the advantage of balanced data distributions.

In the following implementation, we specially adopt the logit loss $L_R(x) = \log(1 + \exp(-x))$ as the empirical loss function due to its retrieval effectiveness and optimization simpleness. But before proceeding we need to decide the value of the shifting parameters α. One idea is choose α to minimize the gaps between the lower bound and the upper bound, i.e., $\min_\alpha[RR_{prox}(f) + RR_{prox}(-f)]/2$ so as to make RR_{prox} a tight approximation for RR'_{reg}. We approach this by utilizing the inequality $L_R(x) + L_R(-x) \leq 2 + |x|$ and thus we can transform the optimization problem into a series of minimization problem w.r.t. each α_i,

---

[2] This is a very general condition with a large family of loss functions satisfied, such as the hinge loss(SVMs), logistic loss and binary loss function.

$$\min_{\alpha_i} \sum_{q_t} \left\{ \sum_{d_j \in D_{q_t}^+} M_D^- |f_i(d_j, q_t) - \alpha_i| + \sum_{d_k \in D_{q_t}^-} M_D^+ |f_i(d_k, q_t) - \alpha_i| \right\}. \qquad (5)$$

The optimal estimator α_i^* can be written as follows,

$$\alpha_i^* = \text{median} \left[\bigcup_{\forall j, t} \left\{ f_i(d_j, q_t) \right\}_{M_D^-} \cup \bigcup_{\forall k, t} \left\{ f_i(d_k, q_t) \right\}_{M_D^+} \right], \qquad (6)$$

where $\{x\}_n$ denote a set of n elements with the same value x. By substituting the optimal α_i^* and the logit loss into Eqn(4), we can proceed to optimize the combination parameter λ_i^* as follows,

$$\min_{\lambda} \sum_{q_t} \left\{ \sum_{d_j \in D_{q_t}^+} M_D^- L_R \left(\sum_i \lambda_i f_{ijt}^* \right) + \sum_{d_k \in D_{q_t}^-} M_D^+ L_R \left(-\sum_i \lambda_i f_{ikt}^* \right) \right\} + \nu \sum_i \lambda_i^2, \ (7)$$

where $f_{ijt}^* = f_i(d_j, q_t) - \alpha_i^*$. The optimal estimation of λ_i can be achieved by using any gradient descent methods such as iterative reweighted least squares(IRLS) algorithm [11]. We also prove in the Appendix that the estimation from Eqn(7) is consistent with the data ranking. In the rest of the paper, we will call this algorithm *ranking logistic regression*(RLR).

5   Experiments

Our experiments are designed based on the guidelines of the manual retrieval task in the TREC video retrieval evaluation(TRECVID), which requires an automatic video retrieval system to search relevant documents without any human feedbacks. To evaluate the proposed learning algorithms, we used TRECVID'03-'05 video collections which officially provide 25 multimodal queries and around 70,000 shots every year[3]. Each of these video collections is split into a development set and a search set chronologically by source. For each query topic, the relevance judgment on the search set was provided officially by NIST and the judgment on the development set was collaboratively collected by several human annotators using the Informedia client [13]. Although we cannot guarantee all the relevant shots can be found in the development set, this collection effort generally provides a high coverage for the relevance data based on our experience. As the building blocks of the retrieval task, we generated a number of ranking features on the search set including 14 high-level semantic features learned from development data (face, anchor, commercial, studio, graphics, weather, sports, outdoor, person, crowd, road, car, building, motion), and 5 uni-modal retrieval experts (text retrieval, face recognition, image-based retrieval based on color, texture and edge histograms). The detailed descriptions on the feature generation can be found in [13].

We compare four different types of algorithms on all three video collections in Table 1, i.e., logistic regression(LR), ranking logistic regression(RLR), full rank-

---

[3] Information about these collections can be found at the TRECVID web site [12].

Table 1. Retrieval performance on TRECVID'03 - '05 data. TrainAP is the mean average precision on the development set. TestAP is the mean average precision on the search set. Prec10, Prec30 and Prec100 indicate the mean precisions at the top 10, 30 and 100 retrieved shots on the search set.

Data	Algorithms	TrainAP	TestAP	Prec10	Prec30	Prec100
t05	F-RLR	0.453	0.217	0.535	0.451	0.341
	RLR	0.447	0.217	0.529	0.433	0.341
	LR	0.389	0.207	0.506	0.433	0.341
	NB	0.409	0.204	0.535	0.410	0.334
t04	F-RLR	0.292	0.143	0.269	0.262	0.192
	RLR	0.283	0.141	0.269	0.264	0.192
	LR	0.261	0.132	0.238	0.241	0.184
	NB	0.236	0.129	0.231	0.215	0.182
t03	F-RLR	0.379	0.189	0.433	0.360	0.221
	RLR	0.371	0.186	0.433	0.342	0.224
	LR	0.358	0.185	0.431	0.358	0.229
	NB	0.348	0.181	0.344	0.338	0.230

ing logistic regression(FRLR) which directly optimizes the pairwise risk function in Eqn(2) and naïve Bayes(NB) [1] which is an example of the generative retrieval models. For each algorithm, we learned the combination weights on a per query basis using the development data. To reduce the learning complexity, we choose the top 1000 shots with the highest text retrieval scores as the training examples. The learned models are evaluated based on the same query using the search set. By averaging the performance on all queries, we report the retrieval performance in terms of the mean average precision(MAP) and precision at top 10, 30 and 100 retrieved shots. To guarantee the learning process being supported by sufficient training data, we intentionally removed the queries with less than 10 positive examples in the training process, which typically decrease the query number to around 20 for each data collection. As shown in Table 1, the discriminative models such as LR are usually superior to the generative model, i.e., NB, in terms of both the training/testing MAP on three collections. Among the discriminative models, the ranking versions of LR provide an additional 3-6% boost on the training MAP and 1% boost on the testing MAP compared with LR, which demonstrated the benefits of ranking-based learning in multimedia retrieval. The less significant improvement in the search set is partially due to the insufficiency of the training data for a single query. Since the difference between RLR and LR is not statistically significant, further experiments might be needed to verify the performance improvement of the proposed methods on other information retrieval tasks. Finally, we also observe that RLR, as an efficient approximation of its fully optimization version FRLR, achieved a fairly close performance to FRLR. Their differences on MAP are always less than 1% on three collections, which demonstrates RLR is a reasonable approximation for its fully optimization counterpart with a ten-fold speedup in the learning process.

6 Conclusions

This paper presents a general margin-based rank learning framework for the information retrieval task, which aims to optimize the number of discordant pairs between the predicted ranking and the target ranking rather than minimizing the classification errors. We also propose an efficient approximation for the margin-based rank learning framework which can significantly reduce the computational complexity with a negligible loss in the performance. Both the exact and approximated rank learning algorithms are able to preserve the rank consistency in the data while the binary classification is not. Our experiments on three TRECVID collections demonstrate the superiority of the proposed rank learning algorithms over the generative/discriminative classification algorithms in the context of retrieval tasks. As the future work, we can consider extending the experiments to the other types of loss functions such as the hinge loss function and other scenarios related to ranking optimization such as collaborative filtering and modeling implicit user feedback.

References

1. S. E. Robertson and K. Sparck Jones, "Relevance weighting of search terms," *Journal of the American Society for Informaiton Science*, vol. 27, 1977.
2. R. Nallapati, "Discriminative models for information retrieval," in *Proc. of the 27th SIGIR conf. on information retrieval*, 2004, pp. 64–71.
3. T. Joachims, "Optimizing search engines using clickthrough data," in *Proceedings of the 8th ACM SIGKDD intl. conf. on knowledge discovery and data mining*, New York, NY, USA, 2002, pp. 133–142, ACM Press.
4. Y. Freund, R. D. Iyer, R. E. Schapire, and Y. Singer, "An efficient boosting algorithm for combining preferences," in *Proc. of the 15th Intl. Conf. on Machine Learning*, San Francisco, CA, USA, 1998, pp. 170–178.
5. C. Burges and et al., "Learning to rank using gradient descent," in *Proceedings of the 22nd intl. conf. on machine learning*, 2005, pp. 89–96.
6. T.-S. Chua, S.-Y. Neo, H.-K. Goh, M. Zhao, Y. Xiao, and G. Wang, "Trecvid 2005 by nus pris," in *NIST TRECVID-2005*, Nov 2005.
7. J. Gao, H. Qi, X. Xia, and J.-Y. Nie, "Linear discriminant model for information retrieval," in *Proceedings of the 28th international ACM SIGIR conference*, New York, NY, USA, 2005, pp. 290–297, ACM Press.
8. R. Herbrich, T. Graepel, and K. Obermayer., "Large margin rank boundaries for ordinal regression," in *Advances in Large Margin Classifiers*, A. J. Smola, P. L. Bartlett, B. Scholkopf, and D. Schuurmans, Eds. MIT Press, 2000.
9. K. Crammer and Y. Singer, "Pranking with ranking," in *Proc. of the Advanced Neural Information Processing Systems (NIPS)*, 2001.
10. T. Hastie, R. Tibshirani, and J. Friedman, *The Elements of Statistical Learning. Springer Series in Statistics*, Springer Verlag, Basel, 2001.
11. M. I. Jordan and R. A. Jacobs, "Hierarchical mixtures of experts and the EM algorithm," *Neural Computation*, vol. 6, pp. 181–214, 1994.
12. A.F. Smeaton and P. Over, "TRECVID: Benchmarking the effectiveness of information retrieval tasks on digital video.," in *Proc. of the Intl. Conf. on Image and Video Retrieval*, 2003.

13. A. Hauptmann, M.-Y. Chen, M. Christel, C. Huang, W.-H. Lin, T. Ng, N. Papernick, A. Velivelli, J. Yang, R. Yan, H. Yang, and H. D. Wactlar, "Confounded expectations: Informedia at trecvid 2004," in *Proc. of TRECVID*, 2004.

Appendix

Theorem 1. *The risk minimization estimators λ^* learned from both the margin-based rank learning framework presented in Eqn(2) and the ranking logistic regression algorithm presented in Eqn(7) are consistent with the data ranking.*

Proof: Let us first consider the Eqn(2). When there is a ranking feature f_a satisfies $f_a(d_j, q_t) \geq f_a(d_k, q_t), \forall q_t, \forall d_j \in D_{qt}^+, \forall d_k \in D_{qt}^-$, we can prove λ_a^* is not lower than 0 by contradiction. Assume $\lambda_a^* < 0$ in this case, since $L(\cdot)$ is monotonically decreasing, we can have

$$L\left(\sum_{i \neq a} \lambda_i f_{ijt} + \lambda_a^* f_{ajt}\right) \geq L\left(\sum_{i \neq a} \lambda_i f_{ijt} + (-\lambda_a^*) f_{ajt}\right), \forall j, t \tag{8}$$

where $f_{ijt} = f_i(d_j, q_t) - f_i(d_k, q_t)$ and $f_{ajt} \geq 0$ with at least one $f_{aj't'} > 0$. Therefore, this leads to a contradiction that λ_a^* is a risk minimization estimator. The case of $f_a(d_j, q) \geq f_a(d_k, q)$ can be proved similarly. This complete the proof for Eqn(2).

Next let us consider the Eqn(7). When there is a ranking feature f_a satisfies $f_a(d_j, q_t) \geq f_a(d_k, q_t), \forall q_t, \forall d_j \in D_{qt}^+, \forall d_k \in D_{qt}^-$, we are sure that the optimal $\alpha_i^* \in [\max(f_a(d_k, q_t)), \min(f_a(d_j, q_t))]$, because there are exactly $M_D^+ \cdot M_D^-$ elements larger than $\min(f_a(d_j, q_t))$ and $M_D^+ \cdot M_D^-$ elements smaller than $\max(f_a(d_k, q_t))$ in the union set of the right hand side of Eqn(6). Therefore, for all d_j, the shifted ranking feature $f_{ijt}^* = f_i(d_j, q_t) - \alpha_i^* \geq 0$. Similarly, for all d_k, the shifted ranking feature $-f_{ikt}^* \geq 0$. This recovers to the setting discussed above and thus we can have $\lambda_a^* \geq 0$. The case of $f_a(d_j, q) \geq f_a(d_k, q)$ can be proved similarly. This complete the proof for Eqn(7).

Theorem 2. *If $2L(x/2) \geq L(x)$, the inequality shown in Eqn(3) holds.*

Proof: We first provide a useful lemma as follows as a basis to prove the inequalities: for any $A, B \in \mathcal{R}$, based on the condition of $2L(x/2) \geq L(x)$ and the convexity of L, we can have $L(A) + L(B) \geq 2L(\frac{A+B}{2}) \geq L(A + B)$. On the other hand, we can slightly modify the lemma to be $L(A + B) + L(-A) \geq L(B)$ and $L(A + B) + L(-B) \geq L(A)$. Summing both inequalities together yields, $L(A+B) \geq \frac{1}{2}(L(A)+L(B)-L(-A)-L(-B))$. Next we go ahead to show the inequalities shown in Eqn(3) holds. If we set $A = f^\alpha(d_j, q) = \sum_{i=1}^n \lambda_i[f_i(d_j, q) - \alpha_i]$ and $B = -f^\alpha(d_k, q)$, both lemmas can be rewritten as,

$$L(f^\alpha(d_j, q)) + L(-f^\alpha(d_k, q)) \geq L(f(d_j, q) - f(d_k, q))$$
$$\geq \frac{1}{2}[L(f^\alpha(d_j, q)) + L(-f^\alpha(d_k, q)) - L(-f^\alpha(d_j, q)) - L(f^\alpha(d_k, q))] \tag{9}$$

By summing all of the cases when $\forall q_t, \forall d_j \in D_{qt}^+, \forall d_k \in D_{qt}^-$ on both sides, we can get $RR_{prox}(f) \geq RR'_{reg}(f) \geq \frac{1}{2}[RR_{prox}(f) - RR_{prox}(-f)]$.

Leveraging Active Learning for Relevance Feedback Using an Information Theoretic Diversity Measure

Charlie K. Dagli, Shyamsundar Rajaram, and Thomas S. Huang

Beckman Institute for Advanced Science and Technology
University of Illinois at Urbana-Champaign
Urbana, IL 61801
{dagli, rajaram1, huang}@ifp.uiuc.edu

Abstract. Interactively learning from a small sample of unlabeled examples is an enormously challenging task. Relevance feedback and more recently active learning are two standard techniques that have received much attention towards solving this interactive learning problem. How to best utilize the user's effort for labeling, however, remains unanswered. It has been shown in the past that labeling a diverse set of points is helpful, however, the notion of diversity has either been dependent on the learner used, or computationally expensive. In this paper, we intend to address these issues by proposing a fundamentally motivated, information-theoretic view of diversity and its use in a fast, non-degenerate active learning-based relevance feedback setting. Comparative testing and results are reported and thoughts for future work are presented.

1 Introduction

An enormous challenge in interactive image and video retrieval is correlating the user-dependent interpretation of image-content with low-level visual descriptors, closing the so-called *semantic gap*. Relevance feedback has garnered much attention in the past decade in attempting to reach this goal [1][2][3][4]. At its heart, relevance feedback suffers from the *small sample learning* problem [5]. Rankers or classifiers must learn in high-dimensional feature spaces with only a handful of labeled training examples. Consequently, many potential discriminating observations go unlabeled. As an additional practical consideration, because these systems have a user in the loop, they must also be quick and robust to change. In recent years, attention has been given to systems that employ *active learning* to address these challenges.

Active learning is a paradigm that proposes ways to incrementally learn from unlabeled data, provided the system has available to it an *oracle*, an entity which knows the correct labeling of all examples [6][7]. Given an initial weak ranker or classifier, the oracle labels a set of points the systems deems to be most informative, the *pool query set*. The information provided from this labeling can then be used to update the system and this process can be repeated indefinitely to improve the accuracy of those points in the returned or *resultant set*. Traditional

H. Sundaram et al. (Eds.): CIVR 2006, LNCS 4071, pp. 123–132, 2006.
© Springer-Verlag Berlin Heidelberg 2006

relevance feedback can be seen as a degenerate case of active learning as the set of top-k returned points serves both as the returned *and* pool query sets. Using a unique pool query set, however, has been shown to improve performance [8].

Whether we use the traditional or active learning-based paradigm, the user is often asked to label examples which are quite similar to one another, often times as a result of examples clustering in the same area of the feature space. In a small-sample setting, especially when the users and systems effort is at a premium, it makes more sense for the user to label a *diverse* set of points for each pool-query rather than many similar points which are, in comparison, much less informative. There have been a handful of techniques which have addressed this issue.

In the traditional relevance feedback scenario, NECs PicHunter [9] cast diversity for image retrieval as matter of *exploration* versus *exploitation*. Utilizing Bayesian relevance feedback techniques, they ask users to label images with low-posterior probability in addition to those with high probability. This notion of diversity relies on the probabilistic modeling for it's calculation, however, which tends to limit its general application. The CLUE system of [10] also realizes that images tend to be semantically clustered in the vicinity of query images. To this end, they propose a local-neighborhood based clustering approach to more efficiently present diverse information for labeling by the user. This clustering must occur for every round of feedback, however, and the computational load of doing so may in some cases outweigh the improved retrieval results.

From a purely active learning viewpoint, one of the first works to incorporate diversity sampling was [11] and subsequently [12] where the notion of angular diversity was investigated for support vector machines (SVMs). The idea of using angular diversity in particular, however, was motivated specifically by the version-space reduction requirements inherent in SVM active learning. It is not clear whether this specialized measure of diversity is suitable for general problems.

In this work, we motivate and introduce a more general notion of diversity based on information-theoretic concepts, and apply it to a fast, *non-degenerate* active learning scheme for relevance feedback based on query-point refinement which, to our knowledge, is a scenario that has not received much attention in the past.

The rest of the paper is organized as follows: Section 2 motivates our measure of diversity and leads into Section 3 which presents the active learning based algorithm built around it. Experimental results and thoughts for future study are presented in Sections 4 and 5 respectively.

2   Information-Theoretic Diversity

To motivate the discussion of our active learning framework, we will first define a basic diversity measure, based on Shannon's entropy [13]. It's intuitively attractive to associate high entropy with diversity, as entropy is essentially a measure of randomness. For any continuous random variable, $\mathbf{X}$, which takes a particular value $\mathbf{x}$, entropy is defined as

$$h(\mathbf{x}) = -\int p(\mathbf{x}) \log (p(\mathbf{x})) = -E\left[\log (p(\mathbf{x}))\right] \tag{1}$$

where $E[\cdot]$ is the expectation (mean) operator. Calculating entropy in practice involves density estimation, as the underlying probabilities are usually not known. Given a set of points, $\{\mathbf{x}_i\}_{i=1}^N$, we can approximate the expectation in (1) by the sample mean so that

$$h(\mathbf{x}) \approx -\frac{1}{N} \sum_{i=1}^N \log (p(\mathbf{x}_i)) \tag{2}$$

which by the Law of Large Numbers approaches the actual mean in the limit as $N \to \infty$. We are still left with the problem of estimating the distribution, $p(x)$. Through Parzen density estimation

$$p(\mathbf{x}) = \frac{1}{N} \sum_{i=1}^N \mathcal{K}(\mathbf{x}, \mathbf{x}_i) \tag{3}$$

where $\mathcal{K}$ is the Parzen window.

Substituting this estimate of the density into (2), we now define a new quantity called *empirical entropy*

$$h_e(\{\mathbf{x}_i\}_{i=1}^N) = -\frac{1}{N} \sum_{i=1}^N \log \left(\frac{1}{N} \sum_{j=1}^N \mathcal{K}(\mathbf{x}_i, \mathbf{x}_j) \right) \tag{4}$$

Expanding this equation, we arrive at the final expression for empirical entropy:

$$h_e(\{\mathbf{x}_i\}_{i=1}^N) = \frac{1}{N} \log(N) - \frac{1}{N} \sum_{i=1}^N \log \left(\sum_{j=1}^N \mathcal{K}(\mathbf{x}_i, \mathbf{x}_j) \right) \tag{5}$$

For all testing and experimentation, we used the Gaussian radial basis kernel

$$\mathcal{K}(\mathbf{x}, \mathbf{x}_i) = \frac{\exp\left(-\frac{1}{2}(\mathbf{x} - \mathbf{x}_i)^T \Sigma^{-1} (\mathbf{x} - \mathbf{x}_i)\right)}{(2\pi)^{-\frac{d}{2}} |\Sigma|^{-\frac{1}{2}}} \tag{6}$$

with isotropic covariance matrix $\Sigma = \sigma \mathbf{I}$.

Before utilizing empirical entropy in an active learning algorithm, it is worth examining this quantity in a bit more detail. To gain better insight into entropy as a general measure of diversity, we present the following theorem.

Theorem 1. *If $h_e(\{\mathbf{x}_i\}_{i=1}^N)$ denotes the empirical entropy of $\{\mathbf{x}_i\}_{i=1}^N$, then a large upper bound on this value corresponds to large distances and angles between mutual paris of points in the sample set $\{\mathbf{x}_i\}_{i=1}^N$.*

Proof. By definition of empirical entropy in Eqn. 4,

$$h_e(\{\mathbf{x}_i\}_{i=1}^N) = -\frac{1}{N}\sum_{i=1}^N \log\left(\frac{1}{N}\sum_{j=1}^N \mathcal{K}(\mathbf{x}_i,\mathbf{x}_j)\right)$$

The logarithm function is concave and applying Jensen's Inequality, we obtain

$$h_e(\{\mathbf{x}_i\}_{i=1}^N) \leq -\frac{1}{N^2}\sum_{i=1}^N\sum_{j=1}^N \log\left(\mathcal{K}(\mathbf{x}_i,\mathbf{x}_j)\right)$$

Assuming $\mathcal{K}(\mathbf{x}_i,\mathbf{x}_j)$ is a Gaussian Kernel as in Equation (6) we obtain,

$$h_e(\{\mathbf{x}_i\}_{i=1}^N) \leq \frac{1}{2N^2}\sum_{i=1}^N\sum_{j=1}^N (d\log(2\pi) +$$

$$\log|\Sigma| + (\mathbf{x}_i - \mathbf{x}_j)^T \Sigma^{-1}(\mathbf{x}_i - \mathbf{x}_j)$$

Observe that the third term on the right-hand side in the above equation is equivalent to the canonical inner product of

$$\langle(\mathbf{x}_i',\mathbf{x}_j')\rangle = (\mathbf{x}_i - \mathbf{x}_j)^T \Sigma^{-1}(\mathbf{x}_i - \mathbf{x}_j) = M(\mathbf{x}_i,\mathbf{x}_j)$$

where $\mathbf{x}_i' = \Sigma^{-1/2}\mathbf{x}_i$, $\mathbf{x}_j' = \Sigma^{-1/2}\mathbf{x}_j$ and the (non-unique) existence of $\Sigma^{-1/2}$ follows from the symmetric, positive semi-definite property of covariance matrix Σ. In the new space induced by $\Sigma^{-1/2}$, the distance between two points $\mathbf{x}_i$ and $\mathbf{x}_j$ is

$$\left\|(\mathbf{x}_i' - \mathbf{x}_j')\right\|^2 = \|\mathbf{x}'_i\|^2 + \|\mathbf{x}'_j\|^2 - 2\|\mathbf{x}_i'\|\|\mathbf{x}_j'\|\cos(\theta)$$

where θ is the angle between $\mathbf{x}_i'$ and $\mathbf{x}_j'$; this follows from the definition of inner product. This expression is largest when $\theta = \pi$, the largest angle between two vectors.   □

The major implication of this analysis is that a large bound on empirical entropy depends on a large mutual distance for points in a sample set, which by the definition of the canonical inner product also implies large mutual angles. In this way, entropic diversity in a general setting is able to capture both these notions of uniqueness, and therefore, in the limit, diversity.

3   Algorithm for Pool-Query Selection

A general active learning algorithm chooses both a resultant and pool-query set to present to the user at each step. We assume that the algorithm narrows down the set of all unlabeled points at each step to a candidate pool-query set. In the case of SVM active learning, these are the unlabeled points which lie in the version space. In a query-point refinement algorithm, one can choose from a large number of points in the neighborhood of the query centroid. We don't want to arbitrarily choose the most diverse points, however. We must keep proper perspective and ensure that these points are still close to the query centroid. To this end, the cost function we minimize is a convex sum of both query point distance and the negative of entropic diversity.

At each round of feedback, then, we must choose from the set of M points (where $M >> k$) closest to the query centroid, $\mathbf{x}_c$, an N point subset known as the *pool-query* set for oracle labeling. Using brute force results in $\binom{M}{N}$ unique N point subsets for which we must compute our empirical entropy diversity measure. Even for moderate sample sizes, however, this number quickly becomes computationally intractable. Instead, we use an adaption of the greedy algorithm in [11] used for calculating angular diversity. Starting with the point closest to the query centroid, $\mathbf{x}_{min}$, at each step we add to the pool-query set PQ that point which most decreases the cost function C.

$1 : \mathbf{x}_{min} = \mathbf{x}_{\underset{i}{\operatorname{argmin}} \|\mathbf{x}_i - \mathbf{x}_c\|}$

$2 : PQ = \{\mathbf{x}_{min}\}$

$3 : \mathbf{do}$

$4 : \quad h_{max} = \underset{i}{\max}(PQ \cup \{\mathbf{x}_i - \mathbf{x}_c\})$

$5 : \quad h_{min} = \underset{i}{\min}(PQ \cup \{\mathbf{x}_i - \mathbf{x}_c\})$

$6 : \quad C(i) = \alpha\|\mathbf{x}_i - \mathbf{x}_c\| + (1 - \alpha)\left[-\dfrac{h_e(PQ \cup \{\mathbf{x}_i - \mathbf{x}_c\})}{h_{max} - h_{min}}\right]$

$\quad \forall i : i \notin PQ$

$7 : \quad PQ \cup \{\mathbf{x}_{\underset{j \notin PQ}{\operatorname{argmin}} C(j)}\}$

$8 : \mathbf{while}|PQ| \leq N$

The mixing parameter, α, allows us to scale up or down the influence of empirical entropy to the cost function. When $\alpha = 1$, the pool-query technique defaults to a nearest neighbour regime completely discounting any diversity information. When $\alpha = 0$, the cost function becomes purely an entropic diversity measure. We will explore the effects of mixing later.

3.1 Biased Discriminant Analysis

In the evaluation of our proposed diversity-framework, we chose to use a small-sample learner especially suited for information-retrieval problems, Biased Discriminant Analysis [5]. BDA casts the problem of relevance feedback from a two-class (positive and negative) to a one-to-many class (one positive, multiple negative) problem. The goal is to find a transformation of the feature space which closely clusters positive examples while pushing away negative ones.

The optimal transformation is obtained by maximizing the following objective function

$$\underset{\mathbf{W}}{\mathrm{argmax}} \left| \frac{\mathbf{W}^T \mathbf{S}_{PN} \mathbf{W}}{\mathbf{W}^T \mathbf{S}_P \mathbf{W}} \right| \tag{7}$$

where $\mathbf{S}_P$ is the intra-class-scatter matrix for all the training examples and $\mathbf{S}_{PN}$ is the inter-class scatter matrix between positive examples and negative training examples, treating each negative example as an individual class.

The optimal value of $\mathbf{W}$ is the solution to the generalized eigenvalue problem presented by the Rayleigh Coefficient in (7). The optimal transformation then becomes

$$\mathbf{A} = \mathbf{\Phi} \mathbf{\Lambda}^{1/2} \tag{8}$$

where $\mathbf{\Lambda}$ is the diagonal eigenvalue matrix and $\mathbf{\Phi}$ is the corresponding eigenvector matrix and $\mathbf{W} = \mathbf{A}\mathbf{A}^T$. The distance between two points in the new space can be computed using the standard Euclidean measure, or in the original space using the distance metric

$$\mathrm{distance}(\mathbf{x} - \mathbf{y}) = (\mathbf{x} - \mathbf{y})^T \mathbf{A}(\mathbf{x} - \mathbf{y}) \tag{9}$$

Although BDA can also be used for feature reduction, in its full form it is essentially a query point refinement algorithm. Each round of user feedback yields a new transformation of the feature space which results in the centroids of both the positive and negative examples being moved.

4   Image Retrieval Experimentation

4.1   Image Features and Testing Procedure

To explore the practical performance of our entropy-based active learning system, we performed extensive tests using a 5000 image subset of the COREL image database. To appropriately model the small-sample scenario, only 1400 images were used for target sets. The target set consisted of 13 unique query concepts.

The first, second and third moments in each channel of the HSV color space, first and second wavelet sub-band moments at three levels of decomposition and a Waterfilling algorithm were used for color, texture and shape features respectively. In total, a 47-dimensional feature vector was extracted from each image.

Initially, the user (oracle) is presented with 20 randomly chosen images. After each round of retrieval, they mark which images they deem to be relevant. The remaining are assumed to be irrelevant. From this information, the systems adjusts its understanding of the query concept using BDA, and returns both the k most similar images and the pool-query set of images to label for active learning.

For each query class, we conducted 25 random feedback sessions of 6 rounds each. In total, there were 325 user-guided sessions, with 1950 total rounds of

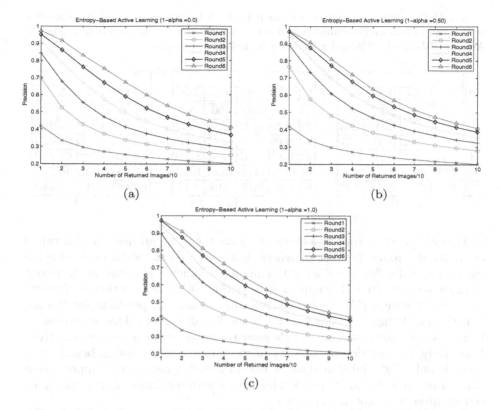

Fig. 1. Effect of α across Feedback Round for (a) $\alpha = 1$, (b) $\alpha = 0.5$, (c) $\alpha = 0$

feedback for each method tested. The size of the pool-query was chosen to reflect a reasonable number of image a human operator could label at one time, 20. Results were averaged across all 325 tests.

4.2   Temporal Role of Diversity

It is reasonable to suspect that diversity is not equally important at every stage of the learning process. Intuition would suggest that at lower feedback rounds, the diversity strategy would be more important as the system has the smallest amount of knowledge and thus needs the most diverse set of labeled examples to learn its query concept. In higher rounds, diversity should be less important as the system should have utilized the information from prior diverse labelings to localize the area in the feature space were most of the relevant images are.

Investigating this intuitive idea, we performed tests using mixing parameter α values of 0, 0.25, 0.5, 0.75 and 1 corresponding to, at the extremes, pure diversity and pure distance (k nearest neighbors). Precision values for oracle-query sets of size 20 were calculated. Figure 1 shows the values of precision versus number of images returned for increasing rounds of feedback, marginalized across query class.

Table 1. Percentage Change in Precision between (a) Entropic Diversity Sampling versus Pure Distance (k-nearest neighbours), α-varying Entropic Diversity versus (b) Angular SVM and (c) Angular Diversity Sampling Techniques

R	α			
	0.75	0.5	0.25	0.0
1	0	0	0	0
2	11.84	11.74	12.00	12.59
3	10.28	11.22	13.10	12.27
4	7.34	6.90	8.21	7.46
5	2.97	2.69	3.42	2.83
6	-0.87	-2.76	-2.49	-2.42

(a)

R	α			
	0.75	0.5	0.25	0.0
1	100	100	100	100
2	42.42	42.32	42.59	43.17
3	29.66	30.60	32.47	31.65
4	21.81	21.37	22.68	21.93
5	15.16	14.89	15.61	15.03
6	9.65	7.77	8.04	8.11

(b)

R	α			
	0.75	0.5	0.25	0.0
1	0	0	0	0
2	3.61	3.22	1.73	0.63
3	2.82	2.46	2.84	0.91
4	2.05	1.78	2.63	0.54
5	2.40	1.50	2.46	1.17
6	2.61	0.31	0.00	0.62

(c)

Trivially, the first round of feedback yields the same precision for all values of α. As the round number increases, however, we can begin to resolve the performance of different values of the mixing parameter. Comparing the purely distance strategy ($\alpha = 1$, Figure 1 (a)) with the first introduction of diversity ($\alpha = 0.5$, Figure 1 (b)) we see marked improvement in precision for Rounds 2-3. (Round 1, initial labeling, is the same for all values.) This improvement increases as we decrease α and weight more toward diversity ($\alpha = 0$, Figure 1(c)). Conversely, the addition of diversity in the final rounds is not as beneficial as there is only slight improvement in Round 5 and a decrease in improvement when using diversity in Round 6. This agrees with our intuition that in higher rounds diversity is not as important.

The exact percentage change in precision between $\alpha = 1.0$, pure distance, and differing degrees of diversity marginalized over different number of returned images can be seen in Table 1 (a).

We can now adjust our entropic diversity pool-query selection scheme to reflect the temporal effect of the mixing parameter. In Round 2, we set $\alpha = 0$ because it yields the largest percent increase, 12.59%. Rounds 3-5 we tune diversity down by changing α to 0.25. Finally, in the last round, we move to a purely distance-based strategy, setting $\alpha = 1$.

4.3   Comparing with Other Relevance Feedback Algorithms

To further investigate the performance of this α-varying, entropic diversity framework, testing with other active learning-based relevance feedback techniques was performed. Comparisons between the proposed system, angular diversity BDA of [14] and a basic version of the angular-diversity SVM framework of [8] and [12] were conducted. (Comparison with plain BDA was unnecessary as it was done already in Section 5.2.) As before, the same batch of 325 user-guided tests using pool-query size of 20 were done. The results of these tests can be summarized in Figure 2.

Looking at Figure2(a)-(b), we can seen that entropy-based diversity yields substantially better results than angular SVM and better results than purely

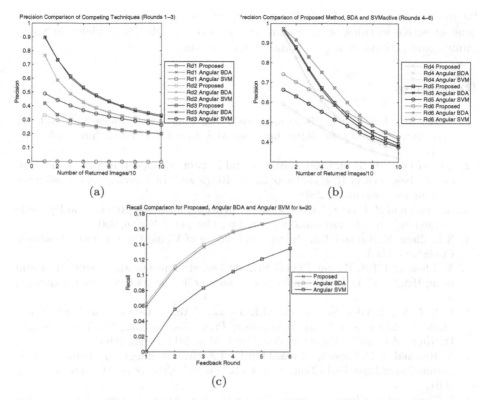

Fig. 2. Precision Comparison for Entropic Diversity BDA, Angular Diversity BDA and Angular SVM for (a) Rounds 1-3 and (b) Rounds 4-6, (c) Recall Comparison for all algorithms (k=20)

angular-based BDA. The recall curves of Figure2(c) also show similar behavior. (Since we are comparing the *algorithms* themselves, the first round of angular-based SVM is zero, since there are two rounds of labeling before the user begins to see results.) Tables 1(a) and 1(b) show specific quantitative results.

As the results show, the incorporation of an information-based diversity measure into a general active learning framework can, indeed, improve performance. Given a weak learner, BDA, we have seen marked improvement over the degenerate case (BDA with nearest neighbors) of at most 12-13% in the lower rounds. In addition, these empirical results also coincide with our notion that an entropic diversity measure should perform as well or better than angular diversity.

5   Summary

In this work, we have proposed a fundamentally motivated, information theoretic view of diversity and incorporated it into a non-degenerate, query-point refinement scheme for relevance feedback. Our results support entropic diversity's viability as a useful tool for pool-query selection in active learning. In the future, we plan to investigate the viability of these types of measures in more general active learning scenarios, as well as looking into these ideas for video mining and active ranking for collaborative filtering.

References

1. Y. Rui and T.S. Huang, "Relevance Feedback Techniques in Image Retrieval," in *Principles of Visual Information Retrieval*, M.S. Lew, Ed. London: Springer-Verlag, 2001.
2. B.C. Ko and H. Byun, Probabilistic Neural Networks Supporting Multi-Class Relevance Feedback in Region-Based Image Retrieval," in *International Conference on Pattern Recognition*, 2002.
3. A. Dong and B. Bhanu, "Active Concept Learning for Image Retrieval in Dynamic Databases," in *International Conference on Computer Vision*, 2003.
4. X.S. Zhou, Y. Rui and T.S. Huang, Exploration of Visual Data, Kluwer Academic Publishers, 2003.
5. X. Zhou and T.S. Huang, "Small Sample Learning during Multimedia Retrieval using BiasMap," in *IEEE Conference Computer Vision and Pattern Recognition*, 2001.
6. D.A. Cohn, Z. Ghahramani and M.I. Jordan, "Active Learning with Statistical Models", *Advances in Neural Information Processing Systems*, Vol. 7, G. Tesauro, D. Touretzky and J. Alspector, Eds. Cambridge: MIT Press, 1995.
7. N. Roy and A. McCallum, "Toward Optimal Active Learning through Monte Carlo Estimation of Error Reduction," in *International Conference on Machine Learning*, 2001.
8. S. Tong and E. Chang, "Support Vector Machine Active Learning for Image Retrieval," in *IEEE International Conference on Computer Vision and Pattern Recognition*, 2001.
9. I.J. Cox, T.P. Minka, T.V. Papathomas and P. N. Yianilos, "Pichunter: Bayesian Relevance Feedback for Image Retrieval," in *International Conference on Pattern Recognition*, 1996.
10. Y. Chen, J.Z. Wang and R. Krovetz "CLUE: Cluster-based Retrieval of Images by Unsupervised Learning," IEEE Transactions on Image Processing, Vol. 14, No. 8, pp. 1187-1201, 2005.
11. K. Brinker, "Incorporating Diversity in Active Learning with Support Vector Machines," in *International Conference on Machine Learning*, 2003.
12. K. Goh, E. Y. Chang, and W.-C. Lai, "Concept-dependent Multimodal Active Learning for Image Retrieval", in *ACM International Conference on Multimedia*, 2004.
13. C.E. Shannon, "A Mathematical Theory of Communication," *Bell System Technical Journal*, Vol. 27, pp. 379-423 and 623-656, 1948.
14. C.K. Dagli, S. Rajaram and T.S. Huang, "Combining Diversity-Based Active Learning with Discriminant Analysis in Image Retrieval," in *IEEE International Conference on Information Technology and Applications*, 2005.

Video Clip Matching Using MPEG-7 Descriptors and Edit Distance

Marco Bertini, Alberto Del Bimbo, and Walter Nunziati

Dipartimento di Sistemi e Informatica - Università degli Studi di Firenze
{bertini, delbimbo, nunziati}@dsi.unifi.it

Abstract. Video databases require that clips are represented in a compact and discriminative way, in order to perform efficient matching and retrieval of documents of interest. We present a method to obtain a video representation suitable for this task, and show how to use this representation in a matching scheme. In contrast with existing works, the proposed approach is entirely based on features and descriptors taken from the well established MPEG-7 standard. Different clips are compared using an edit distance, in order to obtain high similarity between videos that differ for some subsequences, but are essentially related to the same content. Experimental validation is performed using a prototype application that retrieves TV commercials recorded from different TV sources in real time. Results show excellent performances both in terms of accuracy, and in terms of computational performances.

1 Introduction

In many multimedia applications, it is required to compute a similarity measure between video segments taken from (usually large) databases. A natural context is a video retrieval application where the user is allowed to query the system with a small video clip, and the system must return relevant matches. For instance, a company may need to search for its video–commercials (or for other companies' commercials) within an entire day of broadcast transmission, from several TV channels, and without browsing the entire recorded video material. Another relevant applicative scenario is that of finding duplicate clips in large web-based, shared video database, such as Google Video or YouTube. In these applications, users are allowed to upload their video content, hence it is necessary to understand for instance if multiple documents actually refers to the same material, or if a particular document can be made available without raising any copyright or licensing issue.

These are just examples of the general video matching problem, that typically involves the following steps: a) off-line, segment the video streams into basic clip for processing and b) from each segment, extract a *video signature*, that is stored into the database. At run time, a query video signature is compared with all the signatures stored in the database, and most similar results are returned.

This paper concerns the problem of extracting a suitable signature from a video clip, and how to use it to perform matching. There are some general

H. Sundaram et al. (Eds.): CIVR 2006, LNCS 4071, pp. 133–142, 2006.
© Springer-Verlag Berlin Heidelberg 2006

requirements that the signature should meet. First, the signature must be representative of the clip it refers, while being at the same time as compact as possible. Second, the signature must be robust to a wide range of disturb, generated from different encoding schemes, different image formats, etc. Finally, it would be desirable to take advantages of well established, standard image and video descriptors, in order to easily compare videos coming from heterogeneous sources.

Other important considerations are related to the metric used to compare signatures extracted from two different clips. As for all modern multimedia retrieval systems, the metric must be flexible enough to enable similarity matching. Another desirable property would be to allow the user to query the system with a short, "summarized" version of the clip of interest (e.g., the trailer of a movie, or a short version of a commercial), and let the system retrieve the video the clip belongs to.

The proposed method is based on the combination of three MPEG-7 descriptors, namely the *color layout* descriptor, the *edge histogram* descriptor, and the *scalable color* descriptor. These descriptors are collected for each frame, and constitute the clip signature. To match two signatures, the edit distance [14] is employed, in order to cope with clips that may differ for small subsequences. The edit distance, or Levenshtein distance, is a metric widely used in information theory to compute the distance between two strings. It is given by the minimum number of operations needed to transform one string into the other, where an operation is an insertion, deletion, or substitution of a single character. This measure fits naturally in the proposed method, since its applicability requires only that a suitable metric is defined for comparing two "symbols" (in our case, two frame descriptors, which are compared using an appropriate metric).

The rest of the paper is organized as follows: in Sect. 2, we review existing work in the area of video matching, outlining the main differences and the contributions of this paper. Technical aspects and implementation details are presented in Sect. 3, while Sect. 4 presents experimental results, obtained with a prototype application that retrieve TV commercials recorded from various TV sources.

2   Related Work

Given its importance for all kind of video retrieval application, the problem of defining a video clip's signature is currently widely investigated. In early approaches, several researchers have proposed various kind of simple keyframe descriptors, based usually on color and edge cues. In [10], the color coherence vector was used to characterize keyframes of commercials clip. A similar approach was followed in [12], with the addition of the use of the principal components of the color histograms of keyframes for commercial recognition. Recent works along these lines introduced more sophisticated descriptors, or combinations of descriptors. In [4] the combination of color and edge-based features was considered. This work also proposed the use of inverted indices to detect copies of a video clip. In [3], audio features were also used as part of the signature. The author also performed a comprehensive experimental validation on the TRECVID dataset. A hashing mechanism based on color moment vectors to efficiently retrieve repeated video clips was proposed in [16]. In [15], a lookup table was used to store fingerprints based on mean luminance of image blocks. Finally, in [9] color was proposed in combination with the *ordinal measure* (originally proposed for the problem of stereo matching), to define a binary–valued signature of the video.

To overcome limitations of image descriptors, people have proposed to include motion-based feature in the repertoire of descriptors, either at frame level, or at local, object–like level. For instance, in [2], the concept of *video strands* was used to create spatiotemporal descriptions of video data. These video strands encapsulate the movement of objects within half-second segments of a video sequence. In [6], two approaches to video matching based on motion were presented. Both used a single value to represent each frame of the video; In the first approach, simple heuristics were used to find how far particular regions have shifted from one image to the next. In the other, the change in color from one image to the next were reduced to a single scalar. Some motion-based approach analyze DCT coefficients extracted from the compressed stream. In [13], similar shot matching is done using an image signature that is an integer value computed from the low frequency coefficients of the DCT.

While the above mentioned approach proved to perform efficiently on selected datasets, a common limitations is that they rely on ad-hoc features and features' descriptors, which may be difficult to use on existing, large collections of generic videos. Furthermore, and possibly more important, it is not clear how this ad-hoc features perform over collections with high variability, since their effectiveness is usually tested only on a particular domain, at the risk of overfitting the representation over that domain. Our main effort has been to select an effective combination of features and features' descriptors, taken from the well established MPEG-7 standard. Using this descriptors not only allow video content provider to easily index their content with freely available tools, without ambiguity, but also enable to match clips taken from various sources, provided that a suitable, general purpose metric is employed to perform matching.

To this end, we have found the edit distance as an ideal candidate for our goals. The use of the edit distance in the context of video matching is not new, and was initially proposed in [1]. Since then, variations have been proposed over the basic formulation [5]. The main benefit of using a metric belonging to the class of the edit distances, is the possibility to obtain high similarity between videos that may differ for some subsequences, e.g. like those due to re-editing of the original video stored in the database. In the existing literature, features' descriptors are quantized to obtain a sequence of discrete symbols, prior to perform matching. This process has some potential drawbacks, since is not completely clear how one should choose the number of symbols for videos of generic type. In contrast to the existing work, and as a second contribution of this paper, we avoid this discretization step, relying directly on the distance used to compare two descriptors for deciding on the cost of transforming one string into another.

3   Approach

The video clip matching system is performed in two phases. In the first one an indexing process generates the signatures, composed by MPEG-7 descriptors, for the clips that are to be retrieved. In the second phase the target video that has to be analyzed is processed to extract the same features, and these are used to measure similarity with the signatures. There are no special requirements on the video format used to create the index or the target video, since the descriptors are extracted from decompressed frames. Moreover experiments showed that even frame sizes as low as PAL QCIF (192×144) can be used in both phases. The descriptors used capture different aspects of the video content, namely global color, color layout and texture ([11]) and are computationally inexpensive. Motion descriptors have not been used in order to be able to perform recognition in real time. Anyway, the temporal aspects of video are implicitly considered using the edit distance to match the video sequences.

Among the color descriptors defined in the MPEG-7 standard, we have found that an effective combination is given by the *Scalable Color Descriptor* and the *Color Layout Descriptor* for global color and color layout, and by the *Edge Histogram Descriptor* for textures. These features are suited for the creation of fingerprint since they meet the important requirements of fast calculation, compact representation, good discriminative power and tolerance to small differences due to signal degradation. To reduce the space occupation of the stored MPEG-7 descriptors, due to the verbosity of the XML format, it is possible to use the BiM (Binary Format for MPEG-7) framework; in fact BiM enables compression of any generic XML document, reaching an average 85% compression ratio of MPEG-7 data, and allows the parsing of BiM encoded files, without requiring their decompression. In the following we provide a short discussion on these descriptors and the metrics used to match them.

Scalable Color Descriptor (SCD). It is a color histogram in the HSV color space, uniformly quantized into bins according to tables provided in the MPEG-7 standard normative part, encoded using the Haar transform. Its binary representation is scalable since it can be represented with different bits/bins, thus reducing the complexity for feature extraction and matching operations. Increasing the number of bits used improves retrieval accuracy. This descriptor can be extended into the GoF/GoP (Group of Frames/Group of Pictures) color descriptor, thus allowing it to be applied to a video segment. In this case two additional bits allow to define how the histogram is calculated before applying the Haar transform. The standard allows to use average, median or intersection. In the first case, adopted in this work, averaging of the counters of each bin is performed; the result is equivalent to computing the aggregate histogram of the group of pictures and performing normalization. The median histogram is equivalent to compute the median of each counter value of the bins, and may be used to achieve more robustness w.r.t. outliers in intensity values. The intersection histogram requires the calculation of the minimum counter value of each bin, and thus the result is representative of the "least common" color traits of the group of pictures.

SCD descriptors can be matched both in the histogram domain and in the Haar domain using the L1 norm, although it has to be noted that results of the L1 norm-based matching in the Haar domain are not the same of the histogram. Generation of the Haar coefficients is computationally marginal w.r.t. histogram creation, and their matching is equal in complexity to histogram matching, thus to avoid the reconstruction of the histogram from the descriptor we have used matching in the Haar domain, using 128 bits/histogram.

Color Layout Descriptor (CLD). This descriptor represents the spatial distribution of color in an extremely compact form (as low as 8 bytes per image can be used), and thus is particularly interesting for our scope, because of computational cost of matching and space occupation. The input picture is divided in an 8×8 grid and a representative color in the YCrCb color space for each block is determined, using a simple color averaging. The derived colors are then transformed into a series of coefficients using a 8×8 DCT. A few low-frequency coefficients are selected using zigzag scanning and then quantized. Since the calculation of the descriptor is based on a grid it is independent from the frame size.

To match two CLDs ($\{DY, DCr, DCb\}$ and $\{DY', DCr', DCb'\}$) the following distance measure is used [7]:

$$D = \sqrt{\sum_i w_{yi}(DY_i - DY_i')^2} + \sqrt{\sum_i w_{bi}(DCb_i - DCb_i')^2} + \sqrt{\sum_i w_{ri}(DCr_i - DCr_i')^2}$$

where DY_i, DCb_i and DCr_i are the i-th coefficients of the Y, Cr and Cb color components, and w_{yi}, w_{bi} and w_{ri} are the weighting values, that decrease according to the zigzag scan order.

Edge Histogram Descriptor (EHD). This descriptor represents the spatial distribution of five types of edges (four directional and one non-directional). This distribution of edges is a good texture signature even in the case of not homogeneous texture, and its computation is straightforward. Experiments conducted within the MPEG-7 committee have shown that this descriptor is quite effective for representing natural images. To extract it, the video frame is divided into 4×4 blocks, and for each block an edge histogram is computed, evaluating the strength of the five types of edges and considering those that exceed a certain preset threshold. Values of the bins are normalized to $[0, 1]$, and a non linear quantization of the bin values results in a 3 bits/bin representation. Overall the descriptor consists of 80 bins (16 blocks and 5 bins per block), and is thus quite compact.

The simplest method to assess similarity between two EHDs is to consider the 3-bit numbers as integer values and compute the L1 distance between the EHDs.

Video clip matching. Our goal is to be able to perform approximate clip matching, evaluating similarity of video sequences even in case that the original video has been re-edited. This case may happen for example in the case of commercials, where several variations of the same commercial are produced, usually creating shorter versions from a longer one. This may happen also with *video rushes* (the first unedited sequence that is filmed), from which a smaller section is usually selected to be used. Another case may be that of identifying sequences that have a variable length such as those containing anchormen in a news video, those that compose a dialog scene in a movie, or slow motion versions of a sequence like the replay of a sport highlight.

In our approach we extract the features used to create the clip fingerprint from the clip A that has to be analyzed, and consider both its feature vector and the fingerprint of the clip B to be recognized as vectors composed by three strings. All the strings of A will have length m and those of B will have length n.

To evaluate the similarity of the clips we consider each corresponding couple of corresponding strings and calculate an approximate distance. The three distances are used to calculate the Manhattan distance between the clips, and if the distance is bigger than a minimum percentage of the length of the clips then they are matched.

The approximate distance between the strings is evaluated using the Sellers algorithm. This distance is similar to the Levenshtein edit distance, and adds a variable cost adjustment to the cost of gaps, i.e. to insertions and deletions. Using this distance, and tailoring the costs of the edit operation appropriately it is possible to adjust the system to the specific clip matching task. For example if there is need to detect appearances of a long rush sequence, that is likely to be shortened in the video editing process, deletions could be considered less expensive than insertions. A simple dynamic programming implementation of the algorithm, as that shown in [14], is $O(mn)$ in time and $O(min(m,n))$ in space, but other algorithms can reduce time and space complexity. From the edit operations cost formula of [14], and considering the cost matrix C that tracks the costs of the edit operations needed to match two strings, we can then write the cost formula for the alignment of the a_i and b_j characters of two strings as:

$$C_{i,j} = min(C_{i-1,j-1} + \delta(a_i, b_i), C_{i-1,j} + \delta_I, C_{i,j-1} + \delta_D)$$

where $\delta(a_i, b_i)$ is 0 if the distance between a_i and b_i is close enough to evaluate $a_i \approx b_i$ or the cost of substitution otherwise, δ_I and δ_D are the costs of insertion and deletion, respectively. Fig.1 shows a simplified example of edit distance calculation between a part of a commercial and a shortened version of the same commercial, using the CLDs.

The alphabet of the strings has size equal to the dimensionality of features, but it has to be noted that it has no effect in terms of computational time or size on the string similarity algorithm, since only the cost of the edit operations are kept in memory, and the only operation performed on the alphabet characters is the check of their equality, using the appropriate distance described for each feature in the above paragraphs. This approach allows us to overcome a limitation of string matching; in fact usually a difference between symbols is evaluated using the same score, that is the distance between symbol 1 and 2 is the same between

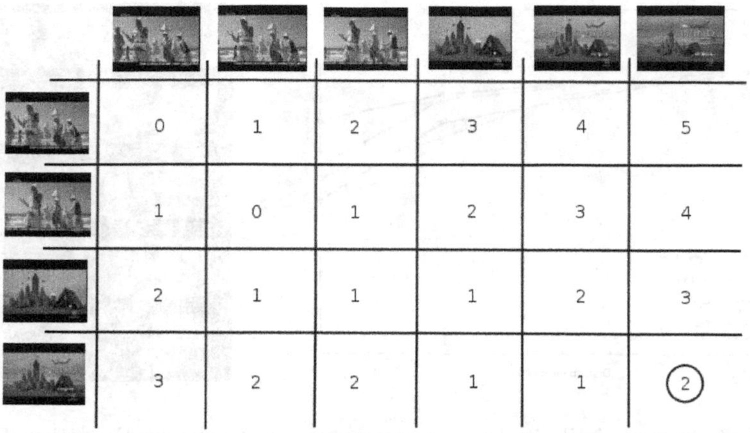

Fig. 1. Simplified example of edit distance calculation performed using CLDs. The top row shows part of a commercial, the left column shows a reduced version. The table contains the $C_{i,j}$ costs, where $\delta(a_i, b_i)$, δ_I and δ_D have value 1. The circled number is the distance between the two sequences.

symbol 1 and 10. In our case instead, when comparing two CLDs, for example, a close match could be evaluated as an equality, without penalizing the distance.

To speed up processing the calculation of similarity can be stopped earlier, when the required similarity threshold has been reached.

4   Experimental Result

The clip matching approach described in the previous section is independent w.r.t. the domain of the videos. According to each domain the most appropriate clip selection algorithm should be used, ranging from simple shot detection (e.g. for news videos) to other methods that may select sequences composed by more shots. In our experiments we have applied our approach to the detection of TV commercials. We have selected this domain since commercials contain highly paced video editing and visual effects that make their detection difficult. Moreover commercials length is often different, since several versions of the same commercial, with different editing, are aired. Lastly, commercials have been used many times in other works on video matching discussed in Sect. 2.

The clip selection algorithm used to extract the commercials to be matched is based on detection of black frames that appear before each commercial, as noted in [10].

About 10 hours of videos were acquired from digital TV signal and from different European and international broadcasters, at PAL frame rate and size, and frame resolution was scaled down to PAL QCIF (192 × 144 pixels). 40 different commercials were selected and added to the test database. Videos were converted to MPEG-1 and 2 format using FFMpeg and Mainconcept MPEG

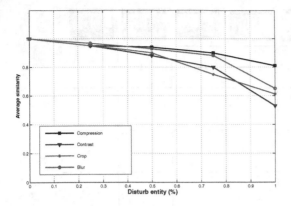

Fig. 2. *Left)* Average similarity between corresponding clips versus the entity of various disturbs on the original signal - *Right)* Keyframes from a sample sequence. The top row shows the reference sequence. Subsequent rows show keyframes taken from the sequence with the maximum level of disturb applied. From top to bottom: original, contrasted, compressed, blurred, and cropped versions.

Pro encoders, at different quality, to test the robustness with respect to compression artifacts and noise. In our prototype application (implemented in C++ under Linux), the system took about five seconds (on average) to extract the signature of a PAL QCIF clip of length 30 seconds. At query time, the system took about half of a second to perform a single comparison between two of such signatures.

Fig. 2 shows the average similarity between pairs of corresponding clips, where one of the clip was corrupted by a range of photometric or geometric disturb. Since we don't have a natural way to express the entity of all the type of disturb, the x-axis represent this measure relatively to the maximum level of the disturb that was applied. Such maximum level is shown in the right column for some sample keyframes of one test sequence. All of the corrupted versions of the clips were obtained using the program Avidemux, on a dataset of about 100 clips taken from various sources. Clips where originally encoded at a frame rate of 1000 kbps, and the maximum compression was obtained setting a fixed bitrate of 50 kbps. The graph shows how similarity gracefully degrades for all kind of disturb. As can be expected, most critical disturb are those that heavily influence the photometric properties, such as large changes in contrast.

Another experiment was conducted on 1 hour of news videos. In this case the goal was to detect similar sequences such as the anchormen shots, interviews, repeated shots used in the news summary and in the newscast. Clips were selected after performing video segmentation using a color histogram intersection technique. Fig. 3 reports the Precision/Recall curve obtained at different similarity values, along with an example of similar anchormen shots retrieved, and an example of news shot that was used to create the initial part of the video and in the newscast.

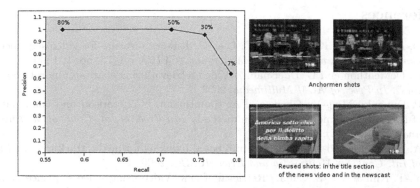

Fig. 3. Precision/Recall curve for news videos. Similarity thresholds are reported over the points. Examples of retrieved similar shots are shown on the right.

In the case of news videos the system has shown some problems in matching sequences with very low contrast due to some foggy scenes, and also to some unusually long anchormen shots, with length ratios that were much longer than those found in the commercials domain. This latter problem could be solved changing the clip selection so that each clip is matched with all the following clips, or simply adding some examples of extremely long anchormen shots to the database. The problem due to low contrast shots is more hard to be solved since it is inherent to the particular domain: in fact producer can not always have complete control over the filming conditions, as it happens when commercials or movies are filmed.

5   Conclusion

We have presented an approximate clip matching algorithm that use robust video fingerprint based on standard MPEG-7 descriptors. The proposed approach can be used to solve different problems related to the general clip matching, such as identification of structural elements like dialogs in movies, appearance of anchorman or interviews in news videos, detection of commercials in TV broadcasts, detection of duplicates in online video sharing services, content-based copy detection. The descriptors used capture several syntactic aspects of videos, are easily computed and compact enough to be used in large databases. Experiments have shown that the approach is suitable for real time recognition.

Use of edit distance as a base for the approximate match allows to cope with re-edited clips (e.g. shorter versions of commercials, or matching of rushes with aired clips), or clips that have different frame rates. While the proposed method can be directly adopted to solve the matching problem efficiently in small databases, additional effort must be made to complete the representation with a suitable indexing scheme, that would make possible matching clips in very large video databases without performing exhaustive search. Our future work will deal mainly with these computational issues, as well as with the use of detected clip repetitions as structural elements of videos, for higher semantic annotation.

References

1. D. A. Adjeroh, I. King, and M. C. Lee, "A distance measure for video sequences". *Computer Vision and Image Understanding (CVIU)*, vol. 75, no. 1, 1999.
2. D. DeMenthon and D. Doermann, "Video retrieval using spatio-temporal descriptors". *In Proc. of ACM Multimedia*, 2003.
3. P. Duygulu, Ming-Yu Chen, and A. Hauptmann, "Comparison and combination of two novel commercial detection methods", *In Proc. of Int. Conf. of Multimedia and Expo (ICME)*, 2004.
4. A. Hampapur and R. Bolle, "Feature based indexing for media tracking". *In Proc. of Int. Conf. on Multimedia and Expo (ICME)*, 2000.
5. Y.-T. Kim and T.-S. Chua, "Retrieval of news video using video sequence matching". *In Proc. of Multimedia Modelling Conference*, 2005.
6. T. C. Hoad and J. Zobel, "Fast video matching with signature alignment". *In Proc. of Workshop on Multimedia Information Retrieval (MIR)*, 2003.
7. E. Kasutani and A. Yamada, "The MPEG-7 Color Layout Descriptor: a Compact Image feature Description for High-Speed Image/Video Segment Retrieval", *IEEE Proc. of International Conference on Image Processing (ICIP 2001)*, vol. I, pp. 674-677, October 2001.
8. E. Kasutani and A. Yamada: "An Adaptive Feature Comparison Method for Real-time Video Identification", *IEEE Proc. of International Conference on Image Processing (ICIP 2003)*, vol. II, pp. 5-8, September 2003.
9. Y. Li, J.S. Jin, and X. Zhou, "Matching commercial clips from TV streams using a unique, robust and compact signature". *In Proc. of Digital Image Computing: Techniques and Applications (DICTA)*, 2005.
10. C. K. R. Lienhart and W. Effelsberg, "On the detection and recognition of television commercials". *In Proc. of Int. Conf. on Multimedia Computing and Systems (ICMCS)*, 1997.
11. B. S. Manjunath, J.-R. Ohm, and V. V. Vasudevan, "Color and Texture Descriptors". *IEEE Transactions on Circuits and Systems for Video Technology*, vol. 11, No. 6, June 2001.
12. R. Mohan, "Video sequence matching". *In Proc. of Int. Conf. on Audio, Speech and Signal Processing (ICASSP)*, 1998.
13. X. Naturel, and P. Gros, "A fast shot matching strategy for detecting duplicate sequences in a television stream". *In Proc. of Int. Workshop on Computer Vision meets Databases (CVDB)*, 2005.
14. G. Navarro, "A guided tour to approximate string matching". *ACM Computing Surveys*, Vol.33, 2001.
15. J. Oostveen, T. Kalker, and J. Haitsma. "Feature extraction and a database strategy for video fingerprinting". *In Proc. of Int. Conf. on Recent Advances in Visual Information Systems (VISUAL)*, 2002.
16. K. M. Pua, J. M. Gauch, S. E. Gauch, and J. Z. Miadowicz. "Real time repeated video sequence identification". *Computer Vision and Image Understanding (CVIU)*, Vol. 93, no. 3, 2004.

Video Retrieval Using High Level Features: Exploiting Query Matching and Confidence-Based Weighting

Shi-Yong Neo*, Jin Zhao, Min-Yen Kan, and Tat-Seng Chua

Department of Computer Science, School of Computing,
National University of Singapore, Singapore, 117543
{neoshiyo, zhaojin, kanmy, chuats}@comp.nus.edu.sg

Abstract. Recent research in video retrieval has focused on automated, high-level feature indexing on shots or frames. One important application of such indexing is to support precise video retrieval. We report on extensions of this semantic indexing on news video retrieval. First, we utilize extensive query analysis to relate various high-level features and query terms by matching the textual description and context in a time-dependent manner. Second, we introduce a framework to effectively fuse the relation weights with the detectors' confidence scores. This results in individual high level features that are weighted on a per-query basis. Tests on the TRECVID 2005 dataset show that the above two enhancements yield significant improvement in performance over a corresponding state-of-the-art video retrieval baseline.

1 Introduction

News video retrieval systems often perform retrieval based solely on automatic speech recognition (ASR) results on the video's audio. This is because ASR, while not fully accurate, is reliable and largely indicative of the topic of videos. Such a transformation of the video retrieval problem into a text-based one has been shown to be effective [1].

To further increase the accuracy and resolution of video retrieval requires analysis and modeling of the video and audio content. The community has investigated this in part by developing specialized detectors that detect and index certain **High-Level Features** (HLFs; e.g., presence of cars, faces and buildings). As such, research retrieval systems incorporate both standard text-based information (from ASR and/or closed captions) with results from an inventory of detectors designed to capture HLFs. In order to carry out a large-scale retrieval of video in a real time environment, most features have to be extracted and preprocessed during offline indexing. In the current state of the art, systems cannot detect and index (or even conceptualize) every possible useful high-level semantic feature. Therefore, it is necessary to carry out inference on a limited set of detectable HLFs that cover and support a wide range of queries. Thus we focus on using only ASR and the HLFs to support news video search.

We offer two extensions to this basic framework that enhance the contributions of HLFs, based on two observations. First, we note that many HLFs have a natural textual description (e.g., "car", "face") that have not been widely utilized for retrieval. We show how to match such feature descriptions with the user's textual query to enhance retrieval

---

* Contact author, supported by the Singapore Millennium Foundation (SMF).

H. Sundaram et al. (Eds.): CIVR 2006, LNCS 4071, pp. 143–152, 2006.
© Springer-Verlag Berlin Heidelberg 2006

performance in a time-dependent manner. We approach this by employing morphological analysis followed by selective expansion using the WordNet [2] lexical database on both the feature descriptions and the user's query. The stronger the match between the descriptions and the query, the more important the HLF is to the query. However as queries are often time-sensitive (featuring new personas, corporations each day, using only the static information in WordNet is not enough. Thus we further employ the use of comparable news articles within the same period of time to further build and expand word-based relationships. Crucially different from previous work that only employs lexical expansion, our method fuses both static lexical information with dynamic correlation by calculating time-dependent mutual information [3].

Secondly, as HLF detectors vary greatly in performance, it is necessary to consider their accuracies in the fusion process. Currently, retrieval systems have used the output of such batteries of detectors "as-is", without considering the confidence of individual detectors. For example, detectors for faces are fairly robust, whereas detectors for cars and animals are not. We introduce a performance-weighted framework which accounts for this phenomenon. Different from previous work, it evaluates the accuracy of individual high-level detectors during training/validation and utilizes probability of correct detection in feature weighting during testing.

We have validated our approach on the TRECVID 2005 dataset [4] and queries. Our experimental results show that the appropriate use of HLFs in retrieval outperforms text-based systems and improves results on a representative state-of-the-art multimodal retrieval systems.

2   Use of High-Level Features in Video Retrieval

Starting from text-based search, video retrieval has incorporated the use of low-level video features (e.g., color, motion, volume) and, more recently, high level features for specific objects or phenomenon (e.g., cars, fire, and applause). To create such high level features, recent work has taken a machine learning approach, where each HLF detector is trained against an annotated corpus of video clips [4,5]. A well-known example is the LSCOM set, which contains approximately 1000 concepts which can be used for video annotation. In TRECVID 2005, the LSCOM-lite set (a LSCOM subset of 39 interesting concepts) have been selected and tagged to provide training examples of approximately 50,000 shots or 70 hours of video. The detectors trained using these examples introduce useful and partial semantics to retrieval systems.

The IBM group used a fusion of low-level features and HLFs based on two learning techniques: Multi-example Content Based Retrieval (a k-NN variant) and support vector machines [6]. Their system automatically maps query text to HLF models. The weights are derived by co-occurrence statistics between ASR tokens and detected concepts as well as by their correlations.

[7] represented the text queries and subshots in an intermediate concept space which contains confidences for each of the 39 concepts. The subshots are represented by the outputs of the concept detectors for each concept, smoothed according to the frequencies of each concept and the reliability of each concept detector. The text queries are mapped into the concept space by measuring the similarity between the query terms and

the terms in the concept's description. This approach was applied to automatic, manual, and interactive searches, yielding high performance for the few topics which have high-performing correlated concepts.

The MediaMill group [8] also extended the LSCOM-lite set by increasing the HLF pool to 101 features, some original as well as some recycled from the previous TRECVID tasks. Other top performing interactive retrieval systems from Informedia [9] and DCU [10] also show effective methods of integrating high level semantic features. One may conclude that even though the HLF detection accuracies are much lower than low level features, HLF have shown to be more useful for semantic queries.

In this work, we use a set of 25 HLFs for news video retrieval. Our primary reason for choosing this set is that the corresponding detectors are readily available and have been trained previously on both the TRECVID 2004 and 2005 HLF task. In addition, they have shown to be useful in retrieval in previous work [11,12]. These 25 features are targeted towards identifying the video genre, objects, backgrounds and actions, as shown in Figure 1. The HLF task requires system to return ranklists of maximum 2000 shots for each HLF. Our system achieves a mean average precision (MAP) of 0.22. In order to maximize the detection accuracy, we combine the best available HLF detection results from various participating groups. We only select ranklists which have a MAP $\geq$ .2 and above (including IBM's HLF detector set [6], which has a .33 MAP). The score of shot S_c containing HLF_k is calculated using the following equation:

$$Score(S_c|HLF_k) = \alpha \sum_j Contains(S_c) + (1-\alpha) \sum_j \frac{maxPos - Pos(S_c)}{maxPos} \quad (1)$$

where $Contains()$ is an indicator function that checks whether a shot is present on the ranklist and the second term produces a normalized score in the range of $[0-1]$ that linearly weights the position (Pos) for the shot on the ranklist. The resulting ranked list achieves a MAP of 0.38.

- Genres: anchorPerson, *commercial, politics, sports, weather, financial*
- Objects: *face, fire, explosion, car, U.S.flag, boat, aircraft, map,* *buildingExterior, prisoner*
- Scene: *waterscape, mountain, sky, outdoor, indoor, disaster, vegetation*
- Action: *peopleWalking, peopleInCrowd*

Fig. 1. High level features used by our system. The ten underlined features indicate the required features from the TRECVID HLFs; italicized features come from LSCOM-lite.

However, having a well-trained, accurate set of HLF detectors is not sufficient for precise retrieval. This is because each HLF detector models a specific phenomenon, and which detectors are useful for particular queries varies greatly. Correctly determining and matching detectors to queries is therefore a critical task. Past systems have done this matching manually or using simple automated methods by unsupervised clustering or simple expansion using dictionaries. In this work, we leverage the textual descriptions of the HLF set for time-dependent matching and also incorporate the confidence of

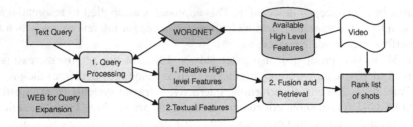

Fig. 2. Retrieval Framework

the detectors in our fusion process. This is illustrated in Figure 2 which shows the placement of both of these modules in our processing framework for large-scale news video retrieval. We describe this two-fold approach in the following two sections.

Note that in the remainder of the paper, system parameters (normally indicated by lowercase Greek letters) that are introduced have all have been optimized by either manual tuning or learned from training.

3   Query Processing for HLF Weighting

As user queries are usually short and contain insufficient context to perform a precise retrieval, we employ previous work on query expansion techniques using external resources [13] and query classification [14] during query processing to expand the user's original query (denoted Q_0) obtain an initial expanded query, Q_1.

WordNet has been a heavily utilized source of ontological lexical information in text retrieval. In text retrieval, systems relate terms by synonymy, hypernymy, hyponymy and overlap in definitions (gloss). We employ a technique close in spirit to the MediaMill group [8] to determine the match between a detector and a query. Both the short one or two word original description of the detector and the user's expanded query (HLF_0 and Q_1) are expanded using WordNet. Both pieces of data are first tagged for part-of-speech using a commercial product, and then closed-class words and words on a 400+ word video domain stopword list are removed.

WordNet expansion. Unlike previous work, we include terms from the WordNet gloss as we have found that the terms extracted from the gloss differs significantly from those extracted from a term's synonyms and the hypernym/hyponym hierarchy. The former sometimes provides visual information about an object – its shape, color, nature and texture; whereas the latter only provides direct relations (e.g., *aircraft* & *airplane*; *fire* & *explosion*). For example, the word *boat* can not be related to *water* by virtue of any relationship link in WordNet, but by its gloss – *"a small vessel for travel on water."*

The expanded terms (Q_2, HLF_1) are then empirically weighted based on an approximate distance from the original terms (Q_1, HLF_0). Expansion terms obtained from synonymy, hyponymy and gloss, where terms obtained from the gloss have a lower weight (due to noise words in the definition).

A final matching phase is done to determine which high level features are most relevant to the query. To match HLF_1 to Q_2 we use the information-content metric of

Resnik [15] (as was done in [16]), which equates similarity with the information content of the pair of words' most specific common ancestor: $Resnik(t_i, t_j) = IC(lcs(t_i, t_j))$ where $lcs(t_i, t_j)$ is the most deeply nested concept in the *is-a* hierarchy that subsumes both t_i and t_j). Here, we factor in the expanded term weights from the previous step.

$$Sim\_Lex(Q_j, HLF_k) = (\sum_{t_q \epsilon Q_j} \sum_{t_f \epsilon HLF_k} Resnik(t_q, t_f))/(|Q_j| \times |HLF_k|)) \quad (2)$$

After summing all such scores for each HLF, the k top scoring HLFs are taken with their weights and used in the final retrieval.

This framework would be fine for video in which the associated text information is aligned exactly to the clip. However, in professionally edited video, speech often comes before the corrsponding visual information. We therefore carry forward β seconds of speech of each preceding shot to its succeeding shot ($\beta = 12$, roughly equivalent to an average shot duration).

Time sensistive expansion. Lexical similarity as computed from static dictionaries may not always be most suitable for news, especially because of news' transient nature. Aside from helping to increase to link named entities to common words, it refines the relations between words already linked by WordNet. For example, although the concept *fire* and *explosion* are associated in WordNet, in news stories the relationship can vary. A chemical factory explosion story is likely to have both terms highly correlated, but a story on forest fires is unlikely to have the *explosion* concept. Similarly, *car, boat* and *aircraft* are related in WordNet as means of transportation, but searches for any of the three usually should not return shots of the other two objects. Thus when systems relies solely on lexical links between words as processed from such dictionaries, they may return spurious results.

To overcome these problems, we sampled external (e.g., non-TRECVID) sources of news to model the dynamic weighting of similarity between HLFs across time. We use the external news articles to calculate the co-occurrence of $feature_1$ and $feature_2$ with respect to time. The relationship between $fire$ and $explosion$ is thus modified according to their co-occurrence in the external articles. If no news articles directly relate $explosion$ and $fire$ during a certain time period t, the link weight between $explosion$ and $fire$ is reduced accordingly. Given a query, the system first retrieves the top relevant shots from the test set. We build a corpus of news articles centered on the timestamp of each retrieved shot. As illustrated in Figure 3, given a period $\delta = 3$ days, all the available news articles for these 3 consecutive days will be used for finding the MI (Mutual Information) of between the word $feature_1$ and $feature_2$. This score is then fused with $Lex\_Sim()$ from above to obtain the time-dependent similarity function $Lex\_Sim_t()$. Equation 3 gives the final, time-sensitive similarity measure.

$$Sim\_Lex_t(Q_j, HLF_k) = \gamma Sim\_Lex(Q_j, HLF_k) + (1 - \gamma)MI(Q_j, HLF_k|t) \quad (3)$$

4   Confidence Fusion and Retrieval

The retrieval step is a text-based retrieval scoring function enhanced with HLF confidence scoring. We use the text scoring function $Text(S_i)$ from [11]. This

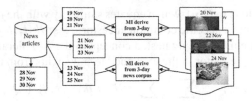

Fig. 3. Dynamic corpora generation for term correlation in video shots

scoring function utilizes the query's class and other additional contextual information to retrieve the relevant documents. In this previous work, it was experimentally shown that irrelevant segments were eliminated while recall was maintained.

As the HLF detectors perform at different accuracy levels, we must consider their precision in retrieval. Using the available training samples, we obtain accuracies for each detector using 5-fold cross validation, in terms of mean average precision. The final score of shot S_i with respect to query Q is given below.

$$Score(S_i) = \zeta * Text(S_i) + (1 - \zeta) * \sum_{HLF_k \in S_i} Conf(HLF_k) \times Sim\_Lex_t(Q, HLF_k)$$

(4)

where $Conf(HLF_k)$ is estimated MAP of the $Detector_k$. The score for each shot will be computed based on the available textual features as well as the HLFs and their detection confidence with respect to the query.

5 Evaluation

The goal of our evaluations is to show the efficacy of both modules: HLF weighting and confidence-based fusion. For the weighting, we can measure how well our automatic weighting scheme agrees with the importance assigned to the HLFs by human subjects. For fusion, we measure the gain in retrieval performance when incorporating confidence in the HLF weighting scheme. We also measure the synergy when employing both modules together in the retrieval framework.

5.1 HLF Weighting Agreement with Human Subjects

We asked 12 paid volunteers to take a survey that assessed how they would weight HLFs in video retrieval. All participants were either university postgraduate or undergraduate students and had not used textual descriptions to search for videos before. We selected 8 queries from past TRECVID queries that were representative of different semantic classes (e.g., "George Bush", "Basketball players on court" and "People entering and leaving buildings"), and asked the participants to first freely associate what types of HLFs would be important in retrieving such video clips, and second, to assign a value on a scale from 1 (important) to 5 (unimportant) of the specific HLF inventory set used in our system (c.f., Figure 1) for the same 8 queries. 5 here refers to a strong positive correlation between the HLF and the query; 1, a negative correlation. In total, we gathered about 2400 judgments.

An analysis of the free association subtask shows that over 90% of the responses are concrete nouns, confirming earlier work that searchers focus on nouns as cues for retrieval. In addition, although only 5% of the features used in our experiments are mentioned explicitly in the free association task, some were later ranked as "Important" by participants in the second subtask. Calculating the interjudge agreement using Kappa (which varies from -1 (no agreement) to 1 (full correlation)), we found only a low agreement ranging from 0.2 to 0.4, which varied with the search task. The low agreement may be partially due to the inexperience of the participants in searching video. We also calculated the standard deviation of a feature's score for each search task, shown in Table 1, which showed results similar to [17].

Table 1. Importance ratings of most HLFs across all 8 search tasks. Blank cells indicate high standard deviations (above 0.7). Features sorted by standard deviation.

Feature (Avg. s.d.)	Map	Tree	Office	Basketball	Ship	Hu Jintao	George Bush	Fire
Fire & Explosion (0.6)		1.4	1.4	1.3		1.3	1.4	5.0
Car (0.7)		1.4	1.2	1.3	1.4		4.4	4.0
Boat (0.8)	1.1	1.5	1.1	1.1	4.5	1.4		
Aircraft (0.9)		1.4	1.2	1.1	1.6			
Face (1.1)	1.2	1.3						
People Walking (1.2)					1.5			
Map (0.7)	4.8		1.4	1.1	1.2	1.5	1.6	1.4
People in Crowd (1.2)								
Sports (0.8)	1.2		1.4	4.7		1.5	1.5	
Weather (0.9)				1.4			1.1	1.4
Disaster (0.9)		1.5	1.4	1.2			1.7	4.5
Building Exterior (1.0)				1.1	1.2			
Waterscape (1.0)	1.5		1.3	1.1	4.1	1.7	1.5	1.3
Outdoor (1.0)	1.6		1.1	3.9				
Indoor (0.9)	1.2	1.2	4.5			1.5		1.5

In some cases, the degree of agreement is high, especially when the search task mentions the feature directly (e.g., the basketball query mentioning "sports"). In fact, a trend of HLF rating stability was observed. Ratings for concrete nouns were most stable, followed by backgrounds and video categories, and with those describing actions being the most variable or unreliable. We also note that negative correlations (scores close to 1.0) are prominent in our dataset. We feel this is quite reasonable, as only a few HLFs are usually relevant per query. We have also computed the Kappa value between the HLF rankings from our system and the ones from the human judges. The value ranges between 0 to 0.25 with a mean value of 0.145. We believe this varying level of agreement is due to the fact that WordNet expansion works well for hypernym and hyponym relations, but less so for other relation types. As a result, the overall agreement is weak. We plan to look into the problem of how to enrich the WordNet so that it is capable of discovering other relations in the near future as an extension to this work.

5.2   Text Retrieval and Query Matching

We follow the evaluation standards in TRECVID 2005 automated search task. A maximum of 1,000 shots are returned for each query; performance is measured by MAP.

We modify our retrieval system [11] to perform the required text retrieval. The text-based retrieval engine uses the text query to retrieve pre-segmented passages of text in the (possibly machine translated) ASR transcripts. These segments correspond to phrase level video segments in the corpus. The video segment associated with the matched phrase and the segment immediately afterwards are retrieved as the retrieved results (because of the aforementioned time lag betweens speech and video). This text-based baseline system also incorporates query expansion using external news resources. The resulting text retrieval system achieves an MAP of 0.063 based on the TRECVID 2005 dataset and queries. In comparison, the top three performers in TRECVID 2005's search tasks yield MAP of 0.067, 0.062, 0.061 respectively (mostly based on common dataset), showing that our text baseline is competitive.

To test the effectiveness of our query matching techniques, we further compare the performance to this system [11] which uses heuristics to weight HLFs to individual queries. When HLFs are integrated into the text-only system [11], the jump in MAP is significant (from 0.063 to 0.104) and validates earlier reported work. To test the effectiveness of the various components in the query matching module, three runs have been carried out.

Table 2. The performance in MAP combining textual features and HLF in retrieval

Technique of Using HLF + Text	MAP (% Gain)
Heuristics weighting by [11] (used as baseline)	0.104
Run1. Automated HLF query matching	0.106 (+1.9%)
Run2. Automated HLF query matching + Gloss (Eqn. 2)	0.110 (+5.8%)
Run3. Automated HLF query matching + Gloss + Temporal MI (Eqn. 3)	0.113 (+8.6%)

The table shows that the use of HLFs during fusion outperformed the text-based retrieval system by more than 50%. This is conclusive as textual feature alone are not reliable enough to pinpoint shots which are relevant to the query. Run1 and Run2 indicates that the use of WordNet glosses is positive as the performance increases from the MAP of 0.106 to 0.110. Run3, which uses all the components obtains a MAP 8.6% better than the baseline system. The main improvement comes from the sport and general queries. Queries which are directly or indirectly related to the available 25 HLFs benefit the most. This suggest that as more HLFs are added, a better performance can be obtained. The MAP performance is higher due to its re-ranking of relevant shots as it takes all 25 HLFs into consideration during fusion. This performance is also better than a similar evaluation run (MAP of 0.070) submitted by IBM [6] which uses only text and HLFs.

5.3 Confidence-Based Fusion and A/V Integration

For the confidence-based fusion, we carried out two more runs to investigate the effects of considering HLF detection accuracy in the retrieval. As Run1 to Run3 uses HLF detection result without considering the accuracy of the various HLF detectors (normal fusion), we added Run4 which applies confidence-based fusion as in Eqn. 4. Run5 is

Table 3. Aggregate MAP of the runs. Percentages indicate performance gain over the baseline system.

Experiment	Normal fusion	Confidence-based fusion (Eqn. 4)
Run4. Text + HLF	0.113 (+8.6%)	0.117 (+12.6%)
Run5. Text + HLF + A/V features[11]	0.127 (+22.1%)	0.131 (+25.9%)

designed to investigate the overall performance of the system by integrating other A/V features including low level features from [11]. The fusion is done by modifying the query-dependent multimodal fusion function in [11] to accommodate Eqn. 4. Results of these experiments are reported in Table 3.

The result shows that the use of confidence-based fusion yields significant improvement over normal fusion. The confidence-based fusion Run4 achieves a MAP of 0.117. This performance is statistically comparable to top performing submissions. The run that incorporate the rest of the A/V features obtains the MAP of 0.127 and 0.131 respectively, which is better than the best published MAP of 0.123 in TRECVID 2005 automated search task. The bulk of improvement come from the general queries as they depend largely on the use of HLFs as evidence of relevancy. Person-oriented queries on the other hand have less significant improvement as textual features and video OCR still constitute the main score. As the confidence-based fusion and the automated HLF to query matching affect different parts of the retrieval system, they can be combined easily, producing largely independent gains on MAP.

6 Conclusion

As video analysis has advanced to building high-level semantic features from low-level ones, schemes that judiciously employ such HLFs are needed. We explore two distinct and complementary approaches to extend the current frameworks of such multimodal retrieval systems. We have investigated methods to automate and expand the matching of HLFs to user query terms. In particular, our query to HLF mapping methods examine 1) the use of dictionary definitions (WordNet's glosses) to help relate terms, and 2) time sensitive mutual information to make sure that the scores are sensitive to the timeframe and story distribution in the video corpus. Overall, our newly Text + HLF retrieval system is able to outperform baseline system and achieve similar results to top performing automated systems reported in TRECVID 2005. This framework is further tested by integrating other A/V features and the resulting performance is better than the best reported result.

References

1. Hauptmann, A., Chen, M.Y., Christel, M., Huang, C., Lin, W.H., Ng, T., Papernick, N., Velivelli, A., Yang, J., Yan, R., Yang, H., Wactlar, H.D.: Confounded expectations: Informedia at TRECVID 2004. In: TRECVID, 2004. (2004)
2. Miller, G.: Wordnet: An on-line lexical database. International Journal of Lexicography (1995)

3. Neo, S., Goh, H., Chua, T.: Multimodal event-based model for retrieval of multi-lingual news video. In: IWAIT. (2006)
4. Over, P., Ianeva, T.: TRECVID 2005: An introduction. In: TRECVID, 2005. (2005)
5. Smeaton, A.F., Kraaij, W., Over, P.: TRECVID - an overview. In: TRECVID, 2003. (2003)
6. Amir, A., Iyengar, G., Argillander, J., Campbell, M., Haubold, A., Ebadollahi, S., Kang, F., Naphade, M.R., Natsev, A.P., Smith, J.R., Tesic, J., Volkmer, T.: IBM research TRECVID-2005 video retrieval system. In: TRECVID, 2005. (2005)
7. Chang, S.F., Hsu, W., Kennedy, L., Xie, L., Yanagawa, A., Zavesky, E., Zhang, D.Q.: Columbia university TRECVID-2005 video search and high-level feature extraction. In: TRECVID, 2005. (2005)
8. Snoek, C.G.M., van Gemert, J., Geusebroek, J.M., Huurnink, B., Koelma, D.C., Nguyen, G.P., de Rooij, O., Seinstra, F.J., Smeulders, A.W.M., Veenman, C.J., , Worring, M.: The Me-diaMill TRECVID 2005 semantic video search engine. In: Proceedings of the 3rd TRECVID Workshop, NIST (2005)
9. Hauptmann, A.G., Christel, M., Concescu, R., Gao, J., Jin, Q., Lin, W.H., Pan, J.Y., Stevens, S.M., Yan, R., Yang, J., Zhang, Y.: CMU Informedia's TRECVID 2005 skirmishes. In: TRECVID, 2005. (2005)
10. Foley, C., Gurrin, C., Jones, G., Lee, H., McGivney, S., O'Connor, N.E., Sav, S., Smeaton, A.F., Wilkins, P.: TRECVid 2005 experiments at dublin city university. In: TRECVID, 2005. (2005)
11. Chua, T.S., Neo, S.Y., Goh, H.K., Zhao, M., Xiao, Y., Wang, G.: TRECVID 2005 by NUS PRIS. In: TRECVID 2005. (2005)
12. Chua, T.S., Neo, S.Y., Li, K., Wang, G., Shi, R., Zhao, M., Xu, H.: TRECVID 2004 search and feature extraction task by NUS PRIS. In: TRECVID 2004. (2004)
13. Yang, H., Chua, T.S., Wang, S., Koh, C.K.: Structured use of external knowledge for event-based open-domain question-answering. In: SIGIR 2003, Canada, Jul 2003. (2003)
14. Neo, S., Chua, T.: Query-dependent retrieval on news video. In: MMIR'05 workshop in SIGIR'05. (2005)
15. Resnik, P.: Semantic similarity in a taxonomy: An information- based measure and its applications to problems of ambiguity in natural language. Journal of Artificial Intelligence Research,11 (1999) 95–130
16. Kennedy, L.S., Natsev, A.P., Chang, S.F.: Automatic discover of query-class-dependent models for multimodal search. In: ACM Multimedia (MM '05). (2005) 882–891
17. Christel, M.G., Hauptmann, A.G.: The use and utility of high-level semantic features in video retrieval. In: Conf. on Image and Video Retrieval, Singapore (2005) 134–144

Annotating News Video with Locations

Jun Yang and Alexander G. Hauptmann

School of Computer Science, Carnegie Mellon University
5000 Forbes Ave., Pittsburgh, PA 15213, USA
{juny, alex}@cs.cmu.edu

Abstract. The location of video scenes is an important semantic descriptor especially for broadcast news video. In this paper, we propose a learning-based approach to annotate shots of news video with locations extracted from video transcript, based on features from multiple video modalities including syntactic structure of transcript sentences, speaker identity, temporal video structure, and so on. Machine learning algorithms are adopted to combine multi-modal features to solve two sub-problems: (1) whether the location of a video shot is mentioned in the transcript, and if so, (2) among many locations in the transcript, which are correct one(s) for this shot. Experiments on TRECVID dataset demonstrate that our approach achieves approximately 85% accuracy in correctly labeling the location of any shot in news video.

1 Introduction

Annotating the geographical location of video scenes is a critical step towards semantic video analysis and retrieval. However, there has been very limited research on this problem [1,3,6]. The goal of this paper is to automatically annotate the location of every shot in broadcast news video. Achieving this goal will leverage high-level retrieval tasks on news video, such as *"Find the scenes showing the flood in California caused by El Nino"*, or *"List the countries that President Bush visited last year and find the scenes of each visit"*.

There have been several efforts on labeling video with locations. One method is to use image characteristics to match the current shot against a set of existing shots with known locations, which has been used by Aoki et al. [1] and Sivic et al. [8]. However, it has limited applicability in news video because the footage contains a huge number of locations with diverse scenes for each one, making the collection of example shots for every location impossible. A separate track of research has used GPS information to determine location [6], which is not available for news video. Christel et al. [3] have successfully used locations extracted from the transcript of news video to create an map-based interface for browsing, but they did not correlate the locations with specific shots. To our knowledge, there is no working approach for annotating the locations of news video shots.

The *general* problem of annotating the locations of video of arbitrary genres is extremely difficult. The *specific* problem we are focusing on, namely annotating locations of broadcast news video, is tractable because news video comes with transcript from closed-captions or speech recognition, which contains most

H. Sundaram et al. (Eds.): CIVR 2006, LNCS 4071, pp. 153–162, 2006.
© Springer-Verlag Berlin Heidelberg 2006

*... fray between the **United States** and **Iraq** ... **U.N.** secretary general Kofi Annan will go to **Baghdad** ... tanks were training in the sands of **Kuwait** ... meeting five permanent members of **U.N.** security council, the **U.S.**, **Russia**, **China**, **France**, and **Britain** ... flexibility by **Iraq** in allowing weapons inspectors ...*

Fig. 1. A sequence of video shots from a news story and the locations in transcript

of the locations shown in the footage. Nevertheless, this specific problem is still challenging for several reasons. First, there are typically more than one location mentioned in the vicinity of each shot, and the true location of the shot is not necessarily the closest one. Second, determining the location from the visual content of a shot is virtually impossible, because one location can have numerous visually different scenes. Last but not the least, some shots do not have a legitimate location, such as the shots showing stock market data, and some have locations that are not worthwhile to be mentioned, such as anchor shots. It is nontrivial to tell if the location of a shot is among those in the transcript.

These difficulties are illustrated in Figure 1, which shows a news story on the Iraqi crisis in 1998, where the locations of the footage switch between Kuwait, United Nations, and Iraq. One difficulty is that the order in which the locations appear in the transcript is different from the order of the shots showing these locations. Moreover, one has to get rid of extra locations such as Russia, China, and France, which are mentioned in the transcript but never shown in the footage. Finally, one needs to tell that the location of the anchor shot is not among those mentioned in the transcript.

As parallel streams of information, *correlations* exist between the mentions of locations in the transcript and the changes of the video scenes to ensure the footage being comprehensible. In this paper, we capture the location-shot associations by exploring clues from different modalities of the news video, including the syntactic analysis of the transcript, temporal video structure, speaker identification, and so on. Machine learning methods are adopted to combine these multi-modal features to solve two sub-problems: (1) is the location of a given shot mentioned in the transcript? and if so, (2) among the many locations in the transcript, which are the correct location(s) of the shot? Experiments on TRECVID dataset demonstrate that our approach achieves 85% accuracy in correctly labeling the location of any shot in news video.

2   An Overview of the Approach

News video footage consists of a series of stories, where each story is a semantically coherent video sequence on a specific news event. A story can be further partitioned into shots, and each shot contains the scene at a specific location.

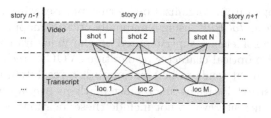

Fig. 2. The formulation of location annotation in news video

Automatic segmentation of stories and shots can be done with high accuracy. Moreover, we can obtain the transcript of news video from its closed-captions (CC) and/or using automatic speech recognition (ASR). All the mentions of locations can be extracted from the transcript (Section 3). ASR text is temporally aligned with the video during its generation process, while CC text can be aligned to video by matching it with ASR text. Thus, the time-stamp of every mention of location in the transcript is known.

As each story is an independent unit, the location of a shot (if mentioned) needs to be searched only among the locations appearing in the transcript of the same story, known as the *candidate locations* of the shot. Figure 2 suggests that location annotation is about finding the correct associations between shots and locations within the boundary of each story. Specifically, we can predict the location of $Shot_i$ by evaluating its probability of being associated with each of its candidate locations $\{Loc_{ij}\}$, denoted as $P(Match|Shot_i, Loc_{ij})$. Each shot-location association is described by a set of multi-modal features that help distinguish the correct/incorrect associations, as will be elaborated in Section 4. Once the probabilities are computed, we can annotate the shot with the location(s) with high probability. Note that one shot can have more than one locations, e.g., California and San Francisco are both valid locations for a shot showing San Francisco. On the other hand, the locations of some shots never appear in the transcript for various reasons, an issue to be further discussed in Section 5.

This formulation leads to a supervised binary classification problem of distinguishing correct and incorrect shot-location associations. Using any existing learning model, we can learn a classifier from example shots that have manually labeled locations, and then use the classifier to predict the probability of each unlabeled shot being associated with each of its candidate locations. We explore two learning approaches in our experiment, namely logistic regression and support vector machine (SVM).

3   Extracting Candidate Locations

The candidate locations are automatically extracted from the video transcript using the BBN named-entity detector [2]. From its output, we take all the terms/phrases recognized as "location" as our candidate locations. Additional locations are mapped from "organization" terms/phrases with self-contained locations, such as *"Capitol Hill"*, using a manually created mapping list. Note that location terms are sometimes superimposed on the video frames, which can be recognized by video optical character recognition (VOCR) techniques [7]. However, the VOCR output tends to be errorful on low-resolution news video, and they offer few *distinct* locations since most of them overlap with those from transcript. Thus, currently we do not include these locations as the candidates, and leave it for future research to utilize such errorful locations.

Two problems need to be addressed to transform the extracted raw locations into those used for annotation: *location synonymity* and *location polysemy*. The synonymity problem arises when there are multiple representations of the same physical location, which can be caused by abbreviations, such as *"NY"* and *"New York"*, specificity, such as *"Long Island"* and *"Long Island, New York"*, canonical names and variants, such as *"Holland"* and *"Netherland"*, etc. By looking up each location term in a a geographical dictionary, or a gazetteer[1], we merge synonymous locations to create a set of distinct candidate locations. The gazetteer has various representations of a location and the hierarchical relationships between locations, which, for example, tells the fact that *"Long Island"* is inside *"New York"*. An item of the gazetteer looks like *"**Paris** – French; Built up area; ...; France; Europe;"*, where it shows the language, coordinate, category, and country and continent of each location.

In contrast, the polysemy problem refers to the case where two or more different physical locations share the same representation. For example, *"London"* can be a city in United Kingdom or a city in Ontario, Canada, and if appearing by itself, it is impossible to tell which city is referred to. We disambiguate such polysemantic location terms by considering the *context* information. For example, if a location term has two possible references, and we find other locations in the same story that either subsumes or is subsumed (based on the gazetteer) by one of the referred locations, we decide that this is the location actually referred to. If no such context clues are found, however, we simply pick the default reference of this location term suggested by the gazetteer.

4   Multi-modal Features for Location Annotation

Features from multiple video modalities are used for classification of correct and incorrect locations. In this section, we discuss the insight behind the use of each modality, and leave the details of all the features to Table 1.

4.1   Temporal Relationships

There is an apparent temporal correspondence between the progress of video shots at different locations and the mentions of location terms in the transcript. For example, generally the location mentioned closest to a shot is mostly likely its true location. We explore such temporal relationships from several aspects:

---

[1] We manually built the gazetteer from the information available at GEOnet Names Server (earth-info.nga.mil/gns/html) and U.S. Geological Survey (www.usgs.gov).

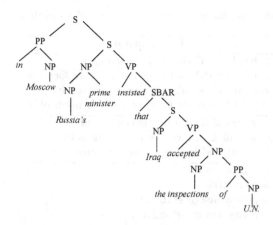

Overlaid: *IRAQ*
VOCR output: *LRAQ*

Edit distances:
France: 0.67
Russia: 1.0
U.S.: 1.0
Iraq: 0.25

Fig. 3. Parse tree of the example sentence   **Fig. 4.** Overlaid location

- *order:* whether a location is mentioned before, within, or after a shot.
- *distance:* the distance (in seconds) between a shot and the nearest mention of a location.
- *closeness rank:* how close a location term is to a shot, compared with the other locations in the same story.

4.2   Syntactic Features

The syntactic roles of a location term in the sentences of the transcript implies whether it is the actual location of the footage. For example, from sentence *"In Moscow, Russia's prime minister insisted that Iraq accepted the inspections of U.N."*, one can easily tell that Moscow is more likely the true location of the video than Iraq or U.N., since it is inside a prepositional phrase *"in Moscow"* which indicates the location of the event. The syntactic roles of a location in a sentence can be obtained from its parse tree. We use Link Grammar Parser [9] to parse sentences into parse trees. Figure 3 shows the parse tree of the above sentence, where it is decomposed into a set of nested *constituents* of several types, such as noun phrase (NP), verb phrase (VP), prepositional phrase (PP), sentence (S), sub-sentence or clause (SBAR). By analyzing the parse tree we can classify the syntactic role of a location term as one of the following:

- *prepositional phrase:* Video locations are often expressed via PPs, such as *"in Moscow"*, so we identify all the location terms occurring in PPs. We also examine the specific preposition used in order to distinguish PPs that do not indicate locations, such as *"of U.N."*.
- *subject/object:* Location terms as the subject or object of a sentence are unlikely references to the actual location, such as *"Iraq"* in above sentence.
- *modifier:* Like Russia in *"Russia's prime minister"*, a location modifying other nouns is usually not the location of the video scene.

Table 1. The feature set describing the association between a shot S and a location L

Modality	Feature	Description
Syntactic Feature	in-loc-pp	L is inside a PP that indicates location
	in-other-pp	L is inside a PP that does not indicate location
	is-subj-obj	L is used as the subject/object of a sentence
	is-modifier	L is used to modify another noun or noun phrase
Temporal Relationship	shot-loc-dist	the temporal distance between S and L
	loc-rank	the rank of L in terms of its closeness to S
	shot-loc-order	L is mentioned before, within, or after S
Location Properties	continent	L is a continent
	country	L is a country
	province	L is a province or state
	city	L is a city, town, or region
	organization	L is an organization
Overlaid Text	vocr-similarity	the similarity between L and VOCR output of S
Speaker Identity	anchor/reporter/ narrator/subject	L is uttered by the anchor, reporter, narrator, or new subjects of the story

4.3   Screen-Overlaid Location (VOCR)

Location terms are occasionally overlaid on video frames to indicate the true location of the current shot. While we choose not to rely on the errorful locations recognized by VOCR [7] (Section 2), they are nevertheless useful due to their similarity to the true location terms. In Fig.4, for example, *Iraq* is recognized as *Lraq*, differing by only one character. Therefore, the string similarity between each candidate location of the shot and the VOCR output indicates which candidate matches the screen-overlaid location, and thus the true location of the shot. The similarity is measured by *edit distance*, defined as the number of insertions, deletions, or substitutions needed to convert one string into another, which is then normalized by the length of the source string. Figure 4 lists the normalized edit distances of some candidate locations to the VOCR output, where the true location *Iraq* has the shortest distance.

4.4   Speaker Identity

The identity of the person who utters a location term is also related to whether this location is shown by the video. The speaker identities of a news story include anchor, reporter, narrator, and news-subjects (i.e., people in news events). Our observation reveals that the true locations are more likely from the speech of the anchor, narrator, and reporter, who are observers of the news, rather than from the news-subjects as the insiders of the story. Speaker identification is a byproduct of the LIMSI speech recognition system [4], which groups the speech segments that are likely to be of the same speaker, with an ID assigned on each group. Although these IDs do not directly indicate the actual identity of each speaker, we can derive that from the distributions of IDs and other clues using

Fig. 5. Various types of shots without specified locations in transcript

the method described in [10]. Once the speaker identity is known, one can tell the identity of the speaker uttering each location by matching their timestamps.

4.5 Location Type

Locations of certain types are simply more (or less) likely to be the real location of a story. For example, when *"White House"* is mentioned, it is dubious whether there are footage showing the actual place, because this phrase is often used to refer to an organization, such as in *"**White House** says today that Iraq must allow the weapon inspectors."*. To capture such information, we classify locations into several types by their specificity and other properties. The type information of a location can be easily read from the gazetteer (Section 3), and is turned into a set of features as shown in Table 1.

5   Distinguishing Shots Without Specified Location

Some shots do not have a legitimate location, such as artificial shots showing maps and stock market data; some have locations but their locations do not appear in the transcript. While it makes no sense to annotate the locations of the shots in the first case, it is extremely difficult to annotate the shots in the second case since their locations can *only* be guessed from the visual content, which is beyond the start-of-the-art of pattern recognition and the focus of this paper. In our approach, we identify the shots *without* specified locations in transcript (i.e., shots in either of the two cases) and dismiss them as "unspecified", leaving the prediction of their specific locations to future work. A close examination reveals that such shots belong to the following types (1) *commercial shots*, (2) *artificial shots*, such as shots showing maps, stock market data, animations, sketches, (3) *studio-setting shots*, including anchor shots and shots showing interviews, (4) *symbolic-scene shots*, which show symbolic scenes whose locations are self-contained, and (5) *general-scene shots*, which show scenes of general types where the specific location is of no interest, such as "people at beach". Figure 5 shows examples of each type of shots.

Given the variety of video shots without specified locations, there is no simple heuristic available to identify all such shots, especially the last two types. Similarly, we formulate it as a supervised binary classification task as to distinguishing shots with specified locations from those without, and apply learning methods such as logistic regression and SVM to it. The features (of each shot) for this task are derived from different modalities of news video. Due to the limited space, we briefly discuss the key features below.

- **Shot category:** Among the aforementioned types, anchor, commercial, and weather-forecast shots can be readily identified by existing concept detectors [5] on news video, whose outputs are incorporated into the feature set.
- **Story topic:** Stories on business, entertainment, health, and technology are more likely to contain scenes without specified locations. Thus, we built a text classifier that predicts based on the transcript the category of each story as *politics, business, health, technology, sports,* and *entertainment,* and the predictions are incorporated as features. The classifier is trained using SVM based on news video transcript with manually assigned topic labels.
- **Motion:** Most artificial and studio-setting shots are close to static. Thus, we use some motion features, such as the average pixel difference between consecutive frames, to help identify such shots.

6   Performance Evaluation

Our experiment is conducted on 10-hour footage of ABC World News Tonight[2] from TRECVID 2004 collection, which consists of 6219 shots. We use a named-entity detector [2] to extract all the location terms from the closed-captions of the footage. It should be noted that our approach can also work with ASR text if closed-captions are unavailable. From the detected locations, we remove the continent names and "United States" since these general locations hardly provide any useful information. The candidate locations of each shot are the locations appearing in the same story as the shot, where the true story boundaries are provided by TRECVID. In average, each shot has 4.02 candidate locations.

To collect the truth, a human annotator gave binary judgment on whether each candidate location is correct or incorrect for a given shot. If a shot has multiple true locations with varying specificity (e.g., *"San Francisco"* and *"California"*), no ranking is enforced and they are considered equally good. If the annotator decided that a shot does not have a legitimate location, or none of the candidate locations is correct, he annotated it as *"unspecified"*. It turned out that 1768 of the 6219 shots are annotated with at least one location, with the remaining labeled as *"unspecified"*. In average, each shot has 1.41 *correct* locations out of 4.02 candidates, making the accuracy of a random annotator about 35%.

For comparison purpose, we implement three heuristic baseline approaches as benchmarks: **WindowLoc** annotates each shot with all the locations found within a temporal window (on the transcript) of 20 seconds centered around that shot, **NearestLoc** labels each shot with the temporally closest location in the corresponding story, and **MaxFreqLoc** annotates each shot with the location

---

[2] Due to time constraint, we are unable to experiment with other types of news video like CNN, but our approach is generally applicable.

Table 2. Performance on location annotation in two settings

Setting		Shots with specified location		All shots	
Metric		ClassAcc	LabelAcc	ClassAcc	LabelAcc
Baseline	**WindowLoc**	0.653	0.480	0.761	0.690
	MaxFreqLoc	0.712	0.576	0.626	0.518
	NearestLoc	0.712	0.641	0.626	0.513
Learning Model	**LogReg**	0.774	0.779	0.853	0.793
	SVM	**0.869**	**0.864**	**0.884**	**0.851**

that appears most frequently in the story. All the three methods annotate a shot as *"unspecified"* if no locations are found in the window or in the story.

The experiment is conducted in two settings. The first one focuses on *only* the 1768 shots with specified locations. The classifier described in Section 2 is applied to predict the probability of every shot being associated with each of its candidate locations, which can be transformed into the (correct/incorrect) labels on these locations. Two performance metrics are computed from the results of 10-fold cross-validation: Classification accuracy (**ClassAcc**) is the ratio of correctly classified candidate locations, while labeling accuracy (**LabelAcc**) is the ratio that the top-ranked candidate location of each shot (i.e., the one with the highest probability) is the correct location. This second metric is practically more meaningful since it represents the chance that users see a shot correctly labeled with at least one location. The left side of Table 2 shows the performance of five methods, including three baselines and the proposed learning methods using **LogReg** (logistic regression) and **SVM**. One can see that the proposed methods significantly outperform the baselines. SVM is the best performer, which achieve 87% accuracy on classifying locations and 86% on labeling shots. The superiority of SVM can be contributed to its RBF kernel which explores the correlations of different features. All the baselines generate results that are better than random, especially the MaxFreqLoc and NearestLoc, implying that heuristics like temporal distance and frequency are useful.

In the second setting, we use all the 6219 shots in order to evaluate our approach for identifying shots without specified locations. For each shot, we first determine whether its location is mentioned in the transcript, using a classifier described in Section 5. If the answer is negative, the shot is labeled as *"unspecified"*, otherwise we predict the location for the shot as in the previous experiment. The result showed that this pre-filtering process classifies 4072 shots as *"unspecified"*, among which only 244 are false-alarms, and it fails to identify 492 shots with unspecified locations. This suggests that our approach can distinguish shots without specified locations with high accuracy (89.7%). Treating *"unspecified"* as a special location, we show the overall accuracy of location annotation on the 6219 shots in the right side of Table 2. The proposed methods achieve 79% (LogReg) and 85% (SVM) accuracy on labeling the locations of shots. This result is very encouraging since this setting is close to the reality where a user has no idea on whether a shot's location is in the transcript or not.

7 Conclusion

This paper has presented a learning-based approach to annotate news video shots with locations based on multi-modal video features. Specifically, we have discussed and solved two problems, namely determining (1) whether the location of a given shot is mentioned in the transcript, and (2) among the locations in the transcript, which are the correct location(s) of the shot. The experiments on TRECVID dataset have shown that our approach can correctly annotate about 85% of the shots with their locations. In future, we plan to evaluate our approach on video data with ASR text to study how imperfect transcript will affect its performance, and include the locations appearing in VOCR text as possible labels of shots. Another challenging future work is to investigate the difficult task of annotating shots whose true locations are not mentioned in the transcript.

Acknowledgement

This work was supported in part by the Advanced Research and Development Activity (ARDA) under contract number H98230-04-C-0406 and NBCHC040037, and by the National Science Foundation under Grant No. IIS-0535056.

References

1. H. Aoki, B. Schiele, and A. Pentland. Recognizing personal location from video. In *Workshop on Perceptual User Interfaces*, pages 79–82, 1998.
2. D. Bikel, S. Miller, R. Schwartz, and R. Weischedel. Nymble: a high-performance learning name-finder. In *Proc. 5th Conf. on Applied Natural Language Processing*, pages 194–201, 1997.
3. M. Christel, A. Olligschlaeger, and C. Huang. Interactive maps for a digital video library. *IEEE MultiMedia*, 7(1):60–67, 2000.
4. J.-L. Gauvain, L. Lamel, and G. Adda. The limsi broadcast news transcription system. *Speech Commun.*, 37(1-2):89–108, 2002.
5. A. Hauptmann and M. Witbrock. Story segmentation and detection of commercials in broadcast news video. In *Advances in Digital Libraries*, pages 168–179, 1998.
6. R. Kumar, H. Sawhney, J. Asmuth, A. Pope, and S. Hsu. Registration of video to geo-referenced imagery. In *Proc. of 14th Int'l Conf. on Pattern Recognition*, volume 2, pages 1393–1400, 1998.
7. T. Sato, T. Kanade, E. Hughes, M. Smith, and S. Satoh. Video OCR: indexing digital new libraries by recognition of superimposed captions. *Multimedia Syst.*, 7(5):385–395, 1999.
8. J. Sivic and A. Zisserman. Video google: A text retrieval approach to object matching in videos. In *Proc. of 9th IEEE Int'l Conf. on Computer Vision, Vol. 2*, 2003.
9. D. Sleator and D. Temperley. Parsing english with a link grammar. In *Third Int'l Workshop on Parsing Technologies*, 1993.
10. J. Yang and A. G. Hauptmann. Naming every individual in news video monologues. In *Proc. of the 12th ACM Intl. Conf. on Multimedia*, pages 580–587, 2004.

Automatic Person Annotation
of Family Photo Album

Ming Zhao[1], Yong Wei Teo[1], Siliang Liu[1], Tat-Seng Chua[1], and Ramesh Jain[2]

[1] Department of Computer Science, National University of Singapore,
21 Lower Kent Ridge Road, Singapore 119077
{zhaom, chuats}@comp.nus.edu.sg
[2] Donald Bren Professor in Information & Computer Sciences
Department of Computer Science
Bren School of Information and Computer Sciences
University of California, Irvine, CA 92697-3425
jain@ics.uci.edu

Abstract. Digital photographs are replacing tradition films in our daily life and the quantity is exploding. This stimulates the strong need for efficient management tools, in which the annotation of "who" in each photo is essential. In this paper, we propose an automated method to annotate family photos using evidence from face, body and context information. Face recognition is the first consideration. However, its performance is limited by the uncontrolled condition of family photos. In family album, the same groups of people tend to appear in similar events, in which they tend to wear the same clothes within a short time duration and in nearby places. We could make use of social context information and body information to estimate the probability of the persons' presence and identify other examples of the same recognized persons. In our approach, we first use social context information to cluster photos into events. Within each event, the body information is clustered, and then combined with face recognition results using a graphical model. Finally, the clusters with high face recognition confidence and context probabilities are identified as belonging to specific person. Experiments on a photo album containing over 1500 photos demonstrate that our approach is effective.

1 Introduction

Digital cameras are widely used by families to produce a huge amount of photos everyday. With vastly growing number of family photos, efficient management tools are becoming highly desirable. To achieve efficient management, photos should be indexed according to when, where, who, what and etc. Although time and location can be available in cameras, the annotation of "who" is left to users, which is a tedious task. In this paper, we assume that the information of time and location in terms of GPS is available and we attempt to automatically annotate family photos with "who".

Intuitively, persons can be annotated with their faces. While current face recognition systems perform well under relatively controlled environments [1], they tend to suffer when variations in pose, illumination or facial expressions

H. Sundaram et al. (Eds.): CIVR 2006, LNCS 4071, pp. 163–172, 2006.
© Springer-Verlag Berlin Heidelberg 2006

are present. As real life family photographs tend to exhibit large variance in illuminations, poses and expressions of face images, it is difficult to detect, align and hence recognize faces in such photographs. Thus, automatic annotation of family photos cannot be solved by face recognition alone.

In fact, the human perception does not make use of facial structure alone to recognize faces. It also uses cues such as color, facial motion, and visual contextual information. Color and motion information have been studied to show their effectiveness in face recognition [2,3]. Visual contextual information has also been successfully used for object and face detection [4], but has not been carefully studied yet for face recognition. In addition, social context is another clues for inferring the presence of specific persons. Social context information takes advantage of the fact that in a family setting, the same group of people tend to appear in the same social events, and they tend to wear the same clothes in the same events. Such information can be used to induce the people's presence when other examples of the same person are recognized or other group members are recognized.

Several semi-automatic annotation systems [5,6,7] have been proposed to help users to annotate faces in each photo by suggesting a list of possible names to choose. Zhang et al. [5] formulated face annotation in a Bayesian framework, in which face similarity measure is defined as the maximum a posteriori (MAP) estimation with face appearance and visual contextual features. With this similarity measure, they generated the name list for a new face based on its similarity to the previously annotated faces. Instead of using the visual content information, Naaman et al. [7] used only the (social) context information including the time and location of persons' occurrence. Based on time and location, clustering is applied to form events. They then proposed several estimators to estimate the probabilities of each person's presence. The name list is generated based on the combined probability. In the mobile phone environment, Davis et al. [8] used time, location, social environment and face recognizer to help automatic face recognition. In particular, they used the identities of mobile phones to detect the presence of specific people in the environment, and used this information for effective person identification. This information, however, is not available in most family photo album environment.

In this paper, we propose a fully automatic framework for person annotation in family photo album. We employ face detection and recognition, in conjunction with visual context and social context to induce the presence of persons in photos. The main contribution in the research is in developing a framework that utilizes all available information for person annotation. The unique features of our system are: (1) Our system is fully automated. This is different from the semi-automatic systems reported in [5,6,7] that suggest a list of probable names for users to select. (2) We improve on face recognition techniques by using eye alignment, delighting and a systematic approach to increasing the number of training samples. This technique helps to maintain the recognition rate even when user is not able to provide sufficient number of training samples. (3) For body detection and recognition, our system uses image segmentation and body clustering, which is more accurate as compared to that reported in [5].

The rest of the paper is organized as follows. The whole framework is described in Section 2. Social context information is discussed in Section 3. Visual information, including face and visual context, is discussed in Section 4. Experiments are performed in Section 5 before conclusions are drawn in Section 6.

2 Automatic Family Photo Album Annotation

This section discusses the overall framework of combining face, visual context (body) and social context (time and location) information for automatic family album annotation.

To obtain face information, we first utilize face recognition to recognize the faces. Even though we use only frontal faces for face recognition, the results for even trained faces are still not very accurate due to the large variation of illumination and expression. However, we know that within a short duration and in nearby places, the same group of people tend to appear together in most pictures and they usually wear the same clothes. This social context information is used to cluster photos into events, so that the visual context (body) of the recognized faces can be used to find other presence of the same person. In fact, both face recognition and body information should be used to complement each other to achieve more reliable results with minimum false detection. In this paper, we propose a graphical model to combine the face and body information. The choice of graphical model is because it provides a natural framework for handling uncertainty and complexity through a general formalism for compact representation of joint probability distribution [9]. The overall framework works as follows:

(1) Cluster family photographs into events according to social context information based on time and location.
(2) Perform face and eye detection, followed by rectification and delighting to provide good alignment and illumination for face recognition.
(3) Perform face recognition on all detected faces.
(4) Extract the visual context information (body) for all detected faces of all persons. For each event, visual context information (body) is first clustered. The resulting clusters are then combined with the face recognition results using a graphical model to provide better person clustering.
(5) Based on face recognition results, build social context estimators, which estimate the probability of people's presence in each photo.
(6) Select the clusters according to the cluster recognition score by combining face recognition and context estimation. For each cluster r, we denote the average face recognition score for person i as $\bar{S}_{FR}(r,i)$ and average context estimation score as $\bar{S}_{CON}(r,i)$. The final recognition score of person i for cluster r is

$$S_C(r,i) = \alpha \bar{S}_{FR}(r,i) + (1-\alpha)\bar{S}_{CON}(r,i) \tag{1}$$

where α is heuristically chosen. This score is used to annotate persons in the photos.

3   Social Context Information

The social context information is used in two ways: first, it is used to cluster photos into events; second, it is used to estimate the probability of people's presence based on the results of face and body recognition.

3.1   Event Clustering

Event is the basic and important organizational unit for family photo album. Although there is not strict definition of event, it usually represents a meaningful happening within a short time duration and in nearby places, such as a birthday party and a visit to the park etc. Event is important as it provides the basis for using the visual context information (body) for person annotation. This is because the visual context information is likely to be consistent within an event, but not so across events. Event is also important for constructing contextual estimators for estimating the probability of the presence of a person in a photo. Figure 1 shows examples of photos in an album event.

Fig. 1. Photo Examples in an Album Event

The automatic organization and categorization of personal photo albums into meaningful events is an important problem intensively explored in recent years [10,11]. In this paper, we adopt an adaptive event clustering method based on time and location. It consists of an initial time-based clustering, and a location-based post-processor that analyzes the location names of photos. Our time-based clustering is heuristic-based, and is based on observations not previously utilized: (a) the probability of an event ending increases as more photos are taken; and (b) the probability of an event ending increases as the time span increases. Photos are processed sequentially in temporal order. A new photo p belongs to cluster C_k if

$$ATD(C_k, p) \leq F(C_k) \tag{2}$$

where $ATD(C_k, p)$ is the average time difference between all photos in C_k and photo p; and $F(C_k)$ is an adaptive function that dynamically predicts the time gap which would possibly indicate the start of a new cluster, here

$$F(C_k) = I - T_w * T_{C_k} - S_w * S_{C_k} \tag{3}$$

where I is the initial value, T_w is the time weight, T_{C_k} is the time span of cluster C_k, S_w is the size weight and S_{C_k} is the size of cluster C_k. Based on observations (a) and (b), with more photos and larger time span of cluster C_k, the chances of adding new photos to this event will be lower as $F(C_k)$ is smaller. Currently, T_w and S_w are heuristically chosen.

3.2   Person Context Estimators

Context information can be used to estimate the probability of person's presence in a photo. We adopt 4 context estimators as proposed in [7]: global, event, time-neighboring and people-rank estimators related to person i. To build the estimators, face recognition results are used in this paper, which is different from [7] where manual annotation results are used. The estimation is based on the following observations:

- Popularity. Some people appear more often than others.
- Co-occurrence. People that appear in the same photos or events may be associated with each other, and have a higher likelihood of appearing together in other photos or events.
- Temporal re-occurrence. Within a specific event, there tend to be multiple photos of the same person.

The first three estimators are modeled in similar ways. The probability of photo p containing person i is modeled as $P_Q(p, i)$:

$$P_Q(p, i) = \frac{\sum_{q \in Q(p)} K_q(i)}{|Q(p)|} \qquad (4)$$

where $Q(p)$ represents the set of photos containing photo p, and $K_q(i)$ is 1 if person i is contained in photo q. The form of $Q(p)$ determines the type of estimator. If $Q(p)$ contains all the photos, $P_Q(p, i)$ is the global estimator. If $Q(p)$ only contains photos of the event of photo p, $P_Q(p, i)$ is the event estimator. If $Q(p)$ contains photos of the neighboring time span of photo p, then $P_Q(p, i)$ is the time-neighboring estimator.

Next, we derive the people-rank estimator by making use of the cooccurrence of persons as

$$PeopleRank(j_2|j_1) = \frac{W(j_1, j_2)}{\sum_{i \in I} W(j_1, i)} \qquad (5)$$

where $W(j_1, j_2)$ is the number of events or photos where person j_1 and j_2 appear together in the training set.

These four estimators are linearly combined as follows:

$$S_{CON}(p, i) = \sum_{j=1}^{3} \alpha_j P_{Q_j}(p, i) + \sum_{j \in I(p,i)} \beta_j PeopleRank(i|j) \qquad (6)$$

where P_{Q_j} represents the global, event, time-neighboring estimators, and $I(p, i)$ is set of persons that appear together with person i in the same photo p or in the same event containing photo p. Currently, we assign the weights heuristically, where higher weights are given to event, time-neighboring and people-rank estimators as the person's presence in a photo is more likely to be inferred from his presence in other photos of the same event or neighboring events, or from related persons' presence in the same event. Further details of the estimators can be found in [7].

4   Visual Information

4.1   Face Recognition with Photograph

Face recognition is a long-studied research topic and many methods have been proposed [1]. However, face recognition is not effective with photos having no restriction on the pose, illumination and expression. So, measures must be taken to circumvent these problems. Face detection [12] is first applied to detect the near frontal faces. To alleviate the pose problem, eye detection is used to rotate the faces so that the two eye are horizontal. The eye detector is trained with AdaBoost, which has been used successfully in face detection [12]. To overcome the illumination problem, we employ the generalized quotient image [13] for delighting. Finally to tackle the pose problem, we use translation and rotation to generate more training faces for three views, *i.e.* left-view, front-view and right-view, for each person.

We then employ the pseudo 2DHMM [14] to perform face recognition. We build three 2DHMMs to model the left-view, front-view and right-view of the face respectively. For each testing face f, the Viterbi Algorithm is used to calculate the recognition probabilities for person i. We consider the top three recognition probabilities P_{M_1}, P_{M_2} and P_{M_3} from models M_1, M_2 and M_3. The face recognition score is

$$S_{FR}(f, i) = 10^3\delta(M_1) + 10^2\delta(M_2) + 10^1\delta(M_3) + (P_{M_1} - P_{M_2})(2\delta(M_1) - 1) \quad (7)$$

where $\delta(M_X)$ is 1 if M_X is one of the three models of the person i, otherwise 0. Further details of the face recognition algorithm can be found in [15].

4.2   Body Detection and Clustering

The body detection uses body mask along with the results of image segmentation, which is performed with mean shift-based feature space analysis [16]. An example of the resulting segmented image is shown in Figure 2(c). With the help of the detected face region in a training data set, a body mask, shown in Figure 2(a), is created to approximate the region of body. For each image segmentation region, we first combine the overlap region between the segmentation region and mask region. We then compute two overlap ratios: the ratios of the overlap region with the segmentation region and the mask region. The eventual body region is extracted based on these two ratios. One example of body detection is shown in Figure 2.

The detected bodies in an event are then grouped into clusters using the constrained clustering method [17]. We employ the affine image matching and feature points matching [18] to identify body regions that are highly similar and should be clustered together. They are the set of "Must-Link" body regions. The set of "Cannot-Link" regions come from the fact that the bodies within the same photo cannot be clustered together as one person cannot appear more than once in a photo. We use LUV color histogram and edge directional histogram

(a) Body Mask   (b) Photograph   (c) Segmentation   (d) Body Detection

Fig. 2. Body Detection

for similarity computation. We employ average-link hierarchical clustering to cluster the body regions. The merging process stops when the average similarity falls below a threshold, which will introduce over-clustering. However, this is better than under-clustering as different persons may have similar contextual information and we want to differentiate the persons. The over-clustered persons will be merged with the help of face recognition information using the graphical model to be discussed in Section 4.3.

4.3   Graphical Model for Combining Face and Body

As discussed in Section 2, body information can help to detect unrecognized faces and reject false recognized faces, and face recognition can help to differentiate persons with similar body information. Obviously, we must combine them to achieve more reliable results. The relationship between face recognition and body information can be properly modeled by graphical model, which is suitable to model the complex relationship between variables. The proposed graphical model for the combined clustering is shown in Figure 3. For a given event k, b_k is the set of body information; c_k is the set of body clusters, i.e. clusters according to body information; f_k is the set of face recognition results while r_k is the resulting clusters combining the body clusters c_k and face recognition results f_k. The reasons for employing this graphical model are as follows:

1) $c_k \rightarrow b_k$: the body clustering provides a set of clusters with relatively small variations for body information.
2) $c_k \rightarrow r_k$: in order to identify the person's cluster, the small clusters in c_k are encouraged to group into larger cluster with face recognition results from f_k.
3) $r_k \rightarrow f_k$: a cluster is encouraged to be split into several clusters if there are several face recognition clusters in it.

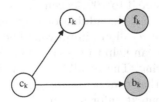

Fig. 3. Graphical Model for Combined Clustering

Given the observation of body information and face recognition results, our goal is to estimate the joint conditional probability of body clustering and combined clustering.

$$p(c_k, r_k | f_k, b_k) = \frac{p(c_k, r_k, f_k, b_k)}{p(f_k, b_k)} \tag{8}$$

To get the optimal clustering results, we maximize the posterior probability:

$$(\hat{c}_k, \hat{r}_k) = \arg \max_{(c_k, r_k)} p(c_k, r_k | b_k, f_k) = \arg \max_{(c_k, r_k)} p(c_k, r_k, f_k, b_k)$$
$$= \arg \max_{(c_k, r_k)} p(c_k) p(b_k | c_k) p(r_k | c_k) p(f_k | r_k) \tag{9}$$

For each cluster $r \in r_k$ in the combined clusters r_k, the average face recognition score for person i is

$$\bar{S}_{FR}(r, i) = \sum_{f \in F(r)} S_{FR}(f, i) / |F(r)| \tag{10}$$

where $F(r)$ is the set of faces contained in cluster r, and $|F(r)|$ is the number of faces; the average context estimation score for person i is

$$\bar{S}_{CON}(r, i) = \sum_{p \in P(r)} S_{CON}(p, i) / |P(r)| \tag{11}$$

where $P(r)$ is the set of photos contained in cluster r, and $|P(r)|$ is the number of photos.

5   Experiments

We evaluate our approach using a personal photo album, containing about 1500 photos with 8 family members. It is taken within 15 months. Each person appears about one hundred times. The album is clustered into 46 events according to the time and location information. The experimental precision/recall results are shown in Figure 4. Four experiments are carried. The curves with "Face" (Equ.(7)), "Face+Body(A)" (Equ.(10)) and "Face+Body(A)+Context" (Equ.(1)) respectively represent the results of employing face recognition only; face recognition with body information; and face recognition with body information plus social context information. The curve with "Face+Body(M)" represents the result of face recognition with manual body clustering. The "Face+Body(M)" is used to provide an indication of upper bound performance if the body information is detected and clustered to 100% accuracy.

It is clear from Figure 4 that the adding of body information to face is very effective. Both precision and recall are improved. The precision is improved because the body information can help to reject the false face recognition through the graphical model clustering. The recall is improved because the body information can get more faces that cannot be recognized by face recognition alone.

The adding of social context information "Face+Body(A)+Context" contributes also to the overall performance. But the improvement is not so big. We

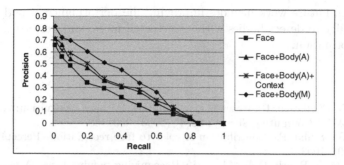

Fig. 4. Recall vs. Precision Performance

can see that its precision is slightly lower than that of "Face+Body(A)" in the low recall range. This is because the contextual information cannot accurately estimate the identity of each detected person. It can only estimate the probability with which each photo contains a person. However, the use of context helps to improve the recall. For example, if no face is recognized by face recognition in an event, the context information can estimate the person's presence if the person appears in nearby events or other related persons appear in this event. Although context estimation will make mistake if "Face+Body(A)" is not accurate, we found that the "Face+Body(A)" detector provides fairly good results, and hence the use of context information improves the overall performance.

We notice that there is a big gap between the manual body clustering and automatic body clustering. This indicates the challenge for body clustering. It also implies that if the body clustering can be improved, the overall performance of person annotation can be improve significantly. Another observation is that the precision becomes zero when the recall reaches about 84%. This is because the face detector can only find about 84% of the presence of persons on average. Again, the improvement in face and body detection results to cover profile faces, faces with sunglasses and backs of bodies etc, would improve the overall performance.

6 Conclusions

In this paper, we proposed an automated method to annotate the names of persons in family photos based on face, content and social context information. The body content information can be used to identify other instances of the recognized persons. Body content information can also improve the recognition accuracy as it can reject falsely recognized faces by performing combined clustering using a graphical model. Also, social context information can be used effectively to estimate the person's presence, though our results indicate that the improvement is minor as it is unable to pinpoint the identity of persons in photo, hence leading to low precision. However, social context information can help to improve the recall. Overall, our results show that the body information is the key to improving the performance of person annotation. However, our current body clustering technique is still preliminary and is far from ideal performance. Future work includes improving the performance of body clustering, the ability to detect bodies without detected faces, and better use of social context information.

References

1. Zhao, W., Chellappa, R., Rosenfeld, A., Phillips, P.: Face recognition: A literature survey. ACM Computing Surveys **35**(4) (2003) 399–458
2. Yip, A.W., Sinha, P.: Contribution of color to face recognition. Perception **31**(5) (2002) 995–1003
3. O'Toole, A.J., Roark, D.A., Abdi, H.: Recognizing moving faces: A psychological and neural synthesis. Trends in Cognitive Science **6** (2002) 261–266
4. Murphy, K., Torralba, A., Freeman, W.T.: Using the forest to see the trees: a graphical model relating features, objects and scenes. In Thrun, S., Saul, L., Schölkopf, B., eds.: Advances in Neural Information Processing Systems 16, Cambridge, MA, MIT Press (2004)
5. Zhang, L., Chen, L., Li, M., Zhang, H.: Automated annotation of human faces in family albums. In: Proceedings of the 11th ACM International Conference on Multimedia. (2003) 355–358
6. Zhang, L., Hu, Y., Li, M., Ma, W.Y., Zhang, H.: Efficient propagation for face annotation in family albums. In: Proceedings of the 11th ACM International Conference on Multimedia. (2004) 716–723
7. Naaman, M., Yeh, R.B., Garcia-Molina, H., Paepcke, A.: Leveraging context to resolve identity in photo albums. In: JCDL. (2005) 178–187
8. Davis, M., Smith, M., Canny, J.F., Good, N., King, S., Janakiraman, R.: Towards context-aware face recognition. In: ACM Multimedia. (2005) 483–486
9. Jensen, F.B.: Bayesian Networks and Decision Graphs. Springer (2001)
10. Cooper, M., Foote, J., Girgensohn, A., Wilcox, L.: Temporal event clustering for digital photo collections. In: Proceedings of the Eleventh ACM Internationl Conference on Multimedia. (2003)
11. Naaman, M., Song, Y.J., Paepcke, A., Garcia-Molina, H.: Automatic organization for digital photographs with geographic coordinates. In: ACM/IEEEE-CS Joint Conference on Digital Libraries. (2004) 53–62
12. Viola, P., Jones, M.: Robust real time object detection. In: IEEE ICCV Workshop on Statistical and Computational Theories of Vision, Vancouver, Canada (2001)
13. Wang, H., Li, S.Z., Wang, Y.: Generalized quotient image. In: Proceedings of IEEE Computer Society Conference on Computer Vision and Pattern Recognition. Volume 2. (2004) 498–505
14. Cardinaux, F., Sanderson, C., Bengio, S.: Face verification using adapted generative models. In: The 6th International Conference on Automatic Face and Gesture Recognition, Seoul, Korea, IEEE (2004) 825–830
15. Zhao, M., Neo, S.Y., Goh, H.K., Chua, T.S.: Multi-faceted contextual model for person identification in news video. In: Multimedia Modeling. (2006)
16. Comaniciu, D., Meer, P.: Mean shift: A robust approach toward feature space analysis. IEEE Trans. Pattern Anal. Mach. Intell **24**(5) (2002)
17. Wagstaff, K., Cardie, C., Rogers, S., Schroedl, S.: Constrained K-means clustering with background knowledge. In: Proc. 18th International Conf. on Machine Learning, Morgan Kaufmann, San Francisco, CA (2001) 577–584
18. Lowe, D.G.: Distinctive image features from scale-invariant keypoints. International Journal of Computer Vision **60**(2) (2004) 91–110

Finding People Frequently Appearing in News

Derya Ozkan and Pınar Duygulu

Bilkent University, Department of Computer Engineering
06800, Ankara, Turkey
{deryao, duygulu}@cs.bilkent.edu.tr

Abstract. We propose a graph based method to improve the performance of person queries in large news video collections. The method
benefits from the multi-modal structure of videos and integrates text and
face information. Using the idea that a person appears more frequently
when his/her name is mentioned, we first use the speech transcript text
to limit our search space for a query name. Then, we construct a similarity graph with nodes corresponding to all of the faces in the search
space, and the edges corresponding to similarity of the faces. With the
assumption that the images of the query name will be more similar to
each other than to other images, the problem is then transformed into
finding the densest component in the graph corresponding to the images
of the query name. The same graph algorithm is applied for detecting
and removing the faces of the anchorpeople in an unsupervised way. The
experiments are conducted on 229 news videos provided by NIST for
TRECVID 2004. The results show that proposed method outperforms
the text only based methods and provides cues for recognition of faces
on the large scale.

1 Introduction

Finding specific people in news videos is important and the challenge is also
acknowledged by NIST in TRECVID video retrieval evaluation [1]. Searching for
the names of the people in the speech transcript text is a common approach for
accessing the related video shots. However, only text based systems are likely to
produce incorrect results since the shots associated with the text may include the
appearances of many other people and especially the anchorperson or reporter
besides the query name. On the other hand, recognizing faces is a long standing
and difficult problem [2,3]. The noisy and complicated nature of news videos
and the variety of poses, expressions and illumination conditions make the face
recognition even more challenging.

Recently, it is shown that the performance of person queries can be improved
by integrating name and face information [4,5,6,7,8]. Yang et al. [9] show that
text-based search results can be improved by modeling the timing between names
and appearances of people in news videos. In [10], Berg et al. proposed a method
for associating the faces in the news photographs with a set of names extracted
from the captions, and then clustering in appropriate discriminant coordinates
to correct the mistakes in labeling and to identify incorrectly labeled faces.

H. Sundaram et al. (Eds.): CIVR 2006, LNCS 4071, pp. 173–182, 2006.
© Springer-Verlag Berlin Heidelberg 2006

In this study, we propose a method for improving the performance of person queries in news videos by combining name and face information. We use the observation that, faces of a query name will appear more frequently when his/her name is mentioned in the speech transcript text, and limit our search space for a query name by choosing the shots around which the name appears. Although, there may be faces in this search space corresponding to other people in the story, or some non-face images due to the errors of the face detection method used, the faces of the query name are likely to be the most frequently appearing ones than any other person in the same space. Our assumption is that, even if the expressions or poses vary, different appearances of the face of the same person tend to be more similar to each other than to the faces of others.

If a similarity measure between any two faces can be assigned, then this measure can be used to find the similarities among all the faces in the search space of a query name. Then, this search space represents a graph structure in which nodes are faces and edges correspond to similarities. The problem transforms into a graph problem in which we aim to find the densest component corresponding to the group of most similar faces, which are the faces belonging to the query name.

In [11], we apply a similar method on news photographs data set collected from the Web by Berg et al. [5]. Due to the higher noise level and lower resolution, news videos is a harder data set to work with. Also, there is usually a time shift between the appearance of a name and the appearance of the face belonging to that name. Therefore, using a single shot temporally aligned with the text may yield incorrect results. Another problem in news videos, which is more important, is that the most frequent face usually corresponds to the anchorperson or reporter rather than the face of the query name (See Fig. 1).

The time shift problem can be handled by taking a window around the name. The solution is, rather than searching the faces only on the shots including the name of the person, also to include the preceding and succeeding shots. In order to handle the problem due to anchorperson faces, we add a mechanism to detect and remove the anchorpeople. Since, the anchorperson are the most frequently appearing people in the news, we take each video separately and apply the densest component algorithm to each of them.

In the following, we first explain the data set used in experiments. Then, we describe the similarity measures and the densest component algorithm. After presenting the method for finding the anchorpeople, the methods for integrating the name and face information for improving the person queries are presented.

2   Data Set

The data set used in the experiments is the broadcast news videos provided by NIST for TRECVID video retrieval evaluation competition 2004 [1]. It consists of 229 movies (30 minutes each) from ABC and CNN news. The shot boundaries and the key-frames are provided by NIST. Speech transcripts extracted by LIMSI [12] are used to obtain the associated text for each shot.

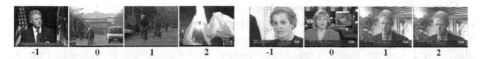

Fig. 1. Key-frames from two different videos. The numbers below each image show the distance to shot, in which the name 'Clinton' is mentioned. Note that in both cases, Clinton does not appear visually in the shot in which his name is mentioned but appears in preceding (left image) or succeeding shots (right image).

For the experiments, we choose 5 people, namely Bill Clinton, Benjamin Netanyahu, Sam Donaldson, Saddam Hussein and Boris Yeltsin. In the speech transcript text, their names appear 991, 51, 100, 149 and 78 times respectively.

The face detection algorithm provided by Mikolajcyzk [13] is used to extract faces from key-frames. Due to high noise levels and low image resolution quality, the face detector produces many false alarms. On randomly selected ten videos, in 2942 images, 1395 regions are detected as faces but only 790 of them are real faces and 580 faces are missed. In total, 31,724 faces are detected over the whole data set.

3   Graph Based Person Finding Approach

Faces of a particular person tend to be more similar to each other than to faces of other people. If we can define a similarity measure among the faces in a set and represent the similarities in a graph structure, then the problem of finding the most similar faces corresponding to the instances of query name's face can be tackled by finding the densest component in the graph. In the following two subsections we explain the similarity measure used and the greedy graph algorithm to find the densest component. The details of the algorithm can be found in [11].

3.1   Constructing the Dissimilarity Graph of Faces

The similarity of faces are defined using the interest points extracted from the detected face areas. Lowe's SIFT operator [14], which have been shown to be successful in recognizing objects and faces, are used for extracting the interest points.

The dissimilarity of two faces are computed based on the matching interest points. To find the matching interest points on two faces, each point on one face is compared with all the points on the other face and the points with the least Euclidean distance are selected. Since this method produces many matching points including the wrong ones, we apply two constraints to obtain only the correct matches, namely the geometrical constraint and the unique match constraint.

Geometrical constraint expects the matching points to appear around similar similar positions on the face when the normalized positions are considered. The matches whose interest points do not fall in close positions on the face are eliminated. Unique match constraint ensures that each point matches to only a single point by eliminating multiple matches to one point and also by removing one-way matches. Example of matches after applying these constraints are shown in Fig. 2.

Fig. 2. Examples for matching points. Note that, even for faces with different size, pose or expressions the method successfully finds the corresponding points.

After applying the constraints, the distance between the two faces is defined as the average distance of all matching points between these two faces. A dissimilarity graph for all the faces in the search space is then constructed using these distances.

3.2   Finding the Densest Component in the Graph

In the dissimilarity graph, faces represent the nodes and the distances between the faces represent the edge weights. We assume that, in this graph the nodes of a particular person will be close to each other (highly connected) and distant from the other nodes (weakly connected). Hence, the problem can be transformed in to finding the densest subgraph (component) in the entire graph. To find the densest component we adapt the method proposed by Charikar [15] where the density of subset S of a graph G is defined as

$$f(S) = \frac{|E(S)|}{|S|},$$

in which $E(S) = \{i, j \in E : i \in S, j \in S\}$ and E is the set of all edges in G and $E(S)$ is the set of edges induced by subset S. The subset S that has maximum $f(S)$ is defined as the densest component.

Initially, the algorithm presented in [15] starts from the entire graph and in each step, the vertex of minimum degree is removed from the set S. The $f(S)$ value is also computed for each step. The algorithm continues until the set S is empty. Finally, the subset S with maximum $f(S)$ value is returned as the densest component of the graph.

In order to apply the above algorithm to the constructed dissimilarity graph, we need to convert it into a binary form, in which 0 indicates no edge and 1 indicates an edge between the two nodes. This conversion is carried out by applying a threshold on the distance between the nodes. For instance, if 0.5 is used as the threshold value, then edges in the dissimilarity graph having higher value than 0.5 are assigned as 0, and others as 1. In other words, the threshold can be thought of an indicator of two nodes being near-by and/or remote.

The success of our algorithm varies with the threshold that is chosen while converting the weighted dissimilarity graph to a binary one. In order to determine a reasonable threshold, we randomly selected 10 videos and recorded recall-precision values of different thresholds for anchorperson detection. These values are plotted in Fig. 3. Further in our experiments, we select the point marked with a cross in the recall-precision curve, which corresponds to threshold of 0.6. The same threshold is used both for anchorperson detection and for person queries.

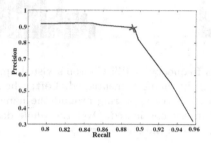

Fig. 3. Recall-precision values for randomly selected 10 videos for threshold values varying between 0.55 and 0.65

4 Integrating Names and Faces

The probability of a person appearing on the screen is high when his/her name is mentioned in the speech transcript text. Thus, looking for the shots in which the name of the query name is mentioned is a good place to start search over people. However, there can be a time shift or there can be some anchorperson/reporter scenes. Anchorpeople can be removed as will be explained in the next section. In order to handle the alignment problem we can also look for also preceding and succeeding shots.

Recently, it has been showed that the frequency of a person's visual appearance with respect to the occurrence of his/her name can be assumed to have a Gaussian distribution [9]. We use the same idea and search for the range where the face is likely to appear relative to the name. As we experimented on "Clinton" query, we see that taking the ten preceding and the ten succeeding shots together with the shot where the name is mentioned is a good approximation to find most of the relevant faces(See Fig. 4).

However, the number of faces in this range (which we refer to as [-10,10]) can still be large compared to the instances of the query name. For better understanding of the distributions, we plot the frequency of faces relative to the

Table 1. Number of faces corresponding to the query name over total number of faces in the range [-10,10] and [-1,2]

Range	Clinton	Netanyahu	Donaldson	Saddam	Yeltsin
[-10,10]	213/6905	9/383	137/1197	18/1004	21/488
[−1,2]	160/2457	6/114	102/330	14/332	19/157

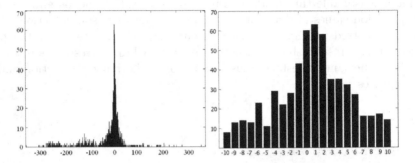

Fig. 4. The figure shows frequency of Bill Clinton's visual appearance w.r.t the distance to the shot in which his name is mentioned. **Left:** when the whole data set is considered, **right:** when the faces appearing around the name within the preceding and the following ten shots are considered. Over the whole data set Clinton has 240 faces and 213 of them appear in the selected range.

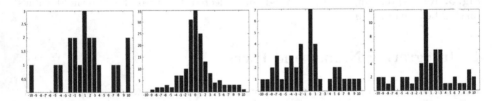

Fig. 5. The relative position of the faces to the name for Benjamin Netanyahu, Sam Donaldson, Saddam Hussein, and Boris Yeltsin respectively

position of the names for the five people that we have chosen for our experiments in Fig. 5. It is seen that taking only one preceding and two following shots (which we refer to as [-1,2]) is also a good choice. Table 1 shows that, most of the correct faces fall into this selected range by removing many false alarms.

5   Anchorperson Detection and Removal

When we look at the shots where the query name is mentioned in the speech transcript, it is likely that the anchorperson/reporter might be introducing or wrapping up a story, with the preceding or succeeding shots being relevant, but not the current one. Therefore, when the shots including the query name are selected, the faces of the anchorperson will appear frequently making our assumption that the most frequent face will correspond to the query name wrong. Hence, it is highly probable that the anchorperson will be returned as the densest component by the person finding algorithm. The solution is to detect and remove the anchorperson before applying the algorithm.

In [6], a supervised method for anchorperson detection is proposed. They integrate color and face information together with speaker-id extracted from the audio. However, this method has some disadvantages. First of all, it highly depends on the speaker-id, and requires the analysis of audio data. The color information is useful to capture the characteristics of studio settings where the anchorperson is likely to appear. But, when the anchorperson reports from another environment this assumption fails. Finally, the method depends on the fact that the faces of anchorpeople appear in large sizes and around some specific positions, but again there may be cases where this is not the case.

In this study, we use the graph based method to find the anchorpeople in an unsupervised way. The idea is based on the fact that, the anchorpeople are usually the most frequently appearing people in broadcast news videos. For different days there may be different anchorpeople reporting, but generally there is a single anchorperson for each day.

We apply the densest component based method to each news video separately, to find the people appearing most frequently, which correspond to the anchorpeople. We run the algorithm on 229 videos in our test set, and obtained average recall and precision values as 0.90 and 0.85 respectively. Images that are detected as anchorperson in ten different videos are given in Fig. 6.

When the anchorpeople are detected, the next step is to remove them from the search space to improve the person queries as will be explained in the following sections.

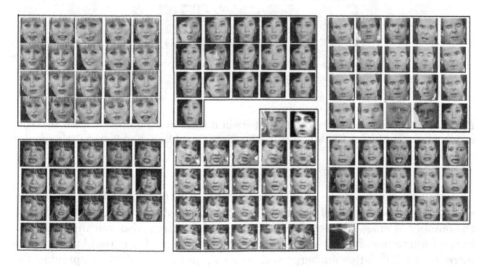

Fig. 6. Detected anchors for 6 different videos

6   Improving Person Queries

After selecting the range where the faces may appear we apply the densest component algorithm to find the faces corresponding to the query name. We have recorded the number of true faces of the query name and total number of images retrieved as in Table 2. The first column of the table refers to total number of true images retrieved vs. total number of true images retrieved by using only the speech transcripts -selecting the shots within interval [-1,2]. The numbers after removing the detected anchorpeople by the algorithm from the text-only results are given in the second column. And the last column is for applying the algorithm to this set, from which the anchorpeople are removed. The precision values are given in Fig. 8. Some sample images retrieved for each person are shown in Fig. 7.

Table 2. Numbers in the table indicate the number of correct images retrieved/ total number of images retrieved for the query name

Query name	Clinton	Netanyahu	Sam Donaldson	Saddam	Yeltsin
Text-only	160/2457	6/114	102/330	14/332	19/157
Anchor removed	150/1765	5/74	81/200	14/227	17/122
Method applied	109/1047	4/32	67/67	9/110	10/57

Fig. 7. Sample images retrieved for five person queries in experiments. Each row corresponds to samples for Clinton, Netanyahu, Sam Donaldson, Saddam, Yeltsin queries respectively.

As can be seen from the results, we keep most of the correct faces (especially after anchorperson removal), and we get reject many of the incorrect faces. Hence the number of images presented to the user is decreased. Also, our improvement in precision values are relatively high. Average precision of only text based results increases by 29% after ancherperson removal, and by 152% after applying the proposed algorithm.

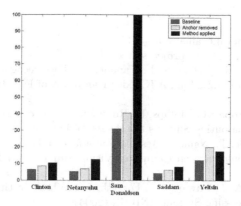

Fig. 8. Precisions values achieved for five people used in our tests

7   Conclusion

This paper addresses the problem of finding a specific person in news videos. We fist use the speech transcripts and select the neighboring shots in which the name of the query name appears to limit our search space. Applying the proposed person finding algorithm on each video separately, we detect the anchorperson in each video. Then, we remove detected anchorperson from the search space of the query name and apply the algorithm to the remaining images.

Experiments are conducted on 229 broadcast news videos archive, which is a difficult set due to large variations in pose, illumination and expressions in data. Experiments show that we improve person search performances relative to only text based results. Average precision values of only text based results are increased by 29% after ancherperson removal, and by 152% after applying the proposed algorithm. The person finding algorithm also performs well for anchorperson detection without requiring any supervision.

In [16] sets of face exemplars for each person are gathered automatically in shots for tracking. A similar approach can be adapted and instead of taking a single face from each shot by only considering the key-frames, face detection can be applied to all frames to obtain more instances of the same. This approach can help to find better matching interest points and more examples that can be used in the graph algorithm.

Acknowledgement

This research is partially supported by TÜBİTAK Career grant number 104E065 and grant number 104E077.

References

1. : Trec video retrieval evaluation
   http://www-nlpir.nist.gov/projects/trecvid/ (2004)
2. Gross, R., Baker, S., Matthews, I., Kanade, T.: Face recognition across pose and illumination. In Li, S.Z., Jain, A.K., eds.: Handbook of Face Recognition, Springer Verlag (2004)
3. Zhao, W., Chellappa, R., Phillips, P., Rosenfeld, A.: Face recognition: A literature survey. ACM Computing Surveys **35**(4) (2003) 399–458
4. Satoh, S., Kanade, T.: Name-it: Association of face and name in video. In: Proceedings of IEEE Conference on Computer Vision and Pattern Recognition(CVPR). (1997)
5. Berg, T., Berg, A.C., Edwards, J., Forsyth, D.: Who is in the picture. In: Neural Information Processing Systems (NIPS). (2004)
6. Chen, M.Y., Hauptmann, A.: Searching for a specific person in broadcast news video. In: International Conference on Acoustics, Speech, and Signal Processing (ICASSP'04), Montreal, Canada (2004)
7. P. Duygulu, A.H.: What's news, what's not? associating news videos with words. In: The 3rd International Conference on Image and Video Retrieval (CIVR 2004) Ireland. (July 21-23, 2004)
8. Ikizler, N., Duygulu, P.: Person search made easy. In: The Fourth International Conference on Image and Video Retrieval (CIVR 2005), Singapore (2005)
9. Yang, J., Chen, M.Y., Hauptmann, A.: Finding person x: Correlating names with visual appearances. In: International Conference on Image and Video Retrieval (CIVR'04), Dublin City University Ireland (2004)
10. Berg, T., Berg, A.C., Edwards, J., Maire, M., White, R., Teh, Y.W., Learned-Miller, E., Forsyth, D.: Faces and names in the news. In: IEEE Conf. on Computer Vision and Pattern Recognition (CVPR). (2004)
11. Ozkan, D., Duygulu, P.: Interesting faces in the news. In: to Appear in IEEE Conf. on Computer Vision and Pattern Recognition. (2006)
12. Gauvain, J., Lamel, L., Adda, G.: The limsi broadcast news transcription system. Speech Communication **37**(1-2) (2002)
13. Mikolajczyk, K.: Face detector. INRIA Rhone-Alpes (2004) Ph.D Report.
14. Lowe, D.G.: Distinctive image features from scale-invariant keypoints. International Journal of Computer Vision **60**(2) (2004)
15. Charikar, M.: Greedy approximation algorithms for finding dense components in a graph. In: APPROX '00: Proc. of the 3rd International Workshop on Approximation Algorithms for Combinatorial Optimization, London, UK (2000)
16. Sivic, J., Everingham, M., Zisserman, A.: Person spotting: video shot retrieval for face sets. In: International Conference on Image and Video Retrieval (CIVR 2005), Singapore. (2005)

A Novel Framework for Robust Annotation and Retrieval in Video Sequences

Arasanathan Anjulan and Nishan Canagarajah

Department of Electrical and Electronic Engineering
University of Bristol, Bristol, UK
{A.Anjulan, Nishan.Ganagarajah}@bristal.ac.uk

Abstract. This paper describes a method for automatic video annotation and scene retrieval based on local region descriptors. A novel framework is proposed for combined video segmentation, content extraction and retrieval. A similarity measure, previously proposed by the authors based on local region features, is used for video segmentation. The local regions are tracked throughout a shot and stable features are extracted. The conventional key frame method is replaced with these stable local features to characterise different shots. Compared to previous video annotation approaches, the proposed method is highly robust to camera and object motions and can withstand severe illumination changes and spatial editing. We apply the proposed framework to shot cut detection and scene retrieval applications and demonstrate superior performance compared to existing methods. Furthermore as segmentation and content extraction are performed within the same step, the overall computational complexity of the system is considerably reduced.

1 Introduction

Video annotation is an active field of research in content based video retrieval and summarization. Typically these systems include three steps: video segmentation, feature extraction and indexing. The existing work in video annotation can be divided into two main groups: video segmentation algorithms and content extraction algorithms. Video segmentation algorithms try to divide the video sequences into meaningful subgroups called shots. Over the years, a number of techniques, varying from colour histogram to block based approaches with motion compensation have been proposed for this purpose[1,2,3,4,5]. However an accurate shot cut detection algorithm which works with all kind of video sequences with a single set of parameters is still a challenging problem. Most of the existing content extraction algorithms select one or more key frames as being representative of each shot; feature extraction techniques such as wavelets or Gabor filters are widely used to then extract features from these frames. An efficient key frame selection method, which works with all kinds of videos with little redundancy, is still a difficult problem. Different imaging conditions and camera and object motions make it nearly impossible to represent a shot by a small number of frames without oversampling and thus increasing the complexity and memory requirements of the system. On the other hand, any attempt to

H. Sundaram et al. (Eds.): CIVR 2006, LNCS 4071, pp. 183–192, 2006.
© Springer-Verlag Berlin Heidelberg 2006

reduce the number of key frames may result in content loss and thus a failure to properly represent the shot. Furthermore, segmentation and content extraction are handled separately in the literature and very little research has been done to perform these two operations within an efficient unified framework. Since each of these techniques use different methods, combining them into a single framework with reasonable computational complexity has been a major problem. In this paper we propose a novel framework for content based indexing and retrieval. This framework allows efficient video segmentation, content extraction and indexing within a single framework.

Early approaches in key frame selection propose to selecting the first frame in each shot as the key frame[6,7]. However one key frame per shot is not always sufficient as there can exist a number of salient changes within a shot due to camera or object motion. Conversely, Ardizzone and Cascia[8] suggest making the number of key frames proportional to the length of the shot. They propose taking a key frame for each second. This approach is likely to oversample the sequence, as the semantic content may not often change that quickly. Zhang et al[9] propose a method to extract key frames based on a similarity measure between adjacent frames. They propose selecting the first frame in a shot as the key frame and compare the following frames with the key frame for content similarity. If a significant change occurs, then that frame is also selected as an additional key frame and this process continues until the end of the shot. The idea behind this method is that any content change between frames suggests significant activity in the shot and should be represented by multiple key frames. Vermaak et al[10] suggest that key frames should be maximally distinct and individually carry the most information. Here the input video is transformed into a sequence of representative feature vectors and this representation is used to define a utility function. A key frame sequence that maximises this function is obtained by a non-iterative dynamic programming procedure.

The initial inspiration of our work is obtained from the work done by Sivic and Zisserman [11,12]. They use local invariant region descriptors to represent key frames. Text retrieval techniques are adapted for fast and efficient retrieval. Local region descriptors are vector quantized into clusters and used as visual "words" in retrieval applications. The regions obtained in key frames are tracked and any region not lasting at least three frames are rejected. In experiments, they show good performance in scene and object matching. However their system is based on key frames and any failure in key frame extraction will affect their system. As they agree that significant change in imaging conditions may limit the performance of the system because of the limited overlapping regions among key frames. This problem however is overcome in our approach by extracting key features throughout a shot rather than extracting them only from key frames.

In our framework, we propose the use of local invariant region features to develop a highly accurate shot cut detection and content extraction method. Stable features are extracted throughout a shot rather than from a small number of key frames. We propose this approach as an alternative to the key frame method. Local regions are tracked throughout a shot with features being ex-

tracted from stable tracks. An efficient method is proposed for region tracking
to avoid possible repetition of the features. The proposed framework is robust
to camera and object motions and can withstand severe illumination changes,
spatial editing and noise. The validity of the framework is established first by
testing with different kinds of video sequences, and then by demonstrating superior performance compared to existing methods using well known test sequences
such as *Run Lola Run* and *Faulty Towers*.

The rest of this paper is organized as follows. The segmentation and content
extraction algorithms are described in section 2. In section 3, we explain the
experiments carried out to demonstrate the performance of our framework with
various video sequences and show superior performance compared to existing
methods. We conclude in section 4 with suggestions for future work.

2   Proposed Framework

In our annotation framework we introduce new methods for cut detection and
content summarisation. A novel approach, which was previously proposed by
the authors[13], is used in cut detection (Local Invariant Region Based cut detection) based on the consistency of the local regions. In Experiments, superior
performance is shown compared to existing cut detection methods. To the best
of our knowledge, all the existing content extraction and retrieval approaches
for video sequences are based on key frames. In this work, however, stable local
features, obtained throughout a shot, are used in content extraction and retrieval
applications. The detected local regions within a shot are tracked based on the
similarity of the region descriptors in adjacent frames. Each new track at any
point within a shot is compared to the existing tracks. This enables regions to be
tracked through occlusions, thus avoiding repetition of the features. Once a shot
cut is detected, the stable tracked regions are summarised based on the length of
the run and used as representative features for that shot. Thus in this method,
a shot is represented by the stable tracked features throughout the shot rather
than the features from one or more key frames. Furthermore both segmentation
and content summarisation are performed simultaneously within a single run
through the video sequences.

Our segmentation and content extraction algorithms are based on the concept of local invariant region descriptors. A brief explantation and performance
evaluation of local region extraction methods can be found in [14]. We choose
Maximally Stable Extremal Regions (MSER) algorithm by Matas et al. [15]
as it performed well with affine and illumination changes. The *Scale Invariant Feature Transform* (SIFT) [16] is used to obtain the region descriptors in
our experiments, as SIFT has been proved to be robust against varying imaging
conditions [17].

2.1   Video Segmentation (LIRB)

We define a new similarity measure between adjacent frames based on the consistency of local descriptors. For each frame, local region descriptors are calculated

independently by using *maximally stable extremal regions* (MSER) and *scale invariant feature transform* (SIFT). The matched descriptors between the adjacent frames are obtained using the greedy algorithm based on a threshold. The consistency measure (CM) between any two adjacent frames is calculated as follows,

$$CM = \frac{N_M}{N_{Max}} \tag{1}$$

where N_M - Number of matches, N_{Max} - Maximum number of regions obtained in any of the frame.

A high consistency value means that most of the selected regions in adjacent frames are matched and a low value means that most of them are dissimilar. If the consistency is less than a threshold value, a shot is declared. As the local region descriptors are highly robust to affine variation caused by motion and illumination changes, the proposed approach can withstand severe camera and object motions. Furthermore local regions are selected across the entire frame which makes the consistency measurement more robust to noise and spatial edits than existing methods. A more detailed explanation of the shot cut algorithm and examples with extreme imaging conditions can be found in [13].

2.2 Content Extraction and Indexing

We extract features from stable local regions throughout the shot, instead of key frames. This is because the key frame method fails when sudden changes occur in camera movement or illumination. Furthermore, features selected from one or more key frames are not robust enough to adequately represent the scenes in a shot.

The extracted local regions are tracked throughout the shot based on the feature matches between adjacent frames. Some of these regions may disappear in particular frames and then reappear later in the shot. This may happen because of occlusion or failure of the MSER algorithm due to extreme conditions. We call these tracks as discontinuous. A real example of a discontinuous track is given in Fig 1 for a shot taken from the video sequence *Tennis*. Fig 1(a) shows the starting frame and the rescaled frame part to highlight the selected region. Fig 1(b) shows the heighlighted regions in the track. The region in question is tracked from frame 585 to 588 and lost in frame 589 because of the movement of the face away from the camera. However the region reappears in frame 608 and is tracked until frame 613. Although these are two different tracks, they represent the same region, thus giving the same content information. In a content extraction system, these two tracks should be joined and considered as one track. This is achieved as follows. Each new starting track at any point in the shot is compared with all the existing tracks within that shot, to avoid possible repetition of the features due to discontinuous tracks. This also enables tracking of regions through occlusions. For example, consider a frame in the middle of a shot with n tracks, $[t_1.........t_n]$; here the length of the track t_i is m_i frames. Track t_i goes through m_i frames and each point in the track contains a 128 element SIFT descriptor vector. Therefore the ith track can be summarised as, $[\mathbf{d}_1.........\mathbf{d}_{m_i}]$. where $\mathbf{d}$ represents the SIFT descriptor. If a region descriptor, $\mathbf{d}$, obtained in the current frame does not have any matches, then it will be compared with the averaged region descriptor of all existing tracks. For the ith track, the averaged descriptor, $\overline{\mathbf{d}}_i$, will be obtained as follows, $\overline{\mathbf{d}}_i = \frac{1}{m_i} \sum_{i=1}^{m_i} \mathbf{d}_i$. The non matched region vector, $\mathbf{d}$ will be compared with all existing averaged tracks to find the closest averaged track. If the distance between $\mathbf{d}$ and the closest averaged track is less than a threshold then it will be considered as a continuation of that track, otherwise a new track will be formed. In the example shown in Fig 1, the new unmatched region in frame 608 matched with the earlier track from frame 585 to 588 as shown in the figure. Therefore these two tracks are joined together and will be considered as a single track.

Once a shot boundary is detected, the feature vectors in the stable tracks throughout that shot will be averaged and stored. The stable tracks are selected based on the length of the tracks through frames. We select a track if it goes through at least 7 frames. If the total selected tracks is greater than 200 for any shot, first 200 most stable tracks are selected. When a query image is presented to the system, the local region descriptors are obtained for that image and compared with the stored shot features. Based on this comparison, the best matched shots will be selected and presented as the matches. If the best match value is less than a threshold value, then no match will be possible.

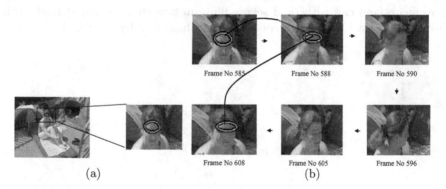

(a)   (b)

Fig. 1. An example of a discontinuous region track through occlusions (a) Starting frame of the track and the rescaled region for more clear view (b) Rescaled regions in the track. The tracked region is lost in frame 589 because of the movement of the face away from the camera. However, it reappears in frame 608 and joined with the earlier track.

3   Results

The proposed framework is applied to firstly video segmentation (see 3.1) and secondly scene matching applications (see 3.2).

3.1   Video Segmentation

The size of the test data for the video segmentation experiments is around 43000 frames with 312 shot positions. The test data contains different kinds of video sequences, varying from movies, TV series, documentaries, sports, wildlife and under water videos. Further details about the test data can be found on[13]. The ground truth shot cut positions were manually defined.

To demonstrate the benefits of our approach, we compare the performance of our algorithm (LIRB) with the following shot detection methods: Pair-wise pixel comparison (PC)[1], Block-based histogram comparison (BH)[3], Likelihood ratio (LR)[1], Average intensity measure[2], Global colour histogram (GCH)[1,3], and Motion based correlation method (MB)[5]. The performance of all the algorithms are compared using well established methods such as Precision-Recall (PR) curves and harmonic mean of recall and precision[18].

Fig 2(a) shows the PR curves obtained for the whole data set. The application of the algorithms to a wide range of media content is important as some algorithms tend to work well with particular type of video and give poor results with other types. For each parameter set, the correctly detected, false and missed number of shots are obtained over the whole data set and the PR curves are plotted. A rescaled version of Fig 2(a) is given in Fig 2(b) to more clearly show the performance near recall value 1. It is clear from these results that our algorithm gives an almost ideal performance and outperforms the rest of the methods. For our approach, the precision value is always greater than 0.98 for any recall value. This is because our algorithm is robust to camera and object movements and can withstand severe illumination changes and spatial editing. Other algorithms fail in such conditions as illustrated by the Fig 2.

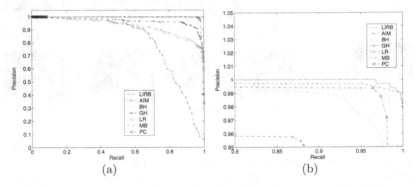

Fig. 2. (a) Performance-Recall curve for the whole data set used in the experiment. (b) A rescaled version of Figure (a) to clearly show the curves near recall value 1.

A good detector should give high values for both precision and recall. A more practical approach to experiment this is to use the harmonic mean (HM) of recall and precision[18], which is defined as,

$$HM = \frac{2P \cdot R}{P + R} \qquad (2)$$

This value varies between 0 and 1. A higher value (near 1) means good performance in both recall and precision and a lower value means poor per-

Table 1. Performance comparison based on harmonic mean. Algorithms are in the decreasing order of performance. Correct - correctly detected shots, False - false alarms, Miss - missed shots.

Algorithm	Correct	Miss	False	Recall	precision	Harmonic Mean
LIRB	312	0	6	1	0.9811	0.9905
MB	312	0	7	1	0.9781	0.9889
BH	312	0	66	1	0.8254	0.9043
GH	312	0	169	1	0.6486	0.7869
LR	312	0	221	1	0.5854	0.7385
PC	312	0	613	1	0.3373	0.5044
AIM	312	0	6807	1	0.0438	0.0840

formance for either recall or precision or both. In applications like video annotation, missing a shot cut is more severe than having false alarms. Therefore, for such applications, recall value should be 1. In Table 1, we compared the precision and harmonic mean value for all the algorithms at this condition. As seen in the table, our algorithm outperforms all other methods. Our algorithm gives equally good results for both recall and precision values. In other words, our algorithm detects all the shot cut positions while avoiding most of the false alarms.

3.2 Scene Retrieval

We next evaluate the retrieval performance of our algorithm based on the stored stable local features. Given a query image, related shots taken of the same scene should be retrieved while avoiding other scenes. The shots may be taken under different imaging or lighting conditions, such as different camera angles, zooming positions and illumination changes. Furthermore a shot may cover a large area varying from one place to another and the system should be able to handle these variations. Scenes appearing in movies *Run Lola Run* and *Groundhog Day* are used in scene retrieval experiments which is often used by other researchers. In these movies, the same scenes were filmed a number of times in different imaging conditions, making these ideal video sequences for scene retrieval experiments. The ground truth of the similar scenes are selected manually throughout the whole movies. If a similar place (building or road) appears in different shots, we conclude them as similar shots. Examples of frames from similar shots are given in Fig 3 (a)-(d). Each sub figure contains frames taken from similar shots. As seen in the figure, the frames vary significantly both in terms of the imaging conditions and the areas covered.

A frame which contains the scene in question is given as the query. The SIFT features are extracted from the selected MSER regions throughout the frame and compared with the features from all the shots. For normalisation the total number of matched features are divided by the number of features obtained from the query frame. If the normalised value is greater than a threshold, it is

(a)   (b)

(c)   (d)

Fig. 3. Examples of frames taken in the same scene. Each of the frame in all the sub figures is taken from different shots taken in the same scene. The frames are varying by imaging conditions and covering different areas.

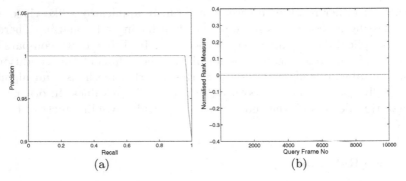

(a)   (b)

Fig. 4. (a) Average Precision-Recall curve obtained in scene matching applications. 10000 randomly selected frames were used in the experiment. (b) Normalised rank value is plotted for all 10000 randomly selected frames used in precision recall experiment. The rank value is 0 for all the 10000 frames which indicates that all the relevant shots are retrieved as first matches for all the query frames.

presented as one of the matched shots and all the matched shots are ordered in the descending order of normalised matched value.

We use the average PR curve and average normalised rank measure [11] to evaluate the performance of our approach. Fig 4(a) shows the average PR curve. We randomly selected 10000 frames (from movies *Groundhog Day* and *Run Lola Run*) as the query image for the system and the matched shots are obtained. The precision value is calculated as the ratio of the number of correctly retrieved shots to the total number retrieved shots; the recall value is calculated as the ratio of the number of correctly retrieved shots to the number of relevant shots in the database. It is important to note that the scene in some of the selected query frames may appear only in one shot. As seen in the Fig 4(a), our algorithm gives a nearly perfect performance (precision value is more than 0.90 for any recall value). Given an image as query, our algorithm picks up all the shots in the same scene while avoiding any false alarms.

The average normalised rank of the relevant shots can be defined as follows,

$$\widetilde{Rank} = \frac{1}{N N_{rel}} (\sum_{i=1}^{N_{rel}} R_i - \frac{N_{rel}(N_{rel}+1)}{2}) \tag{3}$$

where N is the number of total shots, N_{rel} is the number of relevant shots and R_i is the rank of the relevant shot. $\widetilde{Rank}$ is zero if all relevant shots are returned first. The $\widetilde{Rank}$ measure varies between the range 0 and 1 with 0.5 corresponding to random retrieval.

The rank measure is plotted for all 10000 randomly selected frames used in the PR curve experiment, in Fig 4(b). As clearly seen in the figure, the rank value is 0 for all these frames. This indicates that all the relevant shots are retrieved as first matches for all the query frames.

4   Conclusions and Future Work

A novel framework for video annotation based on local region descriptors is proposed. A new similarity measure is developed and the advantages are demonstrated with accurate shot cut detection and scene matching. The proposed method is robust to camera and object motions and can withstand severe illumination changes and spatial editing. The performance is evaluated with different kinds of video sequences and compared with existing methods. The results demonstrate that our method provides significantly improved performance, especially when there are severe object motion, illumination and spatial editing, compared to existing methods. The local regions are tracked throughout a shot and the stable regions are used to form shot representation. The above shot representation gives better results compared to the conventional key frame method and excellent performance is shown in scene matching applications. Future work will consider identifying individual objects in video sequences based on local region descriptors and the current framework provides the foundation for this extension.

References

1. H. J. Zhang and A. Kankanhalli and S. W. Smoliar, *Automatic partitioning of full-motion video*,Multimedia Syetems, vol 1, pp. 10-28, 1993.
2. A. Hampapur and R. Jain and T. Weymouth, *Digital video segmentation*, In Proc. ACM Multimedia, pp. 357-364, 1994.
3. A. Nagasaka and Y. Tanaka, *Automatic video indexing and full-video search for object appearences*, In Proc. Visual database Systems, pp. 113-127, 1992.
4. Y. Yusoff and W. Christmas and J. Kittler, *Video Shot Cut Detection Using Adaptive Thresholding*, In Proc. British Machine Vision Conference, pp. 362-381, 2000.
5. S. V. Porter and M. Mirmehdi and B. T. Thomas, *Video Cut Detection using Frequency Domain Correlation*, In Proc. International Conference on Pattern Recognition, pp. 413-416, 2000.

6. Herng-Yow Chen and Ja-Ling Wu, *A multi-layer video browsing system*, IEEE Trans on Consumer Electronics, vol 44, pp. 842-850, 1995.
7. B. Gunsel and A. M. Tekalp, *Content-based video abstraction*, In Proc. International Conference on Image Processing, pp. 128-132, 1998.
8. E. Ardizzone and M. L. Cascia, *Video indexing using optical flow field*, In Proc. International Conference on Image Processing, pp. 831-834, 1996.
9. H. J. Zhang and Zhong and S. W. Smoliar, *An integrated system for content-based video retrieval and browsing*, Pattern Recognition, vol 30 pp. 643-658, 1997.
10. J. Vermaak and P. Peraz and M. Gangnet and A. Blake, *Rapid summarisation and browsing of video sequences*, In Proc. British Machine Vision Conference, pp. 424-433, 2002.
11. J. Sivic and A. Zisserman, *Video Google: A text retrieval Approach to object matching in videos*, In Proc. International Conference on Computer Vision, 2003.
12. J. Sivic and F. Schaffalitzky and A. Zisserman, *Efficient Object Retrieval from Videos*, In Proc. EUSIPCO, 2004.
13. Arasanathan Anjulan and Nishan Canagarajah, *Invariant Region Descriptors for Robust Shot Segmentation*, Accepted for the Proc. of IS&T/SPIE, 18th Annual Symposium on Electronic Imaging, California, USA, January 2006.
14. K. Mikolajczyk and T. Tuytelaars and C. Schmid and A. Zisserman and J. Matas and F. Schaffalitzky and T. Kadir and L. Van Gool, *A comparison of affine region detectors*, Technical report, University of Oxford, 2004.
15. J. Matas and O. Chum and M. Urban and T. Pajdla, *Robust wide baseline stereo from maximally stable extremal regions*, In Proc. British Machine Vision Conference, pp. 384-393, 2002.
16. D. G. Lowe, *Distinctive image features from scale-invariant key points*, Int. Journal of Computer Vision, vol 60, pp. 91-110, 2004.
17. K. Mikolajczy and C. Schmid, *A performance evaluation of local descriptors*, In Proc. International Conference on Computer Vision and Pattern Recognition, pp. 257-263, 2003.
18. C. J. Van Rijsbergen, *Information Retrieval*, Butterworths, 1979.
19. H. Mullerand and S. Marchand-Maillet and T. Punt, *The truth about corel-evaluation in image retrieval*, In Proc. International Conference on Image and Video Retrieval, pp. 38-49, 2002.

Feature Re-weighting in Content-Based Image Retrieval

Gita Das[1], Sid Ray[1], and Campbell Wilson[2]

[1] Clayton School of Information Technology
Monash University
Victoria 3800, Australia
{Gita.Das, Sid.Ray}@csse.monash.edu.au
[2] Caulfield School of Information Technology
Monash University
Victoria 3800, Australia
Campbell.Wilson@csse.monash.edu.au

Abstract. Relevance Feedback (RF) is a useful technique in reducing semantic gap which is a bottleneck in Content-Based Image Retrieval (CBIR). One of the classical approaches to implement RF is feature re-weighting where weights in the similarity measure are modified using feedback samples as returned by the user. The main issues in RF are learning the system parameters from feedback samples and the high-dimensional feature space. We addressed the second problem in our previous work, here, we focus on the first problem. In this paper, we investigated different weight update schemes and compared the retrieval results. We proposed a new feature re-weighting method which we tested on three different image databases of size varying between 2000 and 8365, and having number of categories between 10 and 98. The experimental results with scope values of 20 and 100 demonstrated the superiority of our method in terms of retrieval accuracy.

1 Introduction

The selection of features e.g. colour, shape, colour-layout etc. and their proper representation e.g. colour histogram, statistical moments etc. are very important for good system retrieval. However, the low level features (e.g. colour, shape) used to represent an image do not necessarily represent the high level semantics and human perception of that image. A solution towards this problem is human intervention in terms of Relevance Feedback [1], [2], [3]. For a given query, the system first retrieves a set of ranked images according to a similarity metric, which represents the distance between the feature vectors of the query image and the database images. Then the user is asked to select the images that are relevant or irrelevant (or non-relevant) to his/her query. The system extracts information from these samples and uses that information to improve retrieval results. A revised ranked list of images is then presented to the user. This process continues until there is no further improvement in the result or the user is satisfied with the result. In classical approach, there are mainly two ways to implement RF

H. Sundaram et al. (Eds.): CIVR 2006, LNCS 4071, pp. 193–200, 2006.
© Springer-Verlag Berlin Heidelberg 2006

namely, query updating and feature re-weighting. In query updating method, the components of the query vector are updated using the average of component values of all relevant samples so that the new query point moves towards the centre of relevant class. In feature re-weighting, the weight factors in the similarity measure are modified using relevant samples. The essence of feature re-weighting is to put more weights on the feature components that discriminate well between relevant and non-relevant images and thus enhances retrieval and to put less weights for the ones that do not help retrieval. Feature re-weighting is found to be very suitable for large size databases and high dimensional feature space [8]. Also, this method is simple to implement and produces fairly good retrieval. However, in order to improve retrieval accuracy we need to use the feedback samples carefully and intelligently. In MARS system [4], they used the inverse of standard deviation of the feature component values for the relevant samples. Most of the work reported in the literature used only relevant samples [5], [6], [7]. In [8], Wu and Zhang proposed a discriminant factor that determines the ability of a feature component in separating relevant images from the irrelevant ones. They showed improvement over the MARS system which used only relevant images. Inspired by their work, we propose a modified weight factor that demonstrated significant improvement over the method in [8]. Both of the query update and the feature re-weighting approaches are based on vector model which originally were used in text retrieval [1]. We used a combination of both methods. We experimented with several weight updating schemes to re-shape the similarity measure and compared the retrieval results.

Sections 2 and 3 describe the proposed approach and experimental results respectively. Section 4 contains conclusions and future directions.

2   Methodology

For rest of the paper, we used the following nomenclature:

N: Number of images in the database
C: Number of semantic categories in the database
N_r: Scope i.e. the number of top retrieved images returned to the user
Q, I: Query image and Database image respectively
k: Number of iterations in RF
M: Number of components in the feature vector
w_i^k: weight factor for i^{th} feature component in k^{th} iteration.

2.1   Feature Representation

In [9], we proposed a compact feature representation based on the elements of Colour Co-occurrence Matrices (CCM) in Hue, Saturation, Value (H,S,V=16,3,3) colour space. We chose HSV colour model as it is known to be perceptually uniform. A Colour Co-occurrence Matrix represents how the spatial correlation of colour changes with distance i.e. pixel positions [10]. So, unlike colour histogram, colour co-occurrence matrix provides spatial information of the image.

We observed that diagonal elements of CCMs are much more in number (about 80%) compared to the non-diagonal elements (about 20%). This observation is in line with that reported in [11]. Also, we have noticed that most of the non-diagonal elements are zero. From the original 148-dimensional feature vector, we constructed a 25-dimensional feature vector with all diagonal elements and Sum-Average [12] of all non-diagonal elements from H,S,V matrices. An increase in feature dimension essentially means an exponential growth in the number of training samples. This limitation, called the Curse of Dimensionality, is a well known fact in Pattern Classification [13]. The reduction in dimension from original higher dimension reduced online computation time and enhanced retrieval accuracy. For more details, see our previous work reported in [9].

As different feature components have different ranges (or values), we normalized them so that they lie within [0,1] and each component contributes equally in the similarity measure. The ith normalized feature component, f_i' is given by [9],

$$f_i' = \frac{f_{i,org} - \mu_i}{3\sigma_i}, \ i = 1, 2, ...M \ . \tag{1}$$

where $f_{i,org}$ is the original i^{th} feature component, μ_i is the mean and σ_i is the Standard Deviation (SD) of $f_{i,org}$. These values are calculated over the entire database of N samples. Under the assumption of Gaussian distribution of values, the term $3\sigma_i$ ensures that at least 99% of the samples are within the range $[-1, 1]$. Any value that is < -1 is set to -1 and > 1 is set to 1. In order to map the normalized values from $[-1, 1]$ to $[0, 1]$, we used the following formula:

$$f_i = \frac{f_i' + 1}{2} \ . \tag{2}$$

2.2   Feature Re-weighting

In CBIR research, a number of distance measures have been used in the past in order to measure the similarity (or dissimilarity) between the query image and the database images. Each one of them has its own merits and demerits. Minkowski distance, of which Manhattan (or City-block) and Euclidean distances are special cases, is probably the most widely used. We chose Manhattan distance because it is computationally very simple and produces fairly good results. Also, as our main focus of this article is on the RF strategy, whatever strength or weakness the similarity measure has got, we assume that it will affect the retrieval of different data sets more or less the same way.

The similarity between I and Q is given by the following weighted Minkowski distance measure:

$$D(I, Q) = \sum_{i=1}^{M} w_i * |f_{iI} - f_{iQ}| \ . \tag{3}$$

where f_{iI}, f_{iQ} are i^{th} feature component of I and of Q respectively and w_i is weight factor. When there is no RF, equal weight values are used for each feature component. With RF, these weights are updated using feedback samples. First, we used the following weight value:

$$weight - type1 : w_i^{k+1} = \frac{\epsilon + \sigma_{N_r,i}^k}{\epsilon + \sigma_{rel,i}^k}, \epsilon = 0.0001 .$$ (4)

Here, $\sigma_{N_r,i}^k$ is standard deviation over the N_r retrieved images and $\sigma_{rel,i}^k$ is the standard deviation over the relevant images in k^{th} iteration. If a feature component has smaller variation over the relevant samples then it should get higher weight as this represents the relevant samples better [4] in the feature space. Similar weight factor is used in [5] and [6], however, there the numerator represented standard deviation over the entire database. In the numerator of eqn (4), we used standard deviation over N_r as the variation over the entire database remains unchanged with iteration and thus does not provide any extra information. However, with each iteration a new set of images is likely to be retrieved and a new $\sigma_{N_r,i}^k$ obtained. A small value of ϵ is used to avoid computational problem of $\sigma_{rel,i}^k$ being zero when no similar image (other than the query itself is retrieved) is retrieved. The value of ϵ is chosen to be 0.0001 so that it does not affect the weight values significantly.

In[8], Wu and Zhang used both relevant and non-relevant images to update weights. They used a discriminant ratio to determine the ability of a feature component in separating relevant images from the non-relevant ones:

$$\delta_i^k = 1 - \frac{\sum_{l=1}^k |\psi_i^{l,U}|}{\sum_{l=1}^k |F_i^{l,U}|} .$$ (5)

where $\sum_{l=1}^k |\psi_i^{l,U}|$ is the no. of non-relevant images located inside the dominant range of relevant samples and $\sum_{l=1}^k |F_i^{l,U}|$ is the total no. non-relevant images among the retrieved images, for the ith feature component. The dominant range of a feature component is found by the minimum and maximum values from the set of relevant samples. The value of δ_i^k lies between 0 and 1. It is 0 when all non-relevant images are within the dominant range and thus, no weight should be given for that feature component. On the other hand, when there is not a single non-relevant image lying within the dominant range, maximum weight should be given to that feature component. They used the following weight factor, for details see [8]:

$$weight - type2 : w_i^{k+1} = \frac{\delta_i^k}{\epsilon + \sigma_{rel,i}^k} .$$ (6)

In order to maximize the benefits in separating relevant images from the non-relevant ones, we introduced weight-type3 where we combined the above discriminant ratio with the weight factor in eqn (4). This resulted in eqn (7) and our experimental results also demonstrated the synergy of the weight-type 1 and weight-type 2.

$$weight - type3 : w_i^{k+1} = \delta_i^k * \frac{\epsilon + \sigma_{N_r,i}^k}{\epsilon + \sigma_{rel,i}^k} .$$ (7)

3   Experiment

To demonstrate the goodness of our weight factor we experimented with three databases of different sizes and different number of semantic categories. All images are of 256×256 pixels size. An image in the retrieved list is considered to be relevant if that image comes from the same category as the query image, otherwise, non-relevant.

We used precision as a measure of system performance which is given by the following formula:

$$precision = \frac{No.\ of\ relevant\ retrieved\ images}{No.\ of\ retrieved\ images}\ . \tag{8}$$

3.1   Image Database and Ground Truth

1. ImageDB2000: This consists of 2000 images from 10 different categories (Flowers, Vegetables and Fruits, Nature, Leaves, Ships, Faces, Fishes, Cars, Animals, Aeroplanes). Each category contains 200 images. We used all 2000 images as query images and calculated performance in terms of Precision after averaging over all query images.
2. ImageDBCaltech: From http://www.vision.caltech.edu website, we obtained the Caltech-101 image database. This consists of 9144 images from 102 categories with 34 to 800 images per category. We omitted all grey scale images including the categories Binoculars, Car-side, Camera and Yin-yang that had mostly grey scale images. Finally, we experimented with 8365 images from 98 categories. As query images, we chose 4 images randomly from each category, thus a total of 392 query images. Results presented are obtained by averaging results over 392 query images.
3. ImageDB2020: This consists of 2020 images from 12 categories. The number of images per category varies from 96 to 376. We measured performance by averaging performance over all 2020 images used as query.

3.2   Result Analysis

Table 1 shows the results for all three data sets for scope 20 and table 2 for scope 100. In figure 1, figure 2 and figure 3, the improvement in precision from 0rf to 1rf are almost the same, however, the improvement in the next iterations is much higher with our weight factor. For scope 20, the improvement in precision with weight-type3 compared to weight-type2 is 5.625 % for ImageDB2000, 1.365% for ImageDBCaltech and 4.52% for ImageDB2020. For scope 100, the precision improvement with weight-type3 compared to weight-type2 is 10.426 % for ImageDB2000, 1.089% for ImageDBCaltech and 5.23% for ImageDB2020.

The significant improvement in precision, for all three weight types, from 0rf to 1rf shows the impact of the use of relevance feedback mechanism. From 1rf to 5rf the improvement is much higher for weight-type3. In other words, the convergence towards the highest possible precision value is higher for this weight

Table 1. Improvement in Precision (%) from 0rf to 5rf, Scope = 20

	weight factor	0rf	1rf	2rf	3rf	4rf	5rf
ImageDB2000	weight-type1	56.002	73.613	75.740	78.488	78.745	79.923
	weight-type2	56.002	71.408	76.605	77.575	78.050	78.235
	weight-type3	56.002	72.455	78.567	82.048	82.980	83.860
ImageDBCaltech	weight-type1	11.811	13.801	14.732	15.242	15.523	15.689
	weight-type2	11.811	13.724	14.592	14.707	14.758	14.834
	weight-type3	11.811	13.801	15.089	15.714	16.110	16.199
ImageDB2020	weight-type1	50.280	63.777	66.381	68.545	68.765	69.639
	weight-type2	50.280	61.399	65.567	66.653	67.037	67.252
	weight-type3	50.280	61.990	67.757	70.250	71.002	71.772

Table 2. Improvement in Precision (%) from 0rf to 5rf, Scope = 100

	weight factor	0rf	1rf	2rf	3rf	4rf	5rf
ImageDB2000	weight-type1	37.264	55.131	56.919	60.060	60.004	61.280
	weight-type2	37.264	53.614	55.054	54.138	53.445	52.877
	weight-type3	37.264	56.259	59.984	62.160	62.465	63.303
ImageDBCaltech	weight-type1	5.526	7.640	8.033	8.607	8.556	8.755
	weight-type2	5.526	7.571	7.982	8.133	8.066	8.077
	weight-type3	5.526	7.793	8.406	8.936	9.074	9.166
ImageDB2020	weight-type1	34.315	48.811	50.579	52.686	52.990	53.611
	weight-type2	34.315	47.467	49.717	49.967	49.787	49.363
	weight-type3	34.315	48.735	52.299	53.862	54.126	54.593

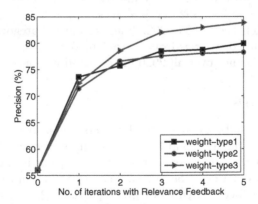

Fig. 1. ImageDB2000: Improvement in precision with RF at scope 20

factor. We reported results up to 5 iterations as after that there is no significant improvement in precision.

It may be worth noting that the precision values for ImageDB2000 and ImageDB2020 are in the range of 50% to 84% whereas for ImageDBCaltech, they

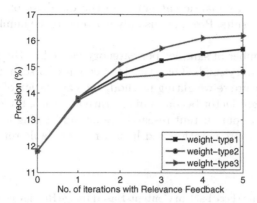

Fig. 2. ImageDBCaltech: Improvement in precision with RF at scope 20

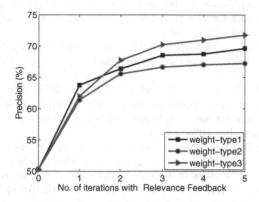

Fig. 3. ImageDB2020: Improvement in precision with RF at scope 20

are in the range of 11% to 16%. This huge difference in precision is clearly explained by the well known result that in the C-category classification problem the classification accuracy is of the order of $\frac{1}{C}$ for random allocation [13]. The effectiveness of feature vector i.e the discriminatory power of feature vector and the inherent separability of classes in the feature space considered are also very important in determining overall precision.

4   Conclusions and Future Directions

To improve system performance with relevance feedback, we used the synergy of weight-type1 and weight-type2 intuitively to obtain weight-type3. For all 3 image databases, weight-type3 performed the best. The experimental results conformed to our expectation. We have also discussed that the convergence towards the highest possible precision value is higher with our weight factor compared to the other two weight factors considered.

Also, the number of semantic categories in the database plays an important role in the retrieval results. Precision usually worsens as the number of categories increases.

In reality, the number of samples per category as well as the number of feedback samples can be very small. The situation becomes worse in high dimensional feature space. In feature re-weighting method, the calculation of standard deviation used in the weight factor becomes inaccurate and thus, the class representation becomes poor. In our current research we are addressing this issue in order to have better class representation and hence, more reliable retrieval results.

References

1. Zhang, H.: Relevance Feedback in Content-Based Image Retrieval, Multimedia Information Retrieval and Management-Technological Fundamentals and Applications, Feng, D.D., Siu, W. C., Zhang, H. (Eds), Chap 3, Springer-Verlog, Germany (2003)
2. Rui, Y., Huang, T. S., Chang, S.: Image Retrieval: Current Techniques, Promising Directions and Open Issues, Journal of Visual Communication and Image Presentation, volume 10, no. 4 (April 1999)
3. Ortega-Binderberger, M., Mehrotra, S.: Relevance Feedback in Multimedia Databases, Handbook of Video Databases: Design and Applications, CRC Press, Chap 23 (2003) 1-28
4. Rui Y., Huang, T.S., Ortega, M., Mehrotra, S.: Relevance Feedback: A Power Tool for Interactive Content-Based Image Retrieval, IEEE Transactions on Circuits and Video Technology, Special issue on Segmentation, Description, and Retrieval of Video Content (September 1998) 644-655
5. Aksoy, S., Haralick, R.M.: A Weighted Distance Approach to Relevance Feedback, International Conference on Pattern Recognition, Barcelona Spain (September 2000)
6. Hore, E.S, Ray, S.: A Sum-result Indexing Algorithm for Feature Combining in Content-Based Image Retrieval, Proceedings of the Fourth IASTED International Conference Signal and Image Processing, Hawaii USA (August 2002) 283-287
7. Ishikawa, Y., Subramanya, R., Faloutsos, C.: MindReader: Querying Databases through Multiple Examples, Proceedings 24th International Conference on Very Large Data Bases (VLDB)(1998)
8. Wu, Y., Zhang, A.: A Feature Re-weighting Approach for Relevance Feedback in Image Retrieval, Special issue on Segmentation, Description, and Retrieval of Video Content, Rochester NewYork (September 2002)
9. Das, G., Ray, S.: A Compact Feature Representation and Image Indexing in Content-Based Image Retrieval, Proceedings of Image and Vision Computing New Zealand 2005 Conference (IVCNZ 2005), Dunedin New Zealand (28-29 November 2005) 387-391
10. Huang, J.: Color-spatial Image Indexing and Applications, PhD Dissertation, Cornell University (1998)
11. Shim, S., Choi, T.: Image Indexing by Modified Color Co-occurrence Matrix, International Conference on Image Processing (September 2003)
12. Haralick, R.M., Shanmugam,K., Dinstein, I.: Textural Features for Image Classification, IEEE Transactions on Systems, Man, and Cybernetics, vol. SMC-3, No.6 (November 1973) 610-621
13. Duda, R. O., Hart, P. E., Stork, D. G.: Pattern Classification, 2nd ed, Wiley-Interscience, New York (2000).

Objectionable Image Detection by ASSOM Competition*

Grégoire Lefebvre[1], Huicheng Zheng[2], and Christophe Laurent[1]

[1] France Telecom R&D
4, Rue du Clos Courtel, 35512 Cesson Sévigné–France
{gregoire.lefebvre, christophe2.laurent}@francetelecom.com
[2] Trinity College Dublin
College Green, Dublin 2–Ireland
zhengh@tcd.ie

Abstract. This article presents a method aiming at filtering objectionable image contents. This kind of problem is very similar to object recognition and image classification. In this paper, we propose to use Adaptive-Subspace Self-Organizing Maps (ASSOM) to generate invariant pornographic features. To reach this goal, we construct local signatures associated to salient patches according to adult and benign databases. Then, we feed these vectors into each specialized ASSOM neural network. At the end of the learning step, each neural unit is tuned to a particular local signature prototype. Thus, each input image generates two neural maps that can be represented by two activation vectors. A supervised learning is finally done by a Normalized Radial Basis Function (NRBF) network to decide the image category. This scheme offers very promising results for image classification with a percentage of 87.8% of correct classification rates.

1 Introduction

In many computer vision applications such as multimedia data mining, pattern recognition, image retrieval, etc., evaluating image content is fundamental. Recognizing harmful images is very challenging in content-based filtering systems.

In the state-of-the-art, different approaches are proposed, focusing on skin color detection. Forsyth et al. use geometric constraints for detecting naked people [1] by reconstructing the human anatomic structure from skin areas. The WIPE system [2] combines Daubechies wavelets, moment analysis and histogram indexing to provide semantically meaningful feature vector matching. Based on the discrete probability distributions obtained from skin and non-skin histograms, Jones and Rehg [3] filter images according to their skin pixel statistics. Other studies [4,5] propose a pornographic image detection system based on skin detection and Multi-Layer Perceptron (MLP) classification.

To avoid inherent skin detection problems, as illumination variations, background interferences, multiple figures, etc., we consider objectionable image filtering as image classification problem in two categories: adult and benign. Image

---

* This work was carried out during the tenure of a MUSCLE Internal fellowship.

H. Sundaram et al. (Eds.): CIVR 2006, LNCS 4071, pp. 201–210, 2006.
© Springer-Verlag Berlin Heidelberg 2006

classification consists in partitioning the input image space into a number of regions separated by decision surfaces and labeled by image classes.

For a given image $\mathcal{I}$, the ultimate goal is to search for a function $f(\cdot) \to \mathcal{J}_{\mathcal{I}}$, $\mathbb{I} \to \mathbb{J}$, where $\mathbb{I}$ is the image space and $\mathbb{J}$ the image label space. However, due to the extremely high dimension of an ordinary image, a direct search of the optimum function $f(\cdot)$ in the original image space $\mathbb{I}$ would generally not be possible.

From this observation, we try to describe the image $\mathcal{I}$ in a more compact way to reduce the dimension of data and obtain the most discriminant informations. In this purpose, we are interested in generating invariant-feature descriptors by using ASSOM neural networks [6].

Adaptive-Subspace Self-Organizing Map (ASSOM) is basically a combination of a subspace method and a competitive selection and cooperative learning as in the traditional SOM [6]. The single weight vectors at map units in SOM are replaced by sets of basis vectors that span some linear subspaces in ASSOM. A long-standing difficulty in the design of feature filters is the variation of input patterns due to typical transformations such as translation, rotation and scaling. By setting filters to correspond to pattern subspaces, some transformation groups can be taken into account automatically.

The input to an ASSOM network is called "episode", which is a sequence of pattern vectors that spans some linear subspace. This sequence is contructed by applying rotation, translation and scaling to the original local signatures. By learning the episode as a whole, ASSOM is able to capture the transformation kernels coded in the episode.

To construct these episodes, we focus our attention on regions of interest (ROI) in the images. Based on some psycho-visual experiments [7], human vision system executes saccadic eye movements between salient locations to capture image content. Likewise, Tversky studies [8] showed that when we compare two images, we detect common and distinct concepts between these regions.

Our method tries to reproduce this extraction and distinction concept with a codebook learning strategy based on ASSOM algorithm. We firstly search salient locations in the images to be compared. Local visual features are then extracted from salient regions and projected onto a set of ASSOM-based learned visual prototypes, resulting in activation vectors.

Finally, we use these activation features to classify the image in adult or benign category with a NRBF neural network.

This method has been experimented for an adult content filtering method where the correct classification rate reaches 87.8%. The database is composed of $1,110$ adult images and $1,200$ benign images downloaded from Internet. The second category, known to be the rest of the world, is mainly constituted of landscapes, portraits and life scenes.

This paper is organized as follows: In Section 2, we first present our image classification scheme based on ASSOM learning from ROI descriptions. Then, Section 3 contributes to some experimental results on the proposed classification schemes. And finally, conclusions are discussed in Section 4.

2 Image Classification Based on ASSOM Learning and Salient Regions of Interest

2.1 Multi-ASSOM Scheme (MAS)

As outlined in [9], a classification scheme is generally composed of three main steps : pre-processing, feature extraction and classification. In this paper, we mainly focus our attention on the two first items, the last being performed by a NRBF neural network.

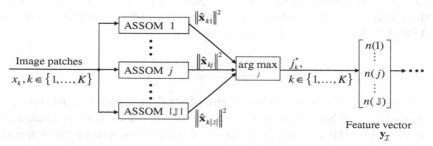

Fig. 1. The construction of the feature vector $\mathbf{y}_\mathcal{I}$ from patches of the image $\mathcal{I}$ in MAS. $|\mathbb{J}|$ ASSOMs compete on these patches and generate a sequence of winning ASSOM index j_k^*, $k \in \{1, 2, \ldots, K\}$. $n(\cdot)$ counts the number of winning times for each ASSOM. The vector $[n(1), \ldots, n(j), \ldots, n(|\mathbb{J}|)]^\mathrm{T}$ forms the final feature $\mathbf{y}_\mathcal{I}$, which is sent to the NRBF neural network.

Our system architecture designs an ASSOM for each category, producing specific ASSOM units for different categories of image patches. This idea was explored in [10] in the recognition of handwritten digits and produced promising results. But in their case, the image size is very small (25×20 pixels), permitting a direct learning through ASSOM. In their work, 10 ASSOMs are employed, one trained for each category of handwritten digits. For digit classification, a test digit is sent simultaneously to all the 10 ASSOMs, which output 10 error values. The ASSOM with the least reconstruction error determines the digit category. An obvious deficiency here is that there is no interaction between the different ASSOMs during the learning phase. An ASSOM learns the features of its own category, however it does not learn to distinguish features of other categories. The optimum decision surface is thus not guaranteed.

In our context, the dealt images have much larger sizes. So, we decide to use a local approach by extracting round image patches at salient locations. RGB patch informations are directly used to describe the local visual features.

Similar strategies have been developped in [11,12]. The principal differences are that the bag-of-keypoints representation is built from a K-means quantization and the classification is made by a Support Vector Machine(SVM).

Here, $|\mathbb{J}|$ ASSOMs are trained on these local descriptions, category by category. $\mathbb{J}$ denotes the number of ASSOM. For filtering use, two ASSOM neural networks are built for adult and benign classes.

To construct the feature vector $\mathbf{y}_\mathcal{I}$ for the final NRBF classification of the image $\mathcal{I}$ (See Figure 1), we operate as follows :

– For each patch $\mathbf{x}_k$, the $|\mathbb{J}|$ ASSOMs compete on it. The jth ASSOM produces an output $\|\hat{\mathbf{x}}_{kj}\|^2$ defined by:

$$\|\hat{\mathbf{x}}_{kj}\|^2 = \max_{i \in I_j} \|\hat{\mathbf{x}}_{k\mathcal{L}_i}\|^2 \ , \tag{1}$$

where I_j is the set of indices of the modules in the jth ASSOM. In words, $\|\hat{\mathbf{x}}_{kj}\|^2$ is the maximum value of the square of the orthogonal projection of the patch $\mathbf{x}_k$ on the subspaces of the modules in the jth ASSOM. The j_k^*th ASSOM with the maximal output wins that patch:

$$j_k^* = \arg\max_{j \in \{1,2,\dots,|\mathbb{J}|\}} \|\hat{\mathbf{x}}_{kj}\|^2 \ . \tag{2}$$

– A counter $n(j_k^*)$ corresponding to this ASSOM network is accordingly increased by 1. When all the patches of the image $\mathcal{I}$ have been presented, the array of ASSOMs produce $|\mathbb{J}|$ counters of the patches won by the respective ASSOM. The feature vector is defined by:

$$\mathbf{y}_\mathcal{I} = [n(1),\dots,n(j),\dots,n(|\mathbb{J}|)]^\mathrm{T} \ , \tag{3}$$

where the components are:

$$\forall j \in \{1,2,\dots,|\mathbb{J}|\}, \quad n(j) = \sum_{k \in \{1,2,\dots,K\}} \delta(j_k^*,j) \ . \tag{4}$$

$\delta(a,b)$ is the pulse function that takes the value 1 when $a = b$ and 0 otherwise.

2.2   Wavelet-Based Salient Point Detection

According to the active vision mechanisms, the goal of salient point detectors is to find perceptually relevant image locations. Many detectors have been proposed in the literature [13,14,15]. The Harris detector [14] aims at locating salient zones on corners by searching for the maxima of a function based on the local autocorrelation matrix of the signal. The detector in [15] proposes to locate salient points in high contrasted area. The salient point detector in [13] uses a wavelet analysis to find pixels on sharp region boundaries.

Working with wavelets in our previous work [13] is justified by the consideration of the human visual system for which multi-resolution, orientation and frequency analysis is of prime importance. In order to extract the salient points, a wavelet transform is firstly performed on the grayscale image. The obtained wavelet coefficients are represented by zerotrees as introduced by Shapiro [16]. This tree is then scanned at a first time from leaves to the root to compute the saliency value at each node. A second scanning occurs in order to determine the salient path from the root to the locations on the original image, where the raw salient points are located. The salient points are listed in order and a threshold τ, $0 < \tau \leq 1$ is set to select the most salient points. By detecting salient points from luminance information only, the points located on boundaries of highlights or shadows are apt to be detected as salient. To remove false salient points caused by lumination conditions, a gradient image is built by using the color invariants proposed by Geusebroek et al. [17].

This salient point detector reaches photometric invariance by combining the detection step with a recently proposed color invariance method [17]. Experimental results in [13] show that the detected points are located on perceptually relevant image areas. Based on the detected salient points, the authors went further to design the salient signature that combines a color histogram with a texture measure. The proposed salient point detector and salient signature are applied to a contented-based retrieval system and the results are quite promising.

In this paper, we will combine the salient point detectors of our previous work with the ASSOM feature selector. Consequently, the ASSOM networks can be trained on small image patches centered on these salient points.

2.3   ASSOM Learning

As mentioned in the introduction, ASSOM is basically a combination of a subspace method and a competitive selection and cooperative learning as in the traditional SOM. ASSOM differs from other subspace methods by permitting to generate a set of topologically-ordered subspaces. That is to say, two units that are close in the map will represent two feature subspaces closed in the total feature space. In ASSOM, the unit is composed of several basic vectors that expand together a linear subspace. This unit is called "module" in an ASSOM neural network. This method aims to learn data features, without assuming any prior mathematical forms of their representation, such as Gabor or wavelet transforms, which are frequently encountered in the traditional image analysis and pattern recognition techniques [6]. In other words, the forms of the filter functions are learned directly from the data.

The input to ASSOM is a group of vectors, called "episode". The vectors in each episode are supposed to be close up to affine transformations.

There are mainly two phases in a learning process of ASSOM:

1. For an input episode, locate the winning subspace from ASSOM modules ;
2. Adjust the winning subspace and its neighbor modules in order to better represent the input episode.

For a linear subspace $\mathcal{L}$ of dimensionality H, one can find a set of basis vectors $\{\mathbf{b}_1, \mathbf{b}_2, \ldots, \mathbf{b}_H\}$, such that every vector in $\mathcal{L}$ can be represented by a linear combination of these basis vectors. Such sets of basis vectors are not unique, however they are equivalent in the sense that they expand exactly the same subspace. For convenience of mathematical measures, the basis vectors are orthonormalized by the Gram-Schmidt process.

The orthogonal projection of an arbitrary vector $\mathbf{x}$ on the subspace $\mathcal{L}$, notated as $\hat{\mathbf{x}}_{\mathcal{L}}$, is a linear combination of its orthogonal projections on the individual basis vectors, and can be computed by:

$$\hat{\mathbf{x}}_{\mathcal{L}} = \sum_{h=1}^{H} (\mathbf{x}^{\mathrm{T}}\mathbf{b}_h)\mathbf{b}_h. \tag{5}$$

If $\hat{\mathbf{x}}_{\mathcal{L}} = \mathbf{x}$, then $\mathbf{x}$ belongs to $\mathcal{L}$, else we can define the distance from $\mathbf{x}$ to $\mathcal{L}$ as $\|\tilde{\mathbf{x}}_{\mathcal{L}}\| = \|\mathbf{x} - \hat{\mathbf{x}}_{\mathcal{L}}\|$, by using the Euclidean norm. When several subspaces exist, the original space is separated from pattern zones and the decision surface between two subspaces, for example $\mathcal{L}_1$ and $\mathcal{L}_2$, is determined by those vectors $\mathbf{x}$ such that $\|\hat{\mathbf{x}}_{\mathcal{L}_1}\| = \|\hat{\mathbf{x}}_{\mathcal{L}_2}\|$. By comparing the distances of a vector to all the subspaces, we can assign this vector to the nearest subspace.

In Kohonen's realization of ASSOM, the subspace is represented by a two-layered neural architecture, as in Figure 2. The neurons in the first layer take the orthogonal projections $\mathbf{x}^{\mathrm{T}}\mathbf{b}_h$ of the input vector $\mathbf{x}$ on the individual basis vectors $\mathbf{b}_h$. The second layer is composed of a single quadratic neuron and makes the output square sum from the first layer neuron.

The output of the whole neural module is then $\|\hat{\mathbf{x}}_{\mathcal{L}}\|^2$, the square of the norm of the projection. It can be regarded as a measure of the degree of matching of the input vector $\mathbf{x}$ with the subspace $\mathcal{L}$ represented by the neural module. In the case of an episode, the distance should be calculated from the subspace of the vectors in the episode and that of the module, which are generally difficult to compute. Kohonen proposed another much easier but robust definition of subspace matching : the *energy* (sum of squares) of orthogonal input vector projections on the module subspace.

Once the first phase occurred, the winning module with its neighbors adjust their subspaces to represent better the input subspace. A neighborhood function $h_c^{(i)}$ is defined on the rectangular or hexagonal lattice (See Figure 3), where c

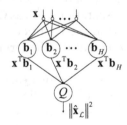

Fig. 2. Neural architecture of orthogonal projection of $\mathbf{x}$ on $\mathcal{L}$

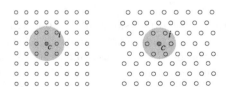

Fig. 3. Left: A rectangular topology. Right: A hexagonal topology. Each empty circle represents a neural module as shown in Fig. 2. The gray areas represent the neighborhood of the winning module indexed by c at a certain learning step.

notates the index of the winning module and i the index of an arbitrary module in the lattice. The neighborhood area defined by $h_c^{(i)}$ shrinks with the learning step. Through this cooperative learning, the map will end at a topologically-organized status, where nearby modules have similar subspaces.

The classical Kohonen's ASSOM learning algorithm works as follows: For the learning step t,

1. Feed the input episode $\mathbf{x}(s)$, $s \in S$, where S is the set of indices of vectors in the input episode. Locate the winning module indexed by c:

$$c = \arg\max_{i \in I} \sum_{s \in S} \|\hat{\mathbf{x}}_{\mathcal{L}_i}(s)\|^2, \tag{6}$$

where I is the set of indices of the neural modules in the ASSOM.

2. For each module i in the neighborhood of c, including c itself, and for each input vector $\mathbf{x}(s)$, $s \in S$, adjust the subspace $\mathcal{L}_i$ by updating the basis vectors $\mathbf{b}_h^{(i)}$, according to the following procedure:

   (a) Rotate each basis vector according to:

$$\mathbf{b}_h^{(i)} = \mathbf{P}_c^{(i)}(\mathbf{x}, t)\mathbf{b}_h^{'(i)} . \tag{7}$$

   In this updating rule, $\mathbf{b}_h^{(i)}$ is the new basis vector after rotation and $\mathbf{b}_h^{'(i)}$ the old one. $\mathbf{P}_c^{(i)}(\mathbf{x}, t)$ is the rotation operator matrix, which is defined by:

$$\mathbf{P}_c^{(i)}(\mathbf{x}, t) = \mathbf{I} + \lambda(t)h_c^{(i)}(t)\frac{\mathbf{x}(s)\mathbf{x}^T(s)}{\|\hat{\mathbf{x}}_{\mathcal{L}_i}(s)\|\|\mathbf{x}(s)\|} , \tag{8}$$

   where $\mathbf{I}$ is the identity matrix, $\lambda(t)$ a learning-rate factor that decreases with the learning step t. $h_c^{(i)}(t)$ is the neighborhood function defined on the ASSOM lattice with the support area shrinking with t.

   (b) Dissipate the components $b_{hj}^{(i)}$ of the basis vectors $\mathbf{b}_h^{(i)}$ to improve the stability of the results [6]:

$$b_{hj}^{\sim(i)} = \text{sgn}(b_{hj}^{(i)})\max(0, |b_{hj}^{(i)}| - \varepsilon), \tag{9}$$

   where ε is the amount of dissipation, chosen proportional to the magnitude of the correction of the basis vectors.

   (c) Orthonormalize the basis vectors in module i.

3   Experiments

In our experiment, the MAS scheme is applied to adult image filtering. There are respectively 733 adult images and 733 benign images in the training set of the image database. The test database is composed of 377 adult images and 467 benign images. The training of each ASSOM for each category takes $T = 200,000$ epochs. The subspace dimension is set to $H = 4$ and the dimension of the

ASSOM arrays is $N = 10 \times 10$. The radius of a image patch is $r = 14.5$ pixels and thus the dimension of the input vector for the ASSOM arrays is $1,971$. These parameters are chosen by experimental results on the training set.

For our experiments, we configure our ASSOM network with the following rules to reach good learning results in terms of accurate input data representation [6]:

- $\lambda(t) = \frac{T}{T+99t}$ forms a monotonically decreasing sequence;
- $h_c^{(i)}(t) = \begin{cases} 1, ||p_c - p_i|| < \mu(t) \\ 0, otherwise. \end{cases}$

The Euclidian norm is chosen and p_i is the 2D location for the ith neuron in the network. $\mu(t)$ specifies the width of the neighborhood decreasing linearly during time t from $\frac{\sqrt{2}}{2}N$ to 0.5 .

The classification performance on the training set is a true positive (TP) rate of 88.5% at a false positive (FP) rate of 13.2%. The TP rate is defined as the proportion of adult images that are correctly classified and the FP rate is the proportion of benign images that are incorrectly classified as adult. On the test set, the TP rate is 89.9% and the FP rate is 13.9%. The confusion matrix is presented in the Table 1. Some examples of correct and incorrect classification are then shown in Figure 4.

The performance is really promising, considering the value 0.9448 for the area under the curve (AUC), drawn in the Receiver Operating Characteristics (ROC) curve in Figure 5.

This multi-ASSOM architecture outperforms with 87.8% of correct classification rates a single ASSOM scheme (85.9%) and a single SOM scheme (78.35%)[1].

Thus, we can see that the competition between an adult ASSOM and a benign ASSOM creates more precise feature vectors for NRBF classification. And the ASSOM algorithm permits to extract more robust features than the basic SOM method.

It is also very interesting to see the filters generated for the adult images and the benign images in Figure 6. We can observe that for the adult images, one of the basis vectors exhibit a orange color tone, and the other one shows obvious orientations. Thus, each final subspace tries to represent the data feature structure. That's why, when an adult image is fed into our scheme the adult ASSOM is stronger activated as shown in Figure 6.

Table 1. Confusion matrix of the MAS classification system with a ASSOM array of dimension 10×10. In this table, A=Adult, B=Benign.

Classified as →	A	B
A	339	38
B	65	402

---

[1] In our experiment, the best configuration for a single ASSOM scheme is : $N = 10 \times 10, H = 4, r = 14.5$; and for a single SOM scheme : $N = 20 \times 20, r = 3.5$.

Fig. 4. The left column presents correctly classified test images. The right column shows examples for misclassification.

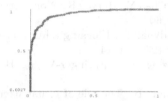

Fig. 5. ROC curve of MAS on classification of adult and benign test images. Horizontal axis represents the FP rate and vertical axis the TP rate.

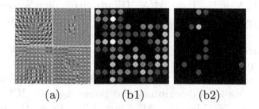

(a)   (b1)   (b2)

Fig. 6. (a)The feature filters generated for adult images and benign images. Top row: The filters generated for adult images. Bottom row: The filters generated for benign images. First column: The first basis vectors. Second column: The second basis vectors. The activation map represents the output energy for each module of adult ASSOM(b1) and benign ASSOM(b2) when an adult test image is proposed to MAS.

4 Conclusion

In this paper, we proposed an original classification system using directly patch information. Based on the three main properties of ASSOM - which are dimension reduction, topology preservation and invariant feature emergence - our scheme filters images in a competitive way. This solution implemented for content-based image filtering gives us very promising results. A further improvement could be to distinguish model portraits from adult images, because this case composes chiefly the false detection. To get efficiency, the adult class training can be achieved with an object-based approach in order to skip background interferences. Furthermore, MPEG7 descriptors may certainly make the performances better than the simple RGB informations.

References

1. Forsyth D.A., Fleck M.M.: Identifying nude pictures. IEEE WACV (1996) 103–108
2. Wang J.Z., Li J., Wiederhold G., Firschein O.: Classifying objectionable websites based on image content. IDMS (1998) 113–124
3. Jones M.J., Rehg J.M.: Statistical color models with application to skin detection. IJCV **46**(1) (2002) 81–96
4. Bosson A., Cawley G.C., Chan Y., Harvey R.: Non-retrieval: Blocking pornographic images. CIVR (2002) 50–60
5. Zheng H., Daoudi M., Jedynak B.: Blocking adult images based on statistical skin detection. ELCVIA **4**(2) (2004) 1–14
6. Kohonen T.: Self-Organizing Maps. Springer-Verlag, Berlin, Heidelberg, New York (2001)
7. Hoffman J.E., Subramanium B.: The role of visual attention in saccadic eye movements. Perception and Psychophysics **57** (1995) 787–795
8. Tversky A.: Features of similarity. Psychological Review **4**(84) (1977) 327–352
9. Duda R.O., Stork D.G., Hart P.E.: Pattern Classification. Wiley Interscience (2000)
10. Zhang, B., Fu, M., Yan, H., Jabri, M.A.: Handwritten digit recognition by adaptive-subspace self-organizing map (assom). IEEE Transactions on Neural Networks **4**(10) (1999) 939–945
11. Csurka, G., Dance, C., Fan, L., Willamowski, J., Bray, C.: Visual categorization with bags of keypoints. ECCV (2004)
12. Quelhas, P., Monay, F., Odobez, J.M., Gatica-Perez, D., Tuytelaars, T., Gool, L.V.: Modeling scenes with local descriptors and latent aspects. ICCV (2005) 883–890
13. Laurent C., Laurent N., Maurizot M., Dorval T.: In depth analysis and evaluation of saliency-based color image indexing methods using wavelet salient features. Multimedia Tools and Application (2004)
14. Harris C., Stephens M.: A combined corner and edge detector. Proc. Fourth Alvey Vision Conf. (1988) 147–151
15. Bres S., Jolion J.M.: Detection of interest points for image indexation. In 3rd Int. Conf. on Visual Information Systems (1999) 427–434
16. Shapiro, J.: Embedded image coding using zerotrees of wavelet coefficients. IEEE Transactions on Signal Processing **12**(41) (1993) 3345–3462
17. Geusebroek, J.M., Boomgrad, R., Smeulders, W.M., Geerts, H.: Color invariance. IEEE Transactions on PAMI **12**(23) (2001) 1338–1350

Image Searching and Browsing by Active Aspect-Based Relevance Learning

Mark J. Huiskes

Centre for Mathematics and Computer Science (CWI),
Amsterdam, The Netherlands
Mark.Huiskes@cwi.nl

Abstract. Aspect-based relevance learning is a relevance feedback scheme based on a natural model of relevance in terms of image aspects. In this paper we propose a number of active learning and interaction strategies, capitalizing on the transparency of the aspect-based framework. Additionally, we demonstrate that, relative to other schemes, aspect-based relevance learning upholds its retrieval performance well under feedback consisting mainly of example images that are only partially relevant.

1 Introduction

For both image and video retrieval, relevance feedback has become a key process in iteratively adapting retrieval results to the user's wishes; [1] and [2] give recent reviews of the state-of-the-art of CBIR relevance feedback. In modern retrieval systems we are increasingly working with large numbers of heterogeneous features. Image descriptions now consist of a combination of low-level features (often various similarity spaces), of segmentation-based features, of learned classifications, and of high-level, possibly context-derived, metadata. The problem that relevance feedback schemes must be able to deal with only few samples in very high-dimensional feature space is thus ever more urgent.

The main inference task is to figure out which feature values, or feature value combinations, lead to high relevance. This essentially comes down to analyzing the clustering behavior of the example images provided in the relevance feedback cycles. However, as we have argued in [3], generalizing from the clustering of the small number of available example images faces a number of serious challenges. First, there is an issue of misleading clustering. Typically there will be many features that are not relevant but this does not mean that examples will not cluster for such features: often they will, namely at feature values with high prior probability. Additionally, selected examples are in practice often only *partially relevant*, especially in the critical initial stages of a searching or browsing session. This means that for the features that are relevant to the user, examples often cluster only to a limited extent. We have shown that for these reasons much can be gained by taking into account database feature value distributions, as this allows us to assess the significance of example clustering. In [3] we proposed aspect-based relevance learning, in which aspects are defined as feature predicates serving as natural units of relevance, for which indeed the significance

H. Sundaram et al. (Eds.): CIVR 2006, LNCS 4071, pp. 211–220, 2006.
© Springer-Verlag Berlin Heidelberg 2006

of associated example clustering can be quantified. This provides a principled method to make sure that feature value regions are only selected as relevant if evidence is sufficiently strong to support the hypothesis that clustering there is not occurring by chance. In section 2 we briefly review this selection procedure, as well as the construction of aspects.

This article has two main contributions. First, in section 3, we extend aspect-based relevance learning with a number of active learning and interaction strategies. Active learning is an increasingly studied topic in image retrieval (e.g. [4,5,6,7]) which aims to reduce the number of images that need to be labeled by the user by presenting him with images that are particularly informative to the system. We propose a method for selecting such images in the aspect-based framework. Furthermore, we discuss interaction strategies which aim to provide the user with a set of tools to (i) obtain a clear insight in the system's inference process, and (ii) improve aspect data during retrieval sessions. All strategies have been implemented in the "Aspect Explorer" retrieval system.

Second, in section 4, we present an experimental study analyzing how well various relevance schemes uphold their retrieval performance under feedback consisting mainly of example images that are only partially relevant. We compare the performance of aspect-based relevance learning to various feature re-weighting schemes as well as to SVM-based methods. Tests are performed using a large commercial database of decoration designs for which a wide variety of low-level and high-level features have been computed.

2   Aspect-Based Relevance Learning

In the following, we assume feedback example selection is implemented by presenting images in a clickable selection display, consisting of a grid of thumbnail images. The number of images inspected per cycle may be larger as the user can leaf through the selection displays. The examples and counterexamples, selected by the user as feedback, are collected in positive and negative *example sets*. At each cycle of the feedback process the user updates the examples in the example sets by either: (i) selecting new images as positive or negative examples, adding them to their respective sets; (ii) removing images from the sets, i.e. the sets are preserved from cycle to cycle unless images are no longer deemed representative enough and are deleted. Based on the example sets a new relevance ranking is determined for display in the next feedback cycle.

2.1   Aspect Selection

In [3] we treat images as sets of aspects, where we understand an "aspect" simply as a property which an image either has or has not, and for which we intend to resolve its effect on perceived relevance as a unit. Aspects can thus be explicitly defined in terms of conditions on feature values, i.e. as derived binary features that model a specific perceptual quality, but can also live solely in the "eye of the beholder". In aspect-based relevance learning the feedback data available at the end of each cycle is used foremost to establish the relevance effect (neutral, positive or negative) of the various aspects.

The main idea is that we must find those aspects for which the user has *actively* selected more examples with that aspect than may be expected to arise by chance only. To this end, we first define the *aspect image frequency* p_{db} as the fraction of images in the database having a certain aspect. Given this frequency, we can model the probability distribution of the number of examples having an aspect when that aspect is neutral, viz. by assuming that it will approximately follow the distribution of aspect occurrence in the database.

In the following we analyze the positive example set; the negative examples are treated analogously. Let n^+ be the current total number of positive examples, and N^+ the number of positive examples that possess an aspect. For each aspect, we consider an *independence hypothesis* H_0^+,

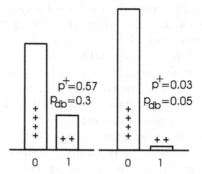

Fig. 1. The significance of example clustering depends on aspect image frequency. Two aspects are shown with bars representing the prior distribution of aspect possession (corresponding to the indicated p_{db} values). For the second aspect the clustering of the two examples with the aspect is more significant than for the first. Note how the method deals with partial relevance: clustering may be significant even if the majority of examples do not have an aspect.

stating that the aspect is neutral to the user. Under this hypothesis we model aspect possession of an example image as a Bernoulli variable with probability p_{db}; consequently, the number of positives with given aspect can be modeled as a binomial variable with parameters n^+ and p_{db}.

An aspect is selected as positive only if the independence hypothesis can be rejected based on an unexpectedly high number of example images with that aspect. The p-value associated with the hypothesis is thus the probability of finding N^+ or more images with aspect in a set of n^+ random images

$$p^+(N^+) = \sum_{i=N^+}^{n^+} \binom{n^+}{i} p_{db}^i (1 - p_{db})^{(n^+ - i)}. \tag{1}$$

We select only those aspects for which their p^+-values are below a certain threshold p_0^+. As Fig. 1 shows, this approach has the benefit that feature selection is not just based on the clustering behavior of the examples. Rather, it analyzes this clustering in its context, viz. the current database. In addition, by taking into account feature value distributions, we are not dependent on negative examples to down-weight positives that cluster at aspects with low saliency. This means negatives can be used to indicate which aspects are not desired, but are not required for the sole purpose of getting sufficient data for classification.

2.2   Aspect Construction

We can divide the methods for constructing aspects from features into supervised and unsupervised types. Unsupervised methods are, for instance, automatic quantization of one-dimensional features and unsupervised clustering methods for higher dimensional feature spaces. Supervised methods may use general classification methods such as SVMs, boosting or prototype-based methods to generate aspects based on sets of annotated sample images. Another supervised method is supervised quantization, by which the user manually selects feature value ranges of interest as aspects. Though unsupervised methods require less work, in general we prefer supervised methods as they tend to lead to aspects that are more perceptually meaningful. Note that binary or discrete features can be converted directly into aspects. For more details, see [3].

3   Active Learning and Interaction

Figure 2 shows the Aspect Explorer retrieval interface.

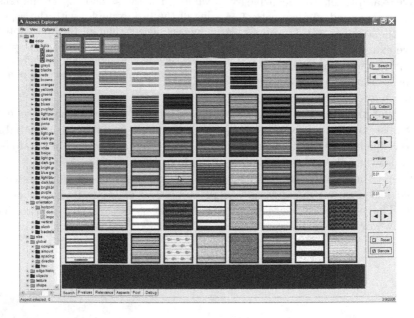

Fig. 2. Aspect Explorer retrieval interface. Selected aspects are highlighted in green (positive) and red (negative; not shown) in the aspect hierarchy on the left. The positive example set is in the green section at the top; negatives in the red section at the bottom. The top part of the selection display, the "relevance display" (RD) shows most relevant images; the lower "information display" (ID) shows images deemed most informative to the system; both displays can be leafed through to browse lower-ranked images.

3.1   Relevance Ranking

The Aspect Explorer system implements the aspect selection scheme detailed above. The main interaction takes place by selection of examples in the "relevance display" (RD). The images displayed there have been determined directly from the selected aspects through a greedy ranking algorithm. Let A^+ and A^- be the index sets of accepted positive and negative aspects, respectively, then the relevance rel_i for image i is defined as $rel_i = \sum_{j \in A^+} M_{ij} - \sum_{j \in (A^-/A^+)} M_{ij}$. Here M is the aspect matrix with boolean variables M_{ij} flagging possession of aspect j for image i.

3.2   Active Learning

The RD shows images inferred to be most relevant to the user given the current example sets. However, these images are not necessarily most informative to the system for improving its retrieval results for the next cycle. Active learning deals with methods to determine images, to be presented to the user for labeling, which allow the system to learn fast. Since, in aspect-based relevance learning, feedback data is used primarily for aspect selection, our aim is to find images that may resolve the status of the most uncertain aspects. The resulting "informative" images will be presented to the user in the "information display" (ID), see Fig. 2. As both selection displays are accessible simultaneously, the ID is designed to show images complementary to images in the RD.

The method proposed here constructs a ranking of images by informativeness on aspects that are uncertain in the sense that their selection p^+-values are close to the threshold. For reasons described below, we focus on aspects with p-values above the threshold, i.e. which have not yet been selected.

An aspect that is not yet selected, but shows promise given its p-value, may be selected in the next cycle if a user selects one or more images with that aspect as positive example. However, simply presenting the user with images having a particular uncertain aspect is not useful as their appearance is generally dominated to a large extent by aspects the user is not interested in. We found that this may be resolved by presenting images that have the uncertain aspect, as well as a relatively high relevance score. Closely related to this, we found that it is important to take into account the *aspect accumulation* of the uncertain aspects. The accumulation is defined as the fraction of images having the particular aspect in the, say 50, top-ranking relevant images. It turns out that it is fairly common for uncertain aspects to already be highly accumulated. The reason is that uncertain aspects often show a correlation with selected aspects. Such accumulated aspects are not interesting for constructing informative images as the user already has sufficient access to such images in the RD.

We conclude that we must present informative images for uncertain aspects that have not yet accumulated in the top-ranking images. To this end, we first sort aspects according to an information score consisting of a weighted combination of the proximity of their p^+-value to the threshold and their accumulation fraction. We found that taking the top-5 of lowest scores provides a suitable set of uncertain aspects. Next, for each uncertain aspect we rank the images having that aspect by relevance. The final information ranking is constructed by inter-leaving the rankings of the uncertain aspects. Images with a high information ranking may still occur in the top images of the RD. These are not repeated in the ID but rather highlighted in the RD (in blue).

Experience with the Aspect Explorer system shows that the informative im-ages, thus constructed, often provide interesting example images as they tend to have promising aspects that are not yet available in the RD. The ID ranking can thus be viewed as a less greedy ranking, for which more than just the selected aspects have been taken into account. An example is shown in Fig. 2, where in the example set there is some evidence that the user may be interested in light colors. In the ID several relevant images with light colors are indeed suggested.

3.3   Advanced Interaction

For interaction scenarios where the emphasis is on ease of use of the interface, e.g. letting customers browse a design collection in a shop, restricting the interface mainly to selection of positive and negative examples from the relevance display (RD) is probably the best choice. For expert users, we can use more advanced features such as the ID, as well as provide insight into the workings of the system. We also discuss a number of interaction strategies that allow the user to correct the system, both at the aspect selection level and the image aspect data level. The latter means that an authorized user may correct aspect data if this proofs merited during the course of a retrieval session.

An important interface component, contributing directly to the transparency of the inference process, is the aspect hierarchy tree, see Fig. 2; its structure is described by a simple XML-file, providing aspect names and their grouping relations. For example, all color aspects are organized in a color group which contains subgroups for specific colors, which, in turn, contain the aspects mod-eling the various levels of importance of that color. The groups serve to organize aspects and to allow modification of the status of many aspects simultaneously. The groups may be aspects themselves, e.g. the aspect "flower" is also a group containing aspects such as "rose" and "tulip".

The aspect tree is used to summarize the state of the inference engine at the end of a feedback cycle in terms of the selected positive and negative aspects, and to allow the user to give direct feedback on this state. Selected positive aspects are highlighted in green, negatives in red. If desired, the user can provide feedback directly in terms of the aspects, both through *soft* and *hard* selection. Soft selection means the aspect is treated as if the selection had occurred from passing the selection hypothesis test. Hard selection is stronger in that possession of the selected aspect becomes binding, restricting the search to a subset of database images having (or not having) the particular aspect. It is also possible to manually "neutralize" aspects selected by the system.

As mentioned, the interaction design has been aimed at making it possible to correct aspect values, whenever a situation is encountered during the retrieval process which shows that a value is in error. We discuss two scenarios. As a first one, consider the situation that the evaluation of a certain aspect as positive, negative, or neutral is surprising to a user. The user may then click this aspect in the aspect tree. This will then highlight all images in the RD, ID and example sets based on the possession of that aspect: green if it has the aspect, red if it does not. Authorized users may then proceed to edit the aspect values in various ways, e.g. by clicking an example image to toggle its value. Other methods use image dragging or pop-up menus to move or copy the image to a different aspect. In the second scenario the user finds an image with an unexpectedly high ranking (to him). In such case, he may inspect its possession of selected aspects, either in a dialog window or the aspect tree; and, again, edit if necessary.

A final useful interaction type is directed at improving aspects in batch-mode. To this end, a separate tab is used to show a selection display divided in two parts: one for images with the selected aspect, one for without; both may be leafed through. This facilitates easy improvement of aspect data by dragging images from one side to the other.

4   Query Simulation Experiments

The main job of a relevance feedback scheme is to produce a relevance ranking of the database images, based on an analysis of the example sets obtained at the end of a feedback cycle. To compare the performance of different schemes we consider the quality of the rankings produced. We will do so for queries represented by simulated example sets. The example sets are simulated in such a way that it is clear what represents a good ranking. Performance is quantified by means of precision-recall graphs for the target images.

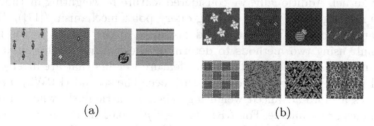

(a)   (b)

Fig. 3. Two simulated example sets, for target aspects "background, large" and "grey, dominant", generated according to the (a) full relevance scenario, and (b) partial relevance scenario

We first select a number of *target aspects*. Each such aspect represents a feature value, or range of feature values, the user is actively interested in. The target aspects are randomly sampled from aspects with a p_{db} value below a given threshold. This assures that the target aspects are saliently present and perceptually relevant. In this study we consider only positive aspects; we do not simulate negative aspects. The target aspects directly correspond to a set of *target images*, viz. those images in the database that possess all target aspects.

We consider two main scenarios for generating the positive example sets. In the *full relevance* scenario we simply sample a subset of the target image set. Fig. 3 (a) shows a generated example set of 4 target images for two target aspects "background, large" and "grey, dominant".

The second scenario is intended to test how well the relevance feedback schemes can deal with example sets consisting of images that are only partially relevant. In this *partial relevance* scenario we generate a fixed number of images for each of the target aspects. The images are randomly sampled from those images that have one target aspect, but do not have the remaining target aspects (or, as few as possible, if no such images exist). Fig. 3 (b) shows such an example set for the same two aspects as before. Observe, for instance, that the last 4 images are grey, but have relatively little background. Compared to the first scenario, where the simulated example sets consist strictly of fully relevant images, this scenario is at the other end of the feedback spectrum, in the sense that feedback is provided here exclusively by means of partially relevant images. In practice, example sets will usually be a mix of these two extreme scenarios. For both scenarios, we test both with and without additional simulated negative examples. Negative examples are randomly sampled from the images that have none of the target aspects. This is mainly for the benefit of the other learning methods as for the aspect-based method they are not needed.

We compared the aspect-based relevance learning method (ARL) to a number of other methods. Two are based on support vector machines, both implemented using [8]. The first (1-SVM) is the one-class SVM method of [9]. The second is a standard ν-SVM method for classifying positive and negative examples, see for instance [10]. We tested both a Gaussian (2-SVM(g)) and a polynomial (2-SVM(p)) kernel. Additionally, we considered feature re-weighting methods with relevance ranking based on the moving query point mechanism ([11]). The relevance ranking follows from the sorted distances of the images to the moving query point, using two methods to determine the feature weights used in the distance measure. The first (FRW1) uses feature weights that are inversely proportional to the example feature value variance. The second (FRW2), proposed in [12], uses a more advanced weighting scheme, particularly when also negative examples are available. For ARL we took $p = 0.01$ as the p-value selection threshold, which is also the default threshold in Aspect Explorer.

Testing is based on aspects (ARL) and features (the other methods) for a large commercial database of decoration designs. To characterize decoration designs we have selected and developed a variety of features suitable for representing both their global appearance (e.g. color, texture, complexity), as well as their elements (shape, size, number, variation, spatial organization). Metadata descriptions in terms of a hierarchy of 42 keywords (e.g. "geometric", "flower") are also used. A detailed description of all features is provided in [13]. Features were computed for 7078 images. From the 161 available features, a total of 585 aspects were derived.

4.1   Experimental Results

Fig. 4 shows precision-recall graphs based on the ranking of the target images for the scenarios outlined above. For each run, 1000 simulations were performed. For the simulations, random target aspects were sampled such that the number of target images was always at least 10, and additionally, the selected aspects corresponded to different features. Only salient aspects with p_{db} value of at most 0.1 were considered as target aspects, and for each aspect 4 example images were selected. Several variations to the experiments have been performed (e.g. taking more example images, increasing the saliency threshold, using a different minimum number of target images, or leaving out various feature groups). These showed roughly the same relative performance between ARL and the other methods.

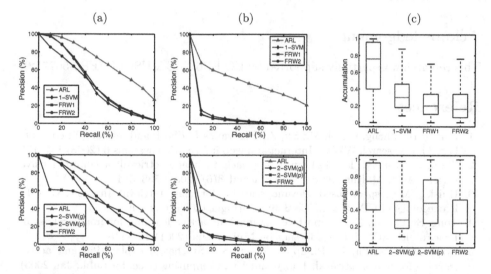

Fig. 4. Target image precision-recall graphs for (a) full relevance scenario, (b) partial relevance scenario; (c) accumulation box-plots for the partial relevance scenario. The top graphs show results for just positive examples; the bottom graphs for both positive and negative examples.

In the full relevance scenario the aspect-based relevance feedback method outperforms the feature re-weighting methods mainly because the re-weighting methods assign too many features with high weights, which leads to poor precision. In the partial relevance scenario the performance of the feature re-weighting methods further deteriorates due to additional difficulty in selecting the correct features as clustering is less clear due to the partial relevance of the examples. For the SVM methods it is interesting to notice that using a polynomial kernel provides a much better performance in the partial relevance scenario than the Gaussian kernel. Fig. 4 (c) demonstrates that ARL leads to a higher accumulation of target aspects in the top ranking images. Shown are the average accumulation fractions (defined in section 3.2) over the target aspects.

5   Conclusion

We have demonstrated that, relative to other schemes, aspect-based relevance learning upholds its retrieval performance well under feedback consisting mainly of example images that are only partially relevant. As a result, the aspect-based approach leads to a natural interaction where generally "what you click is what you get". When this is not the case this is often caused by mistakes in the features or aspects. Several interaction strategies have been presented to correct such mistakes on the fly. Finally, presenting the user with images based on an active learning method was found to provide a useful extension to presenting most relevant images. Such images can resolve uncertainty on whether an aspect should be selected and, by their construction, often have aspects interesting to the user not yet available in the RD.

Acknowledgement

This research was partially supported by EC FP6 NoE MUSCLE (FP6-507752).

References

1. Zhang, H., Zheng, C., Li, M., Su, Z.: Relevance feedback and learning in content-based image search.WWW: Internet and web information systems **6** (2003) 131–155
2. Zhou, X., Huang, T.: Relevance feedback in image retrieval: a comprehensive review. ACM Multimedia Systems Journal **8**(6) (2003) 536–544
3. Huiskes, M.: Aspect-based relevance learning for image retrieval. In Leow, W., ed.: Proceedings of CIVR05, LNCS 3568. Springer (2005) 639–649
4. Tong, S., Chang, E.: Support vector machine active learning for image retrieval. Proc. of 9th ACM Int. Conference on Multimedia (2001) 107–118
5. Cord, M., Gosselin, P., Philipp-Foliguet, S.: Stochastic exploration and active learning for image retrieval. Image and Vis. Computing (Acc. for publ., Jan 2006)
6. Zhou, Z., Chen, K., Jiang, Y.: Exploiting unlabeled data in content-based image retrieval. ECML'04, LNAI 3201 **8**(6) (2004) 525–536
7. Zhang, H., Su, Z.: Relevance feedback in CBIR. In Zhou, X., Pu, P., eds.: Visual and Multimedia Information Systems. Kluwer Academic Publishers (2002) 21–35
8. Canu, S., Grandvalet, Y., Guigue, V., Rakotomamonjy, A.: SVM and kernel methods Matlab toolbox. Perception Syst. et Inf., INSA de Rouen, France (2005)
9. Chen, Y., Zhou, X., Huang, T.: One-class SVM for learning in image retrieval. Proc. IEEE ICIP 2001, Thessaloniki, Greece **1** (2001) 34–37
10. Hoi, C., Lyu, M.: Biased support vector machine for relevance feedback in image retrieval. Proc. Intl. Joint Conf. on Neural Networks, Budapest, Hungary (2004)
11. Rocchio Jr., J.: Relevance feedback in information retrieval. In Salton, G., ed.: The SMART retrieval system: experiments in automatic document processing. Prentice-Hall (1971) 313–323
12. Ciocca, G., Schettini, R.: A relevance feedback mechanism for content-based image retrieval. Information Processing and Management **35**(5) (1999) 605–632
13. Huiskes, M., Pauwels, E.: Indexing, learning and CBR for special purpose image databases. In Zelkowitz, M., ed.: Advances in Computers. Elsevier (2005)

Finding Faces in Gray Scale Images Using Locally Linear Embeddings

Samuel Kadoury and Martin D. Levine

McGill University, Department of Electrical and Computer Engineering,
3480 University Street, H3A 2A7, Montreal, Canada
{sakad, levine}@cim.mcgill.ca

Abstract. The problem of face detection remains challenging because faces are non-rigid objects that have a high degree of variability with respect to head rotation, illumination, facial expression, occlusion, and aging. A novel technique that is gaining in popularity, known as Locally Linear Embedding (LLE), performs dimensionality reduction on data for learning and classification purposes. This paper presents a novel approach to the face detection problem by applying the LLE algorithm to 2D facial images to obtain their representation in a sub-space under the specific conditions stated above. The low-dimensional data are then used to train Support Vector Machine (SVM) classifiers to label windows in images as being either face or non-face. Six different databases of cropped facial images, corresponding to variations in head rotation, illumination, facial expression, occlusion and aging, were used to train and test the classifiers. Experimental results obtained demonstrated that the performance of the proposed method was similar and sometimes better when compared to other face detection methods, while using a lower amount of training images, thus indicating a viable and accurate technique.

1 Introduction

Human face detection has been researched extensively in the past decade due to the recent emergence of applications such as secure access control, visual surveillance, content-based information retrieval, and human/computer interaction. It is also the crucial first task performed in a face recognition system. Simply put, face detection is a two-class decision problem to discriminate facial patterns from background ("non-faces") at every location in an image. This is a challenging task because of the high degree of variability in factors that radically change the appearance of the face [1].

This paper proposes an appearance-based method that detects faces subject to a variety of significant conditions present in a static 2D grayscale image defined in a space of dimension D. These conditions include extreme variations in head rotation, illumination, facial expression, occlusion and aging. The approach is predicated on the hypothesis that the LLE method will intrinsically model the face for each of the six individual variations if a specific database that emphasizes a single particular characteristic is used for training. Once the facial data are transformed into a lower-dimensional space d, Support Vector Regression (SVR) is used to define a mapping from the input to the output space for these data. Thus, the SVR provides a new way to compute the location of a point in d-space, given its location in the input D-space.

H. Sundaram et al. (Eds.): CIVR 2006, LNCS 4071, pp. 221–230, 2006.
© Springer-Verlag Berlin Heidelberg 2006

We demonstrate experimentally that, if this very same SVR is used to map previously unseen *non-face* data, the latter will in general be clustered separately with respect to the specific facial data. An SVM is then used to classify new input patterns as being face or non-face. Six such classifiers were trained using six different databases that were built using different sources. The six decisions were then fused to provide a final decision. Experimental results obtained on common image databases currently referenced in the literature demonstrated that the performance of the proposed method is similar and sometimes better when compared to other face detection methods. The approach described in this paper has the advantage of using significantly less training images than other methods since LLE efficiently models the face space.

2 Locally Linear Embedding (LLE)

LLE was designed to solve the problem of many dimensionality reduction methods [2], such as PCA or *Multi-Dimensional Scaling* (MDS) [3], which would map faraway non-face images to nearby points in the face domain, creating distortions both in the local and global geometry. LLE succeeds by computing a low-dimensional embedding of high-dimensionality data assumed to lie on a non-linear manifold, with the property that nearby face images in the high dimensional space remain nearby, and similarly remain co-located with respect to one another in the low dimensional space.

2.1 LLE Algorithm

The LLE transformation algorithm is based on simple geometric intuitions, where the input data consist of N points X_i, $X_i \in R^D$, $i \in [1,N]$, each of dimensionality D, which were obtained by sampling an underlying manifold. As an output, it provides N points Y_i, $Y_i \in R^d$, $i \in [1,N]$ where $d << D$. The algorithm has three sequential steps:

Step 1. Suppose an adequate number of data points have been acquired so that the underlying manifold can be considered to be "well-sampled". Then each individual data point of this training set and its corresponding neighbors would be sufficiently close to lie within a locally linear patch on the manifold. "Well-sampled" for points on a D-dimensional manifold is assumed to mean that each data point has of order $2d$ neighbors 2, which roughly define a linear patch on the manifold. The K closest neighbors are selected for each point using the Euclidean distance.

Step 2. The second step involves solving for the manifold reconstruction *weights*. Clearly, the local geometry of the patches referred to in Step 1 can be described by linear coefficients that permit the reconstruction of every point from a knowledge of its neighbors. In order to determine the value of the weights, the reconstruction errors are measured by the cost function:

$$\varepsilon(W) = \sum_{i=1}^{N} \left\| X_i - \sum_{j=1}^{N} W_{ij} X_{ij} \right\|^2 \tag{1}$$

where X_i is a data vector and $\varepsilon(W)$ sums the squared distances between all data points and their corresponding reconstructed points. The weights W_{ij} represent the importance of the jth data point to the reconstruction of the ith element.

The most important aspect of this minimization is its respect for point symmetry; that is, any point is invariant to scale, rotation and translation. This property permits the weights to reflect the intrinsic geometric properties of each neighborhood. If the input data lie on a smooth, non-linear manifold of D-dimensions ($d<<D$), then there exists a linear transformation that maps high-dimensional coordinates in D-space to global internal coordinates in d-space. Because the reconstruction weights reflect intrinsic geometric properties, it is expected that the characterization of the local geometry in the original D-dimensional space will be replicated in a lower d- dimensional space. Furthermore, the W_{ij} weights that were used to reconstruct a data point i in D-space will also be valid for reconstructing the embedded manifold in d-space.

Step 3. The final step of the algorithm consists of mapping each high-dimensional X_i to a low-dimensional Y_i, representing the global internal coordinates using a cost function which minimizes the locally linear reconstruction errors:

$$\Phi(Y) = \sum_{i=1}^{N} \left\| Y_i - \sum_{j=1}^{N} W_{ij} Y_{ij} \right\|^2 \tag{2}$$

It is clear that the coordinates Y_i can be translated by a constant displacement without affecting the overall cost, $\Phi(Y)$. This degree of freedom is removed by requiring the coordinates to be centered at the origin, such that $\Sigma Y_i = 0$. The optimal embedding, up to a global rotation of the embedding space, is found by computing the bottom $d + 1$ eigenvectors of the matrix M. The bottom eigenvector of the matrix is the unit vector with all components equal, and represents a free translation mode of eigenvalue zero. This eigenvector is ignored as it enforces the constraint that the embeddings have zero mean. The remaining d eigenvectors form the d embedding coordinates found by LLE.

2.2 Measure for the Intrinsic Dimensionality d

A straightforward manner for estimating the quality of the input-output mapping in terms of the selected intrinsic dimensionality d is to evaluate how well the high-dimensional structure is represented in the embedded space. The residual variance ρ, defined by the distances between pairs of data points, can be used for this purpose. It is given by $\rho = 1 - r^2_{DxDy}$, where r^2_{DxDy} is the standard linear correlation coefficient taken over all entries of D_X and D_Y. D_X and D_Y represent matrices of the Euclidean distances between pairs of points in X (input points in D-space) and Y (output points computed by LLE in d-space). Therefore, the lower the residual variance, the better the high-dimensional data is represented in the embedded space. The best value of the dimension of d-space, d_{opt}, can therefore be found by the absolute minimum of ρ such that $d_{opt} = \arg\min_{d}(\rho)$.

2.3 Selecting the Neighborhood Size K

In [4], the authors present a method for determining the number of neighbors K by using the number of significant reconstruction weights used in LLE. The optimal value for K is determined on the basis of the stability of the resulting embeddings. The number of significant weights $W(K)$ is recorded for each K, $K \in [1, K_{max}]$, where

K_{max} is pre-selected as the maximum possible value. The percent increase of the number of significant weights is defined as:

$$I(K) = \frac{W(K+1) - W(K)}{W(K)} \times 100 \qquad (3)$$

and can be plotted against K. When $I(K)$ stops decreasing consistently with increasing K, the authors in [4] conclude that K is large enough to capture most local contexts and the resulting embedding space is relatively stable. Therefore, the value of K was chosen to satisfy this condition.

When obtaining the reconstruction weights W_{ij} in Step 2 of the LLE algorithm for each neighbor X_j of a data point X_i, the corresponding point X_j is considered to contribute significantly to the reconstruction of X_i, if the parameter W_{ij} satisfies $W_{ij} / W_{ij} > 0.001$. The cutoff value of 0.001 was chosen by the authors on the basis of the stability of the outcome. If this value is too small, the results may be overly sensitive to noise in the data.

2.4 Forward Mapping Using Support Vector Regression (SVR)

Wang et al. [5], in their work on multi-pose face synthesis, have proposed an analytical method based on nonlinear regression to perform mapping from one space to another. Their objective was to determine a *backward* analytical mapping from the embedded space to the original space. However, this approach can also be adapted for the *forward* mapping problem. Suppose the observation data consist of X_i, $(i = 1, 2..N)$, where i is the sample index and N is the number of samples $X_i \in R^D$, $X_i = [x_1, x_2, ..., x_D]^T$, where $x_i \in R(i=1,2,..D)$. The projection of X_i by the LLE algorithm is Y_i , $Y_i \in R^d$, where d is the dimensionality of the embedded space. Suppose each dimension of the embedded data Y_i can be regressed by:

$$Y = [y_1, y_2, ..., y_d]^T = [f_1(X), f_2(X), ..., f_d(X)]^T = F(X) \qquad (4)$$

Equation (4) provides a means of mapping new points in D-space to an embedded lower-dimensional d-space *after* the embedding of each of the six feature databases has been learnt using LLE with the specific training data. The following algorithm describes how the $f_i(X)$ are determined:

Step 1: Using a training set, apply LLE to project the facial images to a d-dimensional space, as described in Sections 2.1-2.3. The training set of facial images is chosen to emphasize a common characteristic (such as head rotation in 3D) and therefore points in the training set should share a similar structure in the observation D-space. The training databases used in our experiments are each parameterized by a different facial attribute, as described in Section 3. Thus, the $f_i(X)$ functions can model the process of dimensionality reduction for the category of faces represented by each training set.

Step 2: The function $f_i(X)$ is defined by the regression model:

$$y_i = f_i(X) = \sum_{j=1}^{N} \alpha_{ij} k(X, X_j) + b \qquad (5)$$

where X_j, $(j=1,2..N)$ are the training data, N is the number of samples in the data set, and $k(X, X_j)$ is the kernel function.

As described in [5], the optimal kernel when using SVR, as well as its corresponding parameters, must be determined in order to provide the best functions for mapping new sample points. Experiments in this study showed that the Radial Basis Function (RBF) kernel was the best for regressing the mapping models. The proper form for $f_i(X)$ can be found using training sets with a sufficient number of facial images. In order to obtain useful information for function and parameter selection, a cost function must again be defined to evaluate regression performance. The entire database is divided into two different sets, one for training (ω_1) which is used for estimating the optimal parameters, and one to evaluate the performance (ω_2). The squared-error function is defined as:

$$\phi(F) = \sum_{j=1}^{N2} \left\| Y_j - F(X_j) \right\| \tag{6}$$

where $Y_j \in j=1,2,..N_2$ and N_2 is the number of samples in the test set. The optimal kernel parameters are determined using this cost function.

Step 3: Once the proper kernel function and parameters are computed, they are considered as the *a-priori* knowledge. Then the optimal values of the parameters α_{ij} and b in Eq. (5) are obtained using SVM regression. For each of the six attribute databases, this gives the set of d functions $f_i(X)$, which denote the forward mapping from a high-dimensional D-space to d-space. The analytical mapping $Y=F(X)$ enables new images to be mapped into an embedded space using SVR. Given a new sample, X_{new}, in D-space, the corresponding point in the lower-dimensional d-space can be computed by the learnt functions:

$$Y_{new} = F(X_{new}) = \left[y_{new1},..., y_{newd} \right]^T = \left[f_1(X_{new}),..., f_d(X_{new}) \right]^T \tag{7}$$

3   Face/Non-face Classification in d-Space Using Support Vector Machines

The analytical mapping to d-space for *faces* can also be used to map *non-faces*, even though the latter were not involved in the training process to this point. The expectation for the *non-faces* is that they will cluster in a different region of d-space, separate from the *faces*. The two categories can be classified by employing an SVM. In this section we briefly sketch the SVM algorithm and its motivation.

Appearance-based methods that employ Support Vector Machines (SVMs) are rooted in learning algorithms, and have attracted much attention recently in the field of face detection, mostly because they have yielded fast and fairly robust empirical results as well as offering excellent discriminability capabilities. The basic insight behind SVM is that linear classification in the input space can be replaced by projecting the data to a higher-dimensional space in the hope of achieving a superior separating plane for the training data. This is achieved by using the so-called "kernel-trick" [6] in which the inner product $<x,x_i>$ is replaced by a kernel function $k(x,x_i)$ in Eq. (8). Since the data vectors are involved only in this inner product, the optimization can be performed in the resulting d-dimensional feature space. The classification weight vector is also defined in this feature space and will thus typically no longer correspond to an image represented by a single vector in the input space. The resulting decision functions are of the more general form:

$$f(x) = \text{sgn}(\sum_{i=1}^{m} {}_i y_i \alpha_i (\Phi(x) \cdot \Phi(x_i)) + b) = \text{sgn}(\sum_{i=1}^{m} {}_i y_i \alpha_i k(x, x_i) + b) \qquad (8)$$

where y_i are the desired outputs for the inputs x_i, α_i are Lagrange multipliers and b is a variable which ensures all constraints in the problem are respected. Figure 1 is a schematic representation of the proposed LLE face detector.

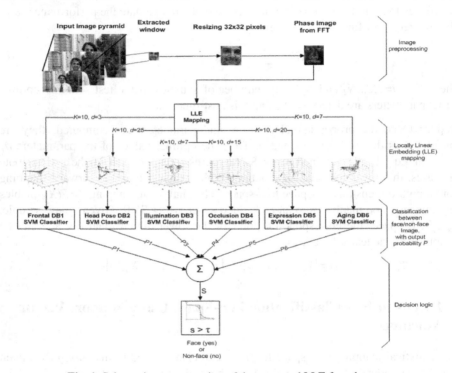

Fig. 1. Schematic representation of the proposed LLE face detector

4   Experiments

Six different facial databases were created corresponding to six feature challenges: a Frontal Database (DB1), a Head Pose Database (DB2), an Illumination Database (DB3), an Occlusion Database (DB4), an Expression Database (DB5), and an Aging Database (DB6) were used in this research, giving a total 2436 cropped images. Figure 2 gives sample facial images from each set along with their source from the Internet. Non-face images for training and testing were taken from the Viola-Jones DB [7].

A pre-processing stage is first applied to normalize and resize all of the training images. Illumination compensation was achieved by using the phase-only image obtained by FFT [12]. Then, all of the training input images (X) in the input D-dimensional space (D=1024) for each database were individually embedded in a

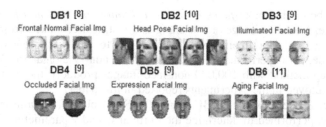

Fig. 2. Sample images in the six facial databases corresponding to six feature challenges

lower d-dimensional space using the LLE algorithm. This created a set of embedded points (Y) in d-space for each database. This mapping was then regressed using the analytical SVR method presented in Section 2.4. The six regressed models (each with a different value for d) were then used to obtain a d-dimensional representation of non-face images by mapping the latter into each of the six d-spaces. The final step was to train a classifier to distinguish between face and non-face images in each of the six d-dimensional spaces given by LLE. Thus, regression and classification models were obtained for each of the six databases in order to embed and classify new sample images. In the proposed face detection system, each of six SVM classifiers outputs a probability P that the input image is a face. The six probabilities $P1, P2, P3, P4, P5,$ and $P6$ are obtained for each input image. In this paper, the method of fusion used was the sum of the probabilities, so that $P=P1+P2+P3+P4+P5+P6$, as in [13].

To obtain the best results, experiments were first conducted on each individual attribute database to obtain the optimal parameters for the LLE (how many K number of neighbors and the best magnitude of d?) and SVM methods (the cost C and the parameters for the Radial Basis Kernel Function). The first experiment varied K while embedding in two dimensions ($d=2$). It turns out that the choice of K is independent of the intrinsic dimension d (see [14] for details). The objective was to determine the best single value of K for all six databases. For each value of K, the increase in the number of significant reconstruction weights $I(K)$ was recorded, as defined in Section 2.3. Results showed that the increase in the number of significant weights fell under 0.5% when $K=10$, thus indicating that the evolution has stabilized and the embedding space is well distributed. The next experiment used residual variance ρ to determine the optimal d-space for each of the six databases, where $d=[1,N]$, $N=30$.

The following test addressed the mapping of images (face and non-face) into the embedded space with $K=10$. This mapping is performed using the SVR analytical mapping. Optimal parameters for the RBF kernel (the C and γ parameters) associated with each database were determined using cross-validation. In this study, a "grid-search" on C and γ was performed, where pairs of (C, γ) were tested and the one with the best cross-validation accuracy was selected. Cross-validation consists of dividing the training data into N ($N=10$ was chosen) disjoint parts of equal size. For each part, a model is created from the N-1 other folds and evaluated on the remaining fold. Optimal cross-validation accuracy was obtained when $C=200$ and $\gamma=0.02$. Note that a separate analytical mapping model is required for each database *based on the individual value of d* for that particular database.

The next experiment evaluated the detection accuracy of the SVM classifier described in Section 3 using a Leave-One-Out (LOO) procedure [15]. This classifier distinguishes between frontal *faces in ambient illumination* and *non-face images* in the LLE space. Non-face images for training and testing were taken from the Viola-Jones database [7]. Experiments were carried out to study the sensitivity of the ultimate face detection performance to the size of the non-face database. It was found that a bootstrap method with 100,000 non-face images produced the best results and these were employed in the experiments reported in this paper.

The last experiment used an RBF kernel for SVM classifier training and cross-validation was performed to determine the optimal C and γ parameters for the two-class problem. Given these optimal parameters, a full comparison between the method reported in this paper and a PCA face detection approach (based on the *Karhunen-Loeve Transform*) was performed. Experiments on each of the six attribute database classifiers showed that the proposed LLE method outperforms the PCA approach in each case (Table 1). In particular, it demonstrates the inability of the PCA method to cope with variations in head pose (DB2), which is clearly not the case for LLE (see [14]).

Table 1. Optimal parameters and detection results for all six facial feature challenges. FPR (false positives rate); FNR (false negatives rate); TPR (true positives rate); TNR (true negatives rate). A comparison of the detection accuracy between LLE and PCA is also presented.

DB	d	K	TPR	TNR	FPR	FNR	Accuracy LLE	Accuracy PCA
DB1	3	10	91.1	99.9	0.1	8.8	99.1	98.2
DB2	25	10	96.5	99.2	3.4	0.8	98.9	94.4
DB3	7	10	100	100	0.0	0.0	100	98.1
DB4	15	10	97.6	100	2.3	0.0	99.7	97.1
DB5	20	10	97.6	100	2.3	0.0	99.6	97.2
DB6	7	10	97.0	100	2.9	0.0	99.6	97.1

5 Face Detection Results

The proposed LLE face detector was tested on the images from the MIT-CMU database [16]. The resulting ROC curve was plotted along with two other results obtained by the Rowley-Kanade system [16] and the Viola-Jones method [7], which have also been tested on the MIT-CMU database. These curves provide an opportunity to assess and compare the performance of the proposed LLE method to other techniques.

The images were scanned at multiple scales and locations. Good results were obtained by increasing the size of the scanning window by a factor of 1.2 at successive scales. For each size, the detector sequentially visited all image locations and the extracted windows were input to the LLE face detector. Sequential locations in an image were obtained by shifting the window by Δ pixels. The scale s of the scanning window affects this shifting process: for example, if the scale of the detector is set at s_l, then the window should be shifted by $s_l\Delta$. The choice of Δ affects both the speed as well as the accuracy of the detector. The authors in [7] showed that $\Delta=1.5$ provided a significant speedup with only a slight decrease in accuracy. In our experiments, 75,081,800 sub-windows were scanned to test the MIT-CMU database.

The ROC curves in Figure 3 shows that the proposed LLE face detection method clearly outperforms the Rowley-Kanade system, which is based on a set of neural

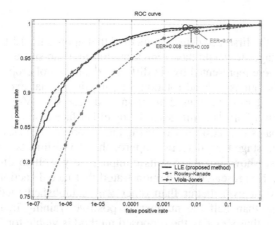

Fig. 3. ROC curves (log scale on the horizontal axis) for the proposed LLE face detector, the Rowley-Kanade system [16] and the Viola-Jones method [7] (on the MIT-CMU DB)

networks, and compares very well with the Viola-Jones face detection method. For a detection rate of 90%, the proposed method generates 71 false alarms, compared to the best system presented by Rowley-Kanade in [16] with 167 false alarms. When comparing at a detection rate of 97%, the LLE method in this paper generates 3750 false alarms, compared to 6520 for the Viola-Jones method. Finally, the proposed LLE method yields a slightly lower Equal Error Rate (EER) compared to the Viola-Jones method (0.08 versus 0.09) (see Figure 3). Furthermore LLE used less than half the number of positive training images used by Viola-Jones (2436 versus 4916), indicating the capability of LLE to efficiently model the face space. Some examples of the performance of LLE on the MIT-CMU database are shown in Figure 4.

It is important to note that perhaps the comparison between LLE and Viola-Jones is not quite appropriate. This database was used in order to make a comparison with the other methods but clearly it does not demand as high a performance level as our LLE method is capable of achieving. This is because of LLE's use of classifiers specifically directed at particular facial image features.

Fig. 4. Results using the proposed LLE face detector

6 Conclusion

This paper presents the first face detection method that applies the LLE algorithm to 2D facial gray scale images to obtain their representation in a sub-space under six different conditions. These were represented by six different databases of cropped facial images, corresponding to variations in head rotation, illumination, facial expression, occlusion and aging. The databases were used to train and test six SVM classifiers which characterized patterns of pixels in images as being either face or non-face.

The paper evaluates the feasibility of using the combined efficacy of the six SVM classifiers in a two-stage face detection approach. Experiments conducted on the MIT-CMU database show that the results compare very well to other popular face detection methods. This research has demonstrated that face detection accuracy using LLE is similar and or even better than other well-established methods, while, for example, using less than half the number of positive training images used in the Viola-Jones method, thus showing the proposed method is viable for face detection.

References

1. M.-H. Yang, D. Kriegman, and N. Ahuja, "Detecting Faces in Images: A Survey", *IEEE Trans. on Pattern Analysis and Machine Intelligence*, 24(1):34-58, 2002.
2. S. Roweis, L. Saul, "Nonlinear Dimensionality Reduction by LLE", *Science*,vol.290, 2000.
3. T. Cox and M. Cox, *Multidimensional Scaling*, Chapman & Hall, London, 1994.
4. F. Katagiri and J. Glazebrook, "Local Context Finder (LCF) reveals multidimensional relationships among mRNA expression profiles of Arabidopsis responding to pathogen infection", *Proc. Natl. Acad. Sci.*, pp. 10842-10847, 2003.
5. J. Wang, Z. Changshui, and K. Zhongbao, "An Analytical Mapping for LLE and Its Application in Multi-Pose Face Synthesis", *14th British Machine Vision Conf.*, 2003.
6. V. Vapnik, *The nature of statistical learning theory*, 2nd Edition, Springer-Verlag, 1997.
7. P. Viola and M. Jones, "Rapid Object Detection Using a Boosted Cascade of Simple Features", *CVPR*, 2001.
8. J. Min, P. Flynn, and K. Bowyer, "Assessment of time dependency in face recognition," *TR-04-12, University of Notre Dame*, 2004
9. A. Martinez and R. Benavente, "The AR face database", *Technical Report 24, Computer Vision Center (CVC)*, Barcelona, Spain, 1998.
10. D.B. Graham and N.M. Allinson, "Characterizing Virtual Eigensignatures for General Purpose Face Recognition", *Face Recognition: From Theory to Applications, Computer and Systems Sciences*, vol. 163, pp. 446-456, 1998.
11. M. Gandhi, "A Method for Automatic Synthesis of Aged Human Facial Images", *Master Thesis,* McGill Univ., 2004.
12. P. Kovesi, "Symmetry and Asymmetry From Local Phase", *Joint Conf. on A.I.*, 1997.
13. A. Ross and A. Jain, "Information fusion in biometrics", *Pattern Recognition Letters 24*, pp. 2115–2125, 2003.
14. S. Kadoury, "Face Detection using Locally Linear Embeddings", *Master Thesis*, McGill Univ., 2005.
15. A. Shilton, M. Palaniswami, D. Ralph, and A. Tsoi, "Incremental Training of Support Vector Machines", *IEEE Trans. on Neural Networks*, 16(1):114-131, 2005.
16. H. Rowley, S. Baluja, and T. Kanade, "Neural Network-Based Face Detection," *IEEE Trans. on Pattern Analysis and Machine Intelligence*, 20(1):23-38, 1998.

ROI-Based Medical Image Retrieval Using Human-Perception and MPEG-7 Visual Descriptors

MiSuk Seo, ByoungChul Ko, Hong Chung, and JaeYeal Nam

Dept. of Computer Engineering, Keimyung University, Daegu, Korea
{forever10047, niceko, hjung, jynam}@kmu.ac.kr

Abstract. In this paper, we present a ROI (Region-Of-Interest)-based medical image retrieval system that is considering combination of feature descriptors and initial weights for similarity matching. For semantic ROI segmentation, we create attention window (AW) to remove the meaningless regions included in the image such as background and propose a quad-tree based ROI segmentation method. In addition, in order to improve the retrieval performance and consider human perception, initial weights for feature distances are also proposed. From, several experiments, we demonstrate that the ROI-based method having different initial weights shows the better performance than previous related methods.

1 Introduction

In a medical field, huge medical images are being digitized as one database with the PACS (Picture Archiving Communication System) and many researches have been focusing on medical image retrieval. Medical image has different meaning according to the eye of the observer and has different color structure according to a dyeing material. Furthermore it has one or more ROIs (Region-Of-Interest), which have important information, and has monotonous background. MPEG-7 Descriptor describes specific feature information of the image and it affects the retrieval performance according to the characteristic of the image. Furthermore because it extracts features and calculate the similarity from overall images, it cannot retrieve medical image efficiently due to the effect of non-ROI parts. Therefore it is necessary to extract ROIs and describe features efficiently through the combination of each descriptor.

There are several medical image retrieval systems using MPEG-7 descriptors. CONTEXT [1] retrieval system represented contours and textures by a vector in order to obtain an effective method for content-based image indexing. Brodatz textures and medical images were used to evaluate retrieval performance. The homogeneous treatment reserved to both contour and texture information made the algorithm elegant and easy to implement and extend. PARIS (Personal Archiving and Retrieving Image System) [2] is a personal photograph library, which includes amount of consumer photographs, metadata description based Dozen Dimensional Digital Content (DDDC) extended MPEG-7 multimedia description schema. Cell

H. Sundaram et al. (Eds.): CIVR 2006, LNCS 4071, pp. 231–240, 2006.
© Springer-Verlag Berlin Heidelberg 2006

Bank System [3] was designed for retrieving breast carcinoma images. This system constructed numeric data of extracted color and texture features of objective properties and then stored them in XML type for MPEG-7 based retrieval standard system. In addition, this system can be used in various applications include breast carcinoma diagnosis, cell characteristic analysis and pathological image training via internet.

In this paper, we present a ROI-based medical image retrieval system using MPEG-7 descriptors. Our ROI-based retrieval system segments multiple ROIs coarsely according to the both attention window and quad-tree, then it extracts color, texture and shape features. Extracted feature vectors are all combined and each ROI has initial important weights for similarity matching according to their saliency intensity.

Figure 1 shows system architecture of the proposed methods.

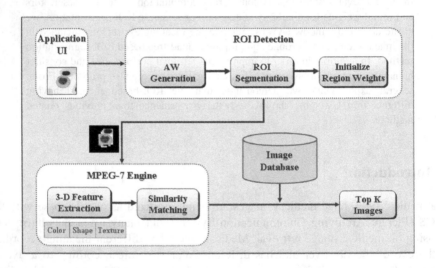

Fig. 1. System architecture of the proposed methods

2   ROI Detection Based on Human-Perception

In general, because object-based image segmentation is beyond current computer vision technique and an object is a group of the related regions, we detect ROIs without image segmentation. To do this, we first create an Attention Window within an image by using both luminance map and saliency points. Itti *et al.* [4] proposed a saliency-based visual attention model and select the most salient area with a WTA (Winner-Take-All) competition. In this paper, we only use luminance feature map among several feature maps to detect ROIs. In medical images, since the intensity is the unique component while color can be changed according to the dyeing material, we do not use color feature map. To generate luminance map ($\overline{L}$), different sized filters $s \in \{11 \times 11, 13 \times 13\}$ are applied to the 1/2 down-sampled gray image L. The filter estimates the center-surround difference between the center-point and the surrounding points within the filter scale s and this difference yields the feature map. In Equation (1), $L(s)$ is the luminance difference map of a down-sampled image between the center-point and the surrounding points with the filter sizes 11x11 and 13x13. When using Equation (1), two feature maps are produced from two filters. These maps are then summed and normalized into one feature map $\overline{L}$, which is then up-sampled to the size of the original image and smoothed with a Gaussian filter to eliminate any pixel-level noise and highlight the neighborhood of influence for the output.

$$\overline{L} = \frac{1}{2}(\sum_{s \in \{11 \times 11, 13 \times 13\}} L \otimes s) \tag{1}$$

In order to create accurate AW, we also extract the saliency points as well as luminance map. Saliency points are a set of "interesting points" within an image that exist in both a corner-like area and a high signal variation occurrence area. We use a wavelet based saliency point detection method [5] to extract saliency points where severe variations occur in an image such as corner and edge.

2.1 Attention Window Creation

After generating the luminance map and extracting the saliency points, the AW needs to be created, which removes useless regions from the image, such as background, thereby reducing the amount of processing time required for segmenting ROIs. As such, the size of the AW is important. In this paper, we propose a top-down AW shrinking method that uses both the luminance map and saliency points. The initial size of the AW is determined as three quarters of the image then this size is reduced until it meets predefined conditions. The initial size of the AW was determined by experiment, where the largest ROI in the experimental database was found to be less than three quarters of the image size. To determine the proper location of the AW, the window with the maximum number of saliency points for the full image is initially chosen then the size of the AW is shrunk to the approximate size of the ROI one pixel at a time. That is, if the boundary position (x, y) of the AW is not the saliency point S_P and if the luminance map value L_m of the boundary position (x, y) is under the predefined threshold T_{L_m}, the size of the AW is repeatedly shrunk from the original AW until it meets the optimal condition from left to right and up to down.

The predefined threshold is estimated based on the mean of L_m within the AW.

```
Top-down AW Shrinking
CAW: Center of AW
1.  Initialize the size of AW
    AWx = 3*width/4;
    AWy = 3*height/4;
2.  Find the candidate position of AW
    AW = Max (SUM (Sp));
3.  T_Lm = Mean_of_Lm;
4.  Repeat
    Shrink one boundary pixel of AW
    Decide a new CAW at center position of AW
    Until Lm_of_xy <T_Lm && Value_xy != Sp
5.  Decide the final position of AW
```

Figure 2-(c) gives some examples of final AWs. In the case of multiple ROIs, the AW that contains all objects is chosen. After the AW is established, ROI segmentation based on quad-tree is applied.

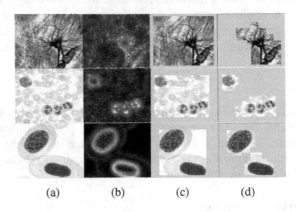

(a)   (b)   (c)   (d)

Fig. 2. ROI segmentation results (a) input image (b) luminance map (c) Attention Window (d) segmented ROIs

2.2 ROI Segmentation Based on Quad-Tree

Even though image segmentation is one of the first steps used in an image analysis, extracting semantic ROI automatically and precisely is still beyond the reach of current computer vision due to the uncontrolled nature of images. Therefore, we use the quad-tree in order to segment coarse ROIs in a shorter time within the AW by using luminance map. Quad-tree was used for image segmentation in previous researches [8-9].

Unlike the previous researches, we only segment ROIs within the limited AW and use the luminance map as a condition of image decomposition. The segmentation steps and conditions are follows:

(1) The average of luminance map is calculated within the AW and the AW is divided into 4x4 scale1 sub-blocks. The average is used for threshold to divide next sub-blocks.
(2) For each sub-block, if the average of luminance map of each sub-block is over the threshold, then sub-block is decomposed into four scale2 sub-blocks again and otherwise that sub-block is removed. That is, if the average of luminance map is below, it means that the sub-block has a lower chance to contain salient regions.
(3) This process is repeated at scale3.
(4) Finally, scale3 sub-blocks merged into adjacent big sub-blocks and they are removed, if they are far from major regions.

Figure 3 shows the process of proposed segmentation method.

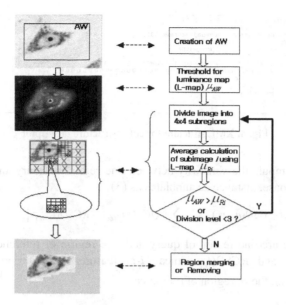

Fig. 3. ROI segmentation steps using a quad-tree

3 MPEG-7 Visual Descriptors

There are several visual descriptors defined by MPEG-7 to describe color, texture, shape of images and video. Color descriptors describe the color distribution, color layout and spatial color structure of an image and show invariant characteristic for image rotation, cropping and distortion. In texture descriptors, an image can be considered as a mosaic of homogeneous textures so that these texture features associated with the regions can be used to index the image data. Shape descriptors can be used in trademark and e-commerce, where it is difficult to use a text index to specify the required shape of the object. In this paper, we use three MPEG-7 descriptors [6] such as Color Structure Descriptors (CSD) for color, Edge Histogram Descriptors (EHD) for texture and Region Shape Descriptor (RSD) for shape from extracted one or more ROIs.

3.1 Color: Color Structure Descriptor (CSD)

Color Structure Descriptor (CSD) represents color distribution of the image similar to a color histogram and the local spatial structure of the color. This feature about color structure makes the descriptor sensitive to certain features to which the color CS is blind. Specifically, the CSD is a 1D array of eight bit-quantized values as (2)

$$CSD = \overline{h}_s(m), \quad m \in \{1,...,M\} \tag{2}$$

Where M is chosen from the set $\{256, 128, 64, 32\}$ and where s is scale of the associated square structuring element.

In this paper, compact 32 bins of CSD are used to describe ROI region. Also, extracted feature vector can be defined as a valid form of MPEG-7 DDL (Description Definition Language) as Figure 4.

```
<?xml version="1.0" encoding="ISO-8859-1" ?>
- <Mpeg7 xmlns="urn:mpeg:mpeg7:schema:2001" xmlns:xsi="http://www.w3.org/2001/XMLSchema-instance"
    xsi:schemaLocation="urn:mpeg:mpeg7:schema:2001 .\Mpeg7-2001.xsd">
  - <Description xsi:type="ContentEntityType">
    - <MultimediaContent xsi:type="ImageType">
      - <Image>
        - <VisualDescriptor xsi:type="ColorStructureType" colorQuant="1">
            <Values>0 0 0 255 0 0 0 248 0 0 0 0 0 0 0 0 0 0 0 0 0 59 0 0 0 0 0 0 0 0</Values>
          </VisualDescriptor>
        </Image>
      </MultimediaContent>
    </Description>
  </Mpeg7>
```

Fig. 4. XML structure for color structure descriptor

In order to compute the similarity between one region of query and one region of reference of database, distance accumulates as (3).

$$Diff\_CSD(qc,rc)_{(Q,R)} = \sum_{i=0}^{31} \left| QCSD(i)_{(qc)} - RCSD(i)_{(rc)} \right| \qquad (3)$$

Where qc and rc are one region of query and one region of reference, respectively. And $QCSD(i)_{(qc)}$ and $RCSD(i)_{(rc)}$ mean i-th feature vectors representing the qc region of query and the rc region of reference.

3.2 Texture: Edge Histogram Descriptor (EHD)

The EHD represents the local edge distribution of edges in each divided sub-image. The image is defined by dividing the image into 4*4 sub-images.

In this paper, 1100 image-blocks are used to extract local edge histogram. 80 bins of EHD describe ROI of the medical images. Extracted feature vector can be defined as a valid form of MPEG-7 DDL (Description Definition Language) as Figure 5.

```
<?xml version="1.0" encoding="ISO-8859-1" ?>
- <Mpeg7 xmlns="http://www.mpeg7.org/2001/MPEG-7_Schema" xmlns:xsi="http://www.w3.org/2000/10/XMLSchema-instance">
  - <DescriptionUnit xsi:type="DescriptorCollectionType">
    - <Descriptor xsi:type="EdgeHistogramType">
        <BinCounts>1 2 3 4 0 0 2 2 2 0 2 0 1 7 1 3 2 3 4 0 2 0 4 0 0 2 0 3 2 3 2 1 3 2 4 1 2 3 7 1 0 1 5 0 0 1 2 3 5 2 1 1 3 3 1 2 2 6 5 5
        0 0 0 0 1 1 4 2 1 0 2 1 3 0 1 4 0 6 3</BinCounts>
      </Descriptor>
    </DescriptionUnit>
  </Mpeg7>
```

Fig. 5. XML structure for edge histogram descriptor

In order to compute the similarity using EHD between one region of query and one region of reference of database, distance accumulates as (4).

$$Diff\_EHD(qc,rc)_{(Q,R)} = \sum_{i=0}^{79} \left| QEHD(i)_{(qc)} - REHD(i)_{(rc)} \right| \qquad (4)$$

Where qc and rc are one region of query and one region of reference, respectively. And $QEHD(i)_{(qc)}$ and $REHD(i)_{(rc)}$ mean i-th feature vectors representing the qc region of a query and the rc region of a reference.

3.3 Shape: Region Shape Descriptor (RSD)

For shape descriptor, we use an Angular Radial Transform (ART). The ART descriptor is defined as a set of normalized magnitudes of complex ART coefficients.

To keep the size to a minimum, quantization is applied to each coefficient and 35 magnitudes are used for ART descriptor [6]. The distance ($Diff\_RSD$) between shape of ROI (qc) and shape of reference region (rc) is calculating using an L-1 norm.

$$Diff\_RSD(qc, rc)_{(Q,R)} = \sum_{i=0}^{34} | M(i)_{(qc)} - M(i)_{(rc)} | \qquad (5)$$

Where $M(i)_{(qc)}$ and $M(i)_{(rc)}$ mean magnitude of query and reference, respectively.

```
<?xml version="1.0" encoding="ISO-8859-1" ?>
- <Mpeg7 xmlns="http://www.mpeg7.org/2001/MPEG-7_Schema" xmlns:xsi="http://www.w3.org/2000/10/XMLSchema-instance">
  - <DescriptionUnit xsi:type="DescriptorCollectionType">
    - <Descriptor xsi:type="RegionShapeType">
        <MagnitudeOfART>13 15 10 11 14 12 12 9 14 12 11 11 8 3 3 7 7 7 3 9 12 4 9 13 5 12 7 0 8 10 3 8 11 7 3</MagnitudeOfART>
      </Descriptor>
    </DescriptionUnit>
  </Mpeg7>
```

Fig. 6. XML structure for shape descriptor

4 Similarity Matching

To evaluate the similarity between two images, their feature vectors must be normalized over a common interval to place equal emphasis on every feature score since the single distance may be defined on widely varying intervals [7]. Three feature vectors (color, texture and shape) are normalized as soon as features are extracted from segmented ROIs, before they are used for distance estimation. For feature normalization, the Gaussian normalization method is used.

After ROIs are extracted, three feature vectors for descriptors are also extracted. Then, one ROI in the query image has $1: N$ distances (for example, in Figure 7, $Q1$ against $Ref1, Ref2,$ and $Ref3$) and only one region that have the smallest distance less than a pre-filtering threshold, is added to a candidate reference set R_c (in Figure 7, $R_c = \{Ref1, Ref3\}$). Therefore, even though some regions are inserted in target image, if their features are not almost the same with query ROI, the number of candidate reference set is the same or less than the number of query set. In addition, if one region is labeled as a candidate region, it is removed from candidate reference set to avoid selecting twice at one time.

After ROIs and their reference set are determined, we estimate the initial important weights (w_i) for feature distance according to their saliency. To determine the saliency between ROIs, we use the luminance map, which is one of characteristics of

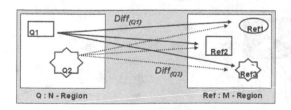

Fig. 7. An example of finding a candidate reference set R_c. Because $Ref2$ has the shorter distance than $Ref2$ and $Ref3$, it is added to R_c. $Ref3$ is added to R_c according to the same manner.

human perception. We first calculate the variation v_i of each ROI using luminance map i. The higher variance means the more important ROI. Then, the relative weights for feature distance are estimated by following Equation (6).

$$w_i = \exp(v_i) \bigg/ \sum_{i=1}^{N} \exp(v_i) \tag{6}$$

Where N represents the number of ROI. The exponential weighting is more sensitive to changes in local feature, and gives rise to a better performance improvement. Finally, each three-feature distance (Equation (7)) is linearly summed into a single measure (S) with their weights (8).

$$Diff_i = Diff\_CSD_i + Diff\_EHD_i + Diff\_RSD_i \tag{7}$$

$$S(q,t) = \frac{1}{N} \sum_{i=1}^{N} (w_i \cdot Diff_i) \cdot \tag{8}$$

5   Experimental Results

In our retrieval system, the actual matching process is to search for the k elements in the stored image set closest to the query image. After a ROI (or ROIs) is segmented, the user queries an image that he/she wants to search. The user can choose just one ROI or multiple ROIs simultaneously. A user can choose color, texture and shape feature constraints in order to search regions more precisely. From the calculated distance, the final distance is estimated by Equation (8) and the top k-nearest images are displayed in ascending order of the final distance $S(q,t)$. Figure 8 shows the user interface of the proposed ROI-based medical image retrieval system.

We have performed extensive experiments using a set of 3459 bio-images covering plant cells, animal cells and histology taken from microscope without pre-selected categories. The experiment is carried out on 28 query images (1~10: plant cells,

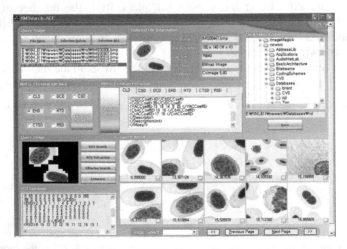

Fig. 8. User interface of the proposed ROI-based medical image retrieval system supporting dynamic feature descriptors

11~19: animal cells, 20~28: histology). Each query image has 14 ground-truths. The ground-truths are a set of visually similar images for a given query image. To measure the retrieval accuracy, we use NMRR (Normalized Modified Retrieval Rank) and ANMRR, which is average version of NMRR instead of Precision/Recall [6]. NMRR considers error between vectors and evaluates order simultaneously and takes a value between 0 and 1. If ANMRR and NMRR values lie close to 0, the performance is better and the performance is worse as it approaches 1.

The experiments are carried out on thirty cell images. First, we compare the retrieval performance between a proposed ROI-based method having the same feature weights with common CBIR methods [1-3] using full image. Two methods are using the same feature descriptors.

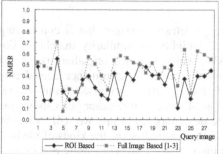 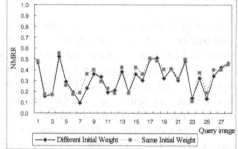

Fig. 9. Performance comparison between proposed ROI-based method and full image-based method

Fig. 10. The NMRR comparison between proposed system with the different initial weights and proposed system with the same initial weights

As we can see from Figure 9, because a ROI-based method removes the meaningless background and retrieve images based on only important regions, it shows better performance. Furthermore, when only one dominant ROI is extracted, the retrieval performance is more efficient because it decreases the error originated from background. However when multiple ROIs are extracted, the performance is almost same with the full image-based method.

Second, we compare the proposed method using three descriptors with proposed method using individual feature descriptor to find out which feature descriptor is most appropriate for medical image. Table 1 shows the combinational representation of features makes image retrieval more efficient and robust even though individual features are attractive for image retrieval descriptors. Among three individual descriptors, EHD shows the best performance and RSD shows the worst performance. However, EHD shows the irregular retrieval performance according to the change of size of ROIs while CSD shows the regular performance regardless of the variation of ROI size.

Third, we test that our initial important weights have an affect on retrieval performance when multiple ROIs are segmented. As we can see from Figure 10, proposed initial weights shows better retrieval performance because it gives semantic initial weights to each ROI and improves the final distance towards a reasonable direction.

Table 1. Average performance comparison between ROI with three descriptors and ROI with individual descriptors

Method	ANMRR
ROI + Three Descriptors	0.3347
ROI + CSD 1-Descriptor	0.4641
ROI + EHD 1-Descriptor	0.4475
ROI + RSD 1-Descriptor	0. 5082
Full image with CSD+EHD Descriptors [1-3]	0.3906

6 Conclusion

This paper presents a ROI-based medical image retrieval system that is considering combination of feature descriptors and initial weights for similarity matching. For semantic ROI segmentation, we proposed AW, which is based on salient point and saliency map. In addition, in order to improve the retrieval performance considering human perception, initial weights for feature distances are also proposed. From, several experiments, we found out that the combination of three feature descriptors shows the best performance than using individual feature descriptor. In future, we will focus our research on more precise ROI segmentation method regardless of the kinds of medical images and relevance feedback method capturing the user's intension more precisely.

Acknowledgement. This work was supported by the grant No. RTI04-01-01 from the Regional Technology Innovation Program of the Ministry of Commerce, Industry and Energy (MOCIE).

References

1. Sistasi, R., nappi, M., Tucci, M., Vitulano, S.: "CONTEXT: A Technique for Image Retrieval Integrating CONtour and TEXTure Information", Image Analysis and Processing (2001) 224-229
2. Kuo P-J and Aoki, T., H.: "PARIS: A Personal Archiving and Retrieving Image System", Information and Telecommunication Technologies, (2005) 122-125
3. Choi H-K, Hwang H-G, Kim M-K and Kim T-Y: "Design of the breast carcinoma cell bank system", Enterprise Networking and Computing in Healthcare Industry, (2004) 88-91
4. Itti L., Koch C. and Niebur E., "A Model of Saliency-based Visual Attention for Rapid Scene Analysis," IEEE Trans. on PAI, Vol.20, (1998) 1254- 1259.
5. Loupias, E., Sebe, N.: Wavelet-based salient points for image retrieval. In Research Report RR 99.11.
6. Manjunath B.S. *et al.*: Introduction to MPEG-7, John Willey&Sons, Ltd (2002).
7. Ko B.C. and Byun H.: "FRIP: A Region-based Image Retrieval Tool Using Automatic Image Segmentation and Stepwise Boolean AND Matching", IEEE Transaction on Multimedia, Vol. 7. Issue 1, (2005) 105-113.
8. Smith J. R. and Chang S-F.: "Quad-tree segmentation for texture-based image query", ACM Multimedia, (1994) 279-286.
9. Chen Y. and Leedham G.: "Decompose algorithm for thresholding degraded historical document images", IEE Proc.-Vis. Image Signal process, Vol. 152, (2005) 702-714.

Hierarchical Hidden Markov Model for Rushes Structuring and Indexing

Chong-Wah Ngo, Zailiang Pan, and Xiaoyong Wei

Department of Computer Science,
City University of Hong Kong, Kowloon, Hong Kong
{cwngo, zerin, xiaoyong}@cs.cityu.edu.hk

Abstract. Rushes footage are considered as cheap gold mine with the potential for reuse in broadcasting and filmmaking industries. However, it is difficult to mine the "gold" from the rushes since usually only minimum metadata is available. This paper focuses on the structuring and indexing of the rushes to facilitate mining and retrieval of "gold". We present a new approach for rushes structuring and indexing based on motion feature. We model the problem by a two-level Hierarchical Hidden Markov Model (HHMM). The HHMM, on one hand, represents the semantic concepts in its higher level to provide simultaneous structuring and indexing, on the other hand, models the motion feature distributions in its lower level to support the encoding of the semantic concepts. The encouraging experimental results on TRECVID'05 BBC rushes demonstrate the effectiveness of our approach.

1 Introduction

In the broadcasting and filmmaking industries, *rushes* is a term for raw footage, which is used to generate the final productions such as TV programs and movies. Only a small portion of the rushes is actually used in the final productions. The "shoot-to-show" ratio, such as in BBC TV, ranges from 20 to 40. The producers see these large amount of raw footage as cheap gold mine. The "gold" refers to *stock* footage which is the "generic" clips with high potentials for reuse. However cataloguing the stock footage is a tedious task, since rushes is unstructured and relatively inaccessible with only a minimum metadata such as program/department name and date. Therefore, it becomes necessary to develop techniques for the structuring, indexing and retrieval of rushes.

In the past decades, researches on video representation and analysis are mainly founded on edited videos, e.g., news, sports and movies. The edited videos are highly structured. More importantly, multiple modalities such as textual, auditory and visual modalities are available for analysis in edited videos. The performance of most state-of-the-art video retrieval systems (e.g, Informedia project [1]) depends on the fusion of these modalities, especially the textual information which mainly comes from the captions and speech transcripts by OCR and ASR respectively. In contrast to edited videos, rushes are characterized by unstructured, natural sounds only and few or no on-screen texts. Thus little textual

H. Sundaram et al. (Eds.): CIVR 2006, LNCS 4071, pp. 241–250, 2006.
© Springer-Verlag Berlin Heidelberg 2006

information can be acquired from rushes. These characteristics present a new aspect of research challenge for rushes retrieval.

In TRECVID'05 [2], several rushes retrieval techniques have been presented in the pilot task of BBC rushes exploration. All of them are mainly based on visual information as other modalities are absent or difficult to obtain. Allen and Petrushin [3] indexed the rushes shots by "visual words" which are the cluster centroid of color, texture and color+texture. The approach proposed by Foley et al [4] considered the color and texture features extracted from each keyframe, as well as the color, texture and shape of the semi-automatically segmented objects. The system allows the user to select features from either frame or object for retrieval. Snoek et al [5] re-attempted their MediaMill system, which is originally trained to index the 101 high-level concepts for news, to analyze the BBC rushes. These approaches basically port the retrieval system developed originally for edited videos directly to the rushes domain. Some issues peculiar to in rushes are not addressed, such as how to detect and manage the redundant footage due to low visual quality or unwanted motion. Ngo et al [6] attempted to solve this problem from the motion point of view. They tested three different approaches, Finite State Machine (FSM), Support Vector Machine (SVM) and Hidden Markov Model (HMM) for the characterization of BBC Rushes.

The main focus of this paper is to locate and index the stock footage. We consider three semantic categories: *stock*, *outtake* and *shaky*. The concept *stock* represents the clips with intentional camera motion which have the potential for reuse, such as capturing an event with still camera and rotating the camera for a panoramic view. In contrast, those clips with intermediate camera motion, which are very likely to be discarded in the final production, are denoted as *outtake*. Examples include a zoom to get more details and a pan to change to another perspective. Beside those two extreme cases, we add another category, *shaky*, to represent the shaky artifacts which may be discarded or used for special effects such as to show a emergent situation. For rushes indexing, shot is usually regarded as the basic unit [3,4,5]. However, since the rushes are raw footage without editing, a shot may consist of different semantic concepts. Thus, in order to index rushes effectively, the temporal structure of rushes needs to be carefully analyzed so that the basic unit can be a subshot, and each subshot contains only one semantic label.

The problem of structuring and indexing is intertwined in rushes. The difficulty comes from the following two aspects. One aspect is that the motion features of the three semantic categories are highly overlapped. For example, a pan motion may come from a *stock* of side view on a moving vehicle, or a *outtake* of perspective change, or a *shaky* of one part of swing. The other aspect is that structuring and indexing rely on each other. Indexing requires the investigation of the temporal structure. As mentioned, an unstructured shot in rushes may be too long to be an appropriate unit for indexing. On the other hand, it is also infeasible to structure the videos without knowing the underlying characteristic of frames. For example, structuring only by motion cannot obtain satisfied performance due to the indiscriminate motion features of the three semantic concepts.

In this paper, we propose a new approach for structuring and indexing the rushes footage by Hierarchical Hidden Markov Model (HHMM) [7,8,9]. HHMM is the generalization of HMM with hierarchical structure. We use a two-level HHMM to encode the three semantic categories and model the sequential changes of their underlying motion features. Higher-level substates represent the semantic concepts, *stock*, *outtake* and *shaky*. Each of these substates is a sub-HMM that has its own substates in the lower level to describe the distribution of the motion features and their transitions. This hierarchical model, on one hand, can alleviate the feature overlap problem by taking into account the temporal constraint. For instance, an *outtake* pan can be distinguished from a *shaky* pan by considering that a *shaky* pan is very likely to have reverse motions before and after. On the other hand, the higher-level substates, which address the semantic concepts, make it possible to simultaneously structure and index the rushes on the whole sequence. The simultaneous decision on the whole sequence provides a way to decouple the interdependency between structuring and indexing.

The remaining of this paper is organized as follows. Section 2 describes our approach for rushes structuring and indexing. We first extract the motion features as the observation for each subshot. A two-level HHMM is then applied to model both the high-level concepts and the low-level motion features to structure and index the rushes. Section 3 presents the experiment results. Finally, Section 4 concludes the paper and discusses future work.

2   Rushes Structuring and Indexing by Hierarchical HMM

Figure 1 illustrates our two-level HHMM structure. On the top is the root state which is an auxiliary substate to make the structure representable by a single tree. The first level is a sub-HMM which has three substates to represent *stock*, *outtake* and *shaky* respectively. Each substate is also a sub-HMM which is further decomposed into several substates in the lower level. Basically a substate in this level models certain aspect of low-level feature to support the encoding of semantic concepts at the higher level. For each semantic concept, we use six substates, *left*, *right*, *up*, *down*, *in* and *out*, to model the six major movements respectively in horizontal, vertical and depth directions. Notice that the substates in each sub-HMM are fully connected. For the simplicity of presenting the figure, we do not show the edges in Figure 1.

In order to facilitate structuring and indexing, a shot in rushes should be partitioned into shorter unit, i.e. subshots. In practice, the subshot string of a shot forms an observation sequence for HHMM. The subshot should not be too long so as not to mix different semantic concepts. Meanwhile, it should not be too short in order to extract robust motion feature. In this paper, we investigate two kinds of subshot: *fixed* and *adaptive*. The former one is obtained through equal partitioning of a shot into segments of fixed length. Adaptive subshots, on the

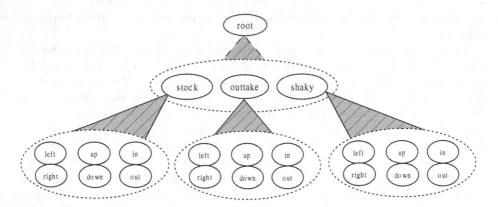

Fig. 1. An illustration of an HHMM of two levels. Solid ellipses denote the substates, while dotted ellipses denote the sub-HMMs of the HHMM structure.

other hand, are obtained by dividing a shot into segments each with consistent motion [10]. Both types of subshots have their strength and weakness. The fixed subshot is easy to obtain in practice, but with inaccurate subshot boundary and motion feature. Intuitively, adaptive subshot may have better performance due to good boundary and motion feature. However, since subshot segmentation by motion itself is a research issue, false and missed detections would introduce under or over segmented subshots that prohibit the finding of underlying semantic labels. For both fixed and adaptive schemes, over-segmentation at early stage can be remedied by HHMM if two adjacent segments have the same semantic labels. Under-segmentation, however, cannot be dealt with by HHMM.

2.1 HHMM Representation

A state in an HHMM actually consists of a string of substates from top to bottom levels. To denote the substate string from top to level d, we use a bar notation,

$$k^d = q_{1:d} = \overline{q_1 q_2 \cdots q_d}, \tag{1}$$

where the subscripts denote the hierarchical levels. We drop the superscript d for abbreviation when there is no confusion. Let D denotes the maximum number of levels and Q denotes the maximum size of any sub-HMM state spaces in HHMM. Then a HHMM can be specified by the following parameters,

$$\Theta = \{\mathcal{A}, \mathcal{B}, \Pi, \mathcal{E}\}. \tag{2}$$

Explicitly, $\mathcal{A}$ denotes the transition probabilities ($\bigcup\limits_{d=1}^{D} \bigcup\limits_{k=1}^{Q^{d-1}} \{a_k^d\}$), where a_k^d is the transition matrix at level d with configuration k^{d-1}. $\mathcal{B}$ is emission parameter which specifies the observation distributions. We assume that the motion features comply with Gaussian distribution $N(\mu, \Sigma)$, then $\mathcal{B} = (\bigcup_{i=1}^{Q^D} \{\mu_i, \Sigma_i\})$. Similarly, let π_k^d and e_k^d denotes the prior and exiting probabilities at level d, then $\Pi = \bigcup_{d=1}^{D} \bigcup_{k_d=1}^{Q^{d-1}} \pi_k^d$ and $\mathcal{E} = \bigcup_{d=1}^{D} \bigcup_{k_d=1}^{Q^{d-1}} e_k^d$ are the prior and existing probabilities for HHMM model.

2.2 Motion Feature Extraction

To obtain the observation sequence for HHMM, we extract three dominant motions, pan, tilt and zoom from each subshot. The inter-frame motion features are firstly estimated from each two adjacent frames. We apply Harris corner detector to extract the image feature points, $\mathbf{x}_t$, from the frame t. Their corresponding points, $\mathbf{x}_{t+1}$, in the next frame $t + 1$, are estimated by the Singular Value Decomposition (SVD) of the 3D tensor structure [10]. Those matched point pairs in each frame pair are assumed to comply with a single camera motion model. Since the dominant features for rushes structuring and indexing is pan, tilt and zoom, 2D camera motion model is sufficient for the representation of these three motion features. Therefore, we use the 2D 6-parameter affine model described as,

$$\mathbf{x}_{t+1} = \begin{bmatrix} a_{11} & a_{12} \\ a_{21} & a_{22} \end{bmatrix} \mathbf{x}_t + \begin{bmatrix} v_1 \\ v_2 \end{bmatrix},$$

where $[a_{11}, a_{12}, a_{21}, a_{22}, v_1, v_2]^T$ are estimated from the matched points in the frame pair using the robust estimator LMedS [11]. RANSAC is not used due to the requirement of inlier threshold which is not easy to set. The parameter v_1 and v_2 characterize the pan and tilt respectively, while the parameter a_{11} and a_{22} describe the zoom motion. We extract a 3-dimensional motion feature vector $f = [v_1, v_2, z = (a_{11} + a_{22})/2]$ for each two adjacent frames. A sequence of motion vector, $\{f\}$, is then obtained from the frame sequence in a subshot. To suppress the outliers, we use the median, instead of average, motion vector as the observation for a subshot, that is,

$$o = \text{median}\{f\}. \tag{3}$$

Then a T-subshot string of a shot forms an observation sequence for HHMM, denoted as $O = (o_1, o_2 \cdots o_n \cdots o_T)$.

2.3 HHMM Parameter Learning by EM Algorithm

Given an observation sequence $O = (o_1, o_2 \cdots o_t \cdots o_T)$, the task of parameter learning is to find Θ^* that maximize the likelihood $L(\Theta)$. This is estimated by the Expectation-Maximization (EM) algorithm as in traditional HMM. Given an old parameter Θ and the missing data $K = (k_1, k_2, \cdots k_t \cdots k_T)$, the expectation of the complete-data likelihood of an updated parameter $\hat{\Theta}$ is written by

$$L(\hat{\Theta}, \Theta) = E(\log p(O, K|\hat{\Theta})|O, \Theta) \tag{4}$$

$$= \sum_K p(K|O, \Theta) \log p(O, K|\hat{\Theta}) \tag{5}$$

$$\propto \sum_K p(O, K|\Theta) \log p(O, K|\hat{\Theta}) \tag{6}$$

The E-step estimates the expectation $L(\hat{\Theta}, \Theta)$, and the M-step finds the value $\hat{\Theta}$ that maximizes the likelihood.

We define the probability of being in state k at time t and in state k' at time $t+1$ with transition happens at level d, given O and Θ, as

$$\xi_t(k, k', d) \stackrel{def}{=} p(k_t = k, k_{t+1} = k', e_t^{1:d} = 0, e_t^{d+1:D} = 1|O, \Theta). \tag{7}$$

Similarly, we define the probability of being in state k at time t, given O and Θ, as follows

$$\gamma_t(k) \stackrel{def}{=} p(k_t = k|O, \Theta). \tag{8}$$

In E-step, these two auxiliary variables are estimated by forward and backward algorithm [8]. Then by marginalizing and normalizing the auxiliary variables ξ and γ in M-step, we can get the updated model parameter $\hat{L}$ as follows,

$$\hat{\pi}_q^d(i) = \frac{\sum\limits_{t=1}^{T-1} \sum\limits_{q'} \sum\limits_{q''} \xi_t(q', \overline{qiq''}, d-1)}{\sum\limits_{t=1}^{T-1} \sum\limits_{q'} \sum\limits_{q''} \sum\limits_{i} \xi_t(q', \overline{qiq''}, d-1)} \tag{9}$$

$$\hat{e}_q^d(i) = \frac{\sum\limits_{t=1}^{T-1} \sum\limits_{q'} \sum\limits_{k'} \sum\limits_{d'<d} \xi_t(\overline{qiq'}, k', d')}{\sum\limits_{t=1}^{T-1} \sum\limits_{q'} \gamma_t(\overline{qiq'})} \tag{10}$$

$$\hat{a}_q^d(i, j) = \frac{\sum\limits_{t=1}^{T-1} \sum\limits_{q'} \sum\limits_{q''} \xi_t(\overline{qiq'}, \overline{qjq''}, d)}{\sum\limits_{t=1}^{T-1} \sum\limits_{q'} \sum\limits_{q''} \sum\limits_{j} \xi_t(\overline{qiq'}, \overline{qjq''}, d)} \tag{11}$$

$$\hat{\mu}_k = \frac{\sum\limits_{t=1}^{T} o_t \gamma_t(k)}{\sum\limits_{t=1}^{T} \gamma_t(k)} \tag{12}$$

$$\hat{\Sigma}_k = \frac{\sum\limits_{t=1}^{T} (o_t - \mu_k)(o_t - \mu_k)^T \gamma_t(k)}{\sum\limits_{t=1}^{T} \gamma_t(k)} \tag{13}$$

2.4 Structuring and Indexing by Viterbi Algorithm

Our final goal is to structure and index rushes with the three semantic categories. Instead of deciding the subshots once at a time, such as using SVM, HHMM can perform simultaneous structuring and indexing upon the whole subshot string. Given an observation sequence of a shot, $O = (o_1, o_2 \cdots o_t \cdots, o_T)$, we apply Viterbi algorithm [8] to obtain the underlying optimal state sequence, $K^* = (k_1^*, k_2^* \cdots, k_t^*, \cdots, k_T^*)$. Each k^* actually has two variables to indicate the sub-states of semantic label and motion feature in the two-level HHMM. The final solution is found the higher-level variable string, $K^{1*} = (k_1^{1*}, k_2^{1*} \cdots, k_t^{1*}, \cdots, k_T^{1*})$, which forms the indices of the semantic concepts for a shot. Meanwhile, the variations in the variable string K^{1*} indicate the locations of the semantic concept boundary. Therefore, by using Viterbi algorithm on the subshot string, the simultaneous structuring and indexing for a rushes shot can be efficiently achieved.

3 Experiments and Results

We randomly select 60 videos (about 400k frames or 4.5 hours) from BBC rushes of TRECVID'05 corpus to evaluate our approach. The videos are manually structured and indexed with the semantic labels: *stock*, *outtake* and *shaky*. We divide the videos equally into two set: 30 videos for training and 30 videos for testing.

We partition each video into shots by [12] and each shot is further decomposed into subshots. For *fixed* subshot, we empirically set the fixed duration to one second. For adaptive subshot, we use the motion-based finite state machine [10] to partition shot into subshots. Each subshot, both fixed and adaptive, is labeled with the three categories based on the ground truth manually marked by human subjects. The two-level HHMM are then trained with EM algorithm. Since only the higher-level labels are available, this is a mixed learning procedure. In other words, the learning at higher level is supervised, while the learning at lower level is unsupervised. For abbreviation, we name the HHMM of fixed and adaptive subshots as F-HHMM and A-HHMM respectively.

We compared the proposed HHMM with our previous work presented in TRECVID'05 [6]. In [6], we experimented three approaches: Finite State Machine (FSM), Hidden Markov Model (HMM) and Support Vector Machine (SVM). Table 1 summaries and contrasts the properties of different approaches. FSM and HMM models are flattened HHMM with only the higher level. FSM is actually a simplified HMM that the fuzzy transitions in HMM become deterministic. SVM, instead of modeling feature distribution, discriminates the three semantic concepts by hyper-plane in feature space. Therefore, from the structure's point of view, HHMM has a two-level hierarchical structure, while the others are flattened. We use Radial Basis Function (RBF) as the kernel for SVM. Meanwhile, Gaussian distribution is used as kernel function in HMM and HHMM. Inside the FSM states, thresholding is used to determine which category an observation belongs to. We applied adaptive subshot detection for FSM and A-HHMM, while using fixed subshot for the others. Notice that we use

Table 1. Comparison of different method's properties

	Subshot	#Structure	#Feature	Kernel
FSM	adaptive	flattened	3	threshold
SVM	fixed	flattened	9	RBF
HMM	fixed	flattened	9	Gaussian
F-HHMM	fixed	hierarchical	3	Gaussian
A-HHMM	adaptive	hierarchical	3	Gaussian

nine-dimensional feature for HMM and SVM. Besides the three motion features (Section 2.2), we also use the motion variations as additional features in order to improve the discriminative power of a flattened structure. The details can be found in [6].

3.1   Rushes Indexing

Table 2 and Table 3 show the indexing results of the training and testing videos respectively. The results are evaluated based on the number of frames being correctly or wrongly classified. The results show that HHMM outperforms the other approaches. Overall, we have about 96% accuracy on *stock*, 40% on *out-take* and 60% on *shaky* in the testing set. The results of SVM indicate that the feature distributions of the three semantic concepts severely overlapped among each other. Thus even the classification accuracy on training set is pretty low. SVM assumes that the observations are independent and neglect the temporal relationship between subshots. For example, a *shaky* tilt is more likely to be followed by a reverse tilt in the same *shaky* segment rather than an *outtake* tilt. By exploiting the temporal relationship, HHMM presents some improvement compared to SVM. Through experiments, hierarchical HMM shows better performance than flat HMM, particularly the accuracy of *shaky* is significantly improved. The reason perhaps lies in the fact that the movement of shaky artifacts usually has patterns such as swinging between left and right. The temporal relationship of the *shaky* can be captured by HHMM as a unique sequential pattern for recognition. The improvement of *outtake*, nevertheless, is less obvious than *shaky*. An *outtake* is usually a single movement, such as a zoom to get details or a pan to get another side of the scene. Thus the amount of sequential information to be captured by HHMM is limited. The sequential pattern of a *shaky* can be more distinctive if the turning points of motion are correctly located. This is why A-HHMM has better *shaky* accuracy than F-HHMM since the adaptively segmented subshots have more expressive power in describing the temporal structure of the *shaky* segments.

3.2   Rushes Structuring

The results of structuring are basically assessed based on the accuracy of the subshot boundaries between the three categories. However, compared to shot boundaries, the subshot boundaries are fuzzy and the exact locations (in term

Table 2. The indexing accuracy on the training video set

	Stock		Outtake		Shaky	
	Recall	Prec.	Recall	Prec.	Recall	Prec.
FSM	0.815	0.981	0.802	0.118	0.011	0.050
SVM	0.827	0.990	0.701	0.162	0.715	0.239
HMM	0.927	0.970	0.329	0.137	0.311	0.339
F-HHMM	**0.977**	**0.980**	**0.602**	**0.512**	**0.440**	**0.497**
A-HHMM	**0.976**	**0.983**	**0.648**	**0.551**	**0.546**	**0.515**

Table 3. The indexing accuracy on the testing video set

	Stock		Outtake		Shaky	
	Recall	Prec.	Recall	Prec.	Recall	Prec.
FSM	0.756	0.968	0.844	0.128	0.000	0.000
SVM	0.778	0.975	0.456	0.120	0.362	0.182
HMM	0.909	0.929	0.375	0.196	0.043	0.067
F-HHMM	**0.959**	**0.953**	**0.489**	**0.342**	**0.328**	**0.523**
A-HHMM	**0.962**	**0.963**	**0.408**	**0.427**	**0.624**	**0.597**

Table 4. The structuring accuracy in both training and testing video set

	Training		Testing	
	Recall	Prec.	Recall	Prec.
FSM	0.614	0.282	0.593	0.279
SVM	0.769	0.281	0.763	0.289
HMM	0.461	0.419	0.395	0.379
F-HHMM	**0.615**	**0.712**	**0.610**	**0.605**
A-HHMM	**0.707**	**0.725**	**0.582**	**0.611**

of frame) are not easy to identify even with careful human inspection. In the experiments, a subshot boundary is counted as correct as long as we can find a matched boundary in the ground-truth within 1-second time frame. In our ground-truth, there are 83.4% of boundaries for transitions between *stock* and *outtake*, 16.3% between *stock* and *shaky* and 0.3% between *shaky* and *outtake*. Table 4 shows the structuring results in both training and testing set. From the table, we can find that HHMM has the best results with about 70% accuracy in training set and 60% in testing set. Compared with other approaches, the precision has more obvious improvement than the recall. This shows that by considering the hierarchal relationship among the features, we can remarkably remove the false alarms while retaining the correct boundaries.

4   Conclusion and Future Work

In this paper, we have presented a novel approach for rushes structuring and indexing, which is one key component to mine the "gold" in rushes for film producers. By taking into account the sequential patterns of the motion features, the proposed two-level hierarchical hidden Markov model is capable of modeling statistical mapping from low-level motion features to high-level semantic concepts: *stock, outtake* and *shaky*. Experimental results show that our approach significantly outperforms other methods based on SVM, FSM and HMM. Currently, we only utilize motion features. Other indicators such as the visual qualities of a film and the cues derived from multi-modal features can be incorporated to further improve the accuracy of locating stock footage.

Acknowledgement

The work described in this paper was fully supported by a grant from the Research Grants Council of the Hong Kong Special Administrative Region, China (Project No. CityU 118905), and a grant from City University of Hong Kong (Project No. 7001804).

References

1. Hauptmann, A.: Lessons for the future from a decade of informedia video analysis research. In: CIVR'05, International Conference on Image and Video Retrieval. (2005)
2. TRECVID: (http://www-nlpir.nist.gov/projects/trecvid)
3. Allen, B.P., Petrushin, V.A.: Searching for relevent video shots in bbc rushes using semantic web techniques. In: Proceedings of the TRECVID Workshops. (2005)
4. Foley, C., et al.: Trecvid 2005 experiments at Dublin City University. In: Proceedings of the TRECVID Workshops. (2005)
5. Snoek, C.G.M., et al.: The mediamill trecvid 2005 semantic video search engine. In: Proceedings of the TRECVID Workshops. (2005)
6. Ngo, C.W., et al.: Motion driven approaches to shot boundary detection, low-level feature extraction and bbc rush characterization. In: Proceedings of the TRECVID Workshops. (2005)
7. Fine, S., Singer, Y., Tishby, N.: The hierarchical hidden Markov model: Analysis and applications. Machine Learning **32** (1998) 41–62
8. Xie, L., et al.: Learning hierarchical hidden Markov models for video structure discovery. Technical report, Columbia University (2002)
9. Murphy, K., Paskin, M.: Linear time inference in hierarchical HMMs. In: Proceedings of Neural Information Processing Systems. (2001)
10. Pan, Z., Ngo, C.W.: Structuring home video by snippet detection and pattern parsing. In: MIR '04: Proceedings of the 6th ACM SIGMM international workshop on Multimedia information retrieval, ACM Press (2004) 69–76
11. Rousseeuw, P.J., Leroy, A.M.: Robust regression and outlier detection. Wiley New York (1987)
12. Ngo, C.W., Pong, T.C., Chin, R.T.: Video partitioning by temporal slice coherency. IEEE Trans. Circuits Syst. Video Technol. **11** (2001) 941– 953

Retrieving Objects Using Local Integral Invariants

Alaa Halawani[1] and Hashem Tamimi[2]

[1] Chair of Pattern Recognition and Image Processing, University of Freiburg,
79110 Freiburg, Germany
halawani@informatik.uni-freiburg.de
[2] Computer Science Dept., University of Tübingen, Sand 1,
72076 Tübingen, Germany
tamimi@informatik.uni-tuebingen.de

Abstract. The use of local features in computer vision has shown to be promising. Local features have several advantages including invariance to image transformations, independence of the background, and robustness in difficult situations like partial occlusions. In this paper we suggest using local integral invariants to extract local image descriptors around interest points and use them for the retrieval task. Integral invariants capture the local structure of the neighborhood around the points where they are computed. This makes them very well suited for constructing highly-discriminative local descriptors. We study two types of kernels used for extracting the feature vectors and compare the performance of both. The dimensionality of the feature vector to be used is investigated. We also compare our results with the SIFT features. Excellent results are obtained using a dataset that contains instances of objects that are viewed in difficult situations that include clutter and occlusion.

1 Introduction

One of the main difficulties in computer vision is to identify objects despite of the changes that may affect the appearance of the object. Possible changes include rotation, translation, changes in scale, changes in illumination conditions, and partial object occlusion. Moreover, objects are usually located in cluttered scenes. It is very important to take these facts into account when designing real-world applications. One of the well-known approaches that deal with object and image retrieval is the use of color histograms [1]. The use of color histograms is simple and fast but it works mainly for non-cluttered scenes or for pre-segmented objects. In [2], Schiele and Crowley proposed using multidimensional receptive field histograms for object recognition. The histograms are constructed from the responses of a vector of local linear neighborhood operators such as gradients, Laplacian, Gabor filters, and Gaussian derivatives. This method is also problematic when dealing with clutter and partial occlusion. Local invariant features computed around interest points have several interesting characteristics. First of all, they are invariant to image transformations like rotation and translation. They are also robust to partial occlusion, clutter,

H. Sundaram et al. (Eds.): CIVR 2006, LNCS 4071, pp. 251–260, 2006.
© Springer-Verlag Berlin Heidelberg 2006

and changes in the background, as only corresponding local features in different scenes should match. This also eliminates the need for any prior segmentation. Schmid and Mohr [3] were among the first to use local image descriptors for the retrieval task. They have used rotation-invariant local feature vectors based on derivative-of-Gaussian local measurements. To identify the interest points, they have used the well-known Harris corner detector [4]. Gout and Boujemaa [5] extended this work to color images using color differential invariants. The feature vectors used in these methods have low dimensionality and are not highly distinctive. Lowe [6] has introduced the SIFT features that are invariant against similarity transformations. The feature vector used in SIFT consists of gradient orientation histograms summarizing the content of a 16×16 region around each point. In this paper we explore the use of local integral invariants for the purpose of retrieving objects located in complex scenes. Integral invariants capture the local structure of the neighborhood around the points where they are computed. Global versions of these features have proven to be robust to independent motion of objects, articulated objects, and topological deformations [7]. In addition to their invariance to Euclidean motion, we explain how it is possible to earn local similarity-invariant features. We study two types of kernels that are used to generate integral invariants. The effect of the dimensionality of the feature vectors is also investigated. A comparison with the SIFT features is also considered.

The paper is organized as follows. In section 2 a summary of the integral invariants is given. Extending the features to be scale invariant is described in section 3. Section 4 gives an overall look on the setup of the system. Results are summarized in section 5 and a conclusion is given in section 6.

2   Integral Invariants

Following is a brief description of the calculation of the rotation- and translation-invariant features based on integration. The idea of constructing invariant features is to apply a nonlinear kernel function, $f(\mathbf{I})$, to a gray-valued image, $\mathbf{I}$, and to integrate the result over all possible rotations and translations (Haar integral over the Euclidean motion):

$$\mathbf{T}[f](\mathbf{I}) = \frac{1}{PMN} \sum_{n_0=0}^{M-1} \sum_{n_1=0}^{N-1} \sum_{p=0}^{P-1} f(g(n_0, n_1, \varphi = p\frac{2\pi}{P})\mathbf{I}) \tag{1}$$

where $\mathbf{T}[f](\mathbf{I})$ is the invariant feature of the image, M, N are the dimensions of the image, and g is an element in the transformation group, $\mathcal{G}$ (which consists here of rotations and translations). Bilinear interpolation is applied when the samples do not fall onto the image grid. The above equation suggests that invariant features are computed by applying a nonlinear function, f, to a circular neighborhood of each pixel in the image, then summing up all the results to get a single value representing the invariant feature. Using several different kernel functions builds up a feature space. To preserve more local information, one can remove the summation over all translations. This results in a map $\mathbf{T}$ that has the same dimensions of $\mathbf{I}$:

$$(\mathbf{T}[f](\mathbf{I}))(n_0, n_1) = \frac{1}{P} \sum_{p=0}^{P-1} f\left(g\left(n_0, n_1, \varphi = p\frac{2\pi}{P}\right)\mathbf{I}\right). \qquad (2)$$

Two types of non-linear kernel function, f, are considered. Invariant features can be computed by applying the monomial kernel, which has the form:

$$f(\mathbf{I}) = \left(\prod_{k=0}^{K-1} \mathbf{I}(x_k, y_k)\right)^{\frac{1}{K}}. \qquad (3)$$

Integral invariants are computed using the monomial kernels by multiplying a constellation of pixels in the circular neighborhood of the center pixel and then averaging the local results. One disadvantage of this type of kernels is that it is sensitive to illumination changes. The work in [8] defines another kind of kernels that are robust to illumination changes. These kernels are called the relational kernel functions and have the form:

$$f(\mathbf{I}) = rel\left(\mathbf{I}(x_0, y_0) - \mathbf{I}(x_1, y_1)\right) \qquad (4)$$

with the ramp function

$$rel(x) = \begin{cases} 1 & \text{if } x < -\epsilon \\ \frac{\epsilon - x}{2\epsilon} & \text{if } -\epsilon \leq x \leq \epsilon \\ 0 & \text{if } \epsilon < x \end{cases}. \qquad (5)$$

Feature calculation using the relational kernels is similar to using the monomial kernels. In the case of the relational kernels, two pixels are compared using the rel-function instead of multiplying them. This kind of kernels is based on the Local Binary Pattern (LBP) texture features [9], which map the relation between a center pixel and its neighborhood pixels into a binary pattern. Equation 5 extends the LBP operator to give values that fall in $[0, 1]$. This is done in order to get rid of the discontinuity of the LBP operator which makes the features sensitive to noise. For more detailed theory about integral invariants, please refer to [7].

3   Scale Invariance

The integral invariants in the form described in Section 2 are invariant to Euclidean motion only and are therefore sensitive to scale changes. Extending the principle of integral invariants to be scale invariant is not easy due to the fact that compact groups are needed, whereas scaling is unbounded [10]. However, if the local scale of each interest point can be determined, we can establish local features that are scale invariant by adapting the local support (the patch size on which the kernel function acts) of the kernels used to the local scale of the point around which they are evaluated. This way, the patch that is used for feature extraction covers always the same details of the image independent of the scale, which consequently means that the extracted feature vector is scale invariant. To achieve this, we use the difference-of-Gaussian (DoG)-based point detector introduced by Lowe in [6], which localizes points in scale and space.

4   Setup

4.1   Dataset

To run the experiments, 11 different objects were chosen. Model images for the objects were recorded. For the purpose of testing, each object was photographed 18 different times resulting in images that show each object in 18 different placements. The placements include rotation, scaling, illumination changes, partial occlusion, and combination of two or more of these situations. All shots were taken in different complex and cluttered backgrounds. The images have a resolution of 480×640 pixels and are stored in JPEG compressed format.

4.2   Feature Extraction

Using the DoG-based detector, the interest points in an image are identified. The detector gives the location and the scale of each candidate point in subpixel resolution. The number of extracted points is between 500 and 2000 depending on the image content. To extract the local integral invariants, we use a set of two-point kernel functions. For an interest point located at (n_0, n_1), each kernel function manipulates (multiplies in the case of monomials or subtracts and compares in the case of relationals) two points that lie on the circumferences of two circles of radii r_1, r_2, respectively, where $r_2 \geq r_1$. A phase shift, θ, between the two points is considered. The radii are adapted to the local scale of each interest point as described in section 3. An example of kernel application is shown in Figure 1. Having a set of V kernel functions, f_i, a V-dimensional feature vector around each interest point, (n_0, n_1), is constructed using:

$$\mathbf{F}(i)\big|_{(n_0,n_1)} = \tfrac{1}{P} \sum_{p=0}^{P-1} f_i \left(g\left(n_0, n_1, \varphi = p\tfrac{2\pi}{P}\right) \mathbf{I}\right), \ i = 1...V.$$

4.3   Retrieval Process

The feature vectors are saved in the database with a pointer to the model image to which they belong. In the retrieval process, a query image is presented to the system. The features of the image are extracted as described above. Each individual feature vector from the query image is compared using the Euclidean distance measure with all the other feature vectors stored in the database of the model images. A kd-tree structure [11] is used to speed up the search. Correspondences between the feature vectors are found based on the method described in [12] which allows for robust matching based on a confidence measure that depends on a uniqueness value assigned to each feature vector. A voting scheme

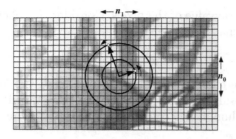

Fig. 1. Evaluation of the monomial kernel $f(\mathbf{I}) = \mathbf{I}(0,3) . \mathbf{I}(6,0)$. The grayvalue of a point on a circle of radius $r = 3$ around (n_0, n_1) is multiplied by the grayvalue of a point on a circle of radius $r = 6$. Notice the phase shift of $\pi/2$ between the two points. Points that do not fall on the grid are interpolated. The same calculation strategy is also valid for the relational kernel function, $f(\mathbf{I}) = rel(\mathbf{I}(0,3) - \mathbf{I}(6,0))$, substituting multiplication with subtraction.

is applied to determine the object model that corresponds to the query image. If a match between a vector from the query image and another from a model image is fired, the model image gets a vote. Finally, the model image that gets the maximum number of matches wins the voting scheme and is returned as the best match to the query image.

4.4   Performance Measures

In addition to the recognition rate, we use two other measures to evaluate the quality of recognition: the *number of matches* and the *match precision*. The match precision gives an indication of how good the matching is, by giving the ratio of correct matches to the total number of matches in the image:

$$\text{Match Precision} = \frac{\text{Number of correct matches}}{\text{Total number of matches}} \times 100\%. \qquad (6)$$

Given two images that contain the same object, a match between a point, $\mathbf{p_1}$, in the first image and a point, $\mathbf{p_2}$, in the second image is considered as a correct match if the error in the relative location of the two points is less that a threshold, τ:

$$\|\mathbf{p_1} - \mathbf{H}\mathbf{p_2}\| < \tau, \qquad (7)$$

where $\mathbf{H}$ refers to the homography. We set $\tau = 3$ pixels following [13].

5   Results

5.1   Monomial vs. Relational Features

The robustness of the features against intensity changes is an important aspect. Local characteristics should not change when lighting conditions change. Monomial type kernels are very sensitive to changes in the intensity since they work directly on the raw grayvalue of the pixels. Consider the following equation that describes the affine change in intensity value, $\mathbf{I}(x, y)$:

$$\gamma(\mathbf{I}(x, y)) = a\mathbf{I}(x, y) + b. \tag{8}$$

Considering a simple monomial kernel that multiplies two grayvalues, $\mathbf{I}(x_1, y_1)$ and $\mathbf{I}(x_2, y_2)$, the result is simply $M = \mathbf{I}(x_1, y_1)\mathbf{I}(x_2, y_2)$. If the image was exposed to change in illumination conditions such that the equation above applies, then we have:

$$\begin{aligned}
M' &= \gamma(\mathbf{I}(x_1, y_1))\gamma(\mathbf{I}(x_2, y_2)) \\
&= a^2\mathbf{I}(x_1, y_1)\mathbf{I}(x_2, y_2) + b[a(\mathbf{I}(x_1, y_1) + \mathbf{I}(x_2, y_2)) + b] \\
&= a^2 M + b\gamma(\mathbf{I}(x_1, y_1) + \mathbf{I}(x_2, y_2)).
\end{aligned}$$

So the result will be scaled by a factor of a^2 and shifted by a factor that is equal to the scaled affine change of the sum of the two grayvalues. The behavior of relational kernels, on the other hand, is different. They are robust against intensity changes as they consider relations between grayvalues of the pixels rather than the raw values themselves. A relational kernel function applied to $\mathbf{I}(x_1, y_1)$ and $\mathbf{I}(x_2, y_2)$ will give a result of $R = rel(\delta)$, where $\delta = \mathbf{I}(x_1, y_1) - \mathbf{I}(x_2, y_2)$ and rel is the fuzzy relation defined in Equation 5. When the intensity changes according to Equation 8, then:

$$\begin{aligned}
R' &= rel(\gamma(\mathbf{I}(x_1, y_1)) - \gamma(\mathbf{I}(x_2, y_2))) \\
&= rel(a\delta). \\
&= \begin{cases} 1 & \text{if } \delta < -\epsilon/a \\ \frac{\epsilon - a\delta}{2\epsilon} & \text{if } -\epsilon/a \le \delta \le \epsilon/a \\ 0 & \text{if } \epsilon/a < \delta \end{cases}
\end{aligned}$$

Clearly, the result is invariant against the shift in the mean luminance. The effect of the scaling parameter, a, depends on the threshold value, ϵ, used in the ramp function, rel. As ϵ approaches zero, a smaller range of δ values will be affected by the scaling parameter a. If ϵ is set equal to zero, then we return to the LBP step operator [9] which is totally invariant to exact monotonic gray scale transformations but sensitive to disturbances. So ϵ is chosen to achieve a good compromise between the robustness against noise and the robustness against gray scale changes. In our experiments, $\epsilon = 0.098$ ($\mathbf{I}(x, y) \in [0, 1]$) was found to give very good results. Two tests were carried out on the database. Once with monomial type features and another with relational type features. In each case, 43 kernels were used to extract a feature vector around each interest point. The results shown in Table 1 depict the tremendous difference in the performance between both types of features. Not only the recognition rate of the monomial features is very low, but also the number of matches per image is small and the percentage of correct matches is low.

Trying to enhance the performance of the monomial-based features, the feature vectors were normalized such that they have a zero mean and a unit variance. A remarkable enhancement in the performance was observed after the

Table 1. Comparison between the results of the tests based on monomial and relational features

	Recognition rate	Avg. # of matches	Avg. match precision
Monomial Features	30.15%	9.94	60.31%
Relational Features	98.99%	72.34	91%

Table 2. Results after normalizing the monomial feature vectors to zero mean and unit variance

	Recog. rate	Avg. # of matches	Avg. match precision
Monomial Features (norm.)	89.45%	36.56	82.1%
Relational Features	98.99%	72.34	91%

Fig. 2. Some query results using relational features

normalization as can be seen in Table 2. Nevertheless there is still a big gap between the performance of the relational-based features and the monomial-based features. Figure 2 shows different example queries for different instances of some objects in the database using relational features. The left part of each example shows the query image of a complex scene that contains an instance of one

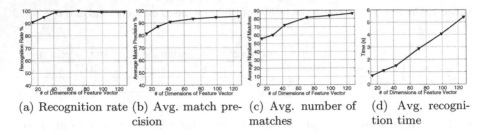

(a) Recognition rate (b) Avg. match pre-   (c) Avg. number of   (d) Avg. recogni-
                       cision   matches   tion time

Fig. 3. Performance as a function of vector dimensionality

object. Different situations like object occlusion, rotation, scaling, and intensity change are shown. The result, expressed by the model image that won the voting scheme, is shown to the right. The outline of the detected object is also shown on the query image. For the sake of clarity, not all matches between the query and the model are displayed. Only randomly selected matches that do not overlap are shown. In the rest of the experiments only relational-based feature vectors are used.

5.2   Dimensionality of the Feature Vectors

Usually, high-dimensional feature vectors convey more information about the local characteristics of a point and lead to better results but at the expense of the storage requirements and the computation and matching complexities. Several experiments were run using feature vectors with dimensionality that ranged between 14 and 127 dimensions. In each case, the recognition rate, the average number of matches and the average match precision were observed. Figure 3 shows the results. The recognition rate and quality (number of matches and match precision) go up as the dimensionality increases. The average match precision shows that, in most cases, most of the matches are correct matches. Only for low dimensionality the average match precision is under 90% (about 82% for dimensionality = 14). It reaches about 95% for 127-dimensional vectors. The time needed for recognition depends on the dimensionality of the feature vector in addition to the number of interest points (the number of feature vectors consequently) found in each image. The average recognition time as a function of the vector dimensionality is shown in Figure 3(d). Utilizing feature vectors with dimensionality of about 40 gives a good compromise between recognition rate and quality from one side and complexity and storage from the other side.

5.3   Comparison with SIFT

We report here the performance achieved when using the well-known SIFT features. Table 3 summarizes the results. More matches and higher match precision are obtained using SIFT. However, the recognition rate achieved using SIFT is the same as that achieved using the relational integral invariants.

It should be noticed that the dimensionality of the used integral invariant vectors (43 dimensions) is much less than that of SIFT (128 dimensions). Moreover,

Table 3. Results using SIFT features

	Recognition rate	Average # of matches	Average match precision
SIFT	98.99%	151.8	96%
Rel. Integral Invariants	98.99%	72.34	91%

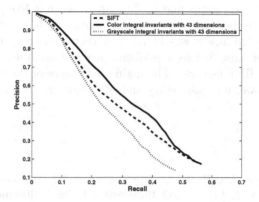

Fig. 4. Precision-Recall graph using 400 queries of the COIL-100 database

in SIFT, about 15% of the points have multiple feature vectors corresponding to multiple orientations assigned to these points. This leads to more storage and matching requirements. This is not the case for the integral invariants. An important advantage of the integral invariants over SIFT is their capability of exploiting color information when needed. SIFT is extracted using grayscale information only. The integral invariants can be extracted from color information by simply applying the kernel functions to the different channels of the color space. To demonstrate this, we carried out some experiments on the COIL-100 database of color objects. In this database, images of 100 different objects were taken at pose intervals of 5 degrees resulting in 72 poses per object. Exploiting color information in such a database is a big plus as the number of points detected in the images of the database is very small (not more than 10 for some objects). Moreover, some objects in the database are similar but with different colors. We tested the performance of the different methods in retrieving objects using 400 query images (4 per object). Figure 4 shows the results in terms of the precision-recall performance measures. The best results were achieved using the color-based integral invariants. SIFT comes in the second place and the grayscale-based integral invariants come third.

6 Conclusion

In this paper we have investigated the use of integral invariants to extract local feature vectors around interest points for the purpose of retrieving objects in complex scenes. The features are by definition invariant to Euclidean motion and can be made similarity invariant by adapting the support of the kernels used to the local support of the interest points. Two types of features were discussed; relational type and monomial type features. Much better results in terms of recognition rate and quality were achieved using the relational type features as they are robust against intensity changes, which is not the case with the monomial type features. Tests were conducted using test images of objects against cluttered backgrounds and in difficult situations like partial object occlusion and intensity changes. Several experiments considering the feature vector length were conducted and it was found that vectors with about 40 dimensions give a good compromise between performance and complexity. We compared our work with the SIFT features. The main advantages of the integral invariants over SIFT is the lower dimensionality and the ability to use color information if needed.

References

1. Swain, M.J., Ballard, D.H.: Color indexing. IJCV **7** (1991) 11–32
2. Schiele, B., Crowley, J.L.: Object Recognition Using Multidimensional Receptive Field Histograms. In: ECCV. Volume 1. (1996) 610–619
3. Schmid, C., Mohr, R.: Local Grayvalue Invariants for Image Retrieval. PAMI **19** (1997) 530–535
4. Harris, C., Stephens, M.: A Combined Corner and Edge Detector. In: Proceedings of The Fourth Alvey Vision Conference. (1988) 147–151
5. Gouet, V., Boujemaa, N.: Object-based Queries using Color Points of Interest. In: CBAIVL, Kauai, Hawaii, USA (2001) 30–36
6. Lowe, D.G.: Distinctive Image Features from Scale-Invariant Keypoints. IJCV **60** (2004) 91–110
7. Schulz-Mirbach, H.: Invariant Features for Gray Scale Images. In: 17th DAGM, Bielefeld (1995) 1–14
8. Schael, M.: Invariant Grey Scale Features for Texture Analysis Based on Group Averaging with Relational Kernel Functions. Technical Report 1/01, University of Freiburg (2001)
9. Ojala, T., Pietikäinen, M., Mäenpää, T.: Gray Scale and Rotation Invariant Texture Classification with Local Binary Patterns. In: ECCV. (2000) 404–420
10. Siggelkow, S.: Feature Historgrams for Content-Based Image Retrieval. PhD thesis, Albert-Ludwigs-Universität, Freiburg (2002)
11. Freidman, J.H., Bentley, J.L., Finkel, R.A.: An Algorithm for Finding Best Matches in Logarithmic Expected Time. ACM Transactions on Mathematical Software **3** (1977) 209–226
12. Biber, P., Straßer, W.: Solving the Correspondence Problem by Finding Unique Features. In: 16th International Conference on Vision Interface. (2003)
13. Mikolajczyk, K., Schmid, C.: A Performance Evaluation of Local Descriptors. In: CVPR. Volume 2. (2003) 257–263

Retrieving Shapes Efficiently by a Qualitative Shape Descriptor: The Scope Histogram

A. Schuldt, B. Gottfried, and O. Herzog

Centre for Computing Technologies (TZI)
University of Bremen, Am Fallturm 1, D-28359 Bremen

Abstract. Efficient image retrieval from large image databases is a challenging problem. In this paper we present a method offering constant time complexity for the comparison of two shapes. In order to achieve this, we extend the qualitative concept of positional-contrast by 86 new relations describing the position of a polygon w. r. t. its line segments. On this basis a histogram of the relations' frequencies is computed for each shape. A useful property of our approach is that, due to the underlying concept of positional-contrast, it can be intuitively decided whether its combination with other features is promising. Especially, retrieval results of about 64% are achieved in the MPEG test with constant time complexity.

1 Introduction

Recent developments show an increasing spread of digital technologies in many areas of economic, scientific, and even personal life. This process often comes along with the application of large image databases. Their management requires feasible search technologies. While a great deal of work addresses issues concerning segmentation, grouping, and feature extraction, less emphasis has been put on the representation of extracted objects so as to support efficient retrieval processes. In this paper we will concentrate on this latter topic bringing forward results in the context of qualitative representations which advance image and video retrieval systems in that they allow objects to be indexed concisely.

While colour and texture have been successfully applied to retrieval systems, shapes pose major difficulties (cf. [11]). Being able to resort to many polygonal approximation algorithms [13], and forming quite a compact description for two-dimensional outlines even with little influence on the perception of shape [2], we shall focus on the description of polygons. We use especially [12], thereby choosing a scale-invariant approximation error of one percent of a polygon's perimeter.

For the search of objects in image databases there are concurrent requirements to be satisfied: On the one hand users demand for adequate responses matching their query, on the other hand users require responses within an appropriate period of time. While the first requirement is well fulfilled for polygons [9], the second one still remains a major difficulty for large image databases due to the

H. Sundaram et al. (Eds.): CIVR 2006, LNCS 4071, pp. 261–270, 2006.
© Springer-Verlag Berlin Heidelberg 2006

time complexity needed when searching for and comparing many objects. Useful are therefore approaches that are based on simple features which only need constant time complexity when comparing objects. Although these features are rather limited for the purpose of object classification, they can be combined in order to improve retrieval results. Examples for such features include moments [8], compactness [3], radius ratio [4], and aspect ratio [3]. In this paper, we propose yet another feature which equally concisely characterises single objects, namely scope histograms, extending the approach which has been introduced in [6]. It shows, that in the MPEG test our new approach outperforms the approaches mentioned above, although still allowing to compare objects with constant time complexity. Due to its completely different representation, it is promising to combine our new approach with the other numerical features. This allows retrieval results of about 64% to be achieved in the MPEG test, staying behind [9] only twelve percentage points. However, they propose a much more complex approach in order to obtain better results, requiring $O(mn^3)$ for comparing two outlines.

In the following section we will shortly review previous work on which scope histograms are based. In Sect. 3 we introduce our new approach, which offers constant time complexity for comparing two shapes. Afterwards, in Sect. 4 the approach is compared and combined with others, and finally, we give a short summary in Sect. 5.

2   Characterising Shapes Using Positional-Contrast

The notion of positional-contrast [6] is based on the extension of the 13 qualitative relations between time intervals [1] to two dimensions. In order to distinguish two-dimensional positions between line segments qualitatively, e. g. positions between line segments of polygons, [6] uses the orientation grid which has been suggested by [15]. The orientation grid is induced by a line segment connecting two points and it consists of three lines: One line passes both points, the other two lines are oriented orthogonally w. r. t. the first one. Each of them passes one of the two reference points. This divides the plane into six sectors, allowing a third point to be located within this grid. Not only single points, but also line segments can be described by their relative position to another reference segment which induces the orientation grid. Every line segment is defined by a start and an end point. Since each of these points can be located in any of the six sectors of the orientation grid, there exist $6^2 = 36$ arrangements between two line segments that can be distinguished qualitatively. According to [5], this number can be reduced to 23, due to symmetries and the omission of intersections. The remaining 23 distinguishable bipartite arrangements, in short $\mathcal{BA}_{23}$, are depicted on the left hand side of Fig. 1. The relations' mnemonic labelling is shown in the centre of Fig. 1.

Applying $\mathcal{BA}_{23}$, it is not only possible to characterise the relative position of two single line segments. Moreover, one can describe the complete course of the polygon w. r. t. a reference segment. This is accomplished by a sequence of n $\mathcal{BA}$ relations describing each of the n line segments, one after another [7]:

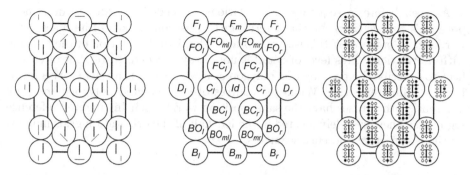

Fig. 1. Left: Example arrangements of $\mathcal{BA}_{23}$ relations. Centre: The relations' mnemonic labels. Right: Iconic representation of the sets describing the relations' scopes.

Definition 1 (Course). *x is a line segment of a simple, closed polygon P. Its course $C(x)$ describes all $\mathcal{BA}$ relations between all lines of P and x:*

$$C(x) \equiv (x_{y_0}, \ldots, x_{y_{n-1}}), x_{y_i} \in \mathcal{BA}, i = 0, \ldots, n-1$$

Up to now, a polygon has only been characterised w. r. t. one of its line segments. In order to gain a complete characterisation, it has to be described w. r. t. each of its segments. In doing so, we obtain a matrix containing n^2 relations. Thus, space complexity for this description is quadratic, $O(n^2)$. Time complexity for the comparison of two polygons which are described this way is even higher. Due to the fact that every matrix can be built up by starting with different reference lines, and that two matrices might be different in size (the second polygon comprises m line segments), time complexity for the comparison of two of these descriptions is $O(mn^3)$. In the following section we shall learn how space and time complexity can be reduced.

3 Reducing Time and Space Complexity

In the following, we elaborate on how time and space complexity of the approach described in the preceding Sect. 2 can be reduced. In our case, space complexity depends on the number of relations, which are needed in order to characterise a polygon. By time complexity we address the cost required for comparing two polygons. In order to reduce the complexity of our description, we start with proposing a new definition for the scope of polygons, which has been introduced in [7]. Later on, this will enable us to compute a histogram of all the scopes which are derivable from a polygon. Since two histograms can be compared with constant time complexity by computing the sum of the distances of their corresponding entries, we obtain a description offering both constant time and constant space complexity. Note that the number of entries in the histogram does not depend on the number of line segments of the polygons but on the number of scopes conceivable, which is a fixed number.

As seen before, a sequence of n relations is needed in order to describe a polygon's course, $C(x)$, by characterising the position of each of its n segments w. r. t. x. In proceeding this way we obtain a detailed description of the polygon with n^2 relations. This level of detail is not always needed. Instead, it often suffices to describe the position of a polygon as a whole w. r. t. a reference segment; Figure 2 illustrates this. While the courses of the depicted polygons are quite different, both courses have the same position w. r. t. their highlighted reference segments: They are solely located in the left half of the orientation grids induced by their respective reference segments.

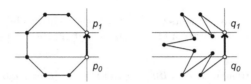

Fig. 2. Two different polygons, both located solely in the left half of the orientation grids induced by their respective reference segments

Instead of taking n relations as before, we now get along with a single relation in order to characterise the polygons. Thus, space complexity for this description is constant. When applied to both polygons depicted in Fig. 2, we obtain the same description, i. e. they cannot be distinguished. At first glance, this seems to be a major loss of information. Although the difference of both polygons is obvious for humans, they would be indistinguishable according to our new description. As we shall see below, this problem can be solved by describing polygons not only w. r. t. one of their line segments. It is rather necessary to use each line segment as a reference segment, inducing the orientation grid to each line segment, one after another. Doing this, we observe that the left polygon in Fig. 2 always lies on the left w. r. t. its reference segments. By contrast, the right example results in many different descriptions.

Hitherto, we described the position of polygons rather at a conceptual level, for instance, having denoted the relation in the preceding example "left". In the following, it is necessary to determine a set of relations which is adequate for our purposes. The $\mathcal{BA}_{23}$ relations introduced in Sect. 2 do not fulfill this requirement. Segments characterised by them only pass through up to four sectors of the orientation grid. Instead, a subset of $\mathcal{BA}_{23}$ containing only atomic bipartite arrangements is worth to be further examined. We classify a $\mathcal{BA}$ relation as being atomic if it either is located in one single sector or if it passes exactly one of the orientation grid's singularities connecting two adjacent sectors. This holds for twelve relations, namely B_l, BO_l, D_l, FO_l, F_l, F_m, F_r, FO_r, D_r, BO_r, B_r, as well as B_m. In the following, these relations will be referred to as $\mathcal{BA}_{12} \subset \mathcal{BA}_{23}$.

3.1   Scope of Bipartite Arrangements

Using the atomic relations identified above, the position of all $\mathcal{BA}_{23}$ relations can be characterised w. r. t. the reference segment. For this purpose, each relation is represented by the set of $\mathcal{BA}_{12}$ relations describing its position. In the following, this set is referred to as the relation's scope σ. The scope of each of the twelve atomic relations is rather simple. It contains only the respective $\mathcal{BA}_{12}$ relation and no further relations. More interesting are the scopes of the remaining non-atomic relations, namely BO_{ml}, BC_l, C_l, FC_l, FO_{ml}, FO_{mr}, FC_r, C_r, BC_r, and BO_{mr}. Since we deal with sets, these scopes can simply be considered as unions of atomic scopes. For instance, the position of C_l is determined by the set $\{B_l, BO_l, D_l, FO_l, F_l\}$. Each scope can be visualised by twelve circles, each of which being located in accordance to its respective atomic relation in the orientation grid. A circle is depicted opaque if its $\mathcal{BA}_{12}$ relation is member of the scope, transparent otherwise. The right hand side of Fig. 1 depicts this iconic visualisation for all $\mathcal{BA}_{23}$ relations.

3.2   Scope of Courses

After having defined the scopes for $\mathcal{BA}_{23}$ relations, we are now prepared to determine the scope of a polygon's course, i. e. for the whole polygon. As seen before, the scope of non-atomic relations can simply be determined by combining their respective atomic relations using the well-known union operation for sets. Extending this to obtain the scope of the complete polygon is straightforward. For the time being, we consider the scope σ' simply as being determined by the union of the scopes of all relations r_i contained in the course $C(x)$:

$$\sigma'(C(x)) \equiv \bigcup_{i=0}^{n-1} \sigma(r_i), r_i \in \mathcal{BA}_{23} \tag{1}$$

Every course of a simple, closed polygon describes a connected sequence of segments. However, while the scopes depicted on the right hand side of Fig. 1 form gapless chains of atomic relations, this does not hold for every scope determined using (1). This observation can be illustrated by taking a closer look at the left hand side of Fig. 1. These visualisations of the $\mathcal{BA}_{23}$ relations show that two relations which pass singularities of the orientation grid can follow each other without being interrupted by the relation in the sector in between. For example, BO_l can be followed directly by FO_l without D_l in between. However, one could argue that D_l has nevertheless been passed through and therefore should be considered in the resulting scope. In order to achieve this, the following auxiliary function is used:

$$close(\sigma') = \{sel(\sigma', 1), sel(\sigma', 2), \ldots, sel(\sigma', 12)\} \tag{2}$$

This function itself uses another auxiliary function:

$$sel(\sigma', i) = \begin{cases} \mathcal{BA}_{12}(i) & \text{if} \quad \mathcal{BA}_{12}(i) \in \sigma' \\ & \text{or} \quad \mathcal{BA}_{12}(i{-}1) \in \sigma' \wedge \mathcal{BA}_{12}(i{+}1) \in \sigma' \wedge odd(i) \\ \{\,\} & \text{else} \end{cases} \tag{3}$$

In order to arrive at a scope having all gaps closed, (2) uses (3) twelve times. The parameters of (3) are the preliminary scope σ' determined with (1) as well as a number from one to twelve. These numbers denote the atomic relations according to their position in the scope as depicted in Fig. 1. Starting with B_l, ending with B_m this allows to denote the atomic relations by $\mathcal{BA}_{12}(1)$ to $\mathcal{BA}_{12}(12)$ instead of their mnemonic labels. Equation (3) first checks whether an atomic relation is part of the preliminary scope. If so, its return value is the atomic relation itself. A second case handles the situation if, instead of the relation itself, both of its adjacent relations are contained in the preliminary scope. If the relation itself additionally has an odd number, it fulfills the condition of being located in one single sector and being left out by its neighbours. In this case, (3) also returns the respective atomic relation. Otherwise it returns an empty set. Applying (2) we get the final definition for the scope of courses:

Definition 2 (Scope). *x is a line segment of a simple, closed polygon and $C(x)$ is its course. The set of atomic relations describing the position of $C(x)$ is called the scope of the course, in short $\sigma(C(x))$. It is defined by:*

$$\sigma(C(x)) \equiv close\left(\bigcup_{i=0}^{n-1} \sigma(r_i)\right), r_i \in \mathcal{BA}_{23}$$

Since every scope is a set of up to twelve atomic relations, in theory $2^{12} = 4096$ different scopes can be distinguished. As outlined above, the scopes realised by simple, closed polygons always form a gapless chain of atomic relations. This restriction leads to an extremely confined number of scopes that actually exist. Each of these chains can contain up to twelve atomic relations. Those chains containing only up to eleven relations can start at each of the twelve atomic positions. If a scope contains all twelve relations its starting point is irrelevant. This scope is referred to as the universal scope. Altogether $11 \cdot 12 + 1 = 133$ gapless scopes can be distinguished. However, it can be observed that 47 of these 133 scopes cannot be realised by simple, closed polygons. This is due to the fact that a realisation of these scopes would require a mathematically negative order of the polygon's points. By restricting ourselves to polygons with a mathematically positive ordering, only $133 - 47 = 86$ scopes can be realised by simple, closed polygons.

To summarise, we are now able to qualitatively characterise the position of any simple, closed polygon w. r. t. a reference segment by a set of twelve atomic relations. This means, that space complexity for this description is constant instead of linear (as before), when characterising a polygon by the position of each of its segments. Thus, we are also able to characterise the polygon w. r. t. all of its segments with linear space complexity instead of quadratic space complexity, as before. In the following section we will see how to reduce this complexity even further.

3.3   Scope of Polygons

In Sect. 2 we recognised that matrices are permutable and that two matrices may not have the same size, which is the reason for the high runtime complexity when comparing two polygons on the basis of this description. In principle, the same holds for a polygon characterised by n scopes as described in Sect. 3.2: The sequence of scopes is permutable and may not have the same length for two polygons. These observations are related to the fact that we deal with an ordered sequence of scopes.

Instead of dealing with ordered sequences, we shall now discard this ordering: The qualitative partitioning into classes by the 86 scopes allows a histogram of frequencies to be computed (Fig. 3). Thus, instead of being linear, space complexity for this description is constant now, since only the frequencies of a fixed number of 86 scopes are to be described. In order to achieve a certain invariance against different approximation results, it makes sense to weight the histogram's entries by the relative length of the respective reference segments. Time complexity also decreases by this procedure, since the distance of two histograms can easily be computed by the sum of the distances of their corresponding entries. Thus, we are now able to characterise polygons with constant space complexity. Furthermore, it is possible to compare two polygons simply by considering the histograms of their scopes. In the following Sect. 4, we shall learn which retrieval results can be achieved by this method.

Fig. 3. Three simple scope histograms and their respective polygons. Left: The square's histogram contains only one entry, since all of its line segments have the same scope relation. Centre: Due to the polygon's regularity, the star's histogram consists of two entries with equal frequency. Right: The bell's scope histogram contains three entries.

4 Comparison with Other Approaches

In order to measure the retrieval performance of our method a comparison to other approaches has been carried out. As an evaluation method, we use the well-known core experiment CE-Shape-1 [10] for the MPEG-7 standard, which allows a comparison of approaches to be accomplished by taking into account only their retrieval results. Part B tests the capability of similarity-based retrieval techniques with a database of 1400 images: These images are semantically grouped into 70 classes of various shapes, each class containing 20 objects. Each image is used as a query, all other images in the database are ordered w. r. t. their similarity by the approach under consideration. For each query the number of images belonging to the same class are counted in the first 40 results. Since every class contains 20 instances, the maximum number of correct matches is 20 for each single query. Altogether, the total number of correct matches for all 1400 queries is 28000. As explained in [10], a retrieval rate of 100% is not possible using only shape knowledge, since some classes contain objects, which are semantically similar but differ significantly regarding their shape. Conversely, using a hypergeometric distribution, it is easy to show that a random ordering of the search results achieves about 2.86% in the MPEG test. This is a lower bound showing how much better an approach is in comparison with mere chance.

Since the scope histogram offers constant time complexity for the comparison of two objects, first of all it makes sense to compare it to other approaches also having this property. This holds for the seven invariant moments proposed by [8]. Applying [14], these moments can directly be computed for polygons like our approach. Even simpler are quantitative numeric features characterising polygons by a single numeric value. An example is the compactness as defined by [3], which corresponds to the ratio $\frac{4\pi A}{P^2}$ of area and perimeter. Further examples are the radius ratio $\frac{R_{min}}{R_{max}}$ of the minimum enclosing circle and the maximal contained circle [4] as well as the aspect ratio $\frac{H_r}{W_r}$ of the minimal enclosing rectangle [3]. Performing the MPEG test for the approaches described before leads to the results listed in Table 1: It shows that the numeric features, namely compactness, radius ratio, and aspect ratio, which characterise a shape by one single number gain results approximately between 16% and 24%. This is already significantly better than when ordering the shapes randomly, which achieves not even three percent correct matches. Even better results can be achieved using the seven Hu moments. Their results are at least ten percentage points better as they retrieve about 34% of the total number of correct matches. The scope histogram introduced in this paper outperforms all other examined approaches and retrieves about 46%. To conclude, using the scope histogram it is possible to achieve a retrieval result which is about 16 times better than a random ordering. Furthermore, our approach outperforms the other examined approaches which also offer constant time complexity.

Table 1. Classification results of compactness (CO), radius ratio (RR), aspect ratio (AR), Hu moments (HU), and scope histogram (SH) for CE-Shape-1 Part B

CO	RR	AR	HU	SH
21.86	16.82	24.12	34.13	**45.52**

After having examined the retrieval results for the scope histogram, the question arises, whether its results can be improved by combining it with one or more of the other approaches with constant time complexity. Table 2 lists the classification results for some of these combinations. It shows that by combining all numeric features, namely compactness, radius ratio, and aspect ratio, a result of about 52% can be achieved; including the Hu moments, we obtain 54%; the scope histogram in combination with the Hu moments, 54%; the scope histogram in combination with the three numeric features, we achieve 64%. When taking all five features together into consideration we achieve a retrieval result of approximately 64%. When comparing the retrieval result of all features (AL) with all but the Hu moments (NS), we learn that the Hu moments do not significantly improve the results. By contrast, a comparison of the retrieval results of all features (AL) and all features excluding our scope histogram (NH) shows that the scope histogram improves the results by about ten percentage points. Eventually, it is worth mentioning that a retrieval result of about 64% is only about twelve percentage points less than the results achieved by the correspondence of visual parts of [9] (which is 76.45%), that has a significantly higher time complexity of $O(mn^3)$ for the comparison of two objects.

Table 2. Classification results for combined features: All numeric features (NF), all numeric features and Hu moments (NH), all numeric features and scope histogram (NS), Hu moments and scope histogram (HS), and all these features together (AL)

NF	NH	NS	HS	AL
51.58	53.99	63.75	53.81	**64.26**

As mentioned above, when performing the complete MPEG test, 1400 queries, each consisting of 1400 comparisons of two objects, have to be processed. Altogether, this results in nearly two million comparisons. In our Java implementation it takes only about 20 seconds to perform the MPEG test for the scope histogram on a computer with Windows XP and an AMD mobile Athlon processor with about 1.5 Gigahertz.

5 Discussion

Using the orientation grid we describe objects by the configuration of their parts, i. e. we obtain self-referring descriptions. In doing so, a certain robustness can be achieved regarding changes of the viewpoint. Our approach is particularly suitable for rigid objects, since they do not change w. r. t. the configuration of their parts. Nevertheless, there exist many areas in which the approach is applicable, that is, there are many domains which deal with rigid artificial objects, and it is the notion of positional-contrast which allows us to intuitively decide whether two object categories can be distinguished. Robustness against noise in the underlying image data is realised by applying approximation algorithms and by using a qualitative approach, completely abstracting from exact quantitative data. Furthermore, it is worth mentioning that the application of an intrinsic reference system brings in invariance against scale, translation, as well as rotation.

Coming to a conclusion, we introduced a new approach offering constant space complexity for the description of a polygon by its scope, which is its relative position w. r. t. one of its line segments. By computing the frequencies of all occurring scopes, it is also possible to describe the whole polygon with constant space complexity. This histogram representation also allows two objects to be compared with constant time complexity. The evaluation results show that our new approach outperforms other approaches which also offer constant time complexity.

Furthermore, due to the underlying concept of positional-contrast it can be intuitively decided, whether it is worth combining it with other approaches, namely with those ones which are not based on the description of the configuration of their parts (e. g. square measures, roundness, etc. — not to mention texture and colour). This combination leads to retrieval results of about 64% in the MPEG test.

References

1. J. F. Allen. Maintaining Knowledge about Temporal Intervals. *Communications of the ACM*, 26(11):832–843, 1983.
2. F. Attneave. Some Informational Aspects of Visual Perception. *Psychological Review*, 61:183–193, 1954.
3. R. O. Duda and P. E. Hart. *Pattern Classification and Scene Analysis*. John Wiley and Sons, Inc., 1973.
4. G. D. Garson and R. S. Biggs. *Analytic Mapping and Geographic Databases*. Sage Publications, Newbury Park, CA, 1992.
5. B. Gottfried. Reasoning about Intervals in Two Dimensions. In *IEEE Int. Conference on Systems, Man and Cybernetics*, pages 5324–5332, The Hague, 2004.
6. B. Gottfried. *Shape from Positional-Contrast — Characterising Sketches with Qualitative Line Arrangements*. Doctoral dissertation, University of Bremen, 2005.
7. B. Gottfried. Querying for Silhouettes by Qualitative Feature Schemes. In *DIAL'06, 2nd IEEE Inter. Conf. on Document Image Analysis for Libraries*, 2006.
8. M.-K. Hu. Visual Pattern Recognition by Moment Invariants. *IRE Transactions on Information Theory*, 8(2):179–187, 1962.
9. L. J. Latecki and R. Lakämper. Shape Similarity Measure Based on Correspondence of Visual Parts. *IEEE PAMI*, 22(10):1185–1190, 2000.
10. L. J. Latecki, R. Lakämper, and U. Eckhardt. Shape Descriptors for Non-rigid Shapes with a Single Closed Contour. In *IEEE CVPR*, pages 424–429, 2000.
11. S. Loncaric. A Survey of Shape Analysis Techniques. *Pattern Recognition*, 31:983–1001, 1998.
12. D. A. Mitzias and B. G. Mertzios. Shape Recognition with a Neural Classifier Based on a Fast Polygon Approximation Technique. *Pattern Recognition*, 27:627–636, 1994.
13. P. L. Rosin. Assessing the Behaviour of Polygonal Approximation Algorithms. *Pattern Recognition*, 36:505–518, 2003.
14. C. Steger. On the Calculation of Arbitrary Moments of Polygons. Technical Report FGBV-96-05, Informatik IX, Technische Universität München, 1996.
15. K. Zimmermann and C. Freksa. Qualitative Spatial Reasoning Using Orientation, Distance, and Path Knowledge. *Applied Intelligence*, 6:49–58, 1996.

Relay Boost Fusion for Learning Rare Concepts in Multimedia

Dong Wang, Jianmin Li, and Bo Zhang

State Key Laboratory of Intelligent Technology and System,
Department of Computer Science and Technology,
Tsinghua University, Beijing, 100084, P.R. China
wdong01@mails.tsinghua.edu.cn,
{lijianmin, dcszb}@mail.tsinghua.edu.cn

Abstract. This paper relates learning rare concepts for multimedia retrieval to a more general setting of imbalanced data. A Relay Boost (RL.Boost) algorithm is proposed to solve this imbalanced data problem by fusing multiple features extracted from the multimedia data. As a modified RankBoost algorithm, RL.Boost directly minimizes the ranking loss, rather than the classification error. RL.Boost also iteratively samples positive/negative pairs for a more balanced data set to get diverse weak ranking with different features, and combines them in a ranking ensemble. Experiments on the standard TRECVID 2005 benchmark data set show the effectiveness of the proposed algorithm.

1 Introduction

The easy video capturing functionalities, rapid increasing of computing, communication and storage capabilities have fostered research to enable semantic retrieval over large video corpora. However, the semantic gap has to be bridged for semantic multimedia retrieval. A promising approach to bridge this gap tries to learn a large vocabulary of generic concepts using machine learning techniques and to establish a mapping between the learned concepts and video semantics. This approach has provided good results in recent TRECVID benchmarks [1].

Generic multimedia concept learning, which is referred to as concept detection in TRECVID benchmark, uses labelled positive and negative instances to train a classifier. Usually negative instances are abundant while positive instances are often rare. This occurs frequently either because the concept is rare or because manual annotation being an expensive process is carried out only on a limited data set. In the learning community, it is called the imbalanced data problem [2].

Concepts are often modelled with classifiers whose optimization objective is the classification error rate not the ranking measure. Unfortunately, they do not coincide under the imbalanced data settings [3]. Algorithms which are designed to minimize the error rate may not lead to the best possible ranking measure. This disparity enforces ranking based performance measures, such as Average Precision (AP), for learning concepts. However, this important aspect is still overlooked by recent approaches, even the most successful concept detection

H. Sundaram et al. (Eds.): CIVR 2006, LNCS 4071, pp. 271–280, 2006.
© Springer-Verlag Berlin Heidelberg 2006

systems in TRECVID 2005, such as [4] and [5]. The former simply increases the cost factor for the positive instances and the latter samples only 20% of the negative instances.

Meanwhile, it is still difficult for the low-level visual features, e.g. color histogram, alone to sufficiently represent the semantic concept. Multiple features provide different, usually not self-sufficient views for describing the same concept. So they should be searched for diverse instances under different representations, in the hope of counterbalancing the imbalanced data.

In this paper, we address the rare concept detection task by resorting to the more basic imbalanced data problem and fuse information from multiple features for it. As a modified version of RankBoost [6], our algorithm, Relay Boost (RL.Boost), directly minimizes the ranking loss, not the classification error. Furthermore, the algorithm iteratively samples important instance pairs to build *weak rankings* (defined in Section 3.1) by using different features, and produces a ranking ensemble. The difference between RL.Boost and RankBoost is that RL.Boost does not search all features with the sampled data set for the best weak ranking due to the formidable computational cost otherwise. We call this algorithm by Relay Boost since these features are chosen in a style similar to the runners in a relay race.

The rest of the paper is organized as follows. Sect. 2 surveys related work from both the imbalanced data and the information fusion perspectives. In Sect. 3, RL.Boost is introduced from three aspects of sampling method, classifier ensemble scheme and multiple feature usage. Sect. 4 demonstrates experimental results, and Sect. 5 discusses the algorithm and concludes our study.

2   Related Work

2.1   Imbalanced Data

A usually adopted approach towards solving the imbalanced data problem is to bias the classifier so that it pays more attention to the instances in the minority class[1]. Biased classifier can be obtained, for example, by increasing the misclassification cost of the positive class relative to the negative class [7].

Another approach is to preprocess the data set by under-sampling the majority class or over-sampling the minority class. Both of these sampling techniques aim at decreasing the overall level of class imbalance in order to create a balanced data set. Advanced sampling techniques like SMOTE [8] are developed. However, these over-sampling techniques make too optimistic an assumption that the areas among nearest positive instances are occupied by positive instances.

A third approach is related to boosting. Boosting algorithms iterative increase the weights associated with the incorrectly classified examples and decrease those associated with the correctly classified ones. Rare classes are more error-prone than common classes [9,10]. It is reasonable to believe that boosting may improve their classification performance because, overall, it will increase the weights of

---

[1] We assume the positive class is the minority class hereafter.

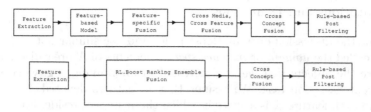

Fig. 1. The processing pipelines for concept detection. The upper part is the basic pipeline and the lower part is the one used by RL.Boost.

the examples associated with rare classes. AdaCost [11], RareBoost [12] and SMOTEBoost [13] are three boosting variants for imbalanced data. See [2] for comprehensive review of the imbalanced data problem.

The RankBoost [6] algorithm is known for boosting the weak ranking functions into a much stronger one. Though not explicitly stated, it is suitable for imbalanced data since it directly minimizes the ranking loss.

2.2   Information Fusion for Concept Detection

An excellent review for concept detection is given in [14]. The common basic framework, which relies on information fusion, comes as follows: build base classifiers independently using different features and take the weighted result as the final output. This common processing pipeline is reproduced and shown in upper part of Fig. 1. Many different kinds of low-level features are used, including visual features, audio features, textual features, and so on. Support Vector Machines (SVMs) are frequently used to build base classifiers for different features for its generalization capability under small sample size. Then these classifiers are fused in two steps of feature specific fusion and cross media, cross feature fusion. This widely accepted fusion scheme is called late fusion since fusion follows classification. Methods for setting weight to each classifier is discussed in 3.4.

The early fusion contrasts the late fusion[15]. It combines the features first and then trains a classifier using the combined feature. Other contrasting schemes like flat/hierarchical fusion, local/global fusion are also possible. See [1,15] for more references on these different schemes. However, these schemes do not explicitly investigate into the imbalanced data problem. In addition, they do not optimize a ranking measure but a classification accuracy in fusion.

3   The RL.Boost Algorithm

In this section, we first present the necessary notations and definitions, and then introduce the algorithm. The sampling method, ranking ensemble and multiple feature usage are discussed subsequently. A heuristic method for choosing feature for each iteration is also discussed in Sec 3.5.

3.1   Notations and Definitions

We follow the discussion on RankBoost in [6] and use similar notations. Let $\mathcal{X}$ be a set called the *domain* or *instance space*. Elements of $\mathcal{X}$ are called instances. These are the objects that we are interested in for ranking, e.g. video shots in the concept detection task. We assume that n features denoted $f_1, \ldots, f_n$ are given and each feature f_i is a space in which the instances reside. Each instance x_i can be represented as $x_i = (x_{i1}, \ldots, x_{in})$, where $x_{is} \in f_s$ is the instance x_i represented in feature f_s.

Let $D(x_0, x_1) \geq 0$ denote the importance that x_1 should be ranked higher than x_0. A pair x_0, x_1 is defined to be *crucial* if $D(x_0, x_1) > 0$. If there is no preference between them, we set $D(x_0, x_1) = 0$. We also set $D(x_0, x_1) = 0$ if the reversed pair x_1, x_0 is crucial and $D(x_1, x_0) > 0$ since the reversed pair provides the same information. In practice, D is normalized with $\sum_{x_0, x_1} D(x_0, x_1) = 1$ so that D is a valid distribution.

A special form of $D(x_0, x_1)$ can be introduced for bipartite problems where there exist disjoint subsets X_0 and X_1 of $\mathcal{X}$ such that, formally, for all $x_0 \in X_0$ and all $x_1 \in X_1$, we have that $D(x_0, x_1) = 1/(|X_0| \cdot |X_1|)$, and $D(x_i, x_j) = 0$ otherwise. For bipartite problems which only cares ranking all instances in X_1 above all instances in X_0, a label y_i is assigned to each instance so that $y_i = +1$ iff $x \in X_1$ and $y_i = -1$ iff $x \in X_0$. Thus, a correspondence is established between the original data label and crucial pairs for ranking and these terms are used interchangeable. In this scenario, $D(x_0, x_1)$ can be decomposed as $D(x_0, x_1) = v(x_0)v(x_1)$ for all crucial pairs x_0, x_1 where $v(x) = 1/|X_0|$ if $x \in X_0$ and $v(x) = 1/|X_1|$ if $x \in X_1$.

The learning algorithm that we study attempts to find a final ranking H with a small weighted number of crucial-pair misorderings, a quantity called the *ranking loss* and denoted $rloss_D(H)$. Formally, the ranking loss is defined as $rloss_D(H) = \sum_{x_0, x_1} D(x_0, x_1)[[H(x_1) \leq H(x_0)]] = Pr_{(x_0, x_1) \sim D}[H(x_1) \leq H(x_0)]$ where $[[\pi]]$ is defined to be 1 if predicate π holds and 0 otherwise.

AP is defined as the performance measure for the ranked list of instances returned. At any given index j, let R_j be the number of relevant instances in the top j instances. Let $I_j = 1$ if the jth instance is relevant and 0 otherwise. AP is defined as $\frac{1}{R} \sum_S^{j=1} \frac{R_j}{j} I_j$ where R is the number of true relevant instances in a set of size S; L the ranked list.

3.2   The Algorithm

RL.Boost is a modified version of RankBoost.B in [6]. Its key idea lies in iteratively sampling instance pairs for different features and combine them in a ranking ensemble. In short, It runs through three stages during the training process, namely initialization, iteration and combination. The sketch of the algorithm is summarized in Fig. 2 and explained as follows. In the initialization step, v_1 is set. In the relayed iterations that follow, D_t is computed as

$$D_t(x_0, x_1) = v_t(x_0)v_t(x_1) \tag{1}$$

Algorithm: **Relay Boost**
Given: disjoint subsets X_0 and X_1 of $\mathcal{X}$.
Initialize:

$$v_1(x_i) = \begin{cases} 1/|X_1| & \text{if } x_i \in X_1 \\ 1/|X_0| & \text{if } x_i \in X_0 \end{cases}$$

For $t = 1, \ldots, T$

- Train weak learner with sampled instances from distribution D_t (as defined by (1)) and feature f_{s_t}.
- Get weak ranking $h_t : \mathcal{X} \to \mathbb{R}$.
- Choose $\alpha_t \in \mathbb{R}$.
- Update:

$$v_{t+1}(x_i) = \begin{cases} v_t(x_i)\exp(-\alpha_t y_i h_t(x_i))/Z_t^1 & \text{if } x_i \in X_1 \\ v_t(x_i)\exp(-\alpha_t y_i h_t(x_i))/Z_t^2 & \text{if } x_i \in X_0 \end{cases}$$

where Z_t^1 and Z_t^2 normalize v_t over X_1 and X_0:

$$Z_t^1 = \sum_{x_i \in X_1} v_t(x_i)\exp(-\alpha_t y_i h_t(x_i)), Z_t^0 = \sum_{x_i \in X_0} v_t(x_i)\exp(-\alpha_t y_i h_t(x_i)).$$

Output the final ranking: $H(x_i) = \sum_{t=1}^{T} \alpha_t h_t(x_{is_t})$.

Fig. 2. The *RL.Boost* algorithm

for all crucial pairs. The crucial pairs are sampled according to D_t. It is easy to verify that $D_{t+1}(x_0, x_1) = v_{t+1}(x_0)v_{t+1}(x_1)$ if $D_t(x_0, x_1) = v_t(x_0)v_t(x_1)$ holds. Then, a separate procedure, the *weak learner* is called with a certain f_{s_t} of these sampled instance pairs to produce a *weak ranking* h_t which is a real-valued function and defines an ordering of all instances. $h_t(x_1) > h_t(x_0)$ means that instance x_1 is preferred to x_0 by h_t. However, if there is only one feature, this feature is used all the time. Finally, these weak rankings are linearly combined.

Though the learner can be any ranking optimizing algorithm, we simply use SVMs with probabilistic output for easy comparison with other state-of-the-art approaches. LIBSVM [16] implementation is used. However, incorporating ranking optimizing learner is important for future work.

The pipeline for concept detection by RL.Boost is also shown in Fig. 1. The three steps in the common processing pipeline are unified in one simple step of cross feature RL.Boost fusion. From the information fusion perspective, RL.Boost is neither pure early feature fusion [17] nor pure late classifier fusion. It unifies both feature specific fusion and cross-feature fusion in the process of producing weak rankings and thus greatly simplifies the processing pipeline.

3.3 Sampling for Weak Ranking

To avoid heavy training burden otherwise, a sampling scheme which samples crucial pairs instead of instances with respect to D_t is introduced. Rejection sampling [18] is a sampling scheme to draw examples independently from a distribution D. In rejection sampling, examples from D are obtained by first drawing examples from $\overline{D}$, and then accepting the examples with probability proportional to D. Assuming a uniform distribution $\overline{D}$, we generate a set of crucial pairs $S_t = \{(x_0, x_1)\}$ which are drawn independently from current ranking loss D_t by running the rejection sampling scheme using D_t and $\overline{D}$. There are two reasons for the sampling. Firstly, $|S_t|$ can be much smaller than $|\mathcal{X}|$ and can be fed into weak learner for more efficient ranking. Secondly, S_t can be used when the weak learner does not accept weights for pairs in $\mathcal{X}$.

We have the following theorem to upper-bound the ranking loss.

Theorem 1. *Assuming the notation of Fig. 2 and without sampling in each iteration, the ranking loss of H is $rloss_D(H) \leq \prod_{t=1}^{T} Z_t$.*

where $Z_t = Z_t^0 Z_t^1 < 1$. The detailed proof can be found in [6]. For the sampling version, theorem 1 also holds with a series of slightly different Z_t due to the sampling induced error variance. Similar analysis applies to the test generalization error [6]. We omit it here for space limitation.

3.4   Weak Ranking Ensemble

Two ensemble methods are often used, namely, average ensemble (AE) and linearly weighted ensemble (LWE). For the general form of the ranking ensemble output $H(x_i) = \sum_{t=1}^{T} \alpha_t h_t(x_{is_t})$, or similarly the late classifier fusion output, AE simply sets each $\alpha_t = 1/T$ when no more information about classifiers is available. This is a robust but conservative ensemble method. Also, numerical methods can be adopted to decide each α_t [6] and heuristic grid search is equally possible [4]. However, a more efficient and principled formula is presented below.

Since we are interested in ranking loss, α_t should be chosen so as to optimize $rloss_{D_1}(H)$. Following theorem 1, α_t can be easily derived as $\alpha_t = \frac{1}{2} \ln \left(\frac{1+r}{1-r} \right)$, where $r = \sum_i v_t(x_i) y_i h_t(x_{is_t})$ [6]. This α_t minimizes an upper bound of Z_t so that $Z_t \leq \sqrt{1 - r^2}$. Note that the expression of r differs subtly from the similar expression of AdaBoost in that different normalization factors are used for different classes. Another difference from AdaBoost is the paired sampling technique.

3.5   RL.BOOST with Multiple Features

When multiple features are present, a certain feature f_{s_t} is selected in each iteration t. This differs from the original RankBoost algorithm in that the weak ranking has to be determined online by training SVMs. The computational cost will be heavy if we search all features for the best ranking, especially when the number of features are large. So we just list the features in the increasing order of their ranking loss under D_1 and use them one-by-one circularly in the iterations to reduce the search time.

From the boosting perspective, this heuristic is surely suboptimal. From the information fusion perspective, however, this heuristic is within a principled approach and simplifies the state-of-the-art fusion pipeline greatly. Not only the intra-feature and inter-feature fusion are unified in one step, but also the combining weights can be given in a principled way. See Fig. 1 for comparison. Also, a very weak ranking h_t resulting from using a suboptimal feature at iteration t will at least not hurt the performance since α_t will be small. h_t is very weak if its ranking does not coincide with the importance defined by D_t induced by v_t. This results in a small $r = \sum_i v_t(x_i)y_i h_t(x_{is_t})$ and subsequently a small α_t.

4   Experiments

In this section, experiments are carried out on TRECVID 2005 (TV05) data set. TV05 contains 170 hours of video. A standard keyframe set of about 170, 000 keyframes are drawn. Please refer to [1] for more details about the data set. 9 out of 10 benchmarking concepts are chosen for our experiments[2]. For each concept, we only use the images annotated consistently by two independent viewers for training, excluding the conflicted or skipped images. The imbalance ratio[3] is calculated as the size ratio of positive/negative instances. As shown in Table 1, nearly all of them are heavily imbalanced.

Three visual features are extracted for each keyframe. They are 166 dimensional Global Color Histogram (CH) in HSV space, Haar Moments Grid (HMG) which is localized texture variances in Haar wavelet subbands and Color Moments Grid (CMG) which is the first 2 moments for localized color, both extracted from a 4×3 grid.

AP is taken as the benchmark measure. Mean AP (MAP) is also calculated to provide a average performance measure over all benchmarking concepts.

4.1   Experiments on Different Sampling and Ensemble Methods

We start with the experiment on different sampling and ensemble methods. Only CMG feature is used so that the counting factors are only sampling and ensemble methods. Four methods are compared, namely using all data for training, randomly sampling the data with AE ensemble, AdaBoost ensemble and RL.Boost ensemble. They are abbreviated as ALL, RAN, ADA, RLB respectively. However, here the AdaBoost ensemble is heuristically modified to apply the sampling technique only on the negative class while keeping all positive instances for each iteration. Otherwise the positive instances being small in size may have strongly skewed error distribution and thus breach the iterations hereafter. This heuristic helps the algorithm performance but surely lacks theoretical soundness. All ensemble methods run 9 iterations, an arbitrarily chosen number. An initial common sub-sampled data set, in which the negative instances is double sized of the

---

[2] "Prisoner" is not a visual concept. So it is excluded since only visual feature are used in the experiments.

[3] It differs from the standard calculation in [1] because we only use images annotated consistently, either positive or negative.

Table 1. Results for different sampling and ensemble methods with the CMG feature

	Build.	Car	Fire	Flag	Maps	Mount.	Sports	Walking	Water	MAP	improved
imbalance ratio	6.51%	3.80%	0.25%	0.50%	0.97%	0.37%	2.68%	1.92%	0.97%	-	-
ALL	0.330	0.213	0.041	0.030	0.369	0.258	0.367	0.154	0.270	0.226	0%
INI	0.290	0.133	0.021	0.025	0.387	0.140	0.231	0.103	0.187	0.168	-
RAN	0.364	0.186	0.033	0.039	0.383	0.164	0.258	0.153	0.225	0.200	-
ADA	0.394	0.234	0.034	0.043	0.392	0.264	0.364	0.161	0.302	0.243	7.64%
RLB	0.406	0.249	0.037	0.042	0.391	0.284	0.386	0.173	0.303	0.252	11.82%
improved	23.16%	17.02%	-11.62%	39.67%	6.11%	10.32%	5.32%	12.36%	12.11%	11.82%	-

positive ones, is used for all iterative methods for fairness. For easy comparison, this initial result is also shown as INI. Then in each iteration, S_t is generated by sampling so that $|S_t| \doteq 2|X_1|$ and the positive instances and negative instances are equally numbered [4]. See Table 1 for details. For SVMs, Gaussian kernel is used and both the variance γ and trade-off factor c are determined by a grid search on a cross-validation set in the INI iteration and kept fixed afterwards. Some concepts are abbreviated for display. See [1] for definitions and original spellings.

As shown in Table 1, ADA and RLB outperform ALL with 8% and 12%. RLB outperform ALL in 8/9 concepts. However, the "Fire" concept need more investigation. Maybe our parameter selection process is too crude for this concept with many representation variations. Although sometimes ADA achieves comparable performance with RLB, RLB is more stable and achieves the same AP earlier than ADA in dynamic iterations as shown in Fig. 3. Comparing ALL and RLB shows that sampling crucial pairs together helps in the imbalanced data settings, but simply random sampling (RAN) does not. Comparing ADA and RLB shows that minimizing rank loss is more preferable than minimizing classification error in the imbalanced data settings.

4.2 Experiments on Single Feature and Multiple Features

RL.Boost with the three individual features is also compared with RL.Boost with all three features. RL.Boost runs 3 iterations for each individual feature. The results are denoted as RLB.feature as shown in Table 2. The only difference between RLB.CMG in Table 2 and RLB in Table 1 is the iteration number. RLB.CMG with only 3 iterations is comparable with RLB with 9 iterations. Using the relay method for multiple features, RL.Boost runs 9 iterations with all three features in their individual MAP order. Shown as RLB.M in Table 2, it outperforms the best individual feature RLB.CMG by 17%. Therefore, the proposed RL.Boost algorithm achieves its best performance when multiple features are incorporated. This verifies that using multiple features boosts the ranking performance when they are combined in a principled way. Also the best result for each concept in TRECVID 2005 is shown as BEST. RLB.M

---

[4] $|S_t|$ is not strictly equal to $2|X_1|$ because of the rejection scheme.

Table 2. Experimental results for ensemble using different features

	Build.	Car	Fire	Flag	Maps	Mount.	Sports	Walking	Water	MAP
RLB.CMG	0.398	0.208	0.026	0.047	0.393	0.258	0.359	0.442	0.201	0.259
RLB.HMG	0.306	0.171	0.043	0.046	0.355	0.208	0.337	0.157	0.274	0.211
RLB.CH	0.154	0.058	0.013	0.010	0.348	0.091	0.179	0.071	0.091	0.113
RLB.M	0.492	0.319	0.074	0.071	0.413	0.332	0.447	0.237	0.333	0.302
BEST	0.511	0.369	0.129	0.141	0.526	0.458	0.521	0.344	0.493	0.388

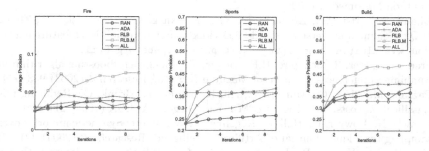

Fig. 3. Dynamic performance of some methods (best view in color)

achieves 78% of BEST using three low-level image features only while excluding the conflicting instances. However, many results in the BEST run, e.g. result of "Flag", are obtained using advanced techniques such as Random Graph Matching [5].

An illustration of the dynamic behavior of some methods is given in Fig. 3 with three randomly chosen concepts. Clearly, RLB.M outperforms all others while RLB behaves more stable than ADA though them have similar AP in the last run.

5   Conclusion

To sum up, this paper relates learning rare concept in multimedia with the more general imbalanced data problem, and proposes RL.Boost to solve it. RL.Boost differs from previous approaches in that it minimizes the ranking loss, not the classification error. RL.Boost iteratively samples crucial pairs of instances and explores multiple features for better ranking performance in a principled fusion style. All these three factors are beneficial to rare concept detection. These assertions are verifies by the large-scale experiments on the standard TRECVID 2005 data set.

There are at least four directions for future work. Adopting some ranking optimizing weak learner may do better. Combining more features of different type, such as fine-grided regional and temporal features, into this algorithm will help. Extending this algorithm to the retrieval scenario is worthwhile. Finally yet importantly, comprehensive comparison with other algorithms will provide us more insight into this algorithm.

References

1. TRECVID: Trecvid home page. http://www-nlpir.nist.gov/projects/trecvid/.
2. Weiss, G.: Mining with rarity: A unifying framework. SIGKDD Explorations **6** (2004)
3. Cortes, C., Mohri, M.: Auc optimization vs. error rate minimization. In: Proc. of NIPS 16. (2003)
4. Natsev, A., Naphade, M.R., Tešió, J.: Learning the semantics of multimedia queries and concepts from a small number of examples. In: Proc. of the ACM SIGMM Int. Conf. on Multimedia. (2005)
5. Chang, S.F., Hsu, W., Kennedy, L., Xie, L., Yanagawa, A., Zavesky, E., Zhang, D.Q.: Columbia university trecvid-2005 video search and high-level feature extraction. www-nlpir.nist.gov/projects/tvpubs/tv.pubs.org.html.
6. Freund, Y., Iyer, R., Schapire, R.E., Singer, Y.: An efficient boosting algorithm for combining preferences. Journal of Machine Learning Research **4** (2003) 933–969
7. Pazzani, M., Merz, C., Murphy, P., Ali, K., Hume, T., Brunk, C.: Reducing misclassification costs. In: Proc. of ICML, San Diego, CA, USA (1994) 217–225
8. Chawla, N., Bowyer, K., Hall, L., Kegelmeyer, W.: Smote: Synthetic minority oversampling technique. Journal of Artificial Intelligence Research **16** (2004) 321–357
9. Yan, R., Liu, Y., Jin, R., Hauptmann, A.: On predicting rare classes with svm ensembles in scene classification. In: Proceedings of the IEEE ICASSP. (2003)
10. Weiss, G.M., Provost, F.: Learning when training data are costly: the effect of class distribution on tree induction. Journal of Artificial Intelligence Research **19** (2003) 315–354
11. Fan, W., Stolfo, S.J., Zhang, J., Chan, P.K.: Adacost: misclassification cost-sensitive boosting. In: Proceedings of the 16th ICML. (1999)
12. Joshi, M.V., Kumar, V., Agarwal, R.C.: Evaluating boosting algorithms to classify rare cases: comparison and improvements. In: Proc. of First ICDM. (2001) 257–264
13. Chawla, N.V., Lazarevic, A., Hall, L.O., Bowyer, K.: Smoteboost: Improving prediction of the minority class in boosting. In: Proceedings of Principles of Knowledge Discovery in Databases. (2003)
14. Naphade, M.R., Smith, J.R.: On the detection of semantic concepts at trecvid. In: Proc. of the ACM SIGMM Int. Conf. on Multimedia. (2004)
15. Snoek, C.G., Worring, M., Smeulders, A.W.: Early versus late fusion in semantic video analysis. In: Proc. of ACM Multimedia. (2005)
16. Chang, C.C., Lin, C.J.: LIBSVM: a library for support vector machines. (2001) Software available at http://www.csie.ntu.edu.tw/~cjlin/libsvm.
17. Naphade, M.R.: The ibm trecvid concept detection: Some new directions and results. www-nlpir.nist.gov/projects/tvpubs/tv.pubs.org.html.
18. von Neumann J.: Various techniques used in connection with random digits. National Bureau of Standards, Applied Mathematics Series **12** (1951) 36–38

Comparison Between Motion Verbs Using Similarity Measure for the Semantic Representation of Moving Object

Miyoung Cho[1], Dan Song[1], Chang Choi[1], Junho Choi[1],
Jongan Park[2], and Pankoo Kim[3]

[1] Dept. of Computer Science
Chosun University, 375 Seosuk-dong Dong-Ku Gwangju 501-759 Korea
irune@chosun.ac.kr, songdan@stmail.chosun.ac.kr,
enduranceaura@gmail.com, spica@chosun.ac.kr
[2] Dept. of Information and Communication Engineering, Chosun University, Korea
japark@chosun.ac.kr
[3] Corresponding author, Dept. of CSE, Chosun University, Korea
pkkim@chosun.ac.kr

Abstract. Most of the researchers have used spatio-temporal relations for retrieval in video. It's just trajectory-based or content-based retrieval. However,
we seldom retrieve information referring to semantics. So, in this paper, we
propose a novel approach for motion recognition from the aspect of semantic
meaning. This issue can be addressed through a hierarchical model that explains
how the human language interacts with human motions. And, in the experiment
part, we evaluate our new approach using trajectory distance based on spatio-
temporal relations to distinguish the conceptual similarity and get the satisfactory results.

1 Introduction

During the last decade, the emerging technology for video retrieval is mainly based
on the content. However, semantic-based video retrieval has become more and more
necessary for the humans especially the naïve users who can only use the human
language during retrieval. So, semantic-based video retrieval research has caused
many researchers' attentions.

Since the most important semantic information for video is based on video motion
research which is the significant factor for video event representation, there has been
a significant amount of event understanding research in various application domains.
One major goal of this research is to accomplish the automatic extraction of feature
semantics from a motion and to provide support for semantic-based motion retrieval.
Most of the current approaches to activity recognition are composed of defining models for specific activity types that suit the goal in a particular domain and developing
procedural recognized by constructing the dynamic models of the periodic pattern of
human movements and are highly dependent on the robustness of the tracking[10].

H. Sundaram et al. (Eds.): CIVR 2006, LNCS 4071, pp. 281–290, 2006.
© Springer-Verlag Berlin Heidelberg 2006

Spatio-temporal relations are the basis for many of the selections users perform when they formulate queries for the purpose of semantic-based motion retrieval. Although such query languages use natural-language-like terms, the formal definitions of these relations rarely reflect the language people would use when communicating with each other. To bridge the gap between the computational models used for spatio-temporal relations and people's use of motion verbs in their natural language, a model of these spatio-temporal relations was calibrated for motion verbs.

In the previous works, the retrieval using spatio-temporal relations is similar trajectory retrieval, it's only the content-based retrieval but not semantic-based. So, in this paper, we put forward a novel approach for mapping the similarity between different motion events(actions) to the similarity between semantic indexes based our new motion model. And, in the experiment part, we evaluate our new approach using trajectory distance based on spatio-temporal relations to distinguish the conceptual similarity and get the satisfactory results. We compare the similarity between motions with similarity between trajectories based on low-level features described by spatial relations in video.

2   Overview for Motion Description

Our proposed abstraction scheme of event in video is as follows. From a video clip, various regions in frames are identified. By using region aggregation, visual objects are constructed and identified. Spatial relations of visual objects in a frame are examined by using bounding contours.

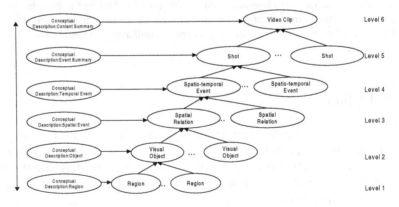

Fig. 1. Abstraction scheme for motion description in video

Spatio-temporal events are the syntactic summary of spatial-relations of visual objects in an interval. Shot is an abstracted description of spatio-temporal events with respect to semantic and syntactic aspects. The highest abstraction level is the video clip. It describes the semantic or syntactic summary of shots. In each level, there are corresponding conceptual descriptions. For instance, a region in a frame has a corresponding conceptual interpretation such as "large blue circle", "brick-textured circular region", etc. In the visual object level, a type or name (i.e., automobile, John Smith) may be assigned to a visual object. The concept mapping procedure in this level requiring complex machine vision technology is not yet mature. Therefore, we enter into manual annotation.

Conceptual description of spatial relation refers to an semantic interpretation of what happens in a certain frame with respect to spatial relations among visual objects Conceptual description of a spatio-temporal event may include information such as "who is (are) doing what during an interval". Conceptual description at the penultimate level tends to describe a topic. In this paper, we focus on level 3 and level 4(computable level) to combine primitive level with semantic level.

3 Similarity Measure Based on Trajectory

In the video data, the trajectory of a moving object plays an important role in video indexing for content-based retrieval. The trajectory can be represented as a spatio-temporal relationship between moving objects, including both their spatial and temporal properties. User queries based on the spatio-temporal relationship are as follows: "Find all objects whose motion trajectory is similar to the trajectory shown in a user interface" or "Finds all shots with a scene that person enter the building "[5].

There have been some researches on content-based video retrieval using spatio-temporal relationships in video data. Most of the researchers retrieve information by directional relation, topological relation. John Z. Li et al.[4] represented the trajectory of a moving object as eight directions. And based on the representations for moving objects' directions, they measure similarity using distance of directional relations between the trajectory of object A and that of object B. Also, Pei-Yi Chen[9] measure velocity similarity by six possible velocity trends.

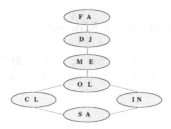

Fig. 2. The graph on topological relations

The figure2 Shows the graph that represents distance among topological relations proposed by Chang[8]. The each node means spatial relation(SA=same, CL=is-inCluded-by, IN=Include, OL=overlap, ME=meet, DJ=Disjoint, FA=Far away). Modeling topological relations is accomplished using a neighborhood graph. The topological relation models attribute the same values at each edge of the neighborhood graphs. The table 1 describes the distance between topological relations. As it shows, distance between same topological relations is 0, the distance between different topological relations is measured by count edge using the shortest distance.

Table 1. The distance between topological relations

	FA	DJ	ME	OL	CL	SA	IN
FA	0	1	2	3	4	5	4
DJ	1	0	1	2	3	4	3
ME	2	1	0	1	2	3	2
OL	3	2	1	0	1	2	1
CL	4	3	2	1	0	1	2
SA	5	4	3	2	1	0	1
IN	4	3	2	1	2	1	0

Considering the relations between two objects, we can measure the distance between them. In the table1, suppose we ignore the difference between FA and DJ, they are the same. So, the maximum distance among these relations is 4. In order to change the motion's distance into similarity, we adopt the following method like the formula shows:

$$sim(m_1, m_2) = S_{max} - distance[m_1, m_2] \tag{1}$$

Where, m_1 and m_2 mean motion to compare. S_{max} is the largest value in similarity matrix about topological relations.

However, most of the researches represent relation based on trajectory of moving object. They cannot describe recognition concept or meaning of motion. So, we cannot retrieve meaning or concept based information through natural language because the researches are not going enough. In this paper, we represent semantic of moving objects in video using motion verbs. The basic idea of proposed method is that we build hierarchical structure on motion verbs by spatio-temporal relations. Also we classify motion verbs using our model.

4 Semantic Representation for Motion

Our final goal is to provide the basis for describing high-level motion verbs using natural-language terms in video retrieval. Specifically, we are concerned the representation of motion verbs based on spatial relations.

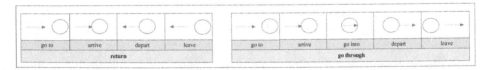

Fig. 3. Semantic representation of motion based on spatio-temporal relations

We apply our modeling which was combined the topological with directional relations to represent the semantic states based on the motion verbs which belong to the 51 classes by Beth Levin[3]. The figure 3 shows semantic representation of motions defined by the basic elements of motion verbs. Specifically, semantic level observable corresponding to objects of interest are mapped directly to general concepts and become elemental terms. This is possible because the semantic meaning of each semantic level observable is clearly defined, and can be mapped directly to a word sense. Moving objects, including moving people, are mapped to verbs. The remaining semantic level information are used as contextual search constraints as described below. This formalism provides a grounded framework to contain motion information, linguistic information and their respective uncertainties and ambiguities.

Table 2. Selected mappings from visual information to semantic terms

Visual information	Element	Attribute
object	person(noun)	-
surrounding	-	none, indoor, outdoor
motion	motion verbs / go through / \ go into go out	-
motion speed	-	none, slow , fast
motion direction	-	north, south, west, east

Elemental terms are very general, and provide entry points for searching motion concept which can be tagged with attribute values indicating that they are visible, capable of motion, and usually located indoors or outdoors. And certain visual information is mapped to attributes and is called attribute terms. As our case, we will introduce motion verbs and visual information to mapping from low-level features to the semantic-level. We define hierarchical description about motion. Figure 4 shows us that 'go into' and 'go out' are subclasses of motion word 'go through' which was set with IS_A relation. But they are different in direction and speed.

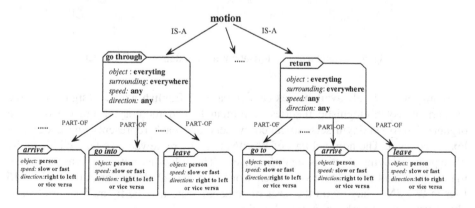

Fig. 4. Hierarchical semantic description for motion verbs

In figure 4, we represent hierarchical structure using both IS_A relation and PART_OF relation. IS_A is the interrelationship which is used to represent specialization(concept inclusion). A concept represented by C_j is said to be a specialization of the concept represented by C_i if C_j is a kind of C_i. In PART_OF relation, a Concept is represented by C_j is PART_OF a concept represented by C_i. if C_i has a C_j (as a part) or C_j is a part of C_i.

We can closely research on hierarchical structure of motion verbs. In the future works, it can be applied to semantic retrieval or indexing. Such as direction changes create the events like; person *'goes right side'* or *'goes left side'*, or *'goes away'* or *'arrives'*. And velocity changes create the events person *'stops'* or *'walks'* or *'starts running'*.

5   Evaluation

As stated above, we omit tracking and detecting work in this section. We define a region that describes a non-moving object, while a line is used to describe the trajectory of a moving object. In order not to hurt accuracy of the experiment results, we consider the WordNet as our research object which is used to compare with our model. WordNet describes relations among concepts using human knowledge.

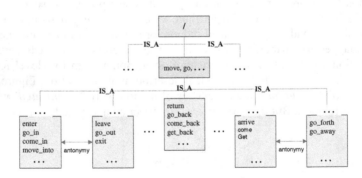

Fig. 5. Hierarchical structure about motion domain in WordNet

WordNet is a freely available lexical database for English whose design is inspired by current psycholinguistic theories of human lexical memory. English words are organized into synonym sets, so-called synsets, and each represents one underlying lexical concept. The nominal part of WordNet can be reviewed as a tangled hierarchy of hypo/hypernymy relations among synsets. The relations between synsets are semantic ones and the relations between words are lexical. Verbs are divided into 15 files in WordNet, largely on the basis of semantic criteria. The figure 5 shows hierarchical structure of verbs in motion domain [1].

5.1 Similarity Measure Based on Semantic Level

There are many features for similarity measure between trajectories. In this experiment, we measure similarity based on low-level features that use only spatial relations which are described in section 3. We got the similarity values by the method which considers the spatial relation according to temporal change.

However, considering motion verbs similarity measures based on the semantic level, there are two widely accepted approaches for measuring the semantic similarity between two concepts in hierarchical structure such as WordNet; the node-based method and the edge-based method. But the edge-based method is a more natural and direct way of evaluating semantic similarity in hierarchical structure.

In the edge-based method, we get the distance measure between c_i and c_j according to the shortest path. And then we need to change from distance between c_i and c_j to similarity.

$$Sim(c_i, c_j) = \frac{1}{D(L_{j \to i})} \tag{2}$$

where, $D(L_{j \to i})$ is a function that returns a distance factor between c_i and c_j. The shorter the path from one node to the other, the more similar they are. So, the distance between two nodes, c_i and c_j, is in inverse proportion to their similarity.

The figure 6 shows the proposed hierarchical model with the PART_OF relations between verbs in vertical direction which are presented by topological relations. We compare our model with motion model in WordNet with the IS_A relations for computing the similarity between them.

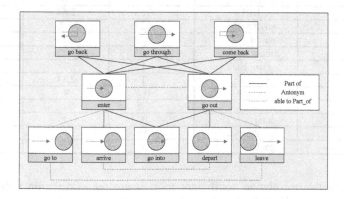

Fig. 6. Hierarchical structure about motion domain in our model

Measuring similarity between motion verbs, we don't consider link type. For example, the shortest path between 'go to' and 'arrive' is 3, and the value of the distance factor is 3. So we get 0.33 as the similarity value.

5.2 Experiment

In the previous works, we describe similarity measure both from high-level and low-level point of view. To evaluate our model that has the good representation for the semantic information, we made a total of 30 motion verbs and motion phrases by the motion classification[3]. The table 3 shows us the similarity values based on Word-Net, trajectory and our model.

Table 3. Word pair semantic similarity measurement

Word pair		Similarity based on WordNet	Similarity based on trajectory	Similarity based on our model
go_to	arrive	0.25	3.5	0.33
approach	depart	0.2	3.5	0.2
go_to	go_into	0.25	2.2	0.33
approach	leave	0.25	4	0.2
go_to	cross	0.25	2.7	0.33
go_to	come_back	0.2	2.7	0.33
approach	go_back	0.25	2.7	0.33
arrive	depart	0.25	3	0.2
reach	enter	0.33	2.5	0.5
arrive	leave	0.33	3.5	0.2
reach	go_through	0.25	2.57	0.33
arrive	return	0.25	2.43	0.33
reach	come_back	0.33	2.43	0.33
arrive	go_back	0.25	2.57	0.33
depart	enter	0.25	2.25	0.25
depart	cross	0.25	2.57	0.33
go_into	leave	0.33	1	0.33
go_into	go_through	0.25	2.29	0.33
enter	return	0.25	2.64	0.5
enter	go_back	0.25	2.64	0.5
leave	go_through	0.25	2.7	0.33
leave	return	0.25	2.29	0.33
leave	come_back	0.25	2.29	0.33
return	come_back	1	4	1
return	go_back	1	2.14	1
go_to	approach	0.2	4	1
arrive	reach	0.5	4	1
go_into	enter	1	4	1
cross	go_through	0.5	4	1
come_back	go_back	1	4	1

We adopt the correlation coefficient to measure the correlation between human judgment(based on WordNet) and machine calculations(based on trajectory and our model). The correlation coefficient is a number between 0 and 1. If there is no relationship between the predicted values and the actual values the correlation coefficient is 0 or very low. A perfect fit gives a coefficient of 1. Thus the higher the correlation is coefficient the better.

Table 4. Summary of experimental results (30 verb pairs)

Similarity Method	Correlation
Trajectory-based Method	0.380
Proposed Method	0.779

The correlation values between the similarity and the human ratings in the Word-Net are listed in Table 4. It indicates that the result of our method is relatively close to the value according to human rating. As our experiment results showed, we cannot get a good correlation coefficient, because WordNet isn't perfect to represent human judgment despite of describing relations among concepts using human knowledge. In addition, we only measure similarity based on edge(only consider IS_A, PART_OF relations) in this experiment but not reflect other relations(antonymy etc.). In the future works, we make a new similarity measurement consider other relations.

6 Conclusions

We introduce a novel model about how to recognize the motion in video using motion verbs. We present hierarchical structure about motion(such as human action) by using spatial relations. In the experiment, we prove our model that has the good representation for the semantic information by adopting the correlation coefficient to measure the correlation between human judgment(based on WordNet) and machine calculations(based on trajectory and our model) and get the satisfactory results.

Acknowledgement

This work was supported by grant No. B1220-0501-0087 from the University fundamental Research Program of the Ministry of Information & Communication in Republic of Korea.

References

1. George A. Miller "Introduction to WordNet: An On-line Lexical Database", International Journal of Lexicography, 1990.
2. http://www.cogsci.princeton.edu/~wn/
3. Beth Levin, "English Verb Classes and Alternations", University of Chicago Press 1993.
4. John Z. Li, M. Tamer Ozsu, Duane Szafron, "Modeling of Moving Objects in a Video Database", In Proceedings of the International Conference on Multimedia Computing and Systems, pp. 336-343 , 1997.
5. Choon-Bo Shim, Jae-Woo Chang, "Spatio-temporal Representation and Retrieval Using Moving Object's Trajectories", ACM Multimedia Workshops 2000: 209-212
6. M. Erwig and M. Schneider, "Query-By-Trace: Visual Predicate Specification in Spatio-Temporal Databases", 5th IFIP Conf. on Visual databases, 2000

7. Z.Aghbari, K.Kaneko, A.Makinouchi, "Modeling and Querying Videos by Content Trajectories", In Proceedings of the International Conference and Multimedia Expo, pp. 463-466, 2000
8. Jae-Woo Chang and Yeon-Jung Kim, "Spatial-Match Iconic Image Retrieval with Ranking in Multimedia Databases", Proceedings of Advances in Web-Age Information Management: Second International Conference, Jul.2001
9. Pei-Yi Chen, Arbee L.P. Chen, "Video Retrieval Based on Video Motion Tracks of Moving Objects", Proceedings of SPIE Volume 5307, 2003, pp. 550-558
10. Somboon Hongeng, Ram Nevatia, Francois Bremond, "Video-based event recognition: activity representation and probabilistic recognition method", Elsevier 2004

Coarse-to-Fine Classification for Image-Based Face Detection

Hanjin Ryu, Ja-Cheon Yoon, Seung Soo Chun, and Sanghoon Sull

Department of Electronics and Computer Engineering, Korea University,
5-1 Anam-dong, Songbuk-gu, Seoul, 136-701, Korea
{hanjin, jcyoon, sschun, sull}@mpeg.korea.ac.kr

Abstract. Traditional image-based face detection methods use a window based scanning technique where the window is scanned pixel-by-pixel to search for faces in various positions and scales within an image. Therefore, they require high computation cost and are not adequate to the real time applications. In this paper, we introduce a novel coarse-to-fine classification method for image-based face detection using multiple face classifiers. A coarse location of a face is first classified by the gradient feature based face classifier where the window is scanned in large moving steps. From the coarse location of a face, the fine classification is performed to identify the local image[1] as a face using the multiple face classifiers where the window is finely scanned. The multiple face classifiers are designed to take gradient, texture and pixel intensity features and trained by back propagation learning algorithm. Experimental results demonstrate that our proposed method can reduce up to 90.4% of the number of scans compared to the exhaustive full scanning technique and provides the high detection rate.

1 Introduction

The automatic detection of face in natural images has been intensively studied and a wide variety of techniques have been proposed so far. Among various face detection techniques, image-based methods recognize face patterns by classifying an image within a fixed size window into face and non-face prototype classes using statistic models, such as neural network [1][2][3][4], principal components analysis [5][6] and support vector machine [7][8]. In order to identify faces in various positions and scales within an image, the fixed size window is scanned at all positions for a pyramid of image that is obtained by sub-sampling the input image by a scaling factor. Therefore, the fixed size window that is the basis unit for classifying a face is scanned for multiple images at various scales. Since the fixed size window is exhaustively scanned to identify face in images at various resolutions, this method is often referred to as the multi-resolution scanning window technique. Although image-based face detection methods based on multi-resolution scanning window technique can provide high detection accuracy on low quality images, they require high computational cost.

Therefore, in order to reduce the computational cost accompanied by the window scanning procedure on the whole input image, some approaches [9][10] use skin color

---

[1] For convenience, the image within a scanning window is called a local image.

H. Sundaram et al. (Eds.): CIVR 2006, LNCS 4071, pp. 291–299, 2006.
© Springer-Verlag Berlin Heidelberg 2006

or motion to provide prior information on the estimate location of face. Although these approaches can reduce much the computational cost, they cannot be applied to gray scale and static images.

Due to this limitation, coarse-to-fine search approaches have been proposed. Approaches proposed in [11][12] made use of grid based search method. In each sub-sampled image, each intersection point of a regular grid was tested by a face classifier. If the output value of the face classifier at the intersection points of a grid was greater than a threshold value, the fine search can be started around those points. The grid based search method heavily relies on the grid step.

The method in [4] proposed a two-stage scheme to overcome the problem of exhaustive full search. In the first stage, a candidate face classifier was used to quickly discard non-face, and in the second stage a more complex classifier was used to perform final classification on the local image that passed from first stage successfully. However, the drawback is that the detection rate is lower than the full search process.

In this paper, we present a novel coarse-to-fine classification method for face detection. The proposed coarse-to-fine classification method is based on the improvement of window scanning process and the design of multiple face classifiers. For the coarse classification, the gradient based face classifier is used to find the coarse location of a face where the window is scanned in large moving steps. For the fine classification, the local image is identified as a face using multiple face classifiers where the window is finely scanned.

The window scanning process is improved by increasing the moving step of scanning window. The moving step of scanning window is empirically determined by the sensitivity analysis of adopted face classifiers. Especially, the translation invariant property of adopted gradient feature contributes to improve the scanning process in coarse classification stage.

The multiple face classifiers, which are taken as a set of different features such as gradient, texture and pixel intensity, are designed to maintain the high detection rate. That is, a weighted sum of the output values of the multiple face classifiers is used for a reliable judgment on the existence of face.

The rest of this paper is organized as follows. Section 2 introduces the system architecture based on multiple classifiers. Section 3 presents the proposed coarse-to-fine classification approach. In order to demonstrate the effectiveness of proposed method, the experimental results are provided in Section 4. In Section 5, the concluding remarks are drawn.

2   The System Architecture Based on Multiple Face Classifiers

In this section, we introduce multiple face classifiers based face detection system and their characteristics including the feature extraction process.

2.1   System Overview

The implemented system is based on multiple face classifiers which are composed of three face classifiers. Each face classifier is trained by back propagation learning algorithm and is taken as a set of different training patterns such as gradient, texture and pixel intensity. Fig. 1 illustrates the proposed overall system architecture. A pyramid of multi-resolution of the input image is obtained by a scaling factor 1.2. Before classification, each local image is converted to gray image and then pre-processed to reduce the intensity variation. In pre-processing step, a face mask is applied to remove any piece of the background image. Subsequently, the intensity normalization which consists of a correct lighting [1] and histogram equalization is used to alleviate the variation of lighting condition within local image. After pre-processing, the features of the local image are extracted and then passed to each face classifier. Each face classifier returns a result between 0.0 and 1.0.

The proposed coarse-to-fine classification is based on improvement of window scanning process and design of multiple face classifiers. In order to find coarse location of a face, the window is scanned in large moving steps and the local image that might contain a face is examined by the gradient based 1st face classifier. From the coarse location of a face, the other face classifiers identify the local image as a face where the window is finely scanned. As a confidence measure for identifying a face, we apply a weighted sum of the output values from two other face classifiers including 1st face classifier. The identified regions in each scale are mapped back to the input image scale.

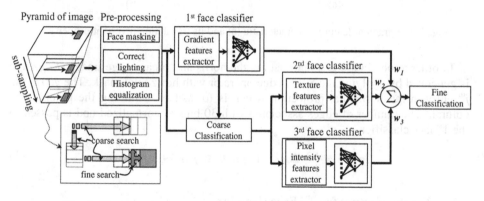

Fig. 1. The overall system architecture based on multiple face classifiers

2.2   Features for Multiple Face Classifiers

It is certain that using mixture of various classifiers may give more reliable judgment for a face than using only single classifier. Thus, we design the multiple face classifiers which are taken different representations of face patterns. The employed gradient and texture features are represented for global face appearance and the pixel intensity feature is for local face appearance. In fine classification, the texture feature compensates for the lack of global appearance in pixel intensity feature. We present, in this section, each feature's characteristics as well as the feature extraction process.

2.2.1   Gradient Feature for 1st Face classifier

The 1st face classifier is based on a gradient feature obtained from the horizontal gradient projection [13]. As shown in Fig. 2(a), the gradient feature contains the integral information of the pixel distribution, which retains certain invariability among facial features. It is noticeable that the positions of facial features are quite stable even under translating the face center regardless of different amount of gradient strength (see Fig. 2(b)). This property provides a clue to improve the window scanning process. That is, if the center of the window falls within permissible bound from the center of face, the 1st face classifier may identify a local image as a face pattern. Therefore, the determination of the permissible bound is a main problem of improving window scanning process, and the solution is described in detail in section 3.

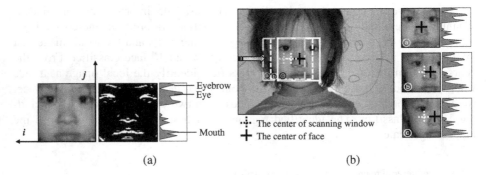

(a)   (b)

Fig. 2. The gradient feature's characteristic (a) and its translation invariant property (b).

In order to obtain the gradient feature, the horizontal binary edge image ($Edge(i,j)$) is generated by applying the Sobel edge operator with horizontal mask. The $g(j)$ is the jth entry in the horizontal projection which is formed by summing the pixels in j^{th} column. The number of edges associated with 30 bins is normalized and is passed to the 1st face classifier.

$$g(j) = \sum_{i=0}^{29} Edge(i, j),\ 0 \le j \le 29,\tag{1}$$

2.2.2 Texture Feature for 2nd Face classifier

Texture is one of the most important defining characteristics of an image. A face image can be thought of a symmetric and regular texture pattern. Although a human face has a distinct texture pattern compared to other objects, the texture feature has not been utilized widely in developing face detection. In our system, the texture feature is derived from gray level co-occurrence matrix [14]. The $(i,j)^{th}$ element of the co-occurrence matrix represents the number of times that a pixel with value i occur, in adjacent distance (d) along a direction (θ), related to a pixel with value j in an image. The texture features are extracted by three measures; correlation, variance and entropy. The correlation is related to the joint probability occurrence of the specified pixel pairs. The variance measures the amount of local variations in an image, whereas the entropy measures the disorder of an image.

When observing the co-occurrence matrix, it is important to observe that the elements are invariant to the distance and direction. Thus, the texture feature extracted from co-occurrence matrix is robust to shift and rotation of pattern in an image. This fact allows the 2nd face classifier to improve the performance in fine classification.

Fig. 3 illustrates an example of computing a co-occurrence matrix for two horizontally ($\theta = 0°$) adjacent pixels ($d=1$). The element $(0,1)^{th}$ and $(1,0)^{th}$ have value two because there are two instances where horizontally adjacent pixels have the values 0 and 1, respectively.

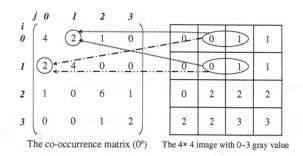

The co-occurrence matrix (0°)   The 4×4 image with 0~3 gray value

Fig. 3. An example of computing a co-occurrence matrix

Feature extraction is processed as follow:

1. The input local image (30×30) is reduced to 10×10 image by applying average filter in 3×3 size.
2. The each pixel is quantized into 25 bins for the computational efficiency.
3. Obtain texture features through the following texture measures;

$$Correlation: \frac{\sum_i \sum_j (i - \mu_x)(j - \mu_y) p(i, j)}{\sqrt{\sigma_x \sigma_y}}, \tag{2}$$

$$Variance: \sum_i \sum_j (i - \mu)^2 p(i, j), \tag{3}$$

$$Entropy: -\sum_i \sum_j p(i, j) \log(p(i, j)), \tag{4}$$

where $p(i, j)$ is the $(i, j)^{th}$ entry of the normalized co-occurrence matrix and $\mu = \mu_x = \mu_y$, because of symmetric matrix.

The extracted 9 texture features (3 measures×3 directions (0°, 45° and 90°)) are passed to the 2nd face classifier.

2.2.3 Pixel Intensity Feature for 3rd Face Classifier

The pixel intensity feature is the most commonly used input format for neural network based object detection. The methods that use pixel intensity have yielded promising detection performance so far. Especially, the regions of facial features such as eyes, nose and mouth have been proven valuable clues for classifying faces.

In our system, the pixel intensity feature is extracted from eye region, because eye region is more reliable than nose and mouth region for determining face pattern.

To extract the feature, a 10×10 smoothed image (Fig. 4(b)) is first reconstructed from the local image (Fig. 4(a)) by sub-sampling the local image with 3×3 average-mask. The normalized pixel intensity values of 40 pixels corresponding to eye region (10×4) are finally obtained (Fig. 4(c)) and are passed to the 3rd face classifier.

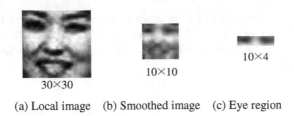

(a) Local image   (b) Smoothed image   (c) Eye region

Fig. 4. Extraction of pixel intensity feature

3   The Proposed Coarse-to-Fine Classification

The proposed coarse-to-fine classification is based on the improvement of window scanning process and design of multiple face classifiers. The problems that must be solved are related to following two matters. The first matter is how to increase the window moving step in the coarse classification and the second is how to reliably identify the local image as a face in the fine classification.

In order to increase the moving step in the coarse classification process, we use the translation invariant property of the gradient feature that is used in 1st face classifier. That is, if we know the permissible bound of translation, we can easily increase the window moving step to find coarse location of a face. For applying the translation invariant property of the 1st face classifier, we analyze the sensitivity of 1st face classifier with respect to the degrees of shift. In order to analyze the detection rate of each classifier for various moving step sizes, we collected a set of 50 images. The images were cropped around center of face in both x and y directions. One example of the test sets is shown in Fig. 5.

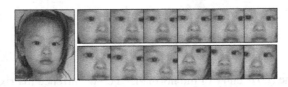

Fig. 5. Original image (left) and an example set of deformed image with respcet to shift (right)

Fig. 6(a) presents the detection rate of the 1st face classifier with respect to shift in both x and y directions when the threshold value was strictly set to 0.8. The detection rate was over 80% when the images were shifted within 10 pixels in x direction and within 4 pixels in y direction. This allows the window moving step for scanning, in the coarse classification process, to be up to 10 pixels in x direction and 4 pixels in y direction.

From the coarse location, the fine search is started where the window is shifted by 2 pixels in both x and y directions. This is based on observations that the 2nd and the 3rd face classifiers have a detection rate of over 80% when the images were shifted by 2 pixels in both x and y directions as shown in Fig. 6(b) and 6(c), respectively.

In the fine classification, a confidence measure is needed for identifying the local image as a face. In our system, a weighted sum of the results from the multiple face classifiers is used to reliably identify the local image as a face. If the weighted sum value is grater than the threshold value (τ), the local image is identified as a face.

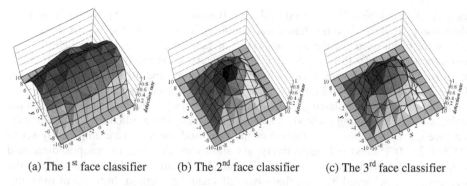

(a) The 1st face classifier   (b) The 2nd face classifier   (c) The 3rd face classifier

Fig. 6. The results of sensitivity analysis with respect to shift images

4 Experimental Results

4.1 Training Face Classifiers

Each face classifier is trained by back propagation learning algorithm and each unit in the network uses a logistic sigmoid activation function. The architectures of 1st, 2nd and 3rd face classifier are shown in Table 1.

Table 1. The architecture of each face classifier

	Input units	Hidden units	Output unit
1st face classifier	30	10	1
2nd face classifier	9	4	1
3rd face classifier	40	12	1

The 1,056 training images of face pattern came from the benchmark face database (Yale [15], AT&T², BioID³, Stirling dataset⁴) and World Wide Web. The face samples were manually normalized to 30×30 rectangle including the outer eye corners and upper eyebrows. In addition, we included the mirror-reverse and two rotation angles (5°, -5°) of each image and produced a total of 4,224 examples of faces. The non-face patterns were collected via an iterative bootstrapping procedure [1]. Before training, we used an initial training set of 2,080 non-face patterns from background images. After bootstrapping process, 15,798 non-face patterns were obtained.

4.2 Results on Several Databases

To evaluate the performance of our proposed method, we compared to an exhaustive full scanning method with several databases which were not used in the training proc-

---

² http://www.uk.research.att.com/facedatabase.html
³ http://www.bioid.com/downloads/facedb
⁴ http://pics.psych.stir.ac.uk/

ess. The test database is consisted of three different test sets (IMM[5], Caltech[6] and AR database [16]). The face databases were publicly available on the World Wide Web and were often used for the benchmarking of face detection algorithm. The images from the IMM (640×480 images) and the AR database (768×576 images) which had a uniform background with various poses, expressions and illuminations, while the Caltech database (896×592 images) varied a lot with respect to background.

Table 2 shows a tabulated comparison for the proposed method and the traditional exhaustive full scanning method on several databases. The applied threshold value (τ) and weight factors (w_1, w_2, and w_3) of the proposed method were empirically set to 0.65, 0.25, 0.35, and 0.4 respectively. As shown in Table 2, the proposed method achieved a detection rate between 93.0% and 95.7% which is almost the same as the detection rate achieved by the exhaustive full scanning method. In terms of the computational cost, we obtained the total number of scans per image used to detect the faces. It can be seen that the proposed method can reduce the number of scans up to 90.4% compared to the exhaustive full scanning method.

To compare to the computational efficiency of our proposed method with other coarse-to-fine method, we analyzed the number of scans required while maintaining similar detection rate achieved by the full scanning method. The proposed method can reduce 97.2% of the number of scans whereas a grid based search method can reduce up to 97.0% of the number of scans in the coarse classification stage. Therefore, the number of scans is similar between the two methods in the coarse classification stage. However, the proposed method requires less number of scans in the fine classification stage, since the window of the proposed method is scanned by 2 pixels in both x and y direction, compared to the grid based search method which employs exhaustive full scanning method in the fine classification stage.

Table 2. Experimental results

| Test DB | Detection results | | | | | | Reduction rates of # of scans |
| | Exhaustive full scanning method | | | Proposed scanning method | | | |
	Detection rate	# of false	# of scans per image	Detection rate	# of false	# of scans per image	
IMM	96.2 %	28	755,418	95.7 %	8	72,273	90.4%
Caltech	94.5 %	12	1,369,067	93.0 %	10	176,674	87.1%
AR	95.7 %	22	1,128,541	95.0 %	6	142,136	87.3%

5 Conclusions

In this paper, we suggest a way to overcome the computational inefficiency of exhaustive full search which is commonly used in image-based face detection. The proposed coarse-to-fine classification for face detection is based on improvement of window scanning process and design of multiple face classifiers. In order to improve

---

[5] http://www2.imm.dtu.dk/~aam/
[6] http://vision.caltech.edu/html-files/archive.html

the window scanning process for computational efficiency, we empirically determined the sub-optimal moving step of scanning window by analyzing the detection rate of each classifier for various moving step sizes. Furthermore, multiple face classifiers were designed for the reliable judgment on existence of face. Experimental results shows that our proposed method can reduce a significant amount of computational complexity with a negligible change in detection rate compare to exhaustive full search method. Therefore, our proposed method would be greatly helpful for putting real-time application into practice.

References

1. Sung, K-K., Poggio, T.: Example based learning for view based human face detection. IEEE Trans. on Pattern Analysis and Machine Intelligence, Vol. 20 (1998) 39-51
2. Burel, G., Garel, D.: Detection and localization of faces on digital images. Pattern Recognition Letter, Vol. 15 (1994) 963-967
3. Juell, P., Marsh, R.: A hierarchical neural network for human face detection. Pattern Recognition, Vol. 29 (1996) 781-787
4. Rowley, H., Baluja, S., Kanade, T.: Neural network based face detection, IEEE Trans. on Pattern Analysis and Machine Intelligence, Vol. 20 (1998) 23-38
5. Kirby, M., Sirovich, L.: Application of K1 procedure for characterization of human faces. IEEE Trans. on Pattern Analysis and Machine Intelligence, Vol. 12 (1990) 103-108
6. Turk, M., Pentland, A.: Face recognition using eigenfaces. Pro. Conf. Computer Vision and Pattern Recognition (1991) 586-591
7. Osuna, E., Freund, R., Girosi, F.: Training support vector machines: an approach to face detection. Pro. Conf. Computer Vision and Pattern Recognition, (1997) 130-136
8. Shih. P., Liu, C.: Face detection using discriminating feature analysis and support vector machine. Pattern Recognition, Vol. 39 (2006), 260-276
9. Yang, J., Waibel, A.: Tracking human faces in real time. Tech. Report CMU-CS-95-210 (1995)
10. Soriano, M., Martinkauppi, B., Hunvinen, S., Laaksonen, M.: Adaptive skin color modeling using the skin lucus for selecting training pixels. Pattern Recognition, Vol. 3 (2003) 681-690
11. Froba, B., Kublbech, C.: Robust face detection at video frame rate based on edge orientation features. Proc. Conf. Automatic Face and Gesture Recognition, (2002) 327-332
12. Feraud, R., Bernier, O. J., Viallet, J-M., Collobert, M.: A fast and accurate face detector based on neural networks. IEEE Trans. on Pattern Analysis and Machine Intelligence, Vol. 23 (2002) 42-53
13. Bebis, G., Uthiram, S., Georgiopoulos, M.: Face detection and verification using generic search. Artificial Intelligence Tools, Vol. 9 (2000) 225-246
14. Peter, R. A., Strickland, R. N: Image complexity metrics for automatic target recognizers. Automatic Target Recognizer System and Technology Conference (1990)
15. Georghiades, A. S., Belhumeur, P. N., Kriegman, D. J.: From few to many: Illumination cone models for face recognition under variable lighting and pose. IEEE Trans. On Pattern Analysis and Machine Intelligence, Vol. 23 (2001) 643-660
16. Martinez, A. M., Benavente, R.: The AR face database. CVC Tech, Report #24 (1998)

Using Topic Concepts for Semantic Video Shots Classification

Stéphane Ayache, Georges Quénot, Jérôme Gensel, and Shin'ichi Satoh

CLIPS-IMAG, LSR-IMAG, NII

Abstract. Automatic semantic classification of video databases is very useful for users searching and browsing but it is a very challenging research problem as well. Combination of visual and text modalities is one of the key issues to bridge the semantic gap between signal and semantic. In this paper, we propose to enhance the classification of high-level concepts using intermediate topic concepts and study various fusion strategies to combine topic concepts with visual features in order to outperform unimodal classifiers. We have conducted several experiments on the TRECVID'05 collection and show here that several intermediate topic classifiers can bridge parts of the semantic gap and help to detect high-level concepts.

1 Introduction

In order to retrieve and browse videos into huge databases, needs for indexing understandable concepts are rapidly growing. The extraction of such concepts is one of the main objectives of the semantic video indexing community. Although using and combining visual and text modalities are expected to improve the performance of high-level concepts classification, new issues arise. Usual approaches, merge directly visual and text features into a single flat classifier. However, even with a clever choice of relevant features, the correlation between such low-level features and high-level concepts is still weak. Such approaches assume that there exists a correlation between uttered speech and high-level concepts to classify high-level features [3, 15, 18]. But, recent TRECVID evaluations [1] have shown the limitations of such approaches: a single classifier cannot bridge this large semantic gap. Furthermore, concerning visual modality, promising results have been obtained by integrating context information based on the merging of intermediate visual concepts [17, 7, 14, 1]. Such a stacked classifier [19] learns implicit relations between intermediate concepts to derive high-level concepts.

In this study, we extend the context based framework we proposed in [1] by exploiting intermediate concepts extracted from textual modality. In order to learn relations between uttered speech and visual content, we propose to classify video shots with several intermediate topic categories, then to combine them for high-level concepts detection. We show that such topic categories provide useful semantic context when combined with visual information. The main idea is that

---

[1] TREC Video Retrieval Evaluation: http://www-nlpir.nist.gov/projects/trecvid/

H. Sundaram et al. (Eds.): CIVR 2006, LNCS 4071, pp. 300–309, 2006.
© Springer-Verlag Berlin Heidelberg 2006

several intermediate classifiers can bridge small parts of the semantic gap in order to improve the detection of high-level concepts. Similarly to the early and late fusion schemes [18], we investigate the combination of intermediate concepts by means of one and two-level fusions. We show the improvement brought by the use of topic concepts for video shots classification through several experiments performed on TRECVID'05 corpora. This paper is structured as follows: in section 2, we argue for the use of intermediate concepts; in section 3, we describe our framework based on intermediate concepts classification; in section 4, we describe and comment some conducted experiments; we finally draw some conclusions in section 5.

2   The Need for Intermediate and Understandable Concepts

Video documents contain visual, textual and audio cues (where text is mainly extracted from speech transcription). Thus, high-level concepts can be extracted from various modalities and can, on the one hand, exploit contexts from other cues while, on the other hand, provide context to them. We have shown that combining intermediate visual concepts offers rich sources of contexts and increase the derivation of high-level concepts [1, 2].

Furthermore, the extraction of understandable concepts is extremely useful for video browsing, since users can use them for expressing non-trivial information needs. Many approaches extract mid-level features by using dimensionality reduction algorithms such as PCA or LSA [13, 5, 11], yielding discriminant features which fit especially well the learned data. However, such eigen-features are hard to interpret and, hence, unusable for other multimedia tasks. Thus, in order to enrich our basis of concepts, we focus on the use of supervised classifiers in order to extract usable intermediate concepts.

2.1   High-Level Concepts

High-level concepts are input devices which allow users to express their information need for video browsing or search tasks. They can be described in terms of other concepts and are independent of the modality in which they are naturally expressed [8]. In this paper, we focus on the 10 high-level concepts defined in TRECVID'05.

2.2   Visual Concepts

We extract visual local concepts from image patches in each keyframe. Intermediate visual concepts provide spatial and semantic knowledge to higher level classifiers. We use a set of 15 visual concepts ('vegetation', 'sky', 'skin/face' ...) selected from the LSCOM ontology [12] which can be extracted from patches and are discriminative enough to help the classification of higher level concept.

2.3 Topic Concepts

We propose to extract a set of topic concepts from speech transcription [6], then to classify shots according to these intermediate concepts. We use 25 categories of the TREC Reuters collection [10] to classify each speech segment. The advantages of extracting such concepts from the Reuters collection are that they cover a large panel of news topics like the TRECVID collection, they are obviously human understandable, and thus they can be used for video search tasks. Examples of such topics are 'Economics', 'Disasters', 'Sports' and 'Weather'. Reuters collection contains about 800000 text news items in the years 1996 and 1997. They are classified among 103 topics, hierarchically structured. We used the 25 top level categories as topic concepts.

3 Video Indexing Framework for High-Level Concepts Classification

In our previous work, we have proposed a context-based approach for automatic image annotation based on intermediate local concepts [1]. Using stacking technique, a multi-layer SVM classifier learns topological and semantic contexts from image content. In the present work, topic concepts and visual global features are expected to enhance the discriminating power of semantic context. We also investigate the use of fusion classifiers in order to merge such intermediate concepts while exploiting the 2 following kinds of context:

- **Topologic context** learns the spatial distribution of a visual local concept and assign a score to the whole image. The idea behind the use of topologic context is that the confidence (or score) of an image performs better by taking into account the confidences obtained for each patch in the image for the same concept.
- **Semantic context** exploits the semantic relations between concepts based on co-occurrences learned by the classifier. The idea is that the confidence of a single concept is computed more accurately by taking into account the confidences obtained for other concepts co-occuring in the same image.

Additionally, we have shown on the TRECVID'05 evaluation that combining both contexts increases the accuracy of high-level concepts classification. By merging all the visual concept scores, a classifier learns **Topologic-Semantic** context associated with the local concepts and the high-level concepts. The classifier can activate or inhibit high-level concepts based on intermediate scores and learned relations [2].

Figure 1 shows a general view of our extended framework. At the intermediate layer, the Local classifier assigns visual local concept scores to each patch of keyframes, while the Topic classifier assigns topic concept scores to each speech segment. Then, the fusion function derives high-level concept scores at shot level, based on both the output of intermediate classifiers and the use of predefined contexts.

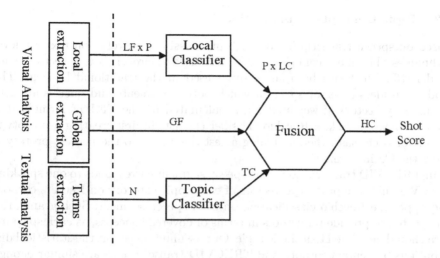

Fig. 1. Extended framework. LF and GF are numbers of Local and Global Low-level Features, P is the number of Patches, LC denotes the number of Visual Local concepts, HC denotes the number of high-level concepts, N is the number of inputs terms and TC the number of Topic Concepts.

3.1 Visual Concepts Classification

We classify each keyframe using intermediate local concepts and global low-level features. One local concept corresponds to the score of one patch according to a visual concept. In order to derive high-level concepts, we merge local concepts using Topologic-Semantic context. Additionally, the use of global low-level features is expected to enhance local only classification.

Visual low-level extraction. As we want to handle the topologic context, we need to compute low-level features for parts of the image, as well as for the whole image. In order to compute local features, many approaches have been proposed. Since the automatic and a priori segmented regions are usually too far from the semantic meaning of image, we have decided to split images into patches. By doing so, we should be far from semantic, but with such granularity one patch is more likely to contain one single concept.

- **Local features:** We first split the image into overlapping patches. In our experiments, we use $P = 20 \times 13$ patches of 32×32 pixels. For each patch, we compute 9 color momentums (3 means + 6 co-variances), 24 Gabor wavelets for texture (3 scales x 8 orientations), and the 2 coordinates of the patches.
- **Global features:** More information can be extracted from a whole image than from a single patch. We extract $4 \times 4 \times 4$ three-dimensional histograms for color features based on RGB channels, Gabor wavelets for texture (5 scales $\times$ 8 orientations), and the first two momentums of motion vectors obtained from optical flow.

3.2   Topic Concepts Classification

Based on speech transcription data, Topic classification relies on text retrieval techniques. The most common and widely used approach is the Vector Space Model [16], which has been successfully used in the traditional IR field. The model considers a vector space in which both documents and queries are represented by vectors of weighted terms calculated by the TF.IDF formula. For the classification task, a Rocchio classifier consists in first creating a prototype vector for each class, then assigning a test document to the nearest prototype using the Cosine similarity.

In TRECVID transcriptions, one speech segment corresponds to one speaking turn. We build the prototype vectors of each topic category on Reuters corpora and apply the Rocchio classification on each speech segment. Such granularity is expected to provide robustness in terms of covered concepts, as each speaking turn should be related to a single topic. Our assumption is that the statistical distributions of Reuters corpora and TRECVID transcriptions are similar enough to obtain relevant results. Finally, we derive high-level concepts by merging outputs of Topic concept classifiers.

Text analysis. We construct a vector representation for each speech segment by applying stop-list and stemming. Also, in order to avoid noisy classification, we reduce the number of input terms. While the whole collection contains more than 250000 terms, we have experimentally found that considering the top 2500 frequently occurring terms gives the better classification results on Reuters collection.

3.3   Combining Intermediate Features

Combining intermediate concepts aims at deriving high-level concepts from several unimodal intermediate concepts. Such strategy leads to a multimodal shot classifier. In order to unify outputs of intermediate classifiers, we report the topic concept scores of speech segments to each keyframe. A given keyframe, corresponding to the time point T, is associated with the speech-segment delimited by the time bounds TB and TE so that $TB \leq T \leq TE$.

We identify two possibilities to merge intermediate features, depending on the abstraction level considered. Similarly to the early and late fusion schemes defined in [18], we use either a one level or a two level fusion schemes, described as follows:

One-level fusion: In a one-level fusion process, intermediate features or concepts are concatenated into a single flat classifier, as in an early fusion scheme [18]. Such a scheme takes advantage of the use of the semantic-topologic context from visual local concepts, and semantic context from topic concepts and visual global features. However, it is constrained by the curse of dimensionality problem. Also, the small numbers of topic concepts and global features compared to the huge amount of local concepts can be problematic: the final score might strongly depend upon the local concepts.

Two-level fusion: In a two-level fusion scheme, we classify high-level concepts from each modalities separately at a first level of fusion. Then, we merge the obtained outputs into a second layer classifier. We investigate the following possible combinations. Classifying each high-level concept with intermediate classifiers, then merging outputs into a second level classifier is equivalent to the late fusion defined in [18]. Using more than two kinds of intermediate classifiers, we can also combine pairwise intermediate classifiers separately, then combine given scores in a higher classifier. For instance, we can first merge and classify global features with topic concepts, then combine the given score with outputs of local concept classifiers in a higher classifier. An other possibility is to merge separately local concepts with global features and local concepts with topic concepts, then to combine the given scores in a higher level classifier. Advantages of such schemes are numerous: the second layer fusion classifier avoids the problem of unbalanced inputs, and keep both topologic and semantic contexts at several abstraction levels.

We compute high-level concept scores for each keyframe using the predefined fusion classifiers. Then, in order to set a score to video shots, we keep the keyframe which has the maximum score, according to the idea that a concept occurs in a shot if one of the sub-shots contains this concept.

4   Experiments

We evaluate the use of visual and topic concepts and their combination for high-level concepts detection in the conditions of the TRECVID'05 evaluation. We show the 10 high-level concepts classification results evaluated with the trec_eval tool using the provided ground truth, and compare our results with the median over all participants. We have used a subset of the training set in order to exploit the speech transcription of the samples. As the quality of TRECVID'05 transcription is quite noisy due to both transcription and translation from Chinese and Arabic videos, some video shots do not have any corresponding speech transcription. In order to compare visual only runs with topic concept based runs, we have trained all classifiers using only keyframes whose transcript is not empty. In average, we have used about 300 positives samples and twice as many negative samples.

It has been shown in [10] that SVM outperforms a Rocchio classifier on text classification. In this experiment, we first show the improvement brought by the topic concepts based classification by comparing with a SVM text classifier based on the uttered speech occurring in a shot after same text analysis as topic classifiers. Then, we give some evidence of the relevance of using topic concepts, by showing the improvement of unimodal runs when combined with the topic concepts. In a second step, we compare one-level fusion with two-level fusion for combining intermediate concepts. We have implemented several two-level fusion schemes to merge the output of intermediate classifiers. Particularly, we show that pairwise combinations schemes can increase high-level concepts classification.

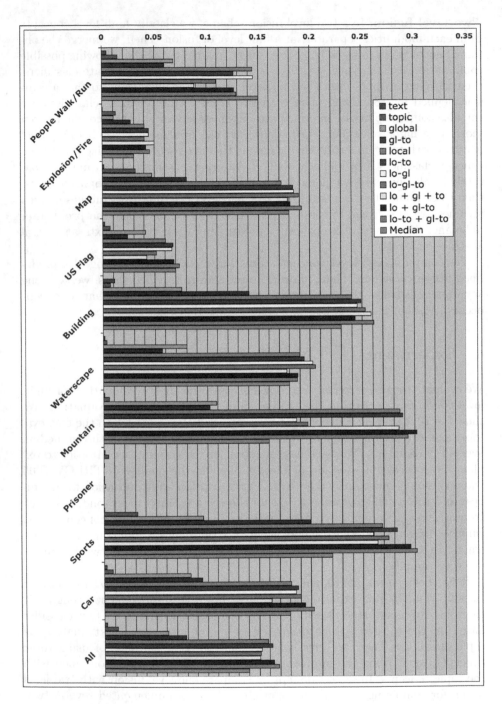

Fig. 2. Mean Average Precision of the 10 high-level concepts of TRECVID'05

We used a SVM classifier with RBF kernels as it has proved good performance in many fields, especially in multimedia classification. LibSVM [4] implementation is easy to use and provides probabilistic classification scores as well as efficient cross validation tool. We have selected the best combination of parameters C and Gamma out of 110, using the provided grid search tool.

Figure 2 shows the Mean Average Precision (MAP) results of the conducted experiments. We compare our results with the TRECVID'05 median result. 'Text', 'Topic' 'Global' and 'Local' experiments refers to the use of unimodal classifiers. On fusion experiments, the sign '-' refers to a one-level fusion and the sign '+' refers to the second-level fusion. For instance, in the run 'lo-to' we have concatenated inputs of the 'Local' and 'Topic' runs, and for the 'lo-to + gl-to' run, we have merged in a second level fusion scheme the classification results of 'lo-to' and 'gl-to' runs.

Topic concepts based classification performs much better than text based classifier, the gain obtained by topic concepts based classification is obvious. It means that despite the poor quality of speech transcription, intermediate topic concepts are useful to reduce the semantic gap between uttered speech and high-level concepts. Each intermediate topic classifier provides significant semantic information despite the differences between Reuters and TRECVID transcripts corpora. It is interesting to notice that the 'Sports' concept is also a Reuters category and has the best MAP value for the Topic concepts based classification.

For 'Global' run, we have directly classified high-level concepts using their corresponding global low level features. When combined with topic concepts, the average MAP increases by 30%, and up to 100% on Sports high-level concept. Also, some high-level concepts which have poor topic based classification MAP cannot benefit from the combination with topic concepts.

The use of the topologic-semantic context in local concepts based classification improves clearly the performance over the global based classifier. However, we observe a non significant gain when combined with topic concepts. This can be explained by the huge numbers of 'Local' inputs compared with the few numbers of 'Topic' inputs. Since we have used RBF kernel, the topic concepts inputs have a very small impact on the euclidian distance between two examples. A solution to avoid such unbalanced inputs could be to reduce the numbers of local concepts inputs using a feature selection algorithm before merging with the topic concepts. Despite this observation, we notice that we obtain better results by combining Local with Topic concepts than combining Local concepts with Global features.

We have conducted several experiments to combine 'Topic' concepts with 'Local' and 'Global' features. Where 'Local' only classification performs very well for some "visual" high-level concepts (Mountain, Waterscape), we can observe an improvement using fusion based runs for most of high-level concepts. The runs 'lo-go-to' and 'lo + go + to', which correspond respectively to the early and late fusion schemes, provide roughly similar results and do not outperform visual local classifier. This is probably due to the relative good performance of 'Local' run compared to other runs.

We have obtained the most significant results using two-level fusion when combining separately topic concepts with local and global features in the first fusion layer. In this case, the duplication of topic concepts at the first level fusion performs better by 10% than other fusion schemes. With such a scheme, topic concepts integrate useful context to visual features and achieve significant improvement, compared to unimodal classifiers, for most of high-level concepts.

5 Conclusion

In this paper, we investigate the use of topic concepts on a generic framework for high-level concepts video shots classification. We show that topic concepts based classification performs much better than a single text classifier to classify high-level concepts. In addition, we show that combined with visual cues, topic concepts can improve shots classification despite the poor quality of speech transcriptions. However, in some case, the 'Local' unimodal classifier does better than other fusion strategies. This could be due to the huge numbers of 'Local' inputs compared to the few numbers of 'Topic' inputs. The RBF kernel used in the presented experiments was not able to handle such unbalanced inputs.

Furthermore, regarding to the 'Sports' classification performance, the choice of topic categories seems to have a direct impact on the high-level concepts classification. Therefore, in future work, we intend to improve the topic based classification by carefully selecting the topic categories and also by appropriately normalizing the texts of Reuters and TRECVID collections. It should be also interesting to evaluate our approach on the TRECVID 2003 and 2004 collections which have better quality transcriptions.

Bibliography

[1] S. Ayache and G. Quénot and S. Satoh. Context-based conceptual image indexing. In ICASSP, 2006.
[2] S. Ayache and G. Quénot and J. Gensel and S. Satoh. CLIPS-LSR-NII experiments at TRECVID 2005. In TRECVID Workshop, 2005.
[3] S. Ayache and G. Quénot and M. Charhad. Video shot classification using lexical context. In European Conference on Information Retrieval, 2005.
[4] C. Chang and C Lin LIBSVM: a library for support vector machines, 2001. Software available at http://www.csie.ntu.edu.tw/ cjlin/libsvm
[5] A Garg, S Agarwal, T.S. Huang. Fusion of Global and Local Information for Object Detection. In 16th International Conference on Pattern Recognition (ICPR'02) - Volume 3, 2002.
[6] J.L. Gauvain, L. Lamel, and G. Adda. The LIMSI Broadcast News Transcription System. Speech Communication, 37(1-2):89-108, 2002.
[7] G. Iyengar and H.J. Nock. Discriminative model fusion for semantic concept detection and annotation in video. MULTIMEDIA '03: Proceedings of the eleventh ACM international conference on Multimedia, 2003.
[8] G. Iyengar and H. Nock and C. Neti and M. Franz. Semantic indexing of multi-mediq using audio, text and visual cues. In IEEE Int. Conference on Multimedia and Expo, 2002.

[9] D. Lewis, F. Li, T. Rose, and Y. Yang. The reuters corpus volume I as a text categorization test collection. In Journal of Machine Learning Research, 2003.

[10] Lewis, D. D.; Yang, Y.; Rose, T.; and Li, F. RCV1: A New Benchmark Collection for Text Categorization Research. Journal of Machine Learning Research, 5:361-397, 2004.

[11] D. A. Lisin, M. A. Mattar, M B. BlMark C. Benfield and E. G. Learned-Miller. Combining Local and Global Image Features for Object Class Recognition. In CVPR, 2005.

[12] LSCOM Lexicon Definitions and Annotations Version 1.0. DTO Challenge Workshop on Large Scale Concept Ontology for Multimedia, Columbia University AD-VENT Technical Report #217-2006-3 , March 2006.

[13] K. Murphy, A. Torralba, D. Eaton and W. Freeman. Object detection and localization using local and global features. Sicily Workshop on Object Recognition. Lecture Notes in Computer Science, 2005.

[14] M. Naphade. On supervision and statistical learning for semantic multimedia analysis. Journal of Visual Communication and Image Representation, 15(3):348369, 2004.

[15] H. J. Nock, G. Iyengar, C. Neti. Issues in speech-based retrieval of video. In ISCA Tutorial Workshop, 2003.

[16] G. Salton. Introduction to Modern Information Retrieval. McGraw-Hill, 1983

[17] C.G.M. Snoek, M. Worring, J.M. Geusebroek, D.C. Koelma and F.J. Seinstra. The MediaMill TRECVID 2004 Semantic Video Search Engine. InTRECVID Workshop, 2004.

[18] C.G.M. Snoek and M. Worring and A.W.M. Smeulders. Early versus Late Fusion in Semantic Video Analysis. Proceedings of ACM Multimedia, 2005.

[19] D.H. Wolpert Stacked Generalization. Neural Networks, Vol. 5, pp. 241-259, Pergamon Press.

A Multi-feature Optimization Approach to Object-Based Image Classification*

Qianni Zhang and Ebroul Izquierdo

Queen Mary, University of London,
Mile End Road, E1 4NS, London, UK
{qianni.zhang, ebroul.izquierdo}@elec.qmul.ac.uk

Abstract. This paper proposes a novel approach for the construction and use of multi-feature spaces in image classification. The proposed technique combines low-level descriptors and defines suitable metrics. It aims at representing and measuring similarity between semantically meaningful objects within the defined multi-feature space. The approach finds the best linear combination of predefined visual descriptor metrics using a Multi-Objective Optimization technique. The obtained metric is then used to fuse multiple non-linear descriptors is be achieved and applied in image classification.

1 Introduction

Content-based image retrieval uses descriptors derived from low-level image features and user relevance feedback to successively find pictures in a database according to a predefined metric in the descriptor space. These approaches rely on low-level analysis for the inference and classification process [1]. For this reason, the retrieval output often has little in common with high-level classification as expected by human observer.

Though low-level feature extraction algorithms are well-studied and able to capture important patterns in visual information [2], the bridge between automatic classification using such low-level primitives and higher level concepts remains an open problem. This challenge is referred to as 'the semantic gap' [3].

In this paper the problem of semantic image classification using multiple descriptors is considered. The emphasis is on single objects rather than on the whole scene depicted in the image. However segmentation is not assumed, since segmenting an image into single object is almost as challenging as the semantic gap problem itself. To deal with objects in images, small image blocks of regular size are considered. This paper focuses on devising an approach for combining the low-level descriptors and finding suitable metrics to represent and measure similarity between semantic objects. It is argued that semantic objects cannot be described by single low-level descriptors and metrics. Their nature is complex and requires a suitable combination of descriptors and multi-feature metric

---

* The work leading to this paper was partially supported by the European Commission under contracts FP6-001765 aceMedia and FP6-027026 K-Space.

H. Sundaram et al. (Eds.): CIVR 2006, LNCS 4071, pp. 310–319, 2006.
© Springer-Verlag Berlin Heidelberg 2006

spaces. But most low-level visual descriptors show non-linear behaviours and their direct combination may become meaningless. Some approaches to combine them have been suggested, like combining descriptor distances by reducing the metric combination to a single selected by a Boolean decision model and application of weighted linear merging of distances where the weights are accumulated from learned examples [4, 5]. A method to measure "visualness" of concepts in introduced in [6]. It performs probabilistic region selection for labeled images and computes an entropy measure of "visualness". In another approach user query is first classified into one of the predefined categories and the retrieval results with query-class associated weights are then aggregated by learning from the development data [7].

The idea of this paper is different from these methods and others in the literature. We propose to combine descriptors and optimize their metrics by analyzing the underlying patterns of low-level visual primitives in the training set. Then the classification of images is done based on the obtained metric. The proposed strategy is based on a Multi-Objective Optimization (MOO) technique, in particular the Pareto Archived Evolution Strategy (PAES) is adopted in this paper as optimization algorithm [8, 9, 10].

The paper is organized as follows: section 2 describes the strategy for block-based concept modeling and feature extraction. Section 3 introduces the proposed technique for building metric in a multi-feature space. Experimental evaluation of the proposed approach is presented in section 4 and the paper closes with conclusions and future work in section 5.

2   A Block-Based Approach to Visual Concept Modeling Using Low-Level Primitives

Usually users are interested in finding single semantically meaningful objects rather than global descriptions of whole scenes such as landscapes, cityscapes, sunsets, or other elements make up the scenes. However current object segmentation technologies are not yet powerful enough to distinguish areas of an object from noisy areas like other objects or backgrounds when multiple objects are overlapping or when the object consists of several parts that are visually very different. Instead of doing segmentations, images can be regarded as mosaics of small building blocks as objects representation. In most cases these building blocks do not represent semantic concepts. But, small blocks of semantic objects should have certain similarity in their visual patterns. In this paper these blocks are referred as 'elementary building blocks', and some of these blocks that, according to professional user's subjective judgment, could best represent the visual patterns of a concept are chosen as 'representative building blocks'. Sets of these representative blocks can be used for visual pattern analysis and extraction. Having a small but very representative set of representative building elements for each semantic concept at hand, a suitable descriptor and its metric in a multiple feature space is sought by using the proposed method described in Section 3.

2.1   Object-Based Approach

In the proposed approach the each image is split into 8x8 blocks of regular size. Among the database of the elementary blocks, a professional user is required to select a set of best representative examples for a concept. Several visual features of the example set are analyzed and used as the training set of finding the most suitable metric space that combines them. An examples of choosing representative elementary building blocks of semantic concepts from one image is illustrated in Fig. 1.

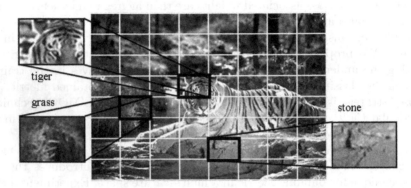

Fig. 1. An image consisting of complex objects is split into elementary building blocks representing single objects

2.2   Feature Extraction and Metric Definition in Multi-feature Space

The primitives used by the proposed analysis are selected from the visual descriptors including MPEG-7 Colour Layout (CLD), Colour Structure (CSD), Dominant Colour (DCD), and Edge Histogram (EHD) [11]. Two texture features are also used as low-level primitives: Texture feature based on Gabor Filters (GF) [12] and Grey Level Co-occurrence Matrix (GLCM) [13]. Additionally, to emphasis invariance to saturation, Hue-Saturation-Value (HSV) [14] color system is also considered.

As mentioned before since most low-level visual descriptors are complex and non-linear, they cannot be combined directly. Thus in this paper a combination of distances with certain metric is used as a similarity measurement. In the very first stage, a step to measure the primitive distances of blocks within different descriptor spaces is conducted. A distance function or metric is defined as

$$d = dist(v_1, v_2) \tag{1}$$

and varies for different descriptors, where v_1, v_2 are the feature vectors for a particular descriptor.

Suppost n descriptors are considered, v_j is the j_{th} descriptor used, $j = [1, n]$. To combine the distance calculated for each elementary block, the most straightforward candidate of possible metrics in the multi-feature space is the linear combination of the distances defined for the descriptors:

$$D(V_1, V_2, A) = \sum_{j=1}^{n} \alpha_j d_j(v_j^{(1)}, v_j^{(2)}) \qquad (2)$$

where D is the sum of a set of distance function as defined (1), and it measures the distance between two sets of feature vectors in a multi-feature space. A is the set of weighting coefficients α we are seeking to optimize. For the specific case given by (2), the optimality problem is regarded in the sense of both concept representation and discrimination power.

The approach to estimate a metric in the underlying multi-feature space relies on comparing different descriptors. Unfortunately, in most cases comparing these functions becomes meaningless. To ensure minimum comparability requirement all distances are normalized using simple *Min-Max Normalization*. This transforms the distance output into the range $[0, 1]$ by applying:

$$d_{j(new)} = \frac{d_j - min_j}{max_j - min_j}. \qquad (3)$$

3   Image Classification in Multi-feature Space

The overall procedure of the proposed approach can be divided into three stages: the pre-processing stage, the learning stage and the classification stage. This is illustrated in Fig. 2. The pre-processing stage includes steps of splitting images into blocks and low-level feature extraction. Besides, in this stage some representative block are selected, their centroid is calculated, and a distance matrix

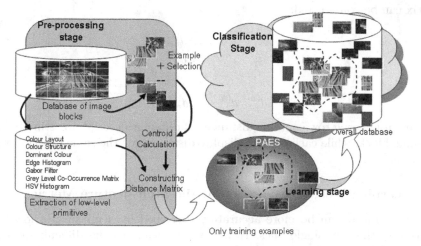

Fig. 2. The overall procedure in a scenario of searching for images of 'tiger' using proposed approach

is constructed. The learning stage uses PAES to define a multi-dimensional similarity metric space. The classification stage uses the learned metric to classify blocks in database.

3.1 The Pre-processing Stage

Initially all images are split into blocks and the visual features of the blocks are extracted. Given a semantic concept that the user would like to retrieve, the first step of the proposed approach is to build up the training group of 'representative building blocks'. It is required for a visual representative element group to be able to represent the nature that the objects of a concept have in common. Besides, it is also required that it possesses the discriminating power of the concept from noise of unrelated elements. Therefore in this paper two types of the representative example are selected and both of the two types are combined in a training set. The first type of representatives is the most relevant examples to a concept in common understanding and they are referred as 'positive examples', while the second are 'negative examples' which, intuitively, should consist of blocks that are visually close to the concept but do not represent the targeting concept.

Let $S = \{s^{(i)} | i = 1, ..., m\}$ be the training set of elementary building blocks containing m elememts in total. For n low-level descriptors, a $m \times n$ matrix is formed in which each element is a descriptor vector. The centroid for each descriptor is calculated by finding the block with the minimal sum of distances to all other blocks in S. All the centroids across different descriptors form a particular set of vectors $\bar{V} = \{\bar{v}_1, \bar{v}_2, ..., \bar{v}_n\}$, in which $\bar{v}_j$ is the centroid vector for all the vectors of the j_{th} descriptor used.

In general $\bar{V}$ does not necessarily represent a specific block of S. Taking $\bar{V}$ as an anchor, for a given concept representing an object the following distance matrix can be constructed:

$$
\begin{matrix}
d_1^{(1)} & d_2^{(1)} & \cdots & d_n^{(1)} \\
d_1^{(2)} & d_2^{(2)} & & d_n^{(2)} \\
\vdots & & \ddots & \\
d_1^{(m)} & d_2^{(m)} & & d_n^{(m)}
\end{matrix}
\tag{4}
$$

is built. In (3) each row contains distances of different descriptors estimated for the same block, while each column display distances for the same descriptor for all blocks.

3.2 Learning Weighting Factors for the Multi-feature Metric

Semantic objects can be more accurately described by a mixture of low-level descriptors than by single ones. However, this leads to the difficult question about how descriptors can be mixed and what is the "optimal" contribution of each feature. In a realistic scenario, an approach based on optimizing a single objective function will not lead to acceptable results because of the complex

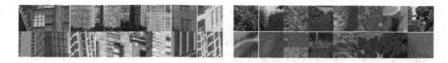

Fig. 3. Examples of image blocks for 'Building' group (left) and 'Flower' group (right)

nature of semantic objects. Often for semantically similar objects, their visual primitives are not similar. Even worse, in many cases different low-level visual features contradict each other. To illustrate the conflicting nature of the objective function presented in (2), an example is considered in Fig 3.

Fig 3 shows Examples of image blocks for 'Building' group (left) and 'Flower' group (right). Blocks selected from images containing buildings ('Building' group) and blocks containing red flower ('Flower' group) are shown in this figure. Considering the 'Flower' group and its intrinsic concept (flower), a colour descriptor identifies blocks in which the red colour is dominant. That is, if single objective optimization is used, say for two descriptors, CLD and EHD, a weight of 1 will be assigned to CLD while a weight of 0 will be assigned to EHD. The retrieval process will mark predominantly red blocks in the database as "Flowers". In this case the edges or textures of the flowers, which also strongly contribute to the semantic concept, will be fully ignored. On the other hand, for the 'Building' group, using a single objective optimization for CLD and EHD, the EHD will dominate the similarity estimation while the CLD or other colour and texture features that are also important for the concept will again be neglected. In order to include all the descriptive characters contained in every single representative building block, each of them should be considered as an objective function in the optimization problem. However, when optimizing a set of contradicting objective functions, usually there is not unique solution achieving an optimum for all objectives at the same time. The solution of the problem at hand is closely related to multiple decision making strategy in which simultaneous optimization of multiple objectives is sought.

In this paper the Pareto Archived Evolution Strategy (PAES) [8] is adopted to optimize the combination metrics. PAES is an evolution strategy employing local search but using a reference archive of previously found solutions to identify the approximate dominance ranking of the current and candidate solution vectors. This will produce a set of set of Pareto Optimal Solutions. Unfortunately none of these pareto-optimal solutions can be identified as better than others without any further consideration, so a second step is required: a higher-level decision-making involving further considerations to choose a single solution.

In this paper the second step is based on finding the minimum solution of

$$F = \frac{sum\ of\ objective\ functions\ of\ all\ positive\ examples}{sum\ of\ objective\ functions\ of\ all\ negative\ examples} \tag{5}$$

considering the that small sums of weighted distances of positive examples means better gathering of all positive points while big sums of weighted distances of negative examples means sparseness of the negative points, which is just the target we are seeking to achieve.

An intensive study as well as comparison with other algorithms in MOO is done in [8]. As a result PAES is a capable multi-objective optimizer across the problems tested.

The problem of finding the suitable metric consists of finding the optimal set of weighting factors α, where optimality is regarded in the sense of both concept representation and discrimination power. This optimization problem can be tackled by minimizing or maximizing one or several objective functions as in (2).

For a given semantic concept and its according distance matrix (3), the optimization is then performed on the set of objective functions like (2):

$$\bar{D}(V, \bar{V}, A) = \begin{cases} D_1(V_1, \bar{V}, A) \\ D_2(V_2, \bar{V}, A) \\ \vdots \\ D_m(V_m, \bar{V}, A) \end{cases} \tag{6}$$

In (5) $\bar{D}$ is the set of objective functions $\{D_i, i = 1, ...m\}$, D_i is the distance vector of the i_{th} block, and A is the collection of weighting factors. The optimal solution is to find the $A = \{a_j | j = 1, ..., n\}$ by which the objectives of positive examples in $\bar{D}$ reaches their minimal values while the objectives of negative examples in $\bar{D}$ reaches their maximal values, subject to constraint $\sum_{j=1}^{n} a_j = 1$. This set of weighting factors is assumed to be the metric that represents the symbolic nature of the concept within a multi visual feature space.

According to the different kinds of examples the way of optimizing the objective functions are different. The optimization process is to simultaneously minimizing the objective functions from the positive representative group and maximizing the objective functions from the negative representative group.

3.3   Classification: The Minimum (Mean) Distance Classifier

The Minimum (Mean) Distance Classifier (MDC) is utilized in this paper for classification within the obtained multi-feature metric space. The reason of choosing it as the classifier is that it is simple to implement and works well when the distance between means is large compared to the spread of each class. What's more, because of its simplicity, it is easy and safe to be transformed into any desired non-linear high-dimensional multi-feature space. Some more intelligent classifier may also be used in future but for now they are avoided despite their various appealing characters, due to the uncertainty of their behaviours when adapted into the transformed metric space.

MDC is a special case of classifiers based on discriminant functions. It is usually applied in linear space, but in this paper, it is adapted to the metric space which combines several non-linear similarity functions of descriptors by the linear weighted function obtained from the PAES algorithm.

The centroid vector as we described in Section 2.2 from the positive examples is used as the mean of the positive class, and is referred later as $\bar{V}_+$. On the other hand a $\bar{V}_-$ that can be obtained by using the same method from the negative examples is used as the mean of the negative class. Using the obtained metric, say $A = \{a_j | j = 1, ..., n\}$, write the distance functions to the two mean values as:

$$D_{i+}(V_+^{(i)}, A) = \sum_{j=1}^{n} \alpha_j d_{j+} \qquad (7)$$

$$D_{i-}(V_-^{(i)}, A) = \sum_{j=1}^{n} \alpha_j d_{j-} \qquad (8)$$

$D_+^{(i)}$ is the distance vector of the i_{th} block to $\bar{s}_+$, and vice versa; while D_{i+} is the similarity estimation of the i_{th} block in the obtained metric space, and vice versa. The decision boundary which separates the positive class from the negative class is given by:

$$D_{i+}(V_+^{(i)}, A) - D_{i-}(V_-^{(i)}, A) = \delta \qquad (9)$$

where δ is a variable that is usually 0 but can be changed for different concepts to fit different requirements.

4   Experimental Evaluation

As stated before current approaches from the conventional literature combine multiple features for image classification using a different model. Usually, classification is done applying single descriptors and fusion of results is performed after the initial mono-feature classification. This makes it difficult to compare our approach with relevant ones from the literature. Even a simple analysis of the final results, for the sake of comparison, is not feasible due to the lack of common test sets. A more critical fact rendering a fair comparative study almost impossible is that software implementation of previously reported approaches is not available and it is not trivial to implement them using only the reported algorithmic steps. For these reasons in this paper only a set of experiments using each single descriptor have also been performed for comparison with the proposed approach.

4.1   Experimental Setup

The test data contains 700 images selected from 'Corel' dataset. The images are labeled manually on 5 predefined concepts as ground truth. The concepts are "building" (141), "cloud" (264), "grass" (279), "lion" (100), and "tiger" (100). The numbers in brackets after concepts are the numbers of images containing the concepts in the test dataset according to ground truth.

As the propose approach classifies images based on their elementary building blocks, we argue that if a block of an image is classified as relevant to a concept, then the image itself is judged as similar to the concept. As a retrieving performance evaluation the MDC is used as a classifier.

4.2 Experimental Results and Evaluation

A group of 10 positive representative blocks and 10 negative representative blocks are manually selected to represent each concept by professional user. For each group (concept) a distance matrix (5) has been computed with the selected blocks and the 7 descriptors used resulting in sets of 7 weighting factors. Using the 7 weighting factors as a combination metric, the accuracy of relevant images classified by the MDC classifier is shown in Table 1, as the first column in each row. The experiments using each single descriptor are also shown in Table 1 for comparison and evaluation.

As it can be observed from Table 1, among the 5 groups of experiments, in the experiments for "cloud", "grass", "lion" and "tiger", the approach using the obtained metric outperforms the approached using any single one of the 7 descriptors. Only in the "building" group the single descriptor EHD slightly outperforms the proposed approach.

Table 1. The accuracy of image classification using obtained metric

%	Obtained metric	CLS	CSC	DCD	EHD	GF	GLCM	HSV
building	70	48	24	20	74	40	38	42
cloud	79	76	70	38	68	28	34	78
grass	92	92	86	28	82	64	88	88
lion	88	50	36	16	50	24	40	66
tiger	60	2	46	7	14	26	34	57

However the results show that the proposed approach using positive and negative representative blocks is generally better than the retrieval based on single descriptors. Even though in some cases specific single descriptors are dominant for a concept, the result from proposed approach is very close to it.

5   Conclusion and Future Work

A technique to estimate optimal linear combinations of predefined metrics by applying a Multi-Objective Optimization is presented. The core strategy uses MOO to optimize the metric in multi-feature space. The proposed approach has been tested for the classification of objects in images. A more comprehensive evaluation of the proposed technique and additional improvements of the method are being undertaken. Immediate work includes adopting more intelligent classifier which can employ the obtained multi-feature metric, as well as extension and evaluation with several other low-level descriptors. Future work will focus on non-linear combinations of descriptors and metrics.

References

1. J. R. Smith and S.Chang. "Visualseek: a fully automated content-based image query system". Proceedings of ACM Multimedia 96, pages 87–98, Boston MA USA, 1996.
2. S.-E Chang and T Sikora, A. Purl, "Overview of the MPEG-7 Standard", IEEE Transactions on Circuits and Systems for Video Technology, Vol. 11, No. 6, pp. 688-695, 2001.
3. J. O'Reilly, ContentEengineering. Electronics Communications Engineering Journal, vol. 14, No. 4, Aug. 2002.
4. H. Eidenberger and C. Breiteneder: "Macro-level Similarity Measurement in ViZir". 2002.
5. Q. Tian, Y. Wu, and T. S. Huang: "Combine User Defined Region-Of-Interest and Spatial Layout for Image Retrieval".IEEE ICIP'2000, pp. 746-749, Vol. 3
6. K. Yanai and K. Barnard, "Image Region Entropy: A Measure of Visualness of Web Images Associated with One Concept". Proc. ACM Multimedia 2005, pp.419-422.
7. R. Yan, J, Yang and A. G. Hauptmann, "Learning QueryClass Dependent Weights in Automatic Video Retrieval". Proc. ACM Multiemdia 2004, pp.548-555.
8. R.E. Steuer: "Multiple Criteria Optimization: Theory, Computation, and Application". New York: Wiley 1986.
9. J. Knowles and D. Corne: "Approximating the Non-dominated front using the Pareto Archived Evolution Strategy". 1999.
10. J. Knowles and D. Corne, "Properties of an adaptive archiving algorithm for storing nondominated vectors", 2002.
11. N. O' Connor and E. Cooke , Le Borgne H., Blighe M., Adamek T. "The aceToolbox: Lowe-Level AudioVisual Feature Extraction for Retrieval and Classification". Proc. of EWIMT'05, Nov. 2005.
12. B.S. Manjunath and W.T. Ma, "Texture features for browsing and retrieval of image data," IEEE Trans. On Pattern Analysis and Machine Intelligence, vol. 18, no. 8, pp. 837-842, August 1996
13. M. Tuceryan and A. K. Jain, Texture Analysis. The Handbook of Pattern Recognition and Computer Vision (2nd Edition), pp. 207-248, World Scien-tific Publishing Co., 1998.
14. M. J. A. Swain and D. H. A. Ballard, "Color indexing" International Journal of Computer Vision, vol. 7, pp. 11-32, 1991.

Eliciting Perceptual Ground Truth
for Image Segmentation

Victoria Hodge, Garry Hollier, John Eakins, and Jim Austin

Advanced Computer Architectures Group, Department of Computer Science,
University of York, York, UK
{vicky, hollier, eakins, austin}@cs.york.ac.uk

Abstract. In this paper, we investigate human visual perception and establish a body of ground truth data elicited from human visual studies. We aim to build on the formative work of Ren, Eakins and Briggs who produced an initial ground truth database. Human participants were asked to draw and rank their perceptions of the parts of a series of figurative images. These rankings were then used to score the perceptions, identify the preferred human breakdowns and thus allow us to induce perceptual rules for human decomposition of figurative images. The results suggest that the human breakdowns follow well-known perceptual principles in particular the Gestalt laws.

1 Introduction

We hypothesise that perception and thus segmentation varies from person to person and also varies with the domain of application (context). This subjectivity is almost inevitably due to culture, education, expectation, domain of application, mood, age etc. but there must be a core set of commonalities across human judgements that we aim to distil out. There is currently no comprehensive theory of human or computational image and shape segmentation. One theory is that humans decompose images along Gestalt principles. There has been widespread investigation including human experimentation of individual Gestalt principles [W23],[K63],[K79],[G72].

Our work forms part of the PROFI (Perceptually-Relevant Retrieval of Figurative Images) project[1]. In PROFI, we aim to develop new techniques for the retrieval of figurative images (i.e. abstract trademarks and logos) from large databases. The techniques will be based on the extraction of perceptually relevant shape features and the matching of these features in the target image against features in the stored images, thereby overcoming many of the limitations of existing methods. In this paper we focus on the perceptual segmentation of raw images and grouping shape elements.

Existing systems, for example trademark search systems, attempt to match a target against stored images such as those shown in Figs. 1-3 in one of two ways: (a) comparing features generated from the images as a whole, or (b) matching features from individual parts of the images [E01].

---

[1] PROFI web page: http://www.cs.uu.nl/profi/

H. Sundaram et al. (Eds.): CIVR 2006, LNCS 4071, pp. 320–329, 2006.
© Springer-Verlag Berlin Heidelberg 2006

Fig. 1. **Fig. 2.** **Fig. 3.**

The principal difficulty in matching by parts is the selection of parts that accurately reflect the image's appearance to a human observer. In Fig. 1 this is reasonably clear (2 triangles and a circle). But in Fig. 2, should the central bars be matched as six individual components, or as two groups of three? And in Fig. 3, should matching be based on a circle and a triangle - neither of which are actually present in the image itself? These are the questions which this current research aims to answer.

For present purposes, therefore, we are primarily interested in clarifying two aspects of human segmentation behaviour: the formation of intermediate-level groupings of image parts; and, the generation of perceived elements not explicitly present in the original image. Our hypothesis is that these will allow us to identify the most salient image elements for matching more accurately than has hitherto been possible.

The seminal decomposition paper for this aspect of the PROFI project is Ren et al. [REB00]. The paper evaluates human participants when segmenting trademark images into their perceived constituent parts. The participants initially breakdown trademark images into a set of components in as many ways as they see fit. These breakdowns are then fed into the second part of the experiment where participants rank these breakdowns by their perceived likelihood. The paper's main discoveries are that humans partition trademark images into disjoint regions most commonly, then into overlapping or nested regions and partition into separate line segments or groups least commonly. The breakdowns generated are similar to the Gestalt principles [W23],[K63],[K79],[G72] of human perceptual organisation. The authors posit that perceptual line grouping, closed-region identification, texture processing, identifying familiar shapes (such as triangles, squares etc.) and uncovering 'hidden' image features (such as figure-ground reversal) are areas requiring further investigation. We aim to augment and complement these results in the current paper and use the results in our development of a computerized image retrieval system.

In current computational approaches, shapes may be segmented using either the shape's boundary or the shape's interior (fill area) but rarely both compared to the holistic viewpoint used by humans. Some examples of shape segmentation approaches, which are founded on geometrical properties, include Hoffman & Richards [HR84] who subdivide shapes based on the notion that concavities arise when two convex parts are joined and hence, divide the surface into parts at loci of negative minima. Siddiqi & Kimia [SK95] proposed a similar approach using limbs and necks: negative curvature minima and local minima of inscribed circles. Singh et al. [SSH99] use minimum distance and skeletal axes to determine segmentation lines between boundaries where at least one boundary is a concave vertex. Tanase & Veltkamp [TV02] also propose a segmentation approach using skeletons. The shape is initially segmented using the skeletal bifurcation points and the boundaries of these segments are then simplified and protrusions removed. Leung & Chen [LC02] aim to unify skeletons and edge detection approaches thus going some way to a boundary-based/fill-area combination technique. The system either performs edge detection or thinning. The authors note that for a solid region where the shape conveys much visual information, edge detection is preferable to thinning as it extracts the contour of the region. However, for a region containing curves, thinning is preferable as it extracts the skeleton and "produces a better representation".

The central premise for the investigations in this paper is to identify how humans decompose images, the degree of commonality across a range of human subjects and to provide a set of ground truth images. These ground truth images may be further analysed to elicit statistics and preference scores regarding the decomposition preferences of humans: i.e., which decomposition is generally preferred for each image, a ranked order of decompositions for each image, how many potential decompositions there should be for each image. We aim to investigate symmetry, texture, singularities and also to some extent the effect of figure/ground phenomena. We note that it is extremely difficult to isolate Gestalt principles within the trademark images. For example, altering an image along symmetrical lines will inevitably alter other Gestalt properties such as familiarity, continuity or perhaps grouping. We attempted to provide as wide a variety of symmetry, texture or singularity alterations as possible. We aim to use the results from our experimental analyses to drive the formation of an integrated computational system that mimics human segmentation. We need to ensure that our resultant computerised technique will not produce too many decompositions for a particular image as multiplicity implies that a Gestalt factor can only be active if it does not produce too many decompositions [DMM04].

In the remainder of this paper we detail the development and implementation of the experimental methodology and provide some analysis.

2 Experimental Methodology

The experimental methodology was developed in conjunction with the Psychology Department at the University of York, UK who advised on methodology, ethical considerations, and best practice and provided general advice and guidance.

We performed an initial pilot study to select suitable trademark or other figurative images and to revise and improve the experimental methodology.

For our experiment, a set of images was presented to University of York staff, students and their relatives and friends. Each image used is 4.5 cm high including any white space. All images are monochrome TIFFs. 28 subjects completed the experiment unsupervised in their own time and 25 subjects attended a 1 hour supervised session giving 53 subjects in total. Each of the 53 subjects received a printed booklet containing: a front sheet and 16 pages with 2 images per page in 2 columns giving 32 images in total in each booklet. The subjects also received a copy of the experiment instructions. The subjects were requested to draw (using pen or pencil) their perceived decompositions of each image in turn on to the booklet and to rank each decomposition (1st, 2nd, 3rd etc.) according to the order in which they perceived that decomposition. All completed booklets were anonymized and labelled with a subject ID number. All subjects who completed the experiment were entered into a prize draw where the prizes were a £200, £50 and 5 x £10 shopping vouchers. The statistics of the subjects are: age range: *14 – 70*; gender: *mixed*; nationality: *mixed international*.

There were 3 sets of **32** images. Each set contains some images present in the other sets to act as controls and thus to verify that the subjects in each group are statistically similar. The trademarks were in pairs (14 pairs in each set, $p_1 .. p_{14}$) along with 4 other images (i1 .. i4). The unpaired images are supplementary control images (i1, i2) and buffer images (i3, i4) in case the subjects do not complete the exercise. The paired images were ordered p_1^1, p_2^1, p_3^1, ... p_{14}^1, i1, i2, p_1^2, p_2^2, p_3^2, ... p_{14}^2, i3, i4. The subjects received the first image of a pair and then later, a second paired image: the same image but altered according to symmetry, texture or singularity principles. These 3 sets of images were further divided into forward and backward sets giving 6 sets in total (A-Forward, A-Reverse, B-Forward, B-Reverse, C-Forward and C-Reverse). The forward and reverse sets have the order of the images reversed to prevent order bias where the order of image presentation affects the perception:

- Forward - $\mathbf{p_1^1}$, $\mathbf{p_2^1}$, $\mathbf{p_3^1}$, ... $\mathbf{p_{14}^1}$, **i1, i2**, $\mathbf{p_1^2}$, $\mathbf{p_2^2}$, $\mathbf{p_3^2}$, ... $\mathbf{p_{14}^2}$, **i3, i4** and then
- Reverse - $\mathbf{p_{14}^2}$, $\mathbf{p_{13}^2}$, $\mathbf{p_{12}^2}$, ... $\mathbf{p_1^2}$, **i1, i2**, $\mathbf{p_{14}^1}$, $\mathbf{p_{13}^1}$, $\mathbf{p_{12}^1}$, ... $\mathbf{p_1^1}$, **i3, i4**.

If all subjects receive p_1^1 before p_1^2 then this may influence their perception of p_1^2.

The first stage of analysing the images was to collate the breakdowns drawn by the subjects and to note the rank ([1st], [2nd], [3rd] etc.). For each image, each breakdown had a list of the ID of the subjects who perceived that breakdown and the rank they awarded it. For each image, if two subjects had drawn identical or extremely similar breakdowns then the breakdowns were marked as the same and the subjects' IDs and the rank they awarded the breakdown added to the list for that specific breakdown. Otherwise, the breakdowns were marked as two separate breakdowns and the subjects' IDs and ranks added to the respective breakdowns' lists. The output from this analysis is a listing of all breakdowns for each image in turn along with a listing of all subjects who drew that breakdown and the rank that each subject gave it.

2.1 Preference Scoring Mechanism

Ren et al. [REB00] used a slightly different experimental methodology compared to us. Ren et al. used subjects to elicit the breakdowns in stage 1 and then used a second set of subjects to rank the breakdowns in stage 2. We collapsed this into a single stage due to time constraints with all **53** subjects drawing and ranking their own breakdowns. This also required a slightly different scoring mechanism.

For 74 of the 84 images, the subjects each drew 1, 2 or 3 breakdowns[2]. The remaining 10 images produced 4 or 5 breakdowns[3]. Therefore, for all images we awarded scores of 3, 2, 1, 0.5 & 0.25 for ranks 1 to 5 respectively.

For each breakdown the scores are totalled and divided by the total of the scores across all breakdowns for that image. This gives the preference score for each breakdown of each image.

---

[2] For 2 images the maximum number of breakdowns drawn by one subject was 1, for 32 images the maximum number was 2 breakdowns and for 40 images the maximum number was 3.

[3] For 7 images the maximum number of breakdowns drawn by one subject was 4. 3 images produced 5 breakdowns. 2 subjects drew most of these 4 or 5 breakdowns per image with another 3 subjects drawing 4 breakdowns per image once each.

3 Overview

Results from the analysis of the perceptions derived from the various sets of subjects indicate that the number of breakdowns perceived varies quite widely from image to image. If the number of human breakdowns is large then the search space required for any computerised shape decomposition system will be large to allow an identical decomposition to be created by the computerised system. The search space will also be large for a computerised system matching components from one image against components in other stored images due to the large potential search space.

One factor that we expect to affect the number of breakdowns is the number of degrees of freedom available within an image. 9 images produced at least 17 breakdowns seen by at least one subject and each of these images had a large number of potential components and a large number of possible arrangements of components. The search space for a computerized decomposition system or image component matching system processing these images would be large.

However, the number of breakdowns seen by 2 or more subjects is much more closely grouped than the number of breakdowns perceived by 1 or more subjects. The mode number of breakdowns perceived by 2 or more people is 3 and only one image had more than 8 breakdowns perceived across all **53** subjects. This indicates that there are individual breakdowns seen by only one person but that there exists a core set of breakdowns that is more tightly grouped which will be seen by 2 or more people. These core breakdowns are the breakdowns we aim to focus on and ensure that any computerized system can reproduce them.

Ren at al. [REB00] had between 1 and 4 breakdowns for each image in their analyses. We found our unrestricted breakdown policy coupled with consolidating Ren et al.'s two-stage experimental process into a single stage allowed more scope for subject variation.

4 Analysis

In the following, we analyse the core set of breakdowns for each image seen by 2 or more subjects. Qualitative analysis of individual results yields a number of insights that we expect to prove useful in subsequent phases of the PROFI project.

From analyzing the **53** subjects' drawings, we noticed that the subjects may be focused purely on eliciting the component breakdowns of each image probably due to the experiment focusing on image decomposition. We feel they may concentrate on the individual components and do not always see the "larger picture". For example, where 6 triangles are arranged in a hexagonal shape many subjects drew 6 triangles but not the overall hexagonal shape. We feel that this should be taken into consideration when using the component breakdowns.

The main empirical findings from the human decompositions produced from our experiments are:

Singularity – changing the orientation of image components changes the perception. This is particularly true for textures where altering the angle of the texture can change the figure/ground perception (see the discussion below regarding figure/ground for an example). Also, familiar image components such as human figures or aircraft (see Table 1) are less often perceived when not in their natural orientation.

Table 1. Showing the image (left column) and modified image (right column) in the top row and the top decomposition for each image (as seen by 2 or more subjects) along with the associated scores in the lower row

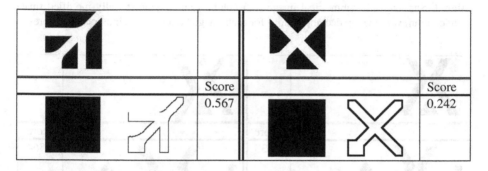

Familiarity – when elements of an image are gradually removed/reorganized so as to destroy familiarity of the image then the human breakdowns change to be based on individual components rather than the entire image and tend to proximity-based grouping as shown in the example in Table 2.

Table 2. Showing the familiar image (left column) and the less-familiar modified image (right column) with the top 3 decompositions and their associated scores below

Symmetry – when symmetry is removed from an image, the human decompositions tend to individual components or image halves. This is particularly true for illusory contours and images where axial symmetry is removed (as shown in the example in Table 3) although there are exceptions where the removal of symmetry has little effect on the decompositions particularly for images that trace the outlines of shapes as seen in Table 4.

Table 3. Showing the symmetrical image (left column) and asymmetrically modified image (right column) with the top decompositions for each image below and their associated scores

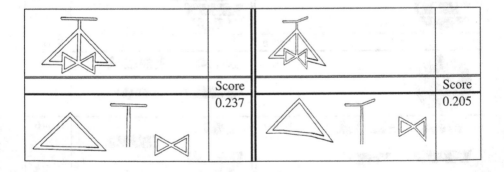

Table 4. Showing the symmetrical image (left column) and asymmetrically modified image (right column), with the top decomposition and associated scores in the lower row

Continuity – reducing the continuity alters the human perceptions with a tendency to proximity grouping and decomposition into individual components. This is particularly true for illusory contours such as Necker cubes where only relatively minor perturbations of the image remove the perception of the cube (see Table 5).

Table 5. Showing the Necker Cube image (left column) and modified discontinuous image (right column) with the top decomposition and associated scores in the lower row

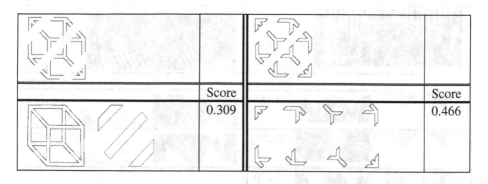

	Score		Score
	0.309		0.466

When continuity is reduced in conjunction with symmetry removal then the decomposition differs from when continuity alone is removed. An asymmetric image promotes the perception of good continuity whereas a symmetric variant of the image promotes proximity grouping as seen in Table 6.

Table 6. Showing the symmetric image (left column) and modified asymmetric image (right column) with the top decomposition for each image below and their associated scores

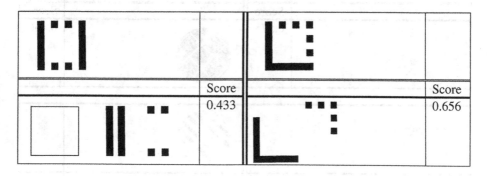

	Score		Score
	0.433		0.656

Figure/ground – if the components of an image are tilted or inverted then the figure/ground perception changes as exemplified in Table 7. If the components are textured with stripes then the figure/ground perception changes from the untextured image and if the texture is strengthened with a darker texture then the figure/ground perception changes even more. This is shown in the example in Table 8. A uniform background enhances the perception of figure/ground reversal whereas familiarity of image components reduces the figure/ground reversal.

Table 7. Showing the image (left column) and modified image (right column) and all decompositions for each image with their associated scores in the lower rows

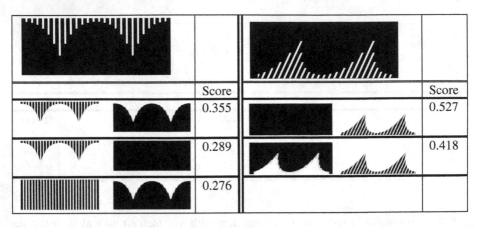

Table 8. Showing the image (top left) and 3 modified textured images coupled with the top decomposition for each image and its associated score

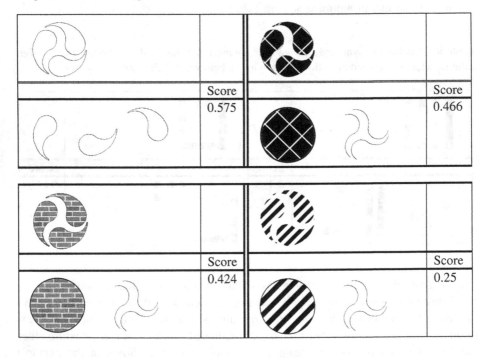

5   Conclusion and Future Work

Our results concur with previous investigations such as [REB00] in that image decomposition appears to follow a set of perceptual principles analogous to the Gestalt laws. The experiments and analyses show that these Gestalt laws interact and possibly conflict as noted by [DMM04]. The experiments also indicate that there are a core set of decompositions for each image perceived by 2 or more people along with a set of decompositions seen only by individuals.

We have identified some possibilities for additional work that would generate useful data. The experimental analyses detailed in this paper are very human-oriented. Humans generate all the breakdowns with no recourse as to whether they are feasible for a computer system to generate. Therefore, after we have used the data from these analyses to develop and refine our computational system, we could use the resultant system to generate a set of breakdowns for further images. We can then present these sets of breakdowns, for each image in turn, to human subjects who can rank them *1 to n* where *n* is the number of images in the set. This will allow us to fine-tune the computational system further using tangible computer-generated breakdowns.

Acknowledgement

This work was supported by E.U. FP6 IST **Project Reference:** 511572 - **PROFI**.

References

[DMM04] Desolneux, A., Moisan, L., and Morel, J.-M. A theory of digital image analysis. 2004. Book in preparation

[E01]   Eakins, J.P. Trademark image retrieval. In M. Lew (Ed.), *Principles of Visual Information Retrieval* (Ch 13). Springer-Verlag, Berlin, (2001).

[G72]   Goldmeier, E. Similarity in Visually Perceived Forms *[1936]*, in Psychological Issues VIII(1), ed. Herbert J. Schlesinger, International Universities Press, 1972.

[HR84]   Hoffman, D.D. and Richards, W.A. Parts of recognition. Cognition, 18:65-96, 1984

[K79]   Kanizsa, G. Organization in Vision: Essays in Gestalt Perception, Praeger, NY, 1979.

[K63]   Koffka, K.. Principles of Gestalt Psychology. Harcourt Brace. New York, 1963.

[LC02]   Leung, W.H. and Chen, T. "Trademark retrieval using contour-skeleton stroke classification", *IEEE Intl. Conf. on Multimedia and Expo.* (ICME 2002), Lausanne, August 2002.

[REB00] Ren, M., Eakins, J. P. and Briggs, P. Human perception of trademark images: implications for retrieval system design. Journal of Electronic Imaging, 9 (4):564-575, 2000.

[SK95]   Siddiqi, K. and Kimia, B. B. Parts of visual form: Computational aspects. Pattern Analysis And Machine Intelligence, 17(3):239-251, March 1995

[SSH99]   Singh, M., Seyranian, G. & Hoffman D.D. Parsing silhouettes: The short-cut rule. Perception & Psychophysics, 61:636-660, 1999.

[TV02]   Tanase, M and Veltkamp, R.C. Polygon Decomposition Based on the Straight Line Skeleton. Theoretical Foundations of Computer Vision 2002: 247-267.

[W23]   Wertheimer, M. Laws of Organization in Perceptual Forms (1923). In, Ellis (ed) A Source Book of Gestalt Psychology, Routledge & Kegan Paul, London 1938.

Asymmetric Learning and Dissimilarity Spaces for Content-Based Retrieval

Eric Bruno, Nicolas Moenne-Loccoz, and Stéphane Marchand-Maillet*

Viper group
Computer Vision and Multimedia Laboratory, University of Geneva
eric.bruno@unige.ch

Abstract. This paper presents novel dissimilarity space specially designed for interactive multimedia retrieval. By providing queries made of positive and negative examples, the goal consists in learning the positive class distribution. This classification problem is known to be asymmetric, *i.e.* the negative class does not cluster in the original feature spaces. We introduce here the idea of Query-based Dissimilarity Space (QDS) which enables to cope with the asymmetrical setup by converting it in a more classical 2-class problem. The proposed approach is evaluated on both artificial data and real image database, and compared with state-of-the-art algorithms.

1 Introduction

Determining semantic concepts by allowing users to iteratively and interactively refine their queries is a key issue in multimedia content-based retrieval. The relevance feedback loop allows to build complex queries made out of positive and negative documents as examples. From this training set, a learning process has to create a model of the sought concept from a set of data features so as to provide relevant documents to the user. The success of this search strategy relies mainly on the representation spaces where data is embedded as well as on the learning machine operating in those spaces.

Various aspects of these problems have been studied with success for the last few years. This includes works on machine learning strategies such as active learning [3], imbalance classification algorithms [13], automatic kernel setting [12] or automatic labelling of training data [10]. All these studies have in common to consider feature spaces to represent knowledge on the multimedia content.

An alternative solution is to represent documents according to their similarities (related to one or several features) to the other documents rather than to a feature vector. Considering a collection of documents, the similarity-based representation, stored in (dis)similarity matrices or some distance-based indexing structures [4], characterizes the content of an element of the collection relatively to a part of or the whole collection. Recent studies have been published for document retrieval and collection browsing by using pre-computed similarities

---

* This work is funded by the Swiss NCCR (IM)2 (Interactive Multimodal Information Management).

H. Sundaram et al. (Eds.): CIVR 2006, LNCS 4071, pp. 330–339, 2006.
© Springer-Verlag Berlin Heidelberg 2006

([1], [7]) The idea is to index elements relatively to their closest neighbours, *i.e.* those who have the best probabilities to belong to the same class providing then a sparse association graph structuring the multimedia collection and allowing fast retrieval of data. As pointed out by authors, the similarity approach provides a convenient way for multimodal data fusion, since adding new features simply consists in adding new distances to the same representation framework. It is also noted that the off-line computation of similarities enables fast accesses and scalable content-based multimedia retrieval systems.

In [2], we proposed a similarity-based representation that goes further the nearest-neighbour model by allowing non-linear mapping of the low-level distance measures to the high-level concept space. Based on Dissimilarity Spaces (DS) introduced by Pekalska *et al* [8], we have defined representation spaces adapted to the *query-by-example* paradigm. These Query-based Dissimilarity Spaces (QDS) have the advantages to be of low-dimension, to allow the direct use of modern non-linear learning techniques (such as SVM or Adaboost) and to ease the fundamental problem of fusion of multimodal sources (*eg* multimodal similarities).

In this paper, we discuss another nice property of the QDS making the approach attractive for content-based retrieval. We demonstrate indeed how QDS overcomes the famous problem of asymmetrical classification due to the ill-definition of the negative class during retrieval. This theoretical study is supported by experimental comparisons with a kernel-based technique and the dedicated Biased Discriminant Analysis approach proposed by Zhou *et al* [13]. The overall results obtain on artificial data and collection of images indicate the validity and the efficiency of QDS for treating asymmetrical classification problem.

2 Query by Example and Asymmetric Classification

In a query by example retrieval system, users formulate complex queries by iteratively providing positive and negative examples in a Relevance Feedback (RF) loop. From this training data, the aim is to perform, at each step of the RF loop, a real-time classification that will select the most relevant documents. Denoting the query as the set T of positive and negative training examples, respectively noted $\mathcal{P}$ and $\mathcal{N}$ with $T = \mathcal{P} \cup \mathcal{N}$, $p = |\mathcal{P}|$ and $n = |\mathcal{N}|$, the problem is to estimate (learn) a ranking function $f(x|T)$ allotting a rank r_i for each element x_i relatively to its relevance to the sought concept.

Because the training set is provided manually by user, through a graphical interface for instance, the number of examples (positive and negative) remains usually small. As a consequence, the learning may be severely undetermined, especially when it consists in estimating complex distributions in high-dimensional space. Moreover, the ill-determination is enforced by the asymmetric nature of the classification problem: To retrieve a concept out of a collection of documents, it is generally assumed that, on the average, the positive elements (representing the sought concept) are close to each other, thus conforming a specific class distribution. On the other hand the negative examples, drawn from the "rest of the world", follow some unknown and complex distributions hardly estimable from the available sparse sampling . The figure 1.a displays an example of such setup. Learning the negative classes (the circular distribution is viewed as an undetermined number of classes) becomes an under-constrained optimization problem when the training sample is small, limiting the efficiency of traditional two-class learning machines.

Dedicated algorithms have been proposed to address the asymmetrical classification [5, 11]. Among all of them, an interesting approach, named *Biased Discriminant Analysis* (BDA) [13], consists in maximizing a criterion which tends to enforce compactness of the positive class while pushing apart negative examples from the positive centroid. It results in a discriminative subspace where query is processed by retrieving nearest elements in the Euclidean neighborhood of the positive centroid. In the following sections, BDA is considered for comparison with the dissimilarity-based solution studied.

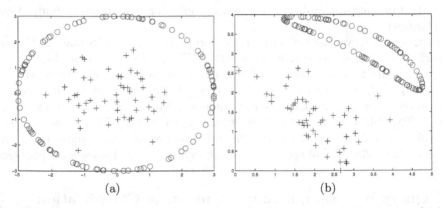

(a)   (b)

Fig. 1. The $1+x$ class problem in feature space (left) and 2D dissimilarity space (right) where the representation objects are two points from the central class (cross)

3   Dissimilarity Space

Let $d(\mathbf{x}_i, \mathbf{x}_j)$ be the distance between elements i and j according to their descriptors $\mathbf{x} \in \mathcal{F}$. $\mathcal{F}$ expresses the original feature space. The dissimilarity space $\mathcal{D}_\Omega$ is defined relatively to a subset $\Omega \subset \mathcal{F}$ by the mapping $\mathbf{d}(\mathbf{x}, \Omega) : \mathcal{F} \to \mathbb{R}^N$

$$\mathbf{d}(\mathbf{x}, \Omega) = [d(\mathbf{x}, \mathbf{x}_1), d(\mathbf{x}, \mathbf{x}_2), \ldots d(\mathbf{x}, \mathbf{x}_N)].$$

The representation set $\Omega = \{\mathbf{x}_1, \ldots, \mathbf{x}_N\}$ is a subset of N objects from which any elements of the collection will be evaluated. The new "features" of an input element are now its dissimilarity values with the representation objects. As a consequence, learning or classification tools for feature representations are also available to deal with the dissimilarities.

The dimensionality of the dissimilarity space is equal to the size of Ω, which controls the approximation made on the original feature space (such an approximation could be computed using projection algorithms like classical scaling [6]).

Increasing the number of elements in Ω increases the representation accuracy. On the other hand, a well-chosen space of low dimension would be more effective for learning processes as it avoids the *curse of dimensionality* problem and reduces the computation load. The selection of a "good" representation set may be driven by considerations on the particular learning problem we are dealing with, as shown in the next section.

4   Query-Based Dissimilarity Space

In this section, we look at how the selection of the set Ω may offer us the possibility to turn the asymmetrical classification problem into a more classical formulation. As stated in section 2, we are facing a $1+x$ class setup where 1 class corresponds to positives while an unknown number x of classes are associated to negative examples. In BDA, this statement consists in finding a subspace where the distances from negatives to positives (*between* scatter) are maximized while inter-positives distances (*within* scatter) are minimized. This may be achieved by seeking some linear or non-linear projections of the original space where the following ratio will be maximized

$$J = \frac{\sum_{i \in \mathcal{P}, j \in \mathcal{N}} d(\mathbf{x}_i, \mathbf{x}_j)^2}{\sum_{i,j \in \mathcal{P}} d(\mathbf{x}_i, \mathbf{x}_j)^2}, \tag{1}$$

Then, defining the Query-based Dissimilarity Space (QDS) $\mathcal{D}_{\mathcal{P}}$ by the mapping

$$\mathbf{d}(\mathbf{x}, \mathcal{P}) = [d(\mathbf{x}, \mathbf{x}_1^+), d(\mathbf{x}, \mathbf{x}_2^+), \dots d(\mathbf{x}, \mathbf{x}_p^+)] \tag{2}$$

and noting that, in QDS, the norm is

$$||\mathbf{d}_i||^2 = \sum_{j \in \mathcal{P}} d(\mathbf{x}, \mathbf{x}_j)^2,$$

the quotient J may be simply rewritten as the ratio between the sum of the negative and the positive vector norms

$$J = \frac{\sum_{i \in \mathcal{N}} ||\mathbf{d}_i||^2}{\sum_{i \in \mathcal{P}} ||\mathbf{d}_i||^2}.$$

As a matter of fact, selecting $\mathcal{P}$ as the representation set naturally embeds the data in an intrinsic discriminative space where the criterion to classify elements is simply the vector norms of elements. Therefore, optimizing any learning machines in that space to separate positive from negative samples will optimize the BDA criterion. In other word, in $\mathcal{D}_{\mathcal{P}}$, the $(1 + x)$-class learning is transformed in a classical binary setup. From a geometrical point of view, the learning task does not consist anymore in estimating a complex distribution composed of x negative classes but a simpler (eventually non-linear) function separating the positive class (close to the origin) to the rest of the space (Figure 1.b).

5   Experiments and Evaluations

5.1   Kernel SVM, BDA and QDS

This experimental section proposes qualitative and quantitative assessment of the retrieval efficiency when operated in QDS, in original feature space and through the BDA algorithm. For QDS and feature space, we have to choose machine learning strategy that will estimate the ranking function introduced in section 2. In both cases, a SVM algorithm is used, where the rank of every element is obtained by sorting the SVM decision function

$$f(\mathbf{x}) = \sum_i \alpha_i k(\mathbf{x}, \mathbf{x}_i) \tag{3}$$

with $\mathbf{x}_i$ the support vectors and α_i their respective weights. The kernel $k(\mathbf{x}, \mathbf{y})$ is chosen linear for QDS in order to facilitate comparison with BDA, but is non-linear (rbf Gaussian kernel) for feature space so as to cope with the $(1 + x)$ classification setup. For all the following retrieval experiments, the Gaussian scale parameter is set by cross-validation.

As far as BDA is concerned, we follow the algorithm presented in [13], where the ranking function is obtained by sorting the euclidean distances between elements and the positive centroid in the discriminative subspace.

5.2   Artificial Data

A Toy Example. The toy example depicted in figure 2.a gives an illustration of how perform the three retrieval approaches considered. In this 2D example, 3 positive and 4 negative examples are provided (∗ markers) to determine a decision function enabling to retrieve the positive samples (+ markers) and discarding negative elements (o markers). Because the problem is 2D, BDA implicitly works within a 1-dimensional subspace, leading to a linear decision function not suited for the problem (figure 2.d). On the other hand, rbf SVM in feature space estimate a non-linear function, but because the $1 + x$ class setup and the small number of training data, the SVM is not able to model well the positive class with respect to the negative one (figure 2.c). For linear SVM in QDS, the use of a Euclidean distance as dissimilarity measure leads also to a non-linear decision function in feature space, but because applied to a 2-class problem, the SVM is able in that case to provide a better estimation of the positive class distribution (figure 2.b).

High-Dimensional 1+x Class Problem. A multidimensional feature space is generated with a positive class of elements x_i^+ drawn from a centered Gaussian distribution $N(0, \sigma_{\mathcal{P}})$ and a negative class x_j^- uniformly distributed with the constraint $|x_j^-| > 10, \forall j$. The set is composed of 250 positive and 750 negatives elements.

In this setup, the positive class is effectively surrounded by negative elements uniformly distributed within the space. The positive scale $\sigma_{\mathcal{P}}$ defines how the

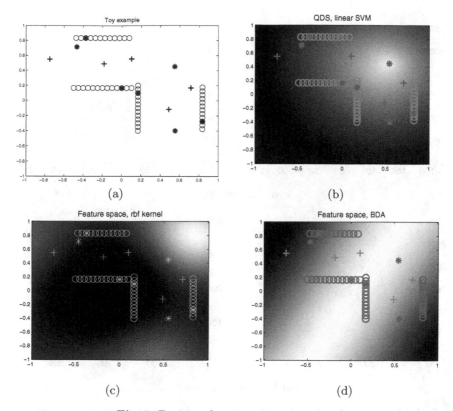

Fig. 2. Decision function on a toy example

two classes overlap each other, making the discrimination more or less difficult to be achieved. The figure 3.a displays a 2D slice of the a 50-dimension feature space for two values of $\sigma_{\mathcal{P}}$.

For the experimentation, an equal number of positive and negative examples is randomly drawn from the two classes. From this training set, an Euclidean QDS is generated by taking positive examples as representation set. The figure 3.b shows QDS built from two positive samples for the corresponding feature spaces. It is worth recalling that the dimensionality of QDS is equal to the number of positive examples p.

The retrieval performance is measured using the Average Precision (AP) [9] computed over the entire ranked list. The measure is repeated 10 times and an averaged value of AP is given for each experimental conditions given below. The figure 4.a presents the AP measures for the three retrieval algorithms and a comparison with the baseline performance given by a random guess of elements. The artificial data are embedded in 50-dimension space and the positive class bandwidth is set to $\sigma_{\mathcal{P}} = 140$. An overlap so important between the two classes does not permit the rbf-SVM to provide results significantly better than the baseline, even when the number of examples becomes large. On the other and, BDA and QDS are able to cope with the asymmetric class setup. However, BDA

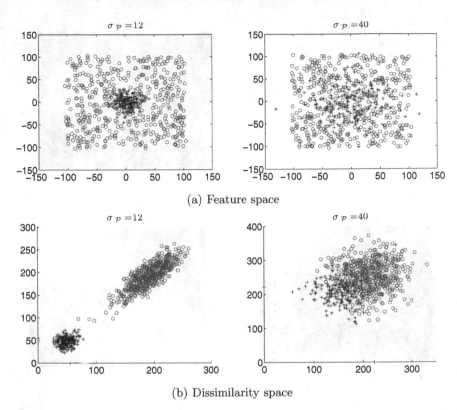

(a) Feature space

(b) Dissimilarity space

Fig. 3. Artificial data composed of positive (+ markers) and negative (o markers) elements in a) Feature space and b) the corresponding QDS build from two positive examples

suffers from the high-dimensionality of the space, especially when the small size of training set leads to a miss-estimation of the *within* and *between* covariance matrices. For QDS, the linear SVM, trained in low-dimensional space, is able to provide an efficient retrieval whatever the number of examples involved.

The second experiment (Figure 4.b) tests the discriminative efficiency as the classes become more and more intricated. In that experiment, 10 positive and 10 negative examples are provided to the machine learning algorithms. Unsurprisingly, the QDS approach outperforms both BDA and rbf SVM. After a certain point however, the three approaches perform just like the baseline, indicating that positive samples are totally scattered within the negative elements.

5.3   Image Retrieval

A last evaluation is conducted on a Corel image subset. The feature space consists in a 64 RGB histogram and embeds 18521 images annotated by several keywords. Symmetrized Kullback-Leibler divergence is taken as the dissimilarity measure for QDS. We get interested by successively retrieving images annotated with the 6 following keywords: 'whale', 'ice', 'wave', 'tulip', 'sunset', 'mountain'.

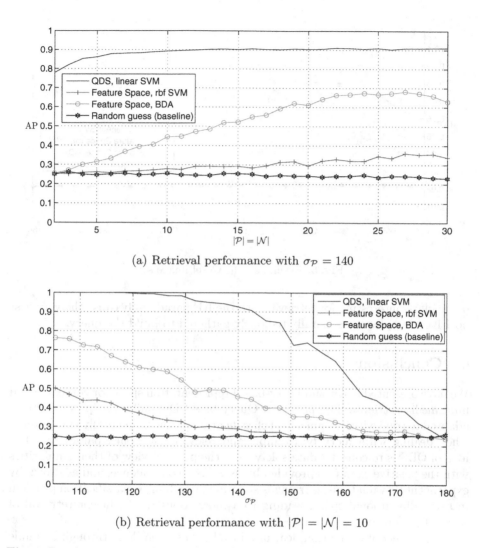

(a) Retrieval performance with $\sigma_P = 140$

(b) Retrieval performance with $|\mathcal{P}| = |\mathcal{N}| = 10$

Fig. 4. Results on artificial data when a.) the number of examples increases and b.) the overlap between the positive and the negative samples growth.

These keywords, somehow correlated with the low-level color descriptors extracted, have been selected to conform with the $1 + x$ classification setup.

For every keyword, 50 queries are made by selecting randomly an equal number of positive (labeled by keyword) and negative (not labeled by keyword) images. The overall evaluation is obtained by taking the mean AP over all queries for all keywords (MAP, [9]).

Figure 5 gives the MAP scores for an increasing training set. The result obtained with QDS outperforms BDA and non-linear SVM, especially when the training set becomes very small ($\backsim 1 - 2$ examples per class). This behavior is

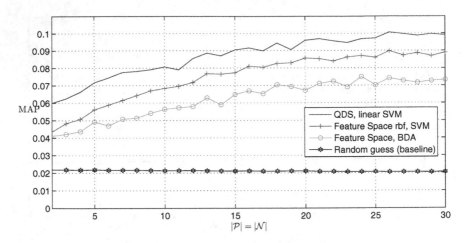

Fig. 5. Results on the Corel image set

particularly interesting for retrieval with the RF paradigm because the very first positive examples are generally tediously gathered to build the query.

6 Conclusion

We have presented a new similarity-based representation space for content-based multimedia retrieval. The proposed Query-based Dissimilarity Space (QDS) is adapted to cope with asymmetrical classification problems generally encountered when dealing with query by example and relevance feedback paradigms. The idea of QDS is to consider data solely from the point of view of their similarities with the positive examples provided by user. As a consequence, and as shown by experimental evaluations, learning is simplified to a binary classification problem in a low-dimensional space, leading to a more robust and efficient retrieval of relevant documents.

For the sake of evaluation, learning in QDS has been done through a simple linear-SVM. However, in order to build an effective multimedia retrieval system as the one we presented in [2], non-linear approaches and more sophisticated strategies may be enlisted to cope with real world non-linearly distributed multimodal documents.

References

1. Liudmila Boldareva and Djoerd Hiemstra. Interactive content-based retrieval using pre-computed object-object similarities. In *Conference on Image and Video Retrieval, CIVR04,* pages 308-316, Dublin, Ireland, 2004.
2. Eric Bruno, Nicolas Moenne-Loccoz, and Stphane Marchand Maillet. Learning user queries in multimodal dissimilarity spaces. In *Proceedings of the 3rd International Workshop on Adaptive Multimedia Retrieval, AMR'05,* Glasgow, UK, July 2005.

3. E. Y. Chang, B. Li, G. Wu, and K. Go. Statistical learning for effective visual information retrieval. In *Proceedings of the IEEE International Conference on Image Processing*, 2003.
4. E. Chávez, G. Navarro, R. Baeza-Yates, and J.L. Marroquin. Searching in metric spaces. *ACM Computing Surveys*, 33(3):273-321, September 2001.
5. Y. Chen, X.S. Zhou, and T.S. Huang. One-class svm for learning in image retrieval. In *IEEE International Conference on Image Processing*, 2001.
6. T.F. Cox and M.A.A. Cox. *Multidimensional scaling*. Chapman & Hall, London, 1995.
7. D Heesch and S Rueger. Nnk networks for content-based image retrieval. In *26th European Conference on Information Retrieval*, Sunderland, UK, 2004.
8. E. Pekalska, P. Paclk, and R.P.W. Duin. A generalized kernel approach to dissimilarity-based classification. *Journal of Machine Learning Research*, 2:175–211, December 2001.
9. A. F. Smeaton, P. Over, and W. Kraaij. Trecvid: Evaluating the effectiveness of information retrieval tasks on digital video. In *Proceedings of the ACM MM'04*, pages 652-655, New York, NY, 2004.
10. R. Yan, A. Hauptmann, and R. Jin. Negative pseudo-relevance feedback in content-based video retrieval. In *Proceedings of ACM Multimedia (MM2003)*, Berkeley, USA, 2003.
11. Ruofei Zhang and Zhongfei (Mark) Zhang. Stretching bayesian learning in the relevance feedback of image retrieval. In *proceedings of the 8th European Conference on Computer Vision (ECCV)*, Prague, Czech Republic, 2004.
12. X.S. Zhou, A. Garg, and T.S. Huang. A discussion of nonlinear variants of biased discriminant for interactive image retrieval. In *Proc. of the 3rd Conference on Image and Video Retrieval, CIVR'04*, pages 353-364, 2004.
13. X.S. Zhou and T.S. Huang. Small sample learning during multimedia retrieval using biasmap. In *Proceedings of the IEEE Conference on Pattern Recognition and Computer Vision, CVPR'01*, volume I, pages 11-17, Hawaii, 2004.

Video Navigation Based
on Self-Organizing Maps

Thomas Bärecke[1], Ewa Kijak[1], Andreas Nürnberger[2], and Marcin Detyniecki[1]

[1] LIP6, Université Pierre et Marie Curie, Paris, France
thomas.baerecke@lip6.fr
[2] IWS, Otto-von-Guericke Universität, Magdeburg, Germany

Abstract. Content-based video navigation is an efficient method for browsing video information. A common approach is to cluster shots into groups and visualize them afterwards. In this paper, we present a prototype that follows in general this approach. The clustering ignores temporal information and is based on a growing self-organizing map algorithm. They provide some inherent visualization properties such as similar elements can be found easily in adjacent cells. We focus on studying the applicability of SOMs for video navigation support. We complement our interface with an original time bar control providing – at the same time – an integrated view of time and content based information. The aim is to supply the user with as much information as possible on one single screen, without overwhelming him.

1 Introduction

Extremely large databases with all types of multimedia documents are available today. Efficient methods to manage and access these archives are crucial, for instance quick search for similar documents or effective summarization via visualization of the underlying structure.

The prototype presented in this paper implements methods to structure and visualize video content in order to support a user in navigating within a single video. It focuses on the way video information is summarized in order to improve the browsing of its content. Currently, a common approach is to use clustering algorithms in order to automatically group similar shots and then to visualize the discovered groups in order to provide an overview of the considered video stream [1,2]. The summarization and representation of video sequences is usually keyframe-based. The keyframes can be arranged in the form of a temporal list and hierarchical browsing is then based on the clustered groups. In this paper, we use one promising unsupervised clustering approach that combines both good clustering and visualization capabilities: the self-organizing maps (SOMs)[3]. In fact, they have been successfully used for the navigation of text [4,5,6,7] and image collections [8,9,10].

The visualization capabilities of self-organizing maps provide an intuitive way of representing the distribution of data as well as the object similarities. As most clustering algorithms, SOMs operate on numerical feature vectors. Thus, video content has to be defined by numerical feature vectors that characterize it. A

H. Sundaram et al. (Eds.): CIVR 2006, LNCS 4071, pp. 340–349, 2006.
© Springer-Verlag Berlin Heidelberg 2006

variety of significant characteristics has been defined for all types of multimedia information. From video documents, a plethora of visual, audio, and motion features is available [11,12]. We rely on basic colour histograms and ignore more sophisticated descriptors, since our primary goal of this study was to investigate the visualisation and interaction capabilities of SOMs for video structuring and navigation.

Our system is composed of feature extraction, structuring, visualization, and user interaction components. Structuring and visualization parts are based on growing SOMs that were developed in previous works and applied to other forms of interactive retrieval [7,13]. We believe that *growing* SOMs are particularly adapted to fit video data. The user interface was designed with the intention to provide intuitive content-based video browsing functionalities to the user. In the following four sections we will describe every system component and each processing step. First we present the video feature extraction. Then we will shortly describe how structuring works with growing self-organizing maps. Afterwards, a detailed description of the visualization component is given. Before concluding, the last section deals with the interaction possibilities of our system.

2   Video Feature Extraction

The video feature extraction component supplies the self-organizing map with numerical vectors and therefore they form the basis of the system. The module consists of two parts, temporal segmentation and feature extraction.

2.1   Temporal Segmentation

The video stream is automatically segmented into shots by detecting cuts. Our temporal segmentation is performed by detecting rapid changes of the difference between colour histograms of successive frames, using a single threshold. It was shown in [14] that this simple approach performs rather well. The colours are represented in the IHS space, because of its suitable perceptual properties and the independence between the three colourspace components. A simple filtering process allows the reduction of the number of false positives. The shots with an insufficient number of frames (usually less than 5), are ignored. However, the number of false positives does not have a great influence on our approach, since similar shots will be assigned to the same cluster, as discussed in the following.

2.2   Feature Extraction

In order to obtain good clustering a reasonable representation of the video segments is necessary. For each shot, one keyframe is extracted (we choose the median frame of a shot) along with its colour histograms using a specified colour space. The system supports the IHS, HSV, and RGB colour models. Apart from a global colour histogram, histograms for the top, bottom left, and right regions of the image are also extracted. The self-organizing map is trained with a vector merging all partial histogram vectors, which is then used to define each shot.

3   Structuring with Growing Self-Organizing Maps

3.1   The Self-Organizing Maps

Self-organizing maps (SOMs) [3] are artificial neural networks, well suited for clustering and visualization of high dimensional information. In fact, they map high-dimensional data into a low dimensional space (two dimensional map). The map is organized as a grid of symmetrically connected cells. During learning, similar high dimensional objects are progressively grouped together into the cells. After training, objects that are assigned to cells close to each other, in the low-dimensional space, are also close to each other in the high-dimensional space.

Our map is based on cells organized in hexagonal form, because the distances between adjacent cells are always constant on the map (see Fig. 1). In fact, in the traditional rectangular topology the distance would depend on whether the two cells are adjacent vertically (or rather horizontally) or diagonally.

The neuronal network structure of SOMs is organized in two layers (Fig. 1). The neurons in the input layer correspond to the input dimensions, here the feature vector describing the shot. The output layer (map) contains as many neurons as clusters needed. All neurons in the input layer are connected with all neurons in the output layer. The connection weights between input and output layer of neural network encode positions in the high-dimensional feature space. They are trained in an unsupervised manner. Every unit in the output layer represents a prototype, .i.e. here the center of a cluster of similar shots.

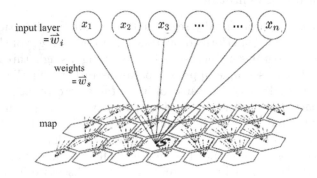

Fig. 1. Structure of a Hexagonally Organized Self-Organizing Map: The basic structure is an artificial neural network with two layers. Each element of the input layer is connected to every element of the map.

Before the learning phase of the network, the two-dimensional structure of the output units is fixed and the weights are initialized randomly. During learning, the sample vectors are repeatedly propagated through the network. The weights of the most similar prototype w_s (winner neuron) are modified such that the prototype moves towards the input vector w_i. As similarity measure usually the

Euclidean distance or scalar product is used. To preserve the neighbourhood relations, prototypes that are close to the winner neuron in the two-dimensional structure are also moved in the same direction. The strength of the modification decreases with the distance from the winner neuron. Therefore, the weights w_s of the winner neuron are modified according to the following equation:

$$\forall i : w_s' = w_s + v(c, i).\delta.(w_s - w_i) \tag{1}$$

where δ is a learning rate. By this learning procedure, the structure in the high-dimensional sample data is non-linearly projected to the lower-dimensional topology.

Although the application of SOMs is straightforward, a main difficulty is defining an appropriate size for the map. Indeed, the number of clusters has to be defined before starting to train the map with data. Therefore, the size of the map is usually too small or too large to map the underlying data appropriately, and the complete learning process has to be repeated several times until an appropriate size is found. Since the objective is to structure the video data, the desired size depends highly on the content. An extension of self-organizing maps that overcomes this problem is the growing self-organizing map [7].

3.2   The Growing Self-Organizing Map

The main idea is to initially start with a small map and then add during training iteratively new units, until the overall error – measured, e.g., by the inhomogeneity of objects assigned to a unit – is sufficiently small. Thus the map adapts itself to the structure of the underlying data collection. The applied method restricts the algorithm to add new units to the external units if the accumulated error of a unit exceeds a specified threshold value. This approach simplifies the growing problem (reassignment and internal-topology difficulties) and it was shown in [7] that it copes well with the introduction of data in low and high dimensional spaces. The way a new unit is inserted is illustrated in Fig. 2. After a new unit has been added to the map, the map is re-trained. Thus, all cluster centers are adjusted and the objects are reassigned to the clusters. This implies that shots may change clusters. This may lead to the emergence of empty clusters, i.e. clusters which "lost" their former objects to their neighbors. This might happen especially in areas where the object density was already small.

3.3   Similarity Between Shots

As in all clustering algorithms the main problem is how to model the similarity between the objects that are going to be grouped into one cluster. We model the difference of two video sequences with the Euclidean distance of the two vectors that were extracted from the video. However, this distance does not necessarily correspond to a perceived distance by a human. In addition, these features represent only a small part of the video content. In any case, there remains a semantic gap between the video content and what we see on the map. However, since for this first prototype study we are mainly interested in

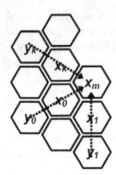

x_i, y_i: weight vectors
x_k: weight vector of unit with highest error
m: new unit
α, β: smoothness weights
Computation of new weight vector for x_m for m:

$$x_m = \left[x_k + \alpha * (x_k - y_k) + \sum_{i=0, i \neq k}^{n} (x_i + \beta * (x_i - y_i)) \right] * \frac{1}{n+1}$$

Fig. 2. Insertion of a new Unit: When the cumulated error of a cell exceeds a threshold, a new unit x_m is added to the map. It is placed next to the unit with the highest error at the border of the map.

the capabilities of the SOMs, this approach seems sufficient, since we are not looking at grouping the shots "purely semantically", but rather at extracting a structure based on visual similarities.

4 Visualization

Our system represents a video shot by a single keyframe and constructs higher level aggregates of shots. The user has the possibility to browse the content in several ways. We combined elements providing information on three abstraction levels as illustrated in Fig. 3. First, there is an overview of the whole content provided by the self-organizing map window (see section 4.1). On each cell, the keyframe of the shot that is the nearest to the cluster centre, i.e. the most typical keyframe of a cluster, is displayed. The second level consists of a combined content-based and time-based visualization. A list of shots is provided for each grid cell (see section 4.2) and a control (see section 4.3) derived from the time-bar control helps to identify content that is similar to the currently selected shot.

4.1 Self Organizing Map Window

The self-organizing map window (see Fig. 4.1) contains the visual representation of the SOM where the clusters are represented by hexagonal nodes. The most typical keyframe of the cluster is displayed on each node. If there are no shots assigned to a special node no picture is displayed. These empty clusters emerge during the learning phase as described above. The background colours of the grid cells are used to visualize different information about the clusters. After learning, shades of green indicate the distribution of keyframes: the brightness of a cell depends on the number of shots assigend to it (see Fig. 4.1a), e.g. a cell containing four shots is displayed in a brighter green than a cell containing only two. Later, the background colour indicates the similarity of the cluster to a selected shot as described below.

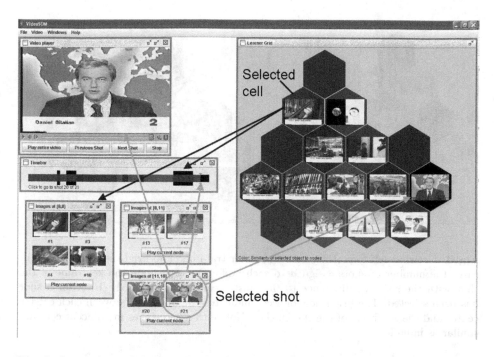

Fig. 3. Screenshot of the Interface: The player in the top left corner provides video access on the lowest interaction level. The time bar and shot list provide an intermediate level of summarized information while the growing self-organizing map on the right represents the highest abstraction level. The selected shot is played and its temporal position is indicated on the time bar whose black extensions correspond to the content of the selected cell (marked with blue arrows).

After this first display, a click on a cell opens a list of shots assigned to the specific cell (see section 4.2). The user can then select a specific shot from the list. As a result, the colour of the map changes to shades of red (see Fig. 4.1b). Here, the intensity of the colour depends on the distance between the cluster centres and the actually selected shot and thus is an indicator for its similarity. For instance, if we select a shot that has the visual characteristics A and B, all the nodes with these characteristics will be coloured in dark red and it will progressively change towards a brighter red based on the distance. This implies in particular that the current node will be automatically coloured in dark red, since by construction all of its elements are most similar. In fact, objects that are assigned to cells close to each other, in the low-dimensional space, are also close to each other in the high-dimensional space.

However, this does not mean that objects with a small distance in the high-dimensional space are necessarily assigned to cells separated by a small distance on the map. For instance, we can have on one side of the map a node with shots with the characteristic A and on another the ones with characteristic B. Then in one of both, let's say A-type, a shot with characteristics A and B.

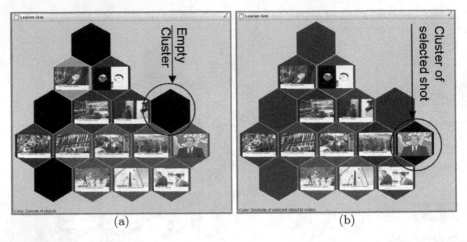

Fig. 4. Growing self-organizing map: (a) After training. The brightness of a cell indicates the number of shots assigned to each node. On each node the keyframe of the shot with the smallest difference to the cluster center is displayed. (b) After a shot has been selected. The brightness of a cell indicates the distance between each cluster center and the keyframe of the chosen shot. Notice that sequences in adjacent cells are similar as intended.

Because of the visualisation schema presented above, starting with a shot that has characteristics A and B, located in a node A, we will easily identify the nodes in which all the shots are rather of type B. This improves significantly the navigation possibilities provided by other clustering schemas.

From user interaction perspective the map is limited to the following actions: select nodes and communicate cluster assignment and colour information to the time bar. Nevertheless it is a very powerful tool which is especially useful for presenting a structured summarization of the video to the user.

4.2   Player and Shot List

The player is an essential part of every video browsing application. Since the video is segmented into shots, functionalities were added especially for the purpose of playing the previous and the next shot. A shot list window showing all keyframes assigned to a cell (Fig. 3) is added to the interface every time a user selects a node from the map. Multiple shot lists for different nodes can be open at the same time. They correspond to the actual selected node in the self-organizing map, as described in section 4.1. When clicking on one of the keyframes, the system plays the corresponding shot in the video. The button for playing the current node starts a consecutive play operation of all shots corresponding to the selected node, starting with the first shot. This adds another temporal visualization method to the segmented video.

4.3   Time Bar

The time bar (Fig. 5) provides additional information and some special interaction possibilities. A green double arrow displays the current temporal position within the video. The main bar is a projection of the colours of the self organizing map into the temporal axis. With this approach, it is possible to see within the same view the information about the similarity of keyframes and the corresponding temporal information. Additionally, corresponding shots of the selected cell are marked by black extensions. This cell can differ from the cluster of the currently selected shot, in which case the black bars correspond to the selected cluster while the colour scheme is based on the selected shot from another cluster. Thus, leading to a possibility to compare a family of similar shots with a cluster. There are two interactions possible with the time bar. By clicking once on any position, the system plays the corresponding shot. Clicking twice, it forces the self organizing map to change the currently selected node to the one corresponding to the chosen frame. And therefore, the background colour schema of the map is recomputed.

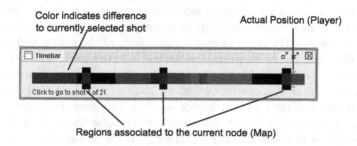

Fig. 5. Time Bar Control: The time bar control provides additional information. The brightness of the colour indicates the distribution of similar sequences on the time scale. Around the time bar, black blocks visualize the temporal positions of the shots assigned to the currently selected node. Furthermore, the two arrows point out the actual player position.

5   User Interaction

The four components presented above are integrated into one single screen (Fig. 3) providing a structured view of the video content. The methods for user interaction are hierarchically organized (Fig. 6). The first layer is represented by the video viewer. The shot lists and timebar visualize the data on the second layer. The self-organizing map provides the highest abstraction level.

The user can select nodes from the SOM and retrieve their content i.e. the list of corresponding keyframes. The time bar is automatically updated by visualizing the temporal distribution of the corresponding shots when the current node is changed. Thus, a direct link from the third to the second layer is established. Furthermore the user views at the same time the temporal distribution

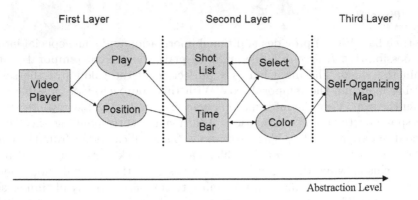

Fig. 6. User Interactions: This figure illustrates the main user interactions that are possible with our system. All listed elements are visible to the user on one single screen and always accessible thus providing a summarization on all layers at the same time.

of similar shots inside the whole video on the time bar, after a certain shot has been selected. In the other direction selecting shots using both the time bar and the list of keyframes causes the map to recompute the similarity values for its nodes and to change the selected node. The colour of the grid cells is computed based on the distance of its prototype to the selected shot. The same colours are used inside the time bar. Once the user has found a shot of interest, he can easily browse similar shots using the colour indication on the time bar or map. Notice that the first layer cannot be accessed directly from the third layer.

Different play operations are activated by the time bar and shot lists. The player itself gives feedback about its current position to the time bar. The time bar is actualized usually when the current shot changes. All visualization components are highly interconnected. In contrast to other multi-layer interfaces, the user can always use all provided layers simultaneously within the same view. He can select nodes from the map, keyframes from the list or from the time bar, or even nodes from the time bar by double-clicking.

6   Conclusions

The structuring and visualization of video information is a complex and challenging task. In this paper we presented a prototype for content-based video navigation based on a growing self-organizing map where the interaction model is hierarchically organized. We perform the clustering ignoring the temporal aspect of video information and reintroduce it in the form of a time bar where we link similar shots with colours. Our interface allows the user to browse the video content using simultaneously several perspectives, temporal as well as content-based representations of the video. Combined with the interaction possibilities between them this allows efficient searching of relevant information in video content.

References

1. Lee, H., Smeaton, A.F., Berrut, C., Murphy, N., Marlow, S., O'Connor, N.E.: Implementation and analysis of several keyframe-based browsing interfaces to digital video. In Borbinha, J., Baker, T., eds.: LNCS. Volume 1923. (2000) 206–218
2. Girgensohn, A., Boreczky, J., Wilcox, L.: Keyframe-based user interfaces for digital video. Computer **34**(9) (2001) 61–67
3. Kohonen, T.: Self-Organizing Maps. Springer-Verlag, Berlin Heidelberg (1995)
4. Lin, X., Marchionini, G., Soergel, D.: A selforganizing semantic map for information retrieval. In: Proc. of the 14th Int. ACM/SIGIR Conference on Research and Development in Information Retrieval, New York, ACM Press (1991) 262–269
5. Kohonen, T., Kaski, S., Lagus, K., Salojärvi, J., Honkela, J., Paattero, V., Saarela, A.: Self organization of a massive document collection. IEEE Transactions on Neural Networks **11**(3) (2000) 574–585
6. Roussinov, D.G., Chen, H.: Information navigation on the web by clustering and summarizing query results. Information Processing & Management **37**(6) (2001) 789–816
7. Nürnberger, A., Detyniecki, M.: Visualizing changes in data collections using growing self-organizing maps. In: Proc. of Int. Joint Conference on Neural Networks (IJCANN 2002), IEEE (2002) 1912–1917
8. Laaksonen, J., Koskela, M., Oja, E.: PicSOM-self-organizing image retrieval with MPEG-7 content descriptors. IEEE Transactions on Neural Network **13** (2002) 841–853
9. Koskela, M., Laaksonen, J.: Semantic annotation of image groups with self-organizing maps. In Leow, W.K., Lew, M.S., Chua, T.S., Ma, W.Y., Chaisorn, L., Bakker, E.M., eds.: Proc. of the 4th Int. Conf. on Image and Video Retrieval (CIVR 2005). Volume 3568 of Lecture Notes in Computer Science., Berlin, Springer-Verlag (2005) 518–527
10. Nürnberger, A., Klose, A.: Improving clustering and visualization of multimedia data using interactive user feedback. In: Proc. of the 9th Int. Conference on Information Processing and Management of Uncertainty in Knowledge-Based Systems. (2002) 993–999
11. Marques, O., Furht, B.: Content-based Image and Video Retrieval. Kluwer Academic Publishers, Norwell, Massachusetts (2002)
12. Veltkamp, R., Burkhardt, H., Kriegel, H.P.: State-Of-The-Art in Content-Based Image and Video Retrieval. Kluwer (2001)
13. Nürnberger, A., Detyniecki, M.: Adaptive multimedia retrieval: From data to user interaction. In Strackeljan, J., Leivisk, K., Gabrys, B., eds.: Do smart adaptive systems exist - Best practice for selection and combination of intelligent methods. Springer-Verlag, Berlin (2005)
14. Browne, P., Smeaton, A.F., Murphy, N., O'Connor, N., Marlow, S., Berrut, C.: Evaluating and combining digital video shot boundary detection algorithms. In: Proc. Irish Machine Vision and Image Processing Conference, Dublin (2000)

Fuzzy SVM Ensembles for Relevance Feedback in Image Retrieval

Yong Rao, Padma Mundur, and Yelena Yesha

Department of Computer Science and Electrical Engineering
University of Maryland, Baltimore County
1000 Hilltop Circle, Baltimore, Maryland, 21250, USA
{yongrao1, pmundur, yeyesha}@csee.umbc.edu

Abstract. Relevance feedback has been integrated into content-based retrieval systems to overcome the semantic gap problem. Recently, Support Vector Machines (SVMs) have been widely used to learn the users' semantic query concept from users' feedback. The feedback is either 'relevant' or 'irrelevant' which forces the users to make a binary decision during each retrieval iteration. However, human's perception of visual content is quite subjective and therefore, the notion of whether or not an image is relevant is rather vague and hard to define. Part of the small training samples problem faced by traditional SVMs can be thought of as the result of strict binary decision-making. In this paper, we propose a Fuzzy SVM technique to overcome the small sample problem. Using Fuzzy SVM, each sample can be assigned a fuzzy membership to model users' feedback gradually from 'irrelevant' to 'relevant' instead of strict binary labeling. We also propose to use Fuzzy SVM ensembles to further improve the classification results. We conduct extensive experiments to evaluate the performance of our proposed algorithm. Compared to the experimental results using traditional SVMs, we demonstrate that our proposed approach can significantly improve the retrieval performance of semantic image retrieval.

1 Introduction

Content-based image retrieval (CBIR) has received much attention from the research communities in the last decade [1]. Relevance feedback has been proposed to bridge the 'semantic gap' between the low-level visual feature vector representation of image content and the high-level user query concept. Various relevance feedback techniques have been proposed [2] and Support Vector Machines [3] have been recently used to learn and classify users' feedback where the system constructs SVM classifiers by training data from user's feedback, and classifies all images in the database into two categories– "relevant" and "irrelevant". However, the relevance feedback procedure is often a tedious and boring step for the users and may result in a small number of positive feedback and degrade the performance of SVM. To increase the number of training samples, several approaches have been proposed. In [4], He, King, Zhang et al proposed to learn a semantic space by learning the users' past relevance feedback history. They called it the 'long-term learning' which is different from 'short-term learning' used to refer to the learning activities in a single retrieval session. In [5],

H. Sundaram et al. (Eds.): CIVR 2006, LNCS 4071, pp. 350–359, 2006.
© Springer-Verlag Berlin Heidelberg 2006

Yoshizawa and Schweitzer proposed a similar "long-term" approach to accumulate semantic groups using past relevant feedback information.

All of the above approaches treat the training samples equally. However, human's perception of visual content is quite subjective and therefore, the notion of whether or not an image is relevant is rather vague and hard to define. Part of the small training samples problem can be thought of as the result of strict binary decision-making in an environment where vagueness occurs in the image content representation, the similarity measure and query concept. While most CBIR systems force users to use binary labeling, some systems provide one more option like 'neutral' as in BlobWorld [6]. In [7] Rui, Huang, Ortega et al let the user assign a score varying from -3 (highly nonrelevant) to 3 (highly relevant) to each retrieved image. The user's feedback is then used to refine the feature weights for the next iteration of retrieval.

Unfortunately, binary labeling, and even multi-level labeling do not reflect the nature of human concepts, which tend to be abstract, uncertain, and imprecise. It is more natural to use a fuzzy membership function to model users' query concept gradually from 'irrelevant' to 'relevant'. In [8], Frigui used Fuzzy set to assign linguistic labels to each image and used Fuzzy Choquet Integral to update the feature weights. In [9], Krishnapuram, Medasani, Jung et al. proposed a fuzzy attributed relational graph (FARG) to represent each image in the database and the user query was translated into a FARG. The image retrieval problem is then converted to a subgraph matching problem. However, in this approach there is no relevance feedback.

In this paper, we propose a Fuzzy SVM (FSVM) technique to overcome the small sample problem. Using FSVM, each sample can be assigned a fuzzy membership to model users' feedback gradually from 'irrelevant' to 'relevant' instead of strict binary labeling. While traditional SVM treats each sample equally, Fuzzy SVM deals with them with different importance. Users can now label the images using natural linguistic variables such as "very relevant", "slightly irrelevant" or "moderately relevant" and so on. Therefore, more feedback can be collected. We propose a new Fuzzy membership function to model those linguistic variables and a FSVM that can classify such Fuzzy samples. In [10], Choi and Lyu assigned a soft label to each training sample and added new training samples from user's query logs. They also designed the soft label SVM to process the samples with different labels. This method is similar to our approach. However, the fuzzy membership value in our approach associated with each sample models users' feedback gradually and naturally. It depends on current session information instead of past user log and is assigned directly by the user.

Recently, it has been reported that using ensemble of SVM classifiers can generate a strong classifier by combining several weak classifiers [11]. In this paper, the method of classifier ensembles is also incorporated into the relevance feedback process to improve the retrieval performance. However, the classifiers in our method are all Fuzzy SVMs that can process samples with fuzzy memberships and we treat the samples differently.

The rest of this paper is organized as follows. Section 2 presents the Fuzzy SVM algorithm, Fuzzy membership function and Fuzzy SVM ensemble technique. Section 3 gives detailed experiments and performance comparison and Section 4 concludes the paper.

2 Fuzzy Support Vector Machines

Training samples in regular SVM are treated equally to impact the decision boundary. However, in the real world, not all samples are of the same importance or confidence. For example, a certain image labeled as "very relevant" should have larger impact than an uncertain image labeled as "slightly relevant". Traditional SVM is very sensitive to those uncertain training data points which are far away from their own classes since they are treated equally with other trusted data. To reduce the risk of such uncertain data, we introduce the FSVM [12,13,14] to deal with the different importance/certainty of each data in our proposed algorithm. In FSVM, each data point x_i has an assigned membership value u_i according to its relative importance in the class. The training set becomes a fuzzy training set S_f :

$$S_f = \{x_i, y_i, u_i\}, i = 1, 2, \cdots, N \tag{1}$$

For positive class ($y_i = +1$), the set of membership values are denoted as u_i^+ . For negative class ($y_i = -1$), the set of membership values are denoted as u_i^- . The two sets of fuzzy membership are assigned independently.

Given a fuzzy training set, FSVM wants to maximize the margin of separation and minimize the classification error. FSVM adds fuzzy membership value u_i to the cost function in order to reduce the effect of less important data points. A parameter m is used to influence the fuzziness of the fuzzified penalty term in the cost function. The objective function becomes

$$\min_{w,b,\xi} \frac{1}{2} \|w\|^2 + C \sum_i u_i^m \xi_i \tag{2}$$

s.t
$$y_i((\Phi(x_i) \cdot w) + b) \geq 1 - \xi_i \tag{3}$$

$$\xi_i \geq 0, i = 1, 2, \cdots, N \tag{4}$$

Now let the Lagrange function be

$$L(w, \xi, b, \alpha, \beta, u) = \frac{1}{2} \|w\|^2 + C \sum_i u_i^m \xi_i$$

$$- \sum_i \alpha_i (y_i (\Phi(x_i) \cdot w) + b) - 1 + \xi_i) - \sum_i \beta_i \xi_i \tag{5}$$

where α_i and β_i are non-negative Lagrange multipliers. Differentiating L with respect to w, b, ξ_i and setting the results equal to zero, we have the following conditions of optimality:

$$\frac{\partial L}{\partial w} = w - \sum_i \alpha_i y_i \Phi(x_i) = 0 \Rightarrow w = \sum_i \alpha_i y_i \Phi(x_i) \tag{6}$$

$$\frac{\partial L}{\partial b} = -\sum_i \alpha_i y_i = 0 \Rightarrow \sum_i \alpha_i y_i = 0 \tag{7}$$

$$\frac{\partial L}{\partial \xi_i} = Cu_i^m - \alpha_i - \beta_i = 0 \Rightarrow 0 \le \alpha_i \le Cu_i^m \tag{8}$$

Substituting Eqs.(6-8) into Eq.(5), the Lagrange is a function of α only. The dual of the optimal problem becomes

$$\min_\alpha \frac{1}{2} \sum_{i,j} \alpha_i \alpha_j y_i y_j K(x_i, x_j) \tag{9}$$

s.t.
$$\sum_i \alpha_i y_i = 0 \tag{10}$$

$$0 \le \alpha_i \le Cu_i^m, i = 1, 2, \cdots, N \tag{11}$$

Then, the decision function can be derived as the form below

$$f(x) = sign(\sum_i \alpha_i y_i K(x, x_i) + b) \tag{12}$$

The only difference between regular SVM and FSVM is the upper bound of Lagrange multipliers α_i in the dual optimization function. The upper bounds of α_i in regular SVM are bounded by a constant C while in FSVM, α_i are bounded by Cu_i^m. The Support Vectors (SVs) with larger membership values will have larger effect on the decision boundary than the SVs with smaller membership values thus reducing the impact of uncertain data.

2.1 Fuzzy Membership Function

The membership values should reflect the relative importance of training data points in their classes. In [12], the fuzzy membership value is defined as the distance to the class center. However, this is impossible when the classes are not available. We define the fuzzy membership function as follows:

$$u_i^+ = \begin{cases} 1 & D(x_i) > 0 \wedge d(x_i) \ge 1 \\ d(x_i), & D(x_i) > 0 \end{cases} \tag{13}$$

$$u_i^- = \begin{cases} 1 & D(x_i) < 0 \wedge d(x_i) \ge 1 \\ d(x_i), & D(x_i) < 0 \end{cases} \tag{14}$$

where $D(x_i)$ is the decision value, $d(x_i)$ is the distance value between a training sample x_i to the optimal separating hyper-plane and is given by $|D(x_i)|/\|w\|$.

From Eq.(13-14), training samples that are closer to the SVM boundary have smaller membership values which means they are less likely to belong to the given class. While the samples that are farther away from the SVM boundary are more likely to belong to the given class and have larger membership values.

2.2 Fuzzy SVM Ensembles

It has been shown that Bagging technique can significantly improve classifier performance. A better classifier can be integrated from multiple weak classifiers which are generated by bootstrapping, i.e. random sampling with replacement on the training samples. In order to further improve our FSVM performance, we adopt a similar asymmetric Bagging strategy as in [11]. Since we have a limited number of positive training samples compared with the number of negative samples, each FSVM classifier is built using the same set of positive feedback and with a set of randomly sampled negative feedback. The number of negative feedback is the same as the positive feedback. One major difference here is that since the samples that have smaller fuzzy membership values are closer to the SVM boundary thus are more "informative", we include N^+ positive and N^- ($N^+ = N^-$) negative samples with the smallest fuzzy membership value in each positive and negative training set. We call them the 'Weak Positive (WP)' and 'Weak Negative (WN)' set. These two sets are included in each classifier. Using balanced number of positive and negative samples and random sampling, the FSVM ensemble approach avoids the un-balanced training sample and over fitting problem of traditional SVMs.

Table 1. Asymmetric Bagging FSVM algorithm

Input: positive fuzzy training set FS^+ ,

  negative fuzzy training set FS^- ,
  weak negative training set (WN),
  weak classifier FSVM,
  integer l (the number of FSVM classifiers)
  x is the test sample

Output: decision value $D(x)$

1. for i = 1 to l
2.   { FS_i^- =(Bootstrap sample from FS^-) $\cup WN$
3. $D_i(x) = FSVM(x, FS^+, FS_i^-)$; }
4. $D(x) = WMV\_Aggregate\{D_i(x), 1 \le i \le l\}$

We use weighted majority voting (*WMV*) method to aggregate the results from individual FSVM classifiers. Let $D_i(x)$ ($i = 1 \cdots l$) be the decision value of i-th individual FSVM classifiers, w_i is the weight associated with each classifier which is determined by its training error ε_i .

$$w_i = \log(\frac{1 - \varepsilon_i}{\varepsilon_i}) \tag{15}$$

w_i is further normalized such that $\sum_i w_i = 1$. The asymmetric bagging FSVM algorithm is listed in Table 1. The fuzzy membership value of each data sample is re-calculated each time when a new decision value is $D(x)$ obtained.

3 Experimental Results

3.1 Data Set and Representation

We use two publicly available data sets for our experiment. The first data set is used in MUVIS [15]. It has 1000 images and we extract 10 categories with 100 images in each category. The other data set is used in SIMPLIcity [16]. We extracted 2000 images for 20 categories and each category has 100 images. Each category has a different semantic label such as food, flower, car, beach, tree, butterfly and so on.

Three types of features, color, shape, and texture are extracted from each image to represent its content. The color feature used in our experiments is color moment. It is a 9-dimension feature vector where 3 moments (color mean, color variance and color skewness) in each color channel (H, S, and V) are extracted from each image. We use edge direction histogram for image shape feature. It is an 18-dimension feature vector. We quantize the edge direction histogram into 18 bins of 20 degree each from the edge image obtained by applying a Canny edge detector on the transformed gray image. The texture feature used is the co-occurrence feature. It is a 20-dimension feature by analyzing the Co-occurrence matrix. Details of these features can be found in [17].

3.2 Experimental Process

In this section, we compare the new FSVM ensembles with existing algorithms through experiments on the two data sets. The experiments are simulated by a computer automatically. A total of K percent of all images are selected randomly as test queries. We set $K = 10$, thus a total number of 100 images are used to test the 10-category data set and 200 images are used to test the 20-category data set. The experiment steps are listed below and the relevance feedback is automatically done by the computer:

1. A query image is randomly selected from the database.
2. Use the Euclidean distance metric to compute distances between the query image and all the other images in the database.
3. 20 images nearest to the query image are returned to the user as the first retrieval results. Mark all relevant images (i.e. images of the same concept as the query image) positive feedback and all others as negative. The initial fuzzy member ship value for all positive and negative feedback is set to 1.
4. Use asymmetric bagging FSVM algorithm to learn an aggregated FSVM classifier and classify all images and get their decision values.
5. Return top 20 images that are farthest from the FSVM boundary to the user as the results. Mark all images of the same concept as the query image with positive feedback and set fuzzy membership value to 1. We call them the "AbsolutePositive (AP)" samples. All other images are marked positive/negative according to their decision value and set their fuzzy membership values using Eq. (13-14). Mark the "Weak Positive (WP)" and "Weak Negative (WN)" samples. Construct positive fuzzy training set FS^+ as all AP samples plus N^+ WP samples:

$$FS^+ = AP \cup WP .$$

Repeat Step 4 until the maximum number of iterations is reached.

We use Average Precision as the performance measure. It is defined as the average ratio of the number of relevant images of the returned images over the number of all returned images. The 95% confidence interval half-widths of the average precision values are also computed accordingly by repeating the simulation process 25 times to demonstrate the statistical significance of the average performance for each algorithm. In the experiments, we compare our proposed relevance feedback algorithm using FSVM ensembles (E_FSVM) over the traditional SVM (SVM) method and single Fuzzy SVM (FSVM) without ensemble technique. All three SVM algorithms are implemented using LIBSVM package [18] with the same RBF kernel and parameters.

3.3 Performance Comparison

Figure 1 and Figure 2 show the average precision values with confidence interval half-widths at each iteration for the three SVM algorithms over the two test data set. The precision curve of Fuzzy SVM ensembles (E_FSVM) outperformed single Fuzzy SVM (FSVM) and regular SVM. The average precision values of FSVM ensemble (E_FSVM) consistently outperform the other two. After 10 iterations, for Top20 returned images, E_FSVM achieved 4.00% improvement over SVM and single FSVM achieved 1.37% improvement over SVM for the 10-category test data. For the 20-category data, the numbers are 6.97% and 2.56% respectively. Table 2 shows the details of the top20 results of the two category data at three iteration steps.

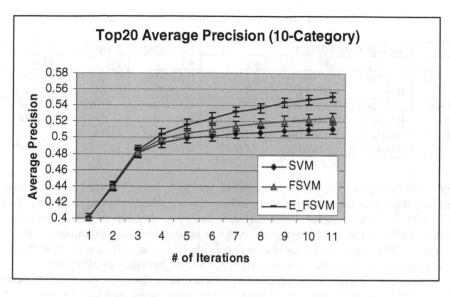

Fig. 1. Experimental results on 10-category data

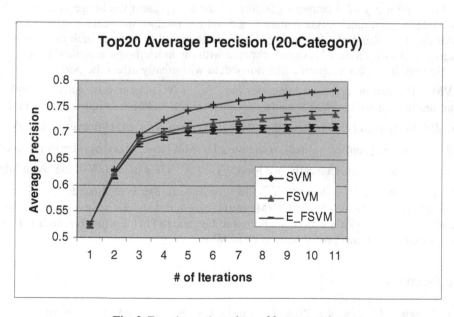

Fig. 2. Experimental results on 20-category data

4 Conclusion

In this paper, we propose to use Fuzzy SVM ensembles to improve the relevance feedback performance in image retrieval. We use Fuzzy membership function to

Table 2. Top 20 Average Precision & Confidence Interval

	10-Category Iteration			20-Category Iteration		
	#1	#6	#11	#1	#6	#11
SVM	0.40126± 0.00468	0.50918± 0.00613	0.51119± 0.00597	0.52461± 0.00679	0.70528± 0.00674	0.71206± 0.00608
FSV M	0.40126± 0.00468	0.50974± 0.00604	0.52491± 0.00615	0.52461± 0.00679	0.71890± 0.00757	0.73761± 0.00608
E_FS VM	0.40126± 0.00468	0.52419± 0.00642	0.55127± 0.00587	0.52461± 0.00679	0.75369± 0.00634	0.78178± 0.00565

gradually model users feedback from 'irrelevant' to 'relevant' instead of strict binary labeling thus more feedback samples can be returned. We propose to use Fuzzy SVM to handle the training samples with different fuzzy membership values. The performance is further improved by using Fuzzy SVM ensembles using asymmetric bagging technique. The experimental results on two publicly available data sets show that the new approach can improve the relevance feedback performance significantly.

Although the experimental results have shown the effectiveness of the proposed Fuzzy SVM ensemble approach, there is some further work that will be done in the near future.

First, we use a 47-d combined feature vector to represent the image content. It is possible to use a much larger feature space and use random sub-space method to deal with the over-fitting problem as in [11]. We will use other features such as color histogram and wavelet-based texture technique with random sub-space method later.

Second, it has been reported that noisy data will greatly affect the performance of SVMs. The current approach integrates the N^+ (N^-) positive (negative) samples that are nearest to the SVM boundary in each iteration. These samples have a much smaller fuzzy membership value thus their impact are reduced. However, when N^+ (N^-) is not appropriately small, some samples with larger fuzzy membership values may act as noisy data. Currently, we limit N^+ (N^-) less than 20% of the 'Absolute Positive' samples. The effect of N^+ (N^-) will be further investigated.

Furthermore, the number of FSVMs in the ensembles should be investigated. Currently, we use 5 FSVMs which is reported to be enough [11]. Further research will be conducted to find the optimal number of FSVMs.

References

1. N. Sebe, M.S. Lew, X.S. Zhou, T.S. Huang, E.M. Bakker. The State of the Art in Image and Video Retrieval, Second International Conference on Image and Video Retrieval, CIVR 2003 Urbana-Champaign, IL, USA, July (2003) 24-25
2. X.S. Zhou, and T.S. Huang. Relevance Feedback in Image retrieval: a comprehensive review. Multimedia Systems, Vol. 8, No. 6, (2003) 536-544
3. V.Vapnik: The Nature of Statistical Learning Theory. Springer-Verlag, New York (1995)

4. X. He, O. King, W.-Y. Ma, M. Li, and H. J. Zhang. Learning a semantic space from user's relevance feedback for image retrieval, IEEE Transactions on Circuits and Systems for Video Technology, Vol,13, No. 1 (2003) 39-48
5. T.Yoshizawa and H. Schweitzer. Long-term learning of semantic grouping from relevance-feedback, Multimedia Information Retrieval, (2004) 165-172
6. C.Carson, S Belongie, H. Greenspan, and J.Malik. Blobworld: Image segmentation using Expectation-Maximization and its application to image querying, EECS department technical report, UC Berkeley (1999)
7. Y. Rui, T. S . Huang, M. Ortega, and S. Mehrotra. Relevance feedback: A power tool in interactive content-based image retrieval, IEEE Transaction on Circuits and Systems for Video Tech., Special Issue on Interactive Multimedia Systems for the Internet, Vol. 8, No. 5 (1998) 644-655
8. H. Frigui, Adaptive Image Retrieval Using the Fuzzy Integral, In Proceedings of North American Fuzzy Information Processing Society Conference, (1999) 575-578
9. R Krishnapuram, S Medasani, SH Jung, YS Choi, R. Content-based image retrieval based on a fuzzy approach, IEEE Transactions on Knowledge and Data Engineering, Vol.16 No.10, (2004) 1185-1199
10. C.-H. Hoi and M. R. Lyu. A Novel Log-based Relevance Feedback Technique in Content-based Image Retrieval. In Proceedings of the 12th ACM International Conference on Multimedia (MM 2004), New York, USA, (2004) 24-31
11. D.Tao, X.Tang. Random Sampling Based SVM for Relevance Feedback Image Retrieval. IEEE Computer Society Conference on Computer Vision and Pattern Recognition (CVPR'04), July(2004) 647-652
12. H.Huang and Y.Liu. Fuzzy Support Vector Machines for Pattern Recognition and Data Mining, International Journal of Fuzzy Systems, Vol. 4, No.3, (2002) 826-925
13. C.Lin and S. Wang. Fuzzy Support Vector Machines, IEEE Transaction on Neural Networks, Vol. 13, No. 2 (2002) 464-471
14. S.Abe and T.Inoue. Fuzzy Support Vector Machines for Multi-class Problems, In Proceedings of European Symposium on Artificial Neural Networks, Bruges (Belgium), 24-26 April (2002) 113-118
15. S. Kiranyaz, K. Caglar, E. Guldogan, O. Guldogan, and M. Gabbouj. MUVIS: a content-based multimedia indexing and retrieval framework, Proc. of the 7th Intl. Symposium on Signal Processing and its Applications, ISSPA 2003, Paris, France, July (2003) 1-8
16. J.Z. Wang, J. Li, G. Wiederhold, SIMPLIcity: Semantics-sensitive Integrated Matching for Picture LIbraries, IEEE Transaction on Pattern Analysis and Machine Intelligence, Vol 23, No.9, (2001) 947-963
17. M. Sonka, V. Hlavac, and R. Boyle. Image Processing, Analysis, and Machine Vision (2nd edition). Thomson-Engineering (1998)
18. Chih-Chung Chang and Chih-Jen Lin, LIBSVM : a library for support vector machines, 2001. Software available at http://www.csie.ntu.edu.tw/~cjlin/libsvm

Video Mining with Frequent
Itemset Configurations

Till Quack[1], Vittorio Ferrari[2], and Luc Van Gool[1]

[1] ETH Zurich
[2] LEAR - INRIA Grenoble

Abstract. We present a method for mining frequently occurring objects and scenes from videos. Object candidates are detected by finding recurring spatial arrangements of affine covariant regions. Our mining method is based on the class of frequent itemset mining algorithms, which have proven their efficiency in other domains, but have not been applied to video mining before. In this work we show how to express vector-quantized features and their spatial relations as itemsets. Furthermore, a fast motion segmentation method is introduced as an attention filter for the mining algorithm. Results are shown on real world data consisting of music video clips.

1 Introduction

The goal of this work is to mine interesting objects and scenes from video data. In other words, to detect frequently occurring objects automatically. Mining such representative objects, actors, and scenes in video data is useful for many applications. For instance, they can serve as entry points for retrieval and browsing, or they can provide a basis for video summarization. Our approach to video data mining is based on the detection of recurring spatial arrangements of local features. These features are represented in quantized codebooks, which has been a recently popular and successful technique in object recognition, retrieval [14] and classification [10]. On top of this representation, we introduce a method to detect frequently re-occurring spatial configurations of codebook entries. Whereas isolated features still show weak links with semantic content, their co-occurrence has far greater meaning. Our approach relies on frequent itemset mining algorithms, which have been successfully applied to several other, large-scale data mining problems such as market basket analysis or query log analysis [1,2]. In our context, the concept of an item corresponds to a codebook entry. The input to the mining algorithm consists of subsets of feature-codebook entries for each video frame, encoded into "transactions", as they are known in the data mining literature [1]. We demonstrate how to incorporate spatial arrangement information in transactions and how to select the neighborhood defining the subset of image features included in a transaction. For scenes with significant motion, we define this neighborhood via motion segmentation. To this end, we also introduce a simple and very fast technique for motion segmentation on feature codebooks.

H. Sundaram et al. (Eds.): CIVR 2006, LNCS 4071, pp. 360–369, 2006.
© Springer-Verlag Berlin Heidelberg 2006

Few works have dealt with the problem of mining objects composed of local features from video data. In this respect, the closest work to ours is by Sivic and Zisserman [5]. However, there are considerable differences. [5] starts by selecting subsets of quantized features. The neighborhoods for mining are always of fixed size (e.g. the 20 nearest neighbors). Each such neighborhood is expressed as a simple, orderless bag-of-words, represented as a sparse binary indicator vector. The actual mining proceeds by computing the dot-product between all pairs of neighborhoods and setting a threshold on the resulting number of codebook terms they have in common. While this definition of a neighborhood is similar in spirit to our transactions, we also include information about the localization of the feature within its neighborhood. Furthermore, the neighborhood itself is not of fixed size. For scenes containing significant motion, we can exploit our fast motion segmentation to restrict the neighborhood to features with similar motions, and hence more likely to belong to a single object. As another important difference, unlike [5] our approach does not require pairwise matching of bag-of-words indicator vectors, but it relies instead on a frequent itemset mining algorithm, which is a well studied technique in data mining. This brings the additional benefit of knowing *which* regions are common between neighborhoods, versus the dot-product technique only reporting *how many* they are. It also opens the doors to a large body of research on the efficient detection of frequent itemsets and many deduced mining methods.

To the best of our knowledge, no work has been published on frequent itemset mining of video data, and very little is reported on static image data. In [3] an extended association rule mining algorithm was used to mine spatial associations between five classes of texture-tiles in aerial images (forest, urban etc.). In [4] association rules were used to create a classifier for breast cancer detection from mammogram-images. Each mammogram was first cropped to contain the same fraction of the breast, and then described by photometric moments. Compared to our method, both works were only applied to static image data containing rather small variations.

The remainder of this paper is organized as follows. First the pre-processing steps (i.e. video shot detection, local feature extraction and clustering into appearance codebooks) are described in section 2. Section 3 introduces the concepts of our mining method. Section 4 describes the application of the mining method to video sequences. Finally, results are shown in section 5.

2   Shot Detection, Features and Appearance Codebooks

The main processing stages of our system (next sections) rely on the prior subdivision of the video into shots. We apply the shot partitioning algorithm [6], and pick four "keyframes" per second within each shot. As in [5], this results in a denser and more uniform sampling than when using the keyframes selected by [6]. In each keyframe we extract two types of affine covariant features (*regions*): Hessian-Affine [7] and MSER [8]. Affine covariant features are preferred over simpler scale-invariant ones, as they provide robustness against viewpoint changes. Each normalized region is described with a SIFT-descriptor [9]. Next, a quantized codebook [10] (also called "visual vocabulary" [5]) is constructed by clustering the SIFT descriptors with the hierarchical-agglomerative technique described in [10]. In a typical video, this results in about 8000 appearance clusters for each feature type.

We apply the 'stop-list' method known from text-retrieval and [5] as a final polishing: very frequent and very rare visual words are removed from the codebook (the 5% most and 5% least frequent). Note that the following processing stages use only the spatial location of features and their assigned appearance-codebook id's. The appearance descriptors are no longer needed.

3   Our Mining Approach

Our goal is to find frequent spatial configurations of visual words in video scenes. For the time being, let us consider a configuration to be just an unordered set of visual words. We add spatial relationships later, in section 3.2. For a codebook of size d there are 2^d possible subsets of visual words. For each of our two feature types we have a codebook with about 8000 words, which means d is typically > 10000, resulting in an immense search space. Hence we need a mining method capable of dealing with such a large dataset and to return frequently occurring word combinations. Frequent itemset mining methods are a good choice, as they have solved analogous problems in market basket like data [1,2]. Here we briefly summarize the terminology and methodology of frequent itemset mining.

3.1   Frequent Itemset Mining

Let $I = \{i_1 \ldots i_p\}$ be a set of p *items*. Let A be a subset of I with l items, i.e. $A \subseteq I, |A| = l$. Then we call A a l-*itemset*. A transaction is an itemset $T \subseteq I$ with a transaction identifier $tid(T)$. A transaction database D is a set of transactions with unique identifiers $D = \{T_1 \ldots T_n\}$. We say that a transaction T *supports* an itemset A, if $A \subseteq T$. We can now define the support of an itemset A in the transactions-database D as follows:

Definition 1. *The support of an itemset $A \in D$ is*

$$support(A) = \frac{|\{T \in D | A \subseteq T\}|}{|D|} \in [0, 1] \qquad (1)$$

An itemset A is called *frequent* in D if $support(A) \geq s$ where s is a threshold for the minimal support defined by the user.

Frequent itemsets are subject to the monotonicity property: all l-subsets of frequent $(l+1)$-sets are also frequent. The well known APriori algorithm [1] takes advantage of the monotonicity property and allows us to find frequent itemsets very quickly.

3.2   Incorporating Spatial Information

In our context, the items correspond to visual words. In the simplest case, a transaction would be created for each visual word, and would consist of an orderless bag of all other words within some image neighborhood. In order to include also spatial information (i.e. locations of visual words) in the mining process, we further adapt the concept of an item to our problem. The key idea is to encode spatial information directly in the items. In each image we create transactions from the neighborhood around a limited subset of selected words $\{v_c\}$. These words must appear in at least f_{min} and at most in f_{max} frames. This is motivated by the notion that neighbourhoods containing a very infrequent word would create infrequent itemsets, neighbourhoods around extremely frequent word have a high probability of being part of clutter. Each v_c must also have a matching word in the previous frame, if both frames are from the same shot. Typically, with these restrictions, about $1/4$ of the regions in a frame are selected.

For each v_c we create a transaction which contains the surrounding k nearest words together with their rough spatial arrangement. The neighbourhood around v_c is divided into B sections. In all experiments we use $B = 4$ sections. Each section covers $90°$ plus an overlap $o = 5°$ with its neighboring sections, to be robust against small rotations. We label the sections $\{tl, tr, bl, br\}$ (for "top-left", "top-right", etc.), and append to each visual word the label of the section it lies in. In the example in figure 1, the transaction created for v_c is $T = \{tl55, tl9, tr923, br79, br23, bl23, bl9\}$. In the following, we refer to the selected words $\{v_c\}$ as *central* words. Although the approach only accomodates for small rotations, in most videos objects rarely appear in substantially different orientations. Rotations of the neighborhood stemming from perspective transformations are safely accomodated by the overlap o. Although augmenting the items in this fashion increases their total number by a factor B, no changes to the frequent itemset mining algorithm itself are necessary. Besides, thanks to the careful selection of the central visual words v_c, we reduce the number of transactions and thus the runtime of the algorithm.

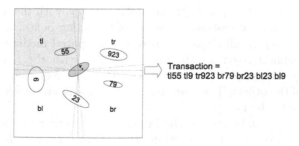

Fig. 1. Creating transaction from a neighborhood. The area around a central visual word v_c is divided into sections. Each section is labeled (tl, tr, bl, br) and the label is appended to the visual word ids.

3.3   Exploiting Motion

Shots containing significant motion[1] allow us to further increase the degree of specificity of transactions: if we had a rough segmentation of the scene into object candidates, we could restrict the neighborhood for a transaction to the segmented area for each candidate, hence dramatically simplifying the task of the mining algorithm. In this case, as the central visual words v_c we pick the two closest regions to the center of the segmented image area. All other words inside the segmented area are included in the transaction (figure 3).

In this section, we propose a simple and very fast motion segmentation algorithm to find such object candidates. The assumption is that interesting objects move independently from each other within a shot. More precisely, we can identify groups of visual words which translate consistently from frame to frame. The grouping method consists of two steps:

Step 1. Matching words. A pair of words from two frames $f(t), f(t+n)$ at times t and $t + n$ is deemed matched if they have the same codebook ids (i.e. they are in the same appearance cluster), and if the translation is below a maximum translation threshold t_{max}. This matching step is extremely fast, since we rely only on cluster id correspondences. In our experiments we typically use $t_{max} = 40$ pixels and $n = 6$ since we operate on four keyframes per second.

Step 2. Translation clustering. At each timestep t, the pairs of regions matched between frames $f(t)$ and $f(t+n)$ are grouped according to their translation using k-means clustering. In order to determine the initial number of motion groups k, k-means is initialized with a leader initialization [12], on the translation between the first two frames. For each remaining timestep, we run k-means three times with different values for k, specifically

$$k(t) \in \{k(t-1) - 1, k(t-1), k(t-1) + 1\} \tag{2}$$

where $k(t-1)$ is the number of motion groups in the previous timestep. $k(t)$ is constrained to be in $[2...6]$. This prevents the number of motion groups from changing abruptly from frame to frame. To further improve stability, we run the algorithm twice for each k with different random initializations. From the resulting different clusterings, we keep the one with the best mean silhouette value [13]. We improve the quality of the motion groups with the following filter. For each motion group, we estimate a series of bounding-boxes, containing from 80% progressively up to all regions closest to the spatial median of the group. We retain as bounding-box for the group the one with the maximal density $\frac{number\ of\ regions}{bounding\ box\ area}$. This procedure removes from the motion groups regions located far from most of the others. These are most often mismatches which accidentally translate similar to the group.

The closest two visual words to the bounding box center are now selected as the central visual word v_c for the motion group. Figure 2 shows detected motion groups for a scene of a music videoclip.

---

[1] Since shot partitioning [6] returns a single keyframe for static shots and several keyframes for moving shots, we can easily detect shots with significant motion.

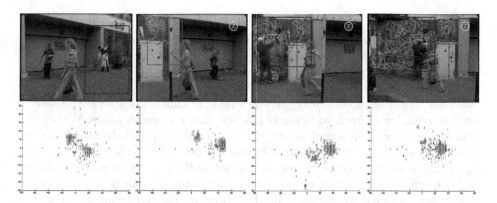

Fig. 2. First row: motion groups (only region centers shown) with bounding boxes. Second row: motion groups in translation space. Note: colors do not necessarily correspond along a row, since groups are not tracked along time.

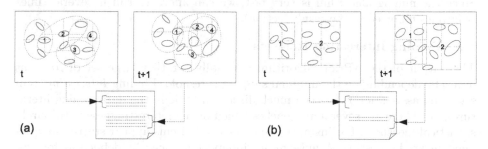

Fig. 3. Creating transactions: (a) static shots: transactions are formed around each v_c from the k-neighborhood. (b) shots with considerable motion: a motion group is the basis for a transaction, thus the number of items in a transaction is not fixed but given by the size of the motion group. With (b) in general fewer transactions are generated.

4 Mining the Entire Video

We quickly summarize the processing stages from the previous sections. A video is first partitioned into shots. For rather static shots we create transactions from a fixed neighborhood around each central word (subsection 3.2). For shots with considerable motion, we use as central words the two words closest to the spatial center of the motion group, and create two transactions covering only visual words within it. For frequent itemset mining itself we use an implementation of APriori from [11]. We mine so called "maximal frequent itemsets". An itemset is called maximal if no superset is frequent. Only sets with four or more items are kept.

Note how frequent itemset mining returns sparse but discriminative descriptions of neighborhoods. As opposed to the dot-product of binary indicator vectors used in [5], the frequent itemsets show *which* visual words cooccur in the mined transactions. Such a sparse description might also be helpful for efficiently indexing mined objects.

4.1　Choosing a Support Threshold

The choice of a good minimal support threshold s in frequent itemset mining is not easy, especially in our untraditional setting where items and itemsets are constructed without supervision. If the threshold is too high, no frequent itemsets are mined. If it is too low, too many (possibly millions) are mined. Thus, rather than defining a fixed threshold, we run the algorithm with several thresholds, until the number of frequent itemsets falls within a reasonable range. We achieve this with a binary split search strategy. Two extremal support thresholds are defined, s_{low} and s_{high}. The number of itemsets is desired to be between n_{min} and n_{max}. Let n be the number of itemsets mined in the current step of the search, and s be the corresponding support threshold. If the number of itemsets is not in the desired range, we update s by the following rule and rerun the miner:

$$s^{(t+1)} = \begin{cases} s^{(t)} + \frac{(s_{high} - s^{(t)})}{2} , \ s_{low} = s^{(t)} \ \text{if} \ n > n_{max} \\ s^{(t)} - \frac{(s^{(t)} - s_{low})}{2} , \ s_{high} = s^{(t)} \ \text{if} \ n < n_{min} \end{cases}$$

Since the mining algorithm is very fast, we can afford to run it several times (runtimes reported in the result section).

4.2　Finding Interesting Itemsets

The output of the APriori algorithm is usually a rather large set of frequent itemsets, depending on the minimal support threshold. Finding *interesting* item sets (and association rules) is a much discussed topic in the data mining literature [16]. There are several approaches which define interestingness with purely statistical measures. For instance, itemsets whose items appear statistically dependent are interesting. A measure for independence can be defined as follows. Assuming independence, the expected value for the support of an itemset is computed from the product of the supports of the individual items. The ratio of actual and expected support of an itemset is computed and its difference to 1 serves as an interestingness measure (i.e. difference to perfect independence). Only itemsets for which this difference is above a given threshold are retained as interesting. This was suggested in [11] and had in general a positive effect on the quality of our mining results.

Another strategy is to rely on domain-specific knowledge. In our domain, itemsets which describe a spatial configuration stretching across multiple sections tl, tr, bl, br are interesting. These itemsets are less likely to appear by coincidence and also make the most of our spatial encoding scheme, in that these configurations respect stronger spatial constraints. The number of sections that an itemset has to cover in order to be selected depends on a threshold $n_{sec} \in \{1 \ldots 4\}$. Selecting interesting itemsets with this criteria is easily implemented and reduces the number of itemsets drastically (typically by a factor 10 to 100).

4.3　Itemset Clustering

Since the frequent itemset mining typically returns spatially and temporally overlapping itemsets, we merge them with a final clustering stage. Pairs of itemsets which jointly appear in more than F frames and share more than R regions are merged. Merging starts from the pair with the highest sum $R + F$. If any of the two itemsets in a pair is already part of a cluster, the other itemset is also added to that cluster. Otherwise, a new cluster is created.

5   Results and Conclusion

We present results on two music videos from Kylie Minogue [17,18]. In particular the clip [17] makes an interesting test case for mining, because the singer passes by the same locations three times, and it even appears replicated several times in some frames. (Figure 4, third row). Hence, we can test whether the miner picks up the reappearing objects. Furthermore, the scene gets more and more crowded with time, hence allowing to test the system's robustness to clutter.

A few of the objects mined from the 1500 keyframes long clip [17] are shown in figure 4. The full miner was used, including motion grouping and itemset filtering with $n_{sec} = 2$. The building in the first row is mined in spite of viewpoint changes, thereby showing this ability of our approach. The street scene in the second row is mined in spite of partial occlusion. Finally, in the third row the singer is mined, based on her shirt. The second video frame of this row is particularly interesting, since the singer appears in three copies and all of them were mined.

Figure 5 shows typical results for mining with a fixed 40-neighborhood, i.e. without motion segmentation, akin to what proposed by [5]. As can be seen in subfigures 5a and 5b, only smaller parts of the large objects from figure 4 are mined. More examples of objects mined at the 40-neighborhood scale are shown in the other subfigures. Comparing these results to those in figure 4 highlights the benefits of defining the neighborhood for mining based on motion segmentation. Thanks to it, objects can be mined at their actual size (number of regions), which can vary widely from object to object, instead than being confined to a fixed, predefined size. Additionally, the singer was not mined when motion segmentation was turned off. The last row of figure 4 shows example objects mined from the clip [18] with a 40-neighbourhood. Our algorithm is naturally challenged by sparsely textured, non-rigid objects. As an example one could mention the legs of the main character. There are few features to begin with and the walking motion strongly changes the configuration of those, thus not the whole body is detected as object.

In table 1 we compare quantitatively mining with motion segmentation, and with a fixed 40-neighborhood for the clip [17]. Note that there are only 8056 transactions when using motion segmentation, compared to more than half a million when using a fixed 40-neighborhood. While the runtime is very short for both cases, the method is faster for the 40-neighborhood case, because transactions are shorter and only shorter itemsets were frequent. Additionally, in the 40-NN case, the support threshold to mine even a small set of only 285 frequent itemsets has to be set more than a factor 10 lower. The mean time for performing motion segmentation matching + k-means clustering) was typically about $0.4s$ per frame, but obviously depends on the number of features detected per frame.

In conclusion, we showed that our mining approach based on frequent itemsets is a suitable and efficient tool for video mining. Restricting the neighborhood by

Fig. 4. Top three rows: results for clip [17]. Each row shows instances from one itemset cluster. Bottom row: results for clip [18].

(a)   (b)   (c)   (d)

Fig. 5. Examples for clip [17] mined at a fixed 40 neighborhood

Table 1. Mining methods compared. *Regions*: number of regions in entire video. #T: number of transactions. t *FIMI*: runtime of frequent itemset mining. s: support threshold. #*FI*: number of frequent itemsets. *FI filt*: number of FI after filtering step with n_{sec} sections. *Clusters*: number of clusters for itemset clustering with parameters F,R.

Method	Regions	#T	t FIMI	s	# FI	# FI filt (n_{sec})	Clusters (F,R)
Motion Seg.	$2.87 * 10^6$	8056	56.12s	0.015	27654	308 (2)	11 (2,2)
40-NN	$2.87 * 10^6$	511626	18.79s	0.0001	285	285 (0)	55 (2,2)

motion grouping has proven to be useful for detecting objects of different sizes at the same time. Future works include testing on larger datasets (e.g. TRECVID), defining more interestingness measures, and stronger customization of itemset mining algorithms to video data.

References

1. Agrawal, R., Imielinski, T., Swami, A.: Mining Association Rules between Sets of Items in Large Databases. Proceedings of the 1993 ACM SIGMOD (1993) (26–28)
2. Mobasher, B., et al.: Effective personalization based on association rule discovery from web usage data. Web Information and Data Management 2001 (9-15)
3. Tešić, J., Newsam, S., Manjunath, B.S.: Mining Image Datasets using Perceptual Association Rules. In Proc. SIAM Sixth Workshop on Mining Scientific and Engineering Datasets in conjunction with SDM 2003.
4. Antonie, M., Zaïane, O., Coman, A.: Associative Classifiers for Medical Images. Lecture Notes in A.I. 2797, Mining Multimedia and Complex Data (2003) (68–83)
5. Sivic, J., Zisserman, A.: Video Data Mining Using Configurations of Viewpoint Invariant Regions. IEEE CVPR (2004), VOL 1, (488–495)
6. Osian M., Van Gool L.: Video shot characterization. Mach. Vision Appl. 15:3 2004 (172–177)
7. Mikolajczyk, K., Schmid, C.: Scale and Affine invariant interest point detectors. IJCV 1(60) 2004 (63–86)
8. Matas, J., Chum, O., Urban, M., Pajdla, T.: Robust wide baseline stereo from maximally stable extremal regions. BMVC 2002 (384–393).
9. Lowe, D.: Distinctive image features from scale invariant keypoints. IJCV 2(60) 2004 (91–110).
10. Leibe, B., Schiele, B.: Interleaved Object Categorization and Segmentation. In Proc. British Machine Vision Conference (BMVC'03).
11. Borgelt, C.: APriori. http://fuzzy.cs.uni-magdeburg.de/~borgelt/apriori.html
12. Webb,A.: Statistical Pattern Recognition. Wiley, 2003.
13. Kaufman, L., Rousseeuw, P.: Finding Groups in Data: An Introduction to Cluster Analysis. Wiley, 1990.
14. Sivic, J., Zisserman, A.: Video Google: A text retrieval approach to object matching in videos. In Proc. ICCV, 2003.
15. Hand, D., Mannila, H., Smyth, P.: Principles of Data Mining. MIT Press 2001.
16. Tan, P., Kumar, V., Srivastava, J.: Selecting the right interestingness measure for association patterns. In Proc. ACM SIGKD 2002.
17. Minogue, K., Gondry, M.: Come Into My World. EMI 2002.
18. Minogue, K., Shadforth, D.: Can't Get You Out Of My Head. EMI 2001.

Using High-Level Semantic Features in Video Retrieval

Wujie Zheng, Jianmin Li, Zhangzhang Si, Fuzong Lin, and Bo Zhang

State Key Laboratory of Intelligent Technology and System
Department of Computer Science and Technology
Tsinghua University, Beijing, 100084, China
idiot00@mails.tsinghua.edu.cn, lijianmin@mail.tsinghua.edu.cn,
scc02@mails.tsinghua.edu.cn, {linfz, dcszb}@mail.tsinghua.edu.cn

Abstract. Extraction and utilization of high-level semantic features are critical for more effective video retrieval. However, the performance of video retrieval hasn't benefited much despite of the advances in high-level feature extraction. To make good use of high-level semantic features in video retrieval, we present a method called pointwise mutual information weighted scheme(PMIWS). The method makes a good judgment of the relevance of all the semantic features to the queries, taking the characteristics of semantic features into account. The method can also be extended for the fusion of multi-modalities. Experiment results based on TRECVID2005 corpus demonstrate the effectiveness of the method.

1 Introduction

The wide availability of digital sensors, the high bandwidth Internet, and the falling price of storage devices have resulted in the increasing growth of unstructured digital media content. Therefore, developing effective information management technologies is a matter of great urgency. Since the last decade, the problem of content-based video retrieval has been actively researched by many communities.

Early research emphasizes on low-level image features such as color, texture and shape. However, "the lack of coincidence between the information that one can extract from the visual data and the interpretation that the same data have for a user in a given situation" [1], which is well known as semantic gap, makes the early retrieval systems disappointing. Moreover, the computation of high dimensional low-level features can lead to poor efficiency. On the other hand, using high-level semantic features for video retrieval allows people to perform search in the semantic level, which is more intuitive. Also, high-level semantic features can integrate additional knowledge of a specific domain as well as low-level features. What's more, they are compact enough so that the retrieval can be performed fast. Though the extraction of high-level semantic features is time consuming, it can be performed offline [11].

To take full advantage of the virtues of high-level semantic features for video retrieval, there are two issues to be addressed: 1) How to extract reliable high-level semantic features. 2) How to use high-level semantic features to describe

H. Sundaram et al. (Eds.): CIVR 2006, LNCS 4071, pp. 370–379, 2006.
© Springer-Verlag Berlin Heidelberg 2006

dataset and queries with relevant retrieval method. The advances in machine learning, and the availability of large annotated information sources, e.g., the TRECVID benchmark, have brought great advances in high-level feature extraction. The lexicon size of semantic features is believed to reach to 1000 in a few years, and the performances of high-level feature extraction in TRECVID 2005 are generally higher than before [5]. However, the performance of video retrieval hasn't benefited much from using high-level semantic features currently. High-level semantic features are considered not useful except a few topics which have well-performing correlated semantic features in [14], and semantic feature sets are used for only 5% of the interactions of interactive retrieval and contribute to negligible improvement [3].

One of the most important causes to the unsatisfying utilization of semantic features is that the issue of interaction between the semantic feature extraction and the search tasks has not been explored enough. Semantic features are mostly treated as complementary elements of other modalities. In most methods only the highly relevant semantic features are chosen, and then fused with other modalities based on complicated analysis of the whole retrieval system. In practice, it is hard to find highly relevant semantic features for most queries, and it is too rude to neglect any semantic feature which is not highly relevant since it may be also helpful for multi-modal fusion. Therefore, we present a method called pointwise mutual information weighted scheme (PMIWS). The method makes a good judgment of the relevance of all the semantic features to the queries, taking the characteristics of semantic features into account. The method can also be extended for the fusion of multi-modalities. Experiment results based on TRECVID2005 corpus demonstrate the effectiveness of the method.

The remainder of this paper is organized as follows. Section 2 gives a brief review of the related work. Then in Section 3, we present details of our approach. Experiments are presented in Section 4. And finally come the conclusions.

2   Related Work

High-level semantic features have been applied in different ways to improve the performance of video retrieval systems. Once semantic features are extracted, shots of dataset can be described by the relevance of them to semantic features, called feature scores. So are queries. With this representation, some machine learning approaches such as SVM are used to classify shots of dataset into two classes: related to the query, not related to the query [6]. The main challenge of this method is that there are a very small number of distinct positive examples and no negative examples. Currently the most popular method is simply the weighted-sum of shot feature scores. In this method, semantic features are assigned with proper weights, which represent the relevance of semantic features to queries. Thus the similarity measurement of shots and a query can be finished by the weighted-sum of shot feature scores.

The techniques for determining weights of features can be divided into three main categories:

1. *Manual methods.* For manual or interactive retrieval, the weights of semantic features can be assigned by human. But as pointed out in [3], it is too ambiguous for people to express a clear, consistent opinion about the relevance of the features to the queries. And it is not realistic while using a large set of semantic features.

2. *Text based methods.* Commonly, the text based methods calculate the feature weights by measuring the similarity between the query text and the concepts' description [14, 15, 16, 18], or using a preprocessed word-concept index [6, 7, 17]. In [15,16], only relevant concepts were utilized. Negative features were also considered in [17] while frequently-used features were added in [18]. More generally, all the semantic features are used in [6, 7, 14].

3. *Semantic feature based methods.* With semantic features already extracted from query as well as shots of dataset, it is natural to make use of them for determining weights of features, yet less work has been done this way [2, 7, 15]. In [2] it is said that the query feature scores are used to construct model vectors followed by appropriate normalization to remove bias and optionally by validity weighting to capture relative concept. But the detail of the normalization is not available. As this kind of methods can benefit more with the improved performances of high-level feature extraction, it needs to be further explored.

To distinguish expected results among hundreds of thousands of different shots, high-level features need to be integrated with other modalities. Though many methods are based on complicated analysis of the whole retrieval system, there are also some valuable works. Iyengar proposed a joint probability model for both the text and the visual components of multimedia documents [8]. Yan proposed to utilize query-class dependent weights within a hierarchical mixture-of-expert framework to combine multiple retrieval results in [10].

3   Our Approach

The task of video retrieval can be modelled as follows. Let D be a specific dataset of video shots, Q be the collection of queries which represent the user's information needs. For a given query $q \in Q$, let Y be the random variable which represents whether a shot $d \in D$ meets the information needs described by q. There are two possible results: meet and not meet, which we can label as y_1 and y_0. It is hard, if possible, to determine the value of Y for shots of D. Actually, the objective of video retrieval is to estimate the probability $p(Y(d) = y_1)$, $d \in D$.

To realize this objective, features which describe different attributes of shots are firstly extracted, and then $p(Y(d) = y_1)$ is estimated using the information provided by the features. In our approach, we model and extract 33 high-level features firstly, and then we present a method called pointwise mutual information weighted scheme (PMIWS) to utilize the information provided by these features. Text retrieval is also performed and the result is fused with semantic features by PMIWS, taking text of the query as another feature Q_{text}. The overview of our video retrieval system is illustrated in Figure 1.

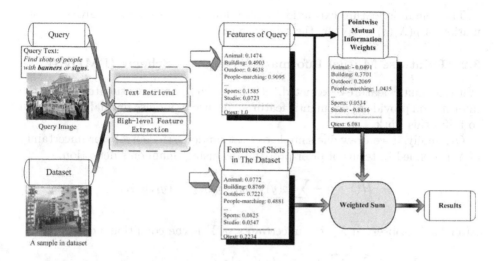

Fig. 1. Overview of the video retrieval system

3.1 High-Level Semantic Feature Extraction

Let $C = \{C_1, C_2, \ldots, C_n\}$ be the semantic feature set. For a given feature $C_i \in C$, let X_i be the random variable which represents the existence of C_i in a shot in D or a query q, where $i \in \{1, 2, \ldots, n\}$. In this case, there are two possible results: exist and not exist, which we can label as x_{i1} and x_{i0}. Generally, in the semantic feature extraction, a detector for the semantic feature C_i is modelled and used to produce confidence scores, which represent the probability $p(X_i(d) = x_{i1})$, Where $d \in D, i \in \{1, 2, \ldots, n\}$.

In our approach, we model and extract 33 high-level features which have support of more than 100 positive samples in the training set of TRECVID2005. The lexicon can refer to [12]. We use SVM as the base classifiers, and propose a Relay Boost approach to fuse the confidence scores produced by the base classifiers. The output of feature C_i for shot $d \in D$ is

$$Confidence_i(d) = \sum_j \alpha_j^i \times conf_j^i(d), j \in \{1, 2, \ldots, m\}$$

where m is the number of base classifiers of C_i, α_j^i is the weight of jth base classifier of C_i, and $conf_j^i(d)$ is the confidence score produced by j^{th} base classifier of C_i, which are mapped from SVM outputs by Platt's conversion method to represent the probabilities of C_i existing in d [13]. Details can be seen in [7]. Divided by the weights of base classifiers of C_i, $Confidence_i(d)$ can be normalized to give an estimation of $p(X_i(d) = x_{i1})$, which we refer to as *Feature Score* for C_i:

$$p(X_i(d) = x_{i1}) = \frac{Confidence_i(d)}{\sum_j \alpha_j^i} = \frac{\sum_j \alpha_j^i \times conf_j^i(d)}{\sum_j \alpha_j^i}, j \in \{1, 2, \ldots, m\}$$

The semantic feature extraction is also done for $q \in Q$, which gives an estimation of $p(X_i(q) = x_{i1})$ by the same formula.

3.2   Pointwise Mutual Information Weighted Scheme (PMIWS)

With semantic features extracted, $p(Y(d) = y_1)$ can be estimated using the information provided by semantic features. We use pointwise mutual information to fulfill this work.

Originally, if we draw one sample of D at random, the entropy or uncertainty of Y is defined in terms of prior probabilities using Shannon's definition:

$$H(Y) = -\sum_y p(y) \cdot log(p(y)), y \in \{y_1, y_0\}.$$

After having observed X_i, the uncertainty of Y is the conditional entropy:

$$H(Y|X_i) = -\sum_{x_i}\sum_y p(y, x_i) \cdot log(p(y|x_i)), y \in \{y_1, y_0\}, x_i \in \{x_{i1}, x_{i0}\}$$

Then the reduction in uncertainty of Y due to knowing about X_i is called mutual information:

$$I(Y, X_i) = H(Y) - H(Y|X_i) = \sum_{x_i, y} p(x_i, y) \cdot log\frac{p(x_i, y)}{p(x_i)p(y)}, y \in \{y_1, y_0\}, x_i \in \{x_{i1}, x_{i0}\}$$

Furthermore, mutual information between two particular points is defined as pointwise mutual information [4]:

$$I(y, x_i) = log\frac{p(x_i, y)}{p(x_i)p(y)} = log\frac{p(x_i|y)}{p(x_i)}, y \in \{y_1, y_0\}, x_i \in \{x_{i1}, x_{i0}\}$$

The pointwise mutual information can be regarded as the amount of information x_i contains about y. The magnitude of $I(y, x_i)$ indicates the power of influence of event $\{X = x_i\}$ to event $\{Y = y\}$, while the sign of $I(y, x_i)$ indicates the direction of influence of event $\{X = x_i\}$ to event $\{Y = y\}$, i.e., increasing or decreasing the confidence of event $\{Y = y\}$ happening. It equals to zero when $\{X = x_i\}$ and $\{Y = y\}$ are independent. Thus, we can use $I(y_i, x_{i1})$ as the weight of semantic feature C_i with linear normalization:

$$weight_{C_i} = Normalize(I(y_1, x_{i1})) = \alpha \cdot log\frac{p(x_{i1}|y_1)}{p(x_{i1})}$$

The normalization coefficient α is the same for all the semantic features. And then we can estimate $p(Y(d) = y_1)$ by the weight sum of $p(X_i(d) = x_{i1})$, where $i \in \{1, 2, \ldots, 33\}$:

$$p(Y(d) = y_1) = \sum_i weight_{C_i} \cdot p(X_i(d) = x_{i1}) = \alpha \cdot \sum_i log\frac{p(x_{i1}|y_1)}{p(x_{i1})} \cdot p(X_i(d) = x_{i1})$$

Here, $p(X_i(d) = x_{i1})$ has been estimated by semantic feature extraction. $p(x_{i1}) = Mean_{d \in D}(p(X_i(d) = x_{i1}))$. And $p(x_{i1}|y_1) \equiv p(X_i(d) = x_{i1}|Y(d) = y_1)$ can be approximated by $p(X_i(q) = x_{i1})$, since q certainly satisfies $Y(q) = y_1$.

The pointwise mutual information weight has grasped two principal issues of high-level semantic features in its expression, i.e., importance and reliability. Firstly, it brings in a term of $p(x_{i1})$, which expresses the underlying importance of different features compared with $p(x_{i1}|y_1)$. It is biased towards infrequent semantic features existing in q. For example, if there is a person and a ship shown in the example of q, then the feature of "ship" is believed to be more important as it is less frequent. However, if the person is George Bush, then the feature of "George Bush", if modelled, is believed to be more important. That is consistent with common usage. But there is also a risk that unreliable detectors of features with less frequency maybe mislead the retrieval. So secondly, it brings in the log factor, which makes it more robust to the unreliable detectors.

3.3   Fusion with Text Retrieval Result

The PMIWS method can not only handle the fusion of multiple semantic features, but also be easy to extend to the fusion of multi-modalities by treating other modalities as one or several kinds of high-level features. We will describe the fusion of high-level semantic features and text retrieval result below.

Our text retrieval system is based on an OKAPI-TF formula using the transcripts from the ASR/MT output provided by NIST. Pseudo feedback is also performed. For shot d the text retrieval system will give a score $T(d)$. Details can be seen in [7]. We treat text of the query as a high-level feature Q_{text}. Let X_{text} be the random variable which represents the existence of Q_{text} in a shot of D. There are two possible results: exist and not exist, which we can label as t_1 and t_0. Similar to aforementioned analysis, we can use $I(y_1, t_1)$ as the weight of Q_{text} by linear normalization:

$$weight_{Q_{text}} = Normalize(I(y_1, t_1)) = \beta \cdot log \frac{p(t_1|y_1)}{p(t_1)}$$

The normalization coefficient β is the same for all the semantic features in place of α. Then $p(Y(d) = y_1)$ can be refined by adding one term of t_1 ($i \in \{1, 2, \ldots, 33\}$):

$$p(Y(d) = y_1) = \beta \cdot \{\sum_i log \frac{p(x_{i1}|y_1)}{p(x_{i1})} \cdot p(X_i(d) = x_{i1}) + log \frac{p(t_1|y_1)}{p(t_1)} \cdot p(X_{text}(d) = t_1)\}$$

Here, $p(X_{text}(d) = t_1)$ is estimated by normalizing the text retrieval result $T(d)$ to 0-1, according to the minimum and maximum value of $T(d)$ in the dataset. And $p(t_1) = Mean_{d \in D}(p(X_{text}(d) = t_1)), d \in D$. While $p(t_1|y_1)$ is assumed to be 1. β can be omitted as it doesn't affect the result for final ranking.

4   Experiments

4.1   Dataset and Evaluation

The experiments are performed on TRECVID2005 dataset provided by NIST. The total amount of news video for the evaluated tasks is about 169 hours, in MPEG-1 format: 43 in Arabic, 52 in Chinese, 74 in English [5]. About 160 hours of them is used for Search Benchmark, the earlier half as development data, and the later half as test data. The data is divided into shots, which are the basic units of video retrieval. For each shot, more than one keyframe is extracted for performing the high-level feature extraction. NIST also provides the English ASR output and machine-translated transcripts for those non English video materials, which are used for text retrieval. We use the 24 multimedia search topics developed by NIST for our experiments. Details of the topics can be seen in [5].

The performances are evaluated by non-interpolated average precision (AP) and mean average precision (MAP) criteria. Non-interpolated average precision is calculated by computing the precision after every retrieved relevant shot and then averaging these precisions over the total number of retrieved relevant/correct shots in the collection for that topic/feature or the maximum allowed result set (whichever is smaller). Average precision favors highly ranked relevant documents. It allows comparison of result sets of different sizes. The topic averages are averaged across all topics to create the non-interpolated mean average precision (MAP). See the TREC-10 Proceedings appendix on common evaluation measures for more information [9].

4.2   Experiment Results

We present four runs of automatic retrieval. The descriptions of the four runs are as follows and the evaluation results are shown in Figure 2, compared with the median effect of automatic retrievals in TRECVID2005.

Run1: This run uses only text retrieval on ASR/MT.
Run2: This run uses high-level feature score weighted sum method, using the feature scores of queries as weights directly.
Run3: This run uses high-level feature score weighted sum method, using PMIWS to calculate weights.
Run4: This run integrates high-level features and text retrieval result with PMIWS.

Observed from Figure 2, using point mutual information as weights of high-level features (Run3) is obviously better than using the feature scores of queries as weights (Run2). We can also find that high-level features are usable for topics which have correlated specific concepts. If the correlation is tight and the correlated specific concepts are well-performing, the results of using high-level features (Run3) can be even better than results of text retrieval (Run1) like 0155(map), 0165(basketball), 0168(road, car), 0170(building), 0171(goal).

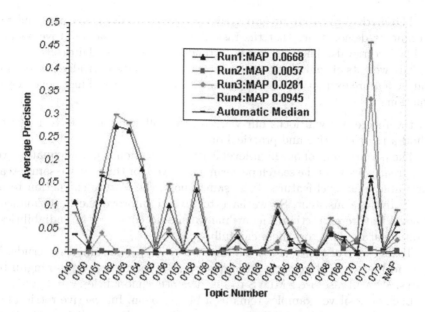

Fig. 2. Performance evaluation results

This validates the effectiveness of PMIWS for judging the relevance of high-level features to queries.

The comparison of individual retrieval runs (Run1 and Run3) and fusion runs (Run4) are also clear in Figure 2. For almost all of the topics, the result of fusion (Run4) is better than the results of using text only (Run1) and using high-level features only (Run3). Note for some topics like the named topics, high-level features are useless by themselves but useful for fusion. This can be explained by regarding high-level features as revisers, which correct the temporal mismatch of the text and the visual content of shots. The MAP of fusion (Run4) is 41.5% higher than using text only (Run1) and 236.3% higher than using high-level features only (Run3). And it is much better than the median effect of automatic retrievals in TRECVID2005 for all topics. This exhibits the effectiveness of PMIWS for multi-modal fusion.

5   Conclusions and Future Works

In this paper, we investigate the issue of how to make good use of high-level semantic features in video retrieval. We focus on determining the relevance of all the semantic features to the query. To achieve this, a method called pointwise mutual information weighted scheme(PMIWS) is presented, which has the following advantages:

1) The method can reflect the exact relevance of semantic features to queries and assigned reasonable weights, by considering the prior distributions of high-level features and referring to information theory.

2) The method gives an integrated view of fusing semantic features and text. Experiments demonstrate that the fusion retrieval has great improvements on individual retrievals. The idea can be extended for other modalities.

3) The weights of semantic features are calculated automatically based on the semantic feature extraction. It is scalable with the advances of high-level feature extraction.

In the future, we will focus our work on the following aspects to make this method a more effective and practical one:

1) The performance of our high-level feature extraction is not adequately well, which greatly restricts the search performance. Even for the positive samples and a correlated high-level feature of the same query, the feature extraction results are not always consistent. So we have to further improve the performance of high-level feature extraction. Meanwhile we should consider the radiabilities of semantic feature detectors more carefully.

2) Taking text of the query as another feature Q_{text} is somewhat crude. We will go further to analyze text of the query and then get more meaningful text features. We will also use PMIWS to fuse the other modalities.

3) Lack of positive examples remains a big problem. Interactive retrieval can be a great help to this with human interaction, and we will investigate the application of PMIWS in an interactive setting to achieve better results.

Acknowledgement

This work is supported by National Natural Science Foundation of China (60135010), National Natural Science Foundation of China(60321002) and the Chinese National Key Foundation Research & Development Plan (2004CB318108).

References

1. AWM Smeulders, M. Worring, S. Santini, A. Gupta, and R. Jain: Content-based image retrieval at the end of the early years. IEEE Transactions on Pattern Analysis and Machine Intelligence, vol.22, no.12, pp.1349-1380, December 2000
2. Apostol Natsev, Milind R. Naphade, John R. Smith: Semantic representation: search and mining of multimedia content. KDD 2004: 641-646
3. Michael G. Christel and Alexander G. Hauptmann: The Use and Utility of High-Level Semantic Features in Video Retrieval. CIVR 2005, 134-144
4. C. D. Manning and H. Schutze : Foundations of Statistical Natural Language Processing. The MIT Press, 1999
5. Paul Over, Tsveta Ianeva, Wessel Kraaij, Alan Smeaton: TRECVID 2005 - An Introduction. Proceedings of TRECVID2005
6. Arnon Amir, Janne Argillandery, Murray Campbellz, Alexander Hauboldz, Giridharan Iyengar, Shahram Ebadollahiz, Feng Kangz, Milind R. Naphadez, Apostol (Paul) Natsevz, John R. Smithz, Jelena Tesicz, Timo Volkmer: IBM Research TRECVID-2005 Video Retrieval System. Proceedings of TRECVID2005

7. Jinhui Yuan, Huiyi Wang, Lan Xiao, Dong Wang, Dayong Ding, Yuanyuan Zuo, Zijian Tong, Xiaobing Liu, Shuping Xu, Wujie Zheng, Xirong Li, Zhangzhang Si, Jianmin Li, Fuzong Lin, Bo Zhang: Tsinghua University at TRECVID 2005. Proceedings of TRECVID2005
8. G.Iyengar, P. Duygulu, S. Feng, P. Ircing, SP Khudanpur, D. Klakow, MR Krause, R.Manmatha, HJ Nock, D. Petkova, B. Pytlik, P. Virga Pages: Joint Visual-Text Modeling for Automatic Retrieval of Multimedia Documents. Proceedings of the 13th ACM international conference on Multimedia, 2005, 21-30
9. TREC-10 Proceedings Appendix on Common Evaluation Measures. http://trec.nist.gov/pubs/trec10/appendices/measures.pdf
10. R. Yan, J. Yang, and A. G. Hauptmann: Learning query-class dependent weights in automatic video retrieval. In Proceedings of ACM Multimedia 2004: 548-555, Oct. 2004.
11. Horst Eidenberger, C. Breiteneder: Semantic Feature Layers in Content-Based Image Retrieval. Proceedings IEEE International Conference on Control, Automation, Robotic and Vision, Singapore, 2002
12. Milind R. Naphade, Lyndon Kennedy, John R. Kender, Shih-Fu Chang, John R. Smith, Paul Over, Alex Hauptmann: A Light Scale Concept Ontology for Multimedia Understanding for TRECVID 2005. IBM Research Report RC23612 (W0505-104), May, 2005
13. J. Platt: Probabilities for SV machines. In Advances in Large Margin Classiers, pages 61-74. MIT Press, 2000.
14. Shih-Fu Chang, Winston Hsu, Lyndon Kennedy, Lexing Xie, Akira Yanagawa, Eric Zavesky, Dong-Qing Zhang: Columbia University TRECVID-2005 Video Search and High-Level Feature Extraction. Proceedings of TRECVID2005
15. Tat-Seng Chua, Shi-Yong Neo, Hai-Kiat Goh, Ming Zhao, Yang Xiao and Gang Wang: TRECVID 2005 by NUS PRIS. Proceedings of TRECVID2005
16. C.G.M. Snoek, J.C. van Gemert, J.M. Geusebroek, B. Huurnink, D.C. Koelma, G.P. Nguyen, O. de Rooij, F.J. Seinstra, A.W.M. Smeulders, C.J. Veenman, M. Worring: The MediaMill TRECVID 2005 Semantic Video Search Engine. Proceedings of TRECVID2005
17. Markus Koskela, Jorma Laaksonen, Mats Sjoberg, Hannes Muurinen: PicSOM Experiments in TRECVID 2005. Proceedings of TRECVID2005
18. A.G. Hauptmann, M. Christel, R. Concescu, J. Gao, Q. Jin, W.-H. Lin, J.-Y. Pan, S. M. Stevens, R. Yan, J. Yang, Y. Zhang: CMU Informedia's TRECVID 2005 Skirmishes. Proceedings of TRECVID2005

Recognizing Objects and Scenes in News Videos

Muhammet Baştan and Pınar Duygulu

Department of Computer Engineering, Bilkent University, Ankara, Turkey
{bastan, duygulu}@cs.bilkent.edu.tr

Abstract. We propose a new approach to recognize objects and scenes in news videos motivated by the availability of large video collections. This approach considers the recognition problem as the translation of visual elements to words. The correspondences between visual elements and words are learned using the methods adapted from statistical machine translation and used to predict words for particular image regions (region naming), for entire images (auto-annotation), or to associate the automatically generated speech transcript text with the correct video frames (video alignment). Experimental results are presented on TRECVID 2004 data set, which consists of about 150 hours of news videos associated with manual annotations and speech transcript text. The results show that the retrieval performance can be improved by associating visual and textual elements. Also, extensive analysis of features are provided and a method to combine features are proposed.

1 Introduction

Due to the rapidly growing quantities of digital image and video archives, effective and efficient indexing, retrieval and analysis of such data have received significant attention. Being an important information source, applications on broadcast news videos are especially challenging. This challenge is also acknowledged by NIST and news videos are chosen as the data set for the TRECVID Video Retrieval Evaluation [2].

It is common to use speech transcript or closed caption text and perform text-based queries to retrieve the relevant information. However, there are cases where text is not available or errorful. Also, text is aligned with the shots only temporally and therefore the retrieved shots may not be related to the visual content. For example, when we retrieve the shots where a keyword is spoken in the transcript we may come up with visually non-relevant shots where an anchor/reporter is introducing or wrapping up a story. An alternative is to use the annotation words, but due to the huge amount of human effort required for manual annotation it is not practical. Recognition of objects and scenes is the ultimate solution but recognition on the large scale is still a challenge.

Recently, it has been shown that large number of objects can be recognized without supervision by using large annotated image collections [3,4,6,7]. In general, the proposed models are based on learning the associations between image regions and annotation words.

H. Sundaram et al. (Eds.): CIVR 2006, LNCS 4071, pp. 380–390, 2006.
© Springer-Verlag Berlin Heidelberg 2006

In this study, we extend these methods to recognize objects and scenes in news videos. To learn the associations, we adapt the translation approach [7] inspired from the models proposed for statistical machine translation [5]. Our method learns the correspondences between visual features extracted from the video shots with the annotation words from a small number of videos. Then the correspondences are used for predicting words for individual regions (**region-labeling**) and for entire images (**auto-annotation**) in the rest of the data.

Methods which use manual annotations to automatically annotate the video shots are also proposed in [9,11]. However, in those methods the associations between image regions and words are not explicitly learned and labeling of individual regions for recognition of objects is not provided.

Since the annotation words are not always available and reliable, as an alternative, we propose to use the speech transcript or closed caption text, which is the main contribution of this work. There is an alignment problem between the text and the visual content, and taking the text temporally aligned with the shot is problematic. One solution is to also use the words aligned with the preceding and following shots as in [8,16]. However, the speech transcript text a few shots before or after may correspond to other stories that are not related with the current shot resulting in association of irrelevant words with the shot.

As a solution, we propose a story-based approach where we treat each story as a document containing associated elements. The translation approach is modified to find the correspondences between the key-frames and the speech transcript words of the story segments. This process, which we refer as **video alignment** enables a textual query to return semantically more accurate images.

While, the effect of features extracted from entire images or from image regions are heavily experimented for automatic annotation, the features extracted around salient points -which are shown to be successful for recognition of objects and scenes- is not well investigated. In this study, we provide an extensive analysis of features by (i)investigating the effect of extracting features from entire images, from fixed sized grids and around interest points, (ii) by experimenting the SIFT descriptors [13] besides the commonly used color, texture and edge features and (iii) applying the bag-of-visterms approach [15] -which has recently been proposed for classification of scenes- to the association problem. Moreover, we propose a new method to combine the features using the prediction probabilities and show that the performance improves.

In this study, we use videos from TRECVID 2004 corpus [2] which consists of over 150 hours of CNN and ABC broadcast news videos provided by NIST. The results show that retrieval performance can be improved by associating the visual elements with words as a way of recognizing objects and scenes on the large scale.

First, we will describe the method to translate visual elements to words briefly and explain our performance evaluation measures. Then, we will present the results for two separate cases: using the manual annotation words and using the speech transcript text. Finally, we will present a detailed analysis of features used in the study.

2   Translating Visual Elements to Words

Learning the associations between visual elements and words can be attacked as a problem of translating visual features into words, as first proposed in [7]. Given a set of training images, the problem is to create a probability table that associates visual elements and words. First, the visual features are transformed into discrete elements, called blobs, using a vector quantization technique such as k-means. The associations between blobs and words are then learned in the form of a probability table (also referred to as translation table), in which each entry indicates the probability that a blob matches with a word. In this study, we use the Giza++ tool [1,14] to learn the probabilities and adapt Model1 of Brown et al. [5] in the form of direct translation. Once learned, the translation table can be used to find the corresponding words for the given test images (**auto-annotation**), to label the image components with words (**region labeling**), and for ranked retrieval of images. For region naming, given a blob corresponding to a region, the word with the highest probability is chosen. For auto-annotation, the word posterior probabilities for an image are obtained by marginalizing the word posterior probabilities of all the blobs in the image and the first N words with the highest posterior probabilities are used to automatically annotate the image.

The translation approach to learn the associations between image regions and annotation words can be modified to solve the **video alignment** problem. Each story is taken as the basic unit, and the problem is turned into finding the associations between the key-frames and the speech transcript words of the story segments. To make the analogy with the association problem between image regions and annotation keywords, the stories correspond to images, the key-frames correspond to image regions and speech transcript text corresponds to annotation keywords. The features extracted from the key-frames are vector quantized using k-means to represent each image with labels which are again called blobs. Then, the translation tables are constructed similar to the one constructed for annotated images. The associations can then be used either to align the key-frames with the correct words or for predicting words for the entire stories.

3   Performance Measurement

We define the annotation performance for an image as the number of correct predictions divided by the number of actual annotation words for that image. The annotation performance is averaged over all test images to obtain the average annotation performance (aap) for an image. We similarly define recall and precision for each word. A word is defined to be predicted correctly, if it matches with one of the actual annotation words. Recall is the number of times that the word is correctly predicted over the number of times that the word is used as an annotation word throughout the entire data set, and precision is the number of times that the word is predicted correctly over the total number of times it is predicted. Average recall and precision are calculated by considering the words that are predicted at least once.

For each image, we can choose to predict as many words as there are in the actual annotation, which we refer to as $case_1$, or a fixed number of words, which we refer to as $case_2$.

The performance of video alignment is measured similarly. We predict N words with the highest probability for a given story and compare them with the actual speech transcript words in that story.

4   Translation Using Manual Annotations

In the TRECVID 2004 corpus, there are 229 videos in the training set and 128 videos in the test set. We use the shot boundaries and the key-frames provided by NIST. On the average, there are around 300 key-frames for each video. 114 videos from the training set are manually annotated with a collaborative effort of the TRECVID participants with a few keywords [12]. In total, there are 614 words used for annotation, most of which have very low frequency, spelling and format errors. After correcting the errors and removing the least frequent words we pruned the vocabulary down to 62 words. We only use the annotations for the key-frames, and therefore eliminate the videos where the annotations are provided for the frames which are not key-frames, resulting in 92 videos with 17177 images, 10164 used for training and 7013 for testing.

We use the manually annotated data set to learn the correspondences between blobs and words for region naming and for auto-annotation. Figure 1 shows some region labeling results. Note that words like female-news-person, female-face, studio-setting, sky and building are correctly predicted.

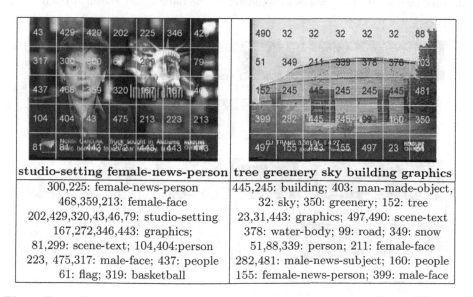

studio-setting female-news-person	tree greenery sky building graphics
300,225: female-news-person	445,245: building; 403: man-made-object,
468,359,213: female-face	32: sky; 350: greenery; 152: tree
202,429,320,43,46,79: studio-setting	23,31,443: graphics; 497,490: scene-text
167,272,346,443: graphics;	378: water-body; 99: road; 349: snow
81,299: scene-text; 104,404:person	51,88,339: person; 211: female-face
223, 475,317: male-face; 437: people	282,481: male-news-subject; 160: people
61: flag; 319: basketball	155: female-news-person; 399: male-face

Fig. 1. Example region labeling results. Manual annotations are shown for comparison.

Fig. 2. Examples for blob-to-word matches

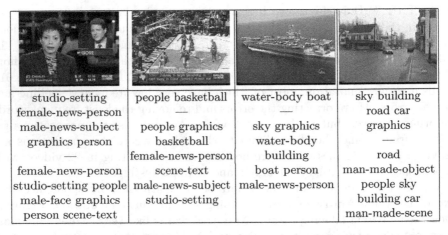

studio-setting	people basketball	water-body boat	sky building
female-news-person	—	—	road car
male-news-subject	people graphics	sky graphics	graphics
graphics person	basketball	water-body	—
—	female-news-person	building	road
female-news-person	scene-text	boat person	man-made-object
studio-setting people	male-news-subject	male-news-person	people sky
male-face graphics	studio-setting		building car
person scene-text			man-made-scene

Fig. 3. Auto-annotation examples. The manual annotations are shown at the top, and the predicted words, top 7 words with the highest probability, are shown at the bottom.

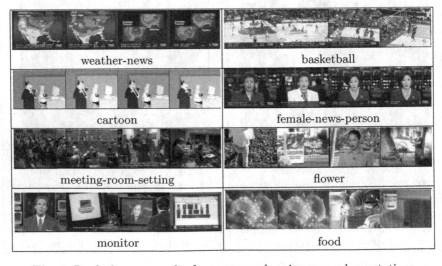

Fig. 4. Ranked query results for some words using manual annotations

Example blobs corresponding to some words with high prediction accuracies are shown in Figure 2.

Some auto-annotation examples are shown in Figure 3. On the average, we obtain an annotation performance around 30%. We should note that the performances are calculated by comparing the predicted annotations with the manual annotations. Since manual annotations are incomplete (for example in the third example of Figure 3, although **sky** is in the picture and predicted it is not in the manual annotations) the calculated values may be lower than the actual ones.

Figure 4 shows query results for some words (with the highest rank). By visually inspecting the top 10 images retrieved for 62 words, the mean average precision (MAP) is determined to be 63%. MAP is 89% for the best (with highest precision) 30 words, and 99% for the best 15 words. The results show that when the annotations are not available the proposed system can effectively be used for ranked retrieval.

5   Translation Using Speech Transcripts in Story Segments

For the experiments using speech transcript text, 111 videos are used for training and 110 videos are used for testing. The automatic speech recognition (ASR) transcripts provided by LIMSI are aligned with the shots on the time basis [10]. The speech transcripts (ASR) are in the free text form and requires preprocessing. Therefore, we applied tagging, stemming and stop word elimination steps and used only the nouns having frequencies more than 300 as our final vocabulary resulting in 251 words.

The story boundaries provided by NIST are used. We remove the stories associated with less than 4 words, and use the remaining 2503 stories consisting of 31450 key-frames for training and 2900 stories consisting of 31464 key-frames for testing. The number of words corresponding to the stories vary between 4 and 105, and the average number of words per story is 15.

The translation probabilities are used for predicting words for the individual shots (Figure 5) and for the stories (Figure 6). The results show that especially for the stories related to weather, sports or economy, which frequently appear in the broadcast news, the system can predict the correct words. Note that, the system can predict words which are better than the original speech transcript words. This characteristic is important for a better retrieval.

An important aspect of predicting words for the video segments is to retrieve the related shots when speech transcript is not available or include unrelated words. In such cases it would not be possible to retrieve such shots with a text based retrieval system if the predicted words were not available. Story based query results in Figure 7 show that the proposed system is able to detect the associations between the words (objects) and scenes. In these examples, the shots within each story are ranked according to the marginalized word posterior probabilities, and the shots matching the query word with highest probability are retrieved; a final ranking is done among all shots retrieved from all stories and all videos and final ranked query results are returned to the user.

| temperature weather forecast | point nasdaq stock | sport time game | jenning people evening |

Fig. 5. Top three words predicted for some shots using the ASR outputs

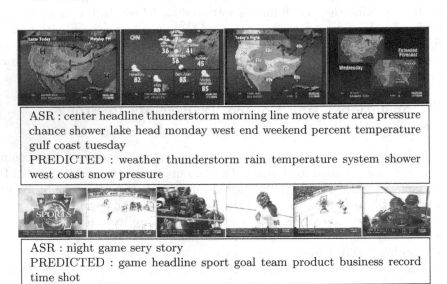

ASR : center headline thunderstorm morning line move state area pressure chance shower lake head monday west end weekend percent temperature gulf coast tuesday
PREDICTED : weather thunderstorm rain temperature system shower west coast snow pressure

ASR : night game sery story
PREDICTED : game headline sport goal team product business record time shot

Fig. 6. For sample stories corresponding ASR outputs and top 10 words predicted

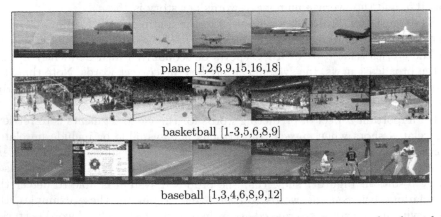

plane [1,2,6,9,15,16,18]

basketball [1-3,5,6,8,9]

baseball [1,3,4,6,8,9,12]

Fig. 7. Ranked story based query results for ASR. Numbers in square brackets show the rank of retrieval.

6   Analysis of Features

For manual annotations and ASR experiments, the key-frames are represented by a set of features including global histograms extracted from entire images, and local statistics extracted from grids or around keypoints.

Color features are extracted for RGB and HSV color spaces, texture is represented as Gabor filter outputs, and Canny edge detector outputs are used for edges. Global features are represented by 64 bin RGB, 162 bin HSV and 16 bin edge histograms from entire images; while local features are extracted from 5x7 fixed sized grids as mean and standard deviation of color, Gabor filter output, and 8 bin Canny edge histogram.

The keypoints are detected and represented using Lowe's SIFT operator[13]. Using the binaries provided by the author, large number of keypoints are extracted. In order to keep the number of features in the order of those extracted from grids, we chose 35 keypoints with maximum scale. In addition to the 128-element SIFT descriptor vectors, mean and standard deviation of color, texture and edge features are also extracted around keypoints similar to features extracted from grids.

We also experimented with the bag-of-visterms approach [15] by taking about 600.000 keypoints extracted from 5 videos, vector quantizing them and forming a keypoint histogram with 1000 bins for each image. The keypoint histograms, as feature vectors for each image, are quantized to obtain the final blobs.

Some words may be predicted better using one feature than others. For example, color is a good cue for commercial and cartoon scenes while edge or texture is good for basketball or studio scenes. If the outputs of multiple features, some of which can predict some words better than others, are combined, then the prediction performance of the system is expected to improve. We combined the outputs of several features at the word prediction step by marginalizing the word posterior probabilities (over all blobs) obtained from several features. If the output one feature is high it is reflected on the final output. As shown in Table 1 and Table 2, on the average, the prediction performance of the system is always improved. The improvement is more notable in the average word precision values.

In Table 1, the results are shown for different features in the form of annotation performance and average word recall and precision values for the case of translation with manual annotations. Note that the performance is always better if the outputs of multiple features are combined as explained above. The performance when SIFT descriptors are used is inferior to the grid based features. Although average word recall and precision values are close to those of other features, the number of words with nonzero prediction is significantly less. The reason is mainly due to the lost color information which is very important for the discrimination of most objects and scenes, and also due to using only the maximum scale 35 keypoints.

Using the number of faces detected per image as additional information does not improve the performance significantly. Increasing the number of blobs improves the performance but the computational cost also increases; therefore, we choose 2500 as an appropriate number.

Table 1. Automatic annotation performances using manual annotations. For details, please see section 3. For $case_2$, 10 words are predicted per image. Numbers 1 through 9 at the top stands for the following features: 1,4,9: mean&std of color, 2,5: mean&std of color + edge, 3,6: mean&std of color + texture, 7: combination of outputs of the first 6 features; 8: SIFT descriptors. In (1-7) features are extracted from 5x7 grids, and in (8-9) features extracted around maximum scale 35 keypoints. In (1-3) HSV and in (4-6,9) RGB is used as the color feature.

case	Performance	1	2	3	4	5	6	7	8	9
$case_1$	aap	0.266	0.267	0.274	0.277	0.276	0.288	0.295	0.235	0.271
$case_1$	recall	0.144	0.149	0.142	0.169	0.170	0.178	0.183	0.155	0.148
	precision	0.218	0.231	0.217	0.294	0.322	0.334	0.390	0.266	0.245
$case_2$	recall	0.323	0.328	0.331	0.327	0.330	0.333	0.344	0.275	0.319
	precision	0.082	0.082	0.081	0.087	0.089	0.089	0.110	0.081	0.079

Table 2. Automatic story annotation performances using ASR. Number of blobs = 1000. For $case_2$, 25 words are predicted per story. Numbers 1 through 7 at the top stands for the features: 1,3: global HSV, RGB histograms, 2,4: global HSV, RGB + Canny edge histograms, 5,6: mean&std of HSV, RGB + texture from 5X7 grids, 7: combination of (1-6), 8: bag-of-visterms approach, 9: combination of (1-6,8).

case	Performance	1	2	3	4	5	6	7	8	9
$case_1$	aap	0.156	0.155	0.172	0.173	0,182	0,183	0,194	0.190	0.200
$case_1$	recall	0.141	0.142	0.160	0.162	0,149	0,150	0,207	0.152	0.170
	precision	0.159	0.164	0.187	0.195	0,207	0,214	0,275	0.226	0.236
$case_2$	recall	0.192	0.193	0.218	0.221	0,169	0,165	0,189	0.200	0.224
	precision	0.102	0.102	0.118	0.119	0,107	0,108	0,136	0.127	0.136

The prediction performances obtained by comparing the predicted words for a given story with the original ASR words for some features are summarized in Table 2. The performance with the bag-of-visterms approach is better compared to the color and texture features although only 5 videos are used in the construction of the bag-of-visterms due to large computational cost. As in the manual annotation case, performance is improved when multiple feature outputs are combined.

7 Conclusion and Future Work

We associate visual features with words using a translation approach, which allows novel applications on news video collections including region naming as a way of recognizing objects, auto-annotation for better access to image databases and video alignment which is crucial for effective retrieval.

In video data, motion information also plays an important role. Usually, moving objects are important than still objects. The regions corresponding to these objects can be extracted using the motion information rather than using any segmentation algorithm. Also, besides associating the visual features such as color, texture and shape with nouns for naming the objects, the motion information can be associated with verbs for naming actions.

Translation approach can also be used as a novel method for face recognition. The correspondence problem that appears between the face of a person and his/her name can be attacked similarly for naming people.

Acknowledgements

This research is partially supported by TÜBİTAK Career grant number 104E065 and grant number 104E077.

References

1. Giza++. http://www.fjoch.com/GIZA++.html.
2. Trec vieo retrieval evaluation. http://www-nlpir.nist.gov/projects/trecvid.
3. K. Barnard, P. Duygulu, N. de Freitas, D. A. Forsyth, D. Blei, and M. Jordan. Matching words and pictures. *Journal of Machine Learning Research*, 3:1107–1135, 2003.
4. D. Blei and M. I. Jordan. Modeling annotated data. In *26th Annual International ACM SIGIR Conference*, pages 127–134, Toronto, Canada, July 28-August 1 2003.
5. P. Brown, S. A. D. Pietra, V. J. D. Pietra, and R. L. Mercer. The mathematics of statistical machine translation: Parameter estimation. *Computational Linguistics*, 19(2):263–311, 1993.
6. P. Carbonetto, N. de Freitas, and K. Barnard. A statistical model for general contextual object recognition. In *Eight European Conference on Computer Vision (ECCV)*, Prague, Czech Republic, May 11-14 2004.
7. P. Duygulu, K. Barnard, N. Freitas, and D. A. Forsyth. Object recognition as machine translation: learning a lexicon for a fixed image vocabulary. In *Seventh European Conference on Computer Vision (ECCV)*, volume 4, pages 97–112, Copenhagen Denmark, May 27 - June 2 2002.
8. P. Duygulu and H. Wactlar. Associating video frames with text. In *Multimedia Information Retrieval Workshop in conjuction with the 26th annual ACM SIGIR conference on Information Retrieval*, Toronto, Canada, August 1 2003.
9. S. Feng, R. Manmatha, and V. Lavrenko. Multiple bernoulli relevance models for image and video annotation. In *the Proceedings of the International Conference on Pattern Recognition (CVPR 2004)*, volume 2, pages 1002–1009, 2004.
10. J. Gauvain, L. Lamel, and G. Adda. The limsi broadcast news transcription system. *Speech Communication*, 37(1-2):89–108, 2002.
11. A. Ghoshal, P. Ircing, and S. Khudanpur. Hidden markov models for automatic annotation and content based retrieval of images and video. In *The 28th International ACM SIGIR Conference*, Salvador, Brazil, August 15-19 2005.
12. C.-Y. Lin, B. L. Tseng, and J. R. Smith. Video collaborative annotation forum:establishing ground-truth labels on large multimedia datasets. In *NIST TREC-2003 Video Retrieval Evaluation Conference*, Gaithersburg, MD, November 2003.
13. D. G. Lowe. Distinctive image features from scale-invariant keypoints. *International Journal of Computer Vision*, 60(2), 2004.

14. F. J. Och and H. Ney. A systematic comparison of various statistical alignment models. *Computational Linguistics*, 1(29):19–51, 2003.

15. P. Quelhas, F. Monay, J.-M. Odobez, D. Gatica-Perez, T. Tuytelaars, and L. V. Gool. Modeling scenes with local descriptors and latent aspects. In *Proc. of IEEE Int. Conf. on Computer Vision (ICCV)*, Beijing, 2005.

16. J. Yang, M.-Y. Chen, and A. Hauptmann. Finding person x: Correlating names with visual appearances. In *International Conference on Image and Video Retrieval (CIVR'04)*, Dublin City University Ireland, July 21-23 2004.

Face Retrieval in Broadcasting News Video by Fusing Temporal and Intensity Information

Duy-Dinh Le[1], Shin'ichi Satoh[1,2], and Michael E. Houle[2]

[1] Department of Informatics,
The Graduate University for Advanced Studies,
2-1-2 Hitotsubashi, Chiyoda-ku, Tokyo, Japan 101-8430
[2] National Institute of Informatics,
2-1-2 Hitotsubashi, Chiyoda-ku, Tokyo, Japan 101-8430
ledduy@grad.nii.ac.jp, satoh@nii.ac.jp, meh@nii.ac.jp

Abstract. Human faces play an important role in efficiently indexing and accessing video contents, especially broadcasting news video. However, face appearance in real environments exhibits many variations such as pose changes, facial expressions, aging, illumination changes, low resolution and occlusion, making it difficult for current state of the art face recognition techniques to obtain reasonable retrieval results. To handle this problem, this paper proposes an efficient retrieval method by integrating temporal information into facial intensity information. First, representative faces are quickly generated by using facial intensities to organize the face dataset into clusters. Next, temporal information is introduced to reorganize cluster memberships so as to improve overall retrieval performance. For scalability and efficiency, the clustering is based on a recently-proposed model involving correlations among relevant sets (neighborhoods) of data items. Neighborhood queries are handled using an approximate search index. Experiments on the 2005 TRECVID dataset show promising results.

1 Introduction

The advancement of digital technology in recent years has made large scale multimedia data more available to users. Therefore, effective and scalable tools for indexing and retrieving video contents are strongly needed. For example, in large scale broadcasting news video, it is desirable for the system to be able to organize the video data into person-involved stories so that users can easily find and browse all events involving a specific person.

Retrieving news video segments related to visual appearance of a specific person from large video datasets is a challenging problem:

- Face appearance varies largely due to intrinsic factors such as aging, facial expressions and make-up styles, and extrinsic factors such as pose changes, lighting conditions, partial occlusion, low quality and resolution. These factors make it difficult to construct good face models. Many efforts have been made in the fields of computer vision and pattern recognition [1], but good results have limited to restricted settings.

H. Sundaram et al. (Eds.): CIVR 2006, LNCS 4071, pp. 391–400, 2006.
© Springer-Verlag Berlin Heidelberg 2006

– Names extracted from video captions and transcripts can be used to find shots containing faces of the person of interest. However, in practice, faces and names may not necessarily appear together [2].
– Detailed visual information often must be represented as high dimensional feature vectors. Evidence suggests that when the representational dimension of feature vectors is high, an effect known as "the curse of dimensionality" causes exact similarity search to access an unacceptably-high proportion of the data elements [3].

Several approaches have been proposed to handle these problems. For example, to eliminate face appearance variations, Sivic et al. modeled a face sequence as a histogram of quantized facial features. Shots containing principal actors of a movie were retrieved using a similarity measure between two histograms. Other work [4,5,6] also showed good face retrieval results for movies. However, compared to news video, the number of persons of interest in movies is much smaller, although they appear more frequently and distinctively.

In [7], low quality results for face recognition, name entity extraction from transcripts and video-caption recognition were integrated with temporal information to boost the overall accuracy of retrieval. However, their experiments were only carried out on a single small-sized video dataset. In [2], video shots related to a named individual were found by exploring various information sources from video data, such as names appearing in transcripts, face information, and most importantly, the temporal alignment of names and faces. Their results were promising, but their use of face information was very limited, and additional reference images of the target face under various conditions were required to be provided in advance. In [8,9], faces were labeled with their corresponding names using supervised learning methods such as SVM and multiple instance learning. With supervised learning methods, good generalization power can only be achieved if large training sets are provided; however, producing and annotating such training sets can be very labor intensive.

To reduce the number of retrieved images presented to users and thereby to improve the precision, clustering can be used to generate representative examples. However, most clustering methods cannot be applied to large, high dimensional datasets such as those typically associated with video image processing. For such applications, k-means has been a favorite method due to its simplicity; however, it suffers from a number of serious drawbacks. First, it cannot be applied to general similarity measures. Second, the number of clusters must be provided in advance. Third, k-means optimizes according to a global criterion, often resulting in the formation of many clusters with relatively poor internal association. Finally, in the case of very large high-dimensional datasets, scalability and convergence problems make it difficult to obtain reasonable results [10].

In this paper, we propose a face retrieval method that is distinguished from previous work by the following features.

First, representative faces are automatically organized in advance and available for users to browse by using the relevant set correlation (RSC) clustering model introduced in [11]. The GreedyRSC clustering heuristic based on this model avoids all the problems of k-means clustering listed above. An overview of the clustering model and heuristics is presented in section 2.

Second, a new similarity measure is proposed integrating both temporal and facial information that allows more accurate retrieval than when only face information is used. It makes use of an RSC reshaping technique to post-process clusters whose initial formation depends only on facial information. The details are presented in section 3.

2   RSC Clustering Model

The clustering strategy employed in this paper is based on the *relevant-set correlation* (RSC) model proposed by Houle [11]. RSC clustering can be viewed as a generalized nearest-neighbor clustering strategy, in which distance information is used only to produce ranked lists of neighbors ('relevant sets') for items in the data set. Under the model, the quality of cluster candidates, the degree of association between pairs of cluster candidates, and the degree of association between clusters and data items are all assessed according to the statistical significance of a form of correlation among pairs of relevant sets and/or candidate cluster sets. In this section, the RSC significance measures are introduced and briefly discussed; full details can be found in [11].

2.1   Internal and External Association

For any data set S, any subset $A \subseteq S$ can be represented as a zero-one set membership vector of length $n = |S|$, where a given coordinate is set to 1 whenever its associated item is present in S. The RSC model assesses the degree of association between two non-empty sets $A, B \subseteq S$ by applying the standard Pearson correlation formula to the sequence of coordinate pairs formed by the set membership vectors, yielding the following *set correlation* formula:

$$\mathrm{R}(A, B) = \frac{|S|}{\sqrt{(|S| - |A|)(|S| - |B|)}} \left(\frac{|A \cap B|}{\sqrt{|A|\,|B|}} - \frac{\sqrt{|A|\,|B|}}{|S|} \right).$$

A set correlation of 1 is achieved only when A is identical to B; otherwise, the correlation value is strictly less than 1.

Intuitively speaking, for an item $v \in A$ to be considered well-associated with the remaining items of A, one would expect those items of S that are highly relevant to v to belong to set A as well. The RSC model assesses the internal association of a candidate cluster set A as the average of the correlations between A and all relevant sets of size $|A|$ based at an item of A. The *self-correlation* of A is thus defined as:

$$\mathrm{SR}(A) \triangleq \frac{1}{|A|} \sum_{v \in A} \mathrm{R}(A, \mathrm{Q}(v, |A|)),$$

where $\mathrm{Q}(v, |A|)$ is the relevant set for item v of size $|A|$. A self-correlation of 1 is achieved when the relevant sets of all members of A perfectly coincide with A.

2.2 Significance of Association

In general, when making inferences involving Pearson correlation, a high correlation value alone is not considered sufficient to judge the significance of the relationship between two variables. When the number of variable pairs is small, it is much easier to achieve a high value by chance than when the number of pairs is large. For this reason, to help interpret correlation scores, statisticians resort to tests of significance (such as the t-test) that account for variation in the number of pairs.

Under the RSC model, associations are measured against a null hypothesis in which all relevant sets of items are assumed to have been produced by means of random selection from the full data set. Under the 'randomness' hypothesis, the mean and standard deviation of the self-correlation score can be calculated. Standard scores (also known as Z-scores) of two actual cluster candidate sets can then be generated and compared. The more significant candidate would be the one whose standard score is higher — that is, the one whose self-correlation score exceeds the expected value by the greatest number of standard deviations.

The RSC significance measure for cluster candidate A is given by:

$$Z(A) = \frac{\text{SR}(A) - \mathbf{E}[\text{SR}(A)]}{\sqrt{\mathbf{Var}[\text{SR}(A)]}} = \sqrt{|A|\,(|S| - 1)}\,\text{SR}(A).$$

Since $|S|$ can be regarded as a constant, using $Z()$ to rank cluster candidates is equivalent to using the following 'normalized-squared' significance statistic:

$$Z_*(A) = \frac{Z^2(A)}{|S|} = |A|\,\text{SR}^2(A).$$

The normalized-squared statistic has the advantage of being easier to interpret. For integer $k > 1$, a significance score of $Z_*(A) = k$ is the level of significance attained by a perfectly-associated cluster of size k — that is, one for which the same-sized relevant set of every member coincides with the cluster.

For inter-set association, testing $\text{R}(A, B)$ against the null hypothesis that set B was generated by random selection from S gives the following standard score:

$$\frac{\text{R}(A, B) - \mathbf{E}[\text{R}(A, B)]}{\sqrt{\mathbf{Var}[\text{R}(A, B)]}} = \sqrt{|S| - 1}\,\text{R}(A, B).$$

Since $|S|$ is regarded as constant, the significance measure used for RSC inter-set association is simply the set correlation $\text{R}(A, B)$ itself.

2.3 Cluster Reshaping

Within any highly-significant set A, the contributions of some relevant sets to the self-correlation may be substantially greater than others. Those items whose relevant sets contribute highly can be viewed as better associated with the concept underlying aggregation A than those whose contributions are small. It turns out that the contributions to the overall significance of A are partitionable among its constituent members according to the formula

$$Z(A) = \frac{1}{\sqrt{|A|}} \sum_{v \in A} Z(A, v), \quad \text{where} \quad Z(A, v) = \sqrt{|S| - 1}\, \text{R}(A, \text{Q}(v, |A|)).$$

Members within a cluster can be re-ranked in order of their contributions $Z(A, v)$, thereby enhancing the power of the underlying similarity measure. This also suggests that candidate A can be improved by modifying its membership to produce a new set A', for which the following significance score is maximized:

$$Z(A, A') = \frac{1}{\sqrt{|A'|}} \sum_{v \in A'} Z(A, v).$$

2.4   Clustering Strategy

The RSC-based clustering method presented in [11] seeks to generate as many clusters as possible, subject to the following restrictions:

- Every selected candidate item set A should meet a minimum threshold value of cluster quality, as measured by $Z(A)$.
- All pairs of selected cluster candidates (A, B) should meet maximum threshold values on cluster similarity, as measured by $\text{R}(A, B)$.

If a region of the data is sufficiently well-associated for a subset to meet or exceed the minimum threshold on cluster quality, then a cluster should be chosen to represent the region. However, if two or more highly-similar cluster candidates arise from within the region, then only one of the candidates should be retained.

The clustering heuristic presented in [11], GreedyRSC, employs a greedy strategy for cluster selection whereby candidates with the highest quality are selected first, and any candidates found to be overly-similar to a previously-selected candidate are declared to be redundant, and then eliminated. GreedyRSC also incorporates the following heuristic design choices:

- The quadratic cost of cluster quality evaluation is avoided by strictly limiting the size of all relevant sets considered to be at most some constant $b > 0$.
- The discovery of clusters of arbitrarily-large size is facilitated by first computing small tentative clusters with respect to a range of data samples of varying sizes. GreedyRSC treats the tentative clusters as *patterns* for the explicit generation of full-sized clusters, by reshaping them with respect to the full dataset as described above.
- The number of candidate clusters is restricted by considering only relevant sets of sample items as the eligible candidate patches or patterns.
- The cost of generating relevant sets in practice is reduced by using approximate neighborhoods as generated using the efficient and scalable SASH similarity search structure [12]. Experiments on a variety of large, very high-dimensional data sets (such as text, protein sequences, and images) have shown that the SASH consistently returns a high proportion of the true k-nearest neighbor set at speeds of roughly two orders of magnitude faster than

sequential search. Furthermore, it offers better performance and significantly better control over the time-accuracy trade-off, than previous approximation methods based on metric indices.

The GreedyRSC heuristic also seeks to reduce the total size and number of candidate cluster sets generated, by eliminating redundant patterns and cluster candidates at intermediate stages of the clustering process.

For more details regarding the GreedyRSC clustering heuristic, its implementation using SASH, and its performance, see [11].

3   Integration of Face and Temporal Information for Cluster Reshaping

Due to large variations in face appearance, with current state of the art techniques in feature extraction and similarity measures, it is difficult to obtain satisfactory results using only intensity information. Experiments in [4,6] indicated that for two face sets for the same individual, it is very difficult to form a single group when the faces are of different expressions. The use of additional temporal information could help in the formation of such groups. Under the assumption that faces appearing in the same video program should be strongly related, we propose the following new distance function resembling the Gaussian probability density function, that integrates temporal information and intensity information to measure the similarity between two faces:

$$dist(F_i, F_j) = e^{\frac{-d^2(F_i, F_j)}{2\sigma_f^2}} (1 + we^{\frac{-d^2(T_i, T_j)}{2\sigma_t^2}}),$$

where $d(F_i, F_j)$ is the Euclidean distance between two faces F_i and F_j in the eigenface space, $d(T_i, T_j)$ is the Euclidean distance between video programs T_i and T_j, and w is a weight describing the contribution of temporal information to intensity information. σ_f and σ_t play the role of standard deviations in the corresponding spaces.

In our system, σ_f was estimated as 25 based on an investigation of $d(F_i, F_j)$ for a total of 300 faces belonging to ten individuals. To normalize the time dimension, the parameter σ_t was arbitrarily set to 7, so as to cover one week with one standard deviation. w was set to 0.015 empirically.

The reshaping process is performed according to the following steps. First, the original dataset is organized into clusters using GreedyRSC together with a similarity measure based only on facial information. Next, for each cluster returned by GreedyRSC, we collect all candidate members from groups of strongly correlated clusters. Then, the process described in section 2.3 is applied to reshape each cluster group. In this reshaping process, the original set consists of the members of the grouped GreedyRSC clusters, and the correlations of the candidate members are computed according to the new facial-temporal similarity measure. The resulting clusters thus consist mainly of members strongly associated according to both temporal and intensity information.

4   Evaluation

4.1   Face Information Extraction

We evaluated the proposed method on the 2005 TRECVID data set [13]. The data set consists approximately 169 hours of video taken from 277 news programs. The channels covered include LBC (Arabic-43 hours), CCTV4, NTDTV (Chinese-52 hours), CNN, NBC, and MSNBC (English-74 hours). A typical news program is 30 minutes long and consists of roughly 54,000 video frames. For efficient management, the news video programs were partitioned into shots, from which 152,500 master key frames were extracted (available at CLIPS-IMAG). A fast and robust face detector [14,15] was used to detect all faces in the key frames. It produced 21,527 faces for which two eyes were clearly visible. Eye positions provided by the face detector were used to align the faces to a predefined canonical pose. To compensate for illumination effects, the subtraction of the best-fit brightness plane followed by histogram equalization was applied as in [16]. Next, the faces were scaled to a size of 64x64 pixels, and an elliptical mask was applied so as to remove the background. The results of these steps are shown in Figure 1.

We then used PCA [17] to reduce the number of dimensions of the feature vectors for face representation. Projection vectors were generated from 3,816 frontal faces with different variations taken from the FERET database [18]. The faces were normalized as described above, and then used to calculate the mean face and the eigenfaces corresponding with the largest 930 eigenvalues. This number was selected so as to retain 97% of the total energy. Some of the eigenfaces are shown in Figure 2.

4.2   Performance of RSC Clustering

The advantages of the RSC clustering model include:

- It can be applied to any dataset for which ranked relevant sets can be efficiently generated whenever a dataset item is treated as a query-by-example. The model does not depend on the precise value of the underlying similarity measure except for the purpose of generating ranked relevant sets.
- Items can appear in more than one cluster. This allows the model to assess the association between two clusters according to the degree of correlation (overlap) between their set memberships.
- The model can assess the quality of internal association of clusters independently from other clusters. The model is not forced to accept a poorly-associated cluster in order to satisfy some global optimization criterion.
- Clustering heuristics based on the model can automatically determine an appropriate number of clusters over a large range of sizes (even as few as 3 or 4 items).

Heuristics based on the RSC model, supported by fast approximate similarity search techniques, have been shown to scale to handle dataset of millions of objects represented in thousands or even millions of dimensions [19,12,11].

Fig. 1. Face extraction from news video - face regions detected by a face detector (top), and faces after normalization (bottom)

Fig. 2. Some eigenfaces used to form the subspace for face representation

Fig. 3. Representative faces of several clusters found by GreedyRSC

Cluster 78 Summary

Cluster ID	Cluster Size	Norm-Squared Significance	Inter-set Correlation
78	36	5.55278	

Related Clusters

Cluster ID	Cluster Size	Norm-Squared Significance	Inter-set Correlation
381	9	5.44343	0.499686

Cluster ID	Cluster Size	Norm-Squared Significance	Inter-set Correlation
687	4	4	0.333085

Fig. 4. An example of GreedyRSC output showing strong inter-cluster correlation

Applying GreedyRSC to the TRECVID faces produced 810 clusters after 10 minutes of execution on a 3.0GHz PC Pentium IV with 2GB RAM. In order to produce approximate k-nearest neighbor lists for use by GreedyRSC, the SASH was tuned for an average accuracy of 98% at a speed of 6 times faster than sequential search.

The resulting clusters had sizes ranging from 4 to 541. To keep the precision high, clusters with more than 100 members were discarded. Of the 21,527 faces, 7,176 faces were not assigned to any clusters. This is not unreasonable since many faces appeared fewer than four times in the dataset. Of the 14,351 faces belonging

Fig. 5. An example of a cluster group both before (left) and after (right) reshaping using temporal information

to at least one cluster, 9,825 faces belong to exactly one cluster. Representative faces of several of the clusters are shown in Figure 3.

The output of the clustering process also provided inter-cluster correlation relationships, examples of which are shown in Figure 4, that can facilitate the navigation and browsing of news video data.

In Figure 5, we show an example from the clustering results that illustrates the impact of temporal information on cluster quality.

5   Discussion

Face identification in real video data (such as broadcast news video) is far more difficult than in controlled environments due to the large variations in face appearance. We have proposed a method to integrate temporal information with intensity information to improve the performance of face identification systems. By using RSC model-based clustering together with fast approximate similarity search, our method has the potential to handle very large scale video datasets effectively and efficiently. In the future, we plan to integrate other information sources from video data such as face positions and name entities extracted from transcripts to further improve the performance. More experiments and evaluations are also needed, particularly on larger datasets.

References

1. Zhao, W., Chellappa, R., Phillips, P.J., Rosenfeld, A.: Face recognition: A literature survey. ACM Computing Surveys **35**(4) (2003) 399–458
2. Yang, J., Chen, M., Hauptmann, A.: Finding person x: Correlating names with visual appearances. In: Proc. Int. Conf. on Image and Video Retrieval (CIVR). (2004) 270–278

3. Weber, R., Schek, H.J., Blott, S.: A quantitative analysis and performance study for similarity-search methods in high-dimensional spaces. In: Proc. Intl. Conf. on Very Large Data Bases (VLDB). (1998) 194–205
4. Fitzgibbon, A., Zisserman, A.: On affine invariant clustering and automatic cast listing in movies. In: Proc. Intl. European Conference on Computer Vision (ECCV). Volume 3. (2002) 304–320
5. Fitzgibbon, A., Zisserman, A.: Joint manifold distance: a new approach to appearance based clustering. In: Proc. Intl. Conf. on Computer Vision and Pattern Recognition (CVPR). Volume 1. (2003) 26–36
6. Arandjelovic, O., Zisserman, A.: Automatic face recognition for film character retrieval in feature-length films. In: Proc. Intl. Conf. on Computer Vision and Pattern Recognition (CVPR). Volume 1. (2005) 860–867
7. Satoh, S., Kanade, T.: Name-it: Association of face and name in video. In: Proc. Intl. Conf. on Computer Vision and Pattern Recognition (CVPR). (1997) 368–373
8. Yang, J., Hauptmann, A.: Naming every individual in news video monologues. In: Proc. ACM International Conference on Multimedia (MM). (2004) 580–587
9. Yang, J., Yan, R., Hauptmann, A.: Multiple instance learning for labeling faces in broadcasting news video. In: Proc. ACM International Conference on Multimedia (MM). (2005) 31–40
10. Kaufman, L., Rousseeuw, P.J.: Finding Groups in Data: an Introduction to Cluster Analysis. John Wiley & Sons (1990)
11. Houle, M.E.: A generic query-based model for scalable clustering. Technical Report NII-2006-008E, National Institute of Informatics (2006)
12. Houle, M.E., Sakuma, J.: Fast approximate similarity search in extremely high-dimensional data sets. In: Proc. Int. Conf. on Data Engineering (ICDE). (2005) 619–630
13. http://www-nlpir.nist.gov/projects/trecvid/.
14. Le, D.D., Satoh, S.: Multi-stage approach to fast face detection. In: Proc. British Machine Vison Conf.(BMVC). Volume 2. (2005) 769–778
15. Le, D.D., Satoh, S.: Fusion of local and global features for efficient object detection. In: Proc. SPIE, Applications of Neural Networks and Machine Learning in Image Processing IX. Volume 5673. (2005) 106–116
16. Rowley, H., Baluja, S., Kanade, T.: Neural network-based face detection. IEEE Transactions on Pattern Analysis and Machine Intelligence 20(1) (1998) 23–38
17. Turk, M., Pentland, A.: Face recognition using eigenfaces. In: Proc. Intl. Conf. on Computer Vision and Pattern Recognition (CVPR). (1991)
18. Phillips, P., Moon, H., Rizvi, S., Rauss, P.: The feret evaluation methodology for face recognition algorithms. IEEE Transactions on Pattern Analysis and Machine Intelligence 22(10) (2002) 1094–1104
19. Houle, M.E.: Navigating massive data sets via local clustering. In: Proc. ACM SIGKDD Int. Conf. on Knowledge Discovery and Data Mining (SIGKDD). (2003) 547–552

Multidimensional Descriptor Indexing: Exploring the BitMatrix*

Catalin Calistru[1,2], Cristina Ribeiro[1,2], and Gabriel David[1,2]

[1] FEUP—Faculdade de Engenharia da Universidade do Porto
[2] INESC—Porto
Rua Dr. Roberto Frias s/n, 4200-465 Porto, Portugal
cmc@inescporto.pt, mcr@fe.up.pt, gtd@fe.up.pt

Abstract. Multimedia retrieval brings new challenges, mainly derived from the mismatch between the level of the user interaction—high-level concepts, and that of the automatically processed descriptors—low-level features. The effective use of the low-level descriptors is therefore mandatory. Many data structures have been proposed for managing the representation of multidimensional descriptors, each geared toward efficiency in some set of basic operations. The paper introduces a highly parametrizable structure called the BitMatrix, along with its search algorithms. The BitMatrix is compared with existing methods, all implemented in a common framework . The tests have been performed on two datasets, with parameters covering significant ranges of values. The BitMatrix has proved to be a robust and flexible structure that can compete with other methods for multidimensional descriptor indexing.

1 Introduction

People need to automatically search on multimedia objects. The retrieval task is characterized by the specification of user queries and the selection of appropriate objects by the system. While textual data allows an easy identification of high-level concepts, images, for instance, do not directly provide such concepts, even if they are subject to state-of-the-art analysis.

Multimedia data has to conform to convenient models in order to be used in retrieval. Extraction techniques are used to analyze the streams, generating higher-level representations of features such as color or texture, in the form of multidimensional descriptors. Descriptors constitute a possible search space on which similarity calculations are required [1].

We concentrate here on the specific task of retrieving objects that satisfy some (sharp) similarity criterion in a database of objects represented by multidimensional descriptors. A BitMatrix is proposed along with methods for searching according to similarity criteria. The BitMatrix is compared with other approaches using an extensible test platform.

---

* Partially supported by FCT under project POSC/EIA/61109/2004 (DOMIR).

H. Sundaram et al. (Eds.): CIVR 2006, LNCS 4071, pp. 401–410, 2006.
© Springer-Verlag Berlin Heidelberg 2006

2   Multimedia Object Models

Multimedia objects typically have a complex structure. It is common for objects to encapsulate parts in different media, to have references to components they do not directly include, and to have complex relationships among them. This is reflected in the models for multimedia objects adopted in recent standards such as MPEG-7 [2]. The goal of our work is to build systems capable of managing structured multimedia objects and offer retrieval functions that range from text-based to structure and content-based browsing and querying. We are using an operational model accounting for the structure of current standards [3] and need to accommodate various descriptors in a flexible way.

As computing power is cheap, it is viable to have image and video processing algorithms analyzing object features and generating large amounts of descriptor data. It is therefore crucial to adopt descriptor representations and indexing methods that, besides accommodating the expected diversity of descriptors, can be effective in the basic retrieval operations. Moreover, as similarity search is a core task for these descriptors, metrics are required and they must be fit for the nature of descriptors. A flexible model for metrics is likely to require a fine-grained representation of the descriptor values and their types.

Multidimensional indexing requires assumptions on the nature of data and the algorithms to search it. Several requirements from the application domain may condition the choice of the indexing method. A common requirement is that updates to the object database are allowed. This will lead to indexing methods able to incrementally update their data structures. Another important aspect is the ability to add new descriptors of varying dimensionality. To meet this requirement, it is necessary to allow varying dimensionality in descriptors, and again to be able to extend the indexing structure piecemeal.

Handling a large number of multidimensional descriptors may be inconvenient in some parts of the retrieval process. Being able to search on a chosen subset is therefore a desirable feature. Metrics can take many forms, and the choice of metric is also important from the point of view of flexibility of the retrieval process.

3   Multidimensional Indexing Methods

The similarity between objects is evaluated with a comparison between their representations. Each object o from the universe of objects $\mathcal{O}$ is characterized by a set $\mathcal{F}$ of **features** (color, motion activity, ...), where each feature f_i is captured as a **feature vector** v_i. In the resulting vector space, with dimensionality N, the similarity between objects is given by a similarity measure which is not necessarily a metric distance. There are, however, distance-only datasets, for which the information available is the distance between the objects. Given a query object o and a metric function $d(o_x, o_y)$, the search task accounts to finding a particular set of objects. Possible results sets are the *Nearest Neighbor Set* $NN(q)$, the set of objects such that $\forall v \in \mathcal{O}, d(q, o) \leq d(q, v)$, the *k- Nearest*

Neighbors Set $NN_k(q)$, a set of k elements closest to q in $\mathcal{O}$, i.e. objects o such that $\forall v \in \mathcal{O}, d(q,v) < d(q,o) \rightarrow v \in NN_k(q)$ and the *approximate Nearest Neighbor Set* $(NN_A(q))$, a set of objects such that $d(q,o) \leq (1+\epsilon)*d(q, NN(q))$ for some $\epsilon > 0$.

Generally, the high-dimensional indexing methods divide the search space in a set of ranges with the goal of pruning them at search time. The remaining partitions have to be exhaustively scanned. A great diversity of indexing methods emerged from the differences in the models of the underlying search space (vectorial or metric), partitioning strategies and similarity measures.

Spatial Access Methods (SAM) are based on a tree data structure with the data nodes (the leaves) grouped in directory nodes. The partitioning strategies of the SAM's can be data partitioning (DP) which uses minimum bounding regions (MBR) such as *R-tree, R*-tree , X-tree*, bounding spheres such as $SS-tree$, MBR and bounding spheres such as $SR-Tree$, generic minimum bounding regions(hyper rectangle, cube, sphere) such as $TV-tree$ and space partitioning methods (SP) such as the $kDB-tree, Hybrid-tree, SH-tree$ [4].

Metric Access Methods (MAM), are distance-based indexing methods, that work with relative distances between the objects rather than their absolute positions. MAM's are also based on tree-structures that recursively partition the data set into subsets (ball partitioning or generalized hyperplane partitioning) at each node level [5]. The applicability of such methods ranges from "native" distance-only datasets to high-dimensional datasets for which conventional SAM's are no longer efficient [6].

Single-Dimensional Mapping techniques map the points in the high-dimensional space to single-dimensional values for which efficient techniques exist. In [7] a spacial data partitioning(DP) technique is applied, followed by a single-dimensional mapping technique within each partition. The mapping process consists of sorting the objects in each partition on the distance to a specific reference point (such as the center). The reference points are then indexed in a B^+-tree structure.

Aggregation algorithms treat each dimension as a separate list, and their goal is to obtain the result of the query by accessing a minimum number of lists and as few objects as possible in each of the visited lists. These methods operate in middleware systems [8], like the Fagin's Algorithm, the Threshold Algorithm, the Quick-Combine [9], or directly on the original data like BOND [10].

Data Approximation Structures make the assumption that a sequential scan is inevitable [11] and construct a vector of approximations (VA-file), significantly smaller than the original data. Each dimension D is divided in k_D ranges, obtaining a grid of approximations. In the first step the approximations are pruned based on their minimum/maximum distance to the query point. For the remaining approximations the corresponding exact data points have to be analyzed.

Using a similar grid of ranges the IGrid [12] maintains separate lists for the objects in each range. The similarity between any two objects uses only the set of dimensions for which the two objects lie in the same range (the *proximity set*). The number of objects that are accessed is kept small as dimensionality increases, at the cost of a large storage overhead (100%) and significant edge-effects. Bitmap variants have been proposed [13,14].

As dimensionality increases, the distances from the query object to the nearest and the farthest objects are harder to distinguish [15]. In such conditions, a query region that includes the nearest neighbor will overlap most of the other partitions, dramatically decreasing selectivity. With low selectivity, the search methods end up accessing all the nodes of their structures, which means pseudo-random access to all the objects in the dataset. Sequential scan therefore becomes a robust competitor. Recent works in this area have established concepts like the *meaningfulness* [15,16], and the *distinctiveness* [17] of the retrieved objects in order to characterize the retrieval process in high-dimensional spaces.

4   The BitMatrix-Based Methods

Given the high cost of random disk access as compared to sequential access, the idea is to construct a collection of signatures that can be sequentially analyzed and used to effectively prune the search space. The BitMatrix method follows a data approximation approach in the spirit of VA-File [11] and IGrid [12], partitioning each of the N dimensions in k ranges . A partition of a dimension D is a set of ranges $\pi_D = \{r_i = [l_i, u_i], i = 1 \ldots k_D\}$, where l_i, u_i are the lower and upper bounds of range i. The partitioning scheme $(k_1, k_2, \ldots, k_N)$ is used to obtain bitmap signatures for all the objects in a dataset $\mathcal{O}$ arranged as lines in a matrix.

4.1   Building the BitMatrix

The first step in the construction of the BitMatrix is to choose a partitioning scheme such as *equi-width*, *equi-depth* or *k-means* partitioning. In the case of equi-width partitioning the ranges have the same length, while in the case of equi-depth the ranges contain an equal number of objects. The k-means partitioning requires a previous k-means clustering step, where k clusters are identified and their centroids calculated and sorted. The bounds of the k ranges are obtained from the centroids: the lower bound for range i is $l_i = (C_{i-1} + C_i)/2$ and its upper bound $u_i = (C_i + C_{i+1})/2$.

Definition 1 (Signature). *Given a partitioning scheme* $(k_1, k_2, .., k_N)$, *an object's signature is a bitmap of length* $\Sigma_{D=1}^{N} k_D$. *For each dimension the signature contains* 1 *for the range where the object belongs and* 0 *for the other ranges.*

The *cardinality* of a signature is the number of bits set to 1. The example in Figure 1 has 2 dimensions ($N = 2$) and 3 ranges per dimension ($k_1 = k_2 = 3$). Object o_2 has signature 001010 as the object lies in range 2 for dimension 1, and in range 1 for dimension 2. Arranging each signature as a line in a matrix we obtain the BitMatrix with $|\mathcal{O}|$ lines and $\Sigma_{D=1}^{N} k_D$ columns.

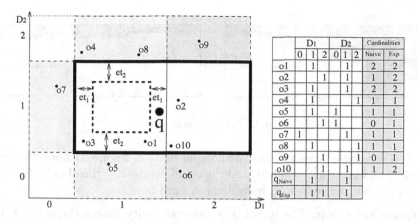

	D1			D2			Cardinalities	
	0	1	2	0	1	2	Naive	Exp
o1		1			1		2	2
o2			1		1		1	2
o3		1			1		2	2
o4	1				1		1	1
o5		1		1			1	1
o6			1	1			0	1
o7	1				1		1	1
o8		1				1	1	1
o9			1			1	0	1
o10			1		1		1	2
q_{Naive}		1			1			
q_{Exp}		1	1		1			

Fig. 1. BitMatrix

4.2 Searching with the BitMatrix

We now propose two algorithms for approximate nearest neighbor, exploring the sequential access to the BitMatrix. The *naïve approach* selects objects based on the cardinality of the bitwise AND between object and query signatures, as follows.

The naïve approach

- *Step 1*: Given a query object $q = [q_1, \ldots, q_N]$, obtain it's signature, i.e. find for each dimension D the range in which the query coordinate q_D lies.
- *Step 2*: Iterate through the objects, performing bitwise AND between their signatures and the query object's signature. If the cardinality of the resulting bitmap is above a predefined **cardinality threshold(ct)** the object is retained for the next phase.
- *Step 3*: Access the full vector values of the remaining objects, compute their exact distance to the query object and rank them.

We will use **cardinality of an object** in the sequel to refer to the cardinality of the bitmap resulting from the bitwise AND between the signatures for the object and the query. In Figure 1, the signature q_{naive}=010010 of the query object is AND'ed with the signatures of all the other objects $o_1, o_2, ..o_{10}$. With the cardinality threshold set to 2 only objects o_1 and o_3 remain for Step 3.

The example above shows that the naïve approach prunes object o_2 which happens to be the nearest neighbor. This effect, known as the *edge-effect* [12] appears because for all dimensions D, only the objects in the same range as q_D are considered. The **range expansion** heuristic is a modification of the naïve approach affecting Step 1: for a dimension in which the query object is close enough to one of the edges, the query's signature is set to 1 for both the query's range and the range next to it. Assuming that q_D lies in range i for dimension D, the expansion takes place to the left if $\|q_D - l_i\| < et_i \|u_i - l_i\|$ or to the right if $\|q_D - u_i\| < et_i \|u_i - l_i\|$, where et_i, the **expansion threshold**, takes values in

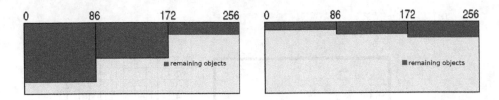

Fig. 2. Subspace selection

[0, 0.5]. The cardinalities column (with expansion) in Figure 1 shows that with the query signature q_{exp}=011010 and the same cardinality threshold, objects o_2 and o_{10} are not pruned, as their cardinalities are now 2.

Subspace selection. The increase of dimensionality makes the task of finding the nearest neighbor harder because the distances between objects become very similar. For the majority of the high-dimensional search methods, the nearest neighbor becomes indistinguishable from the rest of the objects. In order to improve the quality of the nearest neighbor selection, we have considered the *subspace selection* approach, where subsets with smaller dimensionality are successively explored using the BitMatrix algorithms. Let **s** be the number of dimensions of the subspace to be processed in the current iteration:

- *Step 1*: Apply Step 1 and 2 of the naïve or expansion approaches on the selected **s** dimensions ($\Sigma_{D=1}^{s} k_D$ columns of the BitMatrix).
- *Step 2*: Combine the partial result set obtained in this iteration with the previous result set (intersection, union). If *the stop condition* is false repeat Step 1 on the next subspace.
- *Step 3*: Same as Step 3 of the naïve approach.

The stop condition becomes true if enough dimensions have been processed or enough objects have been pruned. Figure 2 illustrates a space with 256 dimensions processed with s=86. In the left part, intersection between the partial result sets is performed, using a low cardinality threshold in each subspace, and in the right part union is performed with a high cardinality threshold.

4.3   Insert, Update, Delete

The insertion of a new object in the BitMatrix, accounts for computing its signature and adding it as a new line in the matrix. The size of the BitMatrix grows linearly with the number of objects and with the dimensionality. The precise size of the BitMatrix is ($\Sigma_{D=1}^{N} k_D$) $* |\mathcal{O}|$ bits. To update an existing object its signature has to be modified through bitwise operations. To delete an object, the corresponding line is removed from the matrix.

5   Experimental Results

One of the difficulties encountered in the evaluation of the various high-dimensional indexing methods was the lack of a common platform on which they

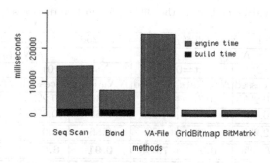

Fig. 3. Time Comparison

can be objectively tested. Indexing methods depend on parameters and storage models, which make them better suited for some domains. This makes them difficult to compare, and the majority of the proposed high-dimensional retrieval methods are only compared to the sequential scan. High-dimensional indexing methods, however, follow common steps such as preprocessing the object data, partitioning the search space, index construction, query processing, searching the index, accessing the remaining objects. A first step in the experimentation work has been to develop a Java framework for the integration and benchmark of the various indexing methods [18]. We have included Sequential Scan, Bond [10], VA-File [11], GridBitmap [13], and the proposed BitMatrix.

The first experiment has been designed to test the time performance of the various methods as memory-based indexing methods. The time columns in Figure 3 have two components: the time to build the index in memory (build time) and the time to search it (engine time). The engine time for the BitMatrix is clearly smaller than the values for Sequential Scan and Bond and is in the same range with the GridBitmap. The time for the VA-file does not do justice to the method as it is tested using the same partitioning scheme as GridBitmap and BitMatrix; with 7 ranges in each of the 256 dimensions, there are 7^{256} cells and the non-empty ones have at most one object.

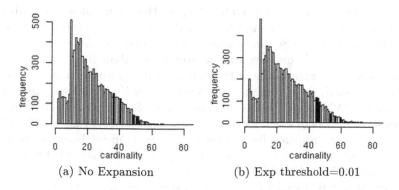

(a) No Expansion   (b) Exp threshold=0.01

Fig. 4. Histogram of cardinalities

Table 1. Testing the BitMatrix on two datasets

ct	Dataset 1 $N = 256, k_D = 7, i = 1 \ldots 256\,(k-means\,partitioning)$							
	NN(q)				$NN_{10}(q)$			
	Naïve(et=0)		et=0,01		Naïve(et=0)		et=0,01	
	NN Rate	accessed	NN Rate	accessed	NN_{10}Rate	accessed	NN_{10}Rate	accessed
0.73	0.6	0.2%	0.7	0.4%	0.39	0.2%	0.48	0.4%
0.67	0.78	0.8%	0.87	1.0%	0.61	0.8%	0.68	1.0%
0.55	0.93	2.9%	0.95	3.8%	0.86	2.9%	0.9	3.8%
0.47	**0.97**	**6.0%**	**0.99**	**7.4%**	**0.91**	**6.0%**	**0.94**	**7.4%**
0.40	**1.0**	**10.9%**	**1.0**	**13.5%**	**0.93**	**10.9%**	**0.96**	**13.5%**

ct	Dataset 2 $N = 80, k_i = 7, i = 1 \ldots 80\,(k-means\,partitioning)$							
	NN(q)				$NN_{10}(q)$			
	Naïve (et=0)		et=0,01		Naïve (et=0)		et=0,01	
0.60	0.24	0.19%	0.25	0.21%	0.08	0.19%	0.09	0.21%
0.50	0.55	1.99%	0.57	2.31%	0.33	1.99%	0.35	2.31%
0.40	0.78	8.16%	0.84	9.32%	0.57	8.16%	0.62	9.32%
0.35	0.90	17.0%	0.93	19.2%	0.77	17.0%	0.80	19.2%
0.30	0.90	32.2%	0.94	34.21%	0.85	32.2%	0.87	34.21%

The second set of experiments was geared toward finding a good parametrization for the BitMatrix. The quality of the parametrization is evaluated comparing the approximate results with the *k-nearest neighbors*. If R is the set $NN_k(q)$ and A is the approximate result ($|A|$ varies with the query object, **ct**, **et**, partitioning scheme, subspace) the quality is computed as $\frac{|A \cap R|}{|R|}$. This measure can be regarded as a formal recall rate, taking R as the relevant set and A as the answer set. The percentage of objects that remain after pruning is also recorded. Two datasets have been used: a dataset of 9908 image histograms with $N = 256$ dimensions obtained from real images (Dataset 1) and a synthetic dataset of 10000 objects with $N = 80$ dimensions IID (Independent Identical Distributed) uniform distribution (Dataset 2). The cardinality threshold was set as a percentage of the maximum cardinality encountered up to that moment for the subspace. The histograms of cardinalities in Fig. 4 use dark bins for the cardinalities of the NN_{10}. On a subspace of 86 dimensions from the original 256, after expansion, all the 10 nearest neighbors have cardinalities larger than 40.

Table 1 shows average values of the two measures (formal recall rate, and % of objects accessed) with respect to $NN(q)$ and $NN_{10}(q)$ across random sets of 100 queries. With a cardinality threshold of 0.55, less than 3% of Dataset 1 is accessed, the average recall rate is 0.93 (relative to NN) and 0.83 (relative to NN_{10}). The experiments have shown that the tradeoff between quality of retrieval and speed can be tuned with the expansion mechanism. For example, with the cardinality threshold 0.47, about 6% of Dataset 1 is accessed, and the average recall rate relative to NN_{10} is 0.91. If expansion is performed the recall is 0.94 at 7.5% accessed, while for a smaller cardinality threshold (ct = 0.4) the recall is 0.93 at 10.9% accessed. Thus, expansion should be preferred in this case. The results for the synthetic IID uniform distributed Dataset 2, (second half of Table 1) show worse performance. Much larger amounts of the Dataset 2 have to be analyzed in order to obtain acceptable recall rates. The expansion mechanism clearly improves the recall rate in this case as well.

6   Conclusions

The purpose of this work has been to study the BitMatrix with as few assumptions as possible on the underlying structure of the descriptors. The BitMatrix is highly parametrizable offering a large space for experimentation: cardinality threshold, expansion threshold, number of dimensions processed in each step, dimension processing order for the case of weighted dimensions. While the majority of the high-dimensional indexing approaches are only compared to Sequential Scan, the current experiments were driven on top of a prototype framework for integration of high-dimensional indexing methods, and include a set of 5 methods: Sequential Scan, Bond, VA-File, GridBitmap, and BitMatrix. The experiments revealed that the BitMatrix retains most of sequential scan's flexibility with good quality of the approximations and a much better time performance. It can be conveniently arranged for efficient sequential access and optimized bitwise operations. It can further be broken into segments for distributed or parallel processing. It supports weighted queries and accommodates query feedback mechanism. Relevant features selection (dimensional reduction) and multiple clustering techniques can be used with the BitMatrix as long as the metric is fixed. Future work includes research on the expansion mechanism, extensive testing with larger collections and integration into a multimedia retrieval system.

References

1. Mojsilovic, A.: Semantic Metric for Image Library Exploration. IEEE Transactions on Multimedia **6** (2004) 828–838
2. MPEG-7 Requirements Group (Editor José M. Martínez): MPEG-7 Overview v.10. ISO/IEC JTC1/SC29/WG11 N6828 (2004)
3. Calistru, C., Ribeiro, C., David, G.: A flexible model for multimedia content structure and description: MetaMedia and its applications. In preparation (2006)
4. Böhm, C., Berchtold, S., Keim, D.A.: Searching in high-dimensional spaces: Index structures for improving the performance of multimedia databases. ACM Comput. Surv. **33** (2001) 322–373
5. Chávez, E., Navarro, G., Baeza-Yates, R., Marroquín, J.L.: Searching in metric spaces. ACM Comput. Surv. **33** (2001) 273–321
6. Digout, C., Nascimento, M.A.: High-dimensional similarity searches using a metric pseudo-grid. In: ICDE Workshops 1174. (2005)
7. Jagadish, H.V., Ooi, B.C., Tan, K.L., Yu, C., Zhang, R.: iDistance: An adaptive B+-tree based indexing method for nearest neighbor search. ACM Trans. Database Syst. **30** (2005) 364–397

8. Carey, M.J., Haas, L.M., Schwarz, P.M., Arya, M., Cody, W.F., Fagin, R., Flickner, M., Luniewski, A.W., Niblack, W., Petkovic, D., Thomas, J., Williams, J.H., Wimmers, E.L.: Towards heterogeneous multimedia information systems: the Garlic approach. In: RIDE '95: Proceedings of the 5th International Workshop on Research Issues in Data Engineering-Distributed Object Management (RIDE-DOM'95), IEEE Computer Society (1995) 124–131

9. Fagin, R., Lotem, A., Naor, M.: Optimal aggregation algorithms for middleware. In: PODS '01: Proceedings of the twentieth ACM SIGMOD-SIGACT-SIGART symposium on Principles of database systems, ACM Press (2001) 102–113

10. Arjen, P.d.V., Mamoulis, N., Nes, N., Kersten, M.: Efficient k-NN search on vertically decomposed data. In: SIGMOD '02: Proceedings of the 2002 ACM SIGMOD international conference on Management of data, ACM Press (2002) 322–333

11. Weber, R., Schek, H.J., Blott, S.: A Quantitative Analysis and Performance Study for Similarity-Search Methods in High-Dimensional Spaces. In: Proc. 24th Int. Conf. Very Large Data Bases, VLDB. (1998) 194–205

12. Aggarwal, C.C., Yu, P.S.: The IGrid index: reversing the dimensionality curse for similarity indexing in high dimensional space. In: KDD '00: Proceedings of the sixth ACM SIGKDD international conference on Knowledge discovery and data mining, New York, NY, USA, ACM Press (2000) 119–129

13. Cha, G.H.: Bitmap indexing method for complex similarity queries with relevance feedback. In: MMDB '03: Proceedings of the 1st ACM international workshop on Multimedia databases, New York, NY, USA, ACM Press (2003) 55–62

14. Goldstein, J., Platt, J.C., Burges, C.J.C.: Redundant Bit Vectors for Quickly Searching High-Dimensional Regions. In: Deterministic and Statistical Methods in Machine Learning. (2004) 137–158

15. Beyer, K., Goldstein, J., Ramakrishnan, R., Shaft, U.: When Is "Nearest Neighbor" Meaningful? Lecture Notes in Computer Science **1540** (1999) 217–235

16. Aggarwal, C.C.: Towards meaningful high-dimensional nearest neighbor search by human-computer interaction. In: Data Engineering, 2002. Proceedings. 18th International Conference on. (2002) 593–604

17. Katayama, N., Satoh, S.: Distinctiveness-Sensitive Nearest Neighbor Search for Efficient Similarity Retrieval of Multimedia Information. In: Proceedings of the 17th International Conference on Data Engineering, Washington, DC, USA, IEEE Computer Society (2001) 493–502

18. Gonçalves, B., Calistru, C., Ribeiro, C., David, G.: Experimental results for multidimensional multimedia descriptor indexing. Submitted for publication (2006)

Natural Scene Image Modeling Using Color and Texture Visterms

Pedro Quelhas[1,2] and Jean-Marc Odobez[1,2]

[1] IDIAP Research Institute
[2] Ecole Polytechnique Federale de Lausanne (EPFL)

Abstract. This paper presents a novel approach for visual scene representation, combining the use of quantized color and texture local invariant features (referred to here as *visterms*) computed over interest point regions. In particular we investigate the different ways to fuse together local information from texture and color in order to provide a better *visterm* representation. We develop and test our methods on the task of image classification using a 6-class natural scene database. We perform classification based on the *bag-of-visterms* (BOV) representation (histogram of quantized local descriptors), extracted from both texture and color features. We investigate two different fusion approaches at the feature level: fusing local descriptors together and creating one representation of joint texture-color visterms, or concatenating the histogram representation of both color and texture, obtained independently from each local feature. On our classification task we show that the appropriate use of color improves the results w.r.t. a texture only representation.

1 Introduction

Viewpoint invariant local descriptors [1,2] (i.e. features computed over automatically detected local areas) have proven to be useful in long-standing problems such as viewpoint-independent object recognition, wide baseline matching, and image retrieval. These feature were designed to have a high degree of invariance. As a result, they are robust to changes in viewpoint and lighting conditions. Furthermore, due to their locality, they provide robustness to image clutter, partial visibility, and occlusion. In addition, the use of *quantized* local invariant features has also proven in recent years to provide a robust and versatile way to model images, leading to good classification [3,4,5], retrieval [6,7] and image segmentation [4,8] performance.

A great advantage of modeling images based on quantized local invariant features for the tasks of retrieval and classification is that the same methodology can be used for different image categories and that performance is often similar if not better than most of the existing task specific state-of-the-art algorithms. This was demonstrated on images of objects [3] and on scenes [4,5]. Moreover, in scene classification, this general approach performed surprisingly well given that only local texture features were used [4,5], while most state-of-the-art techniques [9,10] are based on both texture and color. Nevertheless, in visterm based representations used for scene classification, it seems that by discarding color we

H. Sundaram et al. (Eds.): CIVR 2006, LNCS 4071, pp. 411–421, 2006.
© Springer-Verlag Berlin Heidelberg 2006

are potentially eliminating discriminative information since several scene classes are characterized by specific colors. Thus, it is quite natural and relevant to investigate the use of color in visterm based approaches and address the following related questions: how can color be integrated in the BOV framework and how much is gained by doing so?

In this paper, we propose and present an approach to model scene images using both color and texture visterm representations. More precisely, we first show on a 6-class problem that texture based invariant local features, used to build bags-of-visterm representations, are suitable for natural scene classification. Secondly we show that the inclusion of color improves the classification results. Although not demonstrated in the paper, the representation and methods presented here can be extended for ranking/retrieval [3,4,5].

The rest of the paper is organized as follows. The next Section discusses related work. Section 3 presents the BOV image representation. Section 4 describes the experimental setup. Classification results are provided and discussed in Section 5. Section 6 concludes the paper.

2   Related Work

The problem of image modeling using low-level features has been studied in image and video retrieval for several years [9,10,11,12,13]. Broadly speaking, the existing methods differ by the definition of the target image classes, the specific image representations, and the classification method. In the next paragraphs, we focus our dicussion on the image representation issue.

Image representations based on quantized invariant local descriptors have been used for many tasks, with variations on both local detectors/descriptors and the subsequent image representation. Sivic et. al. [6] applied text retrieval methodologies on quantized local descriptors in a movie keyframe retrieval application. The system was proven to be fast and usable for large image database queries. The exploitation of quantized local descriptors was further extended by Csurka et. al. [3] to object recognition. The authors proposed to represent images using an histogram of the quantized local descriptors (bag-of-visterms). On the Caltech object image database, their system was show to outperform state-of-the-art object recognition techniques. In more recent work Quelhas et. al. [4] and Fei-Fei et. al. [5] have show that this bag-of-visterms representation can be further decomposed into mixtures of latent semantic models. Such latent models enable clustering and ranking of images into meaningfull groups.

On the field of scene image modeling, most works use color and texture information to perform classification/retrieval. Vailaya et al. [9] used histograms of different low-level cues to perform scene classification. Different sets of cues were used depending on the two-class problem at hand: global edge features were used for city vs landscape classification, while local color features were used in the indoor vs outdoor case. More generally scene recognition methods tend to fuse color and texture information. Both Serrano et al. [14] and Szummer et al. [10] propose a two-stage classification of indoor/outdoor scenes, where color and texture features of individual image blocks are computed over a spatial grid layout

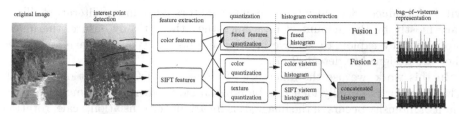

Fig. 1. Schematic representation of our system and of the two alternative fusion approaches: fusion between texture and color information is done either at the feature level before quantization (yellow box) or at the bag-of-visterm level(pink box)

are first independently classified into indoor or outdoor. The local classification outputs are then further combined to create the global scene representation used in the final image classification stage. Vogel and Schiele propose a similar two-stage approach based on a fixed grid layout to perform scene retrieval and classification [15]. Several local features (color and edge histograms, grey-level co-occurence matrix) are concatenated after normalization and weighting into one feature vector. Finally, Boutell et. al. [16] use only Luv color moments in a 7x7 block layout to perform scene multi-label scene classification.

In contrast, methods based on quantized local descriptors use only gray-scale information to create their fundamental features. Although this may be acceptable for some classes it is obvious that for natural scenes, color is important and its use may improve the power of the visterm representation.

3   Image Modeling

In this section we first describe the bag-of-visterms (BOV) image modeling methodology. We then introduce the considered local features used in this paper, and finally introduce the considered fusion schemes.

3.1   Bag-of-Visterms Representation from Local Descriptors

The construction of the BOV feature vector h from an image d involves the steps illustrated in Fig. 1. In brief, interest points are automatically detected in the image, then local descriptors are computed over those regions. These descriptors are quantized into visterms, and the number of occurrences of each specific visterm of the vocabulary are counted to build the image BOV representation. In the following we describe in more detail each step involved in the construction of the BOV representation.

Interest Point Detection. The goal of interest point detectors is to automatically extract characteristic points -and more generally regions- from the image, which are invariant to some geometric and photometric transformations. This invariance ensures that given an image and its transformed version, the same points will be extracted from both and hence, the same image representation will be obtained. Several interest point detectors exist in the literature. They vary mostly by the amount of invariance they theoretically ensure, the image property they exploit to achieve invariance, and the type of image structures they are designed to detect [2,17].

In this work, we use the difference of Gaussians (DOG) point detector [2]. This detector essentially identifies blob-like regions where a maximum or minimum of intensity occurs in the image, it is invariant to translation, scale, rotation and constant illumination variations. This detector was selected for the following reasons. First, it was shown to perform well w.r.t. other detectors [17]. Second, since it defines regions that are homogeneous, it is more adapted to the computation of color descriptors (e.g. mean colors) than, for instance, edge corners (Harris detector). Finally, as an increase of the degree of invariance may remove information about the local image content that is valuable for classification, the DOG detector is preferable than fully affine-invariant ones [1,18].

Local Descriptors. Local descriptors (SIFT or color moments, see next Subsection) are computed on the region around each interest point detected by the local interest point detector.

Quantization and Vocabulary Model Construction. When applying the two preceeding steps to a given image, we obtain a set of real-valued local descriptors. We then quantize each local descriptor into one of a discrete set $\mathcal{V}$ of visterms v according to a nearest neighbor rule:

$$\mathbf{v} \longmapsto Q(\mathbf{v}) = v_i \iff \mathrm{dist}_Q(\mathbf{v}, v_i) \leq \mathrm{dist}_Q(\mathbf{v}, v_j) \qquad \forall j \in \{1, \ldots, N_{\mathcal{V}}\} \qquad (1)$$

where $N_{\mathcal{V}}$ denotes the size of the vocabulary (the set of all visterms). The vocabulary is constructed by applying the K-means algorithm to the set of local descriptors extracted from the training images, and keeping the means as visterms. Except in the fusion case (see Section 3.3), we used the Euclidean distance in the clustering. As for vocabulary size, we used 1000 clusters since it has been shown that little performance can be gained by increasing this number [4,5] when using texture visterms. However, when building a joint color-texture vocabulary, 2000 clusters were considered as detailed in Section 3.3.

Bag-of-Visterms Representation. Finally, the BOV representation of the image is constructed from the local descriptors according to:

$$h(d) = (h_i(d))_{i=1..N_{\mathcal{V}}}, \text{ with } h_i(d) = \mathrm{n}(d, v_i) \qquad (2)$$

where $\mathrm{n}(d, v_i)$ denotes the number of occurrences of visterm v_i in image d. This vector-space representation of an image contains no information about spatial relationship between visterms.

3.2   Local Descriptors

In this work, two local descriptors were considered: SIFT (Scale Invariant Feature Transform) [2], representing local texture/structure information, and Luv color moments. The choice of SIFT was motivated by the findings of several publications [6,17,5], where SIFT was found to work among the best on several tasks. For color, the use of the Luv color space was motivated by the fact that it is a perceptual color space (it was designed to linearize the perception of color distances) and that it has also been known to perform well in both retrieval and recognition applications [9,16]. A description of both features follows:

- **SIFT descriptor $\mathbf{v}_s$:** this descriptor is based on the gray-scale image. SIFT features are local histograms of edge directions computed over different parts of the interest region. They capture the structure of local image regions, which correspond to specific geometric configurations of edges or to more texture-like content. In [2], it was shown that the use of 8 orientation directions and a 4×4 grid gives a good compromise between descriptor size and accuracy of representation. The final feature size is thus 128. Orientation invariance is achieved by estimating the dominant orientation of the local image patch and normalizing for rotation. For a more compact representation, we applied a principal component analysis (PCA) decomposition on this features using training data. By keeping 95% of the energy, we obtain a 44-dimensional feature vector. The PCA step did not increase or decrease performance, but allowed for faster clustering.
- **Luv descriptor $\mathbf{v}_c$:** it is based on 121 Luv values computed on a 11×11 grid normalized to cover the local area given by the interest point detector. From these values, we calculate the mean and standard deviation for each dimension and concatenate the result into a 6-dimensional vector. Each dimension of this vector are then normalized to unit variance so that L (luminance) does not dominate the distance metric.

3.3   Feature Fusion

We investigated two fusion strategies, addressing two different aspects of early fusion [19].

Fusion 1. In this approach, we fused the real valued SIFT and color features before quantization, in order to obtain a joint color/texture vocabulary (see top of Fig 1). The fusion occurs by concatenating the sift feature $\mathbf{v}_s$ and color feature $\mathbf{v}_c$, after normalization, and weighted by a mixing value α according to:

$$\mathbf{v} = (\alpha \mathbf{v}_s^{\star}, (1-\alpha)\mathbf{v}_c^{\star}) \text{ with } \mathbf{v}_s^{\star} = \beta_s \mathbf{v}_s \text{ and } \mathbf{v}_c^{\star} = \beta_c \mathbf{v}_c \qquad (3)$$

The normalization factor β_s (resp. β_c) is learned by setting it to the inverse of the average euclidian distance between 50000 random pairs of SIFT (resp. color) features. These values were found to be: $\beta_s =60$ and $\beta_c =1.6$. As a consequence of this concatenation, using a euclidian distance dist_Q in the Kmeans algorithm, we end up with a weighted distance between the two feature type distances:

$$\text{dist}_Q(\mathbf{v}^1, \mathbf{v}^2) = \alpha \, \text{dist}_Q(\mathbf{v}_s^{\star,1}, \mathbf{v}_s^{\star,2}) + (1-\alpha) \, \text{dist}_Q(\mathbf{v}_c^{\star,1}, \mathbf{v}_c^{\star,2}) \qquad (4)$$

where the distance between feature types is approximately of the same order of magnitude. The value of α is learned through cross-validation on training data.

Fusion 2. Here (bottom part of Fig. 1), we assumed that the two feature types (SIFT, color) were independent, and fused the features by concatenating their BOV representation, again using a mixing value α, i.e. $h = (\alpha h_s, (1-\alpha)h_c)$. The use of the mixing value is necessary to allow the weighting of the different BOV representation in the SVM classifier (see next Section).

4   Experimental Setup

In this section we describe the database we used, the protocol we followed, and the baseline system used for comparison.

4.1   Database

We use the database kindly provided to us by Vogel et. al. [15], and which is constituted of 6 different natural scenes type images. This data set contains a total of 700 images of resolution 720×480 pixels, distributed over the 6 natural scene classes as follows: coasts (142), river/lakes (111), forests (103), plains (131), mountains (179), and sky/clouds (34). We chose this data because of its good resolution and color. Additionally, it is the only available public database we found which contained several natural classes. A drawback, however, is that the database has some non negligeable overlap between classes (e.g. an image belonging to a given class could also easily belong to another class given its content). This is a property originally introduced as part of the database to evaluate human classification performance.

4.2   Classifier and Evaluation Protocol

In all our experiments, we used a multi-class Support Vector Machine (SVM) for classification. To perform experiments, we adopted a 10-fold training/testing protocol. That is, data is split into 10 folds, and for each fold, all parameters (quantization, mixing value α, SVM capacity) are trained on the remaining 90% data, and the learned system is tested on the given fold. The presented class performance corresponds to the averages over the 10 runs, and the overall system performance is the macro average of the class performance.

4.3   State-of-the-Art Baselines

Baseline of [15]. We considered as first baseline the approach introduced along with the database [15]. In that work, the image was divided into a grid of 10×10 blocks, and on each block, a feature vector composed of a 84-bin HSI histogram, a 72-bin edge histogram, and a 24 features grey-level co-occorence matrix was computed. These features were concatenated after normalization and weighting, and used to classify (with an SVM) each block into one of 9 local semantic classes (water, sand, foliage, grass,...). In a second stage, the 9 dimensional vector containing the image occurence percentage of each regional concept was used as

Table 1. Classification performance for the SIFT based BOV representation (left). Sample patches belonging to three visterms.

Class	confusion matrix						performance
coasts	61.3	9.9	1.4	9.2	17.6	0.7	61.3
river/lakes	18.0	30.6	9.9	12.6	24.3	4.5	30.6
forests	0.0	0.0	90.3	2.9	6.8	0.0	90.3
plains	15.3	11.5	6.1	55.7	7.6	3.8	55.7
mountains	10.1	6.1	2.8	6.1	73.7	1.1	73.7
sky/clouds	14.7	2.9	0.0	14.7	0.0	67.6	67.6
overall							63.2

Table 2. Classification results for the Luv color space based BOV representation. Sample patches belonging to three random visterms.

Class	confusion matrix						performance
coasts	49.3	16.9	2.8	12.7	15.5	2.8	49.3
river/lakes	21.6	31.5	9.0	7.2	30.6	0.0	31.5
forests	4.9	8.7	70.9	7.8	7.8	0.0	70.9
plains	9.2	9.2	6.9	53.4	16.8	4.6	53.4
mountains	12.3	12.3	1.7	14.0	59.2	0.6	59.2
sky/clouds	14.7	11.8	0.0	14.7	0.0	58.8	58.8
overall							53.9

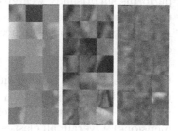

input to an SVM classifier to classify images into one of the 6 scene classes. The reported performance of that approach were good: 67,2%[1].

Color Histogram. In order to compare the results obtained with our color-only visterm BOV representation against a more traditional color histogram approach, we used a concatenated Luv 96-bins linear histogram (32 bins for each dimension: L, u, and v).

5   Results

In this section, we first present the classification performance when using a single information source (texture or color), and then using the fusion schemes.

5.1   SIFT and Color Visterm BOV Classification Performance

Let us first explore the classification results obtained using the BOV representation constructed from each feature type separately.

---

[1] Note however that the approach of [15] requires much more work than ours, as labeled data (image blocks with labels) to train the intermediate regional concept classifier are necessary. In [15], approx. 70000 blocks were manually labeled!

Table 3. Classification results with the first fusion strategy: joint texture/color visterms. Sample patches belonging to three visterms.

Class	confusion matrix						performance
coasts	69.0	8.5	2.1	7.7	10.6	2.1	69.0
river/lakes	21.6	28.8	9.0	11.7	26.1	2.7	28.8
forests	1.9	1.9	85.4	2.9	7.8	0.0	85.4
plains	9.2	9.2	2.3	62.6	12.2	4.6	62.6
mountains	8.4	5.6	1.1	5.6	77.7	1.7	77.7
sky/clouds	5.9	0.0	0.0	14.7	2.9	76.5	76.5
overall							66.7

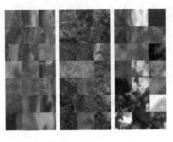

SIFT Features. Table 1 provides the result obtained with the SIFT based BOV representation. While being slightly lower than the baseline, this approach performs surprisingly well given that no color information is used. This is illustrated by the sample patches belonging to 3 different visterms (Table 1, right). As can be seen (and as expected), visterm patches have no coherence in terms of color.

Color Features. Table 2 shows the results obtained using the Luv color visterms. Although significantly smaller than the performance obtain with SIFT visterms, the result is still relatively good given the features' simplicity (6 dimensions). Overall, all classes are affected by the performance degradation. Surprisingly, the forest class gets the most degradation, indicating that there is more reliable information in the local structure than in the color. When observing samples associated to some visterms (Table 2, right), we can see that the goal of color coherence is achieved, but that coherence in terms of texture/structure is mainly lost (there remain some coherence due to the specific interest point detector employed). To further analyse the performance of our BOV approach, we compared it with a simple Luv color histogram (see Section 4.3). The system performance in this latter case exhibited a strong performance drop, achieving a 34.1% recognition rate. This illustrates the necessity for both a data-driven and local approach, embedded in out BOV representation, as compared to global approaches based on more arbitrary color representations.

5.2   Fusion Classification Performance

We now present the classification results combining color and texture information in the BOV representation, as presented in Section 3.3.

Fusion 1. In this approach, local features are concatenated prior to clustering, resulting in a joint texture/color vocabulary of 2000 visterms. The average mixing value α obtained through cross-validation was 0.8, indicating that more importance was given to the SIFT feature. Table 3 displays the results obtained in this case. These results shows an overall improvement w.r.t. those based on the SIFT feature alone, and are very close to the baseline results (67.2%). The

Table 4. Classification results with the second fusion strategy: concatenation of the texture and color BOV representation

Class	confusion matrix						performance
coasts	58.5	13.4	1.4	13.4	10.6	2.8	58.5
river/lakes	20.7	36.0	7.2	9.9	23.4	2.7	36.0
forests	1.9	1.0	89.3	2.9	4.9	0.0	89.3
plains	12.2	6.1	6.9	64.1	7.6	3.1	64.1
mountains	6.1	7.3	3.4	6.7	76.0	0.6	76.0
sky/clouds	14.7	0.0	0.0	11.8	0.0	73.5	73.5
overall							66.2

Fig. 2. Images illustrating the resulting classification of the evaluated systems. Ground-truth is shown on the top left corner. On the bottom are all attributed labels: SIFT BOV, Color BOV, feature fusion and histogram fusion (from left to right).

sky/clouds class is the one that beneficiate mostly from the improvement, with a reduction of its overlap with the coasts class.

When looking at the constructed vocabulary, we observe that visterms have coherence in both texture and color, as illustrated in Table 3. However, since now both features influence the clustering process, we notice an increase of the noise level in both color and texture coherence within the clusters.

Fusion 2. In this second strategy, it is assumed that, at the interest point level, information gathered from color is independent from texture/structure information. This strategy thus works by concatenating the BOV representation of color and texture, after having them weighted by the factor α. Interestingly enough, the optimal α value was again found to be 0.8, showing again an emphasis on information arising from the SIFT features. Table 4 shows the obtained results. These are nearly identical to those obtained with the first fusion strategy, and again very close to those of the baseline.

Overall, the results are encouraging, and demonstrate that the two approaches are valid for the scene classification task. Both fusion approaches performed significantly better than grey-scale BOV representation. The fact that both approaches reach similar results to the baseline may indicate that we are reaching the performance limit that may be obtained in this data when not using any spatial information. Figure 2 shows some images with the labels attributed by each systems we tested. We can see that some labels are subjective. For some images several possible labels could be considered correct. As such some of the errors that the systems produce seem logical. This indicates that the BOV representation captures valid scene properties, however this dataset does not supply a clear enough class definition for the training of the systems.

6   Conclusion

We investigated the use of color information, in addition to texture, to represent scene images with BOV relying on interest point detectors. Two fusion schemes were proposed and tested on a 6 class scene recognition task. They have shown that a small but significant gain in classification performance can be achieved w.r.t. texture only BOV representation. The obtained performances are similar to a state-of-the-art approach that requires much more supervised training. We believe that the proposed fusion schemes can easily be applied to other tasks.

Several extensions to the proposed BOV framework could be investigated to improve scene classification results. For instance, some invariance could be removed in the SIFT descriptor computation: recent studies in object recognition have shown that eliminating the rotation invariance usually leads to better results. Or, as the BOV discards all image spatial information, it would be interesting to reintroduce this information, for instance by computing regional BOV.

Acknowledgements

The authors acknowledge financial support by the Swiss National Center of Competence in Research (NCCR) on Interactive Multimodal Information Management (IM)2, and by the MULTImodal Interaction and MULTImedia Data-Mining (MULTI) project. Both projects are managed the Swiss National Science Foundation on behalf of the federal authorities.

References

1. Mikolajczyk, K., Schmid, C.: Scale and affine interest point detectors. International Journal of Computer Vision **60** (2004) 63–86
2. Lowe, D.G.: Distinctive image features from scale-invariant keypoints. International Journal of Computer Vision **60** (2004) 91–110
3. Willamowski, J., Arregui, D., Csurka, G., Dance, C., Fan, L.: Categorizing nine visual classes using local appearance descriptors. In: Proc. of LAVS Workshop, in ICPR'04, Cambridge (2004)
4. Quelhas, P., Monay, F., Odobez, J.M., Gatica-Perez, D., Tuytelaars, T., Gool, L.V.: Modeling scenes with local descriptors and latent aspects. In: Proc. of IEEE Int. Conf. on Computer Vision, Beijing (2005)

5. Fei-Fei, L., Perona, P.: A Bayesian hierarchical model for learning natural scene categories. In: Proc .of. IEEE Int. Conf. on Computer Vision And Pattern Recognition, San Diego (2005)
6. Sivic, J., Zisserman, A.: Video google: A text retrieval approach to object matching in videos. In: Proc. of IEEE Int. Conf. on Computer Vision, Nice (2003)
7. Sivic, J., Russell, B.C., Efros, A.A., Zisserman, A., Freeman, W.T.: Discovering object categories in image collections. In: Proc. of IEEE Int. Conf. on Computer Vision, Beijing (2005)
8. Dorko, G., Schmid, C.: Selection of scale invariant parts for object class recognition. In: Proc. of IEEE Int. Conference on Computer Vision, Nice (2003)
9. Vailaya, A., Figueiredo, M., Jain, A., Zhang, H.: Image classification for content-based indexing. IEEE Trans. on Image Processing **10** (2001) 117–130
10. Szummer, M., Picard, R.: Indoor-outdoor image classification. In: IEEE International Workshop CAIVD, in ICCV'98, Bombay (1998)
11. Oliva, A., Torralba, A., Guerin-Dugue, A., Herault, J.: Global semantic classification of scenes using power spectrum templates. In: Proc. of the Challenge of Image Retrieval, Newcastle upon Tyne, UK (1999)
12. Paek, S., S.-F., C.: A knowledge engineering approach for image classification based on probabilistic reasoning systems. In: Proc. of IEEE Int. Conference on Multimedia and Expo, New York (2000)
13. Smeulders, A., Worring, M., Santini, S., Gupta, A., Jain, R.: Content-based image retrieval at the end of the early years. IEEE Trans. on Pattern Analysis and Machine Intelligence **22** (2000) 1349–1380
14. Serrano, N., Savakis, A., Luo, J.: A computationally efficent approach to indoor/outdoor scene classification. In: Int. Conf. on Pattern Recognition. (2002)
15. Vogel, J., Schiele, B.: A semantic typicality measure for natural scene categorization. In: Pattern Recognition Symposium DAGM'04, Tübingen, Germany (2004)
16. Boutell, M., Luo, J., Shen, X., C.M.Brown: Learning multi-label scene classification. Pattern Recognition **37** (2004) 1757–1771
17. Mikolajczyk, K., Schmid, C.: A performance evaluation of local descriptors. In: Proc. of IEEE Int. Conf. on Comp. Vision and Pattern Recognition. (2003)
18. Matas, J., Chum, O., Martin, U., Pajdla, T.: Robust wide baseline stereo from maximally stable extremal regions. In: Proc. of the British Machine Vision Conference, Cardiff (2002)
19. Kittler, J., Hatef, M., Duin, R., Matas, J.: On combining classifiers. IEEE PAMI **20** (1998) 226–239

Online Image Retrieval System Using Long Term Relevance Feedback

Lutz Goldmann, Lars Thiele, and Thomas Sikora

Technical University of Berlin, Communication Systems Group,
Einsteinufer 17, 10587 Berlin, Germany

Abstract. This paper describes an original system for content based image retrieval. It is based on MPEG-7 descriptors and a novel approach for long term relevance feedback using a Bayesian classifier. Each image is represented by a special model that is adapted over multiple feedback rounds and even multiple sessions or users. The experiments show its outstanding performance in comparison to often used short term relevance feedback and the recently proposed FIRE system.

1 Introduction

Recently the world wide web has become one of largest repositories of multimedia data, such as images, audio and video. For searching images a large amount of content based image retrieval (CBIR) systems have been proposed.

In the beginning most of them utilized techniques from text retrieval systems and thus relied on textual annotations (keywords). These systems are rather impractical due to the following reasons: On the one hand it is nearly impossible to provide a manual annotation for a large number of images and on the other hand these descriptions are usually incomplete or ambiguious. The latter problem is called the "linguistic gap" that describes the discrepancy between the semantic meaning and the textual description. Thus the direct description of the visual content using visual low level descriptors such as color, texture and shape gained more and more interest[1]. Since these descriptors typically describe only the low level properties of the visual content they can not provide a reliable high level (semantic) description of it. This discrepancy between the visual description and the semantic meaning is known as the "semantic gap". It can be decreased for very restricted applications but remains for general image retrieval tasks. Another problem is the "semantic ambiguity" that describes the varying semantic meaning for different users. Both problems can be handled by incorporating the user into the retrieval process, which is known as relevance feedback (RF).

Existing content based image retrieval systems can be categorized based on several criteria including the year of proposal, the approach (query by example, relevance feedback), if they utilize incremental learning or not, if the images are described globally, locally or based on regions, and what visual features and learning approaches are used. Table 1 gives an overview of recent systems along with the corresponding characteristics. In order to enable a comparison to the other systems, the proposed system is considered as well.

H. Sundaram et al. (Eds.): CIVR 2006, LNCS 4071, pp. 422–431, 2006.
© Springer-Verlag Berlin Heidelberg 2006

Table 1. Overview of available systems

Abbreviation	Year	Appr.	Incr.	Description	Features	Techniques
a-Lip[2]	2003	QE	No	Local	LUV color, Wavelets	2D MHMM
CIRES[3]	2002	QE	No	Global	Color table, Gabor filters, structuring elements	Statical feature weighting
FIRE[4]	2004	RF	No	Global	Invariant feature histogram	Score based
ImageRover[5]	1997	RF	No	Local	Color histogram, texture	Distance based
IRMA[6]	2003	QE	No	Regions	Frequency, texture and structural features	Segmentation, graph matching
MiAlbum[7]	2001	RF	Yes	Global	HSV color histogram, LUV coherence vector, Tamura coarseness and directionality	Bayesian classifier
SIMBA[8]	2001	RF	No	Global	Invariant feature histogram, color and texture features	Manual feature weighting
SIMPLIcity[9]	2001	QE	No	Regions	Wavelets	Segmentation, classification, region matching
Proposed		RF	Yes	Global, local	Edge histogram descriptor, Homogenous texture descriptor, Color layout descriptor, Local average LUV descriptor	Bayesian classifier, Automatic feature weighting

As it can be seen only half of the systems utilize relevance feedback and only very few of them combine it with incremental learning. Only this combination enables users to benefit from previous sessions. Although all system use color and texture features, only some of them consider local or region based features which seems necessary to distinguish images reliably.

Only the "MiAlbum" system developed by Su et al.[7,10] utilizes an approach similar to the proposed system. The main differences are the incremental learning method, the visual low level descriptors and that the proposed system works online[1]. Although we utilize a Bayesian classifier similar to "MiAlbum" the actual learning approach is different. The proposed system is based on MPEG-7 compliant visual descriptors[11] which provide a rich and exchangeable description of the visual characteristics of the images. Furthermore, local and global features are considered, which allow a description on different levels of abstraction. By supporting different initial queries, such as random sample and query by example, the user can influence the session from the beginning depending on the available resources. The combination of these techniques leads to outstanding retrieval results as it will be shown in section 3.

2 System Overview

The proposed system consists of an *offline* and an *online* part. In the former part all the data preprocessing is done, which includes the extraction of the visual descriptors and their normalization. Furthermore their values and informations about the corresponding images are stored in a database to enable efficient and uniform access. In the latter part the actual image retrieval using relevance feedback is done. It starts by offering two different possibilities for the initial

---

[1] http://mpeg7im.nue.tu-berlin.de/imatchRelevance/

search (random sample, query by example) and goes on with the iterative search consisting of user interaction, relevance feedback and display. In the following sessions the most important parts of the overall system are explained.

2.1 Feature Extraction

Each image is represented by a set of features that can be automatically extracted. Both color and texture as well as global and local features are used to obtain a rich description of the image. Beside a novel feature various MPEG-7 descriptors[11] are utilized. The follwing paragraphs describe the descriptors in more detail.

Homogeneous Texture Descriptor (HTD). The HTD is proposed in the MPEG-7 visual standard for describing homogeneous textures in an image. It is based on the human perception of textures and describes them in polar coordinates using 6 orientations and 5 scales. It is extracted using 30 Gabor filters (6 different orientations and 5 different scales), which are applied in the frequency domain. Therefore the image is transformed using a combination of the Radon transform and a one-dimensional Fourier transform. For each of the Gabor filters the energy mean and standard deviation of the filter response with the image is calculated. The final feature vector consists of mean and standard deviation values of the spatial domain and 30 mean and standard deviation values of the frequency domain.

Edge Histogram Descriptor (EHD). The MPEG-7 EHD can be used to describe local edge characteristics. It can be interpreted as multiple localized edge histograms, that describe the amount of certain edge types, such as vertical, horizontal, 45 degree diagonal, 135 degree diagonal and non-directional edges. The image is divided into 4x4 subimages and into 1100 blocks that are assigned to the corresponding subimages. For each of these blocks the edge type is determined using different Haar-like filters which lead to an edge amplitude for each of the possible edges. If the highest edge amplitude is larger than a certain threshold the corresponding edge is assigned to that block. Otherwise the block is considered to contain no edges. For each subimage the ratios of the individual edge types are calculated by averaging all blocks within the subimage. Furthermore 3 semi-global (row, column, block) and 1 global histograms can be calculated by combining the histograms of certain subimages. Altogether this yields a feature vector with 150 elements.

Color Layout Descriptor (CLD. The CLD, defined in the MPEG-7 standard, decribes the global color distribution of the image using the frequency domain. The image is converted into YCbCr color space and subsampled to a 64x64 image. For each channel the discrete cosine transform (DCT) is applied independently leading to a representation where the energy is concentrated in the lower cofficients only. After a zig-zag-scan and a non-linear quantization the first 6 coefficients, corresponding to the low frequencies, are selected as the final features for each channel. Thus the feature vector consists of 18 elements.

Local Average LUV Descriptor (LALD). The proposed LALD provides a straight forward way to describe the local color characteristics using 4x4 subimages, similar to the EHD. First the image is converted into LUV color space, which was chosen due to its closeness to the human perception. For each of the subimages the mean and the variance of the pixels are computed for each color channel independently. This leads to a feature vector of 96 elements.

2.2   Preprocessing

3σ-Normalization. In order to obtain unique ranges for the individual features within a feature vector and over different feature vectors normalization needs to be applied. Since the distributions of each feature x_i can be approximated by a Gaussian distributions with mean μ_i and standard deviation σ_i a 3σ-normalization is applied. Each feature x_i is normalized to $y_i = (x_i - \mu_i)/(3\sigma_i)$ and clipped within the range $y_i \in [-1, 1]$.

Principal Component Analysis. The principal component analysis (PCA) allows to reduce the number of features by finding the optimal decorrelated basis $\mathbf{V}$ of a feature matrix $\mathbf{X}$ and discarding components with less information. This can be useful to avoid the "curse of dimensionality" and decrease the computational complexity in the case of high-dimensional feature vectors. It is based on the eigenvalue decomposition of the covariance matrix $\mathbf{C}_x$ which calculates the eigenvectors $\boldsymbol{v}_i$ and the corresponding eigenvalues λ_i. By sorting λ_i in descending order and discarding the eigenvectors of lower order eigenvalues a reduced basis $\mathbf{V} = (\boldsymbol{v}_1, \boldsymbol{v}_2, \dots)$ can be built. The decorrelated and reduced feature vector $\boldsymbol{y}$ is obtained by projecting $\boldsymbol{x}$ onto $\mathbf{V}$ as $\boldsymbol{y} = \mathbf{V}^T \boldsymbol{x}$.

2.3   Relevance Feedback

In this system relevance feedback is treated as a classification task. Based on the relevant images $j \in J$, selected by the user, a model M is trained that describes the common characteristics of these selected images. This model is compared to all the images $k \in K$ in the database and either the most relevant or most informative images are returned based on the minimum distance criterion $k' = \arg\min_k d_k$. Both non-incremental and incremental learning are considered, depending on whether short term or long term relevance feedback is used.

Minimum Distance Classifier. The minimum distance classifier (MDC) models each class j by the mean vector $\boldsymbol{\mu}_j$ of the provided examples. For an unknown example $\boldsymbol{x}$ the distance $d_j(\boldsymbol{x})$ is simply the Euclidian distance between $\boldsymbol{x}$ and $\boldsymbol{\mu}_j$ which is defined as

$$d_j(\boldsymbol{x}) = \sum_i (x_i - \mu_{ji})^2 \tag{1}$$

The minimum distance classifier is solely used for short term learning.

Bayesian Classifier. An optimal statistical classifier minimizes the probability of missclassifications and can be built by utilizing the maximum a posteriori (MAP) criterion. The posteriori propability $p(j|x)$ of a class j can be calculated from the prior probability $p(j)$ and the likelihood $p(x|j)$ using Bayes rule:

$$p_j(x) = p(j|x) = p(x|j)p(j)$$

Usually a multivariate Gaussian density is used to characterize the distribution of the feature vector x with the probability density function

$$p(x|j) = \frac{1}{(2\pi)^{d/2}|C_x|^{1/2}} \exp(-1/2(x - \mu_j)^T C_j^{-1}(x - \mu_j))$$

With the assumptions that the features x_i are orthogonal and independent to each other, classes having equal prior probabilities and that all images are compared to one class only the logarithmic posterior probability can be calculated as

$$p(x) = -\frac{1}{2}\sum_i \left(\frac{x_i - \mu_i}{\sigma_i}\right)^2$$

Maximizing this probability can also be expressed as minimizing the distance $d(x)$ which is defined as:

$$d(x) = \frac{1}{2}\sum_i \left(\frac{x_i - \mu_i}{\sigma_i}\right)^2 \tag{2}$$

The Bayes classifier is used for short term (non-incremental) and long term (incremental) relevance feedback. The differences between the individual modes is how the model $M = (\mu, \sigma)$ is obtained.

Short Term Relevance Feedback. In short term RF the learning is restricted to the actual round only. That means the actual feedback has no influence on the learning of further rounds or even further sessions. Thus it is also called non-incremental learning. The model $M = (\mu, \sigma)$ solely built based on the joint information of the actual set of relevant images $j \in J$ and is given by

$$\mu_i = \frac{1}{|J|}\sum_j x_{ji}; \; \sigma_i^2 = \frac{1}{|J|}\sum_j (x_{ji} - \mu_i)^2$$

Long Term Relevance Feedback. Here, in contrast to the short term RF, the model M is built from combined information of the set of relevant images and from the individual past of each image j individually. Therefore each image is described by an individual model $M_j = (\mu_j, \sigma_j, n_j)$ with that is updated in every iteration using the following equations

$$n'_j = n_j + |J|$$

$$\mu'_{ji} = \frac{1}{n'_j} \left(n_j \mu_{ji} + n \mu_i \right)$$

$$\sigma'^2_{ji} = \frac{1}{n'_j - 1} \left((n_j - 1)\sigma^2_{ji} + n_j \mu^2_{ji} - n'_j \mu'^2_{ji} + \sum_j x^2_{ji} \right)$$

Finally the parameters of the combined model $M = (\bar{\mu}, \bar{\sigma})$ are calculated by averaging the mean and variance vectors of the updated image models $M'_j = (\boldsymbol{\mu}'_j, \boldsymbol{\sigma}'_j, n'_j)$

$$\bar{\mu}_i = \frac{\sum_j n'_{ji} \mu'_{ji}}{\sum_j n'_{ji}}; \quad \bar{\sigma}_i = \frac{\sum_j n'_{ji} \sigma'_{ji}}{\sum_j n'_{ji}}$$

Weigth Adaption. For each of the feature vectors $f \in \{\text{HTD}, \text{EHD}, \text{CLD}, \text{LALD}\}$ the distance d_f is calculated using equation 2. The overall distance d is then given by

$$d = \sum_f w_f d_f \tag{3}$$

with the weights w_f. These weights can be set according to the selection strategies. For *most relevant* images the feature vector f with the lowest average variance $\tilde{\sigma}$ gets the highest weight. On the other hand for *most informative* images the feature vector f with the highest average variance $\tilde{\sigma}$ gets the highest weight. The average variance $\tilde{\sigma}$ is calculated by averaging all elements of the variance vector $\bar{\sigma}$.

3 Experiments

3.1 Databases

Different image databases are available that can be used to demostrate or evaluate CBIR systems. The following databases have been used: Corel Gallery Magic 65000[2] (Corel), Wangs Subset of the Corel Gallery[3] (Wang), Data Backer Premium Cliparts[4] (DataBecker), The Caltech-101 Object Categories[5] (Caltech) and the Butterfly Database[6] (Butterfly). Table 2 provides an overview of these databases and some of their characteristics.

While all these databases can be used in the online system, the experiments shown here are only based on the Wang database. Nevertheless similar results can be achieved using the other databases.

---

[2] ISBN: K8483417
[3] URL: http://wang.ist.psu.edu
[4] ISBN: 2815868203
[5] URL: http://www.vision.caltech.edu/feifeili/Datasets.htm
[6] http://www-cvr.ai.ai.uiuc.edu/ponce_grp/data

Table 2. Overview of the used databases and their characteristics

Abbreviation	Resolution	Number	Content	Annotation
Corel	384x256	40000	Various	Categories
Wang	384x256	1000	Various	10 categories
DataBecker	ca. 500x900	20000	Various	Multiple keywords
Caltech	Different	9144	Various	101 categories
Butterfly	Different	619	Butterflies	7 categories

3.2 Evaluation Measures

The evaluation of content-based image retrieval systems is usually based on available ground truth data. For the following experiments "Wangs Corel Selection" was used which provides categories that can serve as ground truth data. Based on this well-known measures such as precision P and recall P can be computed. Varying the number of retrieved images N leads to multiple (P, R) pairs that can be visualized as so called precision vs. recall curves. Furthermore, Müller et al.[12] proposed some evaluation measures such as $\widetilde{Rank}$, $P(N)$, $R(P = 0.5)$, $R(N)$ and $R(P = R)$. Both the PR-curves and these supporting measures are considered for the following experiments.

3.3 Results

Normalization. The first set of experiments was conducted to compare the performance of the short term relevance feedback using MDC and BC with or without normalization.

Figure 1 shows the resulting PR-curves. In general normalization improves the results for both approaches. The gain for the BC is much larger than that for the MDC, which shows that normalization is a crucial step for using a BC. In cases where normalization cannot be applied the MDC outperforms the BC. On the other hand the BC is the better choice if the feature vectors are normalized. These facts are supported by the objective measures in table 3.

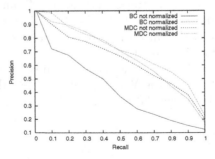

Fig. 1. PR curves for different short term approaches (MDC, BC) with/without normalization

Table 3. Objective measures for different short term approaches (MDC, BC) with/without normalization

	Norm.	Rank	P(N=20)	P(N=50)	P(N=100)	R(P=0.5)	R(N=100)	R(R=P)
MDC	No	0.1063	0.84	0.75	0.61	0.63	0.61	0.61
MDC	Yes	0.0946	0.92	0.80	0.61	0.68	0.61	0.61
BC	No	0.2082	0.71	0.57	0.40	0.27	0.40	0.40
BC	Yes	0.0823	0.91	0.81	0.65	0.64	0.65	0.65

Principal Component Analysis. The goal of this set of experiments was to analyze the influence of the feature reduction using PCA on the performance of the different short term approaches (MDC, BC). Therefore the dimensions of the feature vectors were successively reduced from 100% to 3%. Figure 2(a) and 2(b) show the resulting PR curves for the MDC and the BC respectively. Concerning the reduction of dimensionality it turns out that a reduction to 75% results only in a small performance loss for the MDC and the BC as well. Below that the performance decreases considerably, with the BC dropping faster than the MDC. Table 4 provides a more extensive comparison of the perfomance without applying PCA and utilizing a PCA with 75% of the original dimensions. As it can be seen the performance loss is mainly in the precision which drops about 8% while the recall drops between 1% and 4% depending on the used classifier.

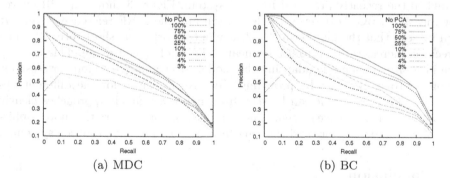

(a) MDC   (b) BC

Fig. 2. PR curves for different approaches and PCA with different dimensions

Table 4. Objective measures for different short term approaches and PCA

	PCA	Rank	P(N=20)	P(N=50)	P(N=100)	R(P=0.5)	R(N=100)	R(P=R)
MDC	No	0.0946	0.92	0.80	0.61	0.68	0.61	0.61
MDC	75%	0.1054	0.84	0.75	0.60	0.64	0.60	0.60
BC ST	No	0.0823	0.91	0.81	0.65	0.64	0.65	0.65
BC ST	75%	0.1110	0.84	0.74	0.61	0.60	0.61	0.61

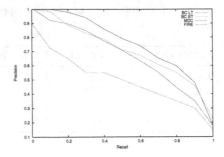

Fig. 3. PR curves for MDC, short and long term BC and FIRE system

Table 5. Objective measures for the short and long term BC and the MDC

	Rank	P(N=20)	P(N=50)	P(N=100)	R(P=0.5)	R(N=100)	R(P=R)
MDC	0.0946	0.92	0.92	0.80	0.61	0.61	0.61
BC ST	0.0823	0.91	0.81	0.65	0.64	0.65	0.65
BC LT	0.0599	0.98	0.87	0.70	0.77	0.70	0.70

Short Term vs. Long Term Relevance Feedback. Finally the performance of the short and the long term relevance feedback based on the BC are compared to each other in order to justify the developed approach. Furthermore it is compared to the recently proposed FIRE[4] system. Figure 3 shows the PR curves for the MDC, BC short term, BC long term and the FIRE reference system. It can be seen that the long term RF clearly outperforms the short term RF. The precision increases by up to 9% for nearly the whole recall range. This justifies the idea of incrementally adapting the models over multiple rounds or sessions. Table 5 proves this fact by providing objective measures for the different approaches. Furthermore it can be seen from figure 3 that all approaches clearly outperform the reference system. The main reason for that are the more sophisticated visual descriptors and the long term RF used in the proposed system.

4   Conclusion

In this paper an original system for content based image retrieval has been proposed, that utilizes a Bayesian classifier combined with an incremental learning strategy to support long term relevance feedback. MPEG-7 descriptors and novel color descriptor are used for describing color and texture characteristics both locally and globally. The experiments show that this combination leads to a very efficient system that clearly outperforms the FIRE reference system.

Future work will consider the use of positive and negative relevance feedback, other learning approaches such as support vector machines and different strategies to incorporate the feedback from different users.

References

1. Crucianu, M., Ferecatu, M., Boujemaa, N.: Relevance feedback for image retrieval: a short survey. (2004)
2. Li, J., Wang, J.Z.: Automatic linguistic indexing of pictures by a statistical modeling approach. (2003)
3. Iqbal, Q., Aggarwal, J.K.: CIRES: A system for content-based retrieval in digital image libraries. In: ICARCV. (2002)
4. Deselaers, T., Keysers, D., Ney, H.: Fire - flexible image retrieval engine: Imageclef 2004. (2004)
5. Sclaroff, S., Taycher, L., Cascia, M.L.: Imagerover: A content-based image browser for the world wide web. In: IEEE Workshop on Content-based Access of Image and Video Libraries. (June 1997)
6. Lehmann, T.M., Glüd, M.O., Thies, C., Plodowski, B., Keysers, D., other: Content-Based Image Retrieval in Medical Applications. Aachen University of Technology (RWTH). (2003)
7. Su, Z., Zhang, H., Ma, S.: Relevance feedback using a bayesian classifier in content-based image retrieval (2001)
8. Siggelkow, S., Schael, M., Burkhardt, H.: SIMBA — Search IMages By Appearance. Lecture Notes in Computer Science (2001)
9. Wang, J.Z., Li, J., Wiederhold, G.: Simplicity: Semantics-sensitive integrated matching for picture libraries. (2001)
10. Su, Z., Zhang, H., Li, S., Ma, S.: Relevance feedback in content-based image retrieval: Bayesian framework, feature subspaces, and progressive learning (2003)
11. Manjunath, B.S., Salembier, P., Sikora, T.: Introduction to MPEG-7. John Wiley & Sons Ltd. (2002)
12. Müller, H., Müller, W., Squire, D.M., Pun, T.: Performance evaluation in content-based image retrieval: Overview and proposals. Technical report, University of Geneva (1999)

Perceptual Distance Functions for Similarity Retrieval of Medical Images

Joaquim Cezar Felipe[1], Agma Juci Machado Traina[2], and Caetano Traina-Jr[2]

[1] Department of Physics and Mathematics, University of São Paulo at Ribeirão Preto
jfelipe@ffclrp.usp.br
[2] Department of Computer Science, University of São Paulo at São Carlos Brazil
{agma, caetano}@icmc.usp.br

Abstract. A challenge already opened for a long time concerning Content-based Image Retrieval (CBIR) systems is how to define a suitable distance function to measure the similarity between images regarding an application context, which complies with the human specialist perception of similarity. In this paper, we present a new family of distance functions, namely, Attribute Interaction Influence Distances (AID), aiming at retrieving images by similarity. Such measures address an important aspect of psychophysical comparison between images: the effect in the interaction on the variations of the image features. The AID functions allow comparing feature vectors using two parameterized expressions: one targeting weak feature interaction; and another for strong interaction. This paper also presents experimental results with medical images, showing that when the reference is the radiologist perception, AID works better than the distance functions most commonly used in CBIR.

1 Introduction

Nowadays images are present in the majority of medical systems. However, to allow effective and suitable use of images, the systems need to provide tools to manage images, including their fast and efficient comparison and retrieval.

The Content-based Image Retrieval (CBIR) techniques use image processing algorithms to automatically extract relevant characteristics (*features*) from the images, which are employed to index them. CBIR techniques use the intrinsic visual features of images, such as color distribution, shape and texture to compare them [1], and take advantage of index structures that use the similarity of features to speed up the retrieval.

Given the current state-of-the-art in Computer Vision [2], the features usually employed to describe images in CBIR systems are restricted to those that can be computed automatically. An important challenge of applying CBIR techniques in any specific application context is to define feature vectors and a distance function that can: (a) precisely discriminate images by content; (b) act as the basis of an index structure to manage the image collection during querying process, and (c) rank the images most similar to a given one in a way resembling the rank possibly defined by an human analyst.

This paper presents two new families of distance functions to compare images using feature vectors that meet these requirements. These families concern with the

H. Sundaram et al. (Eds.): CIVR 2006, LNCS 4071, pp. 432–442, 2006.
© Springer-Verlag Berlin Heidelberg 2006

broader or narrower effects of the interaction of differences in the features when two images are compared.

The remainder of this paper is structured as follows. Section 2 briefly gives a background on distance functions. Section 3 presents the new proposed distance functions. Section 4 discusses the experiments performed in order to corroborate the effectiveness of the new proposed functions, and Section 5 concludes the paper.

2 Background on Distance Functions

The Euclidean distance is the most known and used distance function. It belongs to the Minkowski family, which is based on the Lp norm [3].

Let us consider a set of objects, each one having n attributes. The Minkowski Distance between two objects Q and C, represented by attribute vectors $q=(q_1, q_2, \dots , q_n)$ and $c=(c_1, c_2, \dots , c_n)$, is given by:

$$d(Q,C) = \sqrt[p]{\sum_{i=1}^{n} |c_i - q_i|^p} \tag{1}$$

According to the value of p, specific distance functions are obtained, such as:

$p = 1$: *City Block* or *Manhattan* distance (L_1)
$p = 2$: *Euclidean* distance (L_2)
$p = \infty$: *Infinity* or *Chebychev* distance (L_∞)

The L_2 distance defines the geometric place of all points equidistant from the point representing the query object, that is, in two-dimensional space, it is a circumference centered at the query object. The L_1 distance, on the other hand, defines the geometric place of all points that have the same value of the sum of absolute differences of each attribute, while L_∞ can be approximated by the following expression:

$$d(Q,C) = \max_{i=1}^{n} |c_i - q_i| \tag{2}$$

The region where objects at the same distance from the reference object are placed, considering the most common Minkowski Distances, are shown in Fig. 1.

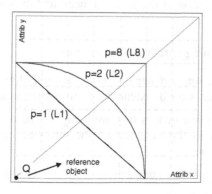

Fig. 1. Geometric places defined by different values of p, considering a 2-dimensional space (only the first quadrant is shown)

Choosing a distance function depends on several characteristics of the related system, such as: a) the descriptors that will be used; b) the statistical nature of the context; c) the data types of each descriptor; d) the pre-processing procedure that will be applied to data; e) the semantic particularities presented by the environment.

Several works concerning the definition and use of new distance functions have been presented in literature. The majority of them focus on specific applications or contexts. Among these distances, we can mention: Mahalanobis distance [4], Kullback-Leibler and Jeffrey divergences [2, 5], $\chi 2$ measure [6, 2], Cosine distance [7], Quadratic distance [8], Histogram intersection [7], Contrast model [9, 10], Perception-based distance [11], Bhattacharyya distance [5], Hellinger distance [6].

3 Proposed Distances

The environment, context, application, purpose and nature of data are some variables that determine what features will be chosen to represent images for similarity retrieval. Different descriptors such as color, shape and texture are commonly used to build the feature vector that represent an image.

For instance, in a specific context we could use texture descriptors – such as *homogeneity* and *entropy* – as representative features of the target images. Even considering that homogeneity and entropy features are independent from each other, there is an important question to be considered when comparing two images: how do these features affect the human perception of similarity when they both vary? In other words, if images Q and C1 present a high difference considering only one feature – for instance, homogeneity – and images Q and C2 present smaller differences considering several other features – for instance, homogeneity and entropy – what image, C1 or C2, is considered more similar to Q? What is the effect of interaction of feature variations on the human judgment of similarity?

Our objective is to answer these questions for a specific context: analysis of medical images. For this purpose, we define two families of distance functions, named *Attribute Interaction Influence Distances* – (*AID*) that allow the user to set parameters and adjust the influence between feature interactions, following more closely the human perception of image differences, and thus achieving a reduction in the semantic gap.

3.1 Distances Concerning Attribute Interaction

For the sake of clarity, we start our discussion using 2-dimensional feature vectors (attributes x and y). Later, we will extend the feature space to any dimension.

Definition: Considering two images that are being compared, **Attribute Interaction (AI)** is the proportion in the variation of the attribute values obtained from the respective feature vectors.

Ex: Attribute Interaction in the comparison of images Q and C, with feature vectors $q=(q_x, q_y)$ and $c=(c_x, c_y)$:

$$AI(Q,C) = \frac{\min(|q_x - c_x|, |q_y - c_y|)}{\max(|q_x - c_x|, |q_y - c_y|)} \tag{3}$$

AI varies from 0 (variation of only one attribute - points on the axes of coordinates in Fig. 1) to 1 (same variation on both attributes - points on the identity line in Fig. 1).

How does the human being perceive variations of similarity when two images present high (near 1) or low (near 0) values of *AI*? Actually, it depends on the context.

Definition 2: **Attribute Interaction Influence (AII)** is the effect of *AI* in the human perception of similarity. In some contexts, high values of *AI* leads to a perceptual effect of high dissimilarity – in this case, we say that the attribute interaction influence *(AII)* is **strong**. In contexts where high values of *AI* leads to a perceptual effect of low dissimilarity, we say that the attribute interaction influence *(AII)* is **weak**.

To deal with weak and strong interaction influence we propose two distance function families: ***Weak Attribute Interaction Influence Distances (WAID)*** and ***Strong Attribute Interaction Influence Distances (SAID)***. Both of them are represented by polynomials of degree 2 that define the geometric place of the objects at the same distance from a reference one. In Fig. 2, all points on the WAID curve are at distance *dw* from Q, while all points on the SAID curve are at the distance *ds* from Q. Taking point C, if we decide to work with WAID, its distance from Q (*dw*) will be smaller than if we decide to work with SAID (*ds*). The use of WAID considers the objects that present high values of *AI* as closer, while the use of SAID considers these objects as farther. Thus, WAID is designed to compare objects in contexts where *AII* is weak, and SAID is designed to compare objects in contexts where *AII* is strong.

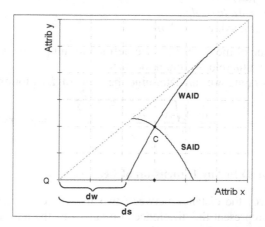

Fig. 2. Curves and distances of WAID and SAID. Only the first octant ($|q_x-c_x|>|q_y-c_y|$) is represented. In the second octant the identity line mirrors the curves.

3.2 Degree of Attribute Interaction Influence

In order to quantify and control the effect of Attribute Interaction Influence (*AII*), we define a parameter *n* that represents the degree of interaction and determines the

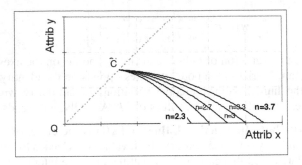

Fig. 3. Family SAID

elongation of the curves. This leads to a family of curves for WAID and another for SAID. Fig. 3 shows examples of curves for the SAID family.

The stronger *AII* the higher the value of *n* of the most suitable SAID curve. The weaker *AII* the higher the value of *n* of the most suitable WAID curve.

3.3 General Expression of SAID[1]

To simplify the notation, we call $|q_x-c_x|$ as x and $|q_y-c_y|$ as y. Considering the first octant, x is always greater than y.

To determine the quadratic expression of SAID, considering $y=f(x)$ a polynomial of degree 2, we use the following constraints:

- $x=d_s$ → $y = f(d_s) = 0$
- $x=d_s/n$ → $y = f(d_s/n) = d_s/n$
- $f'(d_s/n) = 0$ (f maximum at d_s/n)

where d_s is the value of the SAID distance defined for all points on the curve and n is the degree of interaction (elongation of the curve).

With these constraints, we can determine the value of d_s as follows:

$$d_S = \frac{y(n-1)^2 - 2x + (n-1)\sqrt{4x^2 - 4xy + y^2(n-1)^2}}{2(n-2)} \qquad \text{with } n>2 \qquad (4)$$

3.4 Extending SAID to Any Dimension of Feature Space

Expression (4) gives the distance between two images, considering two attributes. Variables x and y represent the differences on values of the attributes. In addition, x represents the maximum difference.

If there are more than two attributes, we should analyze the interaction between x (the maximum attribute difference) and each other attribute in a separate plane, and then gather them into a final expression. To do this, L_1 and $L\infty$ can be very helpful:

---

[1] Due to limitations of space, in this paper we will present the formal definition of SAID but omit the definition of WAID.

$$x = \max attrib = L\infty \tag{5}$$

$$L1 = \sum all\_attribs \tag{6}$$

SAID presents a behavior that is similar to L_1, that is, the attributes are summed up to compose the final distance. Thus, to determine the SAID distance, y will be replaced by the sum of the other attributes values:

$$y = sum\_other\_attribs = \sum all\_attribs - \max attrib \tag{7}$$

thus

$$y = L1 - L\infty \tag{8}$$

Now, replacing the values of x (5) and y (8) in expression (4), we determine the SAID distance between 2 objects in a multidimensional space, as a function of L_1, $L\infty$ and n.

3.5 Composing with Lp Family

A graphical analysis of the *Lp* family shows that L_1, L_2 and $L\infty$ present differentiation regarding attribute interaction. In Fig. 4, looking at these three functions, we can see that the highest difference among them occurs on the identity line, decreasing in the direction of the axes until become zero over the axes. However, this approach presents drawbacks: 1) They are limited by a specific space region; 2) L_1 and $L\infty$ are linear, regarding the proportion of attribute variation; 3) $L\infty$ is not suitable to compare images, since it considers as equal objects that are dissimilar regarding different attributes.

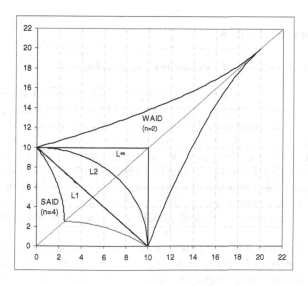

Fig. 4. Composition of *Lp* and AID

The SAID and WAID families can compose with the Lp family to cover the whole feature space, as shown in Fig. 4. The superior limit of SAID is L_1 (SAID with $n=2$) and the inferior limit of WAID is L_∞ (WAID with $n=1$). Actually, the Lp family is not limited by L_1, it can continue in the inferior region, with values of p less than 1, but these measures do not reflect attribute interaction, since the variations that they present along their curves are not consistent with this approach.

3.6 How to Determine the Best Perceptually Fitted Distance Function

Given the AID and Lp families of distance functions, we define a 2-step procedure to determine the best distance for a specific application, as follows.

Step 1: determine the attribute interaction influence. With a training set of images, run similarity tests with distances SAID ($n=3$), L_1, L_2, L_∞ and WAID ($n=3$). Analyze the results of each distance and compare them to the results given by human specialists' evaluations. With the best distance function obtained for this context we determine the attribute interaction influence: if SAID ($n=3$) is the most suitable, then we have a strong attribute interaction context; if WAID ($n=3$) is the best choice, then we have a weak attribute interaction; if one of Lp distances is the best, we have an intermediate attribute interaction context.

Step 2: determine the degree of attribute interaction influence and the best distance function. If the attribute interaction is intermediate, then the best distance function is the one that reached the best results in Step 1. If the attribute interaction is strong, we execute new tests with SAID with different values of n to determine the best one. We execute the same procedure with WAID if the attribute interaction is weak.

This procedure identifies the best perceptual distance function to a specific context, as we will show in the experiments that follow.

4   Experimental Studies

4.1 Perceptual Similarity of Texture for Medical Images

In this experiment, we used a set of 30 images. They consist of Regions of Interest (ROIs) extracted from a set of medical images of Magnetic Resonance, Computerized Tomography and Mammography. Five radiologists (R_1, R_2, R_3, R_4, e R_5) were asked to rank the images in order of similarity with a given reference, comparing the texture presented by the images. Thereafter, we used a texture extractor tool to obtain the features employed to ask for the k-nearest neighbors of the same reference image. The texture descriptors used were *uniformity* and *homogeneity* [12], extracted from the corresponding co-occurrence matrix. The k-nearest neighbor queries were executed for each distance function of the families AID and Lp as described in Step 1 presented in Section 3.6.

Each sequence ranked by the radiologists was then compared to the results from each distance function. In order to analyze the results and evaluate the degree of conformity of the automatic sequences to each radiologist's sequence, we calculated the sequence precision as follows:

- divide the sequences being compared into subsequences of k images;
- count the number *num* of images present simultaneously in both subsequences (the radiologist and the distance function sequences);
- calculate *precision(k)=num/k*;
- vary k from 2 to 29 and calculate *precision(k)*;
- calculate the final precision as the average of *precision(k)*.

Fig. 5 presents the plots of precision achieved with each function.

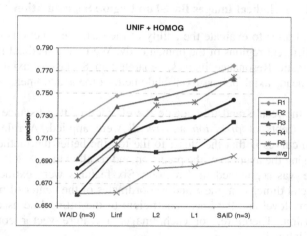

Fig. 5. Precision to evaluate the accuracy of distances. Each curve corresponds to the results for each Radiologist (R_1 to R_5), and their average.

From the analysis of the curves, we can see that despite the large variation between each human specialist, the SAID function consistently reached the best precision. It indicates that this kind of context is characterized by strong attribute interaction.

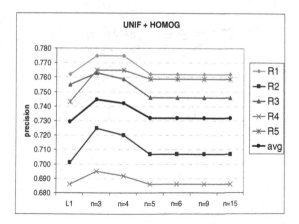

Fig. 6. Precision to determine the best function regarding parameter n (all five radiologists were considered)

In Step 2 of the approach, we applied SAID with different values of *n*, in order to determine its best value. Fig. 6 presents the resulting curves for values of *n* varying from 3 to 15.

Analyzing the curves, we can see that *n*=3 and *n*=4 present similar performances, while for values greater than 4 the performance is reduced. Thus, by the experiments, we conclude that when using these descriptors to represent the image texture, the best distance function is SAID with *n*=3.

4.2 Similarity of Medical Images Based on Region Segmentation

This experiment aims to evaluate the ability of the distance functions to discriminate images from different regions of the human body. We used a medical image database with 704 Magnetic Resonance images, separated in 8 classes: axial head, coronal head, sagittal head, axial pelvis, axial abdomen, coronal abdomen, angiogram and sagittal spine.

To analyze the results and to evaluate the efficacy of the distance functions, the well-known concepts of *precision* and *recall* were applied. A rule of thumb on analyzing such curves is that the closer to the top the better the method. The curves were plotted using the average of the precision and recall values.

Each image was segmented in 5 regions. Six features were extracted from each region: the fractal dimension, the *x* and *y* coordinates of the center of mass, the mass, the average gray level and the linear coefficient of the fitting line used to obtain the Fractal dimension. Therefore, for each image, a feature vector consisting of 30 attributes was defined.

K-nearest neighbor queries were executed taking images from all classes as reference, and using the distance functions of families AID and *Lp*. Individual precision and recall values were calculated and the averages for all classes were used to generate precision vs. recall curves for each distance function. Fig. 7 shows these curves.

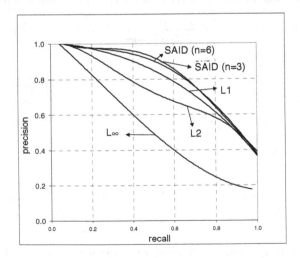

Fig. 7. Precision vs. Recall for image segmentation

In Fig. 7 we can see that the best graph was provided by SAID, so this context is also characterized by strong attribute interaction. We also see that SAID with n=3 is better than SAID with n=6 (we have processed the data with other values of n, but the best results occurred using $n=3$).

5   Conclusions

Two new families of distance functions for image comparison have been presented in this paper. These families – SAID and WAID – take into account the effects of interactions of attribute differences when two images are compared, reflecting the human perception of similarity. Thus, SAID and WAID represent a new way to summarize one aspect of the human perception.

The families of functions have received the mathematical development, in order to define the formal expressions needed to calculate the distance between objects. The composition of AID and Lp families was evaluated, and an experimental approach was described, aiming to determine the most suitable function to perform similarity retrieval in a specific context.

The results from the experiments on the proposed distance function were presented. Using the results of tests employing 5 radiologists, we determined that, for texture representation of medical images, the best function was SAID with coefficient of interaction 3. Another experiment employed a database of segmented images from different human body parts, and the distance functions were evaluated in order to find the best one. Again, the best function regarding discriminative power was SAID with coefficient 3.

Acknowledgments

This research has been supported, in part, by Brazilian National Research Council (CNPq) and the Sao Paulo State Research Foundation (FAPESP).

References

1. Vailaya, A., et al.: Image Classification for Content-based Indexing. IEEE Transactions on Image Processing, 10(1) (2001) 117-130
2. Rubner, Y. and C. Tomasi: Perceptual Metrics for Image Database Navigation. The Kluwer Intl. Series in Eng. and Computer Science. Kluwer Academic Pub. Boston (2001) 137
3. Akleman, E. and J. Chen: Generalized Distance Functions. In: Intl. Conf. on Shape Modeling and Applications. Aizu-Wakamatsu (1999)
4. Theodoridis, S. and K. Koutroumbas: Pattern Recognition. Acad. Press. N. York (1999) 625
5. Vasconcelos, N. and A. Lippman: A Unifying View of Image Similarity. In: Intl. Conf. on Pattern Recognition (ICPR) (2000)
6. Gibbs, A.L. and F.E. Su: On Choosing and Bounding Probability Metrics. International Statistical Review 70(3) (2002) 419-435
7. Zhang, D.S. and G. Lu: Evaluation of Similarity Measurement For Image Retrieval. In: IEEE Int. Conf. on Neural Networks & Signal Processing. Nanjing, China (2003) 928-931

J.C. Felipe, A.J.M. Traina, and C. Traina-Jr

8. Wilson, D.R. and T.R. Martinez: Improved Heterogeneous Distance Functions. Journal of Artificial Intelligence Research 6 (1997) 1-34
9. Tversky, A.: Features of Similarity. Psychological Review 84(4) (1977) 327-352
10. Tversky, A. and I. Gati: Similarity, Separability and the Triangle Inequality. Psychological Review 89(1) (1982) 123-154
11. Chang, E.Y., B. Li, and C. Li: Toward Preception-Based Image Retrieval. In: IEEE Workshop on Content-Based Access of Image and Video Libraries. Hilton Head (2000) 101-105
12. Haralick, R.M., K. Shanmugan, and I. Dinstein: Textural Fetures for Image Classification. IEEE Transactions on Systems, Man and Cybernetics 3(6) (1973) 610-621

Using Score Distribution Models to Select the Kernel Type for a Web-Based Adaptive Image Retrieval System (AIRS)

Anca Doloc-Mihu and Vijay V. Raghavan

University of Louisiana at Lafayette, Lafayette, LA 70504, USA
anca@louisiana.edu, raghavan@@cacs.louisiana.edu
http://www.cacs.louisiana.edu/~axd9917

Abstract. The goal of this paper is to investigate the selection of the kernel for a Web-based AIRS. Using the Kernel Rocchio learning method, several kernels having polynomial and Gaussian forms are applied to general images represented by color histograms in RGB and HSV color spaces. Experimental results on these collections show that performance varies significantly between different kernel types and that choosing an appropriate kernel is important. Then, based on these results, we propose a method for selecting the kernel type that uses the score distribution models. Experimental results on our data show that the proposed method is effective for our system.

1 Introduction

In a Web-based Image Retrieval System, the goal is to answer as well (fast and accurate) as possible with images that meet the user's request. Here, we assume that the database and the query image(s) are represented by color histograms. However, a characteristic of these colors is that they are not independent, but correlated. Moreover, the interaction between colors is stronger for some queries (images) than for other queries. In the former case, a more complex, possibly non-linear, kernel has to be used, whereas in the latter case, a linear kernel may be sufficient. Since we are dealing with real images, and therefore, with complex queries, it is expected that we need to use non-linear kernels to achieve good retrieval results. However, in the literature, "there are currently no techniques available to learn the form of the kernel" [4]. Methods like Relevance Vector Machines [11] assume distribution of data, which might fit or not a real collection. In this study, we learn from real tests the characteristics of our data, and then, we build our kernel selection method.

The paper organization is as follows. Section 2 provides the retrieval model, and the kernel method. Based on the experimental results presented in section 3, section 4 explores a new methodology for selecting the kernel to be used by the Kernel Rocchio learning method in order to improve the performance of an adaptive image retrieval system (AIRS). Finally, section 5 concludes the paper.

H. Sundaram et al. (Eds.): CIVR 2006, LNCS 4071, pp. 443–452, 2006.
© Springer-Verlag Berlin Heidelberg 2006

2 Background

2.1 Retrieval Model

In Image Retrieval, the user searches a large collection of images to find images that are similar to a specified query. The search is based on the similarities of the image attributes (or features) such as colors. A linear retrieval form [2,1] matches image queries against the images from collection

$$F : R^N \times R^N \to R, F(\mathrm{P}, \mathrm{Q}) = \mathrm{P^tQ} .$$

The query image Q contains the features desired by user. The bigger the value of the function F, when applied to a query Q and an image P, the better is the match between the query image Q and the database image P. For representing images by color, we use the histogram representations in RGB and HSV color spaces.

2.2 Kernel Method

The kernel method constitutes a very powerful tool for the construction of a learning algorithm by providing a way for obtaining non-linear decision boundaries from algorithms previously restricted to handling only linearly separable datasets.

In this work, the general form of the polynomial kernels [4,1] is given by

$$K(\mathrm{x}, \mathrm{y}) = (\langle \mathrm{x}, \mathrm{y} \rangle)^{\mathrm{d}}, \mathrm{d} > 0, \tag{1}$$

and the general form of the radial kernels is given by

$$K(\mathrm{x}, \mathrm{y}) = \exp\left(-\frac{\left(\sum_{\mathrm{i}=1}^{N} |\mathrm{x}_{\mathrm{i}}^{\mathrm{a}} - \mathrm{y}_{\mathrm{i}}^{\mathrm{a}}|^{\mathrm{b}}\right)^{\mathrm{c}}}{2\sigma^2}\right), \sigma \in \mathrm{R}^+. \tag{2}$$

Recently, image retrieval systems started using different learning methods for improving the retrieval results. In this work, we use the **Kernel Rocchio** method [1] for learning.

3 Experimental Study of Kernel Type Selection

Since we are dealing with real images, and therefore, with complex queries, it is expected that we need to use non-linear kernels to achieve good retrieval results. Therefore, in this section, we experimentally study, through several test query examples, the possible relationships between the different queries and the different kernels.

3.1 Experimental Setup

For our experiments, we use two test collections of size 5000, which include 10 and 100 relevant images, respectively, for each query image, and one of size 10000, which includes 100 relevant images for each query image. For convenience, we name these sets as 5000_10, 5000_100 and 10000_100. All image collections are quantized to 256 colors in RGB and 166 colors in HSV. We use the same set of 10 images as queries (Q_1, Q_2, ..., Q_{10}) for each experiment.

For evaluation purposes, we use the Test and Control method. The process of obtaining the training and testing sets is described in detail in [6]. For each test collection we create 3 different training sets, each of 300 images (called Set 1, Set 2, Set 3), and one test set. The images in the three training sets and the testing set are randomly distributed. The number of relevant images within the training and the testing sets for each query is given in Table 1. We assume that at each feedback step there are 10 images seen by user. For each test collection (5000_10, 5000_100 and 10000_100), we perform three similar experiments, each one corresponding to a different training set (Set 1, Set 2, Set 3). That is, in total, we performed 9 experiments.

Table 1. Number of the relevant images within the training sets and the testing set

5000_10	Set 1	Set 2	Set 3	Test	5000_100	Set 1	Set 2	Set 3	Test	10000_100	Set 1	Set 2	Set 3	Test
Q_1	0	0	2	4	Q_1	9	8	4	53	Q_1	1	4	2	62
Q_2	1	0	0	4	Q_2	6	5	5	50	Q_2	0	5	4	49
Q_3	0	1	0	7	Q_3	4	8	9	51	Q_3	4	3	2	52
Q_4	0	0	1	7	Q_4	8	5	2	56	Q_4	7	1	5	46
Q_5	1	0	0	7	Q_5	7	8	6	43	Q_5	7	3	3	47
Q_6	0	0	2	4	Q_6	5	9	1	56	Q_6	7	5	3	46
Q_7	0	1	0	5	Q_7	4	7	9	56	Q_7	3	1	4	44
Q_8	1	1	0	4	Q_8	4	5	7	48	Q_8	4	4	5	46
Q_9	0	0	0	2	Q_9	5	5	3	48	Q_9	1	3	1	49
Q_{10}	1	1	0	4	Q_{10}	6	8	9	50	Q_{10}	2	2	2	48

To evaluate the quality of retrieval, we use the R_{norm} measure [3]. We perform the experiments for a set of 12 kernels: 6 polynomials and 6 radial basis, with general forms given respectively by Equations (1) and (2). The values of the parameters (a, b, c, and d) and the names of the kernels used in the experiments are presented in Table 2. In all experiments presented in this work, $\sigma = 1$.

Table 2. Parameters used for the different kernels

d	Name
$d = 1$	Pol_1
$d = 2$	Pol_2
$d = 3$	Pol_3
$d = 4$	Pol_4
$d = 5$	Pol_5
$d = 6$	Pol_6

a) polynomials

a	b	c	name
$a = 1$	$b = 2$	$c = 1$	Rad_1
$a = 1$	$b = 1$	$c = 1$	Rad_2
$a = 0.5$	$b = 2$	$c = 1$	Rad_3
$a = 0.5$	$b = 1$	$c = 1$	Rad_4
$a = 0.25$	$b = 2$	$c = 1$	Rad_5
$a = 0.25$	$b = 1$	$c = 1$	Rad_6

b) radials

Space limitation precludes us from showing all the plots obtained from our experiments. However, as an example, in Figure 1, we present the plots of the kernel values obtained for query Q_1 for 5000_100 image test collection in RGB color space, for the first training set, Set 1.

3.2   Discussion of the Results

In this section, we analyze the possible relationships between the different queries and the different kernels that occur in our experiments.

Selecting the kernel for a given query. In our previous work [6], we found that there is no general best kernel, but there may be a best kernel for each query or groups of queries. Continuing this work, from Figure 1 we notice the different behaviors of the different kernels for query Q_1. Moreover, each query within each of the 9 experiments presents similar behavior. To be able to study the results of our experiments, we need to define our criterion for selecting the best kernel corresponding to a particular query.

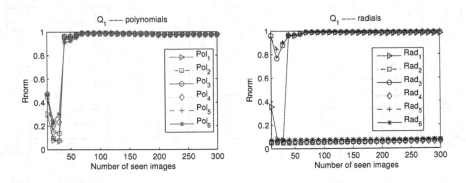

Fig. 1. Kernel results for query Q_1 for 5000_100 in RGB

For this, for each query within each training set of each test collection, we compute the average R_{norm} (over all feedback steps) value corresponding to each kernel, and then, we compare these 12 values. The kernel with the highest average R_{norm} value is chosen as the best initial kernel for the respective query. If for any query there is a kernel more efficient than the initial kernel, whose average R_{norm} value is very close to the initial best kernel (the difference between the two values is less than 0.05), then this kernel is chosen as the best final kernel for that query. The order of our kernels, from the more efficient to the less efficient, is Pol_1, ..., Pol_6, for polynomials and $Rad_2, Rad_1, Rad_4, Rad_6, Rad_3, Rad_5$ for radials. Then, low order polynomials (Pol_1, Pol_2) are always preferred over any radials.

Table 3 presents this process of choosing the best kernel for all 10 queries for 5000_100 collection for the first training set (Set 1) in RGB color space. By using this procedure, we select the best (final) kernels for all runs for all 3 test collections in both color spaces, which we use in our study from now on.

Table 3. Selecting the best (final) kernel for 5000_100 test collection, for Set 1 in RGB

RGB	Q_1	Q_2	Q_3	Q_4	Q_5	Q_6	Q_7	Q_8	Q_9	Q_{10}
Initial	Rad_5	Pol_5	Rad_5	Rad_3	Rad_5	Rad_5	Rad_5	Pol_5	Rad_5	Rad_5
Difference	0.009	0.005	0.007	0.014	0.007	0.025	0.033	0.007	0.006	0.0184
Final	Rad_3	Pol_1	Pol_1	Pol_1	Rad_3	Pol_1	Rad_3	Pol_1	Pol_1	Pol_1

Query groupings based on kernel type. To summarize the results from our experiments, in here, we start by grouping the queries according to their performance with respect to the different best kernels, for each experiment. These groupings are shown in Tables 4 and 5, for 5000_100 and 10000_100 test collections, respectively.

Kernels' behavior in different color spaces. It is known that HSV color space is more attractive, due to its approximately perceptually uniform charac-

Table 4. Query groupings for 5000_100 test collection

Set 1	Rad_2	Rad_3	Pol_1	Pol_2	Pol_3
RGB		Q_1, Q_5, Q_7	$Q_2, Q_3, Q_4, Q_6, Q_8, Q_9, Q_{10}$		
HSV	Q_3, Q_{10}		$Q_2, Q_4, Q_5, Q_7, Q_8, Q_9$	Q_6	Q_1

Set 2	Rad_1	Rad_2	Rad_3	Rad_5	Pol_1	Pol_2
RGB				Q_5	$Q_1, Q_2, Q_3, Q_4, Q_6, Q_7, Q_8, Q_9$	Q_{10}
HSV	Q_1	Q_9		Q_4	$Q_2, Q_3, Q_5, Q_6, Q_7, Q_8, Q_{10}$	

Set 3	Pol_1	Pol_2	Pol_6
RGB	$Q_2, Q_3, Q_4, Q_5, Q_6, Q_7, Q_8, Q_9$	Q_{10}	Q_1
HSV	$Q_1, Q_2, Q_3, Q_4, Q_5, Q_6, Q_7, Q_8, Q_9, Q_{10}$		

Table 5. Query groupings for 10000_100 test collection

Set 1	Rad_2	Rad_3	Rad_5	Pol_1	Pol_3	Pol_5
RGB		Q_1, Q_5, Q_7		$Q_3, Q_4, Q_6, Q_8, Q_9, Q_{10}$	Q_2	
HSV	Q_2		Q_1	$Q_3, Q_4, Q_5, Q_6, Q_8, Q_9, Q_{10}$		Q_7

Set 2	Rad_3	Rad_5	Pol_1	Pol_2	Pol_3
RGB	Q_1, Q_7		Q_2, Q_5, Q_8, Q_9	Q_3, Q_4, Q_6	Q_{10}
HSV		Q_1	$Q_2, Q_3, Q_5, Q_8, Q_9, Q_{10}$		Q_4, Q_6, Q_7

Set 3	Rad_3	Rad_5	Pol_1	Pol_2	Pol_3
RGB	Q_5	Q_7	$Q_1, Q_2, Q_4, Q_6, Q_8, Q_9, Q_{10}$	Q_3	
HSV		Q_7	$Q_2, Q_3, Q_4, Q_6, Q_8, Q_9, Q_{10}$	Q_1	Q_5

teristic, than the RGB color space. In [4] the authors found that, in practice, "the impact of the choice of the color space on performance" is minimal when "compared to the impacts of the other experimental conditions" such as the choice of the kernel type. An explanation is that the classifier does not use any information about the color space after quantization [4]. By using the results presented in the previous tables, we group the queries according to which color space has a more efficient best kernel type in Table 6. As we can see from the table, there are some queries that perform equally well (using the same efficient kernel) in both color spaces (column marked "Same"). Then, there are cases where it seems that it is better to work in RGB color space than in HSV color space (e.g., for the Set 2, for the 10000_100 collection, there are 5 queries in RGB and 3 in HSV), and vice-versa. This result is consistent with the results of [4].

Table 6. Query grouping according to the space representation for Set 2

Set 2	RGB	Same	HSV
5000_10	Q_1, Q_2, Q_7, Q_9	Q_8	$Q_3, Q_4, Q_5, Q_6, Q_{10}$
5000_100	Q_1, Q_4, Q_9	Q_2, Q_3, Q_6, Q_7, Q_8	Q_5, Q_{10}
10000_100	Q_1, Q_4, Q_6, Q_8, Q_9	Q_2, Q_5	Q_3, Q_7, Q_{10}

Kernels' behavior across different collections. In this part, we want to answer the question of whether a query keeps the same best kernel across different test collections or not. From Tables 4 and 5, one can notice that there are queries that keep the same best kernel across both test collections, but only for some training set(s), and not for all 3 training sets of each collection. For example, in RGB, query Q_1 for Set 1 gets Rad_3 as the best kernel across both test collections; and for Set 2, it gets Pol_1 and Rad_3 as the best kernels for 5000_100 and 10000_100 test collections, respectively. As a conclusion, in our experiments, no particular query has a best kernel across different collections.

Kernels' behavior for different training sets. For this study, we perform 3 runs, each corresponding to a different training set (Set 1, Set 2, Set 3), on each test collection. From Tables 4 and 5, one can notice that there are some queries that have the same kernel for all 3 training sets. The other queries, in either color space, have different kernels between the 3 training sets, without a general pattern. In conclusion, since different runs (training sets) include different number of relevant images and cases differ in terms of if they offer enough information or not, the choice of the best kernel between the different training sets depends on how much information (from relevant and non-relevant images) is good enough for the respective query. If this information is equally good between the runs then they show the same best kernel, and conversely.

Influence of the number of relevant images. In here, we analyze the effect of having different number of relevant images in our test collections, or generality [5]. As a statistics: for the 5000_10 test collection, with a generality of 0.002, radial kernels represent 50% in RGB color space, and 40% in HSV; for the

5000_100 test collection, with a generality of 0.02, radial kernels represent 13% in RGB color space, and 17% in HSV; for the 10000_100 test collection, with a generality of 0.01, radial kernels represent 23% in RGB color space, and 13% in HSV. That is, in RGB color space, the smaller the generality fraction, the bigger is the number of queries that present a radial kernel as their best kernel. However, it seems that in HSV color space this rule does not necessarily apply.

From our plots, one can notice that, generally, all polynomial kernels and Rad_3, Rad_5, Rad_1 kernels display the same increasing curves (and behavior) whenever a relevant image is learned. On the other side, the other three radial kernels display, in general, similar behavior, approximately constant. However, there are cases when Rad_2 kernel's curve drops when a relevant image is learned, and cases when Rad_4, Rad_6 curves increase when a relevant image is learned. As a statistics, Pol_1 is the best kernel for the most number of queries (55%), Rad_3 is chosen by 13% of queries, Pol_2 is chosen by 7% of queries, Pol_3 is chosen by 8% of queries, Rad_5 is chosen by 6% of queries, whereas the other kernels are chosen by less than 5% of the queries. From these observations, we can prune down the number of kernels to study from 12 to 5 ($Pol_1, Pol_2, Pol_3, Rad_3, Rad_5$), which answer to approximately 90% of our queries.

4   Using Score Distributions for Kernel Type Selection

Researchers [8,9,7] modeled the score distributions of search engines for relevant and non-relevant documents by using a normal and an exponential distribution, respectively. In this section, we propose a procedure based on this model to select the kernel type for an AIRS.

4.1   Mathematical Model of Image Score Distributions

The score distributions of the relevant documents suggested by researchers [9] are modeled as

$$P(score|R = r) = \frac{1}{\sqrt{2\pi}\sigma} \exp(-\frac{(score-\mu)^2}{2\sigma^2}),$$

where μ is the mean, and σ is the variance of the Gaussian distribution. The score distributions of the non-relevant documents are modeled as

$$P(score|R = nr) = \lambda \exp(-\lambda * score),$$

where λ is the mean for the exponential distribution.

Our experimental results (Section 3.1) support these mathematical models of the score distributions, with some approximation. This analysis was done for 5000_100 and 10000_100 test collections only, since the 5000_10 test collection does not contain sufficient number of relevant images and, therefore, the score distribution models do not fit for this collection. Figure 2 illustrates how the score distributions fit the top 300 images for one query for 3 kernels.

As an observation, the score distributions are different for the different kernel types used in the experiments. This motivates us to seek for a method to select

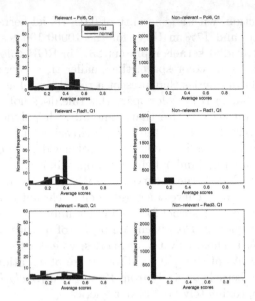

Fig. 2. Score distributions for query Q_1 for 5000_100 and Set 1 in RGB, for Pol_6, Rad_1, Rad_3 kernels

the kernel type by using these differences between the score distributions. Next, we present such a method.

4.2   Kernel Selection Method Based on Image Score Distributions

In image retrieval, the goal is to retrieve as many relevant images and as few non-relevant images as possible. This means, we wish to have a retrieval system capable to rank all the relevant images before the non-relevant ones. In other words, the scores of the relevant images should be as high as possible, whereas the scores of the non-relevant images should be as low as possible.

In our system, these scores are computed by using the different kernels type. Then, logically, the best kernel is the one that is able to distribute the scores of the images such that the relevant images have higher scores than the non-relevant ones. Therefore, we suggest the following procedure for selecting the kernel type:

1. for each kernel type K_i, compute
    (a) the score distribution of the relevant images (ScR_i) by using a Gaussian, and
    (b) the score distribution of the non-relevant images ($ScNR_i$) by using an exponential.
2. compare the results of any two kernel types K_i and K_j; reject those kernels K_j for which there is a kernel K_i with $\sum_{s=1}^{10} ScR_{is} > \sum_{s=1}^{10} ScR_{js}$ and $\sum_{s=1}^{10} ScNR_{is} < \sum_{s=1}^{10} ScNR_{js}$, where $ScR_{is} = NormalizedFreq_{is} * score_{is}$ and s is the score interval.

As an observation, the above procedure can be applied after each feedback step to select the best kernel type to be used for the following feedback step. Another observation is that the model is biased, especially for low scoring images, which do not occur between the top 300 images. However, for high scoring images, the model offers a relatively good estimation [8].

Discussion. Our method of selecting the best kernel tries to fit the score distributions of both relevant and non-relevant images, such that there are as many as possible relevant images with high scores grouped towards the right half of the plot, and less relevant images grouped in the left half side, and vice-versa for the non-relevant images.

For example, in Figure 2, Rad_3 and Pol_6 have better distributions for the non-relevant images than Rad_1 (more non-relevant images get scores of 0 or below). For relevant images, Rad_1, followed by Pol_6, shows the least number of relevant images with scores of 0. But, Rad_3, followed by Pol_6, shows a bigger number of relevant images with bigger scores. As a result, by cumulating these observations, the order for the best kernel is Rad_3, Pol_6, and Rad_1.

If we compare this result with the results from the previous section 3, we can see that these kernels display very close results (Figure 1). However, this result is consistent with our result from the experiments (Table 3). We obtained similar results for most of the queries in all the experiments.

As a conclusion, our method for selecting the kernel type for a particular query is based on score distributions, which are obtained via feedback from user and can be calculated automatically by the system. The method gives the same results as those obtained in Section 3, from extensive experiments, for most of the cases. That is, this method could be a viable solution to automatically select the kernel type in an AIRS.

5   Conclusions and Future Work

Kernel methods offer an elegant solution to increase the computational power of the linear learning algorithms by facilitating learning indirectly in high - dimensional feature spaces. Therefore, kernels are important components that can improve the retrieval system.

This motivates us to investigate several types of kernels in order to improve the performance as well as the response time of our AIRS, which is intended to be a web-based image retrieval application. For this, several kernels having polynomial and Gaussian Radial Basis Function (RBF) like forms (6 polynomials and 6 RBFs) are applied to generic images represented by color histograms in RGB and HSV color spaces.

We implement and test these kernels on image collections of sizes 5000 and 10000. Experimental results on these collections show that an appropriate kernel could significantly improve the system performance. By observing the behavior of the different kernels for several queries, we answer to several questions about the possible characteristics that might influence the kernels' behavior. Then, based on these observations, we propose a kernel selection method that uses score distribution models to select the best kernel for a particular query. The method shows approximately the same results in selecting the best kernel type for most of the queries and parameter settings used in our experiments.

As future work, we plan to investigate whether our kernel selection method works or not when multiple feature types (e.g., color and texture) are used to represent images.

References

1. Doloc-Mihu, A., Raghavan, V., V., Bollmann-Sdorra, P.: Color Retrieval in Vector Space Model. Proceedings of the 26th International ACM SIGIR Workshop on Mathematical/Formal Methods in Information Retrieval, MF/IR (2003)
2. Raghavan, V., V., Wong, S. K. M.: A Critical Analysis of Vector Space Model for Information Retrieval. Journal of the American Society for Information Science **37** (1986) 279-287
3. Bollmann-Sdorra, P., Jochum, F., Reiner, U., Weissmann, V., Zuse, H.: The LIVE Project - Retrieval Experiments Based on Evaluation Viewpoints. Proceedings of the 8th International ACM SIGIR Conference on Research and Development in Information Retrieval (1985) 213-214
4. Chapelle, O., Haffner, P., Vapnik, V.: SVMs for Histogram-Based Image Classification. IEEE Transactions on Neural Networks **5** (1999) 1055-1064
5. Huijsmans, D. P, Sebe, N.: How to Complete Performance Graphs in Content-Based Image Retrieval: Add Generality and Normalize Scope. IEEE Transactions on Pattern Analysis and Machine Intelligence **27** (2005) 245-251
6. Doloc-Mihu, A., Raghavan, V., V.: Selecting the Kernel Type for a Web-based Adaptive Image Retrieval System (AIRS). Internet Imaging VII, Proceedings of SPIE-IS&T Electronic Imaging, SPIE **6061** (2006) 60610H
7. Swets, J., A.: Information Retrieval Systems. Science **141** (1963) 245-250
8. Manmatha, R., Feng, F., Rath, T.: Using Models of Score Distributions in Information Retrieval. Proceedings of the 24th ACM SIGIR Conference on Research and Development in Information Retrieval (2001) 267-275
9. Arampatzis, A., Beney, J., Koster, C., van der Weide, T., P.: Incrementally, Half-Life, and Threshold Optimization for Adaptive Document Filtering. The 9th Text REtrieval Conference (TREC-9) (2000)
10. Cristianini, N., Shawe-Taylor, J.: An introduction to Support Vector Machines and other kernel-based learning methods. Cambridge University Press (2000)
11. Tipping, M., E.: The Relevance Vector Machine. Advances in Neural Information Processing Systems **12** (2000) 652-658

Semantics Supervised Cluster-Based Index for Video Databases[*]

Zhiping Shi[1], Qingyong Li[1,2], Zhiwei Shi[1], and Zhongzhi Shi[1]

[1] Institute of Computing Technology, Chinese Academy of Sciences, Beijing, 100080, China
[2] School of Computer and Information Technology, Beijing Jiaotong University,
100044, Beijing, China
{shizp, liqy, shizw, shizz}@ics.ict.ac.cn

Abstract. High-dimensional index is one of the most challenging tasks for content-based video retrieval (CBVR). Typically, in video database, there exist two kinds of clues for query: visual features and semantic classes. In this paper, we modeled the relationship between semantic classes and visual feature distributions of data set with the Gaussian mixture model (GMM), and proposed a semantics supervised cluster based index approach (briefly as SSCI) to integrate the advantages of both semantic classes and visual features. The entire data set is divided hierarchically by a modified clustering technique into many clusters until the objects within a cluster are not only close in the visual feature space but also within the same semantic class, and then an index entry including semantic clue and visual feature clue is built for each cluster. Especially, the visual feature vectors in a cluster are organized adjacently in disk. So the SSCI-based nearest-neighbor (NN) search can be divided into two phases: the first phase computes the distances between the query example and each cluster index and returns the clusters with the smallest distance, here namely candidate clusters; then the second phase retrieves the original feature vectors within the candidate clusters to gain the approximate nearest neighbors. Our experiments showed that for approximate searching the SSCI-based approach was faster than VA+-based approach; moreover, the quality of the result set was better than that of the sequential search in terms of semantics.

Keywords: High-dimensional index, cluster, video semantics, video database.

1 Introduction

In video database applications, the amount of data is very large and the dimension of data is very high. So it becomes necessary to support efficient retrieval in CBVR systems. Current approaches can be categorized into two general classes: 1) representative size reduction; 2) retrieved set reduction [5]. The dimensionality reduction [1] and VA-based indexing [2,3,4] are examples of representative size reduction. The dimensionality reduction can overcome the curse of dimensionality to a

---

[*] This paper is supported by National Natural Science Foundation of China No. 60435010 and National Basic Research Priorities Programme No. 2003CB317004.

H. Sundaram et al. (Eds.): CIVR 2006, LNCS 4071, pp. 453–462, 2006.
© Springer-Verlag Berlin Heidelberg 2006

degree. However, dimensionality reduction sacrifices some accuracy. The retrieved set reduction can be achieved by limiting search in some semantics range or by cluster-based indexing approaches. Some semantic video classification techniques [6,7,8] are proposed to classify video data into pre-defined semantic classes.

Typically, in video database, there exist two kinds of clues for query: visual features and semantic classes. In general, users of video search engines are interested in retrieving video clips based on semantic concepts such as "shoot events in football games" and so on. However, it is a difficult and expensive manual task to label the video with semantic concepts, and the label process is subjective, inaccurate and incomplete. Users hardly know the semantic classes labeled by video database authors, so video objects are queried by visual feature vectors in CBVR system. Now computers can extract low-level visual features of videos automatically, but there is no efficient index method for large-scale visual features data, and querying video clips based only on visual features usually could not provide satisfied solutions because of the semantic gap.

Intuitively, it is reasonable to develop techniques that combine the advantages of both semantics and visual feature index. However, the visual features of some semantically relevant video clips may not be located very close in the visual feature space, or vice versa, the video objects with similar visual features may come from different semantic classes.

In this paper, we propose a semantics supervised cluster based index approach (briefly as SSCI) to achieve the target. We model the relationship between semantic classes and visual feature distributions of the video data set with the Gaussian mixture model (GMM). The SSCI method proceeds as follows: the entire data set is divided hierarchically by a modified clustering technique into many clusters until the objects within a cluster are not only close in the visual feature space but also within the same semantic class and the cluster here is called as index cluster, in particular, the visual feature vectors in an index cluster are organized adjacently in disk; an index entry (cluster index) including semantic clue and visual feature clue is built for each index cluster.The main character of our technique is that it distinctly improves the search speed and the semantic precision of CBVR.

2   Video Feature Distribution and Modeling

In this section, we discuss the relationship between semantic classes and visual feature distributions of video objects. Intuitively, the semantic gap would be reduced if the relationship between the visual feature vectors and the semantic classes was mined. It is often supposed that the feature vectors within a semantic class follow a single Gaussian distribution [4]. In practice, real data distribution in video databases is complicated, so the feature distribution in a semantic class may be arbitrary shape. Fig. 1(a) abstractly illustrates the complex distributions in the feature space where two arbitrary shaped semantic classes A and B exist. If each semantic class simulated by a single Gaussian model, the Gaussian model for A would cover many objects of B. To alleviate this problem, the distribution of class A in Fig. 1(b) is modeled by a combination of 3 small Gaussian components, which can avoid to cover the objects in class B.

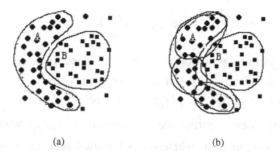

Fig. 1. Feature distribution of two semantic classes. (a) each semantic class with a single Gaussian model; (b) each semantic class with a Gaussian mixed model.

In this paper, we present a reasonable hypothesis: not only the whole data set but also each semantic class follows the Gaussian mixture distribution, and a cluster of feature vectors follow a compact single Gaussian model. In this paper, the expectation maximization (EM) algorithm is used to estimate the GMM parameters.

3   The Semantics Sensitive Approximate NN Search

In this section, we propose a semantics supervised cluster based index (SSCI) approach and approximate NN search method based on the index approach.

3.1   The SSCI Algorithm (SSCI)

We expect to build an index structure based on the following principles: the entire data set is divided into many subsets; the visual feature vectors in a subset are organized together continuously in the disk; an index entry is built for each subset. Supposing that the mean size of the subsets is d, the population of the index file is as $1/d$ as that of the data set. The index file is small enough to fit into memory in a lump. During retrieval, the index file is accessed at first to measure the similarity between the query example and the subsets and only a few most similar subsets are accessed to gain approximate query result. Accessing the several similar subsets from disk takes much less time because the vectors in each subset are stored together.

Now, which objects should be clustered into one subset? We expect that a CBVR system returns semantic relevant results, given a visual feature vector as a query example. If the semantic class of the query could be estimated, we go forward to the expectation. We adopt a Bayes classifier to classify video objects into certain semantic class. Let π_i denote the a priori probability of video semantic class i, $1 \leq i \leq |S|$, where $|S|$ is the number of video semantic class, and $p(x \mid s_i)$ refers to the conditional probability density of x, the feature data point for a video object, given that it belongs to class i. $p(x)$, the probability distribution function of x, is given by $\sum_{i=1}^{|S|} p(x \mid s_i)\pi_i$. The Bayes error that is associated with Bayes classifier is given by:

$$E = \int \left[1 - \max_i \; p(s_i \mid x) \right] p(x) dx \; . \tag{1}$$

Where $p(s_i \mid x)$ is the a posteriori probability of semantic class s_i, $i = 1,2,3,\ldots,|S|$. Because of the complexity of the relation between visual feature distribution and semantic classes (see section 2), $p(s_i \mid x)$ can't be accurate estimated directly. The feature data point space is partitioned into subsets $c_1,\ldots,c_{|C|}$, whose distribution is compact Gaussian component, where $|C|$ is the total number of the subsets. Then, $p(s_i \mid x)$ can be calculated by:

$$p(s_i \mid x) = \sum_{j=1}^{|C|} p(s_i \mid c_j) p(c_j \mid x) \; . \tag{2}$$

Where $p(s_i \mid c_j)$ is the conditional probability density of semantic class s_i given cluster c_j, and the conditional probability density $p(c_j \mid x)$ is the probability of x belonging to cluster c_j and can be given by:

$$p(c_j \mid x) = \frac{p(x \mid c_j) p(c_j)}{p(x)} \; . \tag{3}$$

So the Bayes error E can be written as:

$$E = \int [\sum_j p(x \mid c_j) p(c_j) - \max_i \; \sum_j p(s_i \mid c_j) p(x \mid c_j) p(c_j)] dx \; . \tag{4}$$

Where $p(s_i \mid c_j)$ can be estimated by:

$$p(s_i \mid c_j) = \frac{num(i \mid j)}{num(j)} \; . \tag{5}$$

Where $num(j)$ is the total number of data points in cluster j and $num(i \mid j)$ is the total data points from semantic class i in cluster j.

The above two equations imply that the Bayes error will be lessen to 0 as $\max_i p(s_i \mid c_j)$ increases to 1, to say, when all of data points within a cluster (a single Gaussian component) are from the same semantic class, the error reaches minimum. So all data points within a subset (simulated by a compact Gaussian component) should belong to an identical semantic class. The index entry of a subset takes both visual features and semantic classes into account.

According to what we discussed above, we propose SSCI algorithm to create our expected index structure. The outline of our SSCI is as follows: the entire data set is divided into k clusters (k can be determined by the number of semantic classes involved every time); those clusters which include objects of more than one semantic classes will be divided into sub-clusters moreover until all (or the most of) objects of each cluster belong to an identical semantic class; up to now, the objects of each cluster belong to an identical semantic class; if a cluster's size goes down below the lower threshold, merge the cluster into the nearest neighbor cluster within same semantic class; if a cluster's size goes above the upper threshold, split the cluster into two; at last, the result clusters are index clusters, and an index entry including semantic class identification code and parameters of the Gaussian model (mean and variance) is created for each index cluster. The used clustering algorithm consists of two steps: in first step, K-means cluster algorithm is used to clustering the data into k clusters; in second step, the k clusters are inputted EM algorithm to fine-tuned and the parameters of the Gaussian model for the clusters are obtained.

In practical, we firstly transform the feature space with Karhunen-Loeve Transformation (KLT). After KLT, the covariance matrix becomes a diagonal matrix. Calculation is simplified and more accurate Gaussian clusters can be gained.

The cluster index structure is hierarchical while the semantic concepts in the video database are hierarchical.

3.2 Approximate NN Searching Approach

For the SSCI technique, given a query, the video retrieval algorithm works as follows:

1. Transforming query vector. Transform the query feature vector to KLT space domain.
2. Searching the index file. Read the index file from disk to memory, then compute the distance between the query vector and the index entries based on formula (3) (the probability of the query vector belonging to each cluster).
3. Identifying the query result candidates. Gain the m nearest index clusters and the candidates are the objects within the m clusters.
4. Searching the candidate original feature vectors. The query is answered approximately by k-NN results in the range of the candidates.

The algorithm is marked as Cluster-m.

In the following of this section, we analyze the algorithm complexity of the strategy.

For the large-scale high-dimensional database, the query runtime is dominated by the times of I/O because of memory limitation. On sequential retrieval method, reading the whole database needs many times I/O because of memory limitation. On the proposed algorithm, the accessed portion of data is a small part of the whole data. For the most of practical application, the accessed portion of data can be fixed into memory within one I/O operation. Reasoningly, the efficiency of the SSCI-based searching is higher than that of the VA-based searching [2,3] too. Because the main drawback of the VA-base approaches is that the disk I/O of accessing candidate feature vectors is random, whereas in our SSCI-based approach the disk I/O of accessing candidate feature data is sequential. Obviously, the efficiency of the sequential I/O is much higher than the random I/O, so the SSCI-based approach has better performance. Nevertheless, the SSCI-based approach is only applicable to approximate retrieval. The VA-based methods haven't the limitation.

4 Evaluation

In this section, we evaluate the efficiency and the result quality of the SSCI-based searching approach.

We first describe the data set and the experimental system. The data set is about videos from TV, VCD-ROM, DVD-ROM. We have already collected 150G video files for about 300 hours. We chose about 40 hours videos including 40553 key-frames. We categorized the key-frames based on their video semantics into 20 semantic classes. The 51-dimentional texture histograms [9] of the key-frames were clustered into 3981 clusters, a cluster index entry created for each cluster. For comparison, we employ the VA$^+$-file algorithm, and create 300 bits approximate vector for each 51-dimensional texture feature vector of the data set. Our experiment system is C/S (Client/Server) structure in a local area network of 10 Mbps bandwidth. The client PC is P4 2.4G CPU with 512MB memory. The server PC is P4 1.0GHz×2CPU with 1024MB memory. The data set feature vectors are stored in SQL Server, and the query engine runs on the client PC. The index files are on the client PC.

4.1 Evaluation of Efficiency of the SSCI-Based Searching

In this subsection, we evaluate the speedup achieved by the SSCI-based searching approach compared to the VA$^+$-file based approach. Supposed $k = 90$, we queried 10 times randomly, and the mean times of the two approaches were calculated. Averagely 372 original feature vectors were accessed in the VA$^+$-file based approach. For fairness, we accessed the original feature vectors of top 30 nearest neighbor clusters for the proposed method, noted Cluster-30. The mean number of the visited original feature vectors was 358 in 10 queries. The accessed data sizes of the two methods were nearly equivalent.

Table 1. The mean query times of the two index approaches (the unit is second)

Time Cost	Cluster-30	VA$^+$file
IT_{index}	0.015	0.109
CT_{index}	0.015	1.286
IT_{db}	4.820	5.450
CT_{db}	0.010	
ST	4.860	6.845

Table 1 shows that the efficiency of the SSCI-based approach is higher than that of the VA$^+$-file approach though both methods spend long time because C/S structure and SQL Server were used. Especially, searching the index file of the SSCI-based approach is significantly faster than searching the VA$^+$-file. It is caused by two reasons: first, the population of the index file in VA$^+$-file approach is equal to the population of the original feature data, N, whereas the population of the index file in the SSCI approach is N/m; second, the distances between the query object and the index entries of index file are computed directly in the SSCI-based approach, whereas in the VA$^+$-file based approach, the lower and upper bounds of the distances between the query example and the approximate vectors all need to be calculated. The computing complexity of the latter is obviously higher. At the phase of computing the distance of the original feature vectors, the distance measure of the two approaches are equivalent. The difference is that accessing the original feature vectors is performed at random disk locations in VA$^+$-file but at sequential disk locations in the SSCI-based approach.

4.2 Performance of Approximate k-NN Searching

In this paper, precision is used to measure the performance. In our experiments, an object of result set is correct if and only if the object belongs the same semantic class with the query example. The precision P is defined by $P = c/t$. Where c is the number of the correct result objects, and t is the number of the all result objects.

To evaluate the quality of the approximate result set, we introduce two quality metrics: relative precision ratio and relative distance ratio. Suppose the precision of the approximate k-NN algorithm is p_a and that of the sequential k-NN algorithm is p_s. We define the precision ratio P as relative approximate precision, given by $P = p_a / p_s$. It is intuitive that the bigger P is, the higher the precision of the approximate k-NN search is. If the precision of the approximate k-NN search is higher than that of the sequential k-NN search, P is larger than 1. Or else, P is less than 1.

The precision does not capture important information about the quality of the approximation. Ferhatosmanoglu etc. [5] introduce an error metric. Suppose the approximate k-NN algorithm returns the result set $(a_1, a_2, \ldots, a_k)$ and the real result set computed by the underlying distance function $d_f(q,x)$ is $(r_1, r_2, \ldots, r_k)$. The relative distance ratio D as error metric is given by:

$$D = \frac{\sum_{i=1}^{k} d_f(q, a_i)}{\sum_{i=1}^{k} d_f(q, r_i)} \tag{6}$$

For certainly, $D \geq 1$. Only when the result set of the approximate k-NN algorithm equal to that of the real result set computed by the distance function, the equal sign is tenable. The smaller D is, the closer the result set of the approximate k-NN algorithm is to the real result set.

We compared the proposed method with the VA-LOW-k algorithm. The VA-LOW-k algorithm [10] [5] is an approximate query algorithm based on VA$^+$-file. At first phase, the lower bounds of the distance between the approximate vectors and the query example were figured out. The k nearest neighbor vectors were regarded as the approximate retrieval results. At second phase, only the k original feature vectors were accessed and their accurate distance with the query example were computed for sorting the result objects. We chose 11 semantic classes randomly and do 3 queries for each class randomly, $k = 100$. For the Cluster-m method, the original feature vectors of the top 10 nearest neighbor clusters were accessed to compute the accurate distances, namely Cluster-10. The distance is measured based on the Euclidean distance.

Table 2. Comparison of performances of VA-LOW-k and Cluster-10

Semantic Class	P		D	
	VA-LOW-k	Cluster-10	VA-LOW-k	Cluster-10
Reports	1.0	1.55	3.29	2.62
Weather forecast	0.50	2.75	2.16	1.67
Commercial	0.86	1.05	2.94	1.53
Surf ride	0.52	0.81	2.11	1.71
Basketball	0.45	1.40	2.60	1.42
Running	0.34	1.46	1.90	1.49
Pingpong	0.50	0.73	3.17	1.75
Hockey	0.66	0.91	1.99	1.42
Gymnastics	0.57	1.71	2.80	1.83
Swimming	0.78	1.11	1.69	1.65
Football	0.77	1.33	1.68	1.22
Mean	0.58	1.23	2.19	1.53

The comparisons of performance of VA-LOW-k and Cluster-10 are presented in Table 2 for both the two metrics. On average, the Cluster-10 algorithm achieves an error of $D = 1.53$, whereas the VA-LOW-k algorithm achieves an error level of $D = 2.19$. In terms of total distance of the results, the Cluster-10 algorithm is closer to the sequential retrieval (accurate retrieval). The precision ratios of the Cluster-10 are higher than that of the VA-LOW-k. The mean precision ratio of the Cluster-10 reaches $P = 1.23$, to say, the precision ratio is 1.23 times of that of the sequential retrieval. The mean precision ratio of the VA-LOW-k reaches $P = 0.58$ that is much less than that of the sequential retrieval. Typically, the precision of the approximate retrieval is lower than that of the accurate retrieval. Because the semantic class is taken into account for the SSCI technique to create index, our *approximate* retrieval achieves higher precision than the *accurate* retrieval.

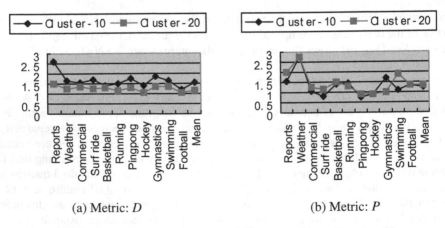

(a) Metric: D (b) Metric: P

Fig. 2. Comparison of performance of Cluster-m with m=10 and m=20

We analyze the improvement of the result quality of our technique as the number of the accessing clusters increases. The result of Cluster-m overlap to that of the accurate retrieval as the value of m increases. Meanwhile, the time cost increases as the size of the accessed original feature data grows. Fig. 2 illustrates the comparison of the performances of Cluster-m with m=10 (Cluster-10) and m=20 (Cluster-20). The D of Cluster-20 is 1.16, whereas the D of Cluster-10 is 1.53 averagely. The P of Cluster-20 and Cluster-10 are average 1.33 and 1.23 respectively. The improvement of the precision is slow as m increases. The clusters with higher condition probability for the query example are relevant to the query semantics with higher probability. Therefore, the higher precision can be gained by accessing a few clusters of original feature vectors using our algorithm.

Comparing to the idea proposed in [5], our approach gives attention to both visual clue and semantic clue of video objects, improving the speed and semantic precision of CBVR systems at same time.

5 Conclusions and Discussions

In this paper, we have proposed an index method based on clustering supervised by semantics to integrate the advantages of both semantic classes and visual features. We analyzed the relation of semantic classes and visual feature distribution of data set and then we modeled the relation with the GMM. We developed the SSCI-based approximate searching technique. The data set is divided into the clusters, in which the objects are similar on visual feature and relevant on semantics. We performed experiments to evaluate our proposed approach. Only accessing original feature vectors within the candidate clusters fastens the query, and higher semantic precision is achieved.

The future work includes finding hidden semantics corresponding to the interim clusters. For example, a cluster including objects of "football" and "grassland" possibly means "green field". This should be helpful to bridge the semantic classes and visual features.

References

1. K. V. R. Kanth, D. Agrawal, and A. Singh, Dimensionality reduction for similarity searching in dynamic databases, in Proc. ACM SIGMOD ICMD, (1998) 166–176
2. R. Weber, H.Schek and S.Blott. A Quantitative Analysis and Performance Study for Similarity-Search Methods in High-Dimensional Spaces. In Proceeding of ACM VLDB (1998)
3. H. Ferhatosmanoglu, E. Tuncel, D. Agrawal, and A. El Abbadi. Vector approximation based indexing for non-uniform high dimensional data sets. In Proceedings of the 9th ACM Int. Conf. on Information and Knowledge Management, McLean, Virginia (2000)202–209
4. Ye H J, Xu G Y. Fast search in large-scale image database using vector quantization. In: International Conference on Image and Video Retrieval, Lecture Notes in Computer Science, vol. 2728, Springer (2003) 458–467

5. H. Ferhatosmanoglu, E. Tuncel, D. Agrawal, and A. El Abbadi. Approximate Nearest Neighbor Searching in Multimedia Databases. In Proceedings of the 17th Int. Conf. on Data Engineering, Wanshington,DC,USA (2001) 503–511
6. S. Fischer, R. Lienhart, and W. Effelsberg. Automatic Recognition of Film Genres. In ACM Multimedia 1995, San Francisco, USA, (1995)295–304.
7. Y. Chen and E. K. Wong. A Knowledge-Based Approach to Video Content Classification. Proceedings of SPIE Vol. 4315:Storage and Retrieval for Media Databases (2001) 292–300
8. A. Mittal, L.F. Cheong. Addressing the problems of Bayesian Network Classification of Video Using High-Dimensional Features. IEEE Trans. On Knowledge and Data Engineering, Vol. 16(2),February(2004)230–244
9. Shi ZP, Hu H, Li QY, Shi ZZ, Duan CL. Texture spectrum descriptor based image retrieval. Journal of Software(Chineses), 16(6),(2005)1039–1045
10. R.Weber, K.Bohm. Trading Quality for Time with Nearest-Neighbor Search. In Proceedings of the 7th International Conference on Extending Database Technology, Konstanz, Germany, March (2000) 21–35

Semi-supervised Learning for Image Annotation Based on Conditional Random Fields

Wei Li and Maosong Sun

State Key Lab of Intelligent Technology and Systems
Department of Computer Science and Technology, Tsinghua University
Beijing 100084, China
wei.lee04@gmail.com, sms@mail.tsinghua.edu.cn

Abstract. Automatic image annotation (AIA) has been proved to be an effective and promising solution to automatically deduce the high-level semantics from low-level visual features. Due to the inherent ambiguity of image-label mapping and the scarcity of training examples, it has become a challenge to systematically develop robust annotation models with better performance. In this paper, we try to attack the problem based on 2D CRFs (Conditional Random Fields) and semi-supervised learning which are seamlessly integrated into a unified framework. 2D CRFs can effectively capture the spatial dependency between the neighboring labels, while the semi-supervised learning techniques can exploit the unlabeled data to improve the joint classification performance. We conducted experiments on a medium-sized image collection including about 500 images from Corel Stock Photo CDs. The experimental results demonstrated that the annotation performance of this method outperforms standard CRFs, showing the effectiveness of the proposed unified framework and the feasibility of unlabeled data to help the classification accuracy.

1 Introduction

Automatic image annotation (AIA) is a crucial step for application areas such as object recognition and semantic scene interpretation, and thus becomes an active research area in computer vision communities. In recent years, many generative models and discriminative approaches have been proposed to automatically annotate images with descriptive textual words to support multi-modal image retrieval using different keywords at different semantic levels. Many of them have achieved state-of-the-art performance. However, most of the approaches may face two key challenges. First, the fundamental problem for image annotation is the ambiguity of label assignment, and contextual constraints are little examined in the annotation process. That is to say, each image component is identified independently without considering the spatial correlations between image components of a scene, which may degrade annotation accuracy due to the ambiguities inherent to visual appearance. For example, like "*sky*" and "*ocean*" region, even for human beings, it is often difficult to identify these two regions accurately without context. In the literature, Random Fields techniques have been used in classification and recognition problems J. Lafferty et al [22] apply CRFs

H. Sundaram et al. (Eds.): CIVR 2006, LNCS 4071, pp. 463–472, 2006.
© Springer-Verlag Berlin Heidelberg 2006

model to segmenting and labeling sequential data, X. He et al [23] and Kumar et al [24] perform image region labeling with the 2D extension. M. Szummer et al [25] present the use of CRFs model to contextual recognition of hand-drawn diagrams. Most of these approaches achieved start-of-the-art performance and motivated us to explore image annotation with the help of their excellent experiences and knowledge. The second challenge is that many hand-labeled images are required to perform the classifier training or parameter estimation. In most cases, however, labeled images are often hard to obtain or create in large quantities, while the unlabeled ones are easier to collect. How to efficiently use the unlabeled images to improve the annotation performance is a key issue for providing an effective and accurate mapping from low-level visual features to high-level semantic concepts. J Fan et al [32] have proposed to use unlabeled data to learn the hierarchical concept model effectively. L. Wang et al [29], Q. Tian et al [30] and Z.-H. Zhou [31] have exploited unlabeled images in relevance feedback to perform query concept learning. Based on the researchers' experiences, our work in this paper focuses on selecting the useful unlabeled images explored by a classification scheme in order to further reduce the human effort and to improve the classification performance.

The main contribution of this paper is two-fold: First, instead of annotating each image components individually, we will annotate them by context-dependent classification scheme. We formulate the image annotation problem as a joint classification task based on 2D CRFs (Conditional Random Fields) model. Compared to generative probabilistic models like Markov Random Fields (MRFs), CRFs can offer some advantages over MRFs. On one hand, CRFs allows the relaxation of conditional independence assumption of the observed image given the class labels usually used in MRF for computational tractability. One the other hand, unlike MRFs, CRFs directly model the conditional distribution of class labels given the observed image so as to avoid the describing the density model, i.e., the distribution of observed data which is complicated and is not needed for classification task. Second, a semi-supervised learning algorithm is introduced to enable the unlabeled images to be exploited to improve the model performance to some degree. Theoretical analysis and experimental results show that our proposed method can outperform the standard CRFs model. To our best knowledge, semi-supervised learning combined with conditional random fields has not been carefully investigated in the task of automatic image annotation.

This paper is organized as follows: Section 2 presents related work. Section 3 first describes the basic theory of Conditional Random Fields; image annotation model based on the 2D extension, and then discusses details of how to use the unlabeled images to improve the model accuracy. Section 4 demonstrates our experimental results and some theoretical analysis. Conclusions and future work are discussed in Section 5.

2 Related Work

Recently, many models using machine learning techniques have been proposed for automatic and semi-automatic image annotation and retrieval, Including hierarchical aspect model [1][2], translation model [3][19], relevance models [4][9][17], classification methods [8][10][12-15] and latent space models [20][21]. Mori et al [5] is the earliest to performance image annotation, they collects statistical co-occurrence information between keywords and image grids and uses it to predict annotated keywords to unseen images. Dyugulu et al [3] views annotating images as similar to a process of translation from "visual information" to "textual information" by the estimation of the alignment probability between visual blob-tokens and textual keywords based on IBM model 2. K. Fang [19] improved IBM model 1 by regularizing the imbalance of keywords distribution in the training set. Barnard et al [1][2] proposed a hierarchical aspect model to capture the joint distribution of words and image regions using EM algorithm. Jeon et al [4] presented a cross-media relevance model (CMRM) similar to the cross-lingual retrieval techniques to perform the image annotation and ranked image. Lavrenko et al [8] proposed continuous relevance model (CRM) to extend the cross-media relevance model using actual continuous-valued features extracted from image regions. This method avoids the clustering and constructing the discrete visual vocabulary stage. S. L. Feng et al [17] improved the CRM model by assuming a multiple Bernoulli distribution to generate the keyword annotations instead of multinomial distribution to model the Blei et al [11] proposed a correspondence LDA and assumes that a Dirichlet distribution can be used to generate a mixture of latent factors that can further relates words and image regions. Wang and Li [8] introduced a 2-D multi-resolution HMM model to automate linguistic indexing of images. Clusters of fixed-size blocks at multiple resolution and the relationships between these clusters is summarized both across and within the resolutions. E. Chang et al [6] proposed content-based soft annotation (CBSA) for providing images with semantic labels using (BPM) Bayesian Point Machine. Cusano C et al [10] proposed using Multi-class SVM to classify each square image region into one of seven predefined concepts of interest and then combine the partial decision of each classifier to produce the overall description for the unseen image. E. Chang, B. Li and K. Goh [12-15] introduced a multi-level confidence-based ensemble scheme to assist the discovery of new semantics and useful low-level perceptual features. F. Monay [20][21] presented to use the latent variables to link image features and words based on the latent semantic analysis (LSA) and probabilistic latent semantic analysis (pLSA). Instead of predicting the annotation probability of a single word given an image, R. Jin et al [18] estimated a coherent language model for each image to infer a set of words with the word-to-word correlation to be considered. J. Fan et al [17] presented a concept hierarchy model and adaptive EM algorithm to deduce multi-level image semantics.

3   The Framework of Automatic Annotation Model

3.1   Conditional Random Fields for Image Annotation

Conditional Random Fields are an instance of undirected graphical models designed for calculating the conditional distribution of class labels given the observed feature vectors. For a given image I, the semantic label and observation of an image are represented as L_I and V_I respectively. (L_I, V_I) is a conditional random field if, when conditioned on V_I , all the random field L_I obey the Markov property $P(L_I(x)|V_I, L_I(y), y \neq x) = P(L_I(x)|V_I, L_I(y), y \in N_x)$, where the set N_x denote the neighboring site of a particular image patch x in Image I. Hence L_I is a random field globally conditioned on observed feature vectors. By using the Hammersley-Clifford theorem, the conditional distribution over the labels L_I given the observations can be defined as.

$$P(L_I|V_I, \theta) = \frac{1}{Z(\theta)} \exp\left(\sum_k \lambda_k S_k(L_I(i), V_I) + \sum_k \sum_{j \in N_i} \mu_k T_k(L_I(i), L_I(j), V_I) \right) \tag{1}$$

where $z(\theta)$ is the normalization factor known as the partition function, λ_k, μ_k are the parameters to be evaluated and S_k, T_k are feature functions to encode the local dependency between observed image data and corresponding semantic labels as well as spatial dependency among the neighboring semantic labels.

Given a training set of annotated images, each image I can be represented by a combined feature vector $I = \{L_{I,1}, L_{I,2}, \cdots, L_{I,m}; V_{I,1}, V_{I,2}, \cdots, V_{I,n}\}$ in a multi-modal feature space including visual appearance and semantic description, where $L_{I,j}$ denotes the labels from a generic predefined vocabulary to describe image semantics, $V_{I,j}$ represents the visual features of each image patch such as color, texture and shape descriptors, m and n are the number of labels and image patches in image I respectively. The goal of our model is to learn the mapping from image data to semantic labels to automatically deduce the image semantics from the observed low-level perceptual features.

3.2 Unigram and Bigram Potential

The key issue for conditional random fields is to select an appropriate neighboring system or clique for each image patch and to define the local clique potentials in the neighborhood. We'd like to employ two kinds of potentials. Firstly, for each node (image patch), we will introduce a unigram potential, which measures the degree of association between one semantic label and visual appearance of the image patch. Secondly, for each edge (label dependence) a bigram potential is provided to measure the pair-wise constraints between the two neighboring labels, conditioned on their associated image patches. Fig. 3.1 illustrates the cliques, i.e., neighboring systems and the two kinds of potential functions defined over the clique.

Fig. 3.1. Cliques and potential functions defined on cliques

3.3 Training and Inference of 2D CRFs

Training and inference are the two essential components of 2D CRFs, and our algorithms for parameter estimation and inferring labels draws heavily from previous work. We also train the 2D CRFs using the conditional Maximum Likelihood criterion, which maximize the following log conditional likelihood:

$$\theta^* = \arg\max_{\theta} \log P(L_I|V_I, \theta) \tag{2}$$

where $\theta = [\mu, \lambda]$ represents the parameters to be estimated

$$\log P(L_I|V_I, \theta) = \sum_k \lambda_k S_k(L_I(i), V_I) + \sum_k \sum_{j \in N_i} \mu_k T_k(L_I(i), L_I(j), V_I) - \log Z(\theta) \tag{3}$$

We need to calculate the expectations under the model distribution which is difficult due to the bottleneck of computing $Z(\theta)$. In this paper, contrastive divergence (CD) [23][34] algorithm is used to compute the expectations which can approximate the gradients in a few steps compared to Markov Chain Monte Carlo sampling method.

Unlike traditional classification methods which infer the class label for an unseen observed data, the problem of inference in 2D CRFs is to find an optimal label configuration given an unlabeled image. Maximum a posterior (MAP) and maximum marginal (MM) solutions are widely used in the literature:

$$L_I^{MAP} = \arg\max_{L_I} P(L_I | V_I, \theta) \qquad L_{I_j}^{MM} = \arg\max_{L_{I_j}} P(L_{I_j} | V_I, \theta) \tag{4}$$

The MAP solution usually finds a globally compatible label configuration, while the MM approach chooses the most likely individual labels which require individual marginal distribution. In the context of image annotation, we would like to minimize the number of individually mislabeled image patches, thus MM criterion is more desirable than MAP solution.

3.4 Learning with the Unlabeled Images

The performance of the image annotation accuracy heavily depends on the size of the labeled training data. Precisely labeled images with explicit correspondence is, however, difficult to create or obtain in large quantities, whereas, unlabeled images are easier to collect. Hence, we propose to use the semi-supervised learning which attempts to exploit the unlabeled images to improve the annotation performance. Suppose we have a small set of labeled images denoted by L, and a large set of unlabeled images denoted by U. The key issue underlying semi-supervised learning is how to select the useful unlabeled images, which aims to optimize the classification performance while minimizing the number of needed labeled images for classifier training. We propose a two-step scheme for effectively training the 2D CRFs from both the labeled and unlabeled images. First, an initial weak 2D CRFs is trained based on the labeled images, and then apply the weak trained model to the unlabeled images to assign semantic labels to each image block. Second, a binary classification approach is employed to select the useful unlabeled data with correct labels which can not only improve the performance of the weak 2D CRFs model, but also reduce the human verification and labeling effort to some degree.

Semi-supervised Conditional Random Fields Learning Algorithm

Input L^T: Labeled data for training 2D CRFs (training set)
L^V: Labeled data for validation (validation set)
U: Unlabeled data
MaxIter: Max number for iteration
Output a trained 2D CRF model λ_*

Algorithm
1. $\tau \leftarrow 0$
2. λ_τ is trained using L^T
3.   apply λ_τ to annotate the images in L^V
4. L^{VP}: positive instances derived from the correctly labeled cliques in L^V
5. L^{VN}: negative instances derived from the incorrectly labeled cliques in L^V
6.   if λ_τ has no improvement on L^V or τ is greater that *MaxIter*
7.   terminate the training
8.   else
9.   apply λ_τ to annotate the images in U
10.   train a binary SVM classifier B based on L^{VP} and L^{VN}
11.   classify the instances (cliques + assigned labels) in U as positive or negative using B
12.   if the instance (cliques + assigned labels) are classified as negative
13.   ignore these cliques as well as the assigned labels from U
14.   else
15.   add the positive instance to U^I
16. $\lambda_{\tau+1}$ is trained from both L^T and U^I
17. $\tau = \tau + 1$
18. return λ_τ as λ_*

The above pseudo-codes describe the outline of the semi-supervised conditional random fields learning algorithm. The labeled set L is first divided into two disjoint sets L^T and L^V, where L^T is used for training the model λ_τ, L^V is used for validation and U is used as the unlabeled images. We use λ_τ to annotate the images in L^V and in U respectively. For the labeled results in L^V, we treat each clique as an independent new instance, that is to say, features and the assigned labels associated with each block in the clique are considered as the instance observation, and the new instance label ranges over $\{-1, +1\}$ depending on whether all the labels are correct or not. These instances are used to generate the sets L^{VP} (positive training instances) and L^{VN} (negative training instances), which are utilized to train a binary SVM classifier B, then B is applied to classify the binary instances derived from the newly labeled images in U into either correctly labeled cliques U^I or incorrectly labeled cliques. Next, a new model is trained from L^T and U^I, where U^I consists of the potential useful training data in U by ignoring those cliques classified as negative using binary SVM classifier B.

4 Experimental Results

Our experiments are carried out using a mid-sized image collection, comprising about 500 images from Corel Stock Photo CDs. In this collection, each image is divided into blocks with the size 28*28 pixels, followed by manually labeling each image block with a predefined semantic label to make explicit correspondence. Some commonly used low-level visual features are computed over each image block such as position, area, HSV color moments and Gabor filters. The predefined textual vocabulary contains 20 keywords including water, sky, airplane, cloud, etc. We evaluate the performance of our proposed methods by comparing with classification approaches as shown in Fig. 4.1.

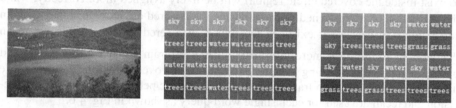

Fig. 4.1. Region labeling for different models

The above figures demonstrate that the region labeling based on 2D CRFs (mid) can significantly outperform the results using SVMs (right most) in terms of spatial dependency, which illustrates the advantage of 2D CRFs in terms of spatial modeling. From the theoretical point of view, SVMs can only predict semantic labels based on the local observation by ignoring the context information, while 2D CRFs can use the Bigram potential to capture the spatial dependency to get a more reasonable and improved label results.

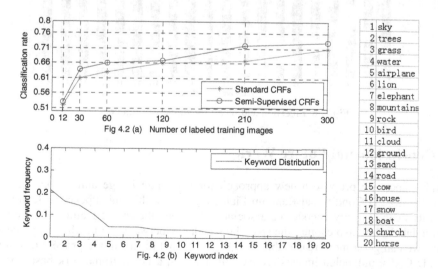

Fig. 4.2. Comparison of classification rate and the keyword distribution

Fig. 4.2(a) shows the effectiveness of training 2D CRFs with the unlabeled images compared with the standard CRFs model and Fig. 4.2(b) illustrates the keyword distribution in the training set. In this experiment, we use different number of labeled training images and apply our semi-supervised learning algorithm to train the CRFs model repeatedly. In each experiment, labeled images are divided into two disjoint sets for training and validation. The current learned 2D CRFs model is applied to assign labels to unlabeled images, and then a classification scheme is used to exploit these newly labeled data in the unlabeled set to select the useful data to train a better CRFs model to reduce the human labeling effort to some degree. For example, λ_0 is assumed to be the trained model and covers a small circle region in the whole observation space, λ_0 will then be used to predict labels for unlabeled data and x^{u_1} (assumed to exist inside the covered circle region) will be likely assigned more correctly, while the prediction of x^{u_2} (assumed to exist outside the covered circle region) may contain some mistakes because it exists in the region uncovered by λ_0. By this we mean that x^{u_2} is more useful or more informative than x^{u_1} to train a better CRFs model and our semi-supervised learning scheme exploits the uncovered region to select more useful data which can help train a better model. For the performance evaluation, precision and recall are used for each single word query as shown in Fig. 4.6.

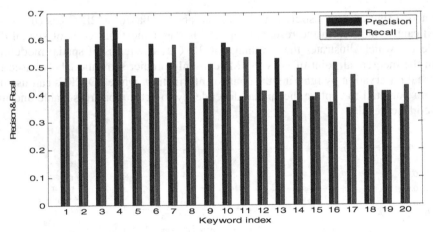

Fig. 4.6. Precision and recall for single word query

5   Conclusion and Future Work

In this paper, we propose a new approach for automatic image annotation and retrieval using 2D Conditional Random Fields together with semi-supervised learning. 2D CRFs can not only encode the association between the image feature and the semantic labels, but also capture the spatial dependency between the neighboring labels. Thus, we can get a more reasonable and accurate label result. In the process of training 2D CRFs, unlabeled images are exploited within a novel framework based on a binary classification scheme to improve the model performance. Compared to the standard 2D Conditional Random Fields, the proposed model gets slightly better annotation and retrieval results, demonstrating the potentials of unlabeled data in training a better model.

In the future, more work should be done to provide more expressive image content representation, efficient algorithms and precise models for semantic image classification using both the labeled and unlabeled images. In addition, language models word-to-word correlations will be taken into consideration as a post-processing step to achieve a more scalable and accurate image-level annotation model.

Acknowledgements

We would like to express our deepest gratitude to Michael Ortega-Binderberger, Kobus Barnard and J.Wang for making their image datasets available. This work would not have been possible without the help of Sanjiv Kumar and Martin Szummer. This research is supported by the National Natural Science Foundation of China under grant number 60321002 and the National 863 Project of China under grant number 2001AA114210-03, and the ALVIS Project co-sponsored by EU PF6 and NSFC.

References

1. K. Barnard, P. Dyugulu, N. de Freitas, D. Forsyth, D. Blei, and M. I. Jordan. Matching words and pictures. Journal of Machine Learning Research, 3: 1107-1135, 2003.
2. K. Barnard and D. A. Forsyth. Learning the Semantics of Words and Pictures. In Proceedings of International Conference on Computer Vision, pages 408–415, 2001.
3. P. Duygulu, K. Barnard, N. de Freitas, and D. Forsyth. Ojbect recognition as machine translation: Learning a lexicon fro a fixed image vocabulary. In Seventh European Conf. on Computer Vision, 97-112, 2002.
4. J. Jeon, V. Lavrenko and R. Manmatha. Automatic image annotation and retrieval using cross-media relevance models. In Proceedings of the 26th intl. SIGIR Conf, 119-126, 2003.
5. Y. Mori, H. Takahashi, and R. Oka, Image-to-word transformation based on dividing and vector quantizing images with words. First International Workshop on Multimedia Intelligent Storage and Retrieval Management, 1999.
6. Edward Chang, Kingshy Goh, Gerard Sychay and Gang Wu. CBSA: Content-based soft annotation for multimodal image retrieval using bayes point machines. IEEE Transactions on Circuts and Systems for Video Technology Special Issue on Conceptual and Dynamical Aspects of Multimedia Content Descriptions, 13(1): 26-38, 2003.
7. J. shi and J. Malik. Normalized cuts and image segmentation. IEEE Transactions On Pattern Analysis and Machine Intelligence, 22(8): 888-905, 2000.
8. J. Li and J. A. Wang. Automatic linguistic indexing of pictures by a statistical modeling approach. IEEE Transactions on PAMI, 25(10): 175-1088, 2003.
9. V. Lavrenko, R. Manmatha and J. Jeon. A model for learning the semantics of pictures. In Proc of the 16th Annual Conference on Neural Information Processing Systems, 2004.
10. Cusano C, Ciocca G, Schettini R, Image Annotation using SVM. Proceedings of SPIE-IS&T Electronic Imaging, 330-338, SPIE Vol. 5304, 2004.
11. D. Blei and M. I. Jordan. Modeling annotated data. In Proceedings of the 26th intl. SIGIR Conf, 127–134, 2003.

12. K.-S. Goh, E. Chang and K.-T. Cheng, SVM binary classifier ensembles for image classification, in Proceedings of the tenth international conference on Information and knowledge management, ACM Press, 2001,pp. 395-402.

13. B. Li and K. Goh, Confidence-based dynamic ensemble for image annotation and semantics discovery, in Proceedings of the eleventh ACM international conference on Multimedia, ACM Press, 2003, pp. 195-206.

14. K.Goh, B. Li and E. Chang, Semantics and feature discovery via confidence-based ensemble, ACM Transactions on Multimedia Computing, Communications, and Applications, 1(2), 168-189, 2005.

15. K.Goh, E. Chang and B. Li, Using on-class and two-class SVMs for multiclass image annotation, IEEE Trans. on Knowledge and Data Engineering, 17(10), 1333-1346, 2005.

16. J. Fan, Y. Gao, and H. Luo, Multi-level annotation of natural scenes using dominant image components and semantic concepts," in *Proc. of ACM MM*, , 540–547, 2004.

17. S. L. Feng, V. Lavrenko and R. Manmatha. Multiple Bernoulli Relevance Models for Image and Video Annotation. In Proceedings of CVPR04, 2004.

18. R. Jin, J. Y. Chai, and L. Si. Effective Automatic image annotation via a coherent language model and active learning. In Proceedings of ACM MM'04, 2004.

19. F. Kang, R. Jin, and J. Y. Chai. Regularizing Translation Models for Better Automatic Image Annotation. In Proceedings of CIKM'04, 2004.

20. F. Monay and D. Gatica-Perez. On image auto-annotation with latent space models. In Proc. of ACM Int. Conf. on Multimedia, Berkeley, Nov. 2003.

21. F. Monay and D. Gatica-Perez. PLSA-based image auto-annotation: Constraining the latent space. In Proc. ACM Int. Conf. on Multimedia, New York, Oct. 2004.

22. J. Lafferty, A. McCallum, and F. Pereira. Conditional random fields: Probabilistic models for segmenting and labeling sequence data. In Proc. ICML01, 282-289, 2001.

23. X. He, R. Zemel, and M. Carreira-Perpinan. Multiscale conditional random fields for image labeling. In *IEEE Conf. CVPR'04*, 695–702, 2004.

24. Kumar, S., & Hebert, M. (2003). Discriminative fields for modeling spatial dependencies in natural images. *NIPS'03*.

25. M. Szummer and Y. Qi. Contextual recognition of hand-drawn diagrams with conditional random fields. *Workshop on Frontiers in Handwriting Recognition*, 2004.

26. X. Zhu, Z. Ghahramani, and J. Lafferty. Semi-supervised learning using Gaussian fields and harmonic functions. In *ICML*, 2003.

27. M. Seeger. Learning with labeled and unlabeled data. Technical report, The University of Edinburgh, 2000.

28. T. Joachims. Transductive learning via spectral graph partitioning. In ICML, 2003.

29. L. Wang, K. L. Chan, and Z. Zhang, Bootstrapping SVM Active Learning by Incorporating Unlabelled Images for Image Retrieval, IEEE Int'l CVPR'03, 2003.

30. Q. Tian, J. Yu, Q. Xue, and N. Sebe, A New Analysis of the Value of Unlabeled Data in Semi-Supervised Learning for Image Retrieval, IEEE Conf. ICME'2004, 2004.

31. Z.-H. Zhou, K.-J. Chen, and Y. Jiang. Exploiting unlabeled data in content-based image retrieval. In *Proc. 15th ECML*, , 2004.

32. J Fan, H Luo, Y Gao. Learning the semantics of images by uing unlabeled samples, IEEE Int'l CVPR'05, 2005.

33. P. Carbonetto, N. de Freitas, and K. Barnard. A Statistical model for general contextual object recognition. In *ECCV*, 350-362, 2004.

34. G. E. Hinton, Training products of experts by minimizing contrastive divergence, *Neural Comp.* 14:1771–1800, 2002.

NPIC: Hierarchical Synthetic Image Classification Using Image Search and Generic Features

Fei Wang and Min-Yen Kan*

Department of Computer Science, School of Computing,
National University of Singapore, Singapore, 117543
{wangfei2, kanmy}@comp.nus.edu.sg

Abstract. We introduce NPIC, an image classification system that focuses on synthetic (e.g., non-photographic) images. We use class-specific keywords in an image search engine to create a noisily labeled training corpus of images for each class. NPIC then extracts both content-based image retrieval (CBIR) features and metadata-based textual features for each image for machine learning. We evaluate this approach on three different granularities: 1) natural vs. synthetic, 2) map vs. figure vs. icon vs. cartoon vs. artwork 3) and further subclasses of the map and figure classes. The NPIC framework achieves solid performance (99%, 97% and 85% in cross validation, respectively). We find that visual features provide a significant boost in performance, and that textual and visual features vary in usefulness at the different levels of granularities of classification.

1 Introduction

Images created entirely by digital means are growing in importance. Such synthetic images are an important means for recording and presenting visual information. The accurate classification of these images – such as icons, maps, figures and charts – is increasingly important. With the advent of the web, images are being used not just to communicate content but also for decoration, formatting and alignment. An image classification system can improve image search and retrieval engines and can act an input filter for downstream web processing as well as image understanding systems.

We introduce NPIC, an image classification system that is specifically trained on synthetic images. The implemented system uses semi-supervised machine learning to create its classifier. It does this by first using class-specific keywords to build a corpus of associated images via an image search engine. Textual features are extracted from the filename, comments and URLs of the images and content-based image retrieval features are also extracted. These features are strung together as a single feature vector and fed to a machine learner to learn a model. The resulting system is able to enhance the performance of text-only based image search, as the addition of visual features allows some spurious image matches to be correctly rejected.

A classifier needs ground truth labels to classify against. Existing image classification taxonomies are a good starting point. However, our dataset comes from the web, and in our opinion, a suitable taxonomy of content images available on the web does not exist. After sampling synthetic images culled from the web, we decided to create

---

* Contact author.

H. Sundaram et al. (Eds.): CIVR 2006, LNCS 4071, pp. 473–482, 2006.
© Springer-Verlag Berlin Heidelberg 2006

our own hierarchy for the classification of web images, loosely based on portions of the Getty Art and Architecture Thesaurus (AAT).

NPIC obtains very good classification accuracy on all three granularities that we have trained the system on. A key point in the analysis of our study shows that although textual features are an immense help to synthetic image classification, their efficacy can be eclipsed by CBIR features at finer granularities.

After reviewing past related work on image classification, we discuss our methodology, including the design for the image hierarchy and how we construct our training data set using the commodity image search engine, Google Image Search. We then inventory both the textual and visual features in Section 4. Finally, we describe our experiments using cross-validation on the training set as well as using another synthetic dataset drawn from the Wikipedia.

2   Related Work

Image classification is a relatively young field of research, with many published systems being created after the year 2000. As of today, although many image categorization systems have been created, most classify against a very general classification scheme. A representative example is [1], who implemented and evaluated a system that performs a two-stage classification of images: first, distinguishing photo-like images from non-photographic ones, followed by a second round in which actual photos are separated from artificial, photo-like images, and non-photographic images are differentiated into presentation slides, scientific posters and comics. The WebSeer system [2] investigates how to classify images into three categories: photographs, portraits and computer-generated drawings. Both schemes are neither exclusive nor exhaustive; many images fall into multiple categories or none. Work has also focused on specific synthetic image classes. [3] and [4] deal only with chart images. These works aim to classify and then extract the data and semantic meaning of several types of charts: such as bar, pie and line charts. Similar to our work, [5]'s system classifies web images found in news sites by their functionality: including classes for story images, advertisements, server host images, icons and logos.

Textual features. Quite a bit of research focuses on the textual features related to an image. [2] and [5] performed classification based on textual features such as the filename, alternate text, hyperlink and text surrounding the image. Both papers deal only with web-accessible images, so hyperlinks are always available to be used. Attempts have also been made to detect and recognize text embedded in images. [6] and [7] use spatial variance and color segmentation techniques to separate text segments from graphics on an image. OCR or similar techniques often can extract the text from regions of the image. Using this technique, [8] detects text on images by examining connected components that satisfy certain criteria. Structure or comment metadata (i.e., MPEG-7) may also provide useful textual features in the future, but currently is not prevalent enough to affect classification performance. Taken altogether, it is probably unsurprising that [9] argues that textual features of images are far more useful in determining which images to return for a search query.

This will not work in cases where an image to be classified does not come from the web. Reliance on textual features might degrade the system performance when an image is not identifiable by these features, yet is easily associated with a category by the image's visual features.

Visual features. Most systems use simple visual features such as the most prevalent color, width-to-height ratio, image file type, among others. Using additional features from the image itself is the focus of Content Based Image Retrieval (CBIR). CBIR systems have progressively advanced, but practically all systems share a body of features based on the image's color histogram, texture, edge shape, and regions. From these low-level features, higher-level features that may have semantic meanings can be identified and built. For single images, region segmentation [10,11] or block segmentation [12] is usually done followed by spatial layout based matching of regions or statistical feature extraction [13]. Feature analysis of the same color, salient points [14], texture and line features can then be assessed for individual regions and matched.

While CBIR has undoubtedly improved much over recent years, it remains a technology that has been mostly omitted from standard image search. This is largely due to the fact that searchers would rather type in a textual description to start. Automatic, content-based blind feedback on the top ranked images also does not seem to work, as text-based search followed by CBIR is computationally expensive.

3 Methodology

Given these observations, one architecture for improved image classification incorporates CBIR visual features with textual ones. This captures both the high accuracy and semantic nuances that textual features can garner, but enables classification based purely on visual features when text is not available.

In a nutshell, NPIC performs its task in three steps. Given a taxonomy of image classification, NPIC: 1) Constructs a dataset of sample images each class using traditional image search engines; 2) Extracts both textual and visual features from each sample image to create feature vectors for learning; 3) Builds discriminative models for each set of sibling classes in the hierarchy that originate from a common parent. Images can then be programmatically classified by generating their feature vector representations (step 2), followed by classification against the inferred models.

While this approach can be applied to any classification, we have specifically trained the NPIC system for synthetic images. We address synthetic images specifically as they often carry semantic content and data that are of interest to scholars and as well as the image analysis and digital library community.

An ontology of synthetic images. What is a proper taxonomy of synthetic images? To our knowledge, few classifications of synthetic images exist. In our exploration of related research, only Lienhart and Hartmann's work [1] addressed synthetic images specifically. In their work, synthetic images found on the web are classified into four distinct categories of photo-like images, presentation slides, scientific posters and comics. Another possible classification is the widely-used Getty Art and Architecture thesaurus [15]. The AAT is used mainly by museums and libraries to catalog visual materials.

It employs a faceted classification for objects, materials, activities, styles and periods (among others) and consists of over 133,000 generic terms.

A successful classification scheme must ensure that it can classify most items and that items clearly belong to distinct classes. For us, a successful classification needs to be simple enough such that an ordinary layman can understand and employ the classification scheme without needing specialist knowledge. Given these criteria, we feel neither Lienhart and Hartmann's classification (covers only certain types of web images) nor the Getty AAT schemes (too complex) work well.

Instead, our classification is based on what types of synthetic images a user encounters during her daily computing tasks. Our classification has five broad categories: *maps*, *figures*, *icons*, *cartoons* and *artwork*. We include *icons* as many images on a computer are icons associated with programs or data files. *Artwork* includes work drawings and pictures representing aesthetic images; *figures* include all types of abstract data representations. In our empirical analysis, this classification covers a large portion of important functional image types that users encounter.

As most images do not come labeled as synthetic or natural, we must include and implement a superordinate classifier to distinguish between *natural* and *synthetic* images for NPIC to be useful. Also, the two classes of *maps* and *figures* can be refined as they are quite general. We use the AAT to refine these two image types. The AAT has classifications for maps based on its form, function, production method, or subject. Based on our analysis, we conflated these schemes to produce a single subordinate classification of five categories: *plans*, *chorographic maps* (i.e., maps of large regions), *relief maps*, *weather maps* and *zip code maps*. Following the same editorial selection of the relevant AAT categories, we construct a categorization of *figures* into seven categories: *block diagrams*, *venn diagrams*, *bar graphs*, *pie charts*, *line graphs*, *tables*, and *illustrations*. Figure 1 shows our resulting classification hierarchy.

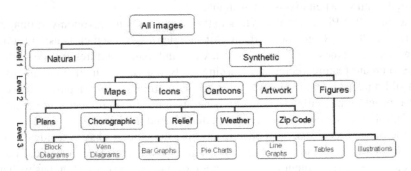

Fig. 1. NPIC's classification hierarchy

We would like to emphasize that the hierarchy developed here constitutes a working attempt to compile a useable and useful classification to typical end users, and should not be construed as a formal model for synthetic image classification. Other image classes or alternate organizations can be also considered; such alternative classification schemes may work equally well in the NPIC framework.

Automatic corpus collection using image search. Given this classification, NPIC needs to collect labeled image samples to extract features for supervised learning. However, publicly available labeled synthetic datasets do not exist and creating one through manual efforts of annotating and selecting clean images is quite costly. However, as most machine learning algorithms are robust to small amounts of noise in their training data, we opt to create an image dataset by automatic means that may contain small amounts of mislabeled data. NPIC thus relies on the ratio of correctly labeled to mislabeled instances in training.

We do this by employing web image search engines. By searching for keywords that are indicative of the desired image category, we can form a noisy collection of images to use in training (hence our method is semi-supervised, as supervision is equated with image search engine relevance). The returned image dataset from any search is noisy, as image search engines occasionally return false matches. As long as the number of false hits is minimal, the image sets should generate useful training features for classification.

We follow this procedure to build image datasets for each of the image classes in the hierarchy. After associating each image class with a set of representative keywords (as shown in Table 1), we input these terms to Google's Image Search to find matching images. We build this dataset from the bottom up, as sample images from each child class can serve as positive examples for its parent. Given a ranked list of images for a class, we programmatically extract the URLs of the images for the first n hits. To help minimize the skew of the dataset, we extract a balanced corpus for each level (10K, 5K and .6K images for each of the three levels, respectively), balancing the number of images extracted from each keyword. We followed this procedure for all of the categories, except for *icons*, as we had access to a clean collection of icons.

Table 1. Some representative keywords for classes in our image hierarchy

Level 1	photograph	aerial, birthday, bedroom, central library, concert, face
Level 2	artwork	painting, drawing, artwork
	icons	*<separate icon collections used>*
	cartoons	cartoon, disney, anime, garfield
Level 3	plans	floor, plan, fire escape
	table	data, excel
	illustration	illustration, DNA molecule, engine

4   Features

Once the corpus was collected, each image was processed to extract textual and visual features for training and testing. As our paper does not focus on the feature creation, we only give a brief inventory of the features used in Table 2. These features have been chosen as they have been shown to be useful for image classification (natural as well as synthetic) in past work, as referenced in the final column of the table. We use standard utilities to extract both sets of features: the `identify` utility from the ImageMagick library to extract image metadata from the header; and for visual features, the OpenCV suite of visual detectors and the `xpm` package to examine the raster data.

A short discussion about the features is necessary. Textual features were created by extracting tokens from the filename, extension, and path information from the URL

Table 2. Features in NPIC. References indicate past published work using this feature.

Feature	Description	Refs.
	Textual Features - via analysis and header metadata	
Filename	Image filename without extension	[2,9,5]
File extension	Extension of the file, if any	[2,9,5]
Comments	Comments in Image metadata header	new
Image URL	URL components of the location of the image on the Web (if applicable)	[2,9,5]
Page URL	URL components of the enclosing page of the image	[2,9,5]
	Visual Features - header information, raster via XPM, or shape detection via OpenCV	
Height	Image dimensions in pixels	[2,1,5]
Width		[2,1,5]
X resolution	Number of pixels per inch (dpi) along X and Y dimensions	new
Y resolution		
C_1	Most common color	[5,2]
C_1 Fraction	Fraction of pixels in the image that have color C_1	[5,2]
$F1$	Fraction of pixels with the neighbor metric greater than zero	[1]
$F2$	Fraction of pixels with the neighbor metric greater than 1/4 of the maximum	[1]
F2/F1	The ratio of F2 to F1	[1]
L1 distance	$L1 = \sum(\lvert h_i - k_i\rvert)$, where $H = \{h_i\}$ is the image histogram, and $K = \{k_i\}$ represents the average histogram in each category	[16]
L2 distance	$L2 = (\sum \lvert h_i - k_i\rvert^2)^{1/2}$	[16]
L-∞ distance	$L\text{-}\infty = (\sum(\lvert h_i - k_i\rvert)^{100})^{1/100}$, a large value of 100 is chosen to represent infinity	[16]
Jeffrey divergence distance	$\sum((h_i log(h_i/m_i) + k_i log(k_i/m_i))$, where $m_i = (h_i + k_i)/2$	[16]
Chi^2 distance	$\sum((h_i - m_i)^2/m_i)$ where $m_i = (h_i + k_i)/2$	[16]
Quadratic distance	$d_A(H, K) = \sqrt{(\mathbf{h} - \mathbf{k})^T \mathbf{A}(\mathbf{h} - \mathbf{k})}$, where $\mathbf{h}$ and $\mathbf{k}$ are vectors that list every entry in $\mathbf{H}$ and $\mathbf{K}$. Cross-bin information is incorporated via a similarity matrix $\mathbf{A} = [a_{ij}]$ where a_{ij} denotes similarity between bins i and j.	[16]
EMD	Earth Movers Distance: $EMD(P,Q) = \dfrac{\sum_{i=1}^{m}\sum_{j=1}^{m} d_{ij}f_{ij}}{\sum_{i=1}^{m}\sum_{j=1}^{m} f_{ij}}$	[17][16]
Rectangles	2 features: Number of rectangles whose sides are parallel to the image frame, fraction of entire image occupied by rectangles	[17]
Circles	Number of circles with certain radius	new
Corners	Number of corners found on the image	new
Lines	5 features: Number of horizontal, vertical and slanted lines; average line length and average line gradient	new

(when available) of the image. For this, simple tokenization was done to create a more meaningful inventory of features (`garfield_2.jpg` → `garfield 2 jpg`) and to reduce problems with sparse data.

We have chosen to use many color features for visual features as they are relatively straightforward to calculate given raster data. We follow the literature and use both the HSV and RGB color spaces for analysis. For neighbor metrics, we create features using the standard RGB and HSV color spaces, as well as reduced HS and H spaces. Color histogram features are calculated using a simplified 9-bit RGB color space. This is done by first obtaining an average histogram over all training samples in a class. Then for each testing image, we calculate the difference between the class average and the image's histogram. A total of n features are generated, where n is the number of classes in the classifier (e.g., 5 for the second level). A number of different distance measures are used: Minkowski-form (L1, L2 and L-∞), Jeffrey Divergence, Chi-square, Quadratic distances as well as EMD.

For the rectangle, line, circle and corner detection features, we need to specific settings for the spatial and scaling constraints of the detectors. Using a *laissez faire* approach, we use a wide variety of parameter settings to create different features and forward these to the learner to decide which group of parameter settings should be used.

5   Evaluation

There are two questions that we would like to answer with our evaluation: 1) how well does NPIC perform? 2) how do the different textual and visual features interact to achieve its performance?

Image datasets. We tested NPIC's performance on two datasets of image data. The first is the original corpus of 15,600 images that was obtained by automatically down-loading pictures from Google Image Search. The second corpus consists of a subset of 1,300 images (200, 500 and 600 images for levels 1, 2 and 3, respectively) retrieved from the Wikipedia Commons. The Wikipedia Commons is a license-free repository of media files free for anyone to use in any way. These datasets are available from our NPIC website, to facilitate further research in the field[1]. These datasets are entirely independent of each other.

Procedure. After obtaining the datasets, each dataset was hand-labeled by the first au-thor (for evaluation only – we rely on the assigned labels from the keyword search in training). For the Google dataset, we performed five-fold cross validation; that is, we used 4/5ths of the data to train a model and 1/5 for testing, and repeated this process five times and averaging the performance. For the Wikipedia dataset, the entire Google dataset was used for training a model, and tested on the Wikipedia set. A boosted deci-sion list learner, BoosTexter [18], was used as the machine learner, as its inferred rules are easy to interpret. The learner was asked to do 300 rounds of boosting (i.e., 300 serial rules inferred) for each classifier. The rules also easily lend themselves to an analysis of which features are helpful. For succinctness, Table 3 shows only the resulting accuracy; precision, recall and F_1 are intentionally omitted.

We observe several trends from the results. First, accuracy increases as we go from the specific Level 3 classifiers towards the Level 1 classifier. This is expected, as the Level 3 classifiers are more fine-grained and are harder, 5- or 7-way decision prob-lems. Second, accuracy on the Wikipedia dataset is lower across the board. Specifically, the textual features are less helpful than the visual ones. This is partially due to the fact that URLs are not available in this dataset and that the filenames are not nearly as indicative of the class as in the Google dataset (after all, filenames are partial evi-dence for relevance in Google's image search, used to construct the dataset). The visual features show roughly the same performance on both data sets. As such, we feel that the test on the Wikipedia dataset is more realistic and representative of what would be encountered in practice. Third, maps are harder to classify than figures, as the figure subcategories have notably different visual features that are captured by the OpenCV detectors. Fourth, icons do extremely well, as their extension in Windows is a fixed .ico and we start with a clean corpus, unlike any of the other sets. Finally, although the performance is not directly comparable with prior reported results (as the problem specifications and datasets differ), the NPIC classifiers show similar performance. The advantage here is that NPIC system uses a set of very general, coarse features that are inexpensive to compute and applicable to a wide range of problems. Classifiers aimed at specific tasks (c.f., [19]) are bound to do better in their stated problem domain.

---

[1] http://wing.comp.nus.edu.sg/npic/

Table 3. Performance of NPIC on the two datasets, with different feature sets

Level	Class	Average C.V. accuracy (Google)			Testing accuracy (Wikipedia)		
		Text (T)	Visual (V)	V + T	T	V	V + T
Level 1	Synthetic	99.4%	95.9%	99.9%	94%	93%	95%
	Natural	99.7%	93.5%	99.9%	90%	92%	94%
	Total	99.6%	94.7%	99.9%	92%	92.5%	94.5%
Level 2	Map	94.3%	87.6%	98.5%	78%	77%	86%
	Figure	90.5%	82.9%	98.7%	74%	78%	90%
	Icon	100.0%	77.6%	100.0%	95%	91%	96%
	Cartoon	89.2%	73.6%	97.6%	69%	84%	81%
	Artwork	92.5%	67.0%	93.2%	73%	74%	79%
	Total	93.3%	77.7%	97.6%	77.8%	80.8%	83.4%
Level 3	Block diagram	84%	86%	84%	72%	82%	86%
(Figure)	Venn diagram	88%	86%	90%	70%	88%	90%
	Bar graph	84%	78%	82%	78%	78%	74%
	Pie chart	82%	86%	90%	80%	86%	86%
	Line graph	80%	78%	80%	66%	74%	76%
	Table	78%	68%	82%	72%	72%	76%
	Illustration	82%	78%	82%	74%	80%	82%
	Total	82.6%	80.0%	84.3%	73.1%	79.9%	81.4%
Level 3	Plan map	86%	76%	86%	82%	78%	84%
(Map)	Chorographic map	86%	80%	88%	78%	82%	82%
	Relief map	90%	68%	84%	70%	70%	72%
	Weather map	84%	64%	84%	74%	66%	72%
	Zip code map	96%	72%	92%	88%	72%	86%
	Total	88.4%	72.0%	86.8%	78.4%	73.6%	79.2%

Given that image search primarily employs textual features, are the improvements by incorporating visual features significant? We compared the textual versus the combined feature judgments using Student's 2-tailed T-test. Our findings indicate a significant ($p < .05$) for both Level 2 classifiers but not the Level 1 or 3 classifiers. We believe the reason for this is simply because there are too few images for the Level 3 classifiers (600 for both Level 3 classifiers) and for the Level 1 Wikipedia classifier (1000).

To assess the efficacy of the feature sets, we explore the resulting classifiers. Table 4 shows the first 100 features used by each of the four inferred models (with repetitions omitted). We see that individual words (each a separate feature) constitute a large fraction the useful features in the Level 1 and 2 classifiers, but a smaller fraction of Level 3 features (validating our earlier claim). We also see that the color histogram distance measures play a larger role in the fined-grained classifiers, and that no one distance measure is best: they all seem to be used by the classifier for discriminating in different instances. Finally, our OpenCV features have been effective for the classes we suspect: circles are used in the *figure* classifier and vertical/slanted lines in the *map* classifier (perhaps for deciding between building plans vs. natural region maps).

For the OpenCV detectors, the learner found optimal settings through cross-validation separation. For the circle detector, a diameter setting of $d = 0.3 \times min$

Table 4. Salient features found in the BoosTexter models

Level	Textual Features	Visual Features
Level 1	jpeg smsu co jennifer friends azoft stylefest gif map painting pie shtml a search drawing areas iconfan serials paris freeyellow online ru tv sponsors sponsors k12 eastburtonhouse	Quantum, C_1, F1/D2, Magick, L-∞, C_1 Fraction, Colors, Height, Background$_H$
Level 2	map painting artwork drawing ico cartoon venn graph diagram disney pie anime garfield maps physics www directory chemistry comics com world artwork art maths archie chem. page street au image tintin gifs sg city hein edu books chinese asp sun moaa gov nr 278 nice chart assembled ga, region	Width, F1/D3, #slantedLines, F2/D1, Quad$_{artwork}$ #HorizontalLines, Quad$_{icon}$, Height, AvgLineLength, Background$_H$, averageLineGradient, F1/D4, F1/D1, Size, F1-F2/D1, EMD$_{diagram}$, JD$_{artwork}$, EMD$_{artwork}$, X-resolution
Level 3 (Figure)	block pie venn bar table diagram data archives illustration 2 barograph none gov charts htm cty us edu venndiagram fag articles hisoftware en cfm 0805rettable pubs	#SlantedLines, #circles, Chi$^2_{block}$, AvgLineGradient, #HorizontalLines, Width, X-resolution, Size, Chi$^2_{diagram}$, #VerticalLines, Colors, AvgLineLength, EMD$_{block}$, Background, Y-resolution, EMD$_{pieChart}$, JD$_{pieChart}$, L1$_{barGraph}$, L2$_{graph}$, EMD$_{block}$, Height, Quad$_{block}$, L-∞_{block}
Level 3 (Map)	weather plan relief noaa gov weather country map us maps com plan wunderground leone scbtvsworld graphics planning wr php province map asp files ca	#SlantedLines, EMD$_{region}$, #HorizontalLines, AvgGradient, #Corners, L1$_{relief}$, EMD$_{relief}$, AvgLineLength, EMD$_{weather}$, L1$_{zipAreaCode}$, L-∞_{relief}, EMD$_{weather}$, L2$_{zipAreaCode}$, JD$_{plan}$, QuadDist$_{zipAreaCode}$, #VerticalLines, Height, EMD$_{plan}$, FractionOccupiedByRectangles, L-$\infty_{weather}$

($height, width$) performed best, as lower settings of d would find many spurious results; the rectangle detector was set to detect only ones parallel to the image frame.

6   Conclusion

We have introduced NPIC, a system specifically trained for synthetic image classification. This system is fully automated and distinguishes between natural vs. synthetic images, and types synthetic images into five classes, of which *maps* and *figures* are further subdivided. We obtain the image datasets by standard text-based image search using keywords highly correlated with each class. This noisily labeled corpus serves as training data, making our classification scheme semi-supervised. In all cases, performance of the classifiers increases when simple color and geometric shape detection features (specifically for particular synthetic image classes) are added. A key result is that visual features make a stronger contribution than the textual ones when fine grained classification is needed.

NPIC is based on a general framework that relies on the scale of image search engines to sift away noise from the training data. Such a framework could be extended to natural image classification, where much of image retrieval research is centered on. We expect to further improve NPIC in the future by 1) using the relevance ranking of the images from search engine in weighting examples for training, and 2) exploring how to find keywords automatically for training data acquisition. We plan to achieve the latter using mutual information which can provide a list of statistically correlated modifiers for a base keyword. We have already done a detailed error analysis on the dataset, and have additional features in mind that may help to improve performance.

References

1. Lienhart, R., Hartmann, A.: Classifying images on the web automatically. Journal of Electronic Imaging **11** (2002)
2. Swain, M.J., Frankel, C., Athitsos, V.: Webseer: An image search engine for the world wide web. In: International Conference on Computer Vision and Pattern Recognition. (1997)
3. Huang, W., Tan, C.L., Loew, W.K.: Model-based chart image recognition. In: Proceedings of the International Workshop on Graphics Recognition (GREC). (2003) 87–99
4. Carberry, S., Elzer, S., Green, N., McCoy, K., Chester, D.: Extending document summarization to information graphics. In: Proceedings of the ACL-04 Workshop. (2004) 3–9
5. Hu, J., Bagga, A.: Functionality-based web image categorization. In: Proceedings of WWW 2003. (2003)
6. Cao, R., Tan, C.L.: Separation of overlapping text from graphics. In: Proc. of the 6th International Conference on Document Analysis and Recognition (ICDAR '01). (2001) 44
7. Zhong, Y., Karu, K., Jain, A.K.: Locating text in complex color images. Pattern Recognition **29** (1995) 1523–1535
8. Zhou, J., Lopresti, D.: Extracting text from www images. In: Proc. of the 4th International Conference on Document Analysis and Recognition. Volume 1. (1997) 248 – 252
9. Munson, E., Tsymbalenko, Y.: To search for images on the web, look at the text, then look at the images. In: Proc. of the 1st international workshop on Web Document Analysis (WDA '01). (2001)
10. Carson, C., Belongie, S., Greenspan, H., Malik, J.: Blobworld: Image segmentation using expectation-maximization and its application to image querying. IEEE Transactions on Pattern Analysis and Machine Intelligence **24** (2002) 1026–1038
11. Ma, W.Y., Manjunath, B.: NaTra: A toolbox for navigating large image databases. In: Proc. IEEE International Conference on Image Processing. (1997) 568–71
12. Smith, J.R., Chang, S.F.: Quad-tree segmentation for texture-based image query. In: Proceedings of the 2nd Annual ACM Multimedia Conference, San Francisco, CA (1994)
13. Wang, J.Z., Li, J., Chan, D., Wiederhold, G.: Semantics-sensitive retrieval for digital picture libraries. D-Lib Magazine **5** (1999)
14. Tian, Q., Sebe, N., Lew, M.S., Loupias, E., Huang, T.S.: Image retireval using wavelet-based salient points. J. of Electronic Imaging **10** (2001) 835–849
15. Getty Institute: Art and architecture thesaurus (2006) http://www.getty.edu/research/ conducting_research/vocabularies/aat/.
16. Rubner, Y., Tomasi, C., Guibas, L.J.: The earth mover's distance as a metric for image retrieval. International Journal of Computer Vision **40** (2000) 99–121
17. Qin, L., Charikar, M., Li, K.: Image similarity search with compact data structures. In: Proc. of the 13th ACM conference on Information and knowledge management, Washington, D.C. (2004)
18. Schapire, R.E., Singer, Y.: Boostexter: A boosting-based system for text categorization. Machine Learning **39** (2000) 135–168
19. Ng, T.T., Chang, S.F., Hsu, J., Xie, L., Tsui, M.P.: Physics-motivated features for distinguishing photographic images and computer graphics. In: Proc. of the ACM Int'l Conf. on Multimedia, Singapore (2005) 239–248

Context-Aware Media Retrieval

Ankur Mani and Hari Sundaram

Arts, Media and Engineering, Arizona State University, Tempe AZ 85282 (USA)
{Ankur.Mani, Hari.Sundaram}@asu.edu

Abstract. In this paper we propose a representation framework for dynamic multi-sensory knowledge and user context, and its application in media retrieval. We provide a definition of context, the relationship between context and knowledge and the importance of communication both as a means for the building of context as well as the end achieved by the context. We then propose a model of user context and demonstrate its application in a photo retrieval application. Our experiments demonstrate the advantages of the context-aware media retrieval over other media retrieval approaches especially relevance feedback.

Keywords: Context modeling, media retrieval, knowledge representation.

1 Introduction

In this paper we propose a representation framework for dynamic multi-sensory knowledge and user context, and its application in media retrieval. There are two fundamental problems in media retrieval: the vagueness of the query and the unavailability of the information about the unique way the user associates the different media elements. The context of the user provides solutions to both these problems at the same time and hence representation and estimation of user context is important.

We interpret the user's interaction with a media retrieval system as a special type of communication in which the user provides messages as query and the system provides messages as retrieved media. In any communication scenario, we define context as *"the finite and dynamic set of multi-sensory and inter-related conditions that influences the exchange of messages between two entities in communication."* This set forms a subset of knowledge that is *"a dynamic set of multi-sensory facts."* Knowledge has three important properties; it is multi-sensory (represented through multiple senses), emergent (new facts are formed) and dynamic (old facts are revised). Context is the dynamic subset of knowledge that is in attention and influences the exchange of messages between the entities in communication. In a media retrieval scenario, the multi-sensory and interrelated information set in the user's short-term memory influences the query provided by the user [2] and at the same time is influenced by the user's activity and the media the user consumes. *This set of multi-sensory and interrelated information forms the user query context.* The organization of the rest of the paper is as such. We propose a user context model for

H. Sundaram et al. (Eds.): CIVR 2006, LNCS 4071, pp. 483–486, 2006.
© Springer-Verlag Berlin Heidelberg 2006

media retrieval in section 2 based upon the above discussion. Section 3 discusses user experiments and finally we discuss conclusions in section 4.

2 Context for Media Retrieval

We now present our context model for media retrieval. The context model consists of two structures: a dynamic multi-sensory knowledge representation consisting of the concepts and the relationships between them, and a temporally evolving context representation in relation to this knowledge. The Knowledge can be subdivided into user knowledge (knowledge about the user), environment knowledge (knowledge about the environment, here limited to the common-sense knowledge from ConceptNet [3]) and application knowledge (media database structure consisting of media and related annotations).

2.1 Knowledge

Knowledge is represented as a graph. The nodes in the graph are the instances of concepts in one modality and the weighted edges (weights represent the similarity between the end nodes along the edge) are the relationships between those instances. The user knowledge model is initialized by an initial set of concepts obtained from the user as their profile and obtaining the neighborhood of this set in the environment knowledge. The user knowledge model grows as the user interacts with the media retrieval system that leads to information exchange between the user and the system. The environment knowledge and the application knowledge are represented similarly.

2.2 User Query Context

User query context is represented as the subset of the nodes and edges in the knowledge graph that are in attention. The attention on concepts and relationship types are represented as weights of the respective concepts and the biases on the types of relationships. The bias on the relationship type along with the weight of relationship determines the similarity between the neighboring concepts demonstrating the relationship. The user context evolves with the interaction and the weights of concepts and the biases on relationship types changes as discussed in [1]. Some important desirable properties of the context dynamics are the stability, controllability and suitable steady-state distribution of weights on concepts. It was proved in [1] that the dynamics has these properties.

2.3 Context-Aware Retrieval

We applied our context model to a photo retrieval system. The system is composed of four components as shown in Figure1: a user context model, a media database, a user interface that allows users to enter text query or select relevant images and a search engine. Given the query as a set of selected images, the context-aware search is performed in the media knowledge space to find the most relevant photographs. The search process first obtains the current context from the context model and modifies it

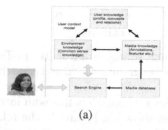

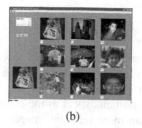

(a)   (b)

Fig. 1. (a) Block diagram of the photo retrieval application and (b) the user interface displays 9 images at a time and allows for query as text and images

using the user information obtained from the query. The modified context is then used to obtain the candidate concepts in the media knowledge space. The images close to the candidate concepts in the media knowledge space form the retrieval results.

3 Experiments

We now discuss the retrieval experiments. To compare the context-aware retrieval with baseline strategies, we performed experiments with three retrieval set-ups namely the random retrieval, relevance feedback based retrieval [4] and the context-aware retrieval. Six graduate students volunteered for the experiments and a database of approximately 4000 images (15% annotated) was made from their shared photo collection. Each user provided a set of at least ten concepts as the seed with which the user knowledge and context were initialized. Then each user searched for one query concept from among a set of choice concepts. Once the images were displayed, the user selected the relevant images that were used to retrieve new set of images without replacement. This process was repeated four times.

Table 1. Number of retrieved images and the mean relevance score for different queries and the % of relevant images in the database

Query	% database	Number of retrieved images; and Mean relevance score		
		Random	Relevance Feedback	Context
Home	10	6; 0.07	12; 0.29	14; 0.32
Birthday	10	4; 0.07	14; 0.24	12; 0.38
Park	20	8; 0.16	20; 0.44	23; 0.51
Office	5	1; 0.02	8; 0.13	10; 0.29

We analyze the experimental results as both cumulative precision of the overall retrieved set and the change in the relevance score with increasing interaction and the personal priorities of different users. We present the cumulative precision results as the number of relevant images that were retrieved in the complete experiment of five iterations and the mean relevance score of the retrieved images in the five iterations. The normalized relevance score for the retrieved set of N images is:

$$S = \frac{2}{N(N+1)} \sum_{j=1}^{N} (N+1-r_j) \; ; \quad \text{where} \quad r_i = \begin{cases} i & i \text{ is relevant to query} \\ 0 & \text{otherwise} \end{cases} \tag{1}$$

The cumulative precisions for three different search strategies are shown in **Table 1**. We observe that the context-aware retrieval gives better cumulative precision than the other retrieval strategies.

An important aspect of the context-based retrieval approach is that with increasing interaction more relevant images are retrieved as shown in Figure 2. The relevance score of the retrieved set is seen increasing with the increasing interaction in the context-based retrieval strategy. The relevance feedback based approach also shows and increasing trend but is not very consistent.

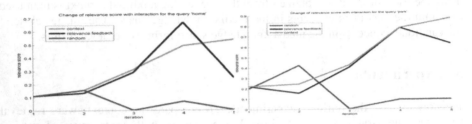

Fig. 2. Plot of relevance score against user interaction for queries 'home' (top) and 'park' (bottom) queries

The improved dynamic performance of the context-based approach against any other approach shows that with increasing interaction, the estimate of the user context becomes more accurate.

4   Conclusions

We presented a representation framework for dynamic multi-sensory knowledge and user context, and its application in media retrieval. Our pilot experiments demonstrated the advantages of context-aware media retrieval. In future along with more experiments, we also plan to expand the representation framework to support the representation of multi-scale and procedural knowledge.

References

1. Mani A., Sundaram H. Modeling User Context with Applications to Media Retrieval. to appear Multimedia Systems Journal, Springer Verlag. summer 2006.
2. Atkinson R. and Shiffrin R. (1968). Human memory: A proposed system and its control processes. The psychology of learning and motivation: Advances in research and theory(eds). New York, Academic Press.
3. ConceptNet http://web.media.mit.edu/~hugo/conceptnet.
4. Rui Y. and Huang T. (1999). A Novel Relevance Feedback Technique in Image Retrieval., Proc. ACM Multimedia 1999, Nov. 1999, Orlando, FL

Estimating the Physical Effort of Human Poses

Yinpeng Chen, Hari Sundaram, and Jodi James

Arts, Media and Engineering, Arizona State University, Tempe, AZ, 85281
{yinpeng.chen, hari.sundaram, jodi.james}@asu.edu

Abstract. This paper deals with the problem of estimating the effort required to maintain a static pose by human beings. The problem is important in developing effective pose classification as wells as in developing models of human attention. We estimate the human pose effort using two kinds of body constraints – skeletal constraints and gravitational constraints. The extracted features are combined together using SVM regression to estimate the pose effort. We tested our algorithm on 55 poses with different annotated efforts with excellent results. Our user studies additionally validate our approach.

1 Introduction

This paper deals with the problem of estimating physical effort for a static human pose. The problem is important in human attention model, dance summary, and pose classification. Human beings routinely are able to distinguish between *human poses that appear to be very similar* by referring to their own physical experience. For example, a standing pose with arm lifting appears similar to a handstand pose. However it is trivial for human beings to see that the handstand pose is very challenging to do for most people. We conjecture that human beings pay *greater attention* to the poses with greater effort, as they are reminded of the difficulty of actually doing the pose. Physical effort is also a useful feature for dance segmentation and summary. Through analyzing the physical effort changing over dance and extracting frames with high effort, we can segment and summary the dance.

Pose classification is a traditional computer vision problem [1,3]. The focus there is appearance based matching or matching in an object based representational space. However, the classification does *not* take the physical experience into account, thus potentially misclassifying poses with different physical effort that appear to be similar. Other related works [4,6] deal with motion quality modals based on Rudolf Laban's Effort Qualities. In Laban Movement Analysis (LMA), effort encompasses qualities of space, weight, time and flow and represents the expressive quality of style within the dynamics of human movement rather than static human poses.

We propose a human pose effort estimation algorithm based on SVM regression. We first extract two kinds of features related to human pose effort: (a) physical constraints and (b) gravity constraints. Then we use SVM regression techniques to combine these features together to estimate effort. We tested our algorithm on an annotated dance pose set with excellent results. We additionally validated our results with user studies.

H. Sundaram et al. (Eds.): CIVR 2006, LNCS 4071, pp. 487–490, 2006.
© Springer-Verlag Berlin Heidelberg 2006

2 Feature Extraction

In this section, we discuss features used for human pose effort. Each pose consists of 35 labeled 3D marker coordinates captured from a marker-based motion capture system. The marker label specifies the location on the body for each marker. We focus on two kinds of constraints related to human pose effort – physical constraints and gravitational constraints. Physical constraints include skeleton structure not related to gravity. Gravitational constraints are introduced due to the force of gravity.

2.1 Features from Physical Constraints

We observe that the physical limitations mainly focus on the joints between limbs. We also observe that arm movements have a wider range of motion in comparison to leg movements, due to the greater mobility of the shoulder joint. Hence, in this paper, we ignore the physical limitations of shoulder and focus on the hip joints.

We use a simple feature, foot distance d_F, to represent inter-leg relationship and four joint angles (1. hip *flexion*, 2. hip *extension*, 3. hip *abduction/adduction* and 4. hip *rotation*) to represent torso-leg relationship. The foot distance and four hip joint angles are shown in Fig. 1. The details on the computation of hip extension (θ_E), hip flexion (θ_F), abduction/adduction (θ_A) and rotation (θ_R) can be found in [2].

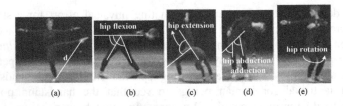

Fig. 1. Five physical constraints. (a) foot distance, (b) left hip flexion and right hip flexion, (c) hip extension, (d) hip abduction/adduction, and (e) hip rotation.

2.2 Features from Gravitational Constraints

Gravitational constraints comprise two factors: (a) *limb torque* and (b) *supporting-limb effort*. In gravity torque computation, we consider three kinds of limbs – *arm*, *leg* and *torso*. The larger the limb gravity torque, the more effort the human needs. We compute the limb gravity torque only if the limb is *not* the supporting limb. This is because limbs in contact with the ground experience a torque due to the normal reaction. This has an effect of canceling the torque of gravity on the limb. The arm, leg and gravity torques are represented by T_A, T_L and T_T respectively. The computation detail can be found in [2].

The supporting limb effort is the effort that the human puts on the limbs in contact with the ground to support the body. This effort is related with the supporting limb power. The supporting limbs that have large supporting power will decrease the amount of effort required holding the pose. We incorporate the supporting power of arms, legs, torso and hip to obtain the supporting limb effort E_s. (See [2] for details)

2.3   Effort Feature Vector

Combining the five physical limitations, three limb torques and supporting-limb effort, we can construct a feature vector for every pose:

$$F = [d_F^\gamma, \theta_F^\gamma, \theta_E^\gamma, \theta_A^\gamma, \theta_R^\gamma, T_A^\gamma, T_L^\gamma, T_T^\gamma, E_s^\gamma]^T \qquad (1)$$

where d_F, θ_F, θ_E, θ_A, θ_R, T_A, T_L, T_T and E_s are foot distance, hip flexion, hip extension, hip abduction/adduction, hip rotation, arm gravity torque, leg gravity torque, torso gravity torque and supporting-limb effort respectively, γ is a constant (γ=1.5).

3   Using SVM Regression

We use SVM regression [5] to combine all features together. In training phrase, each training pose is represented by a feature vector F (eq(1)) and an annotated effort value which is considered as the ground truth G. The goal of SVM regression is to find a function $g(F)$ that has at most deviation ε from the ground truth G for all the training data, and at the same time is as flat as possible. In testing phrase, We extract feature vector F (eq.(1)) of test pose and estimate effort use SVM regression model by:

$$E = g(F) = K(w, F) + b , \qquad (2)$$

where w and b are the solution of SVM regression, $K(\cdot, \cdot)$ denotes a kernel operator.

4   Experiments

We test our human effort estimation algorithm on a dance pose dataset which includes 55 poses. Each pose is annotated with an effort value from zero to five by Professor Jodi James who is an expert in dance and kinesiology. Zero means no effort and five means maximum effort for human to hold a pose. Professor Jodi James made these annotations by her real experience rather than through visual impression of the poses. These 55 poses include 6 levels (0-5), 5 poses for each level (different poses with the same effort) and 5 variations between consecutive levels.

In our experiments, we select one pose as testing data and other 54 poses as training dataset. With 54 training poses, we can train a SVM regression model and apply it on the testing pose to estimate the effort. We repeat this process until every pose is selected as testing data and its effort estimation value is obtained. We use leave-one-out cross validation to evaluate our algorithm:

$$err = \sqrt{\frac{1}{55} \sum_{i=1}^{55} (E_i - G_i)^2} , \qquad (3)$$

where G_i is the ground truth and E_i is the effort estimation result.

In our experiments, we try 3 kernels (linear/polynomial/rbf) in SVM regression. For each kernel, we adjusted SVM regression parameters to minimize the estimation error. The estimation error is minimized when we use polynomial kernel with maximum acceptable deviation ε=10^{-7}, trade-off constant C=27 and polynomial

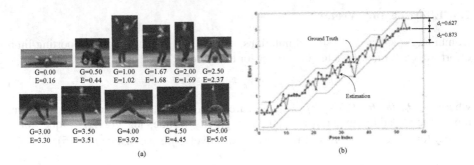

(a)   (b)

Fig. 2. (a) Effort estimation for 11 poses (G is ground truth and E is estimation results, (b) comparisons between ground truth and effort estimation for 55 poses

power=2. Fig. 2(a) shows 11 effort estimation examples and Fig. 2(b) plots the ground truth and effort estimation for all 55 poses. We can see that estimated efforts are close to the ground truth for most poses. The standard deviation (eq. (3)) is 0.295.

We also conducted user studies to determine the relationship between our pose effort measure and human perception and experience. The user studies indicate two clear results (a) our estimation of physical effort is highly correlated with human perception in terms of the effort difference between two poses, (b) the sensitivity to the effort difference is proportional to the effort of the pose that has larger effort [2].

5   Conclusion

In this paper, we have presented a human pose effort estimation algorithm based on SVM regression. There are two key innovations (a) Using both skeletal and gravity constraints to estimate human pose efforts, (b) Using SVM regression to combine features for effort estimation. We evaluated our framework on 55 annotated dance poses with excellent results. In the future, we are planning to incorporate our pose effort framework into human attention model, dance summary and pose recognition.

References

1. S. BELONGIE, J. MALIK, et al. (2002). *Shape matching and object recognition using shape contexts*. IEEE Transactions on Pattern Analysis and Machine Intelligence **24**(24): 509-522.
2. Y. CHEN and H. SUNDARAM (2006). *Using SVM Regression for estimation of Physical Effort*. Arts Media and Engineering Program, ASU, AME-TR-2006-2, Jan. 2006.
3. D. FORSYTH and J. PONCE (2003). Computer vision : a modern approach. Englewood Cliffs, N.J., Prentice Hall.
4. R. LABAN (1971). The Mastery of Movement. Boston, Plays.
5. A. J. SMOLA and B. SCHOLKOPF (2004). *A tutorial on support vector regression*. Statistics and Computing **14**: 199-222.
6. L. ZHAO and N. I. BADLER (2005). *Acquiring and validating motion qualities from live limb gestures*. Graphical Models **67**(1): 1-16.

Modular Design of Media Retrieval Workflows Using ARIA*

Lina Peng[1], Gisik Kwon[1], Yinpeng Chen[1], K. Selçuk Candan[1],
Hari Sundaram[1], Karamvir Chatha[1], and Maria Luisa Sapino[2]

[1] Arizona State University, Tempe, AZ 85287, USA
{lina.peng, gkwon, yinpeng.chen, candan, sundaram}@asu.edu
[2] University of Torino, Italy
mlsapino@di.unito.it

Abstract. In this demo, we present the use of the ARIA platform for modular design of media processing and retrieval applications. ARIA is a middleware for describing and executing media processing workflows to process, filter, and fuse sensory inputs and actuate responses in real-time. ARIA is designed with the goal of maximum modularity and ease of integration of a diverse collection of media processing components and data sources. Moreover, ARIA is cognizant of the fact that various media operators and data structures are adaptable in nature; i.e, the delay, size, and quality/precision characteristics of these operators can be controlled via various parameters. In this demo, we present the ARIA design interface in different image processing and retrieval scenarios.

Keywords: Media retrieval workflows, modular design, image retrieval.

1 Introduction

ARIA [4] is a middleware for describing and executing media processing workflows to process, filter, and fuse sensory inputs and actuate responses in real-time (Figure 1). In this demo, we present the use of the ARIA platform for modular design of media processing and retrieval applications. The objective of ARIA is to incorporate real-time and archived media into live performances, on-demand [4]. This involves development of (1) an adaptive and programmable kernel that can extract, process, fuse, and map media processing workflows while ensuring quality of service guarantees, (2) a specification interface capable of specifying the components of the media processing workflows, and (3) QoS scalable operators.

2 Overview of ARIA

ARIA media processing workflows are modeled as directed graphs where nodes represent sensors, filters, fusion operators, and actuators, while edges represent

---

* This research is funded by NSF grant # 0308268, *"Quality-Adaptive Media-Flow Architectures to Support Sensor Data Management."*

H. Sundaram et al. (Eds.): CIVR 2006, LNCS 4071, pp. 491–494, 2006.
© Springer-Verlag Berlin Heidelberg 2006

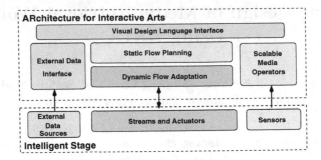

Fig. 1. ARIA modular media processing and retrieval middleware overview

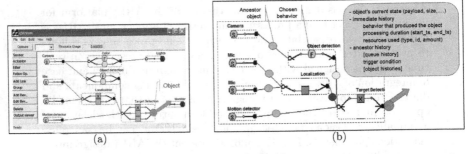

Fig. 2. (a) An example workflow (note that operators have multiple, alternative implementations to choose from) and (b) visual representation of the history of an object

connections that stream objects between components [5]. The basic information unit is a data object (Figure 2(a)). Depending on the task, an object can be as simple as a numeric value (such as an integer denoting the pressure applied on a surface sensor) or as complex as an image component segmented out from frames in a video sequence. Filter and fusion operators provide analysis, aggregation, and filtering semantics. In particular, they may perform complex media processing and database lookup tasks.

Each object in ARIA is annotated with a header, which includes an *object history descriptor*, consisting of the set of *resource usage stamps* and *timestamps* acquired by the object's predecessors as they go through various operators (Figure 2(b)). Among other things, the history descriptor enables the synchronization of objects in the system based on various applicable temporal criteria, queue management decisions, and per-object evaluation of trigger conditions.

Each ARIA operator has a number of input and output queues and a set of behaviors. Each behavior is essentially a different implementation, with different processing delay and quality characteristics. A given behavior of an operator can be executed only when its execution conditions are satisfied. A behavior may not be in an executable state for various reasons, including (but not limited to) resource shortages. The behavior trigger constraints are described in terms of local hardware resources, temporal regulation of the service stream, object property and history (size, precision), and end-to-end workflow conditions (e.g. end-to-end optimization).

When there are multiple behaviors of an operator ready for triggering, it is the job of the ARIA kernel to pick the most appropriate one, based on the quality, delay, or resource constraints [1]. The way the behavior picks its inputs is also governed by resource, time, and quality constraints. Each behavior can sort and use the objects in the input queues based on different criteria (size, quality, recency etc.). When the number of input combinations to consider is larger than the capacity, then system sheds (not the individual queued objects but) combinations of objects that are not promising candidates. Therefore, each behavior also has an input combination shedding model [2].

3   Demo Scenarios

Figure 3 depicts two media retrieval scenarios. In both cases, real-time sensory data are processed, relevant features are extracted through filters, and databases are looked up based on these extracted features. Note that both scenarios include operators with multiple implementations, which will be chosen by the ARIA kernel based on the appropriate optimization and adaptation criteria. Also, the scenarios include user-defined operators as well as system provided operators (such as synchronizers and duplicators).

Figure 4 shows the operator and behavior description interfaces. Note that the operator descriptor is simple in the sense that it only describes the queue

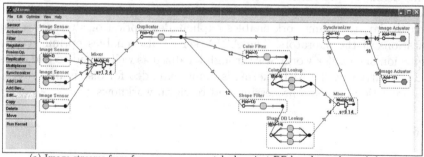

(a) Image streams from four sensors are matched against DB based on color and shape

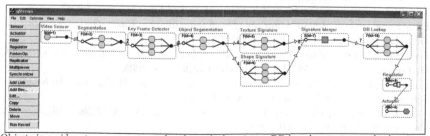

(b) Objects in a video stream are extracted and matched against a DB based on texture and color signatures

Fig. 3. Two media processing and retrieval scenarios

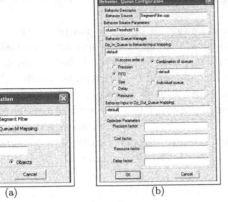

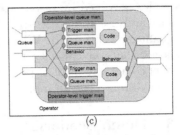

Fig. 4. (a) A filter operator description interface, (b) behavior description interface, and (c) an operator with two behaviors (only one of them active at a time)

properties of the operator. The behavior descriptor, on the other hand, describes the code which implements the behavior, possible input parameters, as well as how a given behavior uses the input queues and default parameters used for optimization and adaptation.

4   Conclusion

In this demo, we present ARIA middleware and its interface for defining media processing and retrieval workflows, especially suitable for sensory applications. In particular, the framework enables explicit description of alternative implementations of the operators. The ARIA kernel also enables optimization and adaptation of complex workflows through localized as well as end-to-end decision making. Currently, the ARIA kernel is being extended for distributed execution and adaptation of media processing and retrieval workflows.

References

1. Lina Peng, *et al. Optimization of Media Processing Workflows with Adaptive Operator Behaviors* accepted for publication at the MTAP Journal, 2005.
2. Lina Peng and K. Selçuk Candan. *Confidence-driven Early Object Elimination in Quality-Aware Sensor Workflows*, DMSN 2005.
3. Lina Peng, *et al. Media Processing Workflow Design and Execution with ARIA.* Demonstration at the ACM Multimedia Conference 2005.
4. Lina Peng *et al. ARIA: An Adaptive and Programmable Media-flow Architecture for Interactive Arts*, ACM MM Inter. Arts Program, 2004.
5. K. Selçuk Candan, G. Kwon, L. Peng, and M.L.Sapino. *Modeling Adaptive Media Processing Workflows.* ICME 2006.

Image Rectification for Stereoscopic Visualization Without 3D Glasses

Jin Zhou and Baoxin Li

Department of Computer Science & Engineering,
Arizona State University,
Tempe, AZ, 85287, U.S.A.
{Jin.Zhou, Baoxin.Li}@asu.edu

Abstract. There exist various methods for stereoscopic viewing of images, most requiring that a viewer wears some special glasses. Recent technology developments have resulted in displays that enable 3D viewing without glasses. In this paper, we present results from our proposed approach to automatic rectification of two images of the same scene captured by cameras at general positions, so that the results can be viewed on a 3D display. Both simulated and real data experiments are presented.

Keywords: Image rectification, stereo, 3-D visualization.

1 Introduction

Recent display technologies have led to various low-cost 3-D displays that enable stereoscopic viewing without inconvenient 3D glasses (see [1] for examples). While the underlying technologies may vary from one manufacture to another, the basic principle of many 3D displays can be illustrated by Fig. 1, where a parallax barrier is used in LCD to direct the light rays from the pixels to the viewer's right and left eyes, respectively. There are many potential applications of this type of displays. However, from Fig. 1, it is obvious that, to enable the stereoscopic viewing capability of a 3D display, one must have the "correct" left and right eye image pair. If the image pair is captured by a standard stereo rig giving proper disparities (i.e., that conforms to the constraints of the display), then this problem is solved. However, true stereo media is scarce, and general consumers rarely use stereo cameras. These unfortunate facts limit the otherwise great potential of the 3D displays.

In this paper, we present results from our algorithms for addressing the following image rectification problem: Given any two images of the same scene from general viewpoint, rectify them so that they look like a true stereo pair like that from a standard stereo rig required by a 3D display. If this problem is solved, we can enable stereoscopic viewing of a lot of media without requiring stereoscopic acquisition. Existing image rectification approaches are mostly for stereo matching rather than forming a true stereo pair, which is our goal.

H. Sundaram et al. (Eds.): CIVR 2006, LNCS 4071, pp. 495–498, 2006.
© Springer-Verlag Berlin Heidelberg 2006

2 Advantages of the Proposed Approach

Detailed description of the proposed algorithm is available through a technical report from cubic.asu.edu. In this section, we highlight the key points of the approach as follows. Firstly, we proposed a new rectification algorithm, starting from the calibrated case. This leads to an intuitive interpretation of the algorithm, which is not available from existing derivations. Secondly, we use a physically meaningful constraint for removing the ambiguity in estimating the required homographies for rectification. The resultant image pair does not have visual distortion that may be present in most existing algorithms such as [3][4]. Thirdly, we designed several practical schemes for shifting the rectified images such that they conform to the disparity requirement preferred by the 3D display.

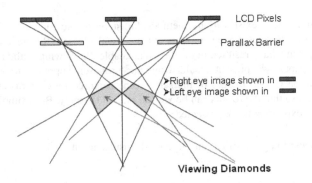

Fig. 1. An illustration of how a parallax-barrier-based 3D display works

3 Demonstration of the Experimental Results

We present three types of experiments to validate the proposed algorithms, as detailed in the following. Note that, although we can only present sample images here, in our experiments, the rectified pairs were further validated by visualizing on a SHARP 15-in 3D display, which will be used in the demo on CIVR 2006.

Experiment I. In the first experiment, we use the data made available on the Internet by the Interactive Visual Media Group at Microsoft Research, which contains accurate camera calibration information and thus allows us to verify the key components of our algorithms without having to use a fundamental matrix estimated from raw data. The data set contains videos captured from 8 different cameras. We select a pair of images from any two cameras (illustrated in Fig. 2, the left column). After applying our rectification algorithm, we got the rectified results as illustrated in Fig. 2 (center column), where the epipolar lines becomes horizontal and also aligned. This satisfied the epipolar constraints. Moreover, we can find that the image do not have obvious visual distortion, demonstrating that the ambiguity in the rectification is removed by the proposed algorithm. As a comparison, we also rectify the pair using the given camera matrices (i.e., using the algorithm for the calibrated case, e.g. see[2]), obtaining the results in Fig. 2 (right column). The shift of the right image is due to the large distance between the two cameras. Other than that, there is no big difference between the results from the calibrated and the uncalibrated algorithms.

Experiment II. In the second type of experiments, we use OpenGL to simulate views from different camera positions, which can be precisely controlled. This provides us

Fig. 2. Left column: original pair. Center column: rectification results based on fundamental matrix. Right column: results based on the proposed method.

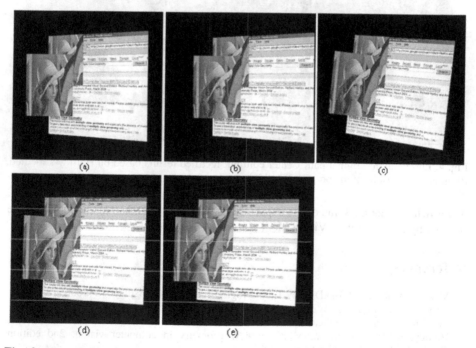

Fig. 3. (a) and (b) are standard stereo pair. (c) is the view after rotating camera on (b)'s position. (d) and (e) are rectified results on (a) and (c) purely based on image. (d) and (e) apparently form a stereo pair.

with virtual stereo pairs of any desired configuration (e.g., any baseline).In the example illustrated in Fig. 35, the scene is made up of two planes at different depth. Fig. 3 (a) and (b) shows a desired stereo pair. Fig. 3 (c) is a view after rotating the camera of (b) (note that this is different from simply rotating the image). We now rectify (a) and (c), with the desired camera configuration as the goal. Ideally, after the rectification, we should have a pair like (a) and (b). Fig. 3 (d) and (e) are the results, which are almost the same as the true stereo images (a) and (b) except for a horizontal translation. Note that in this type of experiments, the algorithm for the uncalibrated case is used, meaning that we have to estimate the fundamental matrix from the synthesized images. The ambiguity of the horizontal translation arises from the fact that our algorithm relies on the fundamental matrix, and thus one of the proposed shifting schemes should be used before visualization on a 3D display.

Experiment III. The third experiments use real images captured by a hand-held camera from different positions. Sample results are given in Fig. 4, in which the left column is the original image pair, the center column the results of the method in ([3]), and the right column our results. It is obvious that there is shear distortion in the center column.

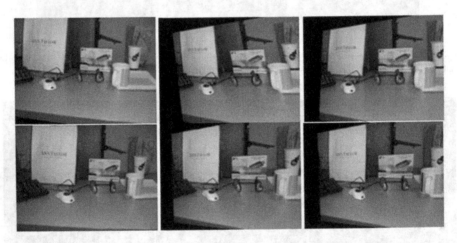

Fig. 4. Left column: original pair. Center column: rectified results based on Hartley's method. Right column: results of the proposed method.

Acknowledgements. Some of the experiments were based on data made public on the Internet by the Interactive Visual Media Group at Microsoft Research.

References

1. May, P.: A Survey of 3-D Display Technologies. Information Display. 32 (2005) 28-33.
2. Fusiello, A., Trucco, E., Verri, A.: A compact algorithm for rectification of stereo pairs. Machine Vision and Applications. 12 (2000), 16-22.
3. Hartley, R., Zisserman, A.: Multiple view geometry in computer vision. 2nd edition. Cambridge University, Cambridge (2003).
4. Loop, C., Zhang, Z.: Computing rectifying homographies for stero vision. Proc. of IEEE Conf. on Computer Vision and Pattern Recogntion (1999), 125-131.

Human Movement Analysis for Interactive Dance

Gang Qian[1,2], Jodi James[1], Todd Ingalls[1], Thanassis Rikakis[1],
Stjepan Rajko[1,3], Yi Wang[1,3], Daniel Whiteley[1,2], and Feng Guo[1,2]

[1] Arts, Media and Engineering Program
[2] Department of Electrical Engineering
[3] Department of Computer Science and Engineering
Arizonoa State University
Tempe, AZ, 85287, USA
{Gang.Qian, Jodi.James, Todd.Ingalls, Thanassis.Rikakis,
Stjepan.Rajko, Yi.Wang.2, Daniel.Whiteley, Feng.Guo}@asu.edu

Abstract. In this paper, we provide a brief overview of the human movement analysis research at the Arts, Media and Engineering program, Arizona State University, and its applications in interactive dance. A family of robust algorithms has been developed to analyze dancers' movement at multiple temporal and spatial levels from a number of perspectives such as marker distributions, joint angles, body silhouettes as well as weight distributions to conduct reliable dancer tracking, posture and gesture recognition. Multiple movement sensing modalities have been used and sometimes fused in our current research, including marker-based motion capture system, pressure sensitive floor and video cameras. Some of the developed algorithms have been successfully used in real life dance performances.

1 Introduction

As a new form of performing arts, interactive dance has attracted increasing interest among choreographers, composers, visual artists as well as computer scientists and engineers [2]. This interest is rooted not only in the freedom that it provides to choreographers and dancers to interact and control the audio and visual feedback, but also in the challenges that composers and visual artists are facing to create feedback engines promptly responsive to the dancers movement. However, to computer scientists and engineers, the biggest challenge is to design robust signal processing and pattern recognition algorithms that can reliably extract movement-related cues that dancers can use to communicate with the feedback engines thus to control the audio and visual feedback.

Interactive dance poses unique challenges for human movement sensing and analysis. In dance performance, there are many factors that can affect the accuracy of the motion analysis, such as the use of costume covering markers, the presence of multiple dancers and complex dance movement. To make interactive dance possible, proper sensing modalities and interactive cues need to be selected and robust motion analysis algorithms are to be designed.

At the Arts, Media and Engineering (AME) Program, we have developed a family of robust algorithms to analyze dancers' movement at multiple temporal and spatial

H. Sundaram et al. (Eds.): CIVR 2006, LNCS 4071, pp. 499–502, 2006.
© Springer-Verlag Berlin Heidelberg 2006

levels, from global tracking and group dynamic analysis of multiple dancers over a long period of time (~20 minutes), to the recognition of static body postures and dynamic gestures. Multiple movement sensing modalities have been used in our movement analysis research, including marker-based motion capture system, pressure sensitive floor and video cameras. The pressure sensitive floor and the marker-based motion capture system have been combined in gesture recognition to improve the recognition spectrum of the analysis engine. Some of the developed algorithms have been successfully used in real life dance performances.

2 Movement Sensing and Analysis

2.1 Dancer Tracking Using Unlabeled Markers

In many dance performances, multiple dancers are present on the stage at the same time [2]. We have developed a robust dancer tracking algorithm [5] using only unlabeled marker data. The reason for the use of unlabeled marker is that since when multiple dancers are present on the stage and the motion capture cameras have to be up and far away from the subjects (to be invisible to the audience), the motion capture system we are using is not able to provide reliable labeled markers in real-time, while reconstruction of the marker 3D coordinates is still reasonable. The tracking algorithm is based on the mean-shift algorithm, by treating dancers with markers as point clouds that have noticeable characteristics. Such characteristics include known marker set, all the markers of one dancer being within an average wingspan. By using these characteristics, a blurring process is used to find the location of the dancers through mode finding. These modes, representing the locations of the dancers, are then tracked using a mean-shift algorithm. This system has been successfully used real life dance performances [2] and reliable tracking results have been obtained.

2.2 Robust Dance Pose Recognition

Robust dance pose recognition algorithms using both the marker-based motion capture systems and video cameras have been developed.

Using the marker-based motion capture system, a series of algorithms for robust dance pose recognition using labeled or unlabeled data have been designed and implemented. To increase both recognition accuracy and computational efficiency, robust pause detection algorithms [4] based on joint angles/shape context are deployed as a filter to identify pauses before recognizing any poses. When most markers are labeled, support vector machines (SVM) using Gaussian kernels are used to recognize the input motion capture frame (i.e. the query pose).

When most markers are unlabeled, pose recognition is cast into an optimization problem through the minimization of the Kullback-Leibler (KL) divergence between the query pose and pre-stored templates, both represented by Gaussian mixture models (GMM). A robust matching algorithm is developed by first rejecting most of the non-matched poses through marginal marker location distribution matching and then localizing possible rotation angles between the query pose and candidate poses using fast Fourier transform. Finally, rotation angle estimates are refined using nonlinear least square minimization through the Levenberg-Marquardt iteration.

Experimental results using real motion capture data show the efficacy of the proposed system. Promising results are also obtained even in the presence of occluded markers. Part of this system has been successfully used in a real life interactive dance performance [2].

Although the marker-based motion capture system has been used fairly successfully in our interactive dance applications, it is still considered as a type of intrusive sensing modality, i.e. passive sensors, such as markers, are needed to be put on the subject' body. We are currently also working on video-based motion capture systems. One of the preliminary results is a pose recognition system using wide-baseline stereo cameras [1]. As shown in Figure 1, a pair of wide-baseline video cameras with approximately orthogonal camera looking directions is used to reduce ambiguities present in pose recognition. Dancer silhouettes extracted from two cameras are represented by GMM and used as features for pose recognition. Relevance vector machine (RVM) is deployed as pose classifiers. The proposed system is trained using synthesized silhouette images created through animation software driven by motion capture data. The experimental results on synthetic and real images have illustrated the efficacy of the system. In addition, the system is easy to set up and there is not need for precise camera calibration.

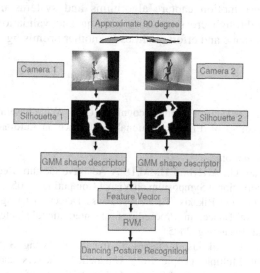

Fig. 1. A block diagram of the video-based pose recognition system, excerpted from [1], © 2006 IEEE

2.3 Dynamic Gesture Recognition

Dynamic body gestures are mostly used by dancers to convey semantics in dance performance. To reliably recognize dynamic gesture, we have developed a hybrid classification method [3], combining hidden Markov models (HMM) and various dynamic programming alignment (DPA) algorithms, such as edit distance, sequence alignment, and dynamic time warping, to improve the computational efficiency and simplify the training process.

Multimodal sensor fusion has also been applied to gesture recognition. Using a marker-based optical motion capture system and a pressure sensitive floor (with a spatial resolution of about 6 sensors one square inch), both joint angles and floor pressure distribution are used to recognize gestures. By placing additional markers on the feet, and calibrating the motion capture coordinates with the floor coordinates, we were able to assign each pressure point detected to either the left foot or the right foot. The fusion of marker-data and floor pressure enables the system to separate gestures that are similar in joint angles but have different weight distributions. This feature allows dancers to express themselves in one more dimension, namely, weight shifting.

3 Conclusions and Future Work

An overview of a family of human movement analysis algorithms for interactive dance is presented. Although encouraging results have been obtained and successful dance performances have been conducted using the presented systems, human movement analysis for dance still remains a challenge, especially using non-intrusive sensing modalities such as video cameras. We expect to see breakthroughs in this area by multimodal fusion, which provides a holistic view of human movement, and helps the design of robust motion capture algorithms and systems using non-intrusive sensing modalities through cross-modality training and validation. In addition, the extraction of Laban shape and effort qualities is another promising research area.

References

1. Guo, F., and Qian, G., Dance Posture Recognition Using Wide-baseline Orthogonal Stereo Cameras, in Proceedings of IEEE International Conference on Automatic Face and Gesture Recognition, 2006
2. http://ame.asu.edu/motione
3. Rajko, S., and Qian, G., A Hybrid HMM/DPA Adaptive Gesture Recognition Method, in Proceedings of International Symposium on Visual Computing, 2005
4. Wang, Y., Qian, G., and Rikakis, T., Robust Pause Detection Using 3D Motion Capture Data For Interactive Dance, in Proceedings of International Conference on Acoustics, Speech, and Signal Processing, 2005
5. Whiteley, D., Qian, G., Rikakis, T., James, J., Ingalls, T., Wang, S., and Olson, L., Real-Time Tracking of Multiple People from Unlabelled Markers and Its Application in Interactive Dance, in Proceedings of British Machine Vision Conference, 2005

Exploring the Dynamics of Visual Events in the Multi-dimensional Semantic Concept Space

Shahram Ebadollahi[1], Lexing Xie[1], Andres Abreu[1], Mark Podlaseck[1], Shih-Fu Chang[2,*], and John R. Smith[1]

[1] IBM T.J. Watson Research Center, Hawthorne, NY, USA
{ebad, xlx, aabreu, podlasec, jrsmith}@us.ibm.com
[2] Department of Electrical Engineering, Columbia University, New York, NY, USA
sfchang@ee.columbia.edu

Abstract. We present a system for visualizing event detection in video and revealing the algorithmic and scientific insights. Visual events are viewed as evolving temporal patterns in the semantic concept space. For video clips of different events, we present their corresponding traces in the semantic concept space as the event evolves. The presentation of the event in the concept space is scored by pre-trained models of the dynamics of each concept in the context of the event, which provides a measure of how well the given event matches the evolution pattern of the target event in the multi-dimensional concept space. Scores obtained for different videos is shown to project them into different parts of the final score space. This presentation walks the user through the entire process of concept-centered event recognition for events such as *exiting car*, *riot*, and *airplane flying*.

1 Introduction

This demo visualizes a novel approach to the problem of event modeling and detection [1]. Events in our approach are regarded as stochastic temporal processes in the semantic concept space. An available pool of semantic concept detectors form the basis of this space. Each concept detector provides its view of the world as depicted in a video clip. The concept-space was formed by 39 LSCOM-lite [2] concept detectors, which were obtained by training Support Vector Machine classifiers over visual features such as grid local color, texture, motion, and edge.

We developed a novel use of this space by modeling the temporal dynamics within. The central assumption in our approach is that during the progression of a visual event, several concurrent concepts evolve in a pattern specific to that event (Figure 1). In [1] we reported such a framework was powerful and could be used to model a large number of events.

In this work, we aim at providing an intuitive display to the process of event recognition in the multi-dimensional semantic concept space, thus providing insights to the algorithm design.

---

* Work performed while visiting IBM T.J. Watson Research Center.

H. Sundaram et al. (Eds.): CIVR 2006, LNCS 4071, pp. 503–505, 2006.
© Springer-Verlag Berlin Heidelberg 2006

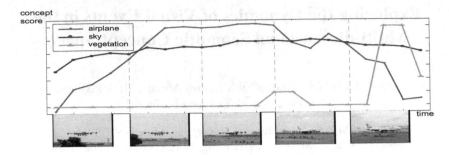

Fig. 1. Example of the dynamics of concepts in the context of the event *airplane landing*

2   Visualizing the Dynamics of Visual Events in the Concept Space

Let's assume that N concept detectors $\Delta = \{\delta_1, \ldots, \delta_N\}$ are available to form the bases of the semantic concept space. Applying each available concept detector to the frames of a video clip results in an array of semantic concept confidence scores $C^n_{1:T} = \{c^n_1, \ldots, c^n_T\}$, where $c^n_t = \delta_n(f_t)$ is the score assigned to the $t-th$ frame by the $n-th$ concept detector. This maps the video clip V into a trajectory in the semantic concept space as depicted in figure 2.

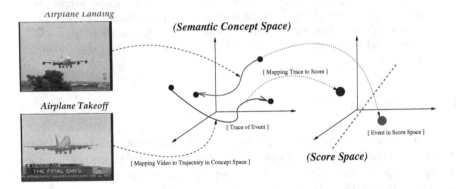

Fig. 2. The process of mapping videos into traces in the semantic concept space and then into the score space. Videos of different events such as *Airplane Landing* and *Airplane Takeoff* display different behaviors in both spaces, whereas videos of the similar event category will display similar evolution characteristics.

The demonstration will illustrate in real-time the trace of the projection of a video clip into the multi-dimensional concept space. Users will be able to see the different traces for videos clips of different types of events.

The projection of the video clip in the concept space is then evaluated by a set of pre-trained HMM thread models to obtain a score. Three different types of scores are used, 1-*Log-Likelihood (LL)*, 2-*State Histogram (SH)*, 3-*Fisher Score (FS)*. These scores collectively project the trace of the video in the concept space into the *score space*. Each dimension of the score space provides a measure of how well the given video clip matches the evolution pattern of exemplar patterns of a particular event. The mapping from the multi-dimensional concept space into the score space is also visualized in the presentation. This will further clarify that example video of differnt events get mapped to different areas in the final score space.

Users will be able to compare multiple video clips taken from the same or different categories of events in real-time, by viewing the sequence, along with their projections into the concept space and score space side-by-side. Figure 2 illustrates the concept of this demonstration.

Acknowledgements

This material is based upon work funded in whole by the U.S. Government. Any opinions, findings and conclusions or recommendations expressed in this material are those of the authors and do not necessarily reflect the views of the U.S. Government. This work was partially supported by DARPA under contract NBCHC050097.

References

1. Shahram Ebadollahi, Lexing Xie, Shih-Fu Chang, and John R. Smith. Visual event detection using multi-dimensional concept dynamics. In *ICME'06: Proceedings of the IEEE international conference on Multimedia and Expo (To be presented)*, 2006.
2. M. R. Naphade, L. Kennedy, J. Kender, S. F. Chang, J. R. Smith, P. Over, and A. Hauptmann. A light scale concept ontology for multimedia understanding for trecvid 2005. Technical report, IBM Research Technical Report, 2005.

VideoSOM: A SOM-Based Interface
for Video Browsing

Thomas Bärecke[1], Ewa Kijak[1], Andreas Nürnberger[2], and Marcin Detyniecki[1]

[1] LIP6, Université Pierre et Marie Curie, Paris, France
thomas.baerecke@lip6.fr
[2] IWS, Otto-von-Guericke Universität, Magdeburg, Germany

Abstract. The VideoSOM sytem is a tool for content-based video navigation based on a growing self-organizing map. Our interface allows the user to browse the video content using simultaneously several perspectives, temporal as well as content-based representations of the video. Combined with the interaction possibilities between them this allows for efficient searching of relevant information in video content.

1 Introduction

The VideoSOM system performs structuring and visualization of video content [1]. It represents a video shot by a single keyframe and constructs higher level aggregates of shots. The user has the possibility to browse the content in several ways. The basic idea is to provide as much information as possible on a single screen, without overwhelming the user.

Before the information is visualized and thus the user can interact with the system, the following steps are performed. First, a shot boundary detection algorithm using a single threshold is applied. Then, each shot is described using its median frame as keyframe. Histograms are extracted for up to four different regions and merged together into a single vector. Finally, a growing self-organizing map algorithm [2,3], clusters the shots into groups ignoring the temporal aspect. The visualization is based on these groups and projects the temporal information on a time bar. Similar objects are linked with colours.

We combined elements providing information on three abstraction levels. First, there is an overview of the whole content provided by the self-organizing map window. On each cell, the most typical keyframe of the corresponding cluster is displayed. The second level consists of a combined content-based and time-based visualization. Furthermore, a list of shots is provided for each grid cell and a control derived from the time-bar control helps to identify content that is similar to the currently selected shot. We evalueted our system on news video from the TRECVID collection.

2 Walkthrough

This section is intended to introduce a chronological walk-through of the Video-SOM tool from the perspective of the user.

H. Sundaram et al. (Eds.): CIVR 2006, LNCS 4071, pp. 506–509, 2006.
© Springer-Verlag Berlin Heidelberg 2006

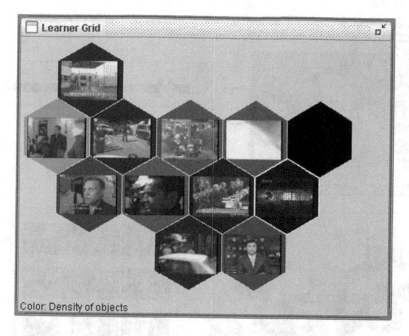

Fig. 1. Growing self-organizing map after learning

2.1 Opening and Pre-processing a Video

First, the data is loaded. This can be either the loading of a new raw video in a supported format, in which case the shot boundary detection and feature extraction steps have to be performed. Alternatively, a video including these information which was pre-processed in a former session can be opened. The user can change important variables of these steps, like the threshold for a shot boundary. Then, the the learning phase of the growing self-organizing map starts. The map has a hexagonal topology and can contain empty clusters. We usually start with a small grid size (2*2 or 3*3) and visualize the evolution of the learning process. The result of this step is illustrated in Fig. 2. The different shades of green indicate the density of shots in a certain cell, i.e. the number of shots assigned to it. The map can be retrained if the obtained clustering seems unsatisfactory.

2.2 Navigating Through a Video

A click on one cell (Fig. 1-1) opens the the corresponding shot list window in the interface. Simultaneously, the temporal position of the shots who are assigned to the chosen cell are projected in the form of black extensions on the time bar. After selecting one keyframe from the shot list (Fig. 1-2), the color of the cells in the map changes from green to shades of red. Now, the colour indicates the distance of the cells from the currently selected shot. Cells being very similar to the selected shot are coloured in dark red while cells being less similar are coloured with a brighter red. A main advantage of self-organizing

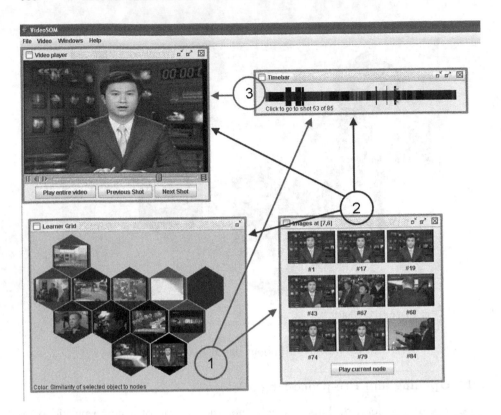

Fig. 2. User Interface with typical interactions. (1) Selection of a cell from the SOM. (2) Selection of a specific shot. (3) Selection of a temporal position.

maps is the fact that objects that are assigned to cells close to each other, in the low-dimensional space, are also close to each other in the high-dimensional space. But this does not mean that objects with a small distance in the high-dimensional space are necessarily assigned to cells separated by a small distance on the map. However, we overcome this problem with the visualisation schema presented above, starting with a specific shot, we will easily identify similar shots in dark red nodes. This improves significantly the navigation possibilities compared to the navigation support provided by other clustering schemas.

From user interaction perspective the map is limited to the following actions (Fig. 1-1): select nodes and communicate cluster assignment and colour information to the time bar. Nevertheless it is a very powerful tool which is especially useful for presenting a structured summarization of the video to the user.

The time bar changes its color synchronously with the map and visualizes the same colors for each shot. Thus, it provides a temporal view of similar keyframes. Furthermore, we added black bars at the positions where the shots of the currently selected cluster are located. The current shot is also played in the video player window. Simultaneously, more shot lists can be obtained by clicking on another cell in the map. The play current node operation merges all shots from the current node into one single video sequence and plays it. Clicking once on the time bar plays the shot at the given position (Fig. 1-3). A double click forces the system to change the currently selected shot resulting in renewing the distances displayed in the self-organizing map and the time bar. In fact, this corresponds to selecting a shot from the shot list but we do not necessarily have to know in which cell the shot is located. Furthermore, the black bars indicating the shots assigned to the currently selected cell are adjusted.

3   System Requirements

VideoSOM is implemented in Java and was tested under Microsoft Windows XP as well as Mandrake Linux operating system. Apart from the Java Virtual Machine, it requires the Java Media Framework (JMF including the mp3plugin) and Java Advanced Imaging (JAI) libraries installed. Although the application itself is platform independent, we recommend to run it under MS Windows using the appropriate Windows Performance Pack versions of these libraries, since the Linux and cross-platform versions do not implement all features, especially the variety of implemented video codecs is reduced significantly. Consequently, all video codecs supported by the libraries can be loaded into VideoSOM. There are no specific hardware requirements, i.e. a standard personal computer is sufficient.

References

1. Bärecke, T., Kijak, E., Nürnberger, A., Detyniecki, M.: Video navigation based on self-organizing maps. In: to appear in Proc. of Int. Conference on Image and Video Retrieval (CIVR 2006), Springer (2006)
2. Kohonen, T.: Self-Organizing Maps. Springer-Verlag, Berlin Heidelberg (1995)
3. Nürnberger, A., Detyniecki, M.: Visualizing changes in data collections using growing self-organizing maps. In: Proc. of Int. Joint Conference on Neural Networks (IJCANN 2002), IEEE (2002) 1912–1917

iBase: Navigating Digital Library Collections

Paul Browne[1], Stefan Rüger[1], Li-Qun Xu[2], and Daniel Heesch[1]

[1] Imperial College London, Department of Computing, South Kensington Campus,
London SW7 2AZ, UK
{paul.browne, s.rueger, daniel.heesch}@imperial.ac.uk
[2] BT Research, Broadband Applications Research Centre, Adastral Park, Ipswich
IP5 3RE, UK
li-qun.xu@bt.com

1 Introduction

The growth of digital image collections in many areas of science and commercial environments has over the last decade spawned great interest in content-based image retrieval. A great variety of methods have been developed to retrieve images based on example queries and techniques to elicit and utilize relevance feedback (e.g. [4, 5]). Often the systems provide a simple framework that permits evaluation of the method and are not intended as full-fledged systems ready to be used in a realistic setting. Also, comparatively little effort has been expended on devising efficient techniques to browse image collections effectively. The few notable exceptions [1, 3, 6] treat browsing internally as a sequence of queries and thus do not leverage the performance benefits associated with pre-computed browsing structures.

2 Our Approach

iBase has been designed to seamlessly integrate the paradigms of text-based search, content-based search with relevance feedback and a recently developed NN^k browsing technique [2] in a unified interface. NN^k browsing takes place along a pre-computed network consisting of images and their nearest neighbours with respect to different feature combinations. In addition to the NN^k approach iBase supports directory and temporal browsing and camera motion, Query by Example and relevance feedback search. It allows fast navigation across a collection, provides a viable alternative to search by example and has proved instrumental for our successful participation in TRECVID [7]. The iBase system is being run successfully on media content from London's Victoria and Albert Museum collection, TRECVID and a personal photo collection from Imperial College London.

The GUI provides each access method with its own tabbed panel. Integration is achieved by building the interface around the notion of a focal image. The user selects an image as the focal one simply by clicking on it. The current focal image is highlighted in each panel and all panels are updated to show results with respect to the new focal image thus ensuring consistency across all views. For example, the NN^k panel shows the nearest neighbours of the focal image, the Content Viewer panel shows an enlarged view of the focal image while the temporal panel (bottom of Figure 2) shows the temporal neighbours of the focal image.

H. Sundaram et al. (Eds.): CIVR 2006, LNCS 4071, pp. 510–513, 2006.
© Springer-Verlag Berlin Heidelberg 2006

3 Running the Demo

The system has been developed as a web application consisting of a Java applet and a servlet running inside Apache Tomcat. To run the client application a computer with Java runtime and Internet connectivity is needed. Figure 1 shows the client application comprising of 8 tabbed panels. The user starts by selecting the required content collection and features from the 'Collection Settings' panel.

Fig. 1. iBase Client Tabbed Panels

The user has a number of options for searching through the collection, they can select the 'NN^k network' panel to view nearest neighbour images (Figure 2), select a category (directory) or search based on Temporal or Emotion information. The NN^k network allows the user to browse the connected neighbours of **all** images in the collection. As the user interacts with other areas of the system (through an image search for example) **any** selected image will have its NN^k neighbours displayed here.

To the right of Figure 2 the 'Hub network' shows the 36 most connected images in the collection. Left of Figure 2 shows the NN^k of the current focal image and controls for browsing the hub network. Exploring the hub network provides an additional search approach for the user.

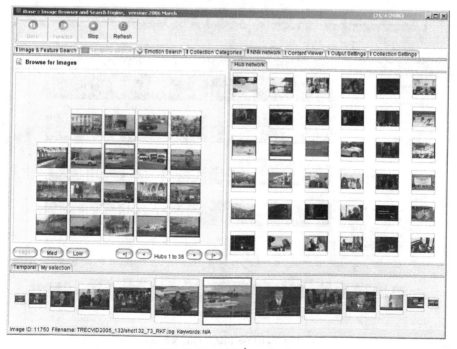

Fig. 2. iBase NN^k network

Figure 3 shows how a user can add an image to their search. An image query can be created or expanded by right clicking on **any** image displayed by the system and adding it to the query. Using this approach the user can provide the system with relevance feedback on their information need. External images can be chosen as query, too.

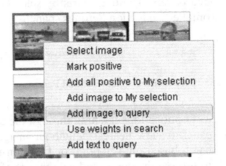

Fig. 3. Adding a query image

Figure 4 illustrates a search using the image selected in the previous section. The users query image(s) are shown in the 'Search images' section on the left of the screen with the search results shown on the right. The user can further refine their query by modifying the feature weighting; this is achieved by adjusting the slidebars (shown just above the 'Search Now' button on the left).

Fig. 4. iBase Image Query Search

The temporal neighbours of any selected image can be seen at the bottom of Figure 2 and 4 while the directory structure of the collection can be browsed from the 'Collection Categories' panel. Both these options provide additional approaches for browsing through the collection.

4 Summary

It is this seamless combination of search and browsing, facilitated by the notion of a focal image, that *sets iBase apart* from other content-based images search engines: the NN^k browsing allows one to identify suitable images for search-by-example, the result of which can be browsed for other relevant material either by NN^k browsing or by temporal or directory browsing.

Additional importance is placed on the design of the GUI. By providing a tight integration of techniques and a rich set of user interactions, we aim to equip the user with substantial navigational power within a straightforward and intuitive interface. Several key concepts of HCI were maintained throughout the design process: (i) consistency (ii) responsiveness and (iii) system progress feedback.

The design of iBase is such that new search approaches that needed to be built into the system like camera motion, hub NN^k network browsing and human emotion feedback were done with relative ease. Demo: http://mmis.doc.ic.ac.uk/demos/ibase.html

References

1. I. Campbell. The ostensive model of developing information-needs. PhD Thesis, University of Glasgow, 2000.
2. D. Heesch and S. Rüger. NN^k networks for content-based image retrieval. In Proc. of ECIR pages 253–266. LNCS 2997, Springer, 2004.
3. Y. Rubner, L. J. Guibas, and C. Tomasi. The earth mover's distance, multidimensional
4. scaling, and color-based image retrieval. In DARPA Image Understanding Workshop, 1997.
5. Y. Rui and T. Huang. Optimizing learning in image retrieval. In Proc. of IEEE Conf. on Computer Vision and Pattern Recognition, 2000.
6. Y. Rui, T. S. Huang, and S. Mehrotra. Content-based image retrieval with relevance feedback in MARS. In Proc. of IEEE Int'l Conf. on Image Processing, 1997.
7. S. Santini and R. Jain. Integrated browsing and querying for image databases. IEEE Multi-Media, 7(3):26–39, 2000.
8. D. Heesch, M. Pickering, S. Rüger and A. Yavlinsky. Video Retrieval using Search and Browsing with Key Frames. TREC Video Retrieval Evaluation, Gaithersburg, MD, 2004. Available at: http://mmir.doc.ic.ac.uk/www-pub/trec2003-nb.pdf.

Exploring the Synergy of Humans and Machines in Extreme Video Retrieval

Alexander G. Hauptmann, Wei-Hao Lin, Rong Yan, Jun Yang, Robert V. Baron, Ming-Yu Chen, Sean Gilroy, and Michael D. Gordon

School of Computer Science, Carnegie Mellon University,
Pittsburgh, PA 15213, USA
{alex+, whlin77, rongy, juny, rvb, mychen,
sgilroy, michael.gordon}@cmu.edu

Abstract. We introduce an interface for efficient video search that exploits the human ability to quickly scan visual content, after automatic retrieval has arrange the images in expected order of relevance. While extreme video retrieval is taxing to the human, it is also *extremely* effective. Two variants of extreme retrieval are demonstrated, 1) RSVP which automatically pages through images with user-control of the paging speed, while the user marks relevant shots and 2) MBRP where the user manually controls paging and adjusts the number of images per page, depending on the density of relevant shots.

1 Interactive vs. Automatic Video Search

When comparing results of fully automated video retrieval to interactive video retrieval [5], one finds a big gap in performance. The fully automated search (no user in the loop) succeeds with good recall for many topics, but relevant shots tend to be distributed throughout the top 3000 to 5000 slots in the ordered shot list, causing the standard metric of average precision for automated search to lag well behind most interactive runs. From this insight, we developed an interface that relies on superior human visual perception to compensate for low precision in automatic search of the visual contents of video [1]. The human user can filter the best automatically generated results and produce a better set that retains the relevant shots, resulting in much greater precision. We named this approach extreme video retrieval (XVR), as it combines the best machine performance with maximal use of human perception skills. Our interface explores two types of approaches to human filtering: rapid serial visual presentation and manually controlled browsing with resizing of pages.

The success of XVR relies heavily on the ability of automatic retrieval systems to recall more relevant at as lower depth as possible. To study the machine extremes of our automatic retrieval system we take a one automatic run [3,4] with query classes and plot MAP over 24 TRECVID 2005 search topics at the depth k of shots, as shown in Figure 1. The automatic run demonstrates respectable performance, achieving MAP of around 0.1 at the depth of 1000 shots commonly chosen in TRECVID. After 1000 shots, MAP reaches a plateau, due to the severe penalty for ranking relevant shots low in the calculation of average precision. However, with an optimal ranking function, the curve becomes the recall at the depth k, and clearly our automatic

H. Sundaram et al. (Eds.): CIVR 2006, LNCS 4071, pp. 514–517, 2006.
© Springer-Verlag Berlin Heidelberg 2006

retrieval systems have decent recall. Figure 1 also shows the best performance of **all** submissions in TRECVID'05. The results suggest that anyone who can browse through the top 2000 shots (merely 2.56% of the test set) per topic in the given 15 minutes could rival the best search performance, with even better performance if she can look deeper/faster!

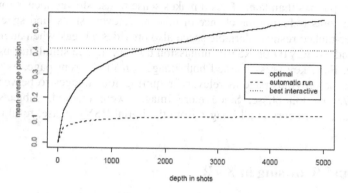

Fig. 1. Mean average precision over 24 TRECVID'05 search topics for our automatic run, the best submitted run (interactive), and a hypothetical run with an optimal re-ranking function

2 Human Extremes – RSVP

Rapid Serial Visual Presentation (RSVP) is a technique of rapidly presenting a series of images, and has been widely used in visualization and psychophysics experiments [2]. The basic version of RSVP, known as the keyhole mode [2], presents a sequence of images in the same position of the screen, where the subsequent image replaces the previous one every n milliseconds, n is thus the interval between two images. Users can vary the presentation speed (adding or subtracting 100ms from n) with two keys A (advance) and S (slow). When a relevant image appears, users press the J key to mark the current image. The previous image is also marked as relevant due to a human reaction time delay after the presentation of the relevant image. Since two images are marked for each relevant key press, a second, *correction phase* is needed to carefully page through all marked images and validate the judgments.

In the TRECVID'05, we submitted one complete run using this variable speed keyhole RSVP interface, where it ranked 4th among all TRECVID 2005 interactive runs [4]. The 24 topics were completed over three consecutive days, with 4 topics in the morning session, and 4 topics in the afternoon session. Before each session, one topic from 2004 was used as practice to "warm up" the participant. We found that subjects can correct around 100 images per minute in the second, *correction phase*, and thus the length of the correction phase was dynamically determined based on the number of relevant shots marked while in the first phase and the total available time.

Even though no existing video retrieval system uses RSVP, several reason argue for it: 1) RSVP is an interface specifically designed to present images rapidly, which matches human ability to quickly react to visual stimuli. 2) Keyhole mode requires no eye movements and therefore optimizes the time a user looks at an image. More complex displays such as grids or collages demand eye movements and extra time for eye fixation on every image. 3) RSVP automatically updates the next image in the sequence without manual paging, which reduces user cognitive load of pressing extra keys for each following display. 4) Variable speed control allows users to adjust the presentation speed. If we take the first derivatives of the optimal curve in Figure 1 we note that the rate of relevant images is not constant. There are more relevant shots in the early, top ranks than later. Thus it makes sense to use slower speeds for the earlier top-ranked shots reducing the chance of missing relevant shots, and speeding up for later, lower-ranked results. Variable speed also provides a break when attention drifts.

A second TRECVID'05 RSVP submission used a 2 image simultaneous display on each page. Each key press marked both images on the current page, as well as two images on the previous page as relevant, requiring four images to be verified in the validation/correction phase. Since more images were marked, subjects were frequently not able to correct all images from the initial RSVP phase, resulting in lower MAP.

3   Manual Browsing in XVR

Manual Browsing with Resizing Pages (MBRP) is a strategy for interactive search, which, unlike RSVP, where the same number of shots per page are used throughout the search, allows adapting the page size according to the (decreasing) percentage of relevant shots. At the beginning when relevant shots are frequent, we use a small page size since multiple relevant shots are likely on one page, which demands more attention (per image) and key presses to label them. Later when relevant shots become infrequent, large page sizes become efficient since it is unlikely that multiple relevant shots will appear even on a large page. MBRP thus reduces the overhead of page turning and the number of necessary key presses for relevant images on a page.

Since the time a user spends browsing each page depends on the page size, the visual complexity of the answer, and the number of correct shots, this time can vary dramatically with different pages. The user may occasionally need to turn back to previous pages to correct erroneous labels. Thus MBRP gains an advantage by letting users turn pages using a forward and backward key press.

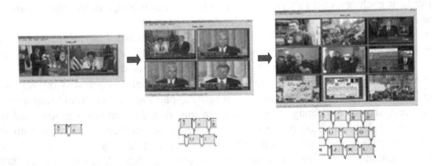

Fig. 2. Manual browsing with different page layouts: 1x2 at the beginning, 2x2 in a later stage, and 3x3 for the rest of the shots. The green bounding boxes indicate the shots labeled relevant, and the keyboard section below a page shows the keys for labeling the respective shots.

Unlike RSVP, where a single key is used to mark all shots in a page, MBRP allows up to 16 keys (in a 4x4 layout on the keyboard) for labeling 16 shots simultaneously, with one key corresponding to each presented image. Moreover, another key can be used to label all the shots on the current page and automatically turn the page.

Although a page could include different layouts of images (e.g., 3x3, 2x5, etc), we use only 1x2, 2x2, and 3x3 for two reasons. First, with practice, one hand can conveniently label any shot(s) in layouts up to 3x3 shots, but not more than 9 shots per page. Second, visually inspecting more than 9 shots per page seemed less time-efficient.

As the user must label as many shots as possible in a fixed time, errors are inevitable due to time pressures. While missed relevant shots cannot be found during the verification phase, usually one or two minutes are used to correct false alarm errors. In addition, if the user is unsure about the relevance of a shot, it can be marked as "maybe"; where all "maybe" shots will be sorted after those ranked as "relevant".

A TRECVID'05 submission using MBRP averaged in looking at about 2000 shots within the 15 minutes per topic. This number is higher for queries that are easily identifiable visually, and vice versa. For example, for the query of "tennis", a user could browse almost 5,000 shots in the allocated 15 minutes time.

The MBRP run achieved the mean average precision (MAP) of 0.408 on the TRECVID'05 evaluation, which ranked second among a total of 50 interactive submissions and was only marginally behind the best run (MAP = 0.414). It also outperformed the submission using the best RSVP method (MAP = 0.366).

Acknowledgments

This work was supported in part by the Advanced Research and Development Activity (ARDA) under contract number H98230-04-C-0406 and NBCHC040037, and by the National Science Foundation under Grant No. IIS-0535056.

References

1. Derthick, M., Interfaces for Palmtop Image Search, JCDL, Portland OR, July 2002, 340-341.
2. Spence, R., Rapid, serial and visual: A presentation technique with potential. Information Visualization, 1(1):13–19, 2002.
3. Yan, R., Yang, J., Hauptmann, A., Learning Query-Class Dependent Weights in Automatic Video Retrieval, ACM Multimedia 2004, New York, NY, pp. 548-555, October 2004
4. A. G. Hauptmann, M. Christel, R. Concescu, J. Gao, Q. Jin, W.-H. Lin, J.-Y. Pan, S. M. Stevens, R. Yan, J. Yang, Y. Zhang, CMU Informedia's TRECVID 2005 Skirmishes, TRECVid 2005 - Text REtrieval Conference TRECVID Workshop, Gaithersburg, MD, Nov. 2005.
5. Over P, Kraaij W and Smeaton A.F. TRECVID 2005 - An Introduction. TRECVid 2005 - Text REtrieval Conference TRECVID Workshop, Gaithersburg, MD, 14-15 Nov. 2005.

Efficient Summarizing of Multimedia Archives Using Cluster Labeling

Jelena Tešić and John R. Smith

IBM T. J. Watson Research Center, Hawthorne NY 10532, USA

Abstract. In this demo we present a novel approach for labeling clusters in minimally annotated data archives. We propose to build on clustering by aggregating the automatically tagged semantics. We propose and compare four techniques for labeling the clusters and evaluate the performance compared to human labeled ground-truth. We define the error measures to quantify the results, and present examples of the cluster labeling results obtained on the BBC stock shots and broadcast news videos from the TRECVID-2005 video data set.

Rapid expansion of availability of multimedia content demands more efficient and effective access of large multimedia repositories. However, in many cases, those repositories have little or no relevant metadata to support effective user search and access. The volume of video data archives is often so great, that there is little opportunity for manual indexing of the content, For example, video blogs, raw or pre-produced video content (B-rolls or rushes) in the domain of broadcast news, home movies, and live Web video feeds often offer little metadata to help to organize and index the content. This category of video data presents additional challenges for automated processing as result of poor picture quality, tendency to be dominated by long shots with repetitive content, minimal speech, high audio noise. The traditional content approaches for video logging rely heavily on shot boundary detection or speech- and text-based indexing for organizing video data. However, to efficiently manage and discover interesting patterns, or groups of scenes in these archives, one must largely rely on the visual content.

The multimedia retrieval system needs to allow the user to efficiently navigate the semantic space of the video repository. However, the information needs of users typically span a range of semantic concepts. Modeling semantics, even the most general semantic concepts, requires investment in creating sufficient amounts of annotated video data for training the models. This is often a costly proposition. Furthermore, the space of semantics of interest to users is much large than the space of semantic concepts that can be modeled and detected by today's systems. The challenges presented by these large repositories requires new scalable methods that enable effective automatic organization on the scale of terabytes of video data. One important tool for video content management is clustering. Unsupervised visual clustering generally performs well for detecting redundant video content, such as when applied to repositories dominated by video rushes. However, when there is a diversity of content, the groupings are often interesting and meaningful, but still present a large space of clusters

H. Sundaram et al. (Eds.): CIVR 2006, LNCS 4071, pp. 518–520, 2006.
© Springer-Verlag Berlin Heidelberg 2006

for users to navigate. Furthermore, the clustering results cannot be leveraged effectively when there is no semantics description associated with the clusters.

We propose to build on visual clustering by aggregating automatically tagged semantics produced by concept detection techniques. The connection between visual cluster information and automatically associated semantics offers a fast and meaningful summarization of large repositories of video data. This approach enables efficient production assistance i.e. allows users to browse, search, classify, and summarize the archives without any previous knowledge of the content. We analyze how well the system groups the video in topics to aid in browsing and discovery of data, and demonstrate examples of the cluster labeling results obtained on the 100 hours of BBC stock shots from the TRECVID-2005 video data set.

Acknowledgments. The BBC 2005 Rushes video used in this work is provided for research purposes by the BBC through the TREC Information Retrieval Research Collection. This material is based upon work funded in part by the U. S. Government. Any opinions, findings and conclusions or recommendations expressed in this material are those of the author(s) and do not necessarily reflect the views of the U.S. Government.

Cluster Labeling Examples

Fig. 1. Cluster in the Local Color Space Labeled: CMG33 - **NOT Indoors** & Sky & Day & Outdoors

Fig. 2. Cluster in the Local Color Space Labeled: CMG58 - NOT Day & **Studio** & Night & NOT Outdoors

Fig. 3. Cluster in the Local Color Space Labeled: CMG10 - **Nature** & NOT Indoors & NOT Building & Greenery

Collaborative Concept Tagging for Images Based on Ontological Thinking

Alireza Kashian[1], Robert Kheng Leng Gay[1], and Abdul Halim Abdul Karim[2]

[1] InfoComm Institute of Singapore, School of EEE,
Nanyang Technological University, Singapore
{alir0001, eklgay}@ntu.edu.sg
[2] School of Communications and Information,
Nanyang Technological University, Singapore
abdu0009@ntu.edu.sg

Abstract. Without textual descriptions or label information of images, searching semantic concepts in image databases is a very challenging task. Automatic annotation techniques for images are aimed to detect objects which are located visually inside images, like a tiger in grass. One challenge which remains to be solved is "Understanding". Image understanding is something beyond automatic annotation scope. The second issue is manual annotation of images. In manual annotation, user contribution is important. In this demo, we have developed an online tool which simulates a collaborative environment to help users to generate several facts for selected images. Ontological thinking led us to devise a method for a simple user interface. We are also studying the construction of synergies out of generated facts for our future work.

1 Introduction

Several methods for image annotation have been proposed. The two main methods are manual and automatic. Automatic annotation techniques usually use signal processing solutions for finding objects inside images or even detecting properties of the objects. The second approach, which is manual annotation, requires human intervention. Users can annotate images in different ways. The output form could be unstructured text or well-formed Meta-data. In this tool, the input form is the point of focus.

We have proposed a new environment for collaborative image tagging which helps users to create, confirm or reject any inferential concept or visual object which exists inside a selected image. We have studied knowledge representation methods and several conceptual theories before designing this tool and scratching the codes. Our tool is based on ontological thinking. Ontology has strong implications for conceptions of reality.

The tool provides a simple interface for user inputs and also assists to build up a collaborative tagging environment. The tool will allow users to select visual area (called regions) in an image and then generate a tag for that region. These tags are basically made for Visual Objects. The second tagging method is inferential tagging which comes from inference capability of human mind. These kinds of tags are not selectable with drawing tools. Tagging, Mapping and Inferring are 3 base actions for this application.

H. Sundaram et al. (Eds.): CIVR 2006, LNCS 4071, pp. 521–524, 2006.
© Springer-Verlag Berlin Heidelberg 2006

2 Collaborative Tagging

The tool is implemented on a server with a central database which records any inputs received from user interaction with the application. Each user would have access to the same pool of images for collaborative tagging. The visual objects in any particular image could be recognized, delineated and tagged with free form user text input. On the other hand, inferential tagging is also available for those kinds of concepts which are not selectable visually.

The collaborative tagging environment has the following benefits:

1. Enables the ranking of each tag based on community consensus.
2. Greater reliability in terms of facts about images.
3. Distributing the job among users. (annotators)
4. Making synergy and easier inference.

1. Ranking the tags: The tool is able to rank each tag based on users' contributions. Each user would confirm or reject any tag which had been created before or even he/she can create a new tag. The confirmation and rejection of a tag would leverage the rank of tag. Several security measures, like caching user IP address and generating cookies are used to prevent any possible abuse.

2. Greater reliability in terms of facts about images: Since the tool is shared among users, contribution of each user would help to strengthen the ranking of each tag.

3. Distributing the job among users: Obviously it takes much time to tag an image especially if and when the depictions are complex. Different people may also be interested in different things in the same image. Thus collaboration is an important element to perform the task of accurately tagging such visualizations.

4. Making synergy and easier inference: Synergy refers to the phenomenon in which two or more discrete influences or agents acting together create an effect greater than the sum of the effects each is able to create independently.

3 User Interface

We have done our best to design a simple user interface which guides users to select, confirm or reject available tags or even generate new tags. The simple design of interface will help user to get hands on with limited knowledge. The latest version of the application has 6 panels for the administration aspect and 4 panels for the annotation purpose. Administration panels are File, User details, Image details, Image lists, Toolbar and Search while annotation section includes Tagging, Mapping, Inferring and Ontologies. Figure 1 illustrates the user interface. In this screenshot you can see that all drawing tools have been used and also we have Terror concept as an inferential tag. Note that we could even use rectangle for selecting microphone instead of arrow.

3.1 Administration Section

The Administration Section has 6 different panels for specific purposes. Loading images and exporting RDF files are done through File panel. There are 4 drawing tools available to users which are: Ellipse, Rectangle, Point and Arrow.

Fig. 1. Screenshot of Collaborative Concept Tagging Tool

The user details panel is used to show some statistics about the current user like his ID, his trust level and also the number of images annotated or the number of tags created by the user.

In the toolbar panel we have 4 main drawing tools. The ellipse and rectangle are helpful when we want to select an area like faces, bodies or information area in an image like the passport number in a digitized passport page. The point will help when we want to talk about a particular spot in the image. The point can even be used to select a pixel. Lastly, the arrow will help to point to a visual object which cannot be selected by rectangle, ellipse or point. For example, in an image of a glass of water, you would choose the glass using a rectangle, but you can use the arrow to point to the water inside the glass.

The image details panel is used to find some statistics about the current image and the image list panel will provide us with a list of all loaded images to application framework. The search panel could be used to find tags in each image or even search for relations between tags. The relation between tags is constructed in mapping panel at annotation section of the application. There is also possibility to map two different tags in two different image files. This brightens the capability of interrelationship of tags among a collection of images.

3.2 Annotation Section

The annotation section includes 4 panels. The first panel is Tagging. It provides a list of all available tags (both visual objects and inferential concepts). There is a button in the tagging panel for creating inferential tags. The inferential tags do not refer to any specific visual object inside an image. There is thus no need to use drawing tools to create inferential tags.

For creating a new visual tag, the user just needs to use a drawing tool. After drawing, a pop-up comes on automatically to ask for the user to assign a description and reference to a resource for that selection. For example if you select your face in a photo, you can give a reference link to your homepage and also put your name as the description.

Another panel is mapping. Mapping will help the user to map two tags to each other. For example we see a boy in our image kicking a ball. Two visual objects are the "boy" and the "ball". In the mapping panel, you can select both tags for boy and ball and then define the relation between them. The final statement would be like: "The Boy <u>kicks</u> the Ball". The linear notation is: [The Boy] ➔ Kicks ➔ [The Ball]. By mapping the tags, we will have more knowledge about the image. The two other panels are aimed to generate new knowledge out of a collection of images or even import different Ontologies and define the relationships between tags and those Ontologies.

4 Future Direction of Research

Interesting issues regarding extraction of knowledge out of images arose from the experience of coming up with this simple tool. One notable issue is knowledge synergy. This involves studying the relationships between groups of images so that we can synergistically arrive at new knowledge out of a combination of images. Importing Ontologies for annotating images and also inference generator is among our interested area and need to be developed in future.

We would like to expand the job to help users export graphical concept maps out of mapped tags in a collection of images which could be useful for educational purposes (especially for small children). As we are gathering information from each individual annotator, we have the opportunity to use data mining methods for the purpose of teaching the system.

References

1. Hai Zhuge. Semantic-Based Web Image Retrieval.
   http://www2003.org/cdrom/papers/poster/p172/p172-zhuge/p172-zhuge.htm
2. J. Wielemaker A.Th. Schreiber, B. Dubbeldam and B.J. Wielinga. Ontology-based photo annotation. IEEE Intelligent Systems, May/June 2001.
3. Siegfried Handschuh and Steffen Staab, editors. Annotation for the Semantic Web. IOS Press, 2003.

Multimodal Search for Effective Video Retrieval*

Apostol (Paul) Natsev

IBM T. J. Watson Research Center
Hawthorne, NY 10532
natsev@us.ibm.com

Semantic search and retrieval of multimedia content is a challenging research field that has drawn significant attention in the multimedia research community. With the dramatic growth of digital media at home, in enterprises, and on the web, methods for effective indexing and search of visual content are vital in unlocking the value of this content. Conventional database search and text search over large textual corpora are both well-understood problems with ubiquitous applications. However, search in non-textual unstructured content, such as image and video data, is not nearly as mature or effective. A common approach for video retrieval, for example, is to apply conventional text search techniques to the associated closed caption or speech transcript. This approach works fairly well for retrieving named entities, such as specific people, objects, or places. However, it does not work well for generic topics related to general settings, events, or people actions, as the speech track rarely describes the background setting or the visual appearance of the subject. Text-based search is not even applicable to scenarios that do not have speech transcripts or other textual metadata for indexing purposes (e.g., consumer photo collections). In addition, speech-based video retrieval frequently leads to false matches of segments that talk about but do not depict the entity of interest. Because of these and other limitations, it is now apparent that conventional text search techniques on their own are not sufficient for effective image and video retrieval, and they need to be combined with techniques that consider the visual semantics of the content. The most substantial work in this field is presented in the TREC Video Retrieval Evaluation (TRECVID[1]) community, which focuses its efforts on evaluating video retrieval approaches by providing common video datasets and a standard set of queries.

Our approach to multimedia search and retrieval addresses non-annotated broadcast news video data, for which speech transcripts may or may not be available. We rely on a set of semantic models that can be applied to image and video content to automatically detect a corresponding set of concepts. Successful concept modeling and detection approaches have been developed in TRECVID, relying predominantly on visual analysis and statistical machine learning methods. Our approach to search and retrieval leverages such concept models to enable or improve video retrieval in scenarios with limited or no textual metadata. In particular, we focus on query analysis and expansion—mapping query words and phrases to concepts—and we

---

* This material is based upon work funded in part by the U. S. Government. Any opinions, findings and conclusions or recommendations expressed in this material are those of the author and do not necessarily reflect the views of the U.S. Government.
[1] http://www-nlpir.nist.gov/projects/trecvid/

H. Sundaram et al. (Eds.): CIVR 2006, LNCS 4071, pp. 525–528, 2006.
© Springer-Verlag Berlin Heidelberg 2006

Fig. 1. Results of speech-based text retrieval using "Basketball" keyword

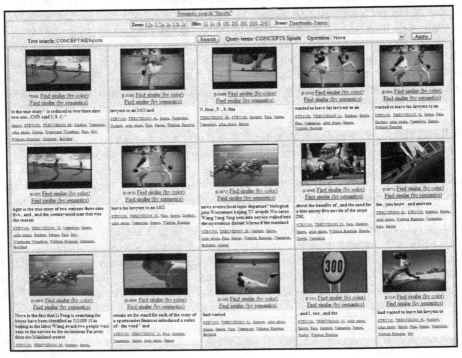

Fig. 2. Results of semantic model-based retrieval using visual "Sports" model

Fig. 3. Results of speech-based retrieval using "Basketball" keyword after filtering with "Sports" model

build a ranked list of matching shots based purely on automatic concept detection scores and automatically computed query-to-concept relevance scores. In addition, when textual metadata is available in the form of annotations, closed caption, automatic speech recognition, or video OCR transcripts, we use the model-based retrieval method to re-rank the purely text-based retrieval results. We also leverage content-based retrieval methods for retrieving results based on visual appearance and similarity matching with respect to one or more image examples relevant to the topic of interest.

In this demonstration, we will present the IBM Research MARVEL[2] system for video retrieval which leverages multiple modalities to improve retrieval effectiveness, integrating text-based retrieval (using metadata and speech transcripts), model-based retrieval (using semantic concept models), and visual content-based retrieval (using colors, textures, edges, and shapes). We will demonstrate the advantages and disadvantages of the various retrieval methods in the context of a sample query scenario. For example, Figures 1 and 2 show retrieval results for text-based and model-based retrieval for the topic of "Basketball". Neither of these is satisfactory on their own since speech-based text retrieval returns documents "mentioning" basketball but not "showing" basketball, while model-based retrieval using the Sports model is too broad for the given query topic. Figure 3 then shows that the

---

[2] http://www.research.ibm.com/marvel/

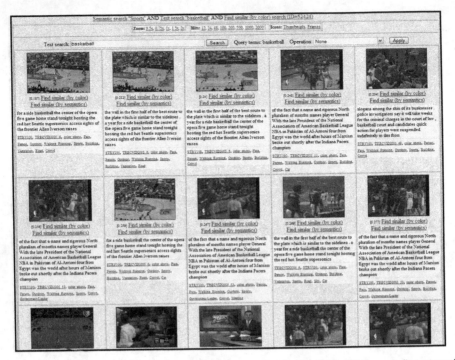

Fig. 4. Combination of speech keyword-based retrieval ("Basketball" keyword), semantic model-based retrieval ("Sports" model) and visual content-based retrieval (from image example) for "Basketball" topic.

combination of the previous two methods returns a more relevant set of results by prioritizing text retrieval matches that are also visually consistent with the Sports model. Figure 4 shows that the result set can then be further refined and improved by also integrating content-based retrieval (i.e., "more like this" scenario) using a relevant basketball image. Figures 1-4 validate the combination hypothesis that for a video retrieval system to achieve a satisfactory level of performance, it needs to effectively combine multiple modalities and retrieval methods.

MediAssist: Using Content-Based Analysis and Context to Manage Personal Photo Collections

Neil O'Hare[1], Hyowon Lee[1], Saman Cooray[1], Cathal Gurrin[1],
Gareth J.F. Jones[1], Jovanka Malobabic[1], Noel E. O'Connor[1,2],
Alan F. Smeaton[1,2], and Bartlomiej Uscilowski[1]

[1] Centre For Digital Video Processing, Dublin City University, Ireland
[2] Adaptive Information Cluster, Dublin City University, Ireland
nohare@computing.dcu.ie
http://www.cdvp.dcu.ie

Abstract. We present work which organises personal digital photo collections based on contextual information, such as time and location, combined with content-based analysis such as face detection and other feature detectors. The MediAssist demonstration system illustrates the results of our research into digital photo management, showing how a combination of automatically extracted context and content-based information, together with user annotation, facilitates efficient searching of personal photo collections.

1 Introduction

Recent years have seen a revolution in photography with a move away from analog film towards digital technologies, resulting in the accumulation of large numbers of personal digital photos. The MediAssist [4] project at the Centre for Digital Video Processing (CDVP) is developing tools to enable users to efficiently search their photo archives. Automatically generated contextual metadata and content-based analysis tools (face and building detection) are used, and semi-automatic annotation techniques allow the user to interactively improve the automatically generated annotations. Our retrieval tools allow for complex query formulation for personal digital photo collection management. Previous work has reported other systems which use context to aid photo management. Davis et al [1] utilise context to recommend recipients for sharing photos taken with a context-aware phone, although their system does not support retrieval. Naaman et al [6] use context-based features for photo management, but they do not use content-based analysis tools or allow for semi-automatic annotation.

2 Content and Context-Aware Photo Organisation

MediAssist organises photo collections using a combination of context and content-based analysis. Time and location of photo capture are recorded and used to derive additional contextual information such as daylight status, weather and indoor/outdoor classification [4]. By using this information the browsing

H. Sundaram et al. (Eds.): CIVR 2006, LNCS 4071, pp. 529–532, 2006.
© Springer-Verlag Berlin Heidelberg 2006

space when seeking a particular photo or photos can be drastically reduced. We have previously shown the benefits of using location information in personal photo management [4]. The MediAssist photo archive currently contains over 14,000 location-stamped photos taken with a number of different camera models, including camera phones. Over 75% of these images have been manually annotated for a number of concepts including buildings, indoor/outdoor, vehicles, animals, babies and the presence and identity of faces, serving as a ground truth for evaluation of our content-based analysis tools.

Our face detection system is built on both appearance-based face/non-face classification and skin detection models [2]. The algorithm detects frontal-view faces at multiple scales, with features supported to detect in-plane rotated faces. We also detect the presence of large buildings in outdoor digital photos, approaching the problem as a building/non-building classification of the whole image using low-dimensional low-level feature representation based on multi-scale analysis and explicit edge detection [5].

3   The MediAssist Web Demonstrator System

The MediAssist Web-based desktop interface allows users to efficiently and easily search through their personal photo collections using the contextual and content-based information described above. The MediAssist system interface is shown in Fig. 1.

Fig. 1. The MediAssist Photo Management System

3.1 Content and Context-Based Search

The user is first presented with basic search options enabling them to enter details of desired location (placenames are extracted from a gazetteer) and time, and also advanced options that allow them to further specify features such as people. Slider bars can be used to filter the collection based on the (approximate) number of people required. In addition, the user can specify the names of individuals in the photo based on a combination of automatic methods and manual annotation, as described below. Time filters allow the formulation of powerful time-based queries corresponding to the user's partial recall of the temporal context of a photo-capturing event, for example all photos taken in the evening, at the weekend, during the summer. Other advanced features the user can search by include weather, light status, Indoor/Outdoor and Builing/Non-Building.

3.2 Collection Browsing

In presenting the result photos, four different views are used. The default view is *Event List* which organizes the filtered photos into events in which the photos are grouped together based on time proximity [3]. Each event is summarized by a label (location and date/time) and five representative thumbnail photos automatically extracted from the event. *Event Detail* is composed of the full set of photos in an event automatically organized into sub-events. *Individual Photo List* is an optional view where the thumbnail size photos are presented without any particular event grouping, but sorted by date/time. *Photo Detail* is an enlarged single photo view presented when the user selects one of the thumbnail size photos in any of the above views. Arrow buttons allow jumping to previous/next photos in this view. In all of the above presentation options, each photo (thumbnail size or enlarged) is presented with accompanying tag information in the form of icons, giving the user feedback about the features automatically associated with each photo.

3.3 Semi-automatic Annotation

MediAssist allows users to change or update any of the automatically tagged information for a single photo or for a group of photos. In *Photo Detail* view, the system can highlight all detected faces in the photo, allowing the user to tidy up the results of the automatic detection by removing false detections or adding missed faces. The current version of the system uses a body patch feature (i.e. a feature modeling the clothes worn by a person) to suggest names for detected faces: the suggested name for an unknown face is the known face with the most similar body patch. The user can confirm that the system choice is the correct one, or choose from a shortlist of suggested names, again based on the body patch feature. Other work has shown effective methods of suggesting identities within photos using context-based data [7]: in our ongoing research we are exploring the combination of this type of approach with both face recognition and body-patch matching to provide identity suggestions based on both content and context.

4   Conclusions

We have presented the MediAssist demonstrator system for context-aware management of personal digital photo collections. The automatically extracted features are supplemented with semi-automatic annotation which allows the user to add to and/or correct the automatically generated annotations. Ongoing extensions to our demonstration system include the integration of mapping tools. Other important challenges are to leverage context metadata to improve on the performance of content analysis tools [8], particularly face detection, and to use combined context and content-based approaches to identity annotation, based on face recognition, body-patch matching and contextual information.

Acknowledgements

The MediAssist project is supported by Enterprise Ireland under Grant No CFTD-03-216. This work is partly supported by Science Foundation Ireland under grant number 03/IN.3/I361.

References

1. S. Ahern, S. King, and M. Davis. MMM2: mobile media metadata for photo sharing. In *ACM Multimedia*, pages 267–268, Singapore, November 2005.
2. S. Cooray and N. E. O'Connor. A hybrid technique for face detection in color images. In *AVSS*, pages 253–258, Como, Italy, September 2005.
3. A. Graham, H. Garcia-Molina, A. Paepcke, and T. Winograd. Time as essence for photo browsing through personal digital libraries. In *ACM Joint Conference on Digital Libraries*, pages 326–335, Portland, USA, July 2002.
4. C. Gurrin, G. J. F. Jones, H. Lee, N. O'Hare, A. F. Smeaton, and N. Murphy. Mobile access to personal digital photograph archives. In *MobileHCI 2005*, pages 311–314, Salzburg, Austria, September 2005.
5. J. Malobabic, H. LeBorgne, N. Murphy, and N. E. O'Connor. Detecting the presence of large buildings in natural images. In *Proceedings of CBMI 2005 - 4th International Workshop on Content-Based Multimedia Indexing*, Riga, Latvia, June 2005.
6. M. Naaman, S. Harada, Q. Wang, H. Garcia-Molina, and A. Paepcke. Context data in geo-referenced digital photo collections. In *ACM Multimedia*, pages 196–203, New York, USA, October 2004.
7. M. Naaman, R. B. Yeh, H. Garcia-Molina, and A. Paepcke. Leveraging context to resolve identity in photo albums. In *ACM Joint Conference on Digital Libraries*, pages 178–187, Denver, CO, USA, June 2005.
8. N. O'Hare, C. Gurrin, G. J. F. Jones, and A. F. Smeaton. Combination of content analysis and context features for digital photograph retrieval. In *EWIMT*, pages 323–328, London, UK, December 2005.

Mediamill: Advanced Browsing in News Video Archives

Marcel Worring*, Cees Snoek, Ork de Rooij, Giang Nguyen,
Richard van Balen, and Dennis Koelma

Intelligent Systems Lab Amsterdam, University of Amsterdam,
Kruislaan 403, 1098 SJ Amsterdam, The Netherlands
worring@science.uva.nl,
http://www.mediamill.nl

Abstract. In this paper we present our Mediamill video search engine. The basis
for the engine is a semantic indexing process which derives a lexicon of 101
concepts. To support the user in navigating the collection, the system defines a
visual similarity space, a semantic similarity space, a semantic thread space, and
browsers to explore them. It extends upon [1] with improved browsing tools. The
search system is evaluated within the TRECVID benchmark [2]. We obtain a top-
3 result for 19 out of 24 search topics. In addition, we obtain the highest mean
average precision of all search participants.

1 Introduction

Despite the emergence of commercial video search engines, such as Google and Blinkx,
video retrieval is by no means a solved problem. Present day video search engines rely
mainly on text in the form of closed captions or transcribed speech. Indexing videos
with semantic visual concepts is more appropriate.

In literature different methods have been proposed to support the user beyond text
search. Some of the most related work is described here. Informedia uses a limited set
of high-level concepts to filter the results of text queries [3]. In [4], clustering is used to
improve the presentation of results to the user. Both [3] and [4] use simple grid based
visualizations. More advanced visualization tools are employed in [5] and [6] based on
collages of keyframes and dynamically updated graphs respectively, but no semantic
lexicon is used there.

In this paper we present our semantic search engine. This system computes a large
lexicon of 101 concepts, clusters and threads to support interaction. Advanced visualization methods are used to give users quick access to the data.

2 Structuring the Video Collection

The aim of our interactive retrieval system is to retrieve from a multimedia archive A,
containing video shots, the best possible answer set in response to a user information
need. Examples of such needs are "find me shots of dunks in a basketball game" or
"find me shots of Bush with an American flag". To make the interaction most effective
we add different indices and structure to the data.

---

* This research is sponsored by the BSIK MultimediaN project.

H. Sundaram et al. (Eds.): CIVR 2006, LNCS 4071, pp. 533–536, 2006.
© Springer-Verlag Berlin Heidelberg 2006

The visual indexing starts with computing a high-dimensional feature vector F for each shot s. In our system we use the Wiccest features as introduced in [7]. The next step in the indexing is to compute a similarity function S_v allowing comparison of different shots in A. For this the function described in [7] to compare two Weibull distributions is used. The result of this step is the *visual similarity space*. This space forms the basis for visual exploration of the dataset.

We employ our generic semantic pathfinder archictecture [8], to create a lexicon of 101 concepts so that every shot s_i is described by a probability vector. Elements in the lexicon range from specific persons to generic classes of people, generic settings, specific and generic objects etc. See [8] for a complete list. Given two probability vectors, we use similarity function S_C to compare shots, now on the basis of their semantics. This yields the *semantic similarity space*.

The semantic similarity space induced by S_C is complex as shots can be related to several concepts. Therefore, we add additional navigation structure composed of a collection of linear paths, called *threads* through the data. Such a linear path is easy to navigate by simply moving back and forth. The first obvious thread is the time thread T^t. A complete set of threads $T^l = \{T^l_1, ..., T^l_{101}\}$ on the whole collection is defined by the concepts in the lexicon. The ranking based on P provides the ordering. Finally, groups are identified by clustering. Each cluster is then linearly ordered using a shortest path algorithm yielding the threads $T^s = \{T^s_1, ..., T^s_k\}$. The *Semantic thread space* is composed of T^t, T^l and T^s.

An overview of all the steps performed in the structuring of the video collection is given in Fig. 1.

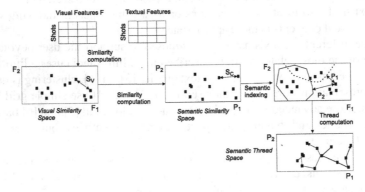

Fig. 1. Simplified overview of the computation steps required to support the user in interactive access to a video collection. Note, for both F and P only two dimensions are shown.

3   Interactive Search

The visual similarity space and the thread space define the basis for interaction with the user. Both of them require different visualization methods to provide optimal support. We developed four different browsers, which one to use depends on the information need. The different browsers are visualized in Fig. 2.

Fig. 2. Top left: the *ConceptBrowser*. Top right: the *CrossBrowser*. Bottom left: the *Sphere-Browser*. Bottom right: the *GalaxyBrowser*.

For many search tasks the initial query is formed by selecting one of the concepts from the lexicon of 101. To aid the user in this selection the *ConceptBrowser* presents the concepts in a hierarchy. Whenever the user comes to a leaf containing the concept j, the single thread T_j^l is shown as a filmstrip of keyframes corresponding to shots. By looking at those keyframes she gets a clear understanding of the meaning of the concept and whether it is indeed relevant to the search topic.

The *CrossBrowser* visualizes a single thread T_j^l based on a selected concept j from the lexicon versus the time thread T^t [8]. They are organized in a cross, with T_j^l along the vertical axis and T^t along the horizontal axis. Except for threads based on the lexicon, this browser can also be used if the user performs a textual query on the speech recognition result associated with the data, as this also leads to a linear ranking. The two dimensions are projected onto a sphere to allow easy navigation. It also enhances focus of attention on the most important element, the remaining elements are still visible, but much darker.

In the *SphereBrowser* the time thread T_j^l is also presented along the horizontal axis [8]. For each element in the time thread, the vertical axis is used to visualize the semantic thread T_j^s this particular element is part of. Users start the search by selecting a current point in the semantic similarity space by taking the top ranked element in a textual query, or a lexicon based query. The user can also select any element in one of the other browsers and take that as a starting point. They then browse the thread space by navigating time or by navigating along a semantic thread.

Browsing visual similarity space is the most difficult task as there are no obvious dimensions on which to base the display. We have developed the *GalaxyBrowser* for this purpose [9] [8]. A short overview is given here. The core of the method is formed by a projection of the high-dimensional similarity space induced by S_v to the two dimensions on the screen. This projection is based on ISOMAP and Stochastic Neighbor

Embedding. However, in these methods an element is represented as a point. In our method great care is taken to assure image visibility by reducing overlap. Two other techniques are used to support the user. Clustering is employed to give users overview of the data and active learning is used to speed up the interaction process based on relevance feedback from the user.

4   Conclusion

We have presented the Mediamill video search engine and its four browsers. The *ConceptBrowser* allows intuitive concept based queries. The *CrossBrowser* is defined for those cases where there is a direct relation between the information need and one of the concepts in the lexicon. If a more complex relation between the need and the lexicon is present, the *SphereBrowser* is most appropriate. Finally, when there is no semantic relation, we have to interact directly with visual similarity space and this is supported in the *GalaxyBrowser*.

References

1. Snoek, C., Worring, M., van Gemert, J., Geusebroek, J., Koelma, D., Nguyen, G., de Rooij, O., Seinstra, F.: Mediamill: Exploring news video archives based on learned semantics. In: ACM Multimedia, Singapore (2005)
2. Smeaton, A.: Large scale evaluations of multimedia information retrieval: The TRECVid experience. In: CIVR. Volume 3569 of LNCS. (2005)
3. Christel, M., Hauptmann, A.: The use and utility of high-level semantic features. In: CIVR, LNCS. Volume 3568. (2005)
4. Rautiainen, M., Ojala, T., Seppnen, T.: Clustertemporal browsing of large news video databases. In: IEEE International Conference on Multimedia and Expo. (2004)
5. Adcock, J., Cooper, M., Girgensohn, A., Wilcox, L.: Interactive video search using multilevel indexing. In: Conference on Image and Video Retrieval, LNCS. Volume 3568. (2005)
6. Heesch, D., Ruger, S.: Three interfaces for content-based access to image collections. In: Conference on Image and Video Retrieval, LNCS. Volume 3115. (2004)
7. Geusebroek, J.: Distinctive and compact color featuress for object recognition (2005) Submitted for publication.
8. Snoek, C., et al.: The MediaMill TRECVID 2005 semantic video search engine. In: Proc. TRECVID Workshop. NIST (2005)
9. Nguyen, G., Worring, M.: Similarity based visualization of image collections. In: Proceedings of 7th International Workshop on Audio-Visual Content and Information Visualization in Digital Libraries. (2005)

A Large Scale System for Searching and Browsing Images from the World Wide Web

Alexei Yavlinsky[1], Daniel Heesch[2], and Stefan Rüger[1]

[1] Department of Computing, South Kensington Campus
Imperial College London, London SW7 2AZ, UK
[2] Department of Electrical and Electronic Engineering, South Kensington Campus
Imperial College London, London SW7 2AZ, UK
{alexei.yavlinsky, daniel.heesch, s.rueger}@imperial.ac.uk

Abstract. This paper outlines the technical details of a prototype system for searching and browsing over a million images from the World Wide Web using their visual contents. The system relies on two modalities for accessing images — automated image annotation and NN^k image network browsing. The user supplies the initial query in the form of one or more keywords and is then able to locate the desired images more precisely using a browsing interface.

1   Introduction

The purpose of this system is to demonstrate how simple image feature extraction can be used to provide alternative mechanisms for image retrieval from the World Wide Web. We apply two recently published indexing techniques — automated image annotation using global features [1] and NN^k image network browsing [2] — to 1.14 million images spidered from the Internet. Traditional image search engines like Google or Yahoo use collateral text data, such as image filenames or web page content, to index images on the web. Such metadata, however, can often be erroneous and incomplete. We attempt to address this challenge by automatically assigning likely keywords to an image based on its content and allowing users to query with arbitrary combinations of these keywords.

As the vocabulary used for automatically annotating images is inherently limited, we use NN^k image networks to enable unlimited exploration of the image collection based on inter-image visual similarity. The idea is to connect an image to all those images in the collection to which it is most similar under *some* instantiation of a parametrised distance metric (where parameters correspond to feature weights). This is unlike most image retrieval systems which fix the parameters of the metric in advance or seek to find a single parameter set through user interaction. By considering all possible parameter sets, the networks provide a rich and browsable representation of the multiple semantic relationships that may exist between images. NN^k networks have proven a powerful browsing methodology for large collections of diverse images [3]. In addition to showing the local graph neighbourhood of an image we extract a number of visually similar

H. Sundaram et al. (Eds.): CIVR 2006, LNCS 4071, pp. 537–540, 2006.
© Springer-Verlag Berlin Heidelberg 2006

subgraphs in which that image is contained thus providing users with immediate access to a larger set of potentially interesting images.

Early experiments with our system are showing promising results, which is particularly encouraging given the 'noisy' nature of images found on the World Wide Web. In the next section we give short, formal descriptions of both indexing frameworks, and we conclude with a number of screenshots.

2 Large Scale Image Indexing

2.1 Automated Image Annotation

We use a simple nonparametric annotation model proposed by [1] which is reported to perform on par with other, more elaborate, annotation methods.

14,081 images were selected from the Corel Photo Stock for estimating statistical models of image keywords, which were then used to automatically annotate 1,141,682 images downloaded from the internet. We compiled a diverse vocabulary of 253 keywords from the annotations available in the Corel dataset.

Global colour, texture, and frequency domain features are used to model image densities. The image is split into 9 equal, rectangular tiles; for each tile we compute the mean and the variance of each of the HSV channel responses, as well as Tamura coarseness, contrast and directionality texture properties obtained using a sliding window [4]. Additionally we apply a Gabor filter bank [5] with 24 filters (6 scales × 4 orientations) and compute the mean and the variance of each filter's response signal on the entire image. This results in a 129-dimensional feature vector for each image. Our choice of these simple features is motivated by results reported in [1] which demonstrate that simple colour and texture features are suitable for automated image annotation. Implementation details of Tamura and Gabor features used in this paper can be found in [6].

2.2 NN^k Networks

NN^k networks were introduced in [2] and analysed in [7] and [8]. The motivation behind NN^k networks is to provide a browsable representation of an image collection that captures the different kinds of similarities that may exist between images. The principal idea underlying these structures is what we call the NN^k of an image. The NN^k of image q are all those images in a collection that are closest to it under at least one instantiation of a parametrised distance metric

$$D(p,q) = \sum_{f=1}^{k} w_f d_f(p,q).$$

where the parameters w are weights associated with feature-specific distance functions d_f. Each NN^k can thus be regarded as a nearest neighbour (NN) of q under a different metric.

Given a collection of images, we can use the NN^k idea to build image networks by establishing an arc from image q to image p if p is the NN^k of q. The number of parameter sets for which p is the NN^k of q defines the strength of the arc. The set of NN^k can be thought of as exemplifying the different semantic facets of the focal image that lie within the representational scope of the chosen feature set.

Structurally NN^k networks resemble the hyperlinked network of the World Wide Web (WWW), but they tend to exhibit a much better connectedness with only a negligible fraction of vertices not being reachable from the giant component. In collections of one million images, the average number of links between any two images lies between 4 and 5. By being precomputed NN^k networks allow very fast interaction.

A soft clustering of the images in the networks is achieved by partitioning not the vertex set but the edge set. An image can then belong to as many clusters as it has edges to other images (for details see [9]).

3   Implementation

The search engine is implemented within the JavaServerPages framework and is served using Apache Tomcat[1]. Figure 1 shows the result of a query 'tower

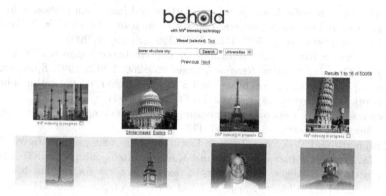

Fig. 1. Initial search using keywords (query: 'tower structure sky')

Fig. 2. Two steps of the NN^k browsing. The circle identifies the currently selected image, other images are its immediate neighbours in the network.

---

[1] A live version of this demo can be found at http://www.beholdsearch.com

structure sky'. Below each image there are two links, one for using the image as a starting point for exploring the NN^k network and the other for viewing different clusters to which the image belongs. Figure 2 shows two steps in the image network after the second search result from the left has been selected as the entry point.

4   Conclusions

Automated image annotation and image network browsing techniques appear to be promising for searching and exploring large volumes of images from the World Wide Web. It is particularly encouraging that representing images using very simple global features often yields meaningful search and visualisation results. Additionally, since most of the computation is done offline, the system is highly responsive to user queries — a desirable attribute for a content based image retrieval system.

References

1. A Yavlinsky, E Schofield, and S Rüger. Automated image annotation using global features and robust nonparametric density estimation. In *Proc Int'l Conf Image and Video Retrieval*, pages 507–517. LNCS 3568, Springer, 2005.
2. D Heesch and S Rüger. NN^k networks for content-based image retrieval. In *Proc European Conf Information Retrieval*, pages 253–266. LNCS 2997, Springer, 2004.
3. D Heesch, M Pickering, A Yavlinsky, and S Rüger. Video retrieval within a browsing framework using keyframes. In *Proc TREC Video*, 2004.
4. H Tamura. Texture features corresponding to visual perception. *IEEE Trans Systems, Man and Cybernetics*, 8(6):460–473, 1978.
5. B Manjunath and W-Y Ma. Texture features for browsing and retrieval of image data. *IEEE Trans Pattern Analysis and Machine Intelligence*, 18(8):837–842, 1996.
6. P Howarth and S Rüger. Evaluation of texture features for content-based image retrieval. In *Proc Int'l Conf Image and Video Retrieval*, pages 326–334. LNCS 3115, Springer, 2004.
7. D Heesch and S Rüger. Three interfaces for content-based access to image collections. In *Proc Int'l Conf Image and Video Retrieval*, pages 491–499. LNCS 3115, Springer, 2004.
8. D Heesch and S Rüger. Image browsing: A semantic analysis of NN^k networks. In *Proc Int'l Conf Image and Video Retrieval*, pages 609–618. LNCS 3568, Springer, 2005.
9. D Heesch. *The NN^k technique for image searching and browsing*. PhD thesis, Imperial College London, 2005.

Embrace and Tame the Digital Content

Gulrukh Ahanger

Tuner Broadcasting Systems
Gulrukh.Ahanger@turner.com

Typically, on a daily basis, large amounts of video content are processed by broad-casting stations. This includes from ingest to cutting packages and eventual trans-mis-sion and storage. New digital broadcast systems are being put in place and these sys-tems are enabling the transition from tape-based to file-based workflow. In addition, news production systems with varying and changing workflows are increasingly be-coming distributed across the bureaus and pushed out into the field. The expectations of news producers and journalists have changed; they want easy access to media for broadcast as well as for package production anywhere in the world, and at anytime. Providing this access to content, when and where needed, significantly impacts the quality of the broadcast product.

Broadcast stations are significantly gaining the ability to move content quickly and efficiently along the digital supply chain throughout the entire production and distribution process. It is being made possible largely due to a file-based environment as the digital file acquisition beings with camera. We need to maximize efficiencies gained from this change in news gathering paradigm; to be of any use, the digital con-tent river coming our way needs not only to be embraced but also to be tamed. Solutions are needed to deliver business value and return on investment through organizing, accessing, distributing, and tracking the flow of vast amounts of the digital media across multiple channels. Technologies and tools are needed that will provide the means of searching, accessing, and sharing content across different location transparently and efficiently.

This talk unlike many of the others you will hear today is not about the wonderful things that I am currently doing, or the amazing projects that are just around the corner. I was invited today to speak to you about a project that we began in 1996 and that continues in various forms well into 2006.

H. Sundaram et al. (Eds.): CIVR 2006, LNCS 4071, p. 541, 2006.
© Springer-Verlag Berlin Heidelberg 2006

Discovering a Fish in a Forest of Trees – False Positives and User Expectations in Visual Retrieval: Experiments in CBIR and the Visual Arts

Marty Harris

Adobe Systems Incorporated
mharris@linkline.com

This talk unlike many of the others you will hear today is not about the wonderful things that I am currently doing, or the amazing projects that are just around the corner. I was invited today to speak to you about a project that I began in 1996 and that continued in various forms well into 2003.

In 1986 I began work for the J. Paul Getty Trust in Los Angeles. I was hired to put together a research and development group, which would focus on the interface between technology and the visual arts. This group became part of a Getty division, the Art History Information Program and over the course of its 13 year life developed information systems and utilities used by many museums and scholarly intuitions. AHIP as our division was called, also was actively involved in researching, prototyping, and implementing systems and tools, which could be used to help humanities research. We focused on seven main areas:

1. Data Standards including early XML work and the application of controlled vocabularies.
2. Relational and entity relational database design.
3. Text searching across heterogeneous databases, relational and text.
4. The design and construction of thesauri and retrieval using these structured vocabularies.
5. Text classification, and contextual searching.
6. Directed web crawling and web search.
7. Content-based image retrieval and its relationship to all of the above.

In 1996 the Getty Art History Information Program partnered with NEC Research Labs to develop one of the earliest web based CBIR systems focused on multiple collections of art and art objects. The system known as Arthur (ART media and text HUb and Retrieval) was based on NEC's Amore CBIR engine, and allowed web users to search across the collections of almost 1000 art institutions, archives and libraries using a visual query-by-example interface. The interface was simple in its presentation and allowed traditional CBIR/QBE interaction. It allowed users to select from a number of image database groups and also supported a Boolean search, which bridged image and text, and included as part of its underlying structure, and thesaurus of art terminology.

Between 1996 and 1999, users of the Getty/Arthur CBIR system logged several million queries from a community, which included art scholars and researchers,

H. Sundaram et al. (Eds.): CIVR 2006, LNCS 4071, pp. 542–543, 2006.
© Springer-Verlag Berlin Heidelberg 2006

archivists, educators, students, k-12 to graduate, librarians, and information scientists. Each group had their own expectations regarding what they were asking for, and the relevance of the resulting retrieval set. Questionnaires and internal usability studies identified several consistent and important questions, which guided the development and growth of the Arthur project. The title of this talk refers to a query and a retrieval set which initiated several usability studies and became the focus of our CBIR group.

Imagine a query, which asked for images, which looked like "this" pine tree. In the resultant retrieval set we find a series of trees, pine, pine, pine, oak, pine, maple, oak, an image of a vertical fish, and several dozen more images of various types of trees. This representative false positive became the irritant, which led to several interesting experiments.

This talk examines some of the issues and lessons learned and describes some steps that where taken to improve both the acceptability of retrieval results and of user satisfaction.

Author Index

Lecture Notes in Computer Science

For information about Vols. 1–3980

please contact your bookseller or Springer

Vol. 4027: H.L. Larsen, G. Pasi, D. Ortiz-Arroyo, T. Andreasen, H. Christiansen (Eds.), Flexible Query Answering Systems. XVIII, 714 pages. 2006. (Sublibrary LNAI).

Vol. 4026: P.B. Gibbons, T. Abdelzaher, J. Aspnes, R. Rao (Eds.), Distributed Computing in Sensor Systems. XIV, 566 pages. 2006.

Vol. 4025: F. Eliassen, A. Montresor (Eds.), Distributed Applications and Interoperable Systems. XI, 355 pages. 2006.

Vol. 4024: S. Donatelli, P. S. Thiagarajan (Eds.), Petri Nets and Other Models of Concurrency - ICATPN 2006. XI, 441 pages. 2006.

Vol. 4021: E. André, L. Dybkjær, W. Minker, H. Neumann, M. Weber (Eds.), Perception and Interactive Technologies. XI, 217 pages. 2006. (Sublibrary LNAI).

Vol. 4020: A. Bredenfeld, A. Jacoff, I. Noda, Y. Takahashi (Eds.), RoboCup 2005: Robot Soccer World Cup IX. XVII, 727 pages. 2006. (Sublibrary LNAI).

Vol. 4019: M. Johnson, V. Vene (Eds.), Algebraic Methodology and Software Technology. XI, 389 pages. 2006.

Vol. 4018: V. Wade, H. Ashman, B. Smyth (Eds.), Adaptive Hypermedia and Adaptive Web-Based Systems. XVI, 474 pages. 2006.

Vol. 4016: J.X. Yu, M. Kitsuregawa, H.V. Leong (Eds.), Advances in Web-Age Information Management. XVII, 606 pages. 2006.

Vol. 4014: T. Uustalu (Ed.), Mathematics of Program Construction. X, 455 pages. 2006.

Vol. 4013: L. Lamontagne, M. Marchand (Eds.), Advances in Artificial Intelligence. XIII, 564 pages. 2006. (Sublibrary LNAI).

Vol. 4012: T. Washio, A. Sakurai, K. Nakajima, H. Takeda, S. Tojo, M. Yokoo (Eds.), New Frontiers in Artificial Intelligence. XIII, 484 pages. 2006. (Sublibrary LNAI).

Vol. 4011: Y. Sure, J. Domingue (Eds.), The Semantic Web: Research and Applications. XIX, 726 pages. 2006.

Vol. 4010: S. Dunne, B. Stoddart (Eds.), Unifying Theories of Programming. VIII, 257 pages. 2006.

Vol. 4009: M. Lewenstein, G. Valiente (Eds.), Combinatorial Pattern Matching. XII, 414 pages. 2006.

Vol. 4008: J.C. Augusto, C.D. Nugent (Eds.), Designing Smart Homes. XI, 183 pages. 2006. (Sublibrary LNAI).

Vol. 4007: C. Àlvarez, M. Serna (Eds.), Experimental Algorithms. XI, 329 pages. 2006.

Vol. 4006: L.M. Pinho, M. González Harbour (Eds.), Reliable Software Technologies – Ada-Europe 2006. XII, 241 pages. 2006.

Vol. 4005: G. Lugosi, H.U. Simon (Eds.), Learning Theory. XI, 656 pages. 2006. (Sublibrary LNAI).

Vol. 4004: S. Vaudenay (Ed.), Advances in Cryptology - EUROCRYPT 2006. XIV, 613 pages. 2006.

Vol. 4003: Y. Koucheryavy, J. Harju, V.B. Iversen (Eds.), Next Generation Teletraffic and Wired/Wireless Advanced Networking. XVI, 582 pages. 2006.

Vol. 4001: E. Dubois, K. Pohl (Eds.), Advanced Information Systems Engineering. XVI, 560 pages. 2006.

Vol. 3999: C. Kop, G. Fliedl, H.C. Mayr, E. Métais (Eds.), Natural Language Processing and Information Systems. XIII, 227 pages. 2006.

Vol. 3998: T. Calamoneri, I. Finocchi, G.F. Italiano (Eds.), Algorithms and Complexity. XII, 394 pages. 2006.

Vol. 3997: W. Grieskamp, C. Weise (Eds.), Formal Approaches to Software Testing. XII, 219 pages. 2006.

Vol. 3996: A. Keller, J.-P. Martin-Flatin (Eds.), Self-Managed Networks, Systems, and Services. X, 185 pages. 2006.

Vol. 3995: G. Müller (Ed.), Emerging Trends in Information and Communication Security. XX, 524 pages. 2006.

Vol. 3994: V.N. Alexandrov, G.D. van Albada, P.M.A. Sloot, J. Dongarra, Computational Science – ICCS 2006, Part IV. XXXV, 1096 pages. 2006.

Vol. 3993: V.N. Alexandrov, G.D. van Albada, P.M.A. Sloot, J. Dongarra, Computational Science – ICCS 2006, Part III. XXXVI, 1136 pages. 2006.

Vol. 3992: V.N. Alexandrov, G.D. van Albada, P.M.A. Sloot, J. Dongarra, Computational Science – ICCS 2006, Part II. XXXV, 1122 pages. 2006.

Vol. 3991: V.N. Alexandrov, G.D. van Albada, P.M.A. Sloot, J. Dongarra, Computational Science – ICCS 2006, Part I. LXXXI, 1096 pages. 2006.

Vol. 3990: J. C. Beck, B.M. Smith (Eds.), Integration of AI and OR Techniques in Constraint Programming for Combinatorial Optimization Problems. X, 301 pages. 2006.

Vol. 3989: J. Zhou, M. Yung, F. Bao, Applied Cryptography and Network Security. XIV, 488 pages. 2006.

Vol. 3988: A. Beckmann, U. Berger, B. Löwe, J.V. Tucker (Eds.), Logical Approaches to Computational Barriers. XV, 608 pages. 2006.

Vol. 3987: M. Hazas, J. Krumm, T. Strang (Eds.), Location- and Context-Awareness. X, 289 pages. 2006.

Vol. 3986: K. Stølen, W.H. Winsborough, F. Martinelli, F. Massacci (Eds.), Trust Management. XIV, 474 pages. 2006.

Vol. 3984: M. Gavrilova, O. Gervasi, V. Kumar, C.J. K. Tan, D. Taniar, A. Laganà, Y. Mun, H. Choo (Eds.), Computational Science and Its Applications - ICCSA 2006, Part V. XXV, 1045 pages. 2006.

Vol. 3983: M. Gavrilova, O. Gervasi, V. Kumar, C.J. K. Tan, D. Taniar, A. Laganà, Y. Mun, H. Choo (Eds.), Computational Science and Its Applications - ICCSA 2006, Part IV. XXVI, 1191 pages. 2006.

Vol. 3982: M. Gavrilova, O. Gervasi, V. Kumar, C.J. K. Tan, D. Taniar, A. Laganà, Y. Mun, H. Choo (Eds.), Computational Science and Its Applications - ICCSA 2006, Part III. XXV, 1243 pages. 2006.

Vol. 3981: M. Gavrilova, O. Gervasi, V. Kumar, C.J. K. Tan, D. Taniar, A. Laganà, Y. Mun, H. Choo (Eds.), Computational Science and Its Applications - ICCSA 2006, Part II. XXVI, 1255 pages. 2006.